Mushrooms
OF THE GREAT LAKES REGION

*The fleshy, leathery, and woody fungi
of Illinois, Indiana, Ohio and the southern half of
Wisconsin and of Michigan*

VERNE OVID GRAHAM

DOVER PUBLICATIONS, INC.

NEW YORK

Published in Canada by General Publishing Company, Ltd., 30 Lesmill Road, Don Mills, Toronto, Ontario.

Published in the United Kingdom by Constable and Company, Ltd., 10 Orange Street, London WC 2.

This Dover edition, first published in 1970, is an unabridged and unaltered republication of the work originally published in 1944 by The Chicago Academy of Sciences and The Chicago Natural History Museum.

The reprint publisher gratefully acknowledges the cooperation of The Chicago Academy of Sciences, which supplied a copy of this work for the purpose of reproduction.

Standard Book Number: 486-22538-0
Library of Congress Catalog Card Number: 74-106484

Manufactured in the United States of America
Dover Publications, Inc.
180 Varick Street
New York, N.Y. 10014

FOREWORD

The manuscript presented here was in large part written and edited at the Chicago Natural History Museum; the plates, based on the author's drawings and the specimens in the Harper collection, were executed in the museum by employees of the Works Progress Administration and printed in the collotype plant of the museum. It was expected that opportunity would be found to publish the entire work in the museum's *Botanical Series*, but on account of the large quantity of unprinted material on hand from all departments this could not be accomplished without long delay. In order to insure its early appearance, the Chicago Academy of Sciences agreed to publish the work under the joint auspices of the two institutions, an arrangement welcomed by this museum as a practical measure of genuine coöperation.

ORR GOODSON, Acting Director,
Chicago Natural History Museum.
(Formerly *Field Museum of Natural History*.)

PREFACE

This book is the outgrowth of studies made in the Great Lakes region during a period of many years. Before the turn of the century (1898) several local botanists interested in the fungi organized the Chicago Mycological Society. Their work resulted in the publication, by the Chicago Academy of Sciences, of Natural History Survey Bulletin No. 7, "The Higher Fungi of the Chicago Region," by Dr. Will Sayer Moffatt, Part 1 in 1909 and Part 2 in 1923. In the autumn of 1927 a course dealing with the fleshy and woody fungi was given by the author at the University of Chicago. Difficulties were encountered in bringing together the scattered publications dealing with the fungi. At that time was born the idea of writing a manual of the fleshy, leathery and woody fungi of the Chicago region in a single volume.

The territory usually studied by Chicago botanists extends beyond the limits of that treated by Moffatt. It has, therefore, seemed advisable to include in the present work not only the species of the immediate vicinity of Chicago but also those which may be found in southern Wisconsin, southern Michigan, and all of Illinois, Indiana, and Ohio. The additions to Moffatt's flora, made necessary by these geographical extensions, increase the number of species from 400 to 1200.

The works of Seaver, Burt, Banker, Kauffman, Neuman, Harper, Peck, Overholts, Murrill, and Coker have been closely followed in the development of this manuscript. Since these monographers have listed the many synonyms of species and specimens in herbaria, it has seemed advisable to save space by omitting many of these data here. No special collection has been preserved as a basis for this work, but the herbarium of E. T. Harper in the Chicago Natural History Museum and the collections of Thelephoraceae and Polyporaceae in the Missouri Botanical Garden have proved very useful. The author, with the help of many others, has examined hundreds of specimens over a period of years. The softer forms, not easily compared with dried specimens, were repeatedly identified and their characteristics checked against the best available descriptions. In many cases additional field notes, helpful for identification, have been included with the descriptions.

Mushrooms are peculiarly different from other plants. One may look with assurance for the higher plants but with much less certainty for a fungus in a particular habitat, even though on previous occasions one may have observed many plants of the kind. This is true for more than one reason: fungi are usually observable in the fruiting stage only, may occur during a single year, and then not again for several years. The irregularity of appearance may in part be due to variations of rainfall. Many fungi fail to appear during seasons of light rainfall but are unusually abundant throughout seasons of much precipitation.

Differentiating details of the vegetative parts of fungi are usually microscopic. The vegetative structure, called the mycelium, is composed of very slender, thread-like hyphae of profuse growth. The nutritive material required for the growth and development of the fungus is absorbed and stored by the mycelium ready for the rapid growth which occurs in the production of the fruiting bodies. The production of fruits by the fungus is so closely dependent on the vegetative growth, and the amount of vegetative growth is so directly dependent on weather conditions, that seasons often pass without the production of fruits.

Fungi play an important part in the science of forestry since many species are parasitic on trees. A particular species of *Fomes* will always grow on one species of tree. It is often more convenient to identify a species of this genus by the kind of tree on which it is growing than from the microscopic features of the fungus. Some species of fungi grow vegetatively for many years within the wood of a tree until the supply of food from wood to fungus diminishes with the death of some of the wood tissue. Then the fungus sends forth the reproductive bodies resulting in fruits. Fruits are often the only structures of the fungus with sufficient differentiating features for identification.

Many species of fungi depend for their growth on the presence of some other living form, which may serve as partial or complete host. Some require a certain acidity or alkalinity of the soil. The majority find the season of the year the most important determiner of their prevalence. That some fungi appear during one year at the appropriate season, but are again not present for several years, is a difficulty encountered by every student of mycology.

The greatest economic value of fungi is in the work accomplished in returning woody tissue to the soil. The world would be piled high with brush from dead trees were it not for the change effected by the growth of fungi on the wood.

To many people mushrooms have but one appeal—edibility. To these a brief review of the fungi may prove valuable. The families Xylariaceae and Pezizaceae have no poisonous species within our area. Many of them are of pleasant flavor. The family Elvelaceae contains *Elvela infula*, which has caused some disagreeable results. Among the Thelephoraceae are some species of texture soft enough for the table. These are not only edible but of fine flavor. The Clavariaceae of this region are all edible, but one white species in the Southeastern States has been found to be dangerous. The Hydnaceae are edible but comparatively rare. All Polyporaceae growing on deciduous wood are edible if soft enough to be eaten. A few species of *Boletus* are poisonous, yet some of our finest mushrooms are in this genus. A study of the entire group should be made before general collection for the table. The Agaricaceae include both the most deadly and some of the best edible species. The deadly *Amanita* is at one extreme and the very fine commercial mushroom at the other. By one well versed in the recognition of these species, hundreds of kinds may be eaten. The Lycoperdaceae are uniformly edible, but should be collected for the table before spore production has changed the color of the interior.

The author suggests that not less than two years be spent in such intensive study that a great many species may be recognized at sight before any student begins to eat the less familiar kinds of wild fungi. When identification may be made with assurance of its correctness by the student himself, he does not need to trust his well being to the judgement of some other person. He also has the assurance of a task well done, and has gained confidence in himself well worth the effort expended.

The author wishes to acknowledge the help rendered by specialists who have read parts of the manuscript. The suggestions of John Dearness and Fred J. Seaver have been especially valuable. B. E. Dahlgren and Francis Drouet have contributed much to the orderly arrangement. The friendly criticisms of Mrs. Cloyd Stifler have proven helpful. T. M. Jelinek, Albert Frey, Tom Hale, and Raymond Taran have worked from the author's original drawings, from selected photographs, and from specimens to prepare the illustrations.

V. O. G.

CONTENTS

MUSHROOMS OF THE GREAT LAKES REGION

KEY TO GENERA

The fungi are divided into three classes: Phycomycetes, Ascomycetes, and Basidiomycetes. The Phycomycetes and the very small species included in the Ascomycetes are not treated here. Fleshy fungi in the orders Sphaeriales and Pezizales of the latter class are represented in this flora. The fleshy and woody Basidiomycetes include three orders: Tremellales, Agaricales, and Lycoperdales. The microscopic Basidiomycetes (rusts and smuts) are omitted.

1   Spores borne in asci, usually eight in each ascus. Among these are the cup-shaped Pezizaceae, the side-saddle-on-a-stem Elvelaceae, the honey-combed Morchellas, and the hard, black, tongue-like Xylariaceae (Ascomycetes)....2

1' Spores borne on basidia, usually four on each basidium. These are the puff balls, gilled mushrooms, polypores, thelephores, gelatinous forms, and those with spores borne on teeth (Basidiomycetes)......28

2   Entirely underground (none included) Tuberales.

2' Above ground, or partly so......3

3   Fruiting bodies discoid to cup-shaped (Pezizaceae).....4

3' Not so shaped......17

4   Substance cartilaginous, apothecium clothed externally with flexuous hairs.................*Pseudoplectania*, p. 23.

4' Flesh soft, apothecium not clothed with hairs......5

5   Flesh waxy, spores warted............*Lamprospora*, p. 23.

5' Flesh not waxy......6

6   Hymenium bright orange.................*Aleuria*, p. 24.

6' Not so colored......7

7   Hymenium scarlet......8

7' Hymenium yellow, brown, gray, white, violet, or black 10

8   Apothecium cup-shaped to shield-shaped......9

8' Apothecium subglobose, then expanding, spores smooth
....*Plectania*, p. 26.

9   Spores sculptured, reticulate, apothecium somewhat asymmetrical, marginal hairs colored............*Melastiza*, p. 24.
9'   Spores not sculptured; apothecium symmetrical, discoid
     ....*Patella*, p. 25.
10   Apothecium or its branches commonly twisted......11
10' Apothecium not twisted......12
11   Dark brown, tough, branched, externally warty, arising
     from a thick sclerotium...................*Wynnea*, p. 28.
11' Yellow-brown, externally furfuraceous, usually unbranched, not arising from a sclerotium....*Scodellina*, p. 27.
12   Apothecium with an internal gelatinous layer......13
12' No such layer present......14
13   Apothecium operculate ....*Bulgaria*, p. 35.
13' Apothecium inoperculate ....*Phaeobulgaria*, p. 22.
14   Margin of apothecium regularly split or crenate......15
14' Margin neither regularly split nor crenate......16
15   Apothecium and hymenium brown-black, 2-6 cm. in diameter ....*Urnula*, p. 28.
15' Apothecium light colored, smaller..........*Geopyxis*, p. 31.
16   Apothecium discoid, symmetrical, externally setose......
     ....*Patella*, p. 25.
16' Apothecium externally tomentose or hairy, usually concave ....*Paxina*, p. 28.
16" Apothecium concave, neither tomentose nor hairy.......
     ....*Peziza*, p. 32.
17   Growing from buried insect larvae or subterranean fungi;
     capitate ....*Cordyceps*, p. 11.
17' Not growing from larvae or underground fungi......18
18   Fruiting bodies hard, firm, mostly colored like charred
     wood (Xylariaceae)......19
18' Soft, not colored like charred wood......21
19   Clavate or cylindrical, sometimes branched....*Xylaria*, p. 14.
19' Globose, convex, or effused, not stalked......20
20   Internally concentrically zoned.............*Daldinia*, p. 13.
20' Not internally zoned...................*Hypoxylon*, p. 13.
21   Clavate, spathulate, or capitate (Geoglossaceae)......22
21' Pileus saddle-shaped, conical, or bell-shaped, and pitted,
     gyrate, or smooth, always with a stem (Elvelaceae)....26
22   Pileus much compressed, spathulate or fan-shaped......
     ....*Spathularia*, p. 20.
22' Clavate......23
22" Capitate......25

33   Stem fleshy, pileus easily separating from stem and of different texture, gills free......34
33′ Pileus and stem of same texture and confluent, fleshy gills attached to stem......35
33″ Stem usually slender, tough or rigid, fragile, with an outer cartilaginous layer......43
34   Volva and annulus present; volva a distinct cup, sometimes nearly adnate, or composed of irregular adnate rings ....*Amanita*, p.157.
34′ Volva present, annulus lacking..........*Amanitopsis*, p.164.
34″ Volva absent, annulus present; nearly all the species with a scaly pileus ....*Lepiota*, p.165.
35   Plants exuding a milky or colored juice when broken.. ....*Lactarius*, p.213.
35′ Not exuding juice......36
36   Stem eccentric or lateral.................*Pleurotus*, p.227.
36′ Stem central......37
37   Annulus present, sometimes inconspicuous and web-like ....*Armillaria*, p. 171.
37′ Annulus lacking......38
38   Parasitic on other mushrooms (especially *Russula*) chlamydospores colored ....*Nyctalis*, p.227.
38′ Not parasitic......39
39   Gills of waxy consistency..............*Hygrophorus*, p.194.
39′ Gills not waxy......40
40   Plants rigid-brittle, tissue short-celled, spores globose, distinctly or obscurely rough.................*Russula*, p.202.
40′ Lacking this combination of characters......41
41   Gills thick on edges, decurrent, forked dichotomously, sometimes anastomosing ....*Cantharellus*, p.224.
41′ Gills thin......42
42   Gills decurrent or broadly adnate..........*Clitocybe*, p.174.
42′ Gills narrowed at stem or emarginate, plants mostly terrestrial ....*Tricholoma*, p.185.
43   Gills decurrent, pileus umbilicate..........*Omphalia*, p.255.
43′ Gills not decurrent......44
44   Pileus campanulate, not expanding but commonly remaining parasol-shaped and thin; plants small....*Mycena*, p.248.
44′ Pileus convex-expanded, the margin at first inrolled; plants mostly small to medium-sized, in a few species large.... ....*Collybia*, p.241.

45   Pileus when dry reviving with moisture; plants small,
fleshy-membranaceous ....*Marasmius*, p. 234.
45'   Pileus similar but with a gelatinous trama. *Heliomyces*, p. 241.
45"   Pileus fleshy-leathery 46

46   Gills split along the edge or blunt and crisped 47
46'   Gills not grooved or split on edge 48

47   Gill-edge split longitudinally .... *Schizophyllum*, p. 233.
47'   Gill-edge obtuse, crisped .... *Trogia*, p. 233.

48   Gill-edge serrated .... *Lentinus*, p. 231.
48'   Gill-edge entire .... *Panus*, p. 230.
48"   Gills more or less anastomosing to daedaloid. . *Lenzites*, p. 130.

49   Gills easily separating from pileus, often anastomosing,
margin of pileus involute .... *Paxillus*, p. 307.
49'   Gills not easily separated from pileus 50

50   Annulus present 51
50'   Annulus absent 52

51   Annulus membranaceous, flaring .... *Pholiota*, p. 283.
51'   Annulus webby or in patches on stem ...... *Cortinarius*, p. 297.

52   Stem lateral or lacking .... *Crepidotus*, p. 308.
52'   Stem central 53

53   Gills free, pileus small, plants sometimes deliquescent....
.... *Bolbitius*, p. 312 , and *Pluteolus*. p. 313.
53'   Gills more or less attached to stem 54

54   Trama brittle, mature spores not smooth 55
54'   Trama not brittle 56

55   Exuding milky or colored juice when broken. *Lactarius*, p. 213.
55'   Not exuding juice .... *Russula*, p. 202.

56   Stem not cartilaginous or rigid-fragile 57
56'   Stem cartilaginous or rigid-fragile 60

57   Inner veil cobwebby; spores rusty or cinnamon-colored
.... *Cortinarius*, p. 297.
57'   Inner veil membranous, fibrous, or floccose 58

58   Growing on wood; gills becoming yellow or rusty yellow
.... *Flammula*, p. 290.
58'   Growing on rotten wood, mosses, earth, etc.; gills ochraceous to brown 59

59   Pileus radiately fibrillose-scaly, plants mostly small....
.... *Inocybe*, p. 292.
59'   Pileus smooth, usually viscid when moist; spores ochraceous; stem commonly dotted toward apex.. *Hebeloma*, p. 279.

60   Gills decurrent .... *Tubaria*, p. 365.
60' Margin of pileus at first incurved, pileus at length convex
     or plane .... *Naucoria*, p. 310.
60" Margin not at first incurved................ *Galera*, p. 314.

61   Volva present, annulus lacking............. *Volvaria*, p. 258.
61' Volva and annulus absent......62

62   Stem lateral or absent, lignicolous......... *Claudopus*, p. 272.
62' Stem central......63

63   Gills free .... *Pluteus*, p. 259.
63' Gills more or less attached to stem......64

64   Stem fleshy or fibrous-fleshy......65
64' Stem tough-cartilaginous or rigid-fragile, slender......66

65   Gills emarginate becoming sinuate.......... *Entoloma*, p. 263.
65' Gills adnate to decurrent, not sinuate........ *Clitopilus*, p. 269.

66   Gills decurrent, pileus usually umbilicate...... *Eccilia*, p. 277.
66' Gills not decurrent......67

67   Sides of pileus at first straight, pileus remaining conical
     or campanulate when mature............... *Nolanea*, p. 275.
67' Margin of pileus at first inrolled, convex at maturity....
     .... *Leptonia*, p. 272.

68   Stem fleshy, free from gills and detachable from pileus;
     annulus present .... *Agaricus*, p. 317.
68' Stem cartilaginous, annulus absent, plants mostly small to
     medium-sized 69
68" Stem fibrous-fleshy, concrete with pileus......71

69   Gills adnate-decurrent .... *Deconica*, p. 333.
69' Gills narrowed toward stem......70

70   Sides of pileus at first straight............. *Psathyra*, p. 331.
70' Sides of pileus at first incurved........... *Psilocybe*, p. 326.

71   Annulus present .... *Stropharia*, p. 321.
71' Annulus absent, remains of veil present on margin of
     pileus .... *Hypholoma*, p. 323.

72   Gills deliquescent, i. e., finally dissolving into an inky
     mass .... *Coprinus*, p. 334.
72' Gills not deliquescent......73

73   Annulus present .... *Anellaria*, p. 343.
73' Annulus lacking......74

74   Gills decurrent........................ *Gomphidius*, p. 343.
74' Gills not decurrent......75

75 Stem long, slender; pileus conical or campanulate, regu-
    lar, not striate; gills variegated in several shades of gray
    ....*Panaeoleus,* p. 341.
75′ Pileus small, striate; gills not variegated; stem cartilagi-
    nous or rigid-fragile ....*Psathyrella,* p. 344.
76 Hymenium of shallow pits formed by anastomosing ridges
    ....*Merulius,* p. 93.
76′ Hymenium leathery or tough or even woody, fleshy in a
    few species, concrete with the context, the spore-bearing
    pores concrete with each other (Polyporeae)......77
76″ Hymenium fleshy-putrescent, easily separable from the
    context; pores deep (Boleteae)......82
76‴ Hymenium as in Boleteae but not easily separable from the
    context; tubes distinctly separate from each other......
    ....*Fistulina,* p. 132.
77 Fruiting body resupinate......78
77′ Fruiting body sessile, stemmed, or effuso-reflexed......79
78 Pores papillate ....*Porothelium,* p. 93.
78′ Pores not papillate, plant like an entirely resupinate
    Polyporus ....*Poria,* p. 96.
79 Pores of unequal depths.................*Trametes,* p. 126.
79′ Pores of uniform depth......80
80 Hymenium on concentric lamellae........*Cyclomyces,* p. 131.
80′ Hymenium on radiating gill-like plates......*Lenzites,* p. 130.
80″ Hymenium labyrinthine (daedaloid)........*Daedalea,* p. 129.
80‴ Hymenium in hexagonal, radially-arranged pores......
    ....*Favolus,* p. 131
80⁗ Hymenium otherwise......81
81 Fruiting-body with as many layers as years of growth..
    ....*Fomes,* p. 121.
81′ Fruiting body annual...................*Polyporus,* p. 101.
82 Pileus bearing floccose cone-shaped scales............
    ....*Strobilomyces,* p. 135.
82′ Pileus not so scaled......83
83 Hymenium with tubes easily separable.......*Boletus,* p. 135.
83′ Hymenium with tubes not easily separated...*Boletinus,* p. 132.
84 Flesh gelatinous ....*Tremellodon,* p. 79.
84′ Flesh soft, corky, leathery, or woody......85
85 Teeth awl-shaped or needle-shaped......86
85′ Teeth growing as warty granules or elevations on the
    resupinate plant......87

86   Flesh either soft or corky.................*Hydnum,* p. 81.
86' Flesh leathery, pileus resupinate to shelf-like...*Irpex,* p. 89.

87   Resupinate, usually radially corrugated or ridged.......
     ....*Phlebia,* p. 91.
87' Resupinate, with warts, granules, tubercles, or short teeth
     on the surface......88

88   With obtuse tubercles....................*Radulum,* p. 90.
88' With crested warts on a base of woven fibers..*Odontia,* p. 92.

89   Hymenium on outer surface of gelatinous plants
     (Tremellales)......90
89' Hymenium otherwise, plants not gelatinous......95

90   Basidia elongate, simple, transversely septate..........
     ....*Auricularia,* p. 76.
90' Basidia subglobose, longitudinally 4-parted......91
90'' Basidia cylindrical or clavate......94

91   Plants erect, spathulate ....*Gyrocephalus,* p. 79.
91' Plants not so shaped......92

92   Plants pulvinate, gyrose ....*Ulocolla,* p. 77.
92' Plants cup-shaped, truncate or irregularly lobed.*Exidia,* p. 77.
92'' Plants neither gyrose nor cup-shaped......93

93   Plants much lobed or brain-like...........*Tremella,* p. 78.
93' Plants convex, with a central hard nucleus.*Naematelia,* p. 79.

94   Plants small, pulvinate, gyrose...........*Dacromyces,* p. 80.
94' Plants substipitate, cup-shaped.............*Guepinia,* p. 81.
94'' Plants substipitate, fusiform ....*Calocera,* p. 81.

95   Hymenium surrounding the upper part of erect, fleshy,
     tender clubs; plants often much branched
     (Clavariaceae)......96
95' Hymenium inferior, on tough plants (Thelephoraceae) 97

96   Plants becoming coriaceous ....*Lachnocladium,* p. 76.
96' Plants not becoming coriaceous ....*Clavaria,* p. 68.

97   Small cistern-shaped fructifications either solitary or some-
     what confluent at bases, from a webby resupinate sub-
     stratum ....*Solenia,* p. 67.
97' Plants otherwise......98

98   Plants fleshy or membranaceous, usually infundibuliform;
     hymenium even, ribbed or wrinkled, the basidia simple
     ....*Craterellus,* p. 65.
98' Plants leathery, hard, or felt-like and resupinate......99

99   Plants erect, often much branched, some resembling *Clavaria* but with more compressed branches; basidia globose or pyriform, longitudinally cruciate, 4-septate.........
................................*Tremellodendron,* p. 61.

99′ Plants resupinate to effused-reflexed and pileate......100

100 Plants resupinate, often ascending weeds or bases of young trees; basidia cruciate as in *Tremellodendron. Sebacina,* p. 61.

100′ Plants mostly resupinate (those of *Stereum* are pileate and in one species infundibuliform), basidia simple......101

101 Plants pileate, the margins commonly torn-fimbriate; spores colored ....*Thelephora,* p. 62.

101′ Plants pileate, usually shelf-like, one included species infundibuliform; spores dull......102

101″ Plants wholly resupinate (the margin slightly elevated and saucer-like in *Aleurodiscus*)......103

102 Hymenium velvety with brown, rigid, even-walled setae; plants pileate to resupinate...........*Hymenochaete,* p. 53.

102′ Hymenium even, plants pileate or reflexed (in one species infundibuliform or flabelliform).............*Stereum,* p. 47.

103 Spores colored, echinulate...............*Hypochnus,* p. 40.

103′ Spores ochraceous, ferruginous, or fuscous, smooth....
....................................*Coniophora,* p. 55.

103″ Spores white or dull......104

104 Subhymenial tissue containing brown, stellate bodies; plants otherwise like *Corticium*........*Asterostroma,* p. 42.

104′ No such bodies present......105

105 Plants resupinate with free and often elevated margin..
....................................*Aleurodiscus,* p. 46.

105′ Plants cup-shaped, hymenium blood-red......*Cytidia,* p. 67.

105″ Margin not elevated, structure compact or hypochnoid 106

106 Cystidia present ....*Peniophora,* p. 56.

106′ Cystidia absent ....*Corticium,* p. 43.

107 Gleba gelatinous, arising from a volva, usually ill-smelling (Phallaceae)......109

107′ Stalk of plant gelatinous, mouth red.......*Calostoma,* p. 361.

107″ Not gelatinous, nor ill-smelling......108

108 Gleba becoming powdery, enclosed in a peridium...... (Lycoperdaceae)......112

108′ Gleba developing into a nest of small peridioles........ (Nidulariaceae)......122

108″ Plant subterranean, gleba in a peridium that breaks up irregularly (Hymenogastraceae).........*Phallogaster,* p. 347.

109   Rosy-colored gleba borne along upper part of stalk, plants ill-smelling .... *Mutinus*, p. 344.

109′   Gleba green or olive...... 110

110   Gleba inclosed by the several apical branches of stalk to which the gleba adheres on their inner and lateral surfaces .... *Anthurus*, p. 345.

110′   Gleba on a more or less conical pileus...... 111

111   A large net-like veil present............ *Dictyophora*, p. 346.

111′   Veil absent .... *Phallus*, p. 346.

112   Stalk slender, several times as long as the diameter of the peridium; plants small.............. *Tylostoma*, p. 359.

112′   Stalk not slender, sometimes absent...... 113

113   Outer peridium splitting and extending outward from the inner peridium in a star-like manner..... *Geaster*, p. 356. and .... *Astraeus*, p. 355.

113′   As above but with several small pores in upper part of inner peridium as in a pepper box .... *Myriostoma*, p. 359.

113″   With other characters...... 114

114   Membranous-coriaceous, peridium usually double, gleba at length a powdery mass of capillitium and spores...... 115

114′   Coriaceous, peridium simple, gleba persistent, capillitium none...... 121

115   Outer peridium splitting equatorially, the lower half subterranean, the inner peridium exposed..... *Catastoma*, p. 361.

115′   Outer peridium not splitting equatorially...... 116

116   Columella extending through peridium to apex........ .... *Secotium*, p. 347.

116′   Columella otherwise...... 117

117   Subgleba prominent as a thickened base in lower part of peridium...... 118

117′   Without a thickened base...... 120

118   Peridium breaking into fragments from apex downward, plants quite large........................... *Calvatia*, p. 348.

118′   Peridium opening by a single apical mouth...... 119

119   Spores sessile .... *Lycoperdon*, p. 350.

119′   Spores stalked, peridium usually flattened above........ .... *Bovistella*, p. 354.

120   Peridium opening irregularly by an apical mouth, capillitium composed of dichotomously much branched threads .... *Bovista*, p. 354.

120′   Peridium very thick, breaking up into areas, almost corky in consistency .... *Mycenastrum*, p. 355.

121   Internally divided into many sac-like cavities (perid-
       ioles) ....*Pisolithus,* p. 363.
121'   Such cavities absent, plants with tough covering........
       ....*Scleroderma,* p. 362.
122   Peridioles (eggs) attached by cords to the inside of pe-
       ridium (nest)......123
122'   Peridioles not attached by cords, but imbedded in
       mucous ....*Nidularia,* p. 365.
123   Peridium cup-shaped, of a single layer, peridioles
       whitish ....*Crucibulum,* p. 364.
123'   Peridium of three layers, peridioles gray or nearly
       black ....*Cyathus,* p. 364.

ASCOMYCETES

HYPOCREACEAE

Perithecia bright colored, rarely whitish, fleshy.

See Seaver, F. J. Mycology 3:207-230, 1911; Mains, E. B. Proc. Amer. Phil. Soc. 74:263-271, 1934.

CORDYCEPS (Fr.) Link. Plate 2.

Stromata growing from sclerotia within the bodies of insects or more rarely in other fungi, simple or branched, at first (Isaria-stage) delicate, protruding conidia, later usually clavate and producing more or less immersed or rarely superficial perithecia which are aggregated into a globose, clavate, or agariciform head supported by a sterile stem and sometimes surmounted by a sterile apex; asci cylindric, 8-spored; spores filiform or subfiliform, many-septate (rarely one-celled), and often breaking into segments in the ascus.

C. militaris (L.) Link. Military Cordyceps. Plate 2, fig. 2.

4-6 cm. high, stem 3-4 cm. x 3-5 mm., head 1-1.5 cm. x 5-7 mm.

Sclerotia formed in pupae of insects, compact, white; stroma at maturity consisting of a slender stem and an ovate-clavate head, bright orange; asci cylindric; spores filiform, many-septate, breaking apart at septa into segments 2-3 μ long; pupa commonly 3 cm. long and 1 cm. in diameter, partially buried.—Rare; North Dakota, New England, Ohio, Virginia, Europe

C. herculea Schw.　Giant Cordyceps.　Plate 2, fig. 1.

5-7 cm. high, stem 3-5 cm. x 1-1.5 cm., head 2-3 x 1-2 cm.

Stromata large; stem dull yellow; head considerably broader than the stem, fertile portion often interrupted, leaving bare patches, terminated by a short, obtuse apex, somewhat roughened by the necks of the perithecia which protrude at the surface; spores filiform, septate, segments 5-8 μ long.—On large, white larvae or pupae.　Illinois to Connecticut and North Carolina.

C. agariciformis Bolt.　Plate 2, fig. 3.

C. capitata Link.

C. canadensis Ell. & Everh.

3-10 cm. high; stem 2-8 x 0.8-1.5 cm.; head 10-15 x 8-16 mm.

Stroma consisting of a sterile stem and an ovoid fertile head; stem sub-equal, cylindrical, fibrous, smooth, dull dingy yellow darkening to almost black in age or in drying; head ovoid or domeshaped (agariciform), reddish-brown becoming blackish, roughened by perithecial necks; asci long-cylindrical; spores filiform 30 x 4 μ. — Parasitic on *Scleroderma* (?) and *Elaphomyces*, on ravine side, Olympia Fields, Illinois, Aug. 1924; Ontario; Maine; Florida.

C. parasitica Willd.

C. ophioglossoides Link.

2-6 cm. high; stem 1-2 mm. broad, enlarging into head 1-2 cm. x 4-5 mm.

Head elliptical, gradually tapering into stem, dark-brown becoming blackish in age or in drying, roughened by perithecia; stem longitudinally striate, olivaceous, becoming dark colored, sending out numerous branching rhizomorphs into soil.—Ontario, Maine, Virginia.

XYLARIACEAE

"Asci long cylindrical, stalks long and filiform, or short, and asci lining the bases and sides of the perithecia; ascospores unicellular, light brown to black, inequilaterally elliptical, fusoid, or globose, uniseriate in ascus; paraphyses thread-like branched, completely filling the perithecial cavity at an early period, and more or less gelatinizing at maturity.　Perithecia membranaceous, seated under a more or less well developed ectostroma, with the bases in entostroma.　Conidiophores hyphomycetous, covering an exposed ectostroma, branched; conidia single or in clusters, minute, borne apically and becoming lateral by continued growth of the conidiophore."　Miller, Mycologia 20:305-339, 1928.　Globose, subglobose. or clavate plants commonly with a burnt-wood appearance, the clavate Xylarias up to several centimeters high.

DALDINIA De Not. Plate 2.

Ectostroma dark purple after conidial layer has disappeared; development similar to that of *Hypoxylon,* but the concentric zonation (as seen in section) is so striking in *Daldinia* that it is separated as a genus. Layers of cells disintegrate as the perithecium develops, but the meristematic hyphae grow upward and around these. A continuation of this action produces from six to forty concentric zones. See J. H. Miller, Mycologia, 20:328. 1928.

D. concentrica (Bolt.) Ces. & De Not. Zoned black fungus, Plate 2, fig. 4.

0.5-3 cm. in diameter, sessile, centrally attached, subglobose, blackish-purple, internally made up of concentric zones also blackish in color; plants sometimes are somewhat stipitate.—On stumps, logs, etc., North Dakota, Maine, Florida.

D. vernicosa (Schw.) Ces. & De Not. Zoned black fungus.

Similar to preceding but laterally compressed, plainly stipitate, and becoming hollow by gelatinization of parts of entostroma.—Northern and eastern United States.

HYPOXYLON Fr. Plate 2.

Stroma globose to pulvinate to effused, erumpent, fleshy when young, leathery, woody, or carbonaceous when mature; perithecia several to many in stroma; paraphyses numerous, thread-like; asci cylindrical, arranged on sides and bottom of perithecium; ascospores brown to black, with an elongate hyaline depression, uniseriate in the ascus; conidial layer formed first on an exposed ectostroma, later developing on old stromata in favorable weather; conidiophores branched, hyphomycetous, hyaline to greenish-brown; conidia minute, borne apically, one to many, becoming lateral by the sympodial growth of the hypha.

H. Howeianum Peck. Brick-colored Hypoxylon.

Stroma 3-12 mm. in diameter, 3-8 mm. high, asci 80-100 μ long, ascospores 6-9 x 3-3.5 μ

Globose, never effused or pulvinate, bright brick-red, finally darkening to almost black.—On species of oak and sometimes on other hosts, throughout our area.

H. rubiginosum Fr. Red Hypoxylon. Plate 2, fig. 5.

Stroma small, effused or pulvinate, bright brick-red or reddish brown, variable in color with moisture, finally black in age; interior of ectostroma always colored, entostroma always dark; asci 70-80 μ

long for spore-bearing part, stalk of ascus 65-80 μ long; ascospores 9-12 x 4-6 μ; in old stromata the ostiole stuffed with a white mycelial growth.—On various deciduous woods, throughout area.

XYLARIA (Hill) Schrank.   Plate 2.

Stromata clavate to cylindrical, usually hard and with an appearance of burnt wood.

1   Plants cylindrical, filiform, on decaying magnolia leaves, rose-colored ....*X. filiformis*
1' Plants clavate..........2
2   Plants velvety or tomentose, at least toward base......3
2' Not as above...........4
3   Two or three times dichotomously branched, velvety at first...
....*X. digitata.*
3' Simple or variously branched, woolly-tomentose at base ....*X. Hypoxylon.*
4   Surface commonly cracked into minute areas, with a spongy tubercular base...........................*X. corniformis.*
4' Not so marked, often lobate-divided at apex..*X. polymorpha.*

X. polymorpha Pers. (edible).   Plate 2, fig. 11.

3-11 cm. high, 1-3 cm. thick, cylindrical, somewhat compressed, often lobate-divided at apex, irregular in shape, long-obovate if un-branched, dark brown to black, hard, firm, the fertile part much longer than the stem; stem enlarged gradually into head; head roughly elliptical in section.—Solitary or caespitose on decaying logs, maple roots, etc., common in temperate North America

X. corniformis Mont.   Horn Xylaria.   Plate 2, fig. 13.

3-5 cm. high, 4-5 mm. thick, clavate, not compressed, obtuse at apex, white then brownish-black, surface commonly minutely areolate-rimose, roughened by papilliform ostioles; plant arising from a spongy tubercular base, two or three commonly connected at base.—Scattered or subgregarious on decaying magnolia and maple logs, etc., Michigan, New York, Texas.

X. digitata Grev.   Plate 2, fig 10.

Height 2-4 cm.; spores 12-16 x 5-6 μ; erect, clavate, dark brown, velvety at first, then glabrate, 2-3 dichotomously divided, at first covered with a white conidial hymenium, narrowed below into a short stem, ending above in a sterile apex; spores dark brown, in one series, overlapping in the ascus, navicular-fusoid.—Caespitose on rotten wood, Indiana, New York, North Carolina, and Texas.

X. Hypoxylon Grev.   Plate 2, fig. 9.

5-8 cm. in height, erect, simple or variously branched, round or compressed, black, woolly-tomentose at base, lanceolate, the tip sterile; stem short, distinct from the fertile head which is roughened by prominent ostioles.—Common on rotton wood, temperate North America.

X. filiformis Alb. & Schw.

On decaying magnolia leaves, rose-colored, 1 mm. thick, cylindrical, 4-7 cm. high.—Probably the range of the host.

GEOGLOSSACEAE.   Plate 2.

Mostly club-shaped or clavate plants, much like the simple Clavarias with which they were placed by early mycologists. Asci arise directly from the surface and form a uniform stratum over it.

See Durand, E. J. Ann. Mycology 6:387-477, pl. 5-22, 1908; Mycology 13:184-187, 1921.

MITRULA Pers.   Plate 2, fig. 14.

Fructifications fleshy, erect, stipitate, clavate, fertile only above, the ascigerous part elliptical to subglobose, recognizable from the stem either by shape or by contrast of color, brightly colored, the stem usually white.

M. irregularis (Peck) Durand.

Geoglossum irregulare Peck.
M. vitellina of most authors.
M. luteola Ellis.
M. crispata Berk.

Plants 1.5-5 cm. high, fertile ½-⅔ of length; asci 90-150 x 5-6 μ; spores 6-10 x 4-5 μ.

Plants clavate, irregular in form, twisted, compressed, obtuse, sometimes lobed, ascigerous (fertile) portion vitelline-yellow; stem tapering downward, pruinose, satiny-white, the substance yellowish-white; spores uniseriate, eight, hyaline, smooth often slightly reniform.—Caespitose or rarely solitary on bare soil and moist mossy ground or among pine needles, Sept.-Nov., New Brunswick to Virginia, west to Minnesota.

M. phalloides (Bull.) Chev.   Plate 2, fig. 14.
M. paludosa Fr.
Leotia elegans Berk.
L. uliginosa Grev.
M. laricina Vill.

Plants 2-6 cm. high; 4-10 mm. wide; stem 1.5-2 mm. thick, 4/5 of plant-height; asci 60-150 x 6-8 μ; spores 10-18 x 3 μ.

Fertile (ascigerous) part clear vitelline-yellow, sharply differentiated from the satiny-white or pinkish stem, solid, becoming vesicled or inflated and hollow when old, elliptic to obovate or pyriform, the apex rounded, somewhat furrowed longitudinally below, often somewhat compressed; the whole plant soft and tremellose; stem terete, often flexuose; spores eight, biseriate, hyaline, smooth.—Solitary or densely gregarious, as many as 10-20 aggregated and cohering at bases, on decaying vegetation, especially on sphagnum in wet places Apr.-June, Ontario, Alabama, to British Columbia.

MICROGLOSSUM Gill.   Plate 2, fig. 15-19.

Plants with the aspect of *Mitrula* or *Geoglossum*, fleshy, erect, stipitate, fertile in upper portion only, brightly colored (yellow, brown, or green); ascus opening by a pore; spores eight, biseriate, elliptical to fusiform, 3-many-septate, paraphyses present.

1   Plants pea-green, stem squammulose..............*M. viride.*
1'   Not so colored..................2
    2   Plants bright yellow........................*M. rufum.*
    2'   Plants yellowish-clay or tawny...............*M. fumosum.*
    2"   Plants cinnamon or olivaceous....3
3   Plants cinnamon-brown.....................*M. longisporum.*
3'   Plants olivaceous or greenish; stem smooth, glabrous
      ....*M. olivaceus.*

M. rufum Underw.   Plate 2, fig. 15.
G. luteum Peck.
M. lutescens Berk.
Leptoglossum luteum (Peck) Sacc.

Plants 2-5 cm. high, 6-12 mm. wide; spores 5-10 septate, 18-38 x 5-6 μ.

Plants clavate, slender; ascigerous portion ⅓-½ length of plant, elliptic-ovate to subcylindrical, obtuse, usually compressed or longitudinally furrowed, distinct from stem, clear vitelline or orange-yellow, rarely dull; stem terete, yellow, squamulose; whole plant drying to dingy-yellowish or reddish-brown.—Solitary to subcaespitose on rotton wood or humus, rarely on mossy banks, frequent, July-Sept., Minnesota, Ontario, Louisiana.

M. fumosum (Peck) Durand. Plate 2, fig. 16.

Plants 2-6 cm. high, 3-12 mm. thick; stem 1-3 cm. long; spores 2-seriate, 20-50 x 5 μ, 7-15-septate.

Plants clavate, robust; ascigerous portion obovate or oblong, with rounded apex, more or less compressed and furrowed, ⅓-½ total length of plant, but little distinct from stem, smoky-yellowish-clay color or tawny; stem terete or slightly compressed, rather fibrous, clay-colored.—Solitary or densely caespitose on much decayed logs or about stumps, July-Aug., northern U. S. Reported from Massachusetts, New York.

M. longisporum Durand. Plate 2, fig. 17.

Plants solitary, gregarious, clavate, often curved or contorted, rich cinnamon brown, 3-6 cm. high; ascigerous portion ⅓-½ of total length, slightly differentiated from stem, oblong to elliptical, obtuse, more or less compressed and longitudinally furrowed, slightly darker than stem, often umber tinted, 1-2.5 cm. long, 4-10 mm. wide; flesh yellowish-brown; stem terete, squamulose, sometimes viscid below, 2-4 cm. long, 2-4 mm. thick, equal.—On the ground among leaves in midst of grasses and sedges, in rich woods and ravines; Aug., New York, North Carolina, Michigan.

M. olivaceum (Pers.) Gill. Plate 2, fig. 18.
Geoglossum olivaceum Pers.
Mitrula olivacea (Pers.) Sacc.

Plants 2-8 cm. high, clavate, regular or twisted; ascigerous part ⅓-½ of total length, not distinct from stem except in color, greenish-brown, compressed, obtuse, up to 3 cm. long, 1 cm. wide; stem terete or compressed above, smooth, shining, hygrophanous, tawny-buff or olivaceous.—Solitary or clustered among fallen leaves or grass in rich woods, May-Sept., northern U. S.

Known by its greenish-buff or smoky tint and fibrous stem.

M. viride (Pers.) Gill. Plate 2, fig. 19.

Plants clavate, up to 5 cm. high; ascigerous part ½ of total length, lanceolate, compressed and furrowed, 3-10 mm. wide, olive-buff or olive-ochraceous; stem slightly compressed, 2-5 mm. thick, conspicuously squamulose, pale-pea-green; crushed flesh pea-green to olive.—Solitary to caespitose on ground in moist woods, June-Oct., eastern U. S.

Recognized by its pea-green color and squamulose stem.

CORYNETES Hazel.

Leptoglossum Cooke.
Xanthoglossum Sacc.

Plants fleshy, erect, stalked, clavate; hymenium black, brownish-black or purplish-black; spores hyaline, smooth, cylindrical, 3-many septate, paraphyses present. It differs from *Geoglossum* in its hyaline spores and from *Microglossum* in the black color of the ascomata.

C. purpurascens (Pers.) Durand.
Geoglossum purpurascens Homsk.
Leotia atropurpurea Corda.
Mitrula purpurascens Pers.

Plants 3-6 cm. high, 1 cm. broad, with a distinct purplish-brown tint on every part when fresh, blackish when dry; crushed flesh vinous-brown; ascigerous portion $\frac{1}{3}$-$\frac{1}{2}$ total length, 1-2 cm. long, 1 cm. wide, irregular, clavate, sometimes forked at apex, more or less compressed; stem cylindrical, minutely squamulose.—Solitary or caespitose on ground or humus, Aug.-Oct., probably throughout northern U. S.

C. robustus Durand.

Plants black or brownish-black, 2.5-8 cm. high, stout; ascigerous portion $\frac{1}{4}$-$\frac{1}{2}$ total length, black tinged with olive-brown, pyriform-elliptical, obtuse, 1-3 cm. long x 6-15 mm. broad, more or less compressed, longitudinally furrowed; flesh dark brown; stem terete or compressed, paler, hygrophanous, 1-4 cm. high, 3-8 mm. thick.—Solitary or gregarious on rich sandy humus among leaves in damp woods, Aug.-Sept., Maine to Mississippi.

GLOEOGLOSSUM Durand.   Plate 2, fig. 22.

"Ascoma viscid-gelatinous, erect, stipitate, clavate, usually ascigerous only in upper portion, black or brownish-black."

"Plants with aspect of *Geoglossum* but of viscid-gelatinous consistency when fresh, and further characterized by the fact that the paraphyses are not confined to the hymenium but continue with unchanged form down the stem to its base thus forming a thick gelatinous ectal layer over it." Durand, Mycol. 6:387-477.

G. glutinosum (Pers.) Durand.   Plate 2, fig. 22.
Geoglossum glutinosum Pers.

Plants 5-8 cm. high, viscid-gelatinous; ascigerous portion clavate, more or less compressed, apex obtuse, 1.5-2.5 cm. long, 5-10 mm. thick, black, not sharply differentiated from stem; stem very smooth and viscid, slightly compressed, brown or brownish-black.—Solitary or clustered on the ground and on rotten wood in rich woods, July-Sept., Ontario, North Carolina.

G. difforme (Fr.) Durand.
Geoglossum difforme Fr.
Plants smooth, viscid, evenly clavate, with no line of demarcation between fertile part and stem, strongly compressed, 3-6 cm. high, 8-14 mm. wide, black, apex obtuse, flesh brown.—Gregarious or solitary on soil, humus, rotten wood, and pine needles in rich woods, July-Sept., Minnesota, Maine, Florida.

GEOGLOSSUM Pers. Plate 2, fig. 26 and 27.

Plants fleshy, erect, stipitate, clavate, hymenium covering the upper portion only, black or brownish-black, not viscid but fleshy; spores dark, elongated, paraphyses not forming a thick coating over stem.

G. glabrum Pers. Plate 2, fig. 26.
G. sphagnophilum Ehrenb.
G. difforme Cooke.
G. simile Peck.
Plants 3-7 cm. high; ascigerous portion black, about ⅓ total length of plant, lanceolate, compressed, 1-3 cm. long, 3-8 mm. thick, obtuse or acute, not sharply delimited from stem; stem terete to slightly compressed, brownish-black, rather slender, densely squamulose, 2-5 cm. high, 1.5-5 (commonly 2) mm. thick.—Solitary on very rotten wood or rarely on soil, July-Sept., Maine, Florida, westward to California.

G. nigritum Cooke. Black Geoglossum. Plate 2, fig. 27.
Plants black or brownish-black; ascigerous portion acute, ½ total length of plant; stem slender, 1-2 mm. thick, almost smooth.—On wet ground among leaves, rarely on rotten wood, Aug.-Oct., Maine to North Carolina and California.

TRICHOGLOSSUM Boud. Plate 2, fig. 6.

Differs from *Geoglossum* in that the stem and hymenium are beset with black, thick-walled, acicular spines or cystidia.

T. velutipes (Peck) Durand. Velvet-stemmed Trichoglossum. Plate 2, fig. 6.
Geoglossum velutipes Peck.
Plants up to 10 cm. high, black or brownish-black; ascigerous portion lanceolate to subrotund, ⅕-⅓ the total length of the plant, 3-10 mm. long, 4-10 mm. thick, more or less compressed, rounded above,

usually distinctly delimited from stem; stem terete-flexuous, 2-3 mm. thick, black, velvety, equal. —Solitary or gregarious on soil, humus, and rotten wood, Aug.-Sept., Vermont to North Carolina, Minnesota.

The species is distinguished also by its tetrasporous asci and 8-11-septate spores.

T. hirsutum Pers.

Plants 3-8 cm. high, velvety-black; ascigerous portion hollow, elliptical to lanceolate, obtuse, more or less compressed, up to 1.5 cm. long and 0.5-0.75 cm. thick, ⅕ as long as stem from which it is rather distinct; stem equal, terete, up to 6 cm. x 2-3 mm.; known from other species of genus by its long, regularly 15-septate spores, tapering toward each end from above the middle.—On rotten wood and humus or among leaves, Ontario to Louisiana and California.

SPATHULARIA Pers.   Plate 2, fig. 7 & 8.

Plants fleshy, erect, stipitate, the spathulate ascigerous portion much compressed, fan-shaped-decurrent on opposite sides of the stem, sharply delimited from stem, brightly colored; ascus clavate, opening by a pore.   The plants differ from those of other genera by their brightly colored ascomata which spread out like fans.

S. clavata (Schaeff.) Sacc.   Plate 2, fig. 7

Plants up to 10 cm. high, pallid, then yellowish or brownish; ascigerous portion much compressed, fan-shaped, usually radiately rugose, irregular, darker than the stem, often twisted, clavate, lobed or almost capitate and decurrent on stem, ⅓-½ of total length of the plant, up to 2.5 cm. wide; stem hollow, 1 cm. in diameter, terete or somewhat compressed, usually gregarious in circles on soil or among needles under pine trees, July-Oct., Maine to California.

S. velutipes (Cooke) Farl.   Velvet-stemmed Spathularia.   Plate 2, fig. 8.

Plants up to 5 cm. high, 1-3 cm. wide; fertile part yellowish to brownish-yellow, decurrent on opposite sides of stem, the margin rounded, often lobed or incised, about 1 cm. high at apex; stem terete or compressed, 2-4 cm. high, 1-1.5 cm. broad above, 3-5 mm. thick at base, solid, bay-brown, minutely velvety, attached to the substratum by the orange mycelium.—Gregarious on rotten logs, among pine needles, and on humus, Aug.-Sept., Minnesota, New Hampshire, North Carolina.

LEOTIA Pers.   Plate 2, fig. 23-25.

Ascoma more or less gelatinous, erect, borne on stems; fertile portion pileate, horizontal, supported in center, the hymenium spread over the upper surface.

L. lubrica (Scop.) Pers.   Plate 2, fig. 23.

Plants 3-6 cm. high, densely clustered, more or less viscid-gelatinous, ochraceous-yellow, often changing in age or in drying to a greenish or olive tint; spore-bearing portion pileate, wrinkled or nodulose, 1-1.5 cm. broad, convex above, the surface often irregularly furrowed, the margin recurved; stem cylindrical or somewhat compressed, the surface often undulate, 1 cm. thick below, 0.5 cm. above, minutely squamulose sometimes with greenish granules; asci narrowly clavate, 130-160 x 10-12 μ; spores 8 in an ascus, hyaline, smooth, subfusiform, 18-28 x 6 μ, becoming 5-7-septate.—Frequent on sandy moss-covered soil in open woods, Iowa, Wisconsin, Ontario, New England, Alabama.

L. stipitata Bosc.   Plate 2, fig 24.

Plants 3-6 cm. or more high, viscid-gelatinous; head 1-2 cm. broad, deep green, whitish below, irregularly nodulose, even, subglobose or much depressed at apex; stem 2-5 cm. x 0.5-1 cm., cylindrical, white or pale-ochraceous, often beset with green squamules.—Infrequent, among mosses, in rich woods, California to Maine, Florida.

Known by its deep blue-green pileus and light yellow stem. It does not intergrade with other species.

L. chlorocephala Schw.   Green Leotia.   Plate 2, fig. 25

Plants 1-5 cm. high; head 2-10 mm. wide; smooth or furrowed, lobed or nodulose, pea-green to aeruginous; stem 1-4.5 cm. x 2-4 mm., cylindrical, firm, the surface densely squamulose with green granules, green changing but little when dried.—Sandy soil in rich woods, Minnesota, New Hampshire, Alabama.

CUDONIA Fr.   Plate 2, fig. 20 & 21.

Ascoma stipitate, erect, fleshy-leathery; fertile portion pileate; hymenium on upper surface, margin acute, incurved.

C. circinans (Pers.) Fr.   Plate 2, fig 21.

Leotia circinans Pers.
Vibrissea circinans Pers.

Plants fleshy, becoming leathery with drying, 2-6 cm. high; ascigerous portion 0.5-2 cm. broad, rather thin, the margin acute, even or wavy, the hymenium convex, even, wrinkled, folded, or twisted, cream-colored with a faint rosy tint, or yellowish or pale-brownish; stem equal or tapering upward, stout; upper pileus striate, the striae prolonged as radiating lines on lower pileus; odor and taste farinaceous.—Solitary or gregarious on rotten wood, humus, or among fallen leaves, July-Sept., Maine to California and northward.

C. lutea (Peck) Sacc. Plate 2, fig. 20.

Plants 1-6 (usually 3) cm. high, fleshy-leathery; pileus convex, margin acute, reflexed; hymenium on upper surface at first covered by a volva-like membrane which cracks irregularly and falls away leaving remnants on margin, deep orange-buff or flesh colored, radiating striae commonly present on lower surface and continuing down the almost terete stem; stem pale yellow, mealy, 1-5 cm. high, 2-5 mm. thick.—Solitary or gregarious on decaying leaves in thickets, Aug.-Sept., Ontario to Tennessee.

INCERTAE SEDIS

PHAEOBULGARIA Seav. Plate 3, fig. 10.

Plant inoperculate, blackish with an internal gelatinous layer; substance thick.

P. inquinans (Fr.) Seav.
Bulgaria inquinans Fr.
Peziza inquinans Pers.
Peziza polymorpha Oed.
Subglobose-expanded to concave, brownish-black, opening by a circular aperture, the margin incurved, 2-5 cm. in diameter, finally shallowly cup-shaped; hymenium a black jelly-like layer about 6 mm. thick.—Attached to decaying sticks and moist logs in wet woods, frequent, Minnesota, New England, and southward.

PEZIZACEAE

Fruiting bodies (apothecia) cup-shaped to discoid or rarely convex, naked to hairy, scarlet, yellow, brown, black cinerous or white, stemmed or sessile; ascus cylindric to oval, opening by a lid (operculate) or by a slit, which makes the apex two-lipped (bilabiate). The hymenium is within the cup or on the upper side of disk. The great majority of these species grow to maturity in May. Many species of small size have not been included in this treatment.

See Dodge, B. O. Trans. Wis. Acad. Sci. Arts and Lettrs. 17:1027-1056, Madison, 1914; Durand, E. J. Bul. Torrey Bot. Club 27:463-495, pl. 27-32, 1900; Graham, V. O. Trans Ill. Acad. Sci. 25:120-121, 1932; Krieger, L.C.C. A Guide to the higher fungi of New York state, Univ. of the state of N. Y., Albany, 1935; Seaver, F. J. North American Cup Fungi (Operculates), 45 pl. the author, 1928.

PSEUDOPLECTANIA Fuckel

Apothecia cup-shaped, fleshy or cartilaginous, blackish, orange, or greenish; externally covered with short, often coiled or twisted hairs; hymenium concave, black or orange; asci cylindrical, each with eight globose spores; paraphyses very slender.

P. fulgens (Pers.) Fuckel. Plate 3, fig. 1.

Plants cup-shaped, regular or irregular in form, sometimes split on one side, 0.5-2.5 cm. in diameter, clothed externally with flexuous hairs, attached to substratum by a dense mass of mycelium, stem short or none; hymenium pale orange, becoming olivaceous or greenish; ascus cylindrical, tapering to a long base, 10 μ in diameter; spores hyaline 6-8 μ, filled with orange granules.—Scattered on soil in coniferous woods; New York to the Pacific Ocean, not common.

P. nigrella Pers. Plate 3, fig. 2.

About the same size and shape as *P. fulgens* and more distinctly stemmed; hymenium brownish-black.—On decaying wood among sphagnum. New Jersey to Manitoba and Alabama.

P. vogesiaca (Pers.) Seav. Plate 3, fig. 3.

Stem about 2 cm. long, 2 mm. in diameter; hymenium dark olive.—Among sphagnum on decaying wood among conifers; New England to Washington.

LAMPROSPORA De Not.

Apothecia at first globose, then spreading to discoid, substance soft and fleshy, waxy, commonly discoid, externally glabrous; hymenium concave, plane, or convex; spores sculptured, spiny or smooth.

L. trachycarpa (Curr.) Seav.
Peziza scabrosa Cooke.
Aleuria trachycarpa Gill.

Crowded, often confluent, forming masses over several centimeters, subglobose-expanding to shallow-cup-shaped with the margin elevated and incurved, sometimes shield-shaped and adhering closely to the substratum, externally paler than hymenium, 2 mm. to 2 cm. in diameter; hymenium dark reddish-brown, becoming black with age; spores warted, pale yellow or smoky, about 16 μ in diameter; ascus cylindrical.—On burnt ground or on charcoal, not uncommon, New England to Rocky Mountains.

ALEURIA Fuckel. Plate 3.

Fruiting body sessile or with stem, externally glabrous or with delicate white hairs; hymenium bright orange or reddish-orange; apothecium plane, cup-shaped, or twisted.

A. aurantia (Pers.) Fuckel. Golden Aleuria. Plate 3, fig. 21.
Peziza aurantia Pers.
Otidea aurantia Mass.

At first globose, gradually expanding to a shallow cup 3-6 cm. in diameter, then becoming irregular and variously twisted or rarely one-sided and split; hymenium bright orange; asci cylindric, 200 x 15 μ; spores in 1 series in the ascus, 12-15 μ long, reticulated.— Gregarious on damp soil in open places, May and autumn, Newfoundland and West Virginia to California, Europe, common.

A. wisconsinensis Rehm. Plate 3, fig. 22.

Becoming discoid, 5-20 mm. in diameter, narrowed at base into a stem-like attachment; margin thick, entire, becoming somewhat convolute, externally light-colored, yellowish, tomentose; hymenium slightly concave or plane, bright orange-red; asci subcylindrical, 200 x 10 μ; spores in 1 series in the ascus, each containing 2 oil-droplets, hyaline, 7 x 15 μ, reticulated.—Gregarious on damp soil in open places, Minnesota, Wisconsin.

A. rutilans (Fr.) Gill. Plate 3, fig. 6.

Closed, later open and turbinate, externally whitish to pale orange, diameter 1 cm.; margin crenate, and fringed with scattered delicate hairs; hymenium orange.—On dead mosses, New England to Iowa.

A. rhenana Fuckel. Plate 3, fig. 7.

Cup-shaped, externally white, tomentose, 1-2 cm. in diameter, half as deep; stems 1-2 cm. long, irregular, clinging together in clumps, arising from a dense mass of white mycelium which binds the leaf mould together; hymenium bright orange; asci cylindric above and tapering and twisted below, 350 x 15 μ; spores in one series in the ascus, 12 x 20 μ, reticulated; paraphyses filled with orange granules. —On soil in conifer woods, Pennsylvania, west to Washington, south to Alabama.

MELASTIZA Boud.

Cup-shaped or shield-shaped; hymenium bright colored, clothed externally with flexuous or bristle-like hairs; spore-surface sculptured or reticulate.

M. Charteri (W. G. Smith) Boud.   Plate 3, fig. 26.

Becoming nearly plane, regular in outline, the margin wavy in age, 1-1.5 cm. in diameter, externally clothed with tufts of poorly developed hairs, pale brown; hymenium bright red; asci cylindric, tapering below, 300 x 12 μ; spores 12 x 18 μ, 1-seriate in the ascus, with reticulated surface, two oil-droplets within.—On bare soil or among mosses, New York to Colorado.

PATELLA Weber

Fruiting body sessile, discoid or shield-shaped, externally setose; hymenium red, yellow, brown, or white, concave or plane; hairs septate; asci usually 8-spored.

1   Hymenium bright red..............2
1' Hymenium white ....*P. albida.*
2   Apothecia fringed with white hairs; on rotten wood.*P. scutellata.*
2' Apothecia fringed with brown hairs; on wet soil. .*P. umbrorum.*

P. scutellata (L.) Morg.
Peziza scutellata L.
Lachnea scutellata Gill

Apothecia few or many, globose then flattened and discoid, 0.6-1.2 cm. in diameter, the margin slightly elevated and fringed with hairs up to 1 mm. long; hymenium bright vermillion-red, fading to pale yellow when dried; spores 12-15 x 20-24 μ, decorated with minute warts.—Common on rotten wood, in swamps and bogs, throughout the United States.

P. umbrorum (Fr.) Seav.
Peziza umbrorum Fr.
Lachnea umbrorum Gill.

In general aspect resembling the preceding species but differing in the color of the fringing hairs; apothecia 0.5-1 cm. in diameter, often crowded, globose then expanding to discoid, appearing dark-brown because of the covering of dark hairs; fringing hairs up to 1 mm. long, dark red-brown; hymenium bright scarlet; spores 13 x 23 μ, decorated with warts.—On damp soil, rarely on rotten wood, New York to Colorado, West Virginia and New Mexico, common.

P. albida (Schaeff.) Seav.
Lachnea hemispherica Gill.

Apothecia scattered, globose and closed then expanding to con-cave-hemispheric, up to 2-3 cm. in diameter, $\frac{1}{2}$ to $\frac{1}{3}$ as deep, externally clothed with tufted hairs which form a fringe on the margin; hymenium white becoming yellowish-brown in dried specimens; spores 1-seriate in the ascus, 12-15 x 25-27 μ.—On soil, occasionally on rotten wood, Maine to Manitoba, Kansas and North Carolina, occasional.

PLECTANIA Fuckel.   Plate 3.

Subglobose then expanding, externally hairy, usually with stem, the margin often incurved; hymenium scarlet; spores smooth.

P. coccinea (Scop.) Fuckel. Scarlet Plectania, scarlet cup (edible). Plate 3, fig. 5.
Peziza coccinea Jacq.
Sarcoscypha coccinea Sacc.
Deep-cup-shaped, with a stem or occasionally sessile, 2-5 cm. in diameter, half as deep, externally white, floccose, with mycelial hairs, the margin usually incurved; hymenium deeply concave, bright scarlet, stem 5 mm. thick and up to 3 cm. long, the length varying with depth of buried sticks; asci 450 x 14 μ, cylindric, tapering to a stem-like base.—Frequent, on sticks in woods Apr. and Nov., New England to Pacific Ocean, south to Virginia.

P. floccosa (Schw.) Seav. Fringed fairy cup. Plate 3, fig. 4.
Peziza floccosa Schw.
Deep-funnel-shaped, narrowed to a stem 2-6 cm. long, 5-15 mm. in diameter and about twice as deep, externally clothed with shaggy hairs which give the margin a fringed appearance; hymenium scarlet; asci 300 x 20 μ, subcylindric and abruptly narrowed to stem-like base; spores 16 x 28 μ, 1-seriate in the ascus.—Gregarious on buried sticks and decaying logs in rich woods, New England to Iowa and Virginia.

P. hiemalis (Nees & Bernst.) Seav. Plate 3, fig. 27.
Peziza cruciata Fr.
Sarcoscypha alpina Ell. & Everh.
Deep-funnel-shaped, 1 cm. in diameter, borne on a stem 3-4 cm. long, at length shallow-cup-shaped with a lobed margin, often reflexed, externally clothed with white, flexuous, soft hairs; hymenium bright red to scarlet; stem 2 mm. in diameter, gradually enlarging into the base of the cup; asci 250 x 20 μ.—Solitary or caespitose on ground in woods, Wisconsin to Colorado, very rare.

P. occidentalis (Schw.) Seav.   Plate 3, fig. 28.
Sarcoscypha occidentalis Sacc.
Peziza hesperidea Cooke & Peck.
Geopyxis hesperidea Sacc.
Shallow-cup-shaped to discoid on a stem up to 3 cm. in length, gregarious or caespitose, externally whitish; hymenium scarlet; spore containing two oil-drops and many granules.—On buried sticks, New England to Nebraska, south to Louisiana.

SCODELLINA S. F. Gray.   Plate 3, fig. 8.

Plants shallow cup-shaped to higher than wide and twisted shell-form, larger or medium sized, often branched and with a short stem-like base, asymmetrical, split on one side, externally furfuraceous.

1 About twice as high as broad. 2
1' Broader than high, externally brownish with a yellowish or olive tinge, growing in conifer woods. . . . .*S. grandis.*
2 Hymenium bright yellow or yellow-brown. . . . .*S. leporina.*
2' Hymenium darker, becoming brownish-black in age. .*S. auricula.*

S. grandis (Pers.) Seav.

Shallow-cup-shaped, the margin incurved, usually split on one side nearly to base, the split edge inrolled, externally pruinose above the tomentose base, dark olive-brown externally, 3-6 cm. in diameter, half as deep; hymenium pale yellow; asci 280 x 12 μ; spores in 1 series in the ascus, 8 x 16 μ.—Caespitose on soil in conifer woods, Wisconsin to New England and southward.

S. leporina (Batsch) S. F. Gray.   Split Peziza.   Plate 3, fig. 8.
Peziza onotica Pers.
Otidea onotica Fuckel.
Strongly elongated on one side, split on opposite side to the base, externally bright brownish-yellow, becoming dull with age, 3-6 cm. high, half as broad; hymenium similar in color; asci 200 x 11 μ; spores 8 x 14 μ, each containing 2 oil-drops.—Scattered on soil in woods, New York to Pacific Ocean, not rare in the spring.

S. auricula (Schaeff.) Seav.
Aleuria auricula Gill.
Peziza auricula Cooke.
Otidea neglecta Mass.
3-5 cm. high, half as broad, spoon-shaped or ear-shaped, elongated on one side, split on opposite side to the base, externally bright yel-

low, becoming brownish-yellow but lighter toward the base; hymenium somewhat darker; asci 250 x 20 μ.—Scattered on ground in woods, Alberta to Wisconsin, south to Florida.

WYNNEA Berk. & Curt. Plate 3, fig. 14.

Firm, subcartilaginous, tough, each branch elongate-ear-shaped, branching from the base, from a buried sclerotium.

W. americana Thaxt. Plate 3, fig. 14.

Sclerotium tough, subgelatinous, to 4 cm. in diameter, main axis divided immediately above sclerotium, the clusters of apothecia of variable number and size, 6-13 cm. high, elongate-ear-shaped, externally black-brown, minutely warty; hymenium dark purple-brown; asci large, 500 x 18 μ.—Caespitose on ground in rich woods, Ohio and Indiana to Tennessee.

URNULA Fr. Plate 3, fig. 11.

Apothecium commonly deeply bowl-shaped or ovoid, tomentose, opening stellate or by a number of radiate slits through apex, the margin crenate.

U. craterium (Schw.) Fr. Plate 3, fig. 11.

Apothecium ovoid, 2-4 cm. in diameter, 4-6 cm. deep, tough and leathery, closed then opening with star-shaped aperture with a crenate, notched, and inrolled margin, externally brownish-black or black, hymenium brownish-black; stem 2-4 cm. long, 5-10 mm. in diameter, attached by black mycelium.—On ground in woods, often near rock outcrops, North Dakota, New York, North Carolina.

PAXINA Kuntze. Plate 3, fig. 12, 13 & 15.

Cup-shaped on a stem, externally hairy or tomentose, substance tough; stem usually stout or sometimes slender, sometimes immersed in ground.

1 Hymenium darker than external part of apothecium...........2
1' Hymenium lighter than outside of apothecium...............9

  2 Stem thick and strongly lacunose or corrugated...........5
  2' Stem slender and little if at all corrugated, apothecium 2-3
    cm. in diameter........3

3 Apothecium roughened by tufts of hair........4
3' Apothecium grayish or whitish-tomentose, stem 3-4 cm.
    long ....*P. hispida.*

4   Apothecium ashy to yellowish-brown, hymenium brownish,
    stem usually smooth......................*P. subclavipes.*
4′ Apothecium yellowish or yellowish-brown, hymenium dark-
    brown to blackish, stem slightly corrugated....*P. Dupainii.*

5   Corrugations extending almost to margin of apothecium
    ....*P. Acetabulum.*
5′ Corrugations extending only to base of apothecium........6
    6   Stem up to 5 cm. long.......................*P. macropus.*
    6′ Stem not over 3 cm. long........7

7   Stem flattened and grooved on opposite sides......*P. platypodia.*
7′ Stem round or angular........8
    8   Apothecium white to ashy, conspicuouly tomentose
        ....*P. leucomelas.*
    8′ Apothecium minutely roughened by hair-clusters, ashy to
        brown ....*P. sulcata.*

9   Stem deeply corrugated; apothecium deep-cup-shaped, large,
    2-5 cm. in diameter, 2-3 cm. deep.................*P. semitosta.*
9′ Stem but slightly corrugated; apothecium 2-3 cm. in diameter,
    1 cm. deep ....*P. fusicarpa.*

P. Acetabulum Kuntze.   Plate 3, fig. 15.

Cup ashy to brownish; 3-6 cm. in diameter, 2-4 cm. deep, on a
stem 1-2 cm. long and 1 cm. in diameter, deeply furrowed and ridged,
lacunose, the ridges much branched and extending up sides of cup to
margin; hymenium darker, brown to brownish-black.—On ground
in open places in woods, Minnesota to New England and Alabama,
May-June.

P. macropus (Clem.) Seav.   Plate 3, fig. 31.

Cup 3-5 cm. in diameter, 1 cm. deep, shallow, ashy white, clothed
especially toward margin with short septate hairs; hymenium darker,
brownish; stem tough, solid, 4-5 cm. long, 5-8 mm. in diameter,
with three or four ribs running lengthwise.—On damp ground, Wisconsin to Colorado, not common.

P. platypodia (Boud.) Seav.
Macropodia platypodia Dodge.

Cup rather shallow, asymmetrical, 2-3 cm. in diameter, 2 cm. deep,
ashy, clothed with conic hair-clusters; hymenium darker, brownish-
black; stem 2-3 cm. long, 4-5 mm. thick, pruinose.—On ground, scattered, Wisconsin.

P. leucomelas (Pers.) Kuntze. Plate 3, fig. 12.

Cup deep, 2-3 cm. in diameter, 2 cm. deep, tomentose externally with conspicuously clustered hairs, whitish; hymenium brownish-black; stem short and thick, up to 1 cm. long, 5-8 mm. thick, strongly ribbed to base of cup; spores 12 x 22 μ, each with 1 large oil-drop.—Gregarious on ground, Wisconsin and westward to California.

P. sulcata (Pers.) Kuntze. Plate 3, fig. 13.

Shallow-cup-shaped on a short stem, 2-3 cm. in diameter, half as deep, externally ashy to brown, minutely roughened by poorly developed hairs; hymenium brownish-black; stem 5-20 mm. long, ribbed to base of cup, yellowish or white; asci 275 x 16 μ, spores 13 x 18 μ, each with one large oil-drop.—Gregarious on ground in woods, New Jersey to Iowa.

P. hispida (Schaeff.) Seav. Plate 3, fig. 30.

Aleuria macropus Gill.

Cup-shaped, 2-3 cm. in diameter, 1 cm. deep, densely white-tomentose; hymenium light-colored, becoming brownish with age; stem slender, 2-4 cm. long, 3-4 mm. in diameter at base, 2 mm. at top, smooth or scarcely lacunose; tomentum of conical bunches of hairs; asci clavate, 250 x 18 μ.—Gregarious on ground in woods, Minnesota to Maine, and southward, also in Colorado.

P. subclavipes (Phill. & Ell.) Seav.

Cup-shaped, up to 2 cm. in diameter, half as deep, ashy to yellowish or rarely olive-brown, rough with hair-clusters; hymenium brownish; stem slender, smooth, 2-10 mm. long, 2 mm. thick; asci 250 x 18 μ, cylindrical.—Gregarious on ground in woods, New York to Iowa, south to Texas and South Carolina.

P. Dupainii (Boud.) Seav.

Cup-shaped, up to 3 cm. in diameter, 1 cm. deep, externally rough with conical hair-clusters, yellow-brown; hymenium very dark brown or blackish; stem yellowish, swollen at base; asci 300 x 15 μ.—On ground, Wisconsin.

P. semitosta (Berk. & Curt.) Seav. Plate 3, fig. 25.

Deep-cup-shaped, 2-5 cm. in diameter, 2-3 cm. deep, brown, densely clothed with brown, flexuous hairs; hymenium creamy-white; stem usually immersed or partly so, deeply lacunose, 1 cm. long. 1-2 cm. in diameter.—Caespitose or gregarious on rich soil or rotten wood, New York to Minnesota and southward.

P. fusicarpa (Ger.) Seav. Plate 3, fig. 24.

Deep-cup-shaped, 2-3 cm. in diameter, 1 cm. deep, clothed with dense flexuous brown hairs; hymenium creamy-white, becoming brownish in age or in drying; stem short, up to 5 mm. long, 3-5 mm. thick, smooth or lacunose, clothed as cup; asci 300 x 20 μ; spores fusiform, 12 x 35 μ, each with 2 large oil-drops.—Gregarious or caespitose on rich soil or rotten wood, Connecticut to Iowa, south to Virginia.

ALEURINA Sacc. & Syd.

Cup-shaped to shield-shaped, fleshy, brownish-black; paraphyses filled with dark granules.

A. atrovinosa (Cooke) Seav.

Deep-cup-shaped, irregularly contorted in age or by mutual pressure, pale brown becoming darker when old, 2-5 cm. in diameter, tapering abruptly to a stem-like base, hymenium darker, with age almost black, tinted olive.—Gregarious or caespitose on ground in woods usually among mosses, Maine to New Jersey and Montana.

GEOPYXIS (Pers.) Sacc. Earth-cup. Plate 3, fig. 17.

Deep-cup-shaped, externally pustulate, with a short slender stem; spores 8 in an ascus, ellipsoid, oil-drops absent.

1   Growing among mosses in conifer-woods.........*G. vulcanalis.*
1' Growing on burned places......................*G. cupularis.*
1" Growing on ground........2
  2   Apothecium covered with coarse warts, bright yellow *G.bronca.*
  2' Apothecium covered with fine warts, dull yellow...*G. catinus.*

G. cupularis Sacc. Earth-cup. Plate 3, fig. 36.

Cup-shaped on a short stem, 3-10 mm. in diameter and depth, margin crenate, dull yellow; stem 3 mm. long, 1 mm. thick; hymenium a little paler.—Gregarious on burned-over ground, New York to Washington, rare.

G. catinus (Homsk.) Sacc. Plate 3, fig. 17.

Deep-cup-shaped on short stem, dull yellow, strongly but finely pustulate, the margin crenate, 2-3 cm. in diameter, 2 cm. deep; hymenium dull yellow; stem 5-10 mm. long, 3-4 mm. thick, nearly smooth or lacunose.—On ground, New York, California.

G. vulcanalis (Peck) Sacc.   Conifer earth-cup.

Funnel-shaped, on short stem, pruinose or glabrate, whitish or yellowish-white, 1-2 cm. in diameter, half as deep, the margin incurved and crenate; hymenium pale orange.—Among mosses or on leaf mould in conifer-woods, Wyoming, Maine, Tennessee.

PEZIZA (Dill.) L.   Plate 3, fig. 16, 18-20, 32-35.

Apothecium cup-shaped, cups medium-sized to large, not tomentose or hairy, usually sessile on ground, rotting wood, or manure; stem short or absent, spores 8 in an ascus.

1 Growing on manure-heaps or manured soil..................2
1' Growing on ground................4
1" Growing on rotten wood.............3

   2 Apothecia large, minutely pustulate, externally
     whitish ....*P. vesiculosa.*
   2' Apothecium small, up to 2 cm. high, externally
     pale brown ....*P. fimeti.*

3 On water-soaked logs, discoid, small, with glistening
   reddish-brown hymenium........................*P. clypeata.*
3' On rotten wood or chip-piles, large, with pale brown
   hymenium ....*P. repanda.*

   4 On humus or debris in woods, apothecium externally
     whitish, hymenium umber-brown or darker.......*P. sylvestris.*
   4' In caves or damp cellars, flesh golden, apothecium white,
     up to 10 cm. high, hymenium white to buff...*P. domiciliana.*
   4" in other situations...............5

5 On burnt ground or charcoal..........6
5' On ground not burned-over..........7

   6 Hymenium violet........................ *P. violacea.*
   6' Hymenium brown or darker, apothecium pustulate,
     margin often crenate......................*P. pustulata.*

7 Flesh golden, hymenium brown, apothecium small and
   externally light-colored, on damp soil in woods......*P. succosa.*
7' Flesh not becoming golden...........8

   8 Hymenium pale rosaceous, apothecium externally
     white-pruinose...........................*P. griseorosea.*
   8' Hymenium brown..............9

9 Hymenium ochraceous-brown; apothecium white, large, on
   damp soil in woods............................*P. Emileia.*
9' Hymenium reddish-brown, or dark-brown.....10

10   Both hymenium and outside of apothecium brown.....11
10' Apothecium externally whitish, hymenium becoming
       venose or reticulate.........................*P. venosa.*
11   Large, with purple pustules, usually caespitose.......*P. badia.*
11' Small, shield-shaped, on ground in damp places.*P. brunneoatra.*

P. badia Pers. Bay Peziza. Plate 3, fig. 16.

Deep-cup-shaped, large, at first globose, symmetrical, infolded, cochleate, rarely one-sided, from tan to dark brown, whitish toward base, pustulate with red-purple warts, 5-10 cm. in diameter, almost as deep; hymenium dark brown, deeply concave; spores 9 x 20 μ. Caespitose or gregarious on ground in open places in woods, New York, Oregon, Alabama, May, June, not rare.

P. brunneoatra Desm

Small, shield-shaped or discoid at maturity, 1-2 cm. in diameter; hymenium concave then plane, or convex-umbilicate, brownish-black with a tinge of green; asci 325 x16 μ, cylindric above. Scattered on ground in damp places, New York to Iowa.

P. succosa Berk. Plate 3, fig. 19.

Hemispheric then shallow-cup-shaped to discoid, symmetrical or contorted, the margin even or lobed, externally whitish or light olivaceous-yellow, 3-4 cm. in diameter; hymenium brown, smooth, often tinted olive by spores; asci 225 x 14 μ, cylindrical.—Gregarious on damp soil in woods, New England, Minnesota, and southward.

P. pustulata (Hedw.) Pers. Plate 3, fig. 18.

Closed, globose, then deep-cup-shaped with incurved and crenate margin, whitish and densely pustulate, dingy with age, 3-5 cm. in diameter; hymenium deep-concave, brown to dark-brown, spores 9 x 16 μ. The pustules give rise to scale-like particles on the mature plant.—New York to Minnesota and southward.

P. Emileia Cooke.

Large, cup-shaped, 6-10 cm. in diameter, at length expanding and repand, even or lobed, white or whitish-mealy; hymenium concave to plane, smooth or undulated, ochraceous-brown; asci 200 x 14 μ. —Gregarious on damp soil in woods, Wisconsin, not common.

P. violacea Pers. Violet Peziza. Plate 3, fig. 34.

Closed and subglobose, expanding to shallow-cup-shaped, discoid, or repand, externally white to pale-violaceous, 3-4 cm. in diameter; hymenium concave, pale violet becoming deep violet or blackish with age, plane, concave, or convex; asci 225 x 14μ.—Gregarious on burned-over ground or on charcoal, New England, North Dakota, southwestward.

P. griseorosea Ger.   Rose-gray Peziza.

Shallow-cup-shaped, pruinose, whitish, thin, fleshy, the flesh grayish-ochre, 2-4 cm. in diameter; hymenium concave, pale-rosaceous to subochraceous; spores 8 x 16 μ, warted.—On the ground, New England to Minnesota, and southwestward.

P. venosa Pers.   Plate 3, fig. 20.

Shallow-cup-shaped with lacunose base, very large, 6-20 cm. in diameter, soon depressed to the substratum with the margin only slightly elevated (the margin entire, then commonly splitting at maturity), externally whitish; hymenium reddish-brown, smooth, then radially convolute or venose-reticulate.—Solitary or gregarious on the ground in woods, especially beech woods, New York to Illinois, and the Southwest.

P. vesiculosa Bull.   Plate 3, fig. 32.

Closed and globose, expanding to deep-cup-shaped, symmetrical or contorted, whitish or yellowish, minutely pustulate, rather large, 5-8 cm. high; hymenium pale brown, paler than outside of cup; spores smooth, 11 x 22 μ.—Gregarious to caespitose on manure-piles or heavily manured fields throughout the United States, common.

P. repanda Pers.   Spreading Peziza (edible).   Plate 3, fig. 35.

Cup-shaped, large, 6-10 cm. high, whitish, becoming expanded and repand, the margin entire, crenate or splitting, often irregularly revolute; hymenium pale brown, becoming darker with age, smooth or convolute; stem short, stout.—On rotten logs or chip-piles, New York, Minnesota, Virginia.

P. fimeti (Fuckel.) Seav.

Subglobose then becoming nearly plane, pale brown, granulose, small, sessile, 1-2 cm. in diameter; hymenium concave to plane, colored as outside; asci 280 x 18 μ.—Scattered on cow-dung, Indiana, Kentucky, Iowa, Colorado.

P. sylvestris (Boud.) Sacc.   Plate 3, fig. 33.

Deep-cup-shaped to nearly discoid, often rather large, 3-8 cm. in diameter, externally whitish, minutely pustulate to smooth, margin entire or crenate; hymenium umber-brown. — Gregarious on rubbish-piles and soil in woods, New England to the Pacific Ocean. Very similar to *P. Cerea* Sowerb.

P. clypeata Schw.
Bulgaria bicolor Peck.
Globose, gradually expanding to shallow-cup-shaped, then discoid, 1-4 cm. in diameter, symmetrical, becoming closely adnate to logs except for the narrow, slightly raised margin; hymenium dark reddish-brown, glistening, later dull and blackish, splitting to form white vein-like markings; substance soft, waxy.—Gregarious on much decayed logs which are saturated with water, New York to Wisconsin and North Carolina.

P. domiciliana Cooke.   Domestic Peziza.
P. odorata Peck.
Concave, soon repand-umbilicate, 3-10 cm. in diameter, asymmetrical, angular in outline because of the folding back of segments, externally white; flesh when broken turning golden-yellow; hymenium at first white, becoming dull buff or brownish; stem up to 1 cm. in length, thick, irregular, white; asci 250 x 15 μ.—Frequent in cellars and mushroom caves, New York to Iowa and Missouri.

BULGARIA Fr

Subglobose to shallow cup-shaped, blackish with an internal gelatinous layer, externally hairy; substance thick.

B. rufa Schw.   Plate 3, fig. 9.
Becoming shallow-cup-shaped, 1-3 cm. in diameter, the margin incurved, externally blackish-brown, clothed with hair-clusters, the jelly-layer several mm. thick; hymenium pale reddish-brown.— Caespitose or gregarious on leaves and buried sticks in woods, Minnesota, New England, North Carolina, not common.

B. melastoma (Sowerb.) Seav.
Subglobose, brownish-black, 1-2 cm. in diameter, tomentose, opening by a circular aperture, the margin remaining incurved; hymenium deeply concave, paler than outside, smooth, glistening.— Attached to sticks in woods, Maine to Washington and West Indies, rare.

ELVELACEAE.   Plate 4.

Ascophore consisting of a distinct stem and pileus; pileus saddle-shaped, subglobose, conical or entirely covering outside of stem; hymenium grooved, pitted, lacunose, gyrose, or smooth.

See Seaver, F. J. North American Cup Fungi (Operculates), 1928.

VERPA Swartz.

Pileus bell-shaped, with a rather long stem attached to central part of lower surface; hymenium covering outside of pileus, yellow to dark brown, smooth or grooved lengthwise.

V. conica (Müll.) Swartz.   Plate 4, fig. 2.
V. digitaliformis Pers.
Pileus bell-shaped, the hymenium dark brown, white beneath, 1-2 cm. long and about 2/3 as broad, smooth or slightly lacunose; stem cylindrical, whitish, 5-6 cm. long, 8-12 mm. in diameter, slightly scaly or flocculose, broadest near the middle; asci tapering below, 300 x 20 μ; spores 18 x 24 μ.—On the ground, May, June, New England and Virginia to Colorado.

V. bohemica (Krombh.) Schröt.   Plate 4, fig. 1.
Morchella bispora Sorok.
Pileus bell-shaped, the hymenium yellow to brownish, white beneath, 2-3 cm. long, 1-2 cm. broad, folded into longitudinal freely anastomosing ribs; stem cylindric, hollow or loosely stuffed, white, 6-8 cm. long, 5-10 cm. thick.—On soil in wet mossy places, May-June, Maine to Minnesota, West Virginia.

MORCHELLA (Dill.) Pers.   Morel.   Plate 4.

Pileus subglobose, elongated, obtuse-conic, the margin usually adnate to stem (more or less free in *M. hybrida*), surface pitted, sponge-like in appearance, the pits irregularly arranged or with radially anastomosing ribs between, lined with hymenium, yellow to dark brown.

1 Ribs of pileus of same color as or lighter than interior of pits.2
1' Ribs of pileus much darker than interior of pits,
smoky-brown ....*M. angusticeps.*

2 Pileus without a margin free from stem...........3
2' Margin of pileus free from stem..................*M. hybrida.*

3 Pileus 2-3 cm. long..........................*M. deliciosa.*
3' Pileus much larger, 4-12 cm. long.............4

4 Plants very large, up to 14 cm. high, the pits large and
shallow; stem bulging toward base..............*M. crassipes.*
4' Plants smaller, the pits deep; stem not so markedly enlarged
at base........................5

5 Pileus subglobose............................*M. esculenta.*
5' Pileus elongated to a conical point..............*M. conica.*

M. crassipes (Vent.) Pers. (edible). Plate 4, fig. 9.

Pileus 6-8 cm. long, 4-6 cm. in diameter, oblong or subconic, yellowish within, the ribs thin, irregularly anastomosing and bounding large shallow pits; stem stout, 10-11 cm. long, 5-6 cm. in diameter at base, elsewhere 4 cm., whitish to yellowish, slightly pubescent.—On the ground under hawthorn trees or in open places and margins of woods, New York, Montana, Illinois, and Iowa.

M. esculenta Pers. Edible Morel, Honeycomb Mushroom (edible). Plate 4, fig. 6.

Pileus subglobose, oblong, sometimes narrowed upward, the base obtuse, 5-9 cm. long, 3-5 cm. broad; pits dull yellowish to brownish, rounded within, asymmetrical, 5-10 mm. in diameter; ribs 1 mm. thick and lighter in color than interior of pits, not longitudinal; stem about 2/3 the diameter of the pileus, sometimes somewhat lacunose toward the somewhat enlarged base, 2-8 cm. long; spores yellowish in mass, 13 x 22 μ.—On ground in woods in open places, common, May-Aug., New England, Minnesota, South Carolina.

M. conica Pers. Conic Morel (edible). Plate 4, fig. 8.

Pileus elongated, subconic, acute, or obtuse at apex, 6-8 cm. long, 3-4 cm. in diameter; pits oblong, more or less rectangular, dull yellow within; ribs longitudinal, connected by cross-ribs and anastomosing, lighter than pits, 1 mm. thick; stem 2/3 the diameter of the base of the pileus, white or dull light yellow, 4-7 cm. long; spores yellowish in mass, 13 x 22 μ.—On ground in open woods, New England to Minnesota and southwestward, also in Washington.

M. deliciosa Fr. Delicious Morel (edible). Plate 4, fig. 5.

Pileus subconic, small, 2-3 cm. long, half as broad; pits elongated, ashy to blackish within; ribs somewhat longitudinally arranged and irregularly anastomosing, 1 mm. thick with rounded edge, much lighter than pits, whitish; stem 1/2 or 2/3 the diameter of the base of the pileus, irregularly lacunose, whitish or dull yellowish.—On the ground in grassy places at edges of woods, etc., New England, Iowa, and southward.

M. angusticeps Peck. Narrow-head Morel (edible). Plate 4, fig. 3.

Pileus narrow-conic, acute at the apex, 2-5 cm. long, half as broad at base; ribs somewhat longitudinally arranged, irregularly anastomosing, less than 1 mm. thick, thin-edged, black on extreme edge, lighter toward apex; pits 5-10 mm. long, half as broad, dull yellow within, smoky-brown at margin; diameter of stem almost equal to that of the pileus.—Sandy soil at borders of woods, not common, in spring, New York, Michigan, Indiana dunes.

M. hybrida (Sowerb.) Pers.   Plate 4, fig. 4.

Morilla semilibera Quel.

Pileus bell-shaped or subconic, 2 cm. long, 1-5 cm. broad, the margin free about halfway up stem; ribs longitudinal or irregularly anastomosing, 1 mm. thick, whitish; pits rounded or oblong, 5 mm. in diameter, dull yellow within; stem white to dull yellow, at first very short, at length 8-10 cm. long, 2 cm. broad at base, narrowed upward; asci 250 x 20 μ; spores hyaline, 13 x 24 μ.—On moist ground at margins of woods, not common, in the spring, New England, North Dakota, and southwestward.

ELVELA L.

Pileus saddle-shaped or subglobose, often irregularly convolute or gyrose-ridged; stem slender or stout, smooth, lacunose, or ribbed, white, yellow or smoky. This name is commonly written"Helvella."

1   Plants white to creamy.............................*E. crispa.*
1' Plants yellow, brown, or blackish........2

2   Stem with sharp-cornered longitudinal ridges, smoky; pileus
    dark colored ....*E. mitra.*
2' Stem not distinctly fluted, smooth or lacunose........3

3   Stem very slender, not over 5 mm. in diameter........4
3' Gyromitra-like, stem usually stout........5

4   Yellowish to dark brown, stem very long............*E. elastica.*
4' Black, pileus 1-3 cm. broad, stem not short............*E. atra.*

5   Pileus red-brown or darker........................*E. infula.*
5' Hymenium chocolate-brown ....*E. Underwoodii.*
5" Hymenium brownish-black, on rotton stumps....*E. sphaerospora.*

E. mitra L.   Black-saddle.   Plate 4, fig. 13.

Pileus dark brownish-black, saddle-shaped to globose, 2-5 cm. in diameter; hymenium smooth or convolute, dark brownish-black; stem 6-10 cm. long, 1-2 cm. in diameter, enlarged below, yellowish to smoky, deeply fluted; asci 8-spored, cylindric, up to 200 x 16 μ; spores 12 to 20 μ, each with one large oil-drop.—On damp soil, New York to British Columbia.

E. crispa (Scop.) Fr.   White-saddle.   Plate 4, fig. 12.

Pileus whitish, most commonly saddle-shaped, irregularly lobed, 3-5 cm. in diameter; hymenium white or cream-colored, smooth or convolute; stem 5-7 cm. long, 2-3 cm. in diameter, entirely white, deeply fluted, in drying cream-yellow; asci 300 x 16 μ; spores 12 x 20 μ, each with one large oil-drop.—On soil in wooded places, New York to Minnesota.

E. atra Oed.
Elvela nigricans Pers.
Pileus mitrate to saddle-shaped, the margin free from the stem when mature; hymenium black; stem slender, larger at base, black except at the white base, 4-5 cm. long, 2-3 mm. in diameter; spores 1-seriate, 12-20 μ, each containing one large oil-drop.—On the ground in the woods, northern Illinois, Wisconsin, and Montana.

E. elastica Bull.   Plate 4, fig. 7.

Pileus irregularly saddle-shaped, the margin reflexed but free from stem, 2-3 cm. broad; hymenium yellow to dark brown or black; stem 5-10 cm. long, 3-10 mm. thick, nearly smooth, never fluted, yellowish, paler than the hymenium.—On the ground in woods, New York to California.

E. infula Schaeff.   Bay Gyromitra (poisonous).   Plate 4, fig. 10.
Gyromitra esculenta Fr
Pileus 4-8 cm. in diameter, reflexed or adnate to stem, saddle-shaped or occasionally subglobose, smooth, contorted, or convoluted, reddish-brown, dark-brown, or almost black; stem 5-8 cm. long, 5-30 mm. in diameter, smooth or lacunose, white to yellowish; asci sub-cylindric, 200 x 14 μ; spores 10 x 21 μ, each with two oil-drops.—On ground or very rotton wood, Maine to British Columbia and southward.

E. Underwoodii Seav.   Brown Gyromitra.   Plate 4, fig. 14.
Gyromitra brunnea Underw.
Pileus much twisted, lobed, folded, anastomose-ridged, 5-10 cm. in diameter, adhering to stem several places, whitish underneath; hymenium chocolate-brown; stem 8-12 cm. long, 2-5 cm. in diameter, white, hollow; spores 14 x 30 μ, each with two large oil-drops.—In rich woods, Ohio to Illinois.

E. sphaerospora Peck.
Gyromitra sphaerospora Sacc.
Pileus wide-spreading, 5-8 cm. in diameter, whitish underneath, slightly tomentose; hymenium smooth or slightly undulated, brown

or brownish-black; stem thick, 2-3 cm. in diameter, 4-8 cm. long, whitish, deeply lacunose or fluted; asci 150 x 11 μ.—On decaying stumps in woods. New England to Manitoba and southward.

UNDERWOODIA Peck.

Pileus fleshy, elongated or columnar, completely covering the stem; hymenium completely covering outer surface, smooth or undulated; stem lacunose or fluted, with several internal longitudinal cavities; asci cylindric, each 8-spored.

U. columnaris Peek. Plate 4, fig. 11.

Pileus clavate, tapering above, or often horn-shaped, light-colored becoming brownish, 6-10 cm. high, 2-3 cm. in diameter; asci 350 x 20 μ; spores warted, 12 x 25 μ.—On the ground among leaves in woods, New York, Michigan, and Manitoba.

THELEPHORACEAE. Plate 1, fig. 26-35.

Fructifications with the smooth hymenial surface borne on the lower surface or surrounding the sterile parts, coriaceous or waxy.

See Burt, E. A. Ann. Mo. Bot. Garden 1:185-228, 1914; 1:327-350, 1914; 2:731-770, 1915; 3:203-241, 1916; 4:237-269, 1917; 4:305-362, 1917; 5:177-203, 1918; 5:301-372, 1918; 6:253-280, 1919; 7:81-248, 1920; 11:1-36, 1924; 12:213-357, 1925; 13:173-354, 1926; Peck, C. H. N. Y. St. Mus. Bul. 2:44-48, 1887.

HYPOCHNUS (Fr.) Burt. Felt-spreads.

Plants resupinate, effused, dry, coriaceous or felt-like, usually composed of loosely interwoven hyphae bearing basidia which sometimes occur in scattered clusters but more usually in a compact hymenium; hymenium smooth or papillose; basidia simple, each bearing two or more spores; spores rough-walled to echinulate, distinctly colored in most species, pale in a few and hyaline in one species.— Growing on decaying wood.

1　Spores distinctly colored as seen under the microscope......2
1'　Spores so pale as to appear hyaline under the microscope....
....H. fumosus.

2　Plants ferruginous......3
2'　Plants of another color......4

3　Non-incrusted cylindrical cystidia protruding from the hymenium; plants growing on conifers....H. canadensis.
3'　Cystidia not present; plants growing on deciduous trees....
....H. ferrugineus.

4   Hyphae nodose-septate......6
4' Hyphae not nodose-septate......5
5   Plants drab to fuscous.................*H. umbrinum.*
5' Plants deep olive-buff.................*H. isabellinus.*
6   Plants brown ....*H. fuligineus.*
6' Plants umber ....*H. spongiosus.*

H. fumosus Fr. Smoky felt-spread.

Plants honey-yellow to drab and fuscous, membranaceous, separable from the substratum, spreading, 3-10 cm. x 1.5-4 cm., 200-400 μ thick, the outer surface covered with intricately anastomosing threads, later granular, the margin whitish or yellowish, flaxy-fibrillose, radiating; spores 4 x 3 μ, minutely echinulate, white; hyphae nodose-septate, 3 μ in diameter, hyaline to slightly fuscous; cystidia absent.—On rotting wood and bark of both conifer and frondose trees, Ontario to North Carolina, westward to the Pacific Ocean, common.

H. canadensis Burt.

Plants small, 1-2 cm. x 0.5-1 cm., membranaceous, ferruginous, easily separable from the substratum, dry, tomentose, two-layered 400-500 μ thick; hymenium smooth or granular with protruding, non-incrusted, cylindrical cystidia.—On wood and bark of conifers on the forest floor, New England to Idaho, not common.

H. fuligineus Burt.

Plants effused, covering an area 4-10 cm. x 2-4 cm., soft, felty-membranaceous, separable from the substratum, pinkish-buff or light fawn, 200-1200 μ thick, margin different in color from hymenial surface; hyphae thick-walled, 5-7 μ in diameter; spores bister, subglobose, 6-8 μ broad.—On rotting frondose wood, New England and Wisconsin, Aug.-Sept., not common.

H. umbrinum (Fr.) Burt.

Plants effused, covering 6-10 cm. x 3-5 cm. of substratum, soft, separable from the substratum, drab to fuscous, 400-600 μ thick; loose hyphae along substratum repeatedly branched to form a compact hymenium.—On rotting conifer and deciduous wood, common, Sept.-Oct., cosmopolitan.

H. isabellinus Fr. Tan Felt-spread.

Plants spreading to 5-10 cm. x 1.5-3 cm. on substratum, deep olive-buff, effused, tomentose, thin, adnate, the margin thinner, of same color, substance 60-200 μ in thickness, with hyphae loose and running along substratum and sending out suberect, loosely interwoven branches; spores and hyphae also olive-buff, the spores echinulate, 7-9 μ broad; hyphae 8-10 μ wide.—On rotting wood of conifer and deciduous trees, Ontario, Florida, Wisconsin, common.

H. ferrugineus (Fr.) Pers.

Plants effused, adnate, 3-6 cm. long, half as wide, 0.3 mm. thick, often suborbicular, thin, brown, dry, tomentose, hypochnoid; hyphae nodose-septate, concolorous with plant; spores subglobose, brown, echinulate, 7 x 8 μ.—Underside of decaying limbs and logs of deciduous trees, July-Oct., occasionally found, throughout our area.

H. spongiosus (Schw.) Burt.   Spongy Felt-spread.

Plants umber to bister, felty-membranaceous, separable from the substratum, 4-10 cm. long, half as wide, 0.2-1.2 mm. thick, margin thinning out, scarcely determinate; hyphae abundantly nodose-septate, widely branching; spores globose, flattened on one side, echinulate, 8 x 7 μ.—On rotten wood of either frondose or conifer trees, July-Nov., common throughout our area.

"If the surface of this plant is viewed with a lens, the component fibers are seen running in all directions, as in felt or blotting paper." Burt, Ann. Missouri Bot. Gard., 3:217, April, 1916.

ASTEROSTROMA Mass.

Plants always resupinate, effused, crustaceous, floccose, fleshy, cartilaginous, coriaceous, or membranaceus; hymenium smooth. In section conspicuous, brown, stellate organs are in evidence. Species will be identified as *Corticium* unless sections are examined.

A. cervicolor Berk. & Curt.

Plants resupinate, thin, spongy, dry, pallid, cinnamon-drab, 150-300 μ thick; stellate organs with 5 unbranched rays; spores echinulate. —On decaying wood, earth, and flower-pots throughout Canada, United States, Mexico, and Japan.

A. bicolor Ell. & Everh.

Plants similar to *A. cervicolor*, but with cobwebby margins and looser structure, covering 1-6 cm. x 4 cm. of the substratum, the hymenium becoming whitish, the rays of stellate organs somewhat branched; spores smooth; cystidia absent.—On rotting wood, especially of conifers, throughout United States, not common.

CORTICIUM Pers.   Plate 1, fig. 34.

Plants always resupinate, effused, waxy-crustaceous or floccose, fleshy, cartilaginous, coriaceous, or membranaceous; hymenium smooth; basidia simple with 2-8 sterigmata, usually 4; basidiospores white in all of our species.   Species of this genus are distinguished from those of *Peniophora* by absence of cystidia.   *C. laeve* has a somewhat reflexed margin and might therefore, as Burt suggests, be placed in *Stereum*.   Some species often considered as members of the genus *Corticium* are to be found in this treatment under *Aleurodiscus, Peniophora,* and *Stereum*.

1   At least 500 μ in thickness in center when mature......2
1' Not over 500 μ in thickness when mature......5

2   Substance of several layers, zonate-stratose..*C. portentosum*.
2' Substance not in stratose layers......3

3   Plants white or cream-colored, waxy, not cracking.*C. galactinum*.
3' Plants cracking, or if not cracking, then colored yellow......4

4   Plants warm-buff to light orange, not cracking..*C. investiens*.
4' Plants cream-colored to wood-brown, cracking into small radial areas ....*C. cremoricolor*.

5   Plants snow-white, the margins arachnoid..*C. arachnoideum*.
5' Plants not snow-white, the margins not arachnoid......6

6   Parasitic on herbs.........................*C. vagum*.
6' Not parasitic......7

7   Plants cracking into small rectangular areas 1-4 per mm.
....*C. calceum*.
7' Plants cracking into areas 1-2 mm. across.....*C. hydnans*.
7" Plants not cracking into areas......8

8   Margin silky or of cottony fibers......9
8' Margin thin but not fibrous......11

9   Plants pruinose, drying buff-pink, the margins silky..*C. roseum*.
9' Plants not pruinose, larger specimens with margins somewhat reflexed ....*C. laeve*.
9" Plants not pruinose, the margins not reflexed......10

10 Plants buff with cottony-fibrous white margins..*C. vellereum*.
10' Plants without cottony fibers on margins......11

11 Plants vinaceous-fawn to wood-brown.......*C. rubellum*.
11' Plants white to buff.....................*C. confluens*.

C. portentosum Berk. & Curt.

Plants coriaceous-soft, rarely cracking, long and widely effused, 4-12 cm. x 2-4 cm., the substance zonate-stratose, of several layers, white, drying buff, 150-1000 μ thick; margin white, pubescent-villose. —On bark and wood of deciduous trees, throughout the world, common.

C. galactinum (Fr.) Burt

Plants coriaceous-soft, long and widely effused, 4-12 x 2-4 cm., 200-1000 μ thick, white to cream colored, waxy, not cracking; margin gradually thinning out, not definitely bounded, the hyphae interwoven.—On roots of living apple and blackberry, on the ground and on rotting logs of frondose or conifer trees, Ontario to Florida, westward to the Pacific Ocean, common.

C. investiens (Schw.) Bres.

Plants yellow, effused, usually thin, 150-300 μ thick, tough, dry, but not cracking, the margin thinning out, covering areas 2-20 x 1-5 cm., texture and color like chamois leather; the yellow hyphae, antler-shaped, branching dichotomously.—On rotting logs and branches of deciduous and conifer trees, very common throughout North America and in Venezuela and Japan, July-Dec. in our area.

C. cremicolor Berk. & Curt.

Plants covering areas 2-10 cm x 1-3 cm., 200-400 μ thick, cream-colored to wood-brown, cracking into radially arranged areas which are small, rectangular, 2-3 mm. in diameter; margin fibrillose, somewhat radiate, narrow.—Frequently found on bark of decaying oak and other frondose trees, Apr.-Dec. Ontario, Florida, and westward to the Pacific Ocean.

C. arachnoideum Berk.

Plants tender, snow-white, 2-6 cm. x 1-3 cm., 100-200 μ thick; cuticle-like hymenium present on sublayer in central part of plant, the arachnoid sublayer forming a sterile, loosely arranged margin.— On humus, leaf fragments, decaying wood, lichens, and mosses, common. Ontario to Louisiana and westward to the Pacific Ocean, also in the West Indies and Hawaiian Islands.

C. vagum Berk. & Curt.

Plants pale olive-buff or cream colored, thin, 5-15 cm. x 5-10 cm. or forming a collar 1-10 cm. long sheathing the bases of living stems, 60-100 μ thick, webby, perforate membranaceous, parasitic, forming minute sclerotia on the host; vegetative part saprophytic in soil and on wood near the ground, arachnoid.—On living stems of potatoes, beans, rhubarb, horse-radish, tomatoes, Amaranthus, etc., near the ground, New Brunswick, Florida, westward to the Pacific Ocean, also in the West Indies, Australia, India, and Europe, common.

C. calceum (Fr.) Burt.

Plants, white to ivory-yellow, floccose-membranaceous, covering areas 3-20 cm. x 1-5 cm., thin, 100-200 μ, cracking into small rectangular masses, 1-4 per mm.; margin mealy.—On lower sides of pine and Arbor Vitae rails, July-Nov., abundant locally, Ontario, Nova Scotia, Wisconsin, British Columbia.

C. roseum Pers.

Plants somewhat membranaceous, pruinose, cream-colored and rose-tinted when fresh, drying buff-pink, finally cracked, 2-3 mm. in diameter, laterally confluent to 1-10 cm. x 1-3 cm.; 250 μ thick; margin white, more or less cottony-fibrous, two-layered; paraphyses antler-shaped.—On bark and wood of poplar, birch, elder, maple, hickory, elm, and other deciduous trees, Ontario, Alabama, west to the Pacific Ocean, also in Europe, common.

C. laeve Pers.

Plants 1-10 cm. x 1-5 cm. membranaceous, 200-500 μ thick, 2-layered, cracking when dried and showing the dark hymenial crust on the white subiculum, drying light pinkish cinnamon to wood-brown and drab; margin on large specimens slightly reflexed as in *Stereum* (where Burt suggests it should be placed).—On bark of fallen limbs of frondose trees, Ontario, Virginia, and westward to the Pacific Ocean, also in Europe.

C. vellereum Ell. & Crag.

Plants white, cream-buff, or pinkish-buff, tender, 200-300 μ thick, rarely cracked, smooth, pulverulent or waxy, covering areas 3-10 cm. in diameter; margin white, cottony fibrous; chlamydospores many, embedded.—On bark and wood of frondose trees, decaying on the ground, Ontario to Texas, westward to the Pacific Ocean, July-March, common.

C. rubellum Burt.

Plants vinaceous-fawn becoming wood-brown when thoroughly dry, smooth, not waxy, 120-500 μ thick, covering areas 5-10 cm. x 1-5 cm., not colored when thin but colored when thick and stratose. —On decorticated wood of dead oak and basswood, Illinois, Florida, and Manitoba, not common.

C. confluens Fr.

Plants whitish to buff or very light pinkish-cinnamon when dried, with few cracks 200-500 μ thick, not stratose, with a spread of 2-8 cm. x 1-3 cm.—On bark of decaying fallen limbs of frondose trees, especially birch, alder and willow, Newfoundland to Florida, Wisconsin, Manitoba, and Washington, also in Africa, Japan, Mexico, and Jamaica, common.

C. hydnans (Schw.) Burt.

Plants long and widely effused, adnate, thin, membranaceous, covering areas 1-10 cm. x 1-3 cm., 100-300 μ in thickness, pinkish buff to cinnamon buff in the herbarium, becoming somewhat tuberculate, cracking into polygonal areas 1-2 mm. in diameter, margin whitish; hyphae longitudinally arranged next the substratum, then ascending and interwoven into the hymenium, not incrusted; spores hyaline, smooth 5-8 x 3 μ.—On decaying limbs on the ground, Apr.-Nov., occasionally found, throughout our area. (After Burt)

This plant was included in Moffatt's Higher Fungi of the Chicago Region as *C. colliculosum* Berk. & Curt.

ALEURODISCUS Rabenh. Plate 1, fig. 32.

Plants resupinate, saucer-shaped, coriaceous in drying, often with margin free; hymenium pulverulent; paraphyses racemose with short branches, or moniliform; basidia simple, large, each with four large sterigmata.

1 Plants disc-shaped or cup-shaped......2
1' Plants entirely resupinate, circular, small.....*A. acerinus.*
1'' Plants normally effuse-reflexed, margin barely showing underside ....*A. candidus.*
2 Plant peziziform, attached by a point.......*A. amorphus.*
2' Plant with edges raised, broadly attached....*A. Oakesii.*

A. candidus (Schw.) Burt.

Plants 3-6 mm. rarely 1-2 cm. in diameter, normally effuse-reflexed, scarcely showing the black color of the lower side of the thickened margins, chalk-white, orbicular, sometimes resupinate, scattered, adnate, following inequalities of bark, pruinose, 800 μ thick; hyphae heavily incrused, much of material in large angular crystalline granules; basidia clavate, 45-60 x 10-15 μ; paraphyses with bushy tips; spores subglobose, 16 x 13 μ.—On bark of living oaks, rarely on ash and maple, New York, Florida, California, and Jamaica, Aug.-Jan.

A. amorphus (Pers.) Rabenh.

Plants 1-4 mm. broad, peziziform, fleshy, drying coriaceous, attached by a central point; hymenium convex, pulverulent, buff-pink drying olive-buff, margin paler.—On fir, spruce and *Thuja plicata,* infrequently found, Newfoundland to New York and Oregon, July-Jan.

A. Oakesii Berk. & Curt.

Plants 1-2 mm. in diameter, confluent into masses 1 x 2 cm. in diameter, peziziform, fleshy, drying coriaceous, with broad attachment, white-tomentose on lower side; hymenium concave, pulverulent, 600 μ thick; paraphyses filiform, racemose, each with about 12 branches or moniliform with 2-3 swellings.—On bark of dead hop hornbeam, oak (*Quercus alba* or *Q. macrocarpa*), willow, and hickory trees, Ontario, Alabama, Missouri, and Manitoba, common.

A. acerinus Pers.

Stereum acerinum Pers

Plants about 3 mm. in diameter rarely elongated to 1 cm., resupinate, crustaceous, adnate, thin, smooth, white, margin abrupt; structure 45-80 μ thick, consisting of densely arranged hyphae, heavily incrusted, rising between the basidia to the surface, loaded with crystalline matter; basidia clavate, 30-45 x 6 μ; spores smooth, hyaline 11 x 7 μ.—On bark and trunks of living maple, oak, etc., throughout the year, not uncommon, throughout our area. (After Burt)

"Forming a thin white crust, generally sterile, surface usually covered with minute particles of lime." (Moffatt, Bul. VII, Nat. Hist. Surv., Chicago Acad. Sci., Part I, p. 136.)

STEREUM Pers.

Plants coriaceous, firm, stipitate, dimidiate, or effused-reflexed: hymenium inferior, smooth, without setae; intermediate layer of longitudinally arranged hyphae normally present; basidia simple; spores smooth. The plants are of shapes similar to those found in the genus *Polyporus,* but the hymenium is smooth. Some have conducting vessels containing latex. Burt calls attention to the wide east and west ranges of the species as compared with those of the north and south.

1   Central-stemmed or in some species lateral-stemmed, more
    or less infundibuliform, coriaceous......2
1' Sessile, dimidiate, some specimens entirely resupinate......3
2   On the ground in deciduous forests, infundibuliform, or
    split and then dimidiate................*S. Burtianum.*

2' On stumps or buried wood, infundibuliform or split and petaloid, obscurely zoned, the margins thin and often lacinate ....*S. pergamenum.*

3 Growing on wood of conifers......15

3' Growing on wood of deciduous trees......4

4 Reflexed part forming a soft pliant pileus, which is brown and felt-like above, white below..................*S. fuscum.*

4' Coriaceous-fleshy, wart-like vinaceous, on poplar..*S. rufum.*

4'' Without this combination of characters......5

5 Pyriform vescicular organs present in the purplish hymenium, plants growing on poplar or birch.*S. purpureum.*

5' Hymenium exuding red milk where wounded; plants villose tobacco-colored, growing on oak.....*S. gausapatum.*

5'' Vescicular organs absent; hymenium not exuding juice......6

6 Upper surface of pileus tomentose or hairy......7

6' Upper surface of pileus glabrous......12

7 Strigose-hairy or hirsute, buff......8

7' Soft-hairy......9

8 Hymenium warm-buff, sometimes pale smoky-gray.... ....*S. hirsutum.*

8' Hymenium pinkish-buff; pileus concentrically sulcate.... ....*S. cinerascens.*

9 Pilei numerous, folded together laterally, zoned, crisped, very thin, shining-cinnamon-buff...........*S. rameale.*

9' Pilei not folded together laterally, not colored as above......10

10 Hymenium yellow; pilei white, villose-tomentose...... ....*S. ochraceo-flavum.*

10' Hymenium at first vinaceous-purple...*S. roseo-carneum.*

10'' Hymenium colored other than as above......11

11 Plants at first effuse-reflexed, shining, glabrous, zones alternating with white tomentose zones.....*S. lobatum.*

11' Plants not usually effuse-reflexed or lobate, more hairy than above ....*S. fasciatum.*

12 Hymenium exuding red milk when broken; pilei multizonate, the margins thick, entire...........*S. rugosum.*

12' Hymenium not exuding red milk; pilei not zonate......13

13 Pileus plane, thin, with a silky luster, growing on Carpinus ....*S. sericeum.*

13' Without this combination of characters......14

14 Plants at first purplish or vinaceous-buff, at length snuff-brown, growing on oak and hickory.......*S. umbrinum.*

14′ Resupinate, woody, crowded-confluent, then broken into frustules (each 3-4 mm. in diameter), growing on ends of logs ....*S. frustulosum.*

15 Shield-shaped, 1-4 mm. in diameter, wood-brown, coriaceous, growing on pine branches...............*S. Pinii.*

15′ Not shield-shaped......16

16 Hymenium exuding red milk when broken; pileus narrowly reflexed, pinkish-buff, not multizonate, growing on conifers ....*S. sanguineolentum.*

16′ Hymenium not exuding red milk......17

17 Pileus velvety or tomentose........18

17′ Pileus glabrous, deeply and concentrically sulcate......... ....*S. sulcatum.*

18 Pileus black and velvety above, hymenium ferruginous and radiately rugose....................*S. radiatum.*

18′ Pileus umber, obscurely zonate, tomentose; hymenium light drab to ashy, pruinose..............*S. abietinum.*

S. Burtianum Peck. Burt's Stereum. Plate 5, fig. 10.

Plants 1-2 cm. high, 0.5-1.5 cm. across, coriaceous, infundibuliform, sometimes dimidiate, the upper surface often with radiating ridges of fibrils, cartilage-buff when fresh, sayal-brown to hazel when dry, thin, the margin lobed; hymenium glabrous, yellow-ochre when fresh, pink-buff to sayal-brown when dry; stem 3-8 mm. long, 1 mm. thick, spores 3-4 μ in diameter.—On ground in woods, New Hampshire, North Carolina, Tennessee, and Japan, July-Oct., rare. This species has the aspect of a *Craterellus* but is thinner, smaller, and more irregular.

S. pergamenum Berk. and Curt.

Plants 1.5-4 cm. high, split and petaloid, obscurely zoned, the margin thin and often laciniate; stem minutely tomentose.—On stumps or buried wood, Ohio, North Carolina, and Mexico.

S. fuscum Schrad.

Plant reflexed from substratum and forming a pileus 1-4 cm. long, 2-5 cm. wide, the resupinate portion 3-10 x 1-3 cm. and 1 mm. thick, membranaceous, spongy, soft, usually becoming conchate-reflexed, often imbricated, villose, at length glabrous, somewhat concentrically sulcate, drying snuff-brown; hymenium white, glabrous, drying cream or mouse-gray, not zonate, the flexuose gloeocystidia 20-60 x 5-7 μ. —On rotting frondose limbs, sometimes on pine, Apr.-Dec., not rare, Ontario, Texas, and Oregon.

S. rufum Fr.

Plants 2-4 mm. broad; 1-2 mm. thick in center, 0.7 mm. on margin, coriaceous fleshy, scattered or gregarious, bursting out from the bark, verruciform, plicate-tuberculose, peltate, vinaceous-brown to hematite-red, under side glabrous, margin free all around; hymenium becoming wrinkled, vinaceous-brown to grayish pruinose; substance of ascending, loosely woven, incrusted, hyaline hyphae; flexuous gloeocystidia 50-90 x 7-10 μ are scattered in or near the hymenium, but not protruding; spores 7 x 2 μ smooth, curved, white.—On dead *Populus tremuloides* timbers, common, northern part of our area (after Burt).

S. purpureum Pers.   Silver-leaf disease.   Plate 5, fig. 11.

Pileus 0.5-2 cm. broad, with lobes 5 mm. broad, the resupinate part 1-2 cm. in diameter, 0.5-0.8 mm. thick, coriaceous, soft, villose-tomentose above, light buff in color, the margin entire, more or less reflexed to form several imbricated pilei; hymenium even, light purple-drab to dark vinaceous-buff, with pyriform vescicular organs 15-30 x 12-25 μ, and no cystidia; spores hyaline, flattened unilaterally, 6 x 3 μ.—On dead stumps and logs of poplar and birch, Newfoundland to Delaware and westward to the Pacific Ocean, June to April, common.   This species is recognized in the field by its buff tomentose pileus and purple hymenium.

S. gausapatum Fr.

Pileus 1 cm. broad, 1-2.5 cm. in diameter, 0.6-0.7 mm. thick, clustered, clothed with a heavy villose coat, tobacco-colored; hymenium dark brown, bleeding when cut.—On oak stumps, Aug.-Mar., common, Ontario to Alabama, west to the Pacific Ocean.

S. sanguineolentum Alb. & Schw.

Pileus with a reflexed margin 0.2-1 cm. broad, the resupinate portion covering an area 1-5 cm. in diameter, 0.4-0.6 mm. thick, coriaceous, thin, villose to silky above, the hairs radially arranged, drying pinkish-buff to olivaceous-buff; hymenium bleeding when wounded, or becoming red-discolored along wounded edge, drying wood-brown. —Frequently found on stumps and logs of conifers, July-Mar., Ontario to Pennsylvania, and to the Pacific Ocean.

S. hirsutum (Fr.) Willd.   Hairy Stereum.

Pileus strigose-hirsute, coriaceous, stiff, rarely wholly resupinate, somewhat concentrically furrowed, cream-buff becoming grayish, the reflexed portion up to 2 cm. broad, 1-2 cm. long, 0.5-0.7 mm. thick; hymenium even, warm-buff becoming pale-smoky.—On birch and beech logs, Newfoundland to the Pacific Ocean, common. As in *S. rameale, S. fasciatum, S. lobatum* and *S. gausopatum,* the hairy covering springs from a thin, golden, horny crust.

S. fasciatum Schw.   Plate 5, fig. 13.

Pileus 2-7 cm. in diameter, the resupinate portion narrow, 0.4-0.7 mm. thick, a dark layer bearing the tomentum of the upper surface; hymenium glabrous, buff to cinnamon-buff, sometimes violet-tinged. —On logs and stumps of oak, common, throughout North America.

S. lobatum Fr.

Similar to the preceding but with lobed margin, thinner context, and tomentose covering; pileus 3-7 cm. long, 2-6 cm. broad, 0.3 mm. thick.—On dead branches of deciduous trees, not common, New York to Wisconsin, south to Brazil.

S. rameale Schw.   Plate 5, fig. 12.

Pileus thin, coriaceous, villose to silky or fibrous-strigose above, soon with glabrous and shining margin with innate fibers radiating from the base, cinnamon-buff to hazel, more or less zoned, 3-10 mm. long, 2-10 mm. broad, 0.3-0.4 mm. thick; hymenium cream-buff, smooth; spores 6 x 2 μ.—On dead twigs and stumps of oak and other trees, our commonest species, Ontario to the Gulf of Mexico and westward to the Pacific Ocean. The plants have the aspect of a small *Polyporus versicolor.*

S. sericeum Schw.   Silky Stereum.

Reflexed portion of the pileus 5-10 mm. broad, 3-10 mm. long, the resupinate portion 1-1.5 cm. in diameter, silvery to pale gray, with silky luster and innate fibrils, lacking the ruddy and ochraceous hues of *S. rameale,* plane, not folded or crisped, coriaceous, small, very thin and papery, 0.25-0.30 mm. thick; hymenium wood-brown or bleached, smooth.—In swampy woods on lower sides of dead twigs of *Carpinus, Liquidambar,* and *Nyssa,* not common, Ontario, Louisiana, and Missouri.

S. radiatum Peck.

Pileus black above, coriaceous, velvety, lobed, 2-8 mm. broad, 1 mm. thick; hymenium bright ferruginous, with shallow broad ridges radiating from center to margin; spores slightly curved, 10 x 4 μ. —On lower sides of conifer wood, not common, Ontario, Pennsylvania, and westward to Montana.

S. ochraceo-flavum Schw.   Plate 5, fig. 14.

Reflexed pileus 3-5 mm. broad, 4 mm. long, 0.2-0.3 mm. thick, conical, coriaceous, white, heavily clothed with long, soft hairs; hymenium bright yellow.—Attached by one side and the umbo to dead branches of deciduous trees, July-May, common, Ontario, Mississippi, west to the Pacific Ocean.

S. abietinum Pers.   Fir Stereum.

Plant coriaceous, spongy, dry, resupinate, rarely reflexed to form a pileus, the resupinate area 2-8 x 2-5 cm., the reflexed portion 3-8 mm. broad, 0.4-0.9 mm. thick, rarely hairy; hymenium cinereous-pruinose.—On wood of fir and pine throughout the ranges of the hosts, local.

S. cinerascens (Schw.) Mass.

Resupinate area of plant 1-10 x 1-2 cm., reflexed pileus 2-8 mm. broad, strigose-hairy, pinkish-buff; cystidia large, incrusted, 100-150 x 12-20 μ, brownish at bases, conical; spores 11 x 6 μ.—On logs of black locust, mulberry, elm, and linden, June to Feb., common, Ontario to Texas and to the Pacific Ocean.

S. sulcatum Burt.

Plants confluent over areas up to 8 x 15 cm.; pileus (the reflexed margin) 3-10 mm. broad, 0.6-1.5 mm. thick, glabrous, bister or light brown, corky, rigid, concentrically sulcate; hymenium ruddy, drying light pinkish-buff, reddish where bruised, tubercular, not polished; incrusted cystidia 30-50 μ long and 8-12 μ thick.—On logs of hemlock, fir, spruce, cypress, Douglas fir, and tamarack, May-Nov., frequently found, Ontario and Texas to Washington.

S. versiforme Berk. & Curt.

Almost entirely effused or resupinate over confluent areas 7 x 1-2 cm., reflexed margin about 1 mm. broad, 0.2-0.4 mm. thick; hymenium Prout's brown, velvety or dull.   The presence in the hymenium of bushy-branched paraphyses among which are scattered large incrusted cylindrical cystidia (45-70 x 12-24 μ) separates this species from *Peniophora cinerea*.—On bark and dead limbs of chestnut birch, and other deciduous trees, July-Feb., common, Ontario and Alabama, westward to Iowa.

S. frustulosum Fr.

Plants woody, resupinate, tuberculose, crowded as if confluent, then broken into frustules, 2-4 mm. in diameter and 1 mm. thick, sometimes with narrowly reflexed or free margins, upper sides black, crust-like, glabrous; hymenium convex, pinkish-buff to whitish-pruinose.—Causing a honey-comb rot on oak wood, common, Ontario, Massachusetts, Texas, Oregon.

S. rosea-carneum Fr.

Plants always resupinate, 3-5 x 2 mm., confluent over areas 6 x 1.5 cm., of an intense fuscous-lilac color, the margin barely free as a pileus with the upper surface tomentose, light pinkish buff; hymenium coriaceous, thin (0.25-0.30 mm. thick), cracking, tesselated, not shining, light vinaceous-purple when young, duller when mature. —On fallen limbs of deciduous trees, not common, Ontario, North Carolina, Wisconsin.

HYMENOCHAETE Lev.   Plate 5, fig. 7

Plants coriaceous, stipitate, dimidiate, effused-reflexed or resupinate; hymenium smooth to velvety, containing conical, colored setae among the unbranched basidia; spores hyaline.   Similar to *Stereum* in structure and appearance, differing in the presence of conical setae.

1 Dimidiate, umbonate-sessile and reflexed, often resupinate......2
1' Resupinate, never reflexed, dimidiate or umbonate......4

2 Hymenium less than 50 μ thick, antique-brown, velvety, margins brown ....*H. Curtisii.*
2' Hymenium more than 50 μ thick, brown; margin yellow, reflexed......3

3 Hymenium cracked radially into systems, one system for about each centimeter of area, tobacco-colored............*H. tabacina.*
3' Hymenium not cracked, velvety, red-brown......*H. rubiginosa.*

4 Infecting two living branches and at length uniting them firmly ....*H. agglutinans.*
4' On dead or decaying branches only......5

5 Tawny-olive, not cracked....................*H. episphaeria.*
5' Antique-brown, not cracked..................*H. cinnamomea.*
5" Argus-brown, cracking in drying.................*H. spreta.*

H. Curtisii Morg.

Plants at first orbicular, then effused, becoming reflexed, up to 10-15 mm. broad, 5 mm. long, confluent in areas 2-25 x 1-3 cm., coriaceous, thin (.14-.24 mm. thick), the layers separable, silky, concentrically ridged, antique-brown, then glabrous and hair-brown when old; setae few and far apart in the velvety and uncracked hymenium.

—Common, Apr.-Dec., on rotting limbs of oak and other frondose trees, Massachusetts, Texas, Oregon.

H. tabacina (Lev.) Sowerb.   Plate 5, fig. 7.

Plants coriaceous, thin (.34-.60 mm. thick) effuse-reflexed (reflexed portion 10-15 x 3-7 mm., resupinate area up to 3 x 30 cm.), often imbricated, sometimes wholly resupinate, antique-brown, silky becoming glabrous and deep-brownish-drab, the margin and middle layer orange-yellow; hymenium tobacco-brown to sepia, often deeply cracked into radiating systems, one system for each cm. of area.— Common northward on dead limbs of deciduous trees, Ontario and Kentucky, to California and Alaska.

H. rubiginosa (Lev.) Dicks

Similar to the preceding, but the pileus rigid, velvety, 3 cm. long, 1-3 cm. broad, 0.5-0.7 mm. thick, concentrically sulcate, and rubiginous (Brussels brown); hymenium dark red, the color intensified by reflected light, the setae more numerous; the margin ochraceous.— On oak logs and stumps, producing pocketed heart-rot in oak lumber, common, widely ranging throughout North America.

H. agglutinans Ell.

Plants 3-7 cm. in diameter, 1-2 mm. thick, resupinate, adnate, orbicular, at first loose texture and buff, later firm, concentrically sulcate, antique brown with thick margin.—On living branches of alder (*Alnus*), spice bush (*Benzoin*), *Acer*, etc., binding two branches which rub together, frequently found, Aug.-Apr., New Hampshire, Florida, westward to Idaho.

H. episphaeria (Schw.) Mass.

Resupinate, effused over areas 2-5 cm. x 1-2 cm., very thin, (up to 90 μ) drying tawny-olive, resembling *H. cinnamomea,* but thinner, lacking hyphal layer, and with setae growing from the substratum and extending through hymenium.—Lower sides of dead deciduous limbs, occasionally found, Illinois, Pennsylvania and Vermont.

H. cinnamomea (Pers.) Bres.

Resupinate, effused, adnate, velvety, not cracked, antique-brown to Brussels-brown, covering areas 3-7 cm. x 1-3 cm., 500-1000 μ thick, of several layers (up to six), each layer containing setae (¼ of seta-length apart).—On bark and decaying frondose and conifer wood, June to Apr., rare, New York to California and British Columbia.

H. spreta Peck.

Resupinate adnate, cracking (rimose) snuff-brown, the margin thinning, velvety when young, covering areas 4-20 cm. x 2-10 cm., 300-500 μ thick, of several layers (each 50-200 μ thick).—On decaying frondose, rarely conifer, wood, Apr.-Jan., common, Ontario to Alabama, westward to the Pacific Ocean.

CONIOPHORA D.C.   Plate 1, fig. 33.

Resupinate, effused, fleshy, subcoriaceous, or membranaceous; hymenium undulate-tubercular-granular or smooth, pulverulent with spores. If the hymenium is nearly smooth the dark color of the spores in mass will separate *Coniophora* from *Corticium* and *Peniophora*.

1   Hymenial surface undulate or gyrose.............*C. cerebella.*
1' Hymenium pulverulent, smooth or slightly tubercular......2
2   On deciduous logs, etc.; margin cottony, composed of radiating mycelium ....*C. polyporoidea.*
2' On conifers or on humus in pine woods......3
3   Plants cream-colored throughout.................*C. byssoidea.*
3' Plants light tawny-olive to olive-brown......4
4   Cystidia protruding to 100 μ; plants buff-citrine to brownish-olive ....*C. olivacea.*
4' Cystidia absent; plants tawny-olive......5
5   Plants tawny-olive with umber shades; hyphae incrusted....
    ....*C. suffocata.*
5' Plants warm-buff to tawny olive; hyphae not incrusted; margin pale ....*C. arida.*

C. byssoidea (Pers.) Fr.

Plants felt-like, covering areas 1-6 cm. in diameter, effused, dry, at first flaxy-hypochnoid, later compact at disk, bright cream to yellow; margin flaxy, 0.15-0.35 mm. thick, composed of loosely woven nodose hyphae which color the plant; hymenium smooth, tomentose. —In pine woods, on wood or ground and humus, June to Dec., common in the northwest and occasional elsewhere, Ontario and Jamaica, to Pacific Ocean.

C. olivacea (Fr.) Karst

Effused, adnate, somewhat felt-like, drying olive or brownish-olive; white disc 0.7 mm. thick, at margin 0.2 mm., covering areas 4-10 cm. x 2-5 cm.; hymenium smooth, tomentose; setae present;

colored hyphae 3-6 μ in diam., not nodose, forming a dense hymenial layer; spores colored, often flat on one side, 9 x 5 μ.—On conifer wood and bark, Ontario and Florida, westward to Idaho.

C. suffocata (Peck.) Mass.

Effused, membranaceous, separable from the substratum when thick, covering areas 2-9 cm. x 1-5 cm., tawny-olive when dry, the margins usually white; hymenium smooth, 60-500 μ thick, composed of loosely arranged incrusted hyphae (each 3-6 μ in diameter).— Common on conifer boards and limbs on the ground, Nova Scotia, Florida, British Columbia. It approaches *C. cerebella* in its tendency to separate from the substratum when thick; it resembles *C. arida* in habit, color, and dry, loose structure.

C. arida (Fr.) Karst.

Plants effused, membranaceous, adnate, warm-buff to tawny-olive, covering areas 4-20 cm. x 1-8 cm., the margins sometimes whitish; hymenium smooth, pulverulent; structure 100-500 μ thick; hyphae loosely woven, hyaline, 2-3 μ in diameter, often collapsing; spores in mass tawny-olive.—Common on limbs, logs, and lower sides of timbers of conifers, Ontario, Louisiana, westward to Idaho.

C. cerebella Pers.

Plants effused, orbicular, fleshy, 300-1000 μ thick, covering round or elongated areas 4-6 cm. x 6-15 cm., light tawny or tawny-olive, the margins white-mucedinous; hymenium undulate or gyrose, with low dome-shaped tubercles, hyphae densely interwoven, smooth-walled, hyaline.—Not rare, on logs and wood of both conifer and deciduous trees; Quebec and Virginia to California.

C. polyporoidea (Berk. & Curt.) Burt.

Effused, membranaceous, separable from the substratum, pink-buff when dry, white margins cottony with radiating mycelial strands; 400-1000 μ thick, composed of loosely interwoven hyphae, covering areas 1-15 cm. x 1-5 cm.; hymenium smooth, pulverulent.—On fallen limbs and wood of frondose trees, occasionally of pine, June to Mar., New Hampshire to Florida, Michigan and Arkansas.

PENIOPHORA Cooke

Fruiting structure waxy, coriaceous, membranaceous, or floccose, smooth, effused, always resupinate; cystidia present, often more or less buried in the hymenium; colored stellate organs absent; basidia simple, each bearing 2-4 white spores.

1 Growing on dead branches and bark of conifers......2
1' Growing on dead branches and bark of frondose trees......5

2 Tobacco-colored ....*P. tabacina.*
2' White or ashy-gray......3

3 On arbor vitae (Thuja) only.....................*P. Thujae.*
3' On other conifers......4

4 Ashy-gray, in appearance like a thin dry coat of paint..*P. cinerea.*
4' White ....*P. gigantea.*

5 Substance not colored......6
5' Substance brown, russet, dark-ashy, or vinaceous......14

6 Plants not separable from the substratum, closely adnate...7
6' Plants separable from the substratum......10

7 Snow-white, granular and pruinose...............*P. Sambucii.*
7' Not snow-white, nor granular and pruinose......8

8 Deep-orange, growing on alder.................*P. aurantiaca.*
8' Not orange......9

9 Plants reddish ....*P. incarnata.*
9' Plants white ....*P. pubera.*

10 Plants minutely velvety, light fawn with white margins....
    ....*P. velutina.*
10' Plants buffy-citrine ....*P. filamentosa.*
10" Not velvety......11

11 Margin radiately fibrillose......12
11' Margin otherwise......13

12 Hyphae granule-incrusted ....*P. laevis.*
12' Hyphae not granule-incrusted. otherwise as in *P. laevis*....
    ....*P. affinis.*
12" Hyphae not granule-incrusted, cracking to show white.*P. mutata.*

13 Margin cobwebby, white; plants cream-colored......*P. cremea.*
13' Margin thin, not cobwebby; plants white............*P. albula.*

14 Substance of hymenium clay-colored..........*P heterocystidia.*
14' Substance dark ....*P. cinerea.*
14" Substance vinaceous-russet ....*P. coccineofulva.*

P. tabacina Burt.

Plants covering several sq. cm., tobacco-colored, not separable from the substratum, in section tawny-olive, 150-400 μ thick, two-layered, the margin thinning; hymenium cracking when dry, and showy concolorous subiculum; cystidia cylindrical, protruding to 80 μ.—On decaying bark of conifers, rare, Wisconsin to the Pacific Ocean.

P. Thujae Burt.

Plants covering several sq. cm., white, drying buff, adnate, thin, 40-150 μ thick; hyphae loosely arranged, suberect and interwoven, 2-3 μ in diameter; cystidia hair-like, somewhat capitate, protruding 20-30 μ beyond the basidia.—On trunks of *Thuja*, more rarely on *Juniperus* and *Pinus Strobus,* occasional, Canada and Massachusetts to Missouri (after Burt).

P. gigantea (Fr.) Mass.

Plants covering large areas, 3-30 cm. in diameter, white, waxy, separable from substratum, drying like parchment, pale pinkish-buff, margin white, fibrillose; substance colorless, 100-500 μ thick; cystidia incrusted, 40-50 μ long and 10 μ thick.—On bark and wood of pine, fir, and hemlock, Europe and most of North America.

P. Sambucii (Pers.) Burt.

Plants covering several sq. cm. by confluence, at first circular and 2-5 mm. across, snow-white, granular and pruinose, drying cream-colored, not cracking, 100-250 μ in thickness, the margin thinning; hyphae erect, thin-walled, incrusted, 3 μ thick; cistidia protruding 10-30 μ beyond the basidia.—Surrounding twigs of and on bark of *Sambucus* (elder), sometimes on other kinds of wood; very common throughout North America.

P. aurantiaca Bres.

Plants covering several sq. cm., deep orange or orange-red, drying light buff or cinnamon, the margin white, radiating, substance 150-250 μ thick; spores large 15 x 10 μ.—Always on *Alnus* (alder), common, Laborador to North Carolina, west to the Pacific Ocean.

P. incarnata (Pers.) Karst.

Plants covering 2-10 x 1-2 cm., reddish, drying pinkish-buff, cracking, the margin paler; substance 100-250 μ thick, with abundant gloeocystidia, some broadly ovoid but usually more slender (30-60 x 8 μ), rarely protruding.—On bark and wood or in warty growths 2-5 mm. in diameter on lenticels, common, Ontario and Alabama to the Pacific Ocean.

P. pubera (Fr.) Sacc.

Plants covering small areas of 2-6 x 1-3 cm., white, drying buff or dirty white, cracking widely when dried, 45-400 μ thick; hymenium even setulose; gloeocystidia large, conical, 45 x 8 μ; cystidia incrusted, conical, fusiform, pointed, 50-90 x 10-20 μ, sometimes protruding 50 μ.—On decaying wood of frondose trees, common, May-Jan., Ontario to Florida, west to Oregon.

P. velutina (D. C.) Cooke.

Plants covering 3-20 x 2-15 cm., light fawn-colored, minutely velvety, the margin whitish, often with extended white threads of mycelium, drying vinaceous fawn, not cracking; 250-500 μ thick, membranaceous; cystidia incrusted 4-100 x 8-15 μ, wholly immersed or protruding to 50 μ.—On decaying limbs of *Fagus* (beech), *Quercus* (oak), *Castanea* (chestnut), *Populus* (poplar), etc., May-Dec., common throughout United States and Canada.

P. laevis (Fr.) Burt.

Plants covering 2-15 x 2-4 cm., whitish, membranaceous, adnate, separable when moistened, drying pinkish-buff to pinkish-cinnamon, subiculum paler; substance 300-400 μ thick; hyphae 3-4½ μ wide, densely crowded, parallel to substratum and then ascending obliquely into the hymenium.—On bark of frondose trees, July-Oct., not common, throughout United States.

P. filamentosa (Berk. & Curt.) Burt.

Plants covering areas 2-10 cm. long, 1-3 cm. wide, 150-400 μ thick. Plants broadly effused, membranaceous, loosely adnate, separable when moistened, soft, drying Isabella color to buffy-citrine, margin and subiculum but slightly paler than the hymenium, often connected with branching mycelial strands; hyphae densely interwoven, incrusted with ochraceous granules; cystidia incrusted, 40-50 x 6-8 μ, protruding up to 40 μ; spores white, smooth, 4 x 2.5 μ.—On decaying wood of deciduous trees, July-Jan., common, throughout our area.

P. affinis Burt.

Plants covering 3-20 x 2-4 cm., whitish, membranaceous, adnate, separable when moistened, drying light buff to pinkish-cinnamon, often cracked and showing the paler subiculum in the cracks, the margin paler and radiately fibrillose, substance 300-500 μ thick; hyphae hyaline, not incrusted, 3-5 μ wide, running parallel to substratum and then ascending obliquely into the hymenium.—On bark of frondose trees, July-Oct., common, New England to Oregon.

P. mutata Peck.

Plants white, covering 3-7 x 1-3 cm., thick, separable from substratum when moistened, membranaceous, drying whitish or buff, cracking in drying and showing white subiculum, substance 300-1000 μ thick, hymenium with radiating folds, tuberculose, margin white, radiately byssoid; gloeocystidia pyriform, 15 x 7 μ.—On bark of decaying branches of *Populus, Tilia,* and *Quercus,* common, Ontario and Alabama, to Idaho.

P. cremea Bres.

Plants covering 4-15 x 2-4 cm., cream colored, separable, cracking when dried and showing white subiculum, 100-300 μ thick, margin cobwebby, white; hyphae branching at wide angles, more or less granular-incrusted; hymenial layer dense, the cystidia protruding and smooth or incrusted at apex.—On bark of frondose trees, not common, throughout the United States.

P. albula Atkins. & Burt.

Plants covering 2-20 x 1-2 cm., or when young in circular areas 3 mm. across, white, adnate, separable in small pieces, light buff and cracked into polygonal areas 1-2 mm. in diameter when dry, substance 200-700 μ thick, margin thinning, not cobwebby; gloeocystidia absent.—On bark of decaying branches of *Alnus, Tilia, Populus,* and other deciduous trees, common, Ontario to Alabama and west to Washington.

P. heterocystidia Burt.

Plants 2-7 cm. in diameter, whitish, drying cinnamon-drab or vinaceous, subtance 200-400 μ thick, two-layered, cracking when dried and loosening from substratum along the cracks; substance of hymenium clay-colored, remainder uncolored; cystidia very large, 40-100 x 20-50 μ; gloeocystidia slender, flexuous, 50 x 5 μ, between the basidia.—On fallen limbs of *Betula, Fagus, Acer, Carpinus,* and *Magnolia,* common, throughout North America.

P. cinerea (Pers.) Cooke.

Plants covering 2-5 x 1 cm., ashy-gray, very thin, closely adnate, in small patches becoming confluent, pruinose, waxy, cracked in drying, substance 50-100 μ thick, brownish and darker near substratum; hyphae densely interwoven, 3 μ in diameter; cystidia incrusted, 25-40 x 4½ μ; spores 6-9 x 2-3 μ.—On decaying limbs of many frondose trees and some conifers, very common throughout North America.

P. coccineofulva (Schw.) Burt.

Plants covering 4-10 x 2 cm., vinaceous-russet, drying russet or brown, margin paler, substance two-layered, 150-400 μ thick; many hyphae incrusted; cystidia incrusted.—On rotting bark and wood of walnut and oak, common, throughout North America.

SEBACINA Tul.

Plants resupinate, floccose, membranaceous, or coriaceous, with habit of *Corticium;* basidia longitudinally septate, sometimes between conidiophores.

S. incrustans (Tul.) Pers.   Incrusting Fungus.

Plants white, on earth and incrusting the bases of living plants, often forming little columns, flaps, or free branches, the apices awl-shaped or fringed, drying warm-buff, 5-7 cm. broad, pileate flaps 0.5-1 cm. long when present, 250-400 μ thick; basidia longitudinally septate, ovoid, 16 x 12 μ.—On ground, logs, plant-bases, and other objects in woods, common, New England and Georgia to Minnesota.

TREMELLODENDRON Atkins.   Plate 5.

Plants erect, Clavaria-like, coriaceous, branched, rarely simple; hymenium inferior or on both sides of flattened branches; basidia longitudinally and cruciately septate; spores smooth, white. The species are indigenous to North America. They have in general the aspect of *Clavaria,* from which they may be distinguished by their tough consistency and lack of brittleness.

1   Plants branched at least when mature......2
1′ Plants simple; stem 1-2 mm. thick, palmately few-branched
....*T. Cladonia.*
2   Plants caespitose, grown together in many places......3
2′ Plants grown together in few places; branches more or less cylindrical; main stem small, 2-10 mm. thick......*T. candidum.*
3   Branches flattened and grown together in many places; cluster of plants commonly 4 cm. or more broad...........*T. pallidum.*
3′ Branches much intertangled, both stems and branches grown together into a close bundle.................*T. merismatoides.*

T. pallidum (Schw.) Burt.   Plate 5, fig. 21.
Thelephora Schweinitzii Peck.
Plants 4 cm. high, up to 15 cm. in diameter, caespitose, arising from a common swollen basal mass, drying buff; stem branching into flattened, furrowed, pileate divisions which fuse at points of contact and form a rosette-like cluster; branches in center somewhat awl-shaped, those toward margin spreading and fimbriate; basidia pyriform, 12-15 x 9 μ; spores white, 11 x 5 μ.—On ground in woods, common, June-Oct., Newfoundland and South Carolina to Missouri and Minnesota.

T. candidum (Schw.) Atkins.

Similar to preceding but in smaller clusters and not so much grown together, 2-5 cm. high, 2-5 cm. broad; stem 2-10 mm. thick, palmately branched with spreading cylindrical branches, the top branches about 1.5 mm. thick; basidia 11 x 8 μ; spores 9 x 5 μ.—On ground in open woods, not common, July-Sept., New England, North Carolina, Missouri, Minnesota.

T. merismatoides (Schw.) Burt.

Plants caespitose, pallid, erect, 2-5 cm. high, 2-3 cm. broad, branchlets few, straight, filiform, angular to round, spreading and fimbriate at apex then splitting into spreading divisions; basidia 11 x 8 μ; spores 10 x 5 μ.—On ground in open woods, not common, June-Aug., Massachusetts and New York to South Carolina and Missouri.

T. Cladonia (Schw.) Burt.

Plants small, 2-5 cm. high by 0.7-2 cm. broad, stem 1-2 mm. thick, pallid, drying buff, erect, soft-coriaceous, branches frequently in threes, cylindrical, some branching again in threes, all arranged in a single plane on the flattened end of one stem, or about the perforate circular end (in which case the branches are channeled).—On ground in woods, not common, Aug.-Sept., Ontario and Mississippi to Missouri and Minnesota.

THELEPHORA Ehrh.   Plate 5, fig. 1-6.

Plants pileate or clavate, sometimes flabelliform with long-fimbriate upper margin, coriaceous; hymenium continuous with and similar to the hymenophore, inferior, smooth or slightly papillose or ribbed; spores colored, typically muricate but smooth, rough-walled in a few species; basidia simple.

1   Erect......2
1' Incrusting various objects, effuse-reflexed or dimidiate....4
2   Pileus divided into very narrow, branching, flattened divisions, 2-6 cm. high.............................*T. palmata.*
2' Pileus infundibuliform, cup-shaped or fan-shaped, often radiately split......3
3   Hymenium brown to fuscous; plant small, 1-3 cm. high....
    ....*T. multipartita.*
3' Hymenium dark; plant large, 3-7 cm. in diameter.......*T. vialis.*
4   Incrusting and ascending small branches and mosses, free branches slender, clustered and flattened at tips......*T. fimbriata.*

4′ Pilei in applanate clusters, effuse-reflexed, or dimidiate......5
5 Hymenium ferruginous-brown to fuscous......6
5′ Hymenium and pileus cinnamon-buff, context spongy, plant 2 mm. or more thick......................*T. albido-brunnea.*
5″ Hymenium drab, pileus pinkish-brown with a broad light margin ....*T. cuticularis.*
6 Pileus zonate, otherwise as *T. terrestris*........*T. griseozonata.*
6′ Pileus not zonate......7
7 Margin fibrous-fimbriate ....*T. terrestris.*
7′ Margin whitish-fimbriate, becoming concolorous and entire ....*T. intybacea.*

T. palmata (Fr.) Scop. Palmate Thelephora, Plate 5, fig. 2.

Plants erect, very much branched, 2-6 cm. high, 1-3 cm. broad, coriaceous, soft, fuscous-purple, drying chestnut-brown, with a fetid odor; pileus with numerous, clustered, flattened divisions, spreading above, with fimbriate, whitish tips; stem simple or soon branched, 1-1.5 cm. long and 1-2 mm. thick; hymenium present on both sides; spores 10 x 7 μ, pale umber, sparingly echinulate.—On moist ground in coniferous woods and in grassy fields, not common, June to Oct., eastern Canada to Illinois and North Carolina.

T. multipartita Schw. Many-parted Thelephora. Plate 5, fig. 3.

Plants erect, 1.5-3.5 cm. high, 1-3 cm. broad, with stem 1-2 cm. long and 1-3 mm. thick, infundibuliform, often cleft unequally into a few lobes and these subdivided into many narrow and spreading divisions, dilated and whitish at apex, coriaceous, fusco-cinereous, sometimes split to the stem and appearing dimidiate; stem erect, equal or tapering upward, villose, drying walnut-brown; hymenium inferior, fawn-colored or vinaceous-drab, smooth, glabrous; spores 7-9 x 5-6 μ, tuberculate, umbrinous under microscope.—Solitary on the ground in frondose (especially oak) woods, not common, July to Sept., Illinois, New York, Alabama (according to Burt).

T. vialis Schw. Plate 5, fig. 4

Plants 2.5-6 cm. high, 2.5-7 cm. broad, of many shapes, often composed of ascending lobes or pilei which arise from a common base and are confluent laterally above to form a cup, or with the interior of the cup filled with numerous small pilei which arise from the upper surface; substance thick, coriaceous, the odor disagreeable in drying; surface dirty-white or pallid-yellowish, sometimes wood-brown at center, fibrillose; stem central or absent; hymenium smoky-yellowish, inferior, rugose; spores olive-buff under microscope, obtusely angular.—On ground in frondose woods, September, not common, Vermont and Illinois to South Carolina.

T. albido-brunnea Schw.   Plate 5, fig. 5.

Plants encircling the bases of shrubs or twigs near the ground, and running up them; pileus sessile or with short stem, coriaceous, thick, spongy when dry, 2-4 cm. broad when circular, or when dimidiate 1-2.5 cm. long by 2-4 cm. broad, often 1 cm. thick at base when dimidiate but usually about 2 mm. thick, uniformly cinnamon-buff, fibrous-tomentose, the margin thick and entire; substance spongy, colored as the upper surface; hymenium smooth, inferior, cinnamon-buff; spores deep olive-buff, echinulate, 8-10 μ x 6-8 μ.—Sometimes in bogs or swampy woods, not common, Louisiana to Quebec and Wisconsin.

T. cuticularis Berk.

Pileus dimidiate or effuse-reflexed, imbricate, 1-1.5 cm. long, 2-4 cm. broad, 1 mm. thick, coriaceous-soft, brown, drying pinkish-buff to cinnamon-brown, with a broad pale margin, the surface radiately rugose, silky-fibrillose, substance concolor, the odor unpleasant in drying; hymenium brown to brownish-drab, inferior, concave, smooth; spores umbrinous, flattened on one side, echinulate, not angular, 8-9 μ x 6-7 μ.—On mossy banks and fallen twigs in woods, June to Aug., not common, Vermont to Missouri and Texas.

T. intybacea (Fr.).   Plate 5, fig. 6.

Clusters up to 5-8 cm. in diameter, sometimes central but more often lateral and triangular, soft, whitish, then rufous-ferruginous, drying chestnut brown, imbricated, fibrous with fibers in matted adnate squamules; pileus 2-4 cm. long and broad, 1 mm. thick, the margin dilated and white-fimbriate at first, finally entire and concolor; hymenium inferior, papillose, concolor; spores concolorous, angular-tuberculate, 7-9 μ x 6-8 μ.—On layers of pine needles, locally common, Ontario to North Carolina and Wisconsin.

T. terrestris (Fr.) Ehrh.

Plant clusters 5-8 cm. in diameter (single pileus 3 cm. x 3 cm., obconic pileus 2-3 cm. in diameter), caespitose, coriaceous, soft, dark-fuscous to fawn-colored, with short stem, dimidiate, or effuse-reflexed, imbricated, often laterally confluent, fibrous-squamulose and usually strigose, thin, the margin lacinate and fibrous-fimbriate; hymenium inferior, papillose, fuscous to fawn-colored; spores angular, pale fuscous, 6-9 μ x 6 μ.—On sandy ground at tree bases, and in pine woods on leaves and fallen twigs, July to Dec., Alaska to Maine and South Carolina.

Burt* observes: "If plants are from sandy soil they are dark fuscous and in flattened imbricated clusters or of the obconic type, from woody material plants are redder and reflexed."

T. fimbriata Schw.   Plate 5, fig. 1.

Plants coriaceous-soft, incrusting and ascending small plants to 1-3 cm., subterete, with many small clusters of branches along sides, the tips fimbriately incised or acute, branches 5-10 mm. long, 1 mm thick, the cluster of branches 5-10 mm. across, pale or whitish, soon rusty-brown; hymenium pruinose, smooth; spores tuberculate, umbrinous, 7-11 μ x 6-9 μ.—In moist places, incrusting mosses and small twigs, locally common, July-Aug., New York to Illinois and South Carolina.

CRATERELLUS Pers.   Plate 5.

Plants fleshy or membranaceous, infundibuliform, tubiform, sometimes clavate, always with a pileus; hymenium continuous, adnate to structure beneath it, waxy, membranaceous, smooth to ridged, often ridged longitudinally, in which case the species approach those of *Cantharellus;* basidia simple; spores white.   None are abundant except very locally.

1   Plants egg-yellow, not smoky......2
1′ Plants smoky or brown......3
2   Stem solid, plants not markedly pliant..........*C. Cantharellus.*
2′ Stem soon hollowed, membranaceous-pliant........*C. odoratus.*
3   Plants clavate to narrow-obconic.................*C. pistillaris.*
3′ Plants tubiform to funnel-form......4
4   Stem slender, flexuous; in swamps and bogs........*C. lutescens.*
4′ Stem short; on ground in the woods......5
5   Pileus tubiform ....*C. cornucopioides.*
5′ Pileus flaring, becoming funnel-form...............*C. dubius.*

C. Cantharellus Schw. (edible).   Plate 5, fig. 18.

Pileus convex, soon infundibuliform, 4-9 cm. high, 3-8 cm. broad, egg-yellow, glabrous, fleshy, firm, drying ochraceous-red, the margin lobed and irregular; stem tapering downward or equal, solid, glabrous, yellow, 2-5 cm. long, 5-10 mm. thick; hymenium wrinkled to

---

*Thelephoraceae of North America, Ann. Missouri Bot. Gard., vol. 1, 1914, p. 219.

smooth, yellow or salmon-tinged; spores 9 μ x 5 μ.—On ground in open woods, especially beech, locally common, June to Sept., Massachusetts to Illinois, southward.

This has the aspect of *Cantharellus cibarius,* from which it differs by the much smoother hymenium.

C. odoratus Schw.   Plate 5, fig. 17.

Plants 3-7 cm. high and broad, convex then depressed-cyathiform, margin curved downward, irregular or lobed, yellow; stem hollow, 2-4 cm. long x 3-7 mm. thick; hymenium wrinkled or smooth, orange with reddish tinge.—In moist woods, rare, June-Oct., Ohio to Missouri and southward.

This plant is more membranaceous than *C. Cantharellus,* thus more pliant. It has the aspect of *Cantharellus cibarius.*

C. cornucopioides (Pers.) L.   Plate 5, fig 16.

Plants 5-8 cm. high, 2-5 cm. broad, tubiform, thin, somewhat membranaceous, smoky-brown, blackish, minutely squamose, the margin lobed, irregular, erect to decurved; stem short, hollow, smooth, concolor, 1-3 cm. long, 3-5 mm. thick; hymenium wrinkled or smooth, ashy; spores hyaline, smooth, 14 μ x 8 μ.—Gregarious or subcaespitose on earth in mixed woods, rare, June-Sept., Ontario to South Carolina, Illinois, and Missouri.

C. dubius Peck.

Plants 5-10 cm. high, 3-6 cm. broad, thin, funnel-form, dark lurid-brown, the margin wavy or lobed; stem short, hollow, ashy, 1-3 cm. long, 3-6 mm. thick; hymenium wrinkled, much anastomosing, ashy; spores 7 μ x 5 μ.—Solitary or caespitose on the ground in rich woods, not common, Ontario to Illinois, Indiana, and New York.

This has a broader and more flaring pileus than *C. cornucopioides.*

C. lutescens (Fr.) Pers.

Plants 3-5 cm. high, 2-3 cm. broad, convex-umbilicate to tubiform or funnel-form, thin, almost membranaceous, smoky-yellow-brown, the margin irregular, lobed; stem equal, flexuous, yellow, slender, hairy at base, 2-4 cm. long, 2-4 mm. thick; hymenium remotely ridged, smooth or wrinkled; spores yellow, smooth, 11 x 7 μ.—On the ground in swamps, Aug.-Oct., not rare, Newfoundland and North Carolina to Michigan.

This resembles *Cantharellus infundibuliformis* in form and color.

C. pistillaris Fr.   Plate 5, fig. 20.

Plants 6-12 cm. high, 2-4 cm. broad, clavate to narrowly obconic, truncate or somewhat convex, yellowish-cinnamon, then smoky-tinged, the margin obtuse; stem solid, paler than the pileus, often bulbous, 3-8 cm. long, 4-12 mm. thick; hymenium corrugated and wrinkled, yellow-cinnamon to fuscous; spores smooth, 11 x 7 μ.— Gregarious on the ground in conifer woods, not common, New England to Michigan.

This plant resembles *Clavaria pistillaris.*

SOLENIA (Pers.) Hoffm. Plate 1, fig. 32.

Without a distinct trama or pileus to join pores and dissepiments together, each pore and its surrounding wall more or less solitary, cylindrical to cistern-shaped, each more easily described as a unit plant; connected by loose hyphae; spores white or wood-colored.— Growing on rotting wood, throughout our area.

Some have placed *Solenia* in the Polyporaceae and interpreted the many separate plants as so many pores on the mycelial substratum.

S. candida Pers. White Solenia.

Plants scattered or solitary, each shaped like a cistern, cylindrical, shining-white, glabrous, 2-3 mm. high; spores smooth, hyaline, 5 x 4 μ.—On moist decaying wood, Aug.-Dec., rare, throughout our area.

S. anomala (Pers.) Fuckel.

S. ochracea Hoffm.

Plants crowded or scattered, each shaped like a cistern, narrowed toward base and apex, turbinate or pyriform, ochraceous, white within, drying snuff-brown, clothed with thick-walled hairs 2½-3 μ in diameter and often rough-walled near their tips; spores smooth, hyaline, cyindrical, curved, 6-11 x 2-4 μ.—On moist decaying wood or bark of dead twigs of deciduous trees, especially *Quercus* and *Salix,* occasionally found, throughout our area.

CYTIDIA Quel.

Fructifications cup-shaped, coriaceous-gelatinous, sessile, scattered to crowded and confluent, resupinate in middle only; hymenium at first smooth and even, becoming somewhat wrinkled or veined; basidia simple; spores white.—Growing on bark and wood.

C. salicina (Fr.) Burt.

Corticium salicina Fr.

Plants 1-3 mm. across, becoming 5-20 mm. by confluence, 400-800 μ thick, pezizoid at first, becoming expanded, affixed by the center only, margin free and upturned, coriaceous, soft, drying rigid and tough; hymenium blood-red to bright brown-red, drying wrinkled; spores hyaline, smooth, cylindrical, curved, 14 x 4 μ.—Growing on dead limbs of *Salix,* common, May-Dec., Indiana dunes, northern half of our area.

CLAVARIACEAE

Hymenium smooth and even, on all sides of the upper parts of erect fleshy clubs or dense branches.

See Burt, E. A., Ann. Mo. Bot. Gardens 19:305-362, 1922; Coker, W. C. The Clavarias of Eastern United States and Canada, 209 p., 92 pl., U. of N. C. Press, 1928.

CLAVARIA L. Coral fungi. Plate 6.

Plants much branched, cylindrical, clavate, or filiform, composed of terete or flattened units, hymenium present on the external surface usually toward the tips of the branches.

Species of *Tremellodendron* are similar to those of *Clavaria* but have more gelatinous substance, and the hymenial surface is confined to one side only of the branch. *Clavaria pistillaris* resembles closely *Craterellus pistillaris.*

1 Plants branched......2
1' Plants simple or confluent at base only......19
1" Plants simple, the bases not confluent......21
2 Plants large, up to 10-15 cm. high; spores colored in mass..3
2' Plants 8 cm. high or smaller......8
3 Branches red-tipped ....*C. botrytoides.*
3' Branches not red-tipped......4
4 Whole plant reddish to red-brown, stem elongated......
  ....*C. holorubella.*
4' Plant pinkish-buff, becoming violet and finally black where
  bruised ....*C. formosa.*
4" Plants not pink or red-tinted......5
5 All branches anastomosing...................*C. densissima.*
5' Branches but slightly or not at all anastomosing......6
6 Plants deep yellow................................*C. flava.*
6' Plants light yellow or white......7
7 Plants white or creamy-yellow, irregularly branching from
  the base ....*C. densa.*
7' Plants ivory or cream-white, dichotomously branched,
  pinkish at base ....*C. Kunzei.*

8   Plant growing on the ground......9
8' Plant growing on wood, 3-10 cm. high......15

9   Plants white, grayish or light tan......10
9' Plants yellow or violet......13

10 Spores colored, flesh slowly acrid then bitter.........*C. albida.*
10' Spores white......11

11 Plants much branched......12
11' Plants but little branched........................*C. rugosa.*

12 Plants ochraceous or yellowish-cinereous..........*C. cinerea.*
12' Plants white, flattened upward, cristate...........*C. cristata.*

13 Plants ochraceous......14
13' Plants apricot-yellow, 3-4 cm. high, little branched......
....*C. corniculata.*
13" Plants lilac, drying yellowish.................*C. amethystina.*

14 Plants growing under pines, 2-4 cm. high.........*C. pinophila.*
14' Plants growing under balsam-fir, globose, 3-5 cm. in diameter, bruises green ....*C. abietina.*
14" Plants growing in deciduous forest, pale yellow, massive..
....*C. crassipes.*

15 Branchlet-tips cup-shaped.......................*C. pyxidata.*
15' Branchlet-tips not cup-shaped......16

16 Tip flattened and encircled with a crown of minute
processes ....*C. coronata.*
16' Tips otherwise......17

17 Plant growing on hemlock logs, becoming cinnamon..*C. tsugina.*
17' Plant not growing on hemlock logs, not cinnamon......18

18 Plant medium-sized, 4-8 cm. high, with strands of white
mycelium at base, the taste bitter...................*C. stricta.*
18' Plant very large, 15 cm. high; stem 2-3 cm. thick.*C. lentofragilis.*

19 Plants bright yellow, branched at base only......20
19' Plants white, branched at base only..........*C. vermicularis.*

20 Plants canary-yellow to cinnabar, hollow...............
..................................*C. aurantio-cinnabarina.*
20' Plants clear canary-yellow, becoming hollow.....*C. fusiformis.*

21 Plants white, with the odor of garlic..............*C. foetida.*
21' Plants orange-yellow ....*C. inequalis.*
21" Plants ochraceous to umber......22

22 Plants slender, 5 mm. or less in diameter......23
22' Plants thicker, 1 cm. in diameter or larger......24

23   Plants brownish, filiform, 5-8 cm. high, 2 mm. in diameter
     ....*C. juncea.*
23' Plants slender, 5-20 cm. high, 2-5 mm. in diameter, larger
     near apex, growing on buried wood..............*C. fistulosa.*
24   Plants large, 5-15 cm. high, 1-5 cm. thick, clavate, larger
     upward, ochraceous-buff ....*C. pistillaris.*
24' Plants medium-sized, 3-7 cm. high, 1 cm. thick toward apex,
     more slender downward, ochraceous ....*C. ligula.*

C. botrytoides Peck (edible).   Plate 6, fig. 1.

Plants 5-10 cm. high, 3-6 cm. across; spores 8 x 5 μ.

Trunk short, buff, divided near base into branches which are repeatedly and irregularly branched, the ultimate branches short, white,
crowded, blunt, with two or more blunt teeth; tips red or pink when
young, soon fading, the flesh white, the taste mild; spores elliptical,
rusty.—On grounds in woods, rare, Massachusetts, South Carolina,
Idaho.

C. holorubella Atkins.   Red Clavaria (edible).   Plate 6, fig. 2.

Plants 9-18 cm. high, 6-12 cm. across.

Trunk stout, 3 cm. in diameter, rooting, the several stout branches
from the trunk branching repeatedly, the entire plant reddish to mad-
der-brown, the flesh reddish, the surface white with bloom composed
of spores.—In woods on ground, rare, eastern part of our area.

C. formosa Pers. (edible).   Plate 6, fig. 3.

Plants 9-18 cm. high, 8-15 cm. across; spores 10 x 5 μ.

Trunk massive, 1-3 cm. in diameter, much branched, fragile, pale
pinkish-buff at first, deeper in color later, the tips blunt, yellowish
or with slight pink tinge, bruising violet then black, the taste slight,
the odor none; branches erect, cylindrical or grooved, 1 cm. in diameter below, 2 mm. near apex; spores ochraceous in mass.—On ground
under beech trees, rare, probably the same range as beech.

C. flava Schaeff.   Golden Clavaria (edible).   Plate 6, fig. 4.

Plants 8-13 cm. high, 5-10 cm. across; spores 11-14 x 5 μ.

Trunk thick, white, fragile, ochraceous or reddish where bruised,
the branching irregular or dichotomous, the branches not flattened,
acute, erect, solid, smooth; spores pale ochraceous in mass.—In conifer and frondose woods, especially of beech, rare, throughout our
area.

C. densa Peck. (edible).   Plate 6, fig. 5.

Plants 5-10 cm. high, 4-8 cm. across; spores 8 x 6 μ.

Trunks clustered from the ground, branching numerously, the branches nearly parallel, crowded, terete, white to cream-colored, the tips dentate, concolorous.—On the ground in woods, rare, August, not with certainty found within our area.

C. densissima Peck. (edible).

Plants 7-10 cm. high, 5-8 cm. wide; spores 9 x 5 μ.

Trunk branched from the base, the branches pale ochraceous to whitish, white within, often compressed, very crowded, sometimes anastomosing, ending in two or more blunt or pointed whitish tips; spores uninucleate, boat-shaped.—On much decayed vegetation in mixed woods, rare, Michigan.

C. albida Peck.   Plate 6, fig. 6.

Plants 5-10 cm. high, 3-8 cm. across; spores 13 x 5 μ.

Plant white, the trunk short, thick, tapering downward or cylindrical, divided at top into a few short, thick, much branched ramuli, the ultimate branches very crowded with tips of a few, short, blunt teeth, the flesh firm, whitish, with slowly acrid then bitter taste; spores pale ochraceous.—On ground in open woods, August, rare, Ohio, probably to be found in the eastern part of our range.

C. crassipes Peck.   Plate 6, fig. 7.

Plants 7-14 cm. high, 5-10 cm. across; spores 15 x 6.5 μ.

Trunk solid, 2-3 cm. thick, firm, glabrous, whitish, tapering downward, bruising smoky-brown, drying tawny-olive, repeatedly branched above, the branches very numerous, crowded, solid, obtusely dentate at the tips, whitish to slightly yellow; spores oblong, uninucleate, each with an oblong apiculus.—On the ground in woods, rare, eastern part of our area.

C. abietina Pers.   Plate 6, fig. 8.

Plants 3-5 cm. high, 3-5 cm. across; spores 8 x 4 μ.

Plants spherical; trunk short, thick, downy, whitish, much branched, the branches dull-ochraceous, becoming greenish in drying or where bruised, compressed, longitudinally wrinkled when dry, the tips pointed or bifid, the branches repeatedly forked, erect, slender, 1-2 mm. thick, the taste bitter, the odor strong; spores deep ochraceous in mass, copious, pip-shaped.—On ground in conifer woods, rare, northern part of area.

C. stricta Pers.

Plants 4-8 cm. high, 3-6 cm. across; spores 8 x 4 μ.

Plants ochraceous, tinged with buff or pinkish-buff, tough, the odor strong and spicy, the taste bitter; trunk distinct, short, thick, tough, root-like, with strands of white mycelium at the base, branching irregularly or dichotomously, the axils acute, the branches erect, slender, cylindrical to compressed, the tips somewhat pointed, solid, slightly incurved; spores ochraceous in mass, pip-shaped.—On rotting wood in woods, common, Sept.-Oct., throughout our area.

C. tsugina Peck.

Plants 4-8 cm. high, 3-6 cm. across; spores 9 x 4 μ.

Plants at first creamy-yellow, the older parts brown or vinaceous-brown, tough, the trunk short, thick, glabrous, branching from the base, solid, the branches few, suberect, flexible, the tips acute; spores ochraceous, elliptic, minutely rough.—On decaying logs of hemlock in woods, rare, northern part of our area.

C. Kunzei Fr.   Plate 6, fig. 12.

Plants 5-12 cm. high, 4-8 cm. across; spores 3 x 4 μ.

Plants ivory to pink, shining, or creamy-white above and pink toward base, brittle, without odor, pleasant in taste, the trunk distinct, 1-2 cm. long, 3-5 mm. thick, loosely branching, with lunate axils, the branching irregularly dichotomous, the branches cylindrical or slightly compressed, often elongated, 2-5 mm. thick, smooth, solid, blunt-pointed, shining-ivory or creamy-white; spores hyaline, globose, minutely apiculate.—In long grass of woods and pastures, not common, northern half of our area.

C. cristata Fr.   Crested Clavaria (edible).   Plate 6, fig. 9.

Plants 3-8 cm. high, 3-6 cm. across; spores 9 x 7 μ.

Plants pure white to pinkish-white, shining, without odor, with a distinct taste, somewhat fragile, numerously branched from base and upward, the branches flattened upward, the branchlets several and short pointed near the tip of the branch, the axils rounded; spores hyaline, smooth, apiculate.—On shaded ground, in woods, frequently covered by fallen leaves, gregarious, common, throughout our area.

C. cinerea Bull.

Plants 3-6 cm. high, 2-5 cm. across; spores 9 x 7 μ.

Plants fragile, ashy-gray or tinged slightly purple, without odor, the flesh white; trunk short, thick, more or less distinct, repeatedly much-branched, the branches cylindrical or compressed, short, stuffed, erect, wrinkled, the apex often toothed, the axils acute; spores hyaline, smooth, copious.—Solitary or gregarious on ground in woods, not common, throughout our area.

C. rugosa Bull.   Plate 6, fig. 15.

Plants 3-8 cm. high, 0.4-1 cm. thick; spores 9 x 7 μ.
Plants club-shaped, very slightly or not at all branched, whitish, tough, solid, thickened upward to 1 cm. in diameter, longitudinally wrinkled, the apex blunt; basidia bearing two sterigmata.—Solitary or gregarious on ground in woods, not common, eastern part of area.

C. pyxidata Pers.   (edible).   Plate 6, fig. 10.

Plants 2-10 cm. high, 2-7 cm. across; spores 3.5 x 2.5 μ.
Plants much branched, white or pallid drying pale tan and somewhat rufescent; trunk slender, glabrous, the branches solid, tiny cups each 1-2 mm. in diameter at or near the apex, the cups radiate-branched, the terminal ones dentate; spores white in mass.—On rotten wood in woods, Sept.-Oct., common throughout our area.

C. coronata Schw.

Plants 2-7 cm. high, 2-6 cm. across; spores 4 x 3 μ.
Plants resembling *C. pyxidata* in color, shape, size, and consistency, differing only in that each ultimate branch is truncate at the apex, and is there encircled with a crown of minute projections.—On rotten wood, not uncommon, throughout our area.

C. pinophila Peck.

Plants small 2-3 cm. high, 1-2 cm. across; spores 11 x 4 μ.
Plants whitish, pale ochraceous, or gray, the trunk short, slender, tufted, much branched, the branches crowded, compressed above and digitately divided, the ultimate branches rather long, and white, subulate and pointed at the tips; spores oblong.—On the ground or sand in thin woods under pines, local, Indiana dunes.

C. lentofragilis Atkins.   Plate 6, fig. 14.

Plants 15 cm. high, 12 cm. across; spores 5 μ in diameter.
Plants large, the trunk gray, 2-4 cm. long, 2-3 cm. thick, dividing into several short white branches, which in turn repeatedly branch dichotomously, the tips short, conical, soft, fragile, white, in dried specimens sepia-colored, the taste and odor little; spores subglobose, white.—On very rotten wood in sphagnous bogs, locally common in the northern part of our area.

C. corniculata Schaeff.   Plate 6, fig. 13.

C. muscoides L.

Plants 2-4 cm. high, 1-2 cm. across; spores 5 μ in diameter.

Plants apricot-yellow, tough, the stem slender, 2-3 mm. in diameter, tapering upward, dividing at half-height into two or four branches which again at half-length may branch into incurving (erect) conical branchlets, the axils rounded; sterigmata 4, spores white, smooth, globose.—On ground in rich moist woods, common, northern part of area.

C. amethystina (Batt.)   Bull.   Plate 6, fig. 11.

Plants 3-4 cm. high, 2-4 cm. across; spores 5-7 μ in diameter.

Plants violet or lilac becoming rapidly yellowish in drying, brittle, with odor and taste of tallow; stem very short, scarcely distinct, the axils not flattened, the branching irregular, the branches 3-5 mm. thick, short, cylindrical, not attenuated, solid, smooth, erect, the tips blunt; spores hyaline, smooth, globose.—Among grass in open woods and pastures, mostly eastern.

Color shades of this species similar to those of *Clitocybe laccata* and its var. *amethystina* are sometimes found.

C. aurantio-cinnabarina Schw.

Plants 4-7 cm. high, 6 mm. thick in middle; spores 5-6 μ in diameter.

Plants club-like, thickest in middle, attenuated above and below, cylindrical when young, becoming compressed and flexuous, golden-yellow or tinted with cinnabar, becoming cinnamon-drab in drying, the base white, pruinose or pulverulent, the apex obtuse.—On ground in woods, not common, Illinois to Vermont and southward.

C. fusiformis Sowerb.   Plate 6, fig. 17.

Differing from the preceding in its bitter taste, acute apex, the clear canary-yellow color, and the fact that it becomes hollow and then flattened.—On ground in wooded ravines, August, west of Chicago.

C. vermicularis Fr.   Plate 6, fig. 23.

Plants 4-10 cm. high, 3-5 mm. in diameter; spores 4 μ in diameter.

Plants unbranched, often slightly flexuous, white, brittle, cylindrical, sometimes hollow, compressed and twisted, the tips acute; spores subglobose.—Often densely clustered on ground in moist wooded ravines, common, Minnesota to Maine and southward.

C. foetida Atkins. Plate 6, fig. 20.

Plants 4-6 cm. high, 2 mm. in diameter; spores 8 x 6 μ.

Plants white to drab, drying yellow, simple, unbranched, broadest near middle, very slender toward base, tapering upward from middle to acute or obtuse apex, the base white, the spore producing part honey-yellow; odor of garlic; spores obovate.—On the ground in woods, rare, New York, probably much more widely distributed.

C. inequalis Müll. Plate 6, fig. 16.
C. similis Boud. & Patoul.

Plants 4-8 cm. high, up to 1 cm. in diameter; spores 4 x 5 μ.

Plants simple, rarely with one or two branches, the largest near middle, round or flattened, in cross-section elongated, oblanceolate, with somewhat wavy contour, the surface smooth or with one or more furrows, bright orange-yellow, the apex acute or obtuse, the flesh whitish, fibrous; spores hyaline to white or slightly ochraceous in mass, subglobose, echinulate.—On ground in woods or among grass, not common, Indiana Dunes State Park to Vermont.

C. pistillaris L. (edible)   Plate 6, fig. 18.

Plants 5-15 cm. high, 1-5 cm. thick above; spores 14 x 8 μ.

Plants simple, oblanceolate or clavate with obtuse sometimes almost truncate apex, solid, whitish then dingy-ochraceous, the flesh white, the taste mild; spores hyaline, ochraceous in mass.—On the ground on the sides of ravines, not common, Minnesota to New York and southward.

C. ligula Schaeff.   Plate 6, fig 19.

Plants 3-7 cm. high, 5-10 mm. thick at widest part; spores 12 x 4 μ.

Plants unbranched, clavate or clavate-spathulate to more slender, broadest above, much narrowed toward base, not hollow, pinkish-buff when young, cinnamon-brown in age; spores hyaline, smooth.—On ground in conifer woods, common locally, Aug.-Oct., New York, Idaho, Missouri.

C. fistulosa Holmsk.   Plate 6, fig. 21.

Plants 5-20 cm. high, 1-5 mm. wide; spores 14 x 7 μ.

Plants almost filiform up to ⅔ of height, then widening to the obovate apex, 5 mm. across, tough, often twisted, smooth, solid, becoming hollow, yellowish then date-brown, villose at base; hyphae much branched, milk-bearing, 6 μ in diameter.—On buried wood in conifer swamps, rare, Sept.-Oct., Wisconsin to New England.

C. juncea Fr.   Plate 6, fig. 22.

Plants 5-8 cm. high, 1 mm. in diameter; spores 10 x 4 μ.

Plants unbranched, filiform, weak, dirty-yellow then tinged rusty or brownish-drab, hollow, hairy at base, with acrid taste and no odor; spores elliptical, smooth, hyaline.—On fallen leaves of deciduous trees, two or three together, abundant locally during wet weather, Wisconsin to New England.

LACHNOCLADIUM Lev.

Fructifications much branched to simple and club-like, like *Clavaria* in shape, coriaceous, more or less hairy-coated.

This genus is separated from *Clavaria* on the basis of its coriaceous consistency and in the presence of the hairy coat.

L. Micheneri Berk. & Curt.
Clavaria fragrans Ell. & Everh.
Plants 2-4 cm. high, 1-1½ cm. broad; spores 6-12 x 3-3.5 μ.

Plants gray, dry, coriaceous; trunk 2-3 mm. in diameter, cylindrical, light buff, tomentose below, arising from mycelial patches on decaying leaves; branches filiform, flexuous, with paler tips, irregular; tomentose patches present at various places on trunk and branches or axils where hymenium has not developed; hymenium glabrous, without cystidia or hairs; spores smooth, hyaline.—On rotting leaves in groves, Canada to New Jersey and westward to Missouri.

AURICULARIACEAE

Gelatinous plants; basidia elongate or fusiform, simple, transversely septate.

See Engler, A. and Prantl, K. Die naturalichen Plantzenfamilien, 6:1-290, 1928.

AURICULARIA Bull.

Plants gelatinous, somewhat cartilaginous, tremulous when moist, hard and tough when dry; basidia transversely septate.

A. auricula (L.) Underw.   Jew's ear.
Tremella auricula L.
Hirneola auricula-Judae Berk.
Auricula Judae Kuntze.
Plants 1-12 cm. high, at first peziza-form then erect and foliaceous, much twisted, slightly ear or shell-shaped, one or several lobed, ses-

sile or substipitate, thin, gelatinous, trembling when moist, sterile surface curling over hymenium, red-brown when moist, yellow-brown to olive-brown when dry, when young glaucous, when older ashy pruinose, irregularly veined; hymenium red-brown when moist, smooth, undulating but not folded or wrinkled, becoming almost black when dried; spores 12 x 5 μ.—Singly or caespitose on logs and stumps, common, throughout our area.

TREMELLACEAE

Gelatinous plants; basidia subglobose at maturity, longitudinally 4-parted.

Engler, A. and Prantl, K. Die naturlichen Planzenfamilien, 6:1-290, 1928; Moffatt, W. S. Higher Fungi of the Chicago region, Bul. 7 (Pt. 1) Nat. Hist. Surv., Chi. Acad. Sci. 1909; Burt, E. A. Ann. Mo. Bot. Gardens 8:361-398, 1921; Gilbert, W. M. Wis. Acad. Sci. Arts & Let. 26:1137-1170, 1910.

EXIDIA Fr.

Plants cup-shaped when young, then gyrose and lobed; spores reniform, producing curved sporidiola on germination.—Growing on tree trunks and branches throughout the year.

E. glandulosa Fr.

Plants 2-8 cm. across, soft and gelantinous when moist, peziza-like in shape, or twisted variously, thick, effused, sometimes pendulous, cup-shaped when young, red-black, blackish-purple or olive-black, translucent when fresh, tasteless, odorless.—Growing on oak, willow, cherry, walnut, and alder, common, winter, throughout our area.

E. albida Bref.

Plants 1-4 cm. across, tough and gelantinous when moist, tough and hard when dried, white, ivory, or tinted lavender, wavy, gyrose, pruinose.—Growing on beech, birch and alder, not common, Sept.-May, throughout our area.

ULOCOLLA Bref.

Plants convex pulvinate, gyrose, cerebriform, gelatinous, rather large; basidia globose, longitudinally 4-parted.—Growing on wood.

U. foliacea Bref.

Plants from 2-9 cm. across, leaf-like, twisted, undulate, and plicate at the base, flaccid, smooth, cinamon-salmon, sometimes yellow-tinted.—Caespitose on stumps of pine, oak, and other trees, common, throughout our area.

TREMELLA Dill. Plate 1, fig. 36.

Plants pulvinate or effused, mesenteriform, cerebriform, incrusting, or tuberculiform, gelatinous, tremelloid, smooth; basidia globose, bifid or trifid, but usually longitudinally 4-parted, each part elongated into a long sterigma.—Mostly on wood, but one species incrusts mosses, etc.

T. fimbriata Pers.

Plants tough-gelatinous, lobes erect, foliaceous, large, wavy-fimbriate, not pruinose with spores, blackish-olive or brown-black.—On dead branches, not common, Wisconsin.

T. frondosa Fr.

Plants large, up to 22 cm. across, tough-gelatinous, lobes foliaceous, gyrose-wavy, plicate at base, smooth, pale yellowish-buff, tinged salmon above, wine-brown toward base, not pruinose with spores.—Growing on stumps and wood of *Fagus* and *Ostrya,* not common, July-Nov., northern part of our area.

T. lutescens Pers.

Plants medium large, up to 4 cm. across, tough gelatinous when partly dried, soft and tremulous when wet, becoming fluid, pale yellow, gyrose-wavy, lobes crowded.—Growing on oak stumps, not common, northern part of our area.

T. mesenterica Retz.

Plants up to 9 cm. across, tough, brain-like, folded-gyrose, smooth, rich orange-yellow, pruinose with white spores.—On dead branches of oak, alder, and beech, common, Jan.-Dec., northern part of our area.

T. intumescens Sowerb.

Plants up to 6 cm. across, soft, brain-like, rounded, conglomerate, twisted and lobed, brown, pruinose with white spores, obscurely punctate.—On fallen limbs, not common, throughout our area.

T. vesicaria Bull.

Plants up to 12 cm. across, firm, brain-like, erect, gyrose, undulate, with swollen bladder-like lobes, wrinkled, buff, pruinose with white spores.—Growing on the ground, rare, throughout our area.

T. epigaea Berk. & Broome.

Plants up to 10 cm. across, effused, thin, gelatinous, gyrose-folded, hyaline then write.—Covering twigs, moss, earth, nuts, etc., rare, Aug.-Nov., northern part of our area.

T. violacea Relh.

Plants up to 1 cm. in diameter, effused, firm, gyrose, violaceous.—
On trunks of pear and other fruit trees, not common, eastern part
of our area.

NAEMATELIA Fr.

Plants firm, subgelatinous, convex, with a firm solid central portion spoken of as the nucleus, not shriveling when dry; basidia longitudinally 4-parted.—Growing on wood.

N. encephala Fr.

Plants 2 cm. in diameter, pulvinate, rugose-plicate, pale flesh-
color, nucleus hard, large, white.—Growing on pine or tamarack
rails, connate for 10 cm., Sept.-Mar., Wisconsin.

N. nucleata Fr.

Plants 0.5 cm. in diameter, sessile, flattened, whitish, becoming
tawny-yellow, nucleus white, 0.5 mm. in diameter.—On decaying oak,
connate to 3 cm., not common, throughout our area.

GYROCEPHALUS Pers.

Plants erect, substipitate, flattened, irregularly spathulate, tremel-
lose-cartilaginous.

G. rufus Bref.

Plants up to 8 x 6 cm. high and wide, erect, subspathulate, orange
to red or dull scarlet above, orange below; hymenium inferior,
smooth.—Terrestrial under pines or on rotting wood, not common,
eastern part of our area.

TREMELLODON Pers. Plate 1, fig. 37

Carpophores gelatinous, pileate, dimidiate to flabelliform or infundibuliform, the spines awl-shaped; stipe very short.—On wood

T. gelatinosum Pers.

Pileous dimidiate, flabelliform or infundibuliform and split down
one side, tinged greenish-brown, covered with small pustules, gelatinous, the spines soft, glaucous, equal; spores irregular, subglobose,
2 μ in diameter.—Growing on wood and sawdust, rare, Sept.-Oct.,
eastern part of our area.

DACRYOMYCETACEAE

Plants gelatinous to horny; basidia cylindrical to clavate.

See Engler, A. and Prantl, K. Die naturlichen Planzenfamilien, 6:1-290, 1928; Moffatt, W. S. Higher Fungi of the Chicago region, Bul. 7 (Pt. 1) Nat. Hist. Surv., Chi. Acad. Sci. 1909.

DACRYOMYCES Nees.

Plants gelatinous, irregular but orbicular, convex, basal portion often root-like and entering the matrix; basidia forked, ending in the tapering sterigmata, terminated each by a cylindrical spore.

1   Plants bursting through the bark....................*D. Ellisii.*
1'   Plants growing on surface......2

2   Plants in connate chains........................*D. abietinus.*
2'   Plants not connate in chains.................*D. deliquescens.*

D. abietinus (Pers.) Schroet.
D. stillatus Nees.
Plants 2 cm. or more x 3 mm. in connate chains, somewhat round, convex, at length plicate, yellow, orange or scarlet; spores 7-septate, colored like the plant body, 15-24 x 6-9 μ.—On pine and other conifer wood, rare, Aug.-Oct., northern part of area.

D. deliquescens (Bull.) Duby.

Plants 1-5 mm. long, 1-3 mm. wide, 1-2 mm. in diameter, small, pulvinate, smoky ochraceous or pale greenish ochraceous, surface wrinkled, flattened and resin-colored when dried; spores smooth, curved, simple becoming 1-3-septate, 10-14 x 4-5 μ.—Growing on much decayed conifer wood, common, Mar.-Nov., throughout our area.

D. Ellisii Coker.
D. Harperi Bres.
Dried plants 3-5 x 2-3 mm., 2 mm. high, fresh plants subglobose or pulvinate, crumpled, firm, gelatinous, orange or wine-colored, fading to olive and drying sepia, surface plicate-gyrose, the base gyrose and buried in the bark; spores hyaline, 12 x 6 μ.—Gregarious, bursting through the bark of dead limbs of alder, oak and other deciduous trees, rare, Oct.-Feb., Illinois and Wisconsin.

GUEPINIA Fr.

Plants unequally cup-shaped, tough-gelatinous; basidia linear, deep-bifurcate; spores curved.—Growing on wood.

G. peziza Tul.

Plants cup-shaped, commonly stipitate, 1 cm. across, yellow; basidia deep-bifurcate; spores curved.—On dead branches, not common, eastern part of area.

CALOCERA Fr.

Plants clavate, cylindrical or awl-shaped, terete, simple or branched, gelatinous, drying horny.

C. palmata Schum.

Plants 12-16 mm. high, simple and subulate, or divaricately branched near the base, branches occasionally divided near the apex, compressed, dilated upward, tremellose-tough, orange-yellow; spores hyaline, curved, 10 x 6 μ.—On fallen branches of oak, sumach, etc., common, throughout our area.

C. cornea Batsch.

Plants 5-6 mm. high, clavate, subulate, connate at base, yellow-orange, smooth, viscid, rooting.—On decaying pine logs, growing in lines out of the cracks in the wood, the bases fused for several cm., often found, range of the pine wood.

HYDNACEAE

Plants variously shaped; context fleshy, coriaceous or woody; hymenium on awl-shaped or other protuberences.

See Banker, H. J. Bul. Torrey Bot. Club 28:199-222, 1901; Mem. Torrey Bot. Club 12:99-194, 1906; Mycologia 4:271-278, 1912; 4:309-318, 1912; 5:12-17, 1913; 5:62-66, 1913; 5:194-205, 1913; 5:293-298, 1913; Coker, W. C. Jour. Elisha Mitchell Sci. Soc. 34:163-197, 1919; Cejp, K. Mycologia 23:130-133, 1931; Univ. Iowa Nat. Hist. Studies 13:3-5, 1931.

HYDNUM L. Plate 7.

Plants central-stemmed, eccentric, or laterally attached, resupinate or effused over the substratum, fleshy-thick to very thin, the substance fleshy to fleshy-fibrous; hymenium projecting as numerous subulate, spine-like, or pendulous aculei; stem when present fleshy-fibrous, more or less cylindrical; spores globose to cylindrical.—Growing on the ground or on decaying wood.

1   Plant pileate......7
1'   Plant resupinate or effused......2
1"   Plant tubercular, or a mass with teeth covering much of the
       surface, or much branched with teeth on the branches.....3

2   Plants white ....*H. pallidum.*
2'   Plants dull, alutaceous..........................*H. Nyssae.*
2"   Plants bright golden-yellow................*H. chryscomum.*
2'" Plants umber to rusty.................*Odontia ferruginea.*

3   Plant white when fresh, branched or tuberculiform......4
3'   Plant partly a resupinate body with concrescent tubercles,
       buff or ochraceous ....*H. croceum.*

4   Plant branched from the base......5
4'   Plant massive, a tubercle or tubercles......6

5   Teeth on ultimate branches only...............*H. coralloides.*
5'   Teeth covering undersides of all branches........*H. laciniatum.*

6   Teeth pendant directly from tubercular body.....*H. erinaceus.*
6'   Teeth pendant from short peripheral branches....*H. caput-ursi.*

7   Pileus on a more or less central stem......11
7'   Pileus dimidiate, sessile, lateral, or resupinate-reflexed......8

8   Pileus less than 8 cm. wide; substance dry, fibrous, tough
       when fresh ....*H. ochraceum.*
8'   Pileus large, fleshy or fleshy-fibrous when fresh......9

9   Stem branching upward to many lateral pilei......*H. adustum.*
9'   Stem absent, pilei imbricated......10

10   Pilei and teeth light-colored to buff.........*H. septentrionale.*
10'   Pilei and teeth dark-colored, brown-black.......*H. strigosum.*

11   Substance of pileus fleshy, brittle......12
11'   Substance of pileus corky, woody, or coriaceous......16

12   Flesh dull-colored, fuscous, rusty, or gray......13
12'   Flesh bright-colored, white, yellow, or orange....*H. repandum.*

13   Pileus glabrous......14
13'   Pileus scaly or tomentose......15

14   Pileus pinkish-gray, stem scabrous..............*H. scabripes.*
14'   Pileus brownish ....*H. laevigatus.*

15   Plants solitary; scales thick, regularly imbricate..*H. imbricatum.*
15'   Plants caespitose, not scaly; stem flexuose......*H. fennicum.*

16   Surface of pileus zonate......22
16'   Surface of pileus not zonate......17

17   Substance of pileus in two layers, the upper compact-felty,
       the lower hard, compact, and continuous with the stem......18

17' Substance of pileus in one layer; color of plant orange; stem central, branched, and bearing several pilei......*H. floriforme.*
18 Lower compact substance black......19
18' Lower compact substance of another color......20
19 Plants azure-blue-black, white-margined..........*H. nigrum.*
19' Plants smoky-brown, not white-margined......*H. albonigrum.*
20 Plants hygrophanous, obscurely zonate, brown.......... ....*H. scrobiculatum.*
20' Plants not hygrophanous, not zonate......21
21 Pileus convex, softly matted; teeth slender......22
21' Pileus convex, teeth coarse...................*H. velutinum.*
21" Pileus depressed, teeth hair-like................*H. Nuttallii.*
22 Pileus reddish-brown, flesh thick.............*H. spongiosipes.*
22' Pileus cinnamon-brown, flesh thin..............*H. zonatum.*

H. croceum Schw. Apple-tree Hydnum.

Plants up to 30 cm. x 20 cm., 2-10 mm. thick; spores 3.5 x 5.5 μ.

Plant a resupinate subiculum, thickened here and there in tuberculous protuberances from which the teeth are pendent, cream-yellow to pinkish-buff, pubescent to tomentose, the margin definite, fimbriate, the substance fibrous, somewhat tough; teeth clustered, bulbous and pubescent at base, terete, acute, the apices flattened, fimbriate, sometimes forked, 5 mm. long; spores white, ovoid, uniguttulate.—On living and dead apple trees, August, not common, eastern part of our area.

H. coralloides Scop. Coral Hydnum (edible). Plate 7, fig. 1.

Plants 4-12 cm. across; spores 5 μ in diameter.

Plants fleshy, cauliflower-shaped, tuberculiform, much branched, pure white becoming yellow-tinged with age, the branches numerous, stem very short, dividing into branches near the base, the larger branches angular or compressed, the terminal branches curved upward and terminating in a crowded, spreading mass of downward-pointing teeth; teeth 4-8 mm. long, fragile, white, pendulous; spores globose, uninucleate, whitish.—On prostrate logs, especially of beech, not common, Aug.-Oct., throughout our area.

H. laciniatum Leers. Plate 7, fig. 2.

Plants 6-15 cm. across; spores 4 x 5 μ.

Plants fleshy, cauliflower-shaped, tuberculiform, much branched, pure white, becoming brown with age, the branches numerous, the ultimate ones 1 mm. thick, the substance fleshy, white; teeth more or less uniformly distributed on the lower surface of the branches, on all sides near tips, terete, acute, 0.5-5 mm. long; spores globose, smooth, white.—On beech and hickory logs, Aug.-Dec., throughout our area.

H. erinaceus Bull.   Plate 7, fig. 3.

Plants 7-20 cm. across.

Plants fleshy, tuberculiform, emarginate, pendulous, or lateral, white becoming yellowish with age or when dried, the large central core unbranched and covered with long pendulous teeth; teeth 1-4 cm. long, equal, straight, downward-pointing.—On trunks and logs of oak and other deciduous trees, Aug.-Oct., occasionally found, throughout our area.

H. caput-ursi Fr.   Bear's-head Hydnum (edible).   Plate 7, fig. 4.

Plants 4-25 cm. across; spores 5 x 6 μ.

Plants fleshy cauliflower-shaped, tuberculiform, pure white pendulous, lateral, or erect, consisting of a large central core with abundant short branches, each clothed with branchlets and awl-shaped teeth, white at first, becoming creamy-alutaceous with age or when dried; teeth 0.8-2 cm. long, downward-pointing; spores globose or subglobose.—On trunks and logs of deciduous trees, occasionally found, summer and autumn, throughout our area.

This plant has been identified as *H. caput-Medusae* Bull., a plant which probably does not occur in the United States. *H. caput-Medusae* is white when fresh and young, becoming gray with age or when dried.

H. repandum L.   Spreading Hydnum (edible).   Plate 7, fig. 7.

Pileus 2-10 cm. broad, 1-2 cm. thick; stem 3-8 cm. x 1-2 cm.; spores 7-8 μ in diameter.

Pileus fleshy, fragile, regular or irregular in outline, convex to plane or somewhat depressed, smooth, variable in color, tawny, buff, rusty-yellow, or reddish, the margin usually wavy and lobed; teeth 5-8 mm. long, white, often tinged pink or yellow; stem cylindrical or thickened above and (or) below, central or eccentric, paler than pileus, short, solid, stout; spores globose, yellowish.—On the ground in woods, not common, July-Oct., throughout our area.

H. scabripes Peck.   Rough-stemmed Hydnum.

Pileus 10-12 cm. broad, 1-2 cm. thick; stem 10-12 cm. x 2-3 cm.; spores 7-8 μ in diameter.

Pileus fleshy, firm, convex, glabrous, pinkish-gray, the decurved margin extending beyond the teeth, the flesh white; teeth whitish or subcinereous, becoming ferruginous-brown, decurrent; stem cylindrical, stout, scabrous-dotted; spores subglobose or irregular, somewhat nodulose.—On the ground under hemlock trees, September, rare, northern, range of hemlock.

H. laevigatum Swartz.   Plate 7, fig. 8.

Pileus 6-15 cm. wide, stem 4-8 cm. x 1-3 cm.; spores 7 x 5 μ.

Plants very large, low, broad, light to dark brown or fuscous; pileus convex to depressed, smooth on the surface, subpubescent or obscurely scaly toward center, the substance fleshy, fragile to tough; stem short, stout, eccentric, solid, subbulbous, concolor; teeth slender, terete, tapering, slightly flexuouse, subdecurrent, brownish with white tips, 3-10 mm. long, 0.5 mm. wide, 2 per square mm.; spores subglobose, coarsely tuberculate, dark-colored.—On ground in woods, Aug.-Mar., not common, eastern part of our area.

H. imbricatum L.   Plate 7, fig. 9.

Pileus 4-10 cm. broad; stem 2-7 x 2-5 cm.; spores 6 x 5 μ.

Pileus umber or brown-umber, zoneless, plane or somewhat depressed or umbilicate, tesselately floccose-scaly, the scales large, the substance fleshy, dingy-white; stem short, thick, concolorous, more or less cylindrical; teeth short or long, ashy-white or grayish-white, decurrent, 8-12 mm. long; spores rough, subglobose, pale yellow.— In mixed woods or in pine woods, autumn, occasionally found, throughout our area.

H. fennicum Karst.   Plate 7, fig. 11.

Pileus 5-10 cm. broad; stem 2-7 cm. long, 1-2.5 cm. thick; spores 4 x 5 μ.

Pileus rough and undulate, at first scaly, brick-colored, the margin undulately lobed, the substance fleshy, white; stem stout, flexuous or curved, acute at the base, concolorous, dark gray within, smooth, white-tomentose; teeth decurrent, pointed, 4 mm. long, white becoming dusky; spores rough, dusky, subglobose.—On sandy soil in woods, rare, eastern part of our area.

H. zonatum Batsch.

Pileus 2-7 cm. broad, stem 2-5 cm. x 0.5-1 cm.; spores 4 x 5 μ.

Pileus rusty-brown, thin, plane to infundibuliform, zoned, radiately rugose, the margin pale, sterile beneath, the flesh uniformly coriaceous; stem slender, tuberous at the base, concolor, cylindrical in some specimens; teeth slender, pallid to rusty; spores subglobose, rough, pale watery-brown.—In sandy woods and borders of swamps, autumn, rare, throughout our area.

H. scrobiculatum Fr.

Pileus 2-4 cm. wide; stem 2-4 cm. x 1-2 cm.

Plants central-stemmed, often confluent in masses, brown throughout; pileus obconical, densely woolly or velvety-pubescent, uneven, rugose, cinnamon-brown, changeable in color with the light, sometimes obscurely zonate, the margin obtuse, sterile, lighter than disk, the juice watery with a slight pinkish tinge; stem slender surrounded by spongy tomentum; teeth 3 mm. long, slender, terete, straight, brown with light tips; spores brown, subglobose, tuberculate; taste disagreeable.—On ground in dark damp forests, August, rare, eastern part of our area.

H. velutinum Fr.

Pileus 1-10 cm. wide; stem 1 cm. long, 1-2 cm. thick.

Plants central-stemmed, dark brown throughout; pileus obconical slightly irregular, strongly convex to depressed, the surface finely tomentose to pubescent, the margin thin, even, substerile, the substance felty-tomentose, cinnamon-brown in upper part of pileus, hard and darker in lower part and extending down the stem; stem short, conical, surrounded at base by a dense mass of felty tomentum, concolor; teeth terete, slender, straight, acute, decurrent to the bulbous base, dark or light brown, the tips lighter; spores coarsely tubercular, subglobose.—On ground in woods, eastern part of our area.

H. Nuttallii Bank.

Pileus 4-6 cm. across, 1 cm. or less thick; stem 4 x 1-2 cm.; spores 4 x 5 μ.

Pileus obconical, deeply depressed, round, thickest in center, thinning uniformly to the margin, the surface radiately rugose or fibrillose, grayish-umber, the margin thin, acute, subfertile with short teeth; stem central, surrounded below by a bulbous mass of felty tomentum; teeth capillary, more or less decurrent, almost black, 7 mm. or less long, 0.2 mm. wide, 2 per mm.; spores brownish, subtuberculate.—On ground in woods, May-July, eastern part of our area.

H. spongiosipes Peck.

Pileus 3-10 cm. broad, stem 3-8 cm. x 1-2 cm.; spores 5 x 6 μ.

Pileus convex, rusty-brown, softly matted-tomentose, the context tough, the lower stratum firmer and fibrous but concolorous; stem hard and corky within, externally spongy-tomentose, concolor, the central substance often transversely zoned, especially toward the apex; teeth slender, 2-4 mm. long, rusty-brown, becoming darker with age; spores subglobose, nodulose, purplish-brown.—On the ground in woods, rare, August, northern part of our area to New York.

H. ferrugineum Fr. is very similar to this species.

H. albonigrum Peck.

Pileus 3-8 cm. broad, 2-5 cm. thick; stem 3-5 cm. x 1-2 cm.; spores 4 x 5 μ.

Pileus convex or nearly plane, broadly obconical, soft, firm, tough, densely tomentose, buff-brown or smoky-brown, often entirely covered with a whitish downy tomentum, sometimes on margin only, the context soft-tomentose and buff-brown in the upper stratum, the lower half hard and black; teeth short, at first white then grayish; stem short, often irregular in shape, blackish to buff-brown, covered with a dense tomentum, the substance black; spores white, globose. —On ground in woods and under trees in dunes, rare, Aug.-Sept., Indiana to New York.

H. nigrum Fr.

Pileus 2-6 cm. broad, 2-5 cm. thick; stem 1-3 cm. x 1-2 cm.

Pileus convex then flattened, plano-depressed, club-shaped when young then obconical or turbinate, azure-blue-black, zoneless but with a white margin when mature, corky-ridged; stem stout, often rooting, often irregular in shape, blackish, tomentose at base, the substance black; teeth awl-shaped, short, slender, white.—On ground under pines in the Indiana dunes, Sept.-Oct., near the Great Lakes.

H. floriforme (Schaeff.) Bank.
H. aurantiacum Alb. & Schw.

Pileus 2.5-12 cm. broad; stem 1-5 cm. long, 1-2.5 cm. thick.

Pileus obconical to turbinate, orange, roughened with small elevation, often clothed with white tomentum, the flesh corky, compact, zoned; stem central, often several united together, orange, short and thick; teeth whitish to orange becoming fuscous, 2-4 mm. long.— On the ground in woods, either of hemlock or deciduous trees, rare, northern part of our area.

H. septentrionale Fr. Plate 7, fig. 13.

Pileus 5-15 cm. long, 5-30 cm. wide, 1-4 cm. thick; spores 3 x 6 μ.

Pilei several from a thick connate body, imbricated, shelf-shaped, sessile, plane, the margin entire or lobed, pallid, gray-brown or whitish, the substance fibrous-fleshy, tough, whitish, the odor strong and unpleasant; teeth cylindrical, crowded, slender, 5-15 mm. long; spores oblong, smooth, apiculate, hyaline.—On elm, maple, beech, black gum, and other deciduous trees, not common, throughout our area.

H. strigosum Swartz.

Pileus 5-20 cm. long and wide, 1-4 cm. thick.

Pilei numerous, imbricated, arising from a fleshy-fibrous connate base, sessile, flabelliform, or shelf-like, dimidiate, subconvex, or deformed when imbricate, fuscous, fuscous-brown, or brown-black, strigose-coated, the substance fibrous, tough; teeth 1-3 cm. long, crowded, slender, whitish at first then dark-colored, forked toward margin.—On deciduous trees, rare, southwest of Chicago.

H. adustum Schw.

Pileus 5-7 cm. broad, stem 2-4 cm. long; spores 12-15 x 7 μ.

Plants large, moist when fresh, bearing many lateral pilei; pileus variable in shape, orbicular and entire to dimidiate or reniform, whitish or pale yellow, the substance coriaceous-tough; stem ascending, unequal, central if unbranched, lateral if one of several branches; teeth 1-3 mm. long, 0.1-0.2 mm. wide, 4 per square mm., pallid or yellowish becoming brown or blackish with age or when dried, slender, tapering, crowded, forking, fimbriate, sometimes flattened and concentric; spores elliptic-oblong.—On moist dead wood, rare, reported from the woods of Glencoe, Illinois.

H. ochraceum Pers.

Pileus 3-15 mm. long, 2-40 mm. wide; spores 3 x 3.5 μ.

Plants pileate, effused-reflexed, sessile, often imbricate, dimidiate, sometimes wholly resupinate, the surface ochraceous to ashy-gray, subrugose, sulcate-zonate, subtomentose, the margin incurved or reflexed, entire, pubescent, sterile for 1 mm. or more, the substance thin, fibrous-tough, 1 mm. or less thick, dry, whitish; hymenium ochraceous, whitish-pubescent; teeth slender, short, compressed to subterete, acute, tough, often forked, shorter toward margin, 1.5 mm. or less long, crowded, 3 per square mm.; spores hyaline, smooth granular.—On dead *Acer, Carpinus, Thuja, Viburnum, Fagus,* throughout the year, not uncommon, throughout our area.

H. pallidum Curt. & Ell.

Plants effused, covering areas 2-30 cm. across, the subiculum membranaceous, soft, white, the margin villous; spines slender, short, 1 mm. long, white, becoming fuscous, crowded.—On undersides of moist decaying deciduous logs, July-Oct., throughout our area.

H. chryscomum Underw.

Plants resupinate, forming areas 2-6 cm. across, bright orange-yellow, the mycelial strands wide-creeping, branched; subiculum thin, whitish-fimbriate on the margin, yellowish or later bright orange-yellow toward center; teeth crowded, 1 mm. in length, often confluent and then appearing flattened, terete when single, obtuse; mycelium consisting of cord-like branching strands 10-20 cm. long penetrating decaying wood, bright orange, its growth finally separating the bark from the wood.—On undersides of decayed logs, Aug.-Nov., not common, throughout our area.

H. Nyssae Berk. & Curt.

Plants effused over areas 3-10 cm. across, copiously pulverulent, alutaceous, the margin indefinite, pulverulent, whitish; teeth awl-shaped, long, crowded, acute, often penciled at tip, concolorous, pubescent, occasionally bearing long hairs at the apex.—On rotting deciduous stumps and moist logs, August, throughout our area.

IRPEX Fr.

Plants resupinate or effused-reflexed, leathery or woody, covering areas several cm. long and wide with or without the edges reflexed to form a pileus, or covering small areas with margin much reflexed to form a relatively large pileus; hymenium composed of teeth, concrete with the pileus or with the leathery or woody subiculum, the teeth often arranged in rows and connected at the base. —Growing on wood.

Some species included here resemble those of *Polyporus* in which the pores become dentate in age.

1 Plants effused-reflexed......2
1′ Plants wholly resupinate......3
2 Pileus white, teeth terete.........................*I. lacteus.*
2′ Pileus tobacco-colored, teeth variously shaped......*I. tabacinus.*
3 Plants white ....*I. ambiguus.*
3′ Plants olive to fawn-colored...................*I. fuscescens.*
3″ Plants whitish, yellowish or pale rusty toward the center..
....*I. nodulosus.*

I. lacteus Fr.

Pileus 1-2 cm. long, 2-3 cm. wide, effused-reflexed, white, villose, somewhat concentrically sulcate; teeth 2-10 mm. long, 0.4-1 mm. in diameter, usually obtusely rounded, sometimes acute, at the tips, terete.—On dead wood of deciduous trees, common, throughout our area.

I. tabacinus Berk. & Curt.

Plants effused, narrowly reflexed, tobacco-colored, subzonate, pubescent; hymenium long-decurrent, bright tobacco-colored, the teeth unequal, often fused in groups, 2-10 mm. long, 0.5-1 mm. in diameter or 4 mm. by fusion.—On decaying poplar in woods, not common, throughout our area.

I. ambiguus Peck.

Plants resupinate over areas several cm. across, adnate, the subiculum very thin, floccose-pruinate, white or whitish; teeth variable in form, subulate to compressed, acute, more or less united at the bases into concentric series, 1-3 mm. long, white becoming pallid.— On decaying wood of deciduous trees, not common, throughout our area.

I. fuscescens Schw.

Plants resupinate, at first orbicular then confluent and covering areas several cm. across, olivaceous becoming cervine, coriaceous-membranaceous, the border narrow, fimbriate; teeth compressed, unequal, 1-8 mm. long, irregular, setulose, cervine then cinnamon with age.—On dead fallen branches, not common, throughout our area.

I. nodulosus Peck.

Plants resupinate forming oval patches 10-25 cm. across, somewhat separable from the substratum, the subiculum thick, tough; hymenium dentate-porous toward the thick and definite margin, centrally nodulose and prolonged into unequal, compressed laciniate, rarely terete teeth, white, centrally ochraceous or pale rusty.—On dead wood, not common, throughout our area.

RADULUM Fr. Plate 1, fig. 12.

Plants resupinate, sometimes reflexed at the margin, effused over bark or wood, often bursting through the bark, coriaceous or membranaceous; hymenium composed of irregular, subcylindrical obtuse tubercles.—On dead sticks and decaying logs.

R. orbiculare Fr.

Plants 5-8 cm. across, 1-4 mm. thick, membranaceous to thick and coriaceous, orbicular, confluent, white becoming yellowish with age, the border byssine but not reflexed; hymenium composed of elongated nearly terete, clustered or scattered tubercles.—On dead sticks in deciduous woods, June-Nov., throughout our area.

During spring the young plant is waxy, flesh-colored, and much softer than when more mature.

R. pallidum Berk. & Curt.

Plants at first orbicular then confluent and effused over areas several cm. across, the margin narrowly reflexed, pallid, tomentose; tubercles pallid, terete, short, unequally formed, scattered or collected in groups or rows.—On decaying oak logs, not common, throughout our area.

PHLEBIA Fr.   Plate 1, fig. 13a.

Plants entirely resupinate, our species red to red-flesh-colored; hymenium amphigenous, waxy-soft, smooth, continuous, from the first wrinkled and usually radiately ridged, the wrinkles crowded, persistent, everywhere bearing spores.—Growing on bark and branches of deciduous trees.

1 Plants villous on undersides, flesh-colored......*P. merismoides*.
1' Plants smooth on both sides......2
2 Plants red-flesh-colored, not concentrically zonate.....*P. radiata*
2' Plants red or orange becoming brownish, zonate...........
......................................*P. strigoso-zonata*.

P. merismoides Fr.

Plants resupinate-effused for several centimeters, flesh-colored fading with age, villous and white on undersides, the border orange, strigose; hymenium with radiating, simple, straight, crowded folds. —On the undersides of fallen decaying branches, Sept.-Oct., not common, throughout our area.

P. radiata Fr.   Plate 7, fig. 15.

Plants resupinate, 1-4 cm. across, waxy-soft, flesh-colored to bright red, somewhat round, smooth on both sides, the border dentate-radiate; hymenium red to red-brown, beset with crowded, radiating folds.—On bark of *Tilia* and on *Quercus* logs, not common, throughout our area.

P. strigoso-zonata (Schw.) Lloyd.
Merulius strigoso-zonatus Schw.
Auricularia strigoso-zonata (Schw.) Lloyd.
Resupinate part 1-5 cm. across; reflexed part 5-15 mm.; spores 7 x 3-4 μ.
Plants resupinate or effused-reflexed, red to orange, drying brown, coriaceous, somewhat imbricated and confluent, concentrically sulcate, somewhat tomentose, zonate, bearing one to three narrow darker

zones; hymenium with crowded, radiating wrinkles which are frequently interrupted, drying smoky-black and suffused with a bloom: spores white, flattened on one side, 6-8 x 3-4 μ.—On poplar, beech, or oak logs and on dead trees, not comon, throughout our area.

ODONTIA Pers.   Plate 1, fig. 13.

Plants entirely resupinate over indefinite areas; subiculum thin, composed of interwoven fibers bearing crested warts or crested spines.—On dead branches or decayed wood.

1 Plants pallid, hymenium composed of minute warts......2
1' Plants umber to rusty, spines slender, long.......*O. ferruginea.*
2 Subiculum fibrous, margin scarcely fimbriate..........*O. tenuis.*
2' Subiculum membranaceous, margin fimbriate.......*O. fimbriata.*

O. tenuis Peck.

Plant effused, very thin, tender, dry, pallid, the margin not clearly fimbriate; hymenium composed of minute verrucae which are borne on the interwoven fibers of the subiculum, the verrucae scarcely visible to the naked eye, subglobose or oblong, scattered or crowded, sometimes entire; mycelium sometimes collected into dingy-yellowish branching slender threads.—On much decayed birch and other woods of deciduous trees, not common, throughout our area.

O. ferruginea (Pers.) Bank.
Hydnum crinale Fr.
Plant effused over areas several cm. long, thin, villous-interwoven, umber; aculei crowded, equal, very slender, rusty-umber, comparatively long.—On bark of rotting logs in woods, October, not common, throughout our area.

O. fimbriata Pers.
Plant effused, membranaceous, seceding, pallid, traversed by rootlike fibers, the border fibrillose-fimbriate; hymenium composed of minute warts in the form of granules, each multifid at the apex. —On dead crab apple, *Ostrya,* or *Crataegus,* June-Sept., not common, throughout our area.

POLYPORACEAE

Hymenium consisting of pores or tubes, usually with the openings facing toward the ground; fructifications resupinate, reflexed, or pileate, with fleshy, coriaceous or woody context.

See Peck, C. H. (*Boletus*) N. Y. Mus. Bul. 8, p. 80-157, 1889; Snell, W. H. Notes on Boletes, Mycologia 24:334-341, 1932; 25:221-232, 1933; 26: 348-359, 1934; 28:13-26, 1936; Murrill, American Boletes, New York, 1914; Neuman, J. J. Wis. Geol. and Nat. Hist. Surv. Bul. 33, Sci. Ser. No. 10, Madison, 1914; Hard, M. E. Mushrooms, edible and otherwise, the Ohio Library Co., 1908; Peck, C. H. (*Boletinus*) N. Y. Mus. Bul. 8:74-80, 1889; Overholts, L. O. Washington Univ. Studies, Vol. 3, Pt. 1, p. 3-98, 1915; Penn. Agri. Exp. Sta. Bul. 298, 1933; Lowe, J. L. N. Y. Col. of Forestry, Tech. publ. 41:142 p., Syracuse, 1934; Baxter, Dow V. Some resupinate Polypores from the region of the Great Lakes, Mich. Acad. Sci. Arts & Let. 14:259-291, 1930; 15:191-228, 1931; 20:273-282, 1934; 21:243-268, 1935; 22:275-296, 1935; 23:285-307, 1936; 24:167-185, 1938; 25:145-170, 1939.

POROTHELIUM Fr.

Plants resupinate, thin, somewhat membranaceous, white, the margin ragged, the papillae crowded toward center, and there becoming confluent, remaining separate and more scattered toward the margin, soon opened.

P. fimbriatum Fr.

Plant covering areas up to 15 x 4 cm., resupinate, white, thin, paper-like, margin thinner and fimbriate-ragged, papillae soon depressed in the center into tubes thus ultimately forming pores.— Growing on underside of decaying logs of both deciduous and conifer species, infrequently found, throughout our area.

MERULIUS Hall. Plate 1, fig. 18.

Plants composed of mucedinous mycelium, resupinate, reflexed or dimidiate, fleshy waxy-soft, almost tremellose in some species; hymenium continuous, waxy-soft, incompletely poroid, becoming gyrose to obscurely irpiciform, at first plane, even, thin, becoming folded and reticulate, the hymenium covering the entire surface.—Mostly on wood.

1 Plants dimidiate, imbricated, coral-pink, tomentose. .*M. rubellus.*
1′ Plants resupinate or effused-reflexed......2
2 Plants effused-reflexed when fully developed......3
2′ Plants always resupinate......5
3 Plants fleshy-tremellose, pores large...........*M. tremellosus.*
3′ Plants not fleshy-tremellose......4

4   Pores 1 mm. across..........................*M. ambiguus.*
4'   Pores 3 per mm...............................*M. corium.*
5   Plants pink to reddish, drying fawn-colored..........*M. rufus.*
5'   Plants yellowish to rusty......6
6   Hymenium bright golden-yellow....................*M. aureus.*
6'   Hymenium duller or rusty......7
7   Hymenium dull yellow, plants growing on conifer wood....
       ....*M. pinastri.*
7'   Hymenium rusty 8
8   Margin thickened ....*M. lacrymans.*
8'   Margin not thickened........................*M. americanus.*

M. pinastri (Fr.) Burt.

Plants covering areas 2-15 cm. across, 1 mm. thick; spores 5-6 x 4-5 μ.

Plants resupinate, effused, membranaceous, soft, yellow at first then olive-ochre, the margin whitish, the flesh soft; hymenium gyrose-porose, becoming toothed as in Irpex by the prolongation of the folds; structure composed of loosely interwoven nodose-septate hyphae, each 4-5 μ in diameter; spores pale ochraceous, smooth, subglobose. —On compost and earth in mushroom beds and greenhouses and on decaying wood and bark, usually of conifers, Oct.-Nov. out of doors, Dec.-Feb. in greenhouses.

M. americanus Burt.
M. lacrymans var. *tenuissimus* Berk.

Plants covering areas 3-15 cm. across, 0.5 mm. thick; spores 9 x 6 μ.

Plants resupinate, effused, membranaceous, separable, thin, yellow-ferruginous drying brown, the margin not thickened; hymenium at first gyrose-porose, the folds elongating into raduloid teeth on an inclined substratum, the pores 1-1.5 mm. in diameter and almost 1 mm. in depth; spores smooth, bone-brown in mass.—Undersides of conifer logs or boards in moist places, not common, throughout our area (after Burt).

M. lacrymans (Fr.) Wulf.
M. destruens Pers.

Plants covering areas 8-15 cm. across, 2-12 mm. thick; spores 10 x 6 μ.

Plants resupinate, effused-reflexed, thick, yellow-rusty, drying brown to sepia, the margin tumid, thickened, tomentose, white, the context 1 mm. thick, spongy, fleshy, moist; hymenium 1-10 mm. thick, soon in large folds, becoming gyrose-dentate, the pores 1-2

mm. across, about 1 mm. deep, the hymenial layer composed of nodose-septate hyphae, some yellowish in color, some hyaline; spores
sepia in mass, citron-yellow under microscope, smooth, flattened on
one side.—Undersides of conifer logs, under floors and beams in
buildings, rare, throughout our area.

M. aureus Fr.

Plants small, 0.5 x 1 cm., 0.3-1.3 mm. thick; spores 4 x 2 μ.

Plants yellow, drying buff-yellow, resupinate-effused, sometimes
effused-reflexed, cottony on the substratum and on the upturned
margin, separable; hymenium golden-yellow drying ochraceous-
orange to russet, radiately plicate-porose, the pores 0.5-1 mm. in diameter, the radiate folds at first more prominent toward the margin, the
edges thin and acute; hyphae loosely interwoven, nodose-septate;
spores small, cylindrical, with slight color.—On decaying pine wood,
rare, Aug.-Nov., throughout our area.

M. rubellus Peck.

Plants covering areas 4-8 cm. long, 2-4 cm. wide, up to 4 mm.
thick; spores 9 x 2 μ.

Plants dimidiate, sessile, mostly imbricated, soft or somewhat
coriaceous, tomentose, coral-pink when fresh, buff when dry, the
margin undulate, often inflexed; hymenium coral-pink drying sal-
mon-buff, the folds much branched, anastomosing to form pores,
up to 3 mm. thick; hyphae 4-5 μ in diameter, sometimes nodose-
septate; spores white in mass, smooth, biguttulate.—On logs of white
oak, beech, birch, and maple, often beneath *Stereum fasciatum,* rare,
throughout our area.

M. ambiguus Berk.

Plants orbicular, 2-6 cm. across, 1 mm. thick; spores 4 x 2 μ.

Plants resupinate with a narrow reflexed, concentrically sulcate,
tomentose margin, white, drying whitish or smoke-gray, the substance coriaceous-soft; hymenium 0.3-0.6 mm. thick, buff, drying
tawny-olive to brown, the folds radiate, flexuose, soon anastomosing
to form shallow angular pores each about 1 mm. across and 0.5 mm.
deep; subiculum up to 100 μ thick, composed of loosely interwoven
hyaline hyphae and a thicker gelatinous layer which bears the hymenium; spores smooth, hyaline.—On pine, rare, May-Nov., throughout
our area.

M. tremellosus Schrad.

Plants 2-6 cm. in diameter, 0.5-2 mm. thick; spores 3 x 1 μ.

Plants resupinate then free and reflexed, sometimes imbricated, white, tomentose, the flesh tremellose; hymenium ruddy, somewhat translucent, drying cinnamon-buff and red, the folds radial then anastomosing to form pores each 1-1.5 mm. across x 0.5 mm. deep, transversely venose; spores smooth, hyaline, allantoid, biguttulate. —On decaying logs and stumps of birch, maple, etc., rarely on conifers, not common, Aug.-Jan., throughout our area (after Burt).

M. corium Fr.

Plants 1-4 cm. across, 0.5 mm. thick; spores 5 x 2 μ.

Plants resupinate, laterally confluent, the reflexed margin 1-3 mm. broad, white, villose, the flesh thin, coriaceous, soft; hymenium pink, reticulately porose, drying pinkish-buff to cinnamon, the pores 3 per mm., shallow; spores smooth, hyaline, cylindrical, flattened on one side.—On bark and dead limbs of deciduous trees, common, throughout the year, throughout our area.

M. rufus Pers.

Plants 1-4 cm. across, 0.5 mm. thick; spores 4 x 2 μ.

Plants resupinate, effused, the margin naked, pink to reddish drying fawn-colored, the flesh waxy-soft; hymenium 100-300 μ thick with folds standing 300 μ higher, fawn-colored to brown, composed of equal angular pores, 2 per mm.; gelatinous layer absent; spores smooth, hyaline, slightly curved.—On decaying pine and hardwood, rare, Illinois.

PORIA Pers. Plate 1, fig. 17.

Plants waxy, corky, leathery, or membranaceous, entirely resupinate, indefinitely spreading over the substratum; hymenium composed of tubes seated on a thin layer of mycelium. In habit the plants look like resupinate parts of *Polyporus*, *Trametes* or *Fomes*.

Key to Species (after Baxter)

1 Context corky, not usually distinct from the tubes...*P. corticola.*
1' Context not corky, subiculum distinct from the tubes......2
2 Plants white......3
2' Plants ashy, smoky, blackish,. violet, yellow, or reddish......19
3 Pore-mouths comparatively large, 1-3 per mm.......4
3' Pore-mouths minute, 4-8 per mm......14

4   Plants growing on cedar, spores echinulate......5
4' Plants not growing on cedar, spores not echinulate......6

5   Margin cobwebby, plant effused.............*P. candidissima.*
5' Margin not cobwebby, well defined; plant in patches......
....*P. papyracea.*

6   Tubes averaging 1 mm. or less in length (see *P. lenis* and
P. medulla panis)......7
6' Tubes longer......8

7   Plants with tinge of lilac, tomentose on the margin........
....*P. semitincta.*
7' Plants snow-white, fragile, not lilac-tinged on the margin
or in the hymenium.........................*P. Vaillantii.*

8   Hymenium becoming sinuous and toothed.........*P. ambigua.*
8' Hymenium not becoming sinuose-toothed......9

9   Plants becoming rubescent where bruised or upon drying,
watery, somewhat gelatinous when fresh......*P. sanguinolenta.*
9' Plants not so colored where bruised or when dry......10

10 Growing on hardwoods......11
10' Growing on conifers......13

11 Hymenium sometimes in layers as in Fomes, dried specimens
separating from substratum at margin...........*P. nigrescens.*
11' Hymenium annual or if perennial not separating at margin....12

12 Plant soft and velvety to the touch..................*P. lenis.*
12' Plant not soft and velvety, hymenium remaining white....
....*P. medulla panis.*

13 Plants coarse, not soft, with long tubes and an acid odor;
spores subglobose ....*P. subacida.*
13' Plants soft and fragile, with short tubes; spores long, curved
....*P. vaporaria.*

14 Spores ovoid or spherical......15
14' Spores allantoid-cylindrical......18

15 Plants soft and fragile, rhizomorphic, snow-white........
....*P. Vaillantii.*
15' Without this combination of characters......16

16 Subiculum indistinct, becoming a chalky mass........*P. crassa.*
16' Subiculum distinct, not friable like chalk......17

17 Tubes usually long, pore-mouths fringed; plant usually
growing on conifers...........................*P. subacida.*
17' Tubes short, 2 or 3 mm. long; plant usually growing on
black ash ....*P. undata.*

18   Plants white, pores sulphurous within....*P. xantha* var. *calcea*.
18' Plants with snow-white hymenium, drying white to brownish
     ....*P. xantha*.
19   Plants brownish-black; pore-mouths minute, 4-6 per mm.
     ....*P. nigra*.
19' Plants violet, yellow, or reddish......20
20   Plants light pink or vinaceous-buff, very thin (less than 1
     mm.) ....*P. attenuata*.
20' Plants at first white or subochraceous, becoming purplish
     ....*P. purpurea*.
20'' Plants dull yellow or bright yellow......21
21   Plants bright-colored, yellow, brownish-yellow, or orange-
     cinnamon; pores formed on only part of the well-formed
     soft subiculum......22
21' Plants dull yellow when fresh, becoming buff; tubes shallow
     ....*P. myceliosa*.
22   Subiculum cobwebby to felty, plant growing on conifers..
     ....*P. albolutescens*.
22' Subiculum not cobwebby or felty but thin and soft, plant
     growing on poplar..........................*P. vitellina*.
22'' Pores minute, orange-cinnamon when fresh........*P. spissa*.

P. corticola (Fr.) Cooke.

Plants resupinate, whitish, the context corky, not distinct from the
tubes as a layer, trametes-like, arid; hymenium light brown, the
tubes 0.5-4 mm. long, usually shallow, and less than 3 mm. long;
cystidia conspicuous, often incrusted; spores 5 x 3 μ.—On hardwoods, according to Baxter.

P. candidissima (Schw.) Cooke

Plants resupinate, white, effuse, thin, not corky or trametes-like,
not arid, the margin cobwebby; hymenium white, distinct from context, the pores 1-3 per mm.; spores echinulate, 2-3 x 3-4 μ.—Usually
on arbor vitae, northern part of our area.

P. papyracea (Schw.) Cooke.

Plants resupinate, white, not effuse, thin, not corky or arid, the
margin narrow and well defined, not arachnoid; hymenium white,
distinct from context, the pores 1-3 per mm.; spores echinulate, 5 x
10 μ.—In patches on cedar branches.

P. semitincta (Peck) Cooke.

Plants resupinate, thin, white, the margin tomentose and with a tinge of lilac; hymenium typically poroid, white to lilac, 1 mm. thick, the tubes 1-3 per mm., less than 1 mm. long; spores oblong, smooth, 4 x 1-2 μ.—Usually on oak.

P. Vaillantii Fr.
P. mollusca Bres.

Plants snow-white, thin, soft, resupinate, margin often rhizomorphic or tomentose; hymenium at length breaking up into teeth, snow-white, the pores lacerate in age, collected in centers, less than 1 mm. in length, small, thin-walled; spores ovoid, 3.5 x 5.5 μ.—On charred pine, northern half of area.

P. ambigua Bres.

Plants resupinate, covering large portions of stumps and dead trunks, whitish; hymenium 1-4 mm. thick, the pores becoming sinuose-toothed, tuberculate or nodulose; spores obovate to oblong 3 x 6 μ.—On dead wood of deciduous trees, common, throughout our area.

P. sanguinolenta (Alb. & Schw.) Cooke.

Plants resupinate, white, becoming rubescent where bruised or upon drying, watery, somewhat gelatinous when fresh, becoming brown or blackish and membranaceous when dried, the pores 1-6 mm. long, 3-6 per mm.; spores 5 x 3 μ.—On wood of deciduous trees.

P. nigrescens Bres.

Plants perennial, frequently exhibiting several layers as in *Fomes*, separating from the substratum about the margin, when dried flesh colored, or lighter when fresh, darkening with age or in drying; pores 5 per mm.; spores 4-7 μ in diameter.—On hardwood stumps or logs.

P. lenis Karst.

Plants tinted yellowish at times, usually white or whitish, soft; hymenium soft, the partitions thin, the tubes 1-1.5 mm. long; spores comma-shaped 1 x 4 μ.—On wood of either conifer or deciduous trees.

P. medulla panis (Pers.) Cooke.

Plants thin, covering large surfaces, resupinate, inseparable from the substratum, leathery or hardened, white to buff-yellow; tubes 0.5-3 mm. long, pore-mouths always entire, never becoming lacerate or breaking up into teeth; hyphae much branched; spores 3-5 μ.—On wood of deciduous trees, common, throughout our area.

P. subacida (Peck) Sacc.

Plants effused, separable from the substratum, tenacious, flexible, uneven, strong and subacid in odor, the margin free from rounded depressed spots, downy, narrow, pure white; hymenium white to dingy-yellowish, pale tan or dull cream-colored, the pores with thin walls, often dentate, short to long, 0.5-9 mm. long, mostly 2-4 mm.; spores 3-5 x 5 μ.—On hardwoods and conifers.

P. vaporaria Fr.

Plants widely effused, innate, bordered with white mycelial threads which creep into the wood, white, floccose; hymenium white becoming pallid, firm, the pores large, angular, 2 to 4 per mm., unequal in size.—On rotten wood in moist places in woods, throughout our area.

P. crassa Karst.

Plants effused, soon arid, pulverizing between the fingers like chalk, the subiculum indistinct, fusing at the base of tubes as a friable mass; tubes 5-7 mm. long, the mouths glistening, 5 per mm.; spores 3 x 5 μ.—On conifers, northern part of area.

P. undata (Pers.) Bres.

Plants effused, ivory-yellow, cream-colored, not soft to the touch, becoming horny and more or less separated from substratum when dried; hymenium ivory-yellow becoming gray-flesh-colored when dried, the pores 1-4 mm. long, 4 per mm.; spores 5 x 5 μ.—Spreading widely on black ash logs, throughout our area.

P. xantha Lind.

Plants effused over areas 12 x 3 cm., 1 mm. thick, rugose, subplicate, hard, the margin undulate, minutely velvety; hymenium snowwhite drying brownish, the pores minute, 4 per mm., round; spores 5 x 1-1.5 μ, slightly curved.—Commonly spreading on logs of deciduous trees.

P. xantha var. **calcea** (Lind.) Romell.

Differing from the typical variety in that the plants are white, the pores sulphur-colored within.—On decaying logs.

P. nigra Berk.

Plants effused, always dark-colored, brownish-black; pores small, 4-6 per mm., 1-5 mm. long; spores 7 x 5 μ.—On hard woods, around the Great Lakes.

P. purpurea Fr.

Plants effused, thin, white or yellowish, later purplish then red-purple or darker, the border of plant narrow, pubescent, white or pink; hymenium 0.5 mm. thick, the pores small, 2-4 per mm., thin-walled; spores cylindrical, 7 x 2 μ.—On hardwoods, northern part of our area.

P. myceliosa Peck.

Plants effused, warm buff-clay-colored when dry, pale yellow when fresh; hymenium thin, about 1 mm. thick, the pores usually 0.5 mm. deep, 3 per mm.; spores 2-3 x 3-4 μ.—On conifer wood, northern part of our area.

P. albolutescens Romell.

Plants neither becoming horny nor separating from the substratum when dried, yellow, with thin, cobwebby to felty subiculum; hymenium thin, 1 mm. thick, the pores 0.5-1 mm. long, 3 per mm., well formed, angular, thin-walled, drying light ochraceous-buff to tawny. —On conifer logs, northern part of area.

P. vitellina (Schw.) Cooke.

Plants thin, soft to the touch, the subiculum thin, soft, but not particularly felty, yellow or bright egg-yellow, the margin radiate-fibrillose; tubes fragile, delicate, 0.5 mm. or less long, 3 per mm.; spores strongly curved, 2 x 5 μ.—On poplar, showing strands of yellow mycelium penetrating the wood, throughout our area.

P. spissa (Schw.) Cooke.

Plants widely effused, perennial, hard, immersed, cinereous-brown, the margin very narrow, inflexed; pores minute, 5 per mm., the mouths, angular, obtuse, entire, orange-cinnamon to hazel or seal-brown when dry, the tubes 0.5-1.5 mm. long, the pore-surface lustrous; spores 5 x 1 μ.—On branches of *Prunus, Juglans, Quercus,* and sometimes on conifers, throughout our area.

P. attenuata (Peck.) Cooke.

Plants resupinate, pinkish-ochre effused, less than 1 mm. thick, separable from the substratum, the margin whitish; hymenium thin, less than 0.5 mm. thick, vinaceous-buff or light pinkish, the pore-mouths 5 per mm., minute, subrotund, thin-walled; spores 4 x 3 μ.—On dead wood of oak, throughout our area.

POLYPORUS (Fr.) Michel.   Plates 8 and 9.

Plants coriaceous, corky, fleshy, producing but one layer of pores; pileus orbicular, reniform, flabelliform, dimidiate, spathulate, or resupinate-effused-reflexed; hymenium coriaceous, corky or fleshy, composed of tubes in one layer only, 0.5 mm. to 3 cm. long, the mouths minute (8 per mm.) to large and angular (3 mm. in diameter), stem usually absent but when present central, eccentric, lateral, or attached to center of upper side of pileus; spores mostly hyaline, smooth, minute, long elliptical to globose.

Polyporus tulipifera has caused some controversy. This species, so common on basswood in the Chicago area, is mostly resupinate with the margin reflexed to form pilei; the large resupinate hymenial areas are at first poroid but soon break up into small circular areas of teeth, superficially resembling those of *Irpex*.

1   Context brown or brownish......56
1′ Context white, yellow, or reddish......2

2   Pore-surface red or purple-red......3
2′ Pore-surface not red......5

3   Pore-surface waxy, hymenium a thin elastic layer.........
    ....*P. dichrous*, p. 107
3′ Pores not waxy, context reddish, hymenium red......4

4   Pileus 2-5 mm. thick..................*P. sanguineus*, p. 110
4′ Pileus thicker ....*P. cinnabarinus*, p. 109

5   Pileus red-varnished above, sometimes orange or black varnished......6
5′ Pileus not varnished......8

6   On hemlock or other conifers...............*P. Tsugae*, p. 114
6′ On or about trunks or stumps of deciduous trees......7

7   Pileus ochraceous in part, margin truncate....*P. Curtisii*, p. 115
7′ Pileus reddish to chestnut-colored, margin rounded......
    ....*P. lucidus*, p. 115

8   With a simple central, eccentric, or lateral stem......9
8′ With numerous pilei from a short fleshy stem or tubercle.23
8″ With pileus sessile, dimidiate or effused-reflexed......28

9   Plants small, less than 1 cm. high, on oak......*P. pocula*, p. 113
9′ Plants much larger......10

10 Context composed of two differing layers; plant twisted and distorted, then the entire surface porous....*P. distortus*, p. 114
10′ Context uniform, plants not distorted......11

11 Stem black at base......12
11′ Stem not black at base......15

12 Attached to buried wood, on the ground, stem radicating..
    ....*P. radicatus*, p. 117
12′ On wood above ground, stem not radicating......13

13   Pileus bearing large scales; pores very large, often 2-4 mm. broad; stem short; plant usually on willow. *P. squamosus*, p. 114

13' Pores minute, 4-6 per mm.......14

14   Pileus tan, smooth, 2-5 cm. broad...........*P. elegans*, p. 114

14' Pileus dark chestnut, smooth, 4-20 cm. broad. .*P. picipes*, p. 114

15   Growing from the ground or buried wood......16

15' Growing on wood above ground......17

16   Pileus smooth, yellow when fresh........*P. Peckianus*, p. 116

16' Pileus-surface cracking into areas..........*P. cristatus*, p. 116

16" Pileus gray-brown, clothed with erect hairs; stem lateral or eccentric ....*P. hirtus*, p. 117

17   Plant with central or eccentric stem......18

17' Plant with short lateral stem......20

18   Pores long-decurrent on stem........*P. pennsylvanicus*, p. 117

18' Pores not at all or but slightly decurrent......19

19   Pores large, 1 mm. broad, angular; plants common in spring ....*P. arcularis*, p. 117

19' Pores small, ½ mm. broad; plants common from July to November ....*P. brumalis*, p. 118

20   Pileus thin, arising from a shallow cup around which concentric flat zones are added; plants on dead elm or Ostrya branches ....*P. conchifer*, p. 111

20' Pileus not arising from a cup-shaped center......21

21   Pileus globular, 2-4 cm. across; pores at first covered by a membrane; plants growing on conifers......*P. volvatus*, p. 108

21' Pileus neither globose nor volvate......22

22   Margin of pileus projecting 5 mm. or more beyond hymenium, incurved; plants growing on birch....*P. betulinus*, p. 108

22' Pileus not so margined......23

23   Plants large, 10-20 cm. broad; hymenium bright sulphur-yellow when fresh ....*P. sulphureus*, p. 109

23' Plants smaller, or hymenium not bright-sulphur......24

24   Plants lateral-stemmed, each arising from a short (2 cm. long) central stem, several forming a rosette............ ....*P. floriformis*, p. 115

24' Stem short and thick, branching and giving rise to a large fruiting body composed of 2 to many fleshy pilei......25

25   Pilei small, less than 5 cm. broad......26

25' Pilei much larger......27

26   Pilei regular, circular, each central-stemmed............. ....*P. umbellatus*, p. 115

26' Pilei laterally attached, irregular..........*P. frondosus*, p. 116

27   Plants arising from an underground tuber, pilei eccentric, thin, brown or yellow-brown..............*P. Berkeleyi,* p. 116
27' Plants arising from a short thick stem; pilei thin, gray, drab, or black, flabelliform or spathulate........*P. giganteus,* p. 117
28   Growing on conifer wood......29
28' Growing on wood of deciduous trees......32
29   Context of pileus less than 1 mm. thick......30
29' Context more than 1 mm. thick..........*P. guttulatus,* p. 108
30   Pileus orange, orange-red, or pink......34
30' Pileus of another color......31

31   Growing on limbs of red cedar, pileus not over 1.5 mm. thick, tubes white to brown.................*P. pinsitus,* p. 108
31' On other conifers; pileus up to 2 mm. thick; tubes white, bay or violaceous.......................*P. abietinus,* p. 108
32   Pileus brown to black......33
32' Pileus tan, gray, ashy, or white......36
33   Pileus 8 mm. or more thick, fleshy to rigid..*P. resinosus,* p. 109
33' Pileus about 1 mm. thick, coriaceous........*P. planellus,* p. 109
34   On conifers......35
34' An oak or chestnut, pileus buff or orange, pores small..... ....*P. croceus,* p. 109

35   Pileus pinkish-brown, regular in outline, the margin thin; hymenium pink, composed of minute pores............ ....*Trametes carnea,* p. 128
35' Pileus brown-pink, tubes distinctly stratified, the margin thick ....*Fomes roseus,* p. 124

36   Hymenium smoky-colored......37
36' Hymenium not smoky......39
37   Hymenium blackish from first, context thin......38
37' Hymenium gray or smoky-gray, becoming darker where bruised; context 2.5-10 mm. thick; tubes 1.5-4 mm. long.. ....*P. fumosus,* p. 107
38   Margin of pileus wavy and crisped, strigose toward base.. ....*P. crispus,* p. 107
38' Margin entire, not wavy, pileus short-tomentose........ ....*P. adustus,* p. 107

39   Pileus glabrous when mature, or thick, soft, and watery..45
39' Pileus tomentose to hirsute, thin, coriaceous......40
40   Context less than 1 mm. thick, pileus with shining zones of many colors........................*P. versicolor,* p. 110
40' Context thicker or pileus not multicolor-zonate......41

41 Context very thin, less than 1 mm. thick; pores breaking up
    into teeth 42
41' Context thicker, pores not breaking up into teeth......43
42 Hymenium rosy to violaceous then pale...............
    ....*P. pergamenus*, p. 110
42' Hymenium always white...............*P. tulipiferus*, p. 110
43 Pileus hirsute; pore-walls thick and entire, whitish, bearing
    concentric furrows ....*P. hirsutus*, p. 110
43' Pileus not hirsute; pore-walls thin, sometimes dentate or
    torn......44
44 Pileus bearing colored zones...............*P. zonatus*, p. 110
44' Pileus not distinctly zoned, coriaceous, fleshy, tough; plants
    usually on beech.......................*P. pubescens*, p. 111
45 Pileus thin, spongy, mostly resupinate...*P. semipileatus*, p. 111
45' Pileus thin, coriaceous, silky-fibrillose.......*P. biformis*, p. 111
45'' Pileus thick, soft and watery, or firm and corky, never
    zonate, usually more than 1 cm. thick......46
46 Context firm and hard when dry, firm when fresh or if soft
    then the odor disagreeable......47
46' Context not hard when dry, odor not disagreeable......48
47 Context soft, very hard when dry; odor disagreeable....
    ....*P. Spraguei*, p. 111
47' Context soft, drying hard; pileus narrowed to a stem-like
    base; odor not disagreeable................*P. osseus*, p. 115
48 Growing on living black locust........*P. robiniophilus*, p. 112
48' Growing on dead wood......49
49 Pores large, 0.5 mm. or more in diameter......50
49' Pores smaller......51
50 On oak trees only, margin of pileus thick.....*P. obtusus*, p. 113
50' On other wood, margin of pileus thinner...*P. delectans*, p. 113
51 Pileus pubescent, hispid, or strigose......52
51' Pileus glabrous or nearly so......54
52 Pileus pubescent, flesh bluish where bruised...*P. caesius*, p. 112
52' Pileus hispid or strigose, not staining blue......53
53 Plants with sweet odor, pileus densely strigose..........
    ....*P. galactinus*, p. 113
53' Plants without odor, pileus hispid, pores collapsing, margin
    incurved ....*P. spumeus*, p. 113
54 Pileus gray when fresh...............*P. tephroleucus*, p. 112
54' Pileus pure white or yellowish when fresh......55

55 Tubes 1-3 mm. long......................*P. chioneus,* p. 112
55′ Tubes 4-9 mm. long.......................*P. albellus,* p. 112

56 Plant more or less red-varnished......57
56′ Plant not red-varnished......58

57 On hemlock or other conifers..............*P. Tsugae,* p. 114
57′ On deciduous wood......................*P. lucidus,* p. 115

58 With a distinct stem......59
58′ Sessile or effused-reflexed......64

59 Growing on the ground, pileus very thin, context about 1 mm. thick......60
59′ On wood or attached to buried wood, context 3 mm. or more thick......62

60 Pileus radiate-fibrillose with shining silky fibrils, commonly on clay banks......................*P. cinnamomeus,* p. 118
60′ Pileus-surface not shining......61

61 Pores rather small, 3 per mm..............*P. perennis,* p. 118
61′ Pores large, 1 mm. or more in diameter......*P. focicola,* p. 118

62 Pileus covered with a thin easily indented crust...........
....*Fomes lobatus,* p. 122
62′ Pileus not incrusted, plants associated with pines......63

63 Context duplex ....*P. circinatus,* p. 118
63′ Context not duplex, large; plants on or about pine trees....
....*P. Schweinitzii,* p. 119

64 Plant composed of a large solid central core, with many crowded overlapping pilei attached......*P. graveolens,* p. 119
64′ Plant not so constructed......65

65 Plants rusty or brown-yellow, large, on pines............
....*P. Schweinitzii,* p. 118
65′ Plants on or about wood of deciduous trees......66

66 Context very light brown, pileus-surface velvety-brown...
....*P. resinosus,* p. 109
66′ Context rusty, yellow-brown or smoky-brown......67

67 Pileus thin or thick, umber to cinnamon, margin bruising violaceous when fresh.................*P. nidulans,* p. 119
67′ Pileus 2-10 cm. thick......68
67″ Pileus seldom as thick as 2 cm.......69

68 Pileus covered with a dense hispid tomentum..*P. hispidus,* p. 119
68′ Pileus soft-tomentose or scabrous, context with a central globose core ....*P. Rheades,* p. 120

69   Pileus covered with a wooly tomentum, 3-10 mm. thick....
..................................*P. cuticularis,* p. 120
69'   Pileus not so clothed......70
70   Hymenium ferruginous-brown......71
70'   Hymenium greenish-yellow becoming brown...........
..................................*P. glomeratus,* p. 120
71   Pileus radiately wrinkled, margin lobed.....*P. radiatus,* p. 120
71'   Pileus rough, uneven, not radiately wrinkled, the margin
smooth ....*P. gilvus,* p. 120

P. dichrous Fr.   Plate 9, fig. 1.

Pileus 1-3 cm. long, 1-4 cm. wide, 0.1-0.5 cm. thick; spores 4 x 1 μ.

Pileus conchiform, thin, pliant, dimidiate, sessile, convex, velu-
tinous to glabrous, white, the context white, 1-4 mm. thick; hymenium purple-red, waxy, separable as a layer from context, the tubes
less than 1 mm. long, circular, small, 5 per square mm.; spores
allantoid.—On dead wood of deciduous trees, occasionally found,
throughout our area.

P. crispus (Fr.) Pers.   Plate 9, fig. 2.

Pileus 2-7 cm. long, 1-5 cm. wide, 0.1-4 cm. thick.

Pileus sessile or effused-reflexed, closely imbricate, coriaceous,
gray, light brown or clay-colored, strigose toward base, fibrillose
toward margin, the margin radiate-lined, crisped or wavy, the context white, 1-3 mm. thick; hymenium gray-black, the pores small,
3-6 per mm., 1-3 mm. long.—On deciduous wood, not very common,
throughout our area.

P. adustus (Fr.) Willd.

Pileus 1-6 cm. long, 3-8 cm. wide, 0.1-0.6. thick.

Pileus somewhat fleshy to corky, dimidiate, sessile or effused-
reflexed, scarcely imbricate, thin, white, smoky, or pale tan, finally
tomentose to short-villose, the context 1-4 mm. thick, the margin
thin, not crisped, often black; hymenium almost black or smoky, the
tubes short, less than 2 mm. long, minute, 6 per mm.—On dead wood
of deciduous species, common throughout our area.

P. fumosus (Fr.) Pers.

Pileus 2-10 cm. long, 3-15 cm. wide, 2 cm. thick.

Pileus somewhat fleshy to corky, dimidiate, sessile or effused-
reflexed, white to pale tan, the context 2.5-10 mm. thick, always
separated from hymenium in cross section by a dark line, anise-
scented or disagreeable in odor; hymenium pale smoky-colored, the

pores 1.5-4 mm. long, 3 per mm.—On dead wood of deciduous trees, usually elm, common throughout our area.

P. abietinus (Fr.) Dicks. Plate 9, fig. 3.

Pileus 0.5-5 cm. long, 0.5-5 cm. wide, 0.1-0.2 cm. thick; spores 6 x 2 μ.

Pileus effused-reflexed or sessile, coriaceous, thin, white, ashy or blackish with age, villous, zonate, the context white, up to 1 mm. thick; hymenium white, bay, or violaceous, the pores 2-3 per mm., 2-3 mm. long, rarely breaking into teeth, sometimes seriate and more or less gilled; spores cylindrical, hyaline.—On conifer wood, especially of pine, not common, mostly in northern part of our area.

P. pinsitus Fr.

Pileus 1-4 cm. long, 2-6 cm. wide, 0.5-1.5 mm. thick; spores 4 x 2 μ.

Pileus effused-reflexed or sessile, coriaceous, very thin, ashy to pale brown, hirsute to tomentose, multizonate, the context white, up to 0.5 mm. thick; hymenium light tan to brown or smoky-brown, the tubes less than 1 mm. long, 2 per mm.; spores hyaline, smooth.—On dead wood of red cedar, not common, in the southern half of our area.

P. guttulatus Peck. Plate 9, fig. 7.

Pileus 4-7 cm. long, 6-10 cm. wide, 5-15 mm. thick; spores 3 x 4 μ.

Pileus sessile or with short stem, soft, fleshy, of cheesy consistency, yellowish-white marked with darker zones and watery spots, glabrous, the context white, 4-10 mm. thick; hymenium white to yellowish, the tubes minute, 4 per mm., 1-5 mm. long; spores hyaline.—On conifer wood, occasionally found in the northern part of our area.

P. volvatus Peck. Plate 9, fig. 10 and 11.

Pileus 2-4 cm. long, 2-4 cm. wide, 1-3 cm. deep, spores 8 x 5 μ.

Pileus subglobose, fleshy, firm, smooth, flattened behind and attached by a small point, whitish or tinged brown, the cuticle continuous, covering the hymenium like a coriaceous volva, at length rupturing by a round enlarging opening and revealing the pores, the context white, 2-15 mm. thick; hymenium white to brownish, the pores small, 3 per mm., 2-5 mm. long; spores elliptical, flesh-colored.—On dead wood of conifers, northern part of our area.

P. betulinus Fr. Plate 8, fig. 17.

Pileus 5-14 cm. long, 6-24 cm. wide, 1-4 cm. thick.

Pileus large, reniform, fleshy becoming corky, azonate, glabrate, covered with a thin, separable, gray, gray-brown, or tan cuticle, the context white, the margin obtuse-rounded, involute, projecting beyond the hymenium and forming a border 5 mm. or more wide;

hymenium white, plane and smooth, the tubes small, 3 per mm., 4-8 mm. long; spores smooth, white.—Growing on birch trunks, locally common, northern Indiana, northern Illinois, Wisconsin, and Michigan.

P. sulphureus (Fr.) Bull. Sulphur polypore (edible). Plate 8, fig. 20.

Single pileus 8-16 cm. long, 10-30 cm. wide, 1-3 cm. thick.

Pilei numerous, densely clustered, closely overlapping, grown together toward base, bright sulphur, with salmon tinge, to orange, moist, soft, broadly and irregularly dimidiate, the margin thick, obtuse; hymenium sulphur-yellow, the tubes small, short; spores hyaline, smooth, oval.—On trees and stumps of oak and other deciduous trees, common throughout our area.

P. resinosus (Fr.) Schrad.

Pileus 6-25 cm. long, 8-45 cm. wide, 1-4 cm. thick; spores 6 x 2 μ.

Pileus large, fleshy, smoky-brown or cinnamon, zonate, flocculose-pruinose, the context very light brown; hymenium white or pale, the tubes small, 4-6 per mm., 1-6 mm. long; spores cylindrical or allantoid.—On deciduous and conifer wood, common throughout our area.

P. planellus Murr.
Polystictus planus Peck.
Pileus 1-3.5 cm. long, 1-3 cm. wide, 0.5-1 mm. thick.

Pileus sessile, thin, coriaceous, plane, suborbicular, dorsally attached, light brown to umber, minutely villose or velvety with narrow darker glabrous zones, the mragin whitish, the context papery-thin, whitish; hymenium whole or yellowish, the pores angular, 5 per mm.—On dead limbs of deciduous trees, rare, in the northwestern part of our area, Wisconsin, Iowa.

P. croceus (Fr.) Pers. Plate 9, fig. 17.
P. Pilotae Schw.
Pileus 4-10 cm. long, 5-12 cm. wide, 1-4 cm. thick; spores 4 x 3 μ.

Pileus thick, almost ungulate in thick specimens, buff to crimson-orange, watery, spongy, fibrous, dry, hard and corky, the substance zonate, the context 0.7-2 cm. thick; hymenium orange, the tubes small, 4 per mm., 5-20 mm. long; spores hyaline, smooth.—On wood of oak, rare, but found throughout our area.

P. cinnabarinus (Jacq.) Fr. Plate 8, fig. 22.
Pileus 2-5 cm. long, 3-10 cm. wide, 0.5-1 cm. thick; spores 5 x 2.5 μ.

Pileus sessile, coriaceous, rigid, rugulose, pubescent to glabrous, cinnabar fading to buff-brown; hymenium bright cinnabar-red, the pores angular to slightly daedaloid, 2-4 per mm., 1-4 mm. long; spores smooth, hyaline.—On dead wood of many kinds, common throughout our area.

P. sanguineus (Fr.) L.   Plate 9, fig. 18.

Pileus sessile, coriaceous, rigid, thin, similar in size and color to *P. cinnabarinus,* 0.2-0.5 cm. thick, the margin very thin.—On dead wood of deciduous trees, common in the southern part of our area.

P. versicolor (L.) Fr.   Plate 8, fig. 15.

Pileus 1-4 cm. long, 2-6 cm. wide, 0.1-0.3 cm. thick; spores 6 x 1.5 μ.

Pileus sessile, dimidiate, coriaceous, thin, rigid, depressed behind, smooth, velvety, shining, bearing diversely-colored zones; pores minute, round, acute, lacerate, white then pale yellowish; spores hyaline.—On all kinds of dead wood, our commonest polypore, throughout our area.

P. zonatus Fr.

Differing from *P. versicolor* in its larger pores and thicker pileus. —Probably throughout our area, not common.

P. pergamenus Fr.   Plate 9, fig. 5.

Pileus 1-5 cm. long, 1-6 cm. wide, 0.1-0.3 cm. thick; spores 6 x 2 μ.

Pileus resupinate, sessile, thin, dimidiate, flabelliform or triangular and narrowed toward base, whitish, ashy or brownish with age, concentrically sulcate; pores seriate, rosy or violaceous, 2-3 per mm., 1-3 mm. long, changing to very thin toothed gills; spores smooth, cylindrical or allantoid, hyaline.—On dead wood of deciduous trees, common throughout our area.

P. tulipiferus (Overh.) Schw.

Pileus 0-1 cm. long, 1-3 cm. wide, 0.1-0.6 cm. thick.

Pileus thin, coriaceous, rigid, sessile, resupinate or effused-reflexed, whitish, villose-zonate; pores white or yellowish, 2 per mm., 1-5 mm. long, soon breaking up into teeth; cystidia scattered, hyaline, incrusted, 35-45 x 6-7 μ.—On deciduous dead wood, especially basswood, throughout our area.

P. hirsutus (Schrad.) Fr.   Plate 9, fig. 20.

Plants 2-5 cm. long, 2-7 cm. wide; 0.2-1 cm. thick; spores 6 x 2 μ.

Pileus coriaceous, rigid, convex, plane, rough with rigid hairs of one color, whitish, zonate with concentric furrows, the margin sometimes dark-colored, the context white, 1-6 mm. thick; hymenium white to yellowish or slightly smoky, the pores 3 per mm., 1-4 mm. long, the walls thick and entire; spores cylindrical, smooth, hyaline.—On dead deciduous wood, common, throughout our area.

P. pubescens (Fr.) Schum.

Plants 2-4 cm. long, 3-5 cm. wide, 0.4-1 cm. thick; spores 5 x 2 μ.

Pileus dimidiate, sessile, leathery, tough, soft villose-tomentose, azonate, white, often radiate-rugose, the margin acute, entire, the context 1-5 mm. thick, white; pores white, yellowish or umber, small, angular, acute, becoming torn, 1-4 mm. long, 3 per mm.; spores hyaline, cylindrical or allantoid.—On dead wood of deciduous trees, common, throughout our area.

P. conchifer Schw.   Plate 8, fig. 14.

Pileus 1-3 cm. long, 1-4 cm. wide, 0.2-0.3 cm. thick; spores 7 x 2 μ.

Pileus at first cup-shaped, growing by the addition of concentric zones around the cup, coriaceous, thin, white, smooth, shining, the cup dark brown marked with shining zones which soon fade, the context white, 1 mm. or less thick; pores white or yellowish, 1-2 mm. long, 3 per mm., appearing first on rim of the cup then below as the lower edge of cup grows.—Usually on dead elm branches, sometimes on *Ostrya*, common, throughout our area.

P. biformis Klotzsch.

Pileus 1-4 cm. long, 1-6 cm. wide, 0.2-1.4 cm. thick; spores 8 x 2.5 μ.

Plants effused-reflexed; pileus imbricate, sessile, coriaceous, soft and pliant when fresh, white to alutaceous, roughened with fibrils, otherwise glabrous, often radiately wrinkled and concentrically sulcate, the context white, 1-5 mm. thick; hymenium white to yellowish, the pores circular, angular, or somewhat daedaloid, then torn and broken into teeth, 1-2 per mm., 2-5 mm. long; spores hyaline.—On dead wood of deciduous trees, throughout our area.

P. semipileatus Peck.

Pileus up to 1.5 cm. long, 0.7-3 cm. wide, 0.1-0.4 cm. thick; spores 1 x 4 μ.

Pileus spongy and watery when fresh, effused-reflexed, often entirely resupinate, the context white, 1-3 mm. thick; hymenium whitish, greenish, or slightly violaceous, the tubes 1-2 mm. long, small, angular, 5 per mm.; spores hyaline, smooth.—On decaying wood, Iowa, Michigan and Kentucky.

P. Spraguei Berk. & Curt.
P. sordidus Cooke.

Pileus 4-10 cm. long, 5-15 cm. wide, 0.5-3 cm. thick; spores 4 x 5 μ.

Pileus watery, soft, firm, fleshy, irregularly dimidiate, sessile or effused-reflexed, narrowed behind, velvety, sordid-fuliginous or gray, blackening when dry, the margin glabrous, the context white, zonate, very hard when dry, the odor when fresh disagreeable; hymenium whitish, the tubes small, 4 per mm., 3-10 mm. long.—On dead wood of oak and beech, not common, throughout our area.

P. robiniophilus (Lloyd) Murr.

Pileus 3-10 cm. long, 5-15 cm. wide, 1-4 cm. thick; spores 7 x 5 μ.

Pileus watery but firm when fresh, sessile, dimidiate, white, ashy or yellowish, glabrous, the context thick, white, soft and punky, with sweet odor when first dried, 0.5-3 cm. thick; hymenium white, the pores 5 per mm., 3-10 mm. long.—On deciduous trees, especially black locust, hackberry, and maple, not common, throughout our area.

P. chioneus Fr.   Plate 9, fig. 13.

Pileus 2-6 cm. long, 1-6 cm. wide, 0.5-1.5 cm. thick; spores 4 x 1 μ.

Pileus hygrophanous, white, soft, fleshy, watery, smooth, glabrous, azonate, covered by a thin gray or yellowish pellicle, the margin incurved, the context 2-7 mm. thick, light, soft, and brittle when dry; pores regular, 2-3 mm. long, 3 per mm,; spores hyaline.—On dead wood, deciduous and conifer, especially common during wet weather, throughout our area.

P. albellus Peck.   Plate 9, fig. 14.

Pileus 1-8 cm. long, 1-8 cm. wide, 1-5 cm. thick; spores 4 x 1 μ.

Pileus white or yellowish, soft, fleshy, watery, triangular in section, very thick, glabrous, with a thin yellow pellicle, the odor sweet when fresh, the context 0.5-3.5 cm. thick, soft, white; hymenium white or yellowish, the pores 4-10 mm. long, 3 per mm.; spores cylindrical, smooth, hyaline.—On dead wood of deciduous trees, common during wet weather, throughout our area.

P. tephroleucus Fr.   Plate 9, fig. 15.

Pileus 2-6 cm. long, 4-8 cm. wide, 0.5-1.5 cm. thick; spores 4 x 1 μ.

Pileus gray, soft, watery, glabrous, sessile, narrow-triangular in section or applanate, the context white; hymenium white, the pores small, 4 per mm., 3-9 mm. long, angular; spores hyaline, smooth.— On dead wood of deciduous trees, throughout our area.

P. caesius (Fr.) Schrad.   Plate 9, fig. 16.

Pileus 2-4 cm. long, 2-4 cm. wide, 1-2 cm. thick; spores 3 x 1 μ.

Pileus white or grayish, soft and watery when fresh, somewhat triangular in section, villous-pubescent or strigose, the context white, becoming bluish where bruised, 5-12 mm. thick; hymenium white or bluish-gray, the pores comparatively large, 1-3 per mm., thin-walled, becoming torn, 3-7 mm. long; spores cylindrical or allantoid, smooth, hyaline.—On dead wood of deciduous trees, not common, throughout our area.

P. galactinus Berk.

Pileus 4-7 cm. long, 6-9 cm. wide, 1-3 cm. thick; spores 4 x 3 μ.

Pileus white or yellowish, soft and watery when fresh, sessile, tomentose, strigose toward base, narrow-triangular in section, the context white, hard and often resinous when dry, 3-20 mm. thick, zonate, odorous when fresh; pores 5-10 mm. long, minute, angular, 4-6 per mm.; spores smooth, hyaline.—On logs near streams, on flood plains, not common, throughout our area.

P. spumeus Sowerb.

Pileus 5-6 cm. long, 7-20 cm. wide, 2-6 cm. thick; spores 5 x 4 μ.

Pileus white to reddish-straw-colored, soft and watery when fresh, sessile, narrow-triangular in section, matted-strigose to strigose-tomentose, the context white; pores white or yellowish, angular, averaging 2-4 per mm., the walls thin and acute, collapsing, 5-15 mm. long; spores hyaline, subglobose, smooth.—Growing from wounds of living deciduous trees, occasionally on logs, not common, throughout our area.

P. delectans Peck.

Pileus 3-10 cm. long, 4-15 cm. wide, 1.5-4 cm. thick; spores 5 x 4 μ.

Pileus white becoming yellowish, sessile or effused-reflexed, soft and watery, firm, glabrous or finely tomentose, the context white, sometimes duplex when dry, 5-20 mm. thick; hymenium concolor, the pores 5-15 mm. long, large, 1-2 per mm.; spores hyaline, subglobose.—On living and dead hardwood trees, not common, throughout our area.

P. obtusus Berk.

Pileus 3-8 cm. long, 4-12 cm. wide, 3-6 cm. thick; spores 5 x 7 μ.

Pileus white or yellowish, becoming brownish, fleshy, spongy, firm, sessile, convex or ungulate, hirsute tomentose, the margin obtuse, the context white, 1-3 cm. thick; pores 15-30 mm. long, 1 mm. or more wide, compound; spores hyaline, smooth, ellipsoid.—Usually on oak wood, not common, throughout our area.

P. pocula (Berk. & Curt.) Schw.

Pileus 1-5 mm. long and broad, 1-3 mm. thick.

Pileus short-stipitate, coriaceous when fresh, becoming rigid when dry, white to brownish, pruinose, the context white, the stem dorsally attached and expanding toward the pileus, 1-5 mm. long; hymenium concolor, the pores minute, 0.5 mm. long.—On under-sides of dead branches, especially oak, central and southern part of our area.

P. picipes Fr.   Plate 8, fig. 11.

Pileus 3-12 cm. long, 4-20 cm. broad, 2-8 mm. thick; spores 6 x 2 μ.

Pileus chestnut-brown or darker, smooth, reniform infundibuli-form, tough, leathery, thin, the context white, 1-7 mm. thick; hymenium pure white, drying brown, decurrent, the tubes 1-2 mm. long, minute, 6 per mm.; stem central or eccentric, black at base, glabrous, 2-7 cm. long, 5-20 mm. thick; spores hyaline, smooth, long-elliptical. —On deciduous stumps and logs, common, throughout our area.

P. elegans (Fr.) Bull.

Pileus 2-4 cm. long, 3-6 cm. broad, 0.5 cm. thick; spores 7 x 3 μ.

Pileus usually reniform, orange or dull orange, smooth tough, leathery, thin, the context white, 1-4 mm. thick; hymenium white, long-decurrent, the tubes 1-3 mm. long, minute, 4-5 per mm.; stem central to lateral, 2-6 cm. long, 0.5 cm. thick, black at base, pruinose or glabrous; spores cylindrical, smooth, hyaline.—On dead wood of deciduous trees, throughout our area.

This plant is very similar to, though not as common as, *P. picipes*. Some consider it a small form of that species.

P. squamosus (Fr.) Huds.   Plate 8, fig. 18.

Pileus 4-12 cm. long, 5-20 cm. wide, 1-3 cm. thick; spores 11 x 5 μ.

Pileus large, fleshy, heavy, whitish to dingy-yellow or light brown, covered with large black appressed scales, the context white; hymenium pure white when fresh becoming yellowish, decurrent, the pores shallow, large and angular, 1-3 mm. across; spores oblong, hyaline, smooth.—Growing on living willows and other deciduous trees, not common, throughout our area.

P. distortus (Fr.) Schw.

Pileus 2-8 cm. long and broad, 5-10 mm. thick; spores 6 x 4 μ.

Pileus orbicular, light tan, coriaceous-fleshy, tough, with a two-layered context which by unequal shrinkage causes twisting; hymenium in much twisted plants present on the entire outer surface, white, the pores 2-5 mm. long, 2 per mm.; stem 0-5 cm. long, usually just a tubercle; cystidia hyaline, blunt, 20-40 x 6-10 μ.—About stumps, not common, throughout our area.

P. Tsugae (Overh.) Murr.   Plate 8, fig. 7.

Pileus 6-18 cm. long, 8-30 cm. wide, 1-3 cm. thick; spores 10 x 6 μ.

Pileus reniform or flabelliform, stipitate, red-mahogany to black, shining as though varnished, glabrous, usually sulcate, the context whitish, 0.5-2 cm. thick; hymenium white becoming brown, the tubes minute, 5 per mm., 4-8 mm. long; stem 3-20 cm. long, 2-3 cm. thick, the color and context like that of pileus; spores light brown, ovoid; hyphae irregular and much branched, up to 15 μ broad.—On living hemlock and on dead hemlock and pine, throughout our area.

P. Curtisii Berk.   Plate 8, fig 9.

Pileus 3-10 cm. long, 4-15 cm. wide, 1-2 cm. thick; spores 10 x 6 μ.

Pileus reniform or flabelliform, stipitate, mahogany to ochraceous, glabrous, zonate, the margin usually truncate, the context soft, whitish above, brown near the tubes; hymenium white to brown, the tubes .5-12 mm. long, minute, 5 per mm.; stem 2-15 cm. long, 1-2 cm. thick, with color and context like that of the pileus; spores ovoid.—On deciduous stumps, common, southern half of our area.

P. lucidus (Fr.) Leyss.   Lucid bracket.   Plate 8, fig. 8.

Pileus 3-15 cm. long, 5-20 cm. wide, 1-2.5 cm. thick; spores 11 x 6 μ.

Pileus reniform or flabelliform, sessile or stipitate, red-mahogany to chestnut-colored, incrusted, glabrous, zonate, the context composed of an upper white and a lower brown layer, 0.5-1.5 cm. thick; hymenium white to umber-brown, the tubes 2-15 mm. long, 4 per mm.; stem eccentric or lateral, 2-15 cm. long, 0.5-2 cm. thick, like pileus in color and context; spores ovoid.—On stumps of deciduous trees, common, throughout our area.

P. osseus Kalchb.   Bone bracket.

Pileus 1-5 cm. long, 2-7 cm. wide, 0.3-2 cm. thick.

Plants imbricate, multipileate; pileus whitish to gray, dimidiate, concave, tough, elastic, very rigid, hard and firm when dried, the flesh white; hymenium 1-3 mm. thick, firm when fresh, hard when dry, the pores minute, 6 per mm.—On dead wood, especially pine, rare, northern part of our area.

P. floriformis Quel.

Pileus 2-3 cm. long, 2-4 cm. wide, 1-3 mm. thick.

Pilei white or gray, soft, sessile or dimidiate or very short-stemmed, many in a rosette, each narrowed at the base, growing from a central stem-like point of attachment, the context white, 1-2 mm. thick, disagreeable in odor; hymenium whitish or yellowish, the pores small, 3 per mm., 2 mm. long.—On deciduous wood, rare, northern part of our area.

P. umbellatus (Pers.) Fr.   Plate 8, fig. 10.

Plant 8-25 cm. in diameter, pileus 1-5 cm. in diameter; 1-3 mm. thick.

Plant fleshy, with a stem which branches repeatedly giving rise to numerous central-stemmed pilei, each orbicular, white to smoky-brown, the context thin; hymenium white, the tubes small, 3 per mm., 2 mm. long; stem arising from an underground tuber-like sclerotium. —About stumps of deciduous trees, rare, throughout our area.

P. frondosus (Fr.) Dicks. (edible).   Plate 9, fig. 21.

Plants 3-10 cm. long, 2-7 cm. wide, 2-10 mm. thick, spores 8 x 5 μ.
Plants composed of many-branched stems, each branch bearing a pileus, plants composed of ten to fifty, rarely more pilei, forming a large group, roughly a globe from 6-40 cm. in diameter; pileus flabelliform or spathulate, becoming tough, thick, grayish, drab or brownish black, almost glabrous, substance white; tubes 2-4 mm. long, decurrent, mouths 0.5 mm. across, white, small, angular; spores ovoid to elliptical.—On partly buried wood or stumps of deciduous trees, common, throughout our area.

P. Berkeleyi (Fr.) Berk. (edible).   Plate 8, fig. 4.

Pileus 8-20 cm. in diameter, 4-20 mm. thick.
Plant composed of 2-5 large pilei or but one centrally depressed pileus; pileus tough-fleshy, yellow-brown to whitish, glabrous, more or less zoned, orbicular to reniform, the context white; hymenium 2-8 mm. thick, decurrent, white, the pores angular, unequal, small or large, 3 per mm. up to 1 mm. across; stem short and thick, somewhat tubercular, often arising from an underground sclerotium.— About tree bases and stumps, often found, throughout our area.

P. Peckianus Cooke.

Pileus 4-10 cm. across, 2-5 mm. thick.
Plant composed of one to several pilei on a stipe; pileus yellow, glabrous, depressed or infundibuliform, stipitate, the context white; hymenium white to pale yellow, decurrent, the tubes 1-3 mm. long, the pores 4 per mm.; stem central or eccentric, sometimes branched, glabrous, 3-5 cm. long, 5-20 mm. thick.—On the ground attached to buried wood, not common, northwestern part of our area.

P. cristatus (Fr.) Pers.   Plate 8, fig. 3.
P. flavovirens Berk. & Raven.
P. poripes Fr.
Pileus 5-20 cm. in diameter, 3-12 mm. thick; spores 6 x 4 μ.
Pileus orbicular or irregular, fleshy, stipitate, yellowish-green or yellowish-brown, often yellow in the center and brown toward the margin, becoming cracked into areas; hymenium whitish or yellowish,

deeply decurrent, 1-5 mm. thick, the pores large, 2 per mm.; stem about 5 cm. long, 15 mm. thick.—On ground in deciduous woods, not common, throughout our area.

P. giganteus (Fr.) Pers.

Pileus 8-20 cm. in diameter, 3-5 mm. thick; spores 5 μ in diameter.

Plants stipitate, of 1-5 dimidiate, flabelliform or spathulate pilei, each gray to black, tomentose, the margin thin, drying involute, the context white, 2 mm. thick; hymenium white, black where bruised and when dried, 1-3 mm. thick, the pores angular, becoming torn, 6 per mm.; stem short and thick; spores hyaline, smooth, globose.— Growing on the ground about stumps, not common, throughout our area.

P. radicatus Schw.   Plate 8, fig. 6.

Pileus 5-30 cm. broad, 2-4 cm. thick; stem 6-14 cm. long, 1-5 cm. thick; spores 13 x 7 μ.

Pileus brown, convex or depressed, irregularly orbicular, thin toward margin, thick on disk, the margin at first incurved; hymenium white or yellowish, 1-5 mm. thick, decurrent, the pores angular or sinuous, 3 per mm.; stem central, velvety, tapering to a long black root.—On the ground, attached to buried wood, occasionally found, throughout our area.

P. hirtus Quel.

Pileus 5 x 7 cm. broad, 5-15 mm. thick; stem 3 cm. long, 1 cm. thick; spores 14 to 5 μ.

Pileus brown, roughened by short, erect, stiff hairs, the context white; hymenium white, 2-5 mm. thick, the pores 2 per mm., round, the walls thin, toothed; stem clothed and colored as pileus, lateral or eccentric; spores fusiform, smooth, hyaline.—Attached to buried wood about stumps, not common, northern part of our area.

P. pennsylvanicus Sumst.

Pileus 5 cm. broad, 4 mm. thick; stem 3 cm. long, 8 mm. thick; spores 12 x 5 μ.

Pileus pale tan, orbicular, umbilicate or depressed, glabrous, the flesh white, the odor sweet; hymenium 3 mm. thick, yellowish, decurrent, the pores angular, large, 1 mm. in diameter; stem central or eccentric, glabrous, pallid; spores oblong, smooth, hyaline.—On rotting wood of deciduous trees, not common, southern half of our area.

P. arcularis (Fr.) Batsch.   Plate 8, fig. 1.

Pileus 2-6 cm. in diameter, 2-3 mm. thick; stem 4 cm. x 4 mm.; spores 8 x 3 μ.

Pileus orbicular, convex, umbilicate or depressed, dark brown, squamulose, tough, the context white; hymenium white or yellowish, 1-2 mm. thick, the pores large, angular, hexagonal, up to 1 mm. in diameter; stem central, cylindrical, brown or darker, squamulose to glabrous; spores smooth, hyaline.—On dead wood, Apr.-June, common, throughout our area.

P. brumalis (Fr.) Pers.   Plate 8, fig. 2.

Pileus 2-6 cm. in diameter, 3 mm. thick; stem 3 cm. x 3 mm.; spores 3 x 9 μ.

Pileus orbicular, convex or umbilicate, brown to almost black, minutely hispid to glabrous, tough, the context white; hymenium slightly decurrent, whitish, the pores round or angular, small, 2-3 per mm.; stem central, cylindrical, gray or brown, minutely hispid; spores smooth, hyaline.—On dead wood, common, July-Oct., throughout our area.

P. cinnamomeus (Fr.) Jacq.   Plate 8, fig. 13.

Pileus 1-3 cm. in diameter, 2-3 mm. thick; stem 1-4 cm. x 1-3 mm.; spores 7 x 4 μ.

Pileus orbicular, convex to umbilicate or depressed, shining, cinnamon to yellowish-brown, radiate-silky-fibrillose, striate, the context thin, brown; hymenium reddish-cinnamon, 1-2 mm. thick, the pores 3 per mm.; stem concolor, velvety; spores smooth, ovoid.—Among moss on clay banks, local, throughout our area.

P. perennis (Fr.) L.   Plate 8, fig. 12.

Pileus 1-5 cm. in diameter; 1-3 mm. thick; stem 1-4 cm. x 1-5 mm., spores 7 x 5 μ.

Pileus orbicular, convex, umbilicate, or depressed, gray-brown to rusty-brown, zonate, tomentose, coriaceous, the context brown, thin, 1 mm. thick; hymenium gray-brown to rusty-brown, 2 mm. thick, the pores 3 per mm.; stem cylindrical, central, brown-velvety; spores smooth, ovoid.—On sandy soil and burned-over earth, not common, throughout our area.

P. focicola Berk. & Curt.

Differing from *P. perennis* in its larger pores (1 mm. in diameter). —On burned-over ground in woods, eastern part of our area.

P. circinatus Fr.   Plate 11, fig. 2.

Pileus 3-10 cm. in diameter, 3-20 mm. thick; stem 1-5 cm. x 0.5-2 cm.; spores 5 x 3 μ.

Pileus irregularly orbicular to flabelliform, whitish when young,

becoming ochraceous then umber-brown, soft-velvety, the context
ochraceous to brown, soft and spongy, firm near the hymenium; hymenium 1.5-4 mm. thick, brown with white tinge, the pores angular, 3
per mm.; stem central to lateral or eccentric, brown, tomentose, often
rudimentary; dark brown setae abundant.—On the ground in woods,
more common where conifers are present, northern third of our area.

P. Schweinitzii Fr.   Plate 8, fig. 16.
Pileus 10-30 cm. across, 0.5-2 cm. thick; spores 7 x 4 μ.
Pileus rusty-brown to rusty-ochraceous, large, sessile or stipitate,
circular and central-stemmed if attached to a root, strigose-hairy to
glabrous, the context spongy or corky, yellowish to rusty-brown;
hymenium yellowish, darker when old or where bruised, 1-6 mm.
thick, the pores 3 per mm.; stem central, eccentric or absent, 0-7 cm.
long, 1-3 cm. thick; cystidia present, clavate, 50 x 10 μ.—Growing
under pines, attached to roots or on sides of trees or stumps, local
throughout our area.

P. graveolens Schw.   Plate 8, fig. 5.
Plant 4-25 cm. in diameter; pileus 1-2 cm. long and wide, 3-6 mm.
thick; spores 10 x 3 μ.
Plant composed of 20-30 overlapping pilei arising from a central
core, usually oblong in shape, the long axis vertical; pilei gray-brown
to cinnamon, laterally confluent, the content fibrous; hymenium 2-4
mm. thick, dark gray-brown, the pores small, 4 per mm., round;
spores long, oblong, smooth.—On trunks and logs of deciduous trees,
rare, throughout our area.

P. nidulans Fr.
Pileus 2-5 cm. long, 3-7 cm. wide, 0.5 cm. thick; spores 2 x 3 μ.
Pileus spongy, very soft when fresh, effused-reflexed to sessile,
cinnamon to tawny-brown or smoky-tinged, fibrillose to glabrous, the
margin purplish where bruised, the flesh concolorous with pileus;
hymenium hoary or yellowish or brick-colored, 2-7 mm. thick, the
pores 3 per mm., angular or sinuous; spores subglobose, hyaline,
smooth.—Usually on oak logs or stumps, somewhat common, throughout our area.

P. hispidus (Fr.) Bull.
Pileus 5-20 cm. across, 2-5 cm. thick; spores 9 x 7 μ.
Pileus thick, soft and watery, large, sessile, yellow-brown or rusty,
covered with dense soft hispid tomentum, the context light yellow-
brown above, dark reddish-brown toward hymenium; hymenium
4-12 mm. thick, yellowish-brown becoming darker with age or where

bruised, the pores 3 per mm.; spores broadly ovoid, smooth, yellow-brown.—On living deciduous trees, not common, throughout our area.

P. Rheades (Fr.) Pers.

Pileus 3-12 cm. long, 5-20 cm. wide, 2-8 cm. thick; spores 5 x 7 μ.

Pileus very thick, fleshy, firm, gray-brown to reddish-brown, pubescent then scabrous, finally glabrous, sessile, often subglobose or tubercular, with a central granular core, often permeated with white strands; hymenium cinnamon-brown, 0.3-3 cm. thick, the pores 2 per mm.; spores subglobose, smooth, brown.—Usually on living oak, cottonwood, and willow, not common, throughout our area.

P. cuticularis (Fr.) Bull.

Pileus 3-6 cm. long, 3-8 cm. wide, 0.3-1 cm. thick; spores 7 x 5 μ.

Pileus dimidiate, often thin, spongy, fleshy, firm when fresh, yellow-rusty-brown, compact, sessile, woolly-tomentose, the flesh of the same color; hymenium of the same color or hoary-tinged, 2-6 mm. thick, the pores minute, 4 per mm.; spores smooth, subglobose, yellow-brown in mass.—On stumps and logs of deciduous trees, not common, throughout our area.

P. glomeratus Peck.   Green-pored bracket.

Pileus 3-4 cm. long, 5-7 cm. wide, 5-15 mm. thick; spores 5 x 6 μ.

Pileus dimidiate, sessile, or effused-reflexed, corky, dark tawny, the surface uneven, velvety, the context tawny; hymenium 3-7 mm. thick, greenish-yellow when fresh becoming brown when dry, the pores angular, minute, 6 per mm.; spores subglobose, smooth, yellow. —On maple wood, rare, Michigan and Ohio.

P. radiatus (Fr.) Sowerb.

Pileus 3-5 cm. long, 4-7 cm. wide, 4-15 mm. thick; spores 4 x 5 μ.

Pileus dimidiate, rigid, sessile, yellow-rusty-brown, velvety soon glabrous, usually zoned, the context rusty-yellow, corky; hymenium rusty-brown with a hoary tinge, 1-8 mm. thick, the pores 5 per mm.; spores elliptic-globose, smooth.—Usually on dead trunks of birch and alder, northern half of our area.

P. gilvus (Fr.) Schw.   Plate 8, fig. 21.

Pileus 2-6 cm. long, 3-10 cm. wide, 3-18 mm. thick; spores 6 x 4 μ.

Pileus firm and rigid, yellow-rusty-brown, dimidiate, sessile or effused-reflexed, the surface rough-uneven, zonate, the context bright rusty-yellow; hymenium 1-6 mm. thick, reddish-brown to dark brown, the pores minute, 6 per mm.; spores smooth, broadly oblong; setae abundant, brown, subulate.—On hardwood, common, throughout our area.

FOMES (Gill.) Fr.

Plants sessile, woody, corky, or spongy, some incrusted, perennial by adding a new layer of tubes each year; hymenium poroid.—Growing on living or dead wood.

1   Context of pileus dark brown or rusty......2

1' Context flesh or rose, white or pale......12

2   Crust of pileus easily indented, the new pileus growing beneath that of the preceding year..................*F. lobatus.*

2' Crust of pileus not easily indented, pileus perennial by addition of a new stratum of pores each year......3

3   Context rust-colored......6

3' Context brown......4

4   Plants growing on Prunus, small, 4-5 cm. in diameter.... ....*F. fulvus.*

4' Plants on other hosts, larger......5

5   Pileus several times as broad as thick; pores pure white, scratching brown ....*F. applanatus.*

5' Pileus hoof-shaped, pores rusty.............*F. fomentarius.*

6   Pileus large, growing on trunks of black locust....*F. rimosus.*

6' Pileus medium or small, growing on red cedar.......... ....*F. juniperinus.*

6'' Pileus medium to large, growing on other trees......7

7   On bushes, gooseberry or Symphoricarpos...........*F. Ribes.*

7' On other trees, living or dead......8

8   Context 5 mm. or less thick......9

8' Context much thicker......10

9   Context tawny, plant growing on conifers.............*F. Pini.*

9' Context brown, plant usually on willows.........*F. conchatus.*

10 Setae present, spores brown, context 1-5 cm. thick, pileus rarely hoof-shaped, remaining brown on margin......... ....*F. Everhartii.*

10' Setae absent, spores hyaline, pileus often ungulate......11

11 Context 1-3 cm. thick, tubes not white-stuffed, plant growing on birch wood.............................*F. Bakeri.*

11' Context 0.5-1 cm. thick, tubes of older layers conspicuously white-stuffed or incrusted ....*F. igniarius.*

12 Context tinted red......13

12' Context white or pallid......14

13 Tubes pink, distinctly in layers; small plants, not incrusted, on conifers ....*F. roseus.*

13'   Tubes pallid or flesh colored, often in one layer; large plants, with thin hard crusts, usually on ash......*F. fraxineus.*

14   Usually on conifers, large plants......15

14'   On deciduous trees......16

15   At first covered with reddish resinous crust, older zones gray to black ....*F. pinicola.*

15'   Entire plant whitish, generally confined to larch....*F. officinalis.*

16   Pileus small, not over 2 cm. in diameter, on alder and witch-hazel ....*F. scutellatus.*

16'   Pileus much larger......17

17   Context woody; pileus soon dark and rimose, on living or dead ash or on Shepherdia.................*F. fraxinophilus.*

17'   Context soft and corky; pileus soon yellow or gray-black, on living or dying maple......................*F. connatus.*

F. lobatus (Cooke) Schw.

Pileus 5-14 cm. long, 5-17 cm. wide, 1-3 cm. thick; spores 6-8 μ. Pileus large but relatively thin, shelf-like, perennial by reviving for 2-4 years and producing a new pileus each year beneath and adherent to the old one, rusty brown, with a thin, distinct, easily indented crust, the context soft, punky, brown; hymenium white to umber-brown, the tubes 4-10 mm. long, the mouths minute, 4 per mm.; spores minutely echinulate.—On rotting stumps and logs of deciduous trees, rare, throughout our area.

F. fulvus (Gill.) Scop.

Pileus 1-5 cm. long, 3-6 cm. wide, 0.5-2 cm. thick; spores 4-6 μ. Pileus if sessile often ungulate, orbicular if attached to underside of branch, or oblong in outline, with reflexed margins, the context woody, brown; hymenium in one to several layers, each 1-4 mm. thick, brown, the tube-mouths minute, 5 per mm., the older layers not incrusted; setae present.—Growing on trunks and branches of plum or cherry, common, throughout our area.

F. applanatus (Wall.) Pers.   Artist's Fomes.   Plate 9, fig. 19, Plate 11, fig. 11.

Pileus 5-40 cm. long, 8-60 cm. wide, 2-8 cm. thick; spores 6 x 4 μ. Pileus large, dimidiate, plane or convex, gray, with a thick horny crust, the context punky, brown; hymenium with a pure white surface, scratching brown, the pores minute; spores ovoid with truncate bases.—On rotting stumps and logs of frondose trees, very common, throughout our area.

F. fomentarius (Gill.) L.   Plate 11, fig. 12.

Pileus 4-12 cm. long, 6-18 cm. wide, 4-12 cm. thick; spores 14 x 5 μ.

Pileus convex to hoof-shaped, gray-brown or almost black, covered by a thick horny crust, zonate, sulcate, the context brown, punky, 5-25 mm. thick; hymenium gray to brown, the pores minute, 3 per mm., 4-20 mm. long; spores cylindrical.—On living deciduous trees, common, throughout our area.

F. rimosus Berk.

Pileus 3-25 cm. long, 6-40 cm. wide, 2-10 cm. thick; spores 4-5 μ.

Pileus convex to ungulate, uniformly brown, soon black, sulcate and rimose with age, the context yellow-brown or rusty, 5-30 mm. thick; tubes 1-4 mm. long each year, minute, 5 per mm., hymenial surface brown.—On living trunks of black locust, southern half of our area.

F. juniperinus Von Schrenk.

Pileus 4-6 cm. long, 2-6 cm. wide, 2-5 cm. thick; spores 6 x 4 μ.

Pileus small, ungulate, orange, gray-black with age, the margin remaining orange or yellow, smooth becoming very much cracked in age, the context tawny or reddish-orange, 5-10 mm. thick; hymenium yellowish to brown, tubes 6 mm. long, 3 per mm.—On trunks of Juniperus, not common, southern half of our range.

F. Ribes (Gill.) Schum.

Pileus 2-8 cm. long, 2-7 cm. wide, 0.5-1.4 cm. thick.

Pileus thin, convex or plane, zoned or sulcate, small, brown, becoming gray-black with age, the context punky, brown, 3-6 mm. thick; tubes short, minute, brown, 1-3 mm. long, 5 per mm.—On bushes, especially living stems of *Ribes* (gooseberry) and *Symphoricarpos* (snowberry and coral berry), rare, throughout our area.

F. Pini (Lloyd) Thore.

Pileus 8-16 cm. long, 10-20 cm. wide, 2-8 cm. thick.

Pileus convex, often ungulate, at first tawny, with raised zones of tomentum, becoming gray-black and cracking or irregular on surface, the context thin, less than 5 mm. thick, woody, ochraceous to tawny; hymenium ochraceous-orange to orange-brown, the tubes angular to daedoloid, about 4 mm. long, 2 per mm.—On wood of living or dead conifers, rare, northern part of our area.

F. conchatus (Gill.) Pers.

Pileus 0-8 cm. long, 4-10 cm. wide, 0.2-3 cm. thick.

Fruiting body often mostly resupinate, the reflexed portion thin and shell-shaped, sessile, yellow-brown or gray then blackish, neither incrusted nor rimose, the context brown, 15-25 mm. thick; hymenium fulvous to dark brown, the pores minute, short, 5 per mm., 1-2 mm. long.—On dead deciduous wood, especially willow, not common, throughout our area.

F. Everhartii Ell. & Gall.

Pileus 2-12 cm. long, 5-20 cm. wide, 2-12 cm. thick; spores 4 x 3 μ.

Pileus usually convex, uniformly brown, gray-black in age especially behind, the margin remaining brown, tomentose, usually concave toward margin, the surface not incrusted but becoming rough and cracked in age, the context woody, rusty-brown, 1-4 cm. thick; pores brown, 4-6 mm. long each year, small, 5 per mm.; setae present. —On living trees, especially oak, not common, throughout our area.

F. Bakeri (Sacc.) Murr.

Pileus 3-8 cm. long, 5-15 cm. wide, 2-6 cm. thick; spores 5-6 μ.

Pileus convex to short-ungulate, blackish with a gray-brown margin, not incrusted, large specimens sulcate, the context brown, woody, 1-3 cm. thick; tubes minute, brown, 5 per mm., 4 mm. long each year; spores subglobose, hyaline.—On trunks of birch, throughout our area.

F. igniarius (L.) Gill.

Pileus 3-10 cm. long, 5-15 cm. wide, 2-12 cm. thick; spores 5 x 4 μ.

Pileus convex to ungulate, gray-black, not incrusted, sometimes cracking in age, the context hard, woody, brown, thin, 5-10 mm. thick; tubes minute, 4 per mm., brown with silvery sheen by reflected light, 2-5 mm. long each year, older layers conspicuously stuffed or incrusted; spores subglobose; setae present.—On living trunks of deciduous trees, especially oak, common, throughout our area.

F. roseus (Cooke) Alb. & Schw.

Pileus 2-6 cm. long, 3-8 cm. wide, 1.5-3 cm. thick; spores 8 x 3 μ.

Pileus ungulate, brownish-pink, often black in age, not incrusted, furrowed on margin, small, the context rose-colored, corky, 2-10 mm. thick; tubes 2-3 mm. long each year, minute, 4 per mm., rosy; spores long.—Usually on conifer wood, not common, northern part of our area.

F. fraxineus (Fr.) Bull.

Pileus 4-12 cm. long, 5-20 cm. wide, 1-6 cm. thick; spores 6 x 7 μ.

Pileus plane or convex, medium to large, light colored, reddish-brown stained or entirely reddish, somewhat zoned and covered with hard thin crust, the context punky, 4-30 mm. thick, red-tinted; hymenium whitish to flesh-colored, the tubes 5 per mm., minute, 3-10 mm.

long each year, commonly in a single layer; spores subglobose.—
Usually on ash, sometimes on poplar, not common, throughout our
area.

F. pinicola (Cooke) Swend.

Pileus 5-20 cm. long, 7-30 cm. wide, 3-10 cm. thick.

Pileus regular, convex to broadly ungulate, the younger surface
with reddish resinous crust, the older gray to black, sulcate in age,
the context corky to woody, pale wood-colored, 0.5-2.5 cm. thick;
tubes whitish to light umber, small, 4 per mm., 4 mm. long each
year.—Usually but not always on wood of conifers, common, northern part of our area.

F. officinalis Fr.

Pileus 5-10 cm. long, 7-15 cm. wide, 6-25 cm. thick.

Pileus ungulate, white, whitish, or yellowish, sometimes incrusted
with yellowish, chalky substance, brittle, the taste bitter, the odor
farinaceous, the context 2-5 cm. thick, white; tubes small, 4 per mm.,
3-8 mm. long, white.—On trunks of conifers, especially tamarack
and arbor vitae, not common, northern part of our area.

F. scutellatus (Cooke) Schw.

Pileus 0.5-2 cm. long, 0.5-2 cm. wide, 0.2-0.6 cm. thick.

Pileus small, convex to broadly ungulate, or attached by vertex
and subcircular in outline, dark brown when mature, the context
corky, 2 mm. thick; tubes pallid, small, 4 per mm., short, 1-2 mm.
long.—Usually on alder or witch hazel, not common, throughout
our area.

F. fraxinophilus Peck

Pileus 3-30 cm. long, 5-40 cm. wide, 2-10 cm. thick.

Pileus large, convex to broadly ungulate, at first white, soon gray
or black, sometimes sulcate, sometimes rimose in age, the context
woody, 5-15 mm. thick; tubes 2-4 mm. long each year, indistinctly
stratified, small, 3 per mm., the pore-surface white to light brown.
—On living or dead ash, not common, throughout our area.

F. connatus (Gill.) Weinm.

Pileus 4-8 cm. long, 5-12 cm. wide, 1-3 cm. thick.

Pileus convex, white to yellow, tawny, or gray-black, the surface
smooth, rarely sulcate, the context corky, light-colored, 3-10 mm.
thick; hymenium pale yellowish with a silvery sheen by reflected
light, the tubes minute, 4 per mm., 3-5 mm. long each year, distinctly
stratified by tramal layers between the layers of tubes.—On living
maple trees, usually near the ground, common, throughout our area.

TRAMETES Fr.   Plate 1, fig. 19.

Pileus annual, sessile, rigid, coriaceous or corky, small or medium-sized, the context white, brown, or pink, the hymenium composed of pores which sink unequally deep into the substance (a cross section shows a jagged boundary between context and hymenium) ; cystidia none, spores hyaline, averaging 6-10 x 3-5 μ.

1   Context rosy, pinkish, or flesh-colored.................*T. carnea.*
1' Context white or brownish......2

2   Pileus more than 1 cm. thick......3
2' Pileus less than 1 cm. thick......4

3   Context white, pores large, plant growing on dead or dying
    willow ....*T. suaveolens.*
3' Context light brown ; pores large, 1 mm. in diameter, on wil-
    low and poplar ; pileus bearing hispid hairs...........*T. Peckii.*

4   Context white......5
4' Context brownish......7

5   Pileus brown......6
5' Pileus white, commonly on structural timbers........*T. sepium.*

6   Pores large ....*T. serialis.*
6' Pores small ....*T. variiformis.*

7   Context rusty or yellow-brown......8
7' Context light brown......9

8   Setae absent................poroid form of *Lenzites sepiaria.*
8' Setae present ....*Fomes Pini.*

9   Pileus densely hirsute or hispid......10
9' Pileus merely tomentose or glabrous......11

10 Pileus less than 5 mm. thick, leathery...............*T. rigida.*
10' Pileus more than 5 mm. thick, commonly more than 1 cm.,
    the context punky or corky......................*T. Peckii.*

11 Substance of pileus very thin (less than 1 mm.), pileus almost
    black ....*T. mollis.*
11' Substance 2-5 mm. thick, the pileus pallid.........*T. malicola.*

T. suaveolens (Fr.) L.

Pileus 1-4 cm. long, 2-8 cm. wide, 1-3 cm. thick ; spores 10 x 3.5 μ.
Pileus sessile, whitish or yellowish, villous to glabrate, not zoned, the context 5-20 mm. thick ; hymenium white to dusky, pores 1-3

per mm., 3-15 mm. long.—On dead or dying willow, common, throughout our area.

T. Peckii Kalchb.   Plate 11, fig. 13.
Pileus 1-5 cm. long, 2-10 cm. wide, 5-20 mm. thick.
Pileus usually sessile, clothed with a dense brown strigose or hirsute covering, the context 2-10 mm. thick; hymenium gray-brown or dark, pores 3-10 mm. deep, large, angular, 1 per mm.—On wood of willow and poplar, common, throughout our area.

T. sepium Berk.
Pileus 0.5-1 cm. long, 1-3 cm. wide, 2-8 mm. thick.
Pileus sessile or effused-reflexed, white, not zoned, glabrate, the context very thin, less than 1 mm. thick; hymenium whitish, pores medium-sized, 1-2 per mm., 2-5 mm. in length, circular to slightly sinuous.—On wood of frondose trees, not common, throughout our area.

T. variformis Peck.
Pileus 0-1 cm. long, 1-6 cm. wide, 1-2 mm. thick; spores 6 x 2.5 μ.
Plants often resupinate, the pileus when present narrow, cinnamon-brown or tawny, glabrate, zoned, the context very thin, less than 1 mm. thick; hymenium whitish, composed of medium-sized tubes, 1-2 per mm., 1-2 mm. long.—On wood of frondose and conifer trees, not common, throughout our area.

T. serialis Fr.
Pileus 0-1 cm. long, 1-5 cm. wide, 3-8 mm. thick; spores 8 x 2.5 μ.
Plants often resupinate, the pileus when present narrow, uniformly brown-colored, zoned, glabrate, the context thin, less than 1 mm. thick; hymenium whitish composed of small pores, 3 per mm., 2-6 mm. long.—On dead wood of frondose trees, not common, throughout our area.

T. rigida Berk. and Mont.
Pileus 0-3 cm. long, 2-5 cm. broad, 1-3 mm. thick.
Plants sessile varying to resupinate, the pileus hispid-zonate, light brown to ashy; hymenium light brown or white composed of very short pores 2-3 per mm., up to 1 mm. long.—On dead wood, not common, throughout our area.

T. mollis (Fr.) Sommerf.
Pileus up to 2.5 cm. long, 2-4 cm. wide, 1-5 mm. thick; spores 9 x 3.5 μ.
Plants effused-reflexed to entirely resupinate, the pileus dark um-

ber-brown, zonate, the context very thin, less than 1 mm. thick;
hymenium gray to brown, the tubes angular to sinuous, 1-3 per mm.,
2-3 mm. long.—On dead wood of frondose trees, not common,
throughout our area.

T. malicola Berk. and Curt.

Pileus up to 1 cm. long, 1-6 cm. wide, 3-8 mm. thick; spores 8 x 3 μ.
Plants effused-reflexed to entirely resupinate, the pileus wood-
brown or light brown, glabrate, not zoned, the context 2-4 mm.
thick; hymenium light brown, composed of pores 2-4 mm. long,
sometimes in a few layers, the mouths circular to sinuous, 1-2 per
mm.—On dead wood of frondose trees, not common, throughout
our area.

T. carnea (Cooke) Nees

Pileus 2-8 cm. long, 2-5 cm. wide, 0.7 cm. thick.
Pileus brownish-pink, black with age, rigid, regular in contour,
circular to dimidiate, firm; hymenium rose-colored to pink, composed
of minute pores, 4 per mm., 1-3 mm. long.—On wood of conifers,
not common, throughout our area.

DAEDALEA (Fr.) Pers.   Plate 11.

Plants annual or rarely persisting for two or three years; pileus coriaceous, corky or somewhat woody, dimidiate to flabelliform, sessile or effused-reflexed, never incrusted, the context white or pallid, fibrous or corky; hymenium typically labyrinthine, with tube mouths curved and sinuous but sometimes poroid, toothed, or lamellate; spores hyaline.

1   Plants white, context white.....................*D. ambigua.*
1' Plants darker......2
2   Pileus very thin, densely hairy, often colored by algae....
....*D. unicolor.*
2' Pileus thicker, glabrate......3
3   Pore walls not obtuse, plants growing on willow or poplar
....*D. confragosa.*
3' Pore walls obtuse, plants growing on oak or chestnut....
....*D. quercina.*
3" Pore walls obtuse, plants growing on red cedar....*D. juniperina.*

D. unicolor (Bull.) Fr.   Plate 11, fig. 6.

Pileus 3-6 cm. long, 3-7 cm. wide, 0.2-0.5 cm. thick.

Pileus sessile or effused-reflexed, often dimidiate, thin, flexible, white, ashy or brownish, densely villose or hirsute, often green with a covering of algae, the context white, 1 mm. or less thick; hymenium white, yellowish or smoky-colored, labyrinthine, the sinuous tube-mouths soon breaking up into teeth.—On dead wood of deciduous trees, common, throughout our area.

D. ambigua Berk.

Pileus 3-15 cm. long, 4-20 cm. wide, 0.4-1 cm. thick.

Pileus sessile or substipitate, somewhat dimidiate, white, blackened toward base, glabrous or minutely velvety-tomentose, the context corky to leathery, rigid, milk-white, the margin thin; hymenium white or yellowish, the mouths small, sinuous to round, 2 per mm., 3 mm. long, thick-walled.—On dead trunks and stumps of deciduous trees, occasionally found, throughout our area.

"*D. albida* Fr. as reported by Neuman from Wisconsin is certainly this species." (Overholts, Polyporaceae of Middle-Western United States, p. 73.)

D. confragosa (Bolt.) Fr.   Plate 11, fig. 8.

Pileus 2-8 cm. long, 4-12 cm. wide, 0.3-2 cm. thick.

Pileus sessile, dimidiate, convex-plane, rough, reddish-brown, obscurely zonate, coriaceous or almost woody, the context corky, whitish; hymenium white, gray, or light flesh-colored, darker where bruised, the pores labyrinthine, 1-10 mm. long, about 1 mm. in diameter.—On living or dead trees, especially willow, common, throughout our area.

D. quercina (L.) Fr. Plate 11, fig. 9.

Pileus 3-10 cm. long, 5-12 cm. wide, 1-5 cm. thick.

Pileus sessile, dimidiate, very thick, rigid, whitish, smoky or almost black, glabrous, the context corky, pallid, 1 cm. or less thick, the margin thick, obtuse; hymenium whitish to smoky-colored, the tubes 1-4 cm. long, thick-walled, obtuse at mouth, the mouths 1-2 mm. broad. —On oak and chestnut wood, not common, throughout our area.

D. juniperina Murr.

Pileus 2-8 cm. long, 3-10 cm. wide, 1-3 cm. thick.

Pileus sessile, dimidiate, decurrent, very thick, rigid, gray to blackish, glabrous, the context corky or punky, pallid, 1 cm. thick, the margin obtuse; hymenium daedaloid to almost lamellate, the walls thick, obtuse, pallid, the mouths 1 mm. across.—On *Juniperus virginiana*, not common, southern half of our area.

LENZITES Fr.

Plants resupinate, reflexed on margin to form shelf-like pilei, or sessile, coriaceous or hard and rigid, the context thin, white to brown; hymenium lamellate, poroid or daedaloid, coriaceous in texture or rigid; spores hyaline.—Growing on wood, widely distributed.

1 Context white, hymenium often composed of whitish lamellae
   ....*L. betulina.*
1' Context brown, hymenium colored......2
2 Pileus nearly glabrous, hymenium poroid............*L. vialis.*
2' Pileus strigose-tomentose, hymenium somewhat lamellate..
   ....*L. saepiaria.*

L. betulina (Fr.) L.

Pileus 2-5 cm. long, 3-8 cm. wide, 4-8 mm. thick; spores 6 x 2 μ.

Pileus rigid or coriaceous, sessile, gray or gray-brown, multicolor-zonate, tomentose, the context white, 1 mm. thick; hymenium typically lamellate sometimes poroid, white or whitish, the lamellae separated, 1 mm. apart, each 3-7 mm. wide; cystidia hair-like; spores hyaline, smooth, cylindrical.—On dead wood of deciduous trees, common, throughout our area.

L. vialis Peck.

Pileus 1-3.5 cm. long, 2-6 cm. wide, 3-6 mm. thick; spores 7 x 3 μ.

Pileus shelf-like, sessile or effused-reflexed, glabrous, gray-brown to cinnamon, the context corky-coriaceous, rigid, brown, 1-3 mm. thick; hymenium more or less daedaloid or poroid, rarely approaching lamellate, brown, the pores 2 per mm. or the lamellae separated by 1-2 mm.; spores long-oblong, hyaline, smooth.—On dead wood of conifer and deciduous trees, common, throughout our area.

L. saepiaria Fr.   Plate 11, fig. 10.

Pileus 1-5 cm. long, 3-8 cm. wide, 3-8 mm. thick; spores 9 x 3 μ.

Pileus shelf-like to dimidiate, sessile or effused-reflexed, bright orange-rusty to dark rusty, strigose-tomentose, zonate, the context rusty-yellow to rusty, 1-4 mm. thick; hymenium 2-4 mm. thick, lamellate, sometimes daedaloid or poroid, brown, the lamellae 1 mm. apart, thick; spores long-oblong, hyaline, smooth.—On conifer wood, common, throughout our area.

CYCLOMYCES Fr.

Pileus plane and circular, on a central stem, the context floccose to fibrous, brown; hymenium concentrically poroid, finally broken up into concentric lamellae.

C. Greenei Berk.   Plate 8, fig. 19.

Pileus 2-9 cm. broad; stem 2-7 cm. x 7-20 mm.

Pileus orbicular, plane or depressed, yellowish brown, to rusty or darker, 0.5-2 cm. thick, tomentose to glabrous, somewhat zoned, the context fulvous to cinnamon, 5-10 mm. thick; hymenium at first composed of tubes with concentrically elongated mouths, soon breaking up to form concentric lamellae; stem central, velvety, fulvous to rusty.—On the ground in woods, rare, throughout our area.

FAVOLUS Fr.

Fructification composed of a more or less stipitate pileus, with the stipe typically laterally attached; hymenium composed of large angular pores, usually arranged radially from the stem.—Growing on wood.

F. canadensis Klotsch.   Plate 11, fig. 1.

Pileus 1-4 cm. long, 1-8 cm. broad, 1-7 mm. thick; stem 0-3 mm. long; spores 10 x 4 μ.

Pileus dimidiate, fleshy-tough, reddish brown becoming cream-colored to white, innately fibrillose, context very thin, 1 mm.; pores

1-3 mm. deep, 1 mm. across, radiating from the stem and widest in the radial direction.—On dead branches, common, throughout our area.

F. rhipidium Berk.

Pileus 1-1.5 cm. broad, 1-3 mm. thick; stem 0.5-2.5 cm. long x 2 mm. in thickness.

Pileus reniform to spathulate, coriaceous, orange-red, brick-red, or tan, minutely squamulose or mealy, context white, 1 mm. thick; pores more or less waxy, whitish, denticulate, 1-2 mm. across; stem lateral, pruinose.—Growing on dead wood, rare, northern and eastern part of our area.

FISTULINA Bull.   Plate 11, fig. 3.

Pileus dimidiate or flabelliform, smooth, shining above, fleshy; hymenial surface at first papillate-warty, the warts developing into cylindrical tubes that remain distinct and free from each other. Compare with *Polyporus.*

F. hepatica (Huds.) Fr.   Oak tongue mushroom, beefsteak mushroom.   Plate 11, fig. 3.

Pileus 3-6 cm. long, 2-4 cm. wide, 0.5-1 cm. thick; spores 6 x 4 μ.

Pileus subspathulate or dimidiate, substipitate, blood-red, viscid, smooth, fleshy, soft, the flesh juicy, streaked with red, the tubes pallid to red; stem lateral, short or absent; spores subglobose, salmon-colored.—Solitary on oak, chestnut, and other deciduous stumps and logs, not common, throughout our area.

F. pallida Berk. and Raven.   Pale beefsteak mushroom.

Pileus 2.5 cm. long, 2-5 cm. wide, 0.5-1 cm. thick.

Pileus reniform, pallid-red, puberulent, the margin inflexed, the tubes somewhat decurrent; stem lateral, striate, up to 4 cm. in length by 1 cm, in diameter.—On dead wood, chiefly of oak, rare, southern half of our area.

BOLETINUS Kalchb.   Plates 10 and 11.

Pileus orbicular to reniform, fleshy, thick, putrescent; stem sometimes lateral or eccentric; hymenium of radiating gills which are connected by anastomosing partitions forming large angular radiating pores or tubes which are not readily separated from each other or from the pileus, yellowish; spores pale yellowish.

1   Stem lateral or eccentric......2
1' Stem central......3
2   Tube-mouths honey-yellow, with irregular cross-veining....
....*B. merulioides.*
2' Tube-mouths deep yellow, composed of anastomosing gills
....*B. porosus.*
3   Stem hollow ....*B. cavipes.*
3' Stem solid......4
4   Pileus red or adorned with red scales......5
4' Pileus pale yellow or buff......................*B. decipiens.*
5   Pileus remaining red, stem slender......6
5' Pileus becoming yellow, adorned with red-squamules...*B. pictus.*
6   Without an annulus.............................*B. paluster.*
6' With an annulus...............................*B. spectabilis.*

B. decipiens (Berk. and Curt.) Peck.   Deceptive Boletinus.
Pileus 4-8 cm. broad; stem 5-7 cm. x 6-8 mm.; spores 9 x 4 μ.
Pileus conical then convex-plane, minutely silky, pale buff; flesh buff, 8 mm. thick; hymenium plane or somewhat concave, yellow, consisting of large, radiating, unequal tubes of anastomosing lamellae; stem solid but spongy, equal; veil floccose, disappearing, at first clinging to pileus-margin; spores rusty-yellow, oblong.—In open woods, rare, Wisconsin to North Carolina.

B. porosus (Berk.) Peck.   Plate 10, fig. 1.
Pileus 5-12 cm. broad; stem 1-2 x 0.5-1 cm.
Pileus kidney-shaped to orbicular, fleshy, thick, viscid when moist, shining reddish-brown; flesh thick above stem, thin on margin, soft, smooth; tubes deep-yellow, formed by radiating gills which are branched and connected, 1-2 mm. in diameter, angular; stem lateral, tough, spreading into pileus, reticulated above by decurrent tube-walls, concolor; spores ovate.—On ground in rich woods, especially in wooded ravines, frequent, Minnesota to Maine and North Carolina.

B. cavipes Kalchb.   Hollow-stemmed Boletinus
Pileus 3-5 cm. broad; stem 3-7 cm. x 6-12 mm.; spores 9 x 4 μ.
Pileus broadly convex, often subumbonate, tawny-brown, sometimes tinged with reddish or purplish, rather tough, flexible, soft; flesh yellowish; tubes slightly decurrent, pale-yellow then darker and tinged green, dingy in age; stem hollow, tawny, equal, fibrillose, slightly ringed, yellowish at apex, striate with decurrent tubes, white within; veil whitish, part adhering to margin, evanescent.—In swamps among mosses, under tamarack trees, Illinois, Wisconsin, New York and northward.

B. pictus Peck. (edible).   Plate 11, fig. 7.

Pileus 5-10 cm. broad; stem 4-8 cm. x 6-12 mm.; spores 10 x 5 μ.

Pileus yellow, convex or nearly plane, covered when young with red fibrillose tomentum, which divides into small scales; flesh yellow, sometimes slowly changing to dull red where wounded; tubes pale yellow becoming dingy-ochraceous with age, concealed when young by a copious white webby veil; stem subequal, concolor, solid, slightly annulate with an evanescent veil, the apex yellowish; spores ochraceous.—In low gravelly soil and mossy swamps, autumn, rare, Wisconsin to New England, Pennsylvania.

B. paluster Peck.   Swamp Boletinus. (edible).

Pileus 2-5 cm. broad; stem 2.5-5 cm. x 4-6 mm.; spores 9 x 4 μ.

Pileus broadly convex, plane or slightly depressed, thin, often with a small umbo, bright red, floccose; tubes very large-mouthed, yellow becoming dingy-ochraceous, slightly decurrent; stem slender, red, yellowish toward apex, solid, glabrate; spores pinkish-brown.—In sphagnum swamps, Minnesota to Maine and Pennsylvania.

B. merulioides Schw.

Pileus 5-12 cm. broad; context 5-10 mm. thick; stem 1-2 cm x 0.5-1 cm.

Pileus thin, irregularly lobed, depressed when mature, minutely tomentose, dry, dull red-brown, slowly tinging blue-green where wounded; tubes decurrent, honey-yellow, composed of radiating and anastomosing lamellae 2-3 mm. apart, branched and connected by irregular veins; stem eccentric or lateral.—Gregarious in woods, Canada and Wisconsin to Alabama.

B. spectabilis (Peck) Murr.   Plate 10, fig. 2.

Pileus 5-10 x 1.5-2.5 cm.; stem 8-12 x 1 cm.; spores 14 x 6 μ.

Pileus broadly convex, covered with red tomentum, then scaly, viscid, red, the scales becoming gray-red, brown, or yellowish; flesh white or pale yellow; tubes yellow, large, angular, adnate, concealed at first by a glutinous, reddish membrane which breaks and forms a red, or red and yellow annulus toward stem apex; stem yellow above annulus, red or red with yellow stains below; spores purplish-brown; tubes about 6 mm. x 1 mm.—In swamps and bogs, common, August and September, Illinois to New York, northward to Canada.

STROBILOMYCES Berk.

Pileus orbicular, hemispherical to convex, margin appendiculate.
Pileus and stem distinctly rough with large floccose scales, regular in shape, central-stemmed; tubes not easily separable from the hymenophore, large; flesh tough.—Growing on the ground in woods.

S. strobilaceus Berk. Cone Boletus (edible).

Pileus 5-10 cm. x 1-2 cm.; stem 7-12 x 1-2 cm.; spores 11 μ in diameter.

Pileus hemispherical or convex, dry, blackish, covered with thick floccose blackish or brownish-black projecting scales, the margin appendiculate with hanging veil remnants; flesh whitish becoming first reddish then blackish where wounded; tubes adnate, whitish, becoming brown or blackish with age, mouths large, angular, changing in color as does the flesh; spores globose, rough, blackish-brown. —Common in open woods throughout temperate North America.

BOLETUS Dill. Plates 10 and 11.

Pileus fleshy, putrescent, central-stemmed to eccentric, orbicular; hymenium composed of pores which are connected as a layer but are easily separated from each other and from the pileus; tube-mouths round or angular, simple or compound, yellows, white, rusty-brown, or red, or changing to blue or green where wounded. Species of the genus *Boletus* are distinguished from *Polyporus* and *Boletinus* by the easily separating tubes, and from *Polyporus* by the soft, putrescent texture and the almost invariably terrestrial habitat.

Key to Tribes (after Peck)

1   Pileus and stem yellow-pulverulent, stem not reticulated with
    veins.........Pulverulenti (*B. auriflammeus* to *B. Ravenelii*).
1' Pileus and stem not yellow-pulverulent, or if so, then the
    stem is reticulated with veins......2
2   Tubes of one color or mouths not reddish......3
2' Tubes yellowish with reddish or reddish-brown mouths
    ....Luridi (*B. Satanus* to *B. Sullivantii*).
3   Stem lacunose-reticulated and lacerated................
    ....Laceripedes (*B. Russelli* to *B. Betula*).
3' Stem reticulated with veins, not lacerated......4
3" Stem neither reticulated nor lacerated......6
4   Tubes white, becoming flesh-colored...................
    ....Hyporhodii (*B. felleus* to *B. gracilis*).
4' Tubes not becoming flesh-colored......5

5 Tubes free, or if adnate then stuffed when young......Edules.
5' Tubes adnate, not stuffed when. young.................
....................Calopodes (*B. Peckii* to *B. modestus*).
6 Pileus viscid or glutinous when moist......7
6' Pileus dry, not viscid......8
7 Tubes adnate..Viscipelles (*B. sphaerosporus* to *B. sanguineus*).
7' Tubes free or nearly so, yellowish.....................
........................Edules (*B. separans* to *B. affinis*).
7'' Tubes free or nearly so, whitish.......................
.................Versipelles (*B. duriusculus* to *B. sordidus*).
8 Stem solid......9
8' Stem spongy within, soon cavernous...................
....Cariosi (*B. cyanescens* to *B. castaneus*).
9 Tubes becoming flesh-colored....................Hyporhodii.
9' Tubes not becoming flesh-colored......10
10 Tubes adnate......11
10' Tubes free or nearly so......12
11 Pileus subtomentose ....
........Subtomentosus (*B. chrysenteron* to *B. subtomentosus*).
11' Pileus glabrous or pruinose...........................
............Subpruinosi (*B. miniato-olivaceus* to *B. pallidus*).
12 Tubes yellowish, or else stuffed when young..........Edules.
12' Tubes whitish, not stuffed.....................Versipelles.

Key to Species

1 Pileus viscid at least when moist......2
1' Pileus not viscid......8
2 Plant yellow-pulverulent, stem not reticulated, pileus dull red, tubes yellow ....*B. Ravenelii*, p. 147
2' Plant not covered with yellow powder......3
3 Tubes yellow, with red mouths......4
3' Tubes not with red mouths......5
4 Flesh violet-tinted; stem ventricose-ovate, red-reticulate upward ....*B. Satanus*, p. 146
4' Flesh yellow, stem reticulate or punctate....*B. luridus*, p. 146
5 Stem lacunose-reticulate and lacerate......6
5' Stem not lacerate......7
6 Stem red in depressions.................*B. Morgani*, p. 145
6' Stem pale yellow.........................*B. Betula*, p. 145
7 Stem roughened with points...............*B. scaber*, p. 149
7' Stem not so roughened, solid, not bulbous, lacerate or reticulate......47

8   Plant yellow-pulverulent, stem not reticulate with veins....9
8' Plant not yellow-powdered or if so the stem
    reticulate......10
8" Stem lacunose-reticulate and lacerate.......*B. Russelli*, p. 145

9   Plants bright golden-yellow except for scarlet-tube mouths;
    growing on ground.................*B. auriflammeus*, p. 147
9' Plants golden-yellow; growing on wood; tubes yellow, the
    mouths large, angular, becoming red-brown.............
    ....:.....*B. hemichrysus*, p. 147
9" Plants growing on ground, the center of the pileus reddish
    ....*B. Ravenelii*, p. 147

10   Tubes yellow with red or brown mouths......11
10' Tubes white, soon flesh-colored......14
10" Tubes of one color or not becoming flesh-colored......17

11   Plant bright blood-red....................*B. Frostii*, p. 147
11' Plant not so colored......12

12   Pileus bearing alveolar depressions in the tube surface, stem
     rough, flesh white becoming blue where bruised........
     ....*B. alveolatus*, p. 146
12' Pileus bearing no such hymenium-depressions......13

13   Flesh white, becoming blue where bruised; stem
     smooth ....*B. vermiculosus*, p. 146
13' Flesh scarcely changing color when bruised.*B. Sullivantii*, p. 147

14   Stem slender, long.......................*B. gracilis*, p. 155
14' Stem comparatively stout......15

15   Pileus and stem blackish.................*B. nigrellus*, p. 155
15' Pileus lighter in color, plants large......16

16' Plants with mild taste, ochre-brown........*B. indecisus*, p. 155
16   Plants with very bitter taste...............*B. felleus*, p. 155

17   Stem ventricose, soon cavernous; plants dull buff quickly
     changing to blue where bruised..........*B. cyanescens*, p. 156
17' Without this combination of characters......18

18   Tubes white......19
18' Tubes yellow......30

19   Pileus red-brown, stem stuffed or hollow....*B. castaneus*, p. 156
19' Pileus not red-brown, or if so then the stem solid......20

20   Tubes soon yellow, green when bruised......21
20' Tubes not becoming green......22

21   Pileus glabrous ....*B. edulis*, p. 150
21' Pileus scaly or tomentose.................*B. varipes*, p. 150

22   Stem brownish-lilac or chocolate-colored......23
22'   Stem black ....*B. alboater*, p. 148
22"   Stem of another color......24

23   Stem reticulate ....*B. separans*, p. 149
23'   Stem not reticulate, furfuraceous..........*B. eximius*, p. 150

24   Tubes becoming blue where bruised, minute; stem white, streaked with brown.....................*B. pallidus*, p. 153
24'   Tubes not becoming blue where bruised......25

25   Pileus yellow-brown tufted with red points, stem striate upward ....*B. Roxanae*, p. 154
25'   Without this combination of characters......26

26   Stem yellow at base...................*B. chromapes*, p. 148
26'   Stem not yellow at base......27

27   Pileus margin bearing remnants of the veil..*B. versipellis*, p. 148
27'   Pileus not appendiculate......28

28   Stem scabrous or dotted with squamules......*B. scaber*, p. 149
28'   Stem smooth......29

29   Pileus white ....*B. albellus*, p. 149
29'   Pileus dark brown......................*B. sordidus*, p. 149

30   Stem stuffed or hollow; entire plant minutely velvety tomentose, cinnamon or reddish-brown......*B. castaneus*, p. 156
30'   Stem not stuffed or hollow......31

31   Tubes becoming blue where bruised......32
31'   Tubes becoming green where bruised......38
31"   Tubes not becoming blue or green where bruised......39

32   Pileus red at least when young......33
32'   Pileus of another color......35

33   Stem red, pileus fading to buff-brown, margin remaining red ....*B. Peckii*, p. 151
33'   Stem partly yellow......34

34   Stem yellow sometimes with red stains; pileus glabrous, vermillion becoming olivaceous....*B. miniato-olivaceus*, p. 152
34'   Plants large, stem reticulate.............*B. speciosus*, p. 151
34"   Plants of medium size, stem not reticulate, pileus dark red becoming yellow-stained ....*B. bicolor*, p. 152

35   Flesh red beneath cuticle....36
35'   Flesh not red beneath cuticle......37

36   Flesh golden ....*B. chrysenteron*, p. 153
36'   Flesh whitish, stem smoky-brown........*B. fumosipes*, p. 154

37   Stem 5 cm. long, radicating by tapering downward; margin
     of pileus thin, involute....................*B. radicans,* p. 154
37' Stem 5-10 cm. long, ovate-bulbous, reticulate, red and yel-
     low-variegated ....*B. pachypus,* p. 151
38   Pileus not spotting white, glabrous...........*B. edulis,* p. 150
38' Pileus not spotting, not glabrous; stem reticulate.......
     ....*B. variipes,* p. 150
39   Parasitic on the tough-skinned puffball (Scleroderma)....
     ....*B. parasticus,* p. 153
39' Not parasitic......40
40   Tubes greenish-yellow, pileus cushion-shaped............
     ....*B. alutaceus,* p. 153
40' Tubes not greenish......41
41   Tubes golden-yellow, stem viscid or glutinous when moist
     ....*B. auriporus,* p. 153
41' Without this combination of characters......42
42   Stem reticulate, scabrous or ribbed......43
42' Stem smooth, pileus and stem chestnut-tawny..*B. affinis,* p. 151
43   Stem scabrous or ribbed, tubes large-angular, flesh whitish
     ....*B. subtomentosus,* p. 154
43' Stem scabrous with black points, stem large and fusiform
     ....*B. duriusculus,* p. 148
43" Stem reticulate......44
44   Stem thick, ventricose; pileus velvety, yellow-brown......
     ....*B. crassipes,* p. 150
44' Stem not markedly ventricose....45
45   Stem yellow, beautifully reticulated; pileus brown.......
     ....*B. ornatipes,* p. 152
45' Stem brown, chocolate, or red-brown......46
46   Plants small, 2-4 cm. in diameter, the yellowish-brown tubes
     short, angular ....*B. modestus,* p. 152
46' Plants large, chocolate or red-brown; flesh white........
     ....*B. separans,* p. 149
47   Stem with an annulus......48
47' Stem without an annulus......51
48   Stem dotted above the persistent, membranous annulus....
     ....*B. luteus,* p. 142
48' Stem dotted both above and below annulus..*B. subluteus,* p. 142
48" Stem not dotted......49
48'" Stem squamose, reticulate above annulus.....*B. viscidus,* p. 141

B. sphaerosporus Peck. Plate 10, figure 3.

Pileus 7-20 cm. broad x 2-3 cm. thick; stem 2-8 x 1-3 cm.; spores 8 μ in diameter.

Pileus hemispherical then convex, reddish-brown or chestnut, or at first creamy-yellow, glabrous, viscid, thick; the flesh pale yellow; the tubes 6 mm. long, angular, grouped, 1-2 mm. in diameter, large, yellow becoming brown, covered for much of the life of the pileus with a thick membranous persistent concolorous veil, which finally breaks by a small opening and at length completely contracts, part toward the stem as an annulus and part toward the margin of the pileus; stem stout, cylindrical, smooth or reticulate upward, central or eccentric, occasionally lateral, spores globose or broadly elliptical. —In ravines and sandy places, not uncommon, Minnesota to Wisconsin and Iowa.

B. Clintonianus Peck.   Clinton's Boletus (edible).

Pileus 5-12 broad x 1-2 cm. thick; stem 5-12 x 1-2 cm.; spores 10 x 4.5 μ.

Pileus convex, golden-yellow, orange, or chestnut, very viscid or glutinous, glabrous, soft, shining, with thin margin, the flesh pale yellow, dingy where exposed; the tubes pale yellow, small, plane, adnate or subdecurrent, changing to brown or purplish-brown where bruised; stem cylindrical, yellow above, red-brown below the annulus, the annulus white or yellow, forming a thick band around the stem; spores brownish-ochraceous.—On mossy ground in woods or near tamaracks, or on grassy open ground, Wisconsin to New England and New Jersey.

This species is typically with reddish-brown pileus, yellowish where found in open places; it differs from *B. elegans* in its thick persistent annulus. Its smaller tubes and persistent annulus separate it from *B. flavus*.

B. Elbensis Peck.

Pileus 5-10 cm. broad x 1 cm. thick; stem 7-12 cm. x 8-12 mm.; spores 11 x 4.5 μ.

Pileus convex, dingy-gray, tinged pink or brown, spotted or streaked with innate fibrils, glabrous, viscid, the flesh thin, white, the tubes white becoming brownish-ochraceous, large, angular, plane, up to 1 mm. in diameter, adnate or slightly decurrent; stem white above annulus, dingy-gray below, the apex sometimes reticulate; spores rusty-brown.—In tamarack swamps and under spruces, rare, Wisconsin to New York and northward.

B. viscidus L.

Pileus 5-10 cm. broad; stem 4-8 cm. x 7-12 mm.

Pileus convex-plane, dirty-yellow or greenish-stained, very glutinous-viscid, pulvinate, soft, glabrous, 1-2 cm. thick, the flesh white, the tubes about 7 mm. long, adnate, white or greenish, large, angular, unequal; stem white, annulate, reticulate above annulus, viscid, becoming yellow or brown-stained; spores fuscous.—In deciduous forests, not common, October, Wisconsin to New York.

B. laricinus Berk.

Pileus lacking green shades, viscid rather than gluten-smeared, the tubes larger; spores brown, 12 x 4-5 μ.—In tamarack bogs, October, locally common, Wisconsin to New York.

B. luteus L. (edible).   Plate 10, fig. 5.

Pileus 5-12 cm. broad; stem 2-5 x 1-2 cm.; spores 7 x 3.5 μ.

Pileus convex, gibbous, brownish becoming yellow-brown and virgate-spotted, covered with brown gluten which separates and exposes yellow colors; the flesh white, the tubes yellow, minute, adnate, simple, darkened with age; stem stout, yellowish and dotted above the large, membranous, brownish-white annulus, brownish or yellow below; spores fusiform, yellow-brown.—Under pines and on sandy soil, not common, Maine to Minnesota and southward.

B. flavus With.

Pores large, angular, otherwise very similar to the preceding.— Rare in the United States.

B. subluteus Peck.   (edible)

Pileus 3-7 cm. broad x 1 cm. thick; stem 3-6 cm. x 4-8 mm.; spores 9 x 4 μ.

Pileus convex-plane, dull or dingy-yellow, often brownish or rusty-tinged, often obscurely virgate-spotted, viscid, the flesh white to dull yellow, the tubes ochraceous, small, subrotund, adnate, often plane; stem slender, dull yellowish, dotted above and below annulus with brown or red dots, the annulus at first glutinous and covering the tubes, collapsing to form a narrow whitish or brownish band about the stem; spores rusty-ochraceous.—On sandy soil beneath pines, common, autumn, New England to Minnesota, Indiana and Maryland.

B. punctipes Peck.

Pileus 5-8 cm. broad; stem 5-8 cm. x 6-10 mm.; spores 10 x 4-5 μ.

Pileus convex to plane, thin toward margin, yellow, gray-pulverulent toward margin when young, glutinous, the margin becoming upturned in age, the tubes brownish then dirty-ochraceous, short, small, subrotund, nearly plane, adnate, bearing glandules; stem tapering upward, yellowish, rhubarb yellow, glandular-dotted, rather long. —In mixed woods, rare, autumn, Wisconsin to Ontario and New York.

B. americanus Peck. (the caps edible).   Plate 10, fig. 4.

Pileus 2-7 cm. in diameter x 1-1.5 cm. thick; stem 4-6 cm. x 4-8 mm.; spores 10 x 4-5 μ.

Pileus convex, plane, thin, sometimes with an umbo, yellow, dingy with age, sometimes streaked with red, soft, very viscid, slightly tomentose on margin when young, the flesh pale yellow, pinkish-gray or dull where exposed, the tubes rather large about 1 mm. broad, angular, pale yellow becoming sordid-ochraceous, plane or convex; stem slender, not annulate, firm, yellow, brown toward base, yellow within, adorned from apex almost to the base with red or brown persistent glandular dots; spores rusty-ochraceous.—Under pines in open places in sand, or in swampy places, common, Sept.-Oct.. Minnesota to Maine and Indiana.

B. hirtellus Peck.

Pileus 5-10 cm. broad; stem 5-8 cm. x 8-12 mm.; spores 10 x 4-5 μ.

Pileus broadly convex, golden-yellow, adorned with numerous minute hair-tufts or fibrils, soft, viscous, the flesh pale yellow; stem stout, yellow, adorned with glandular dots; spores pale ochraceous-brown.—Somewhat caespitose on sandy soil under pine trees, rare, September, Wisconsin to New York and Alabama.

B. subaureus Peck. (edible).

Pileus 5-10 cm. broad; 4-6 cm. x 8-12 mm.; spores 9 x 4 μ.

Pileus convex to plane, pale yellow, the young margin slightly grayish-tomentose, sometimes with darker spots, viscous, the flesh pale yellow, the tubes small to medium, angular, clear pale yellow, exuding yellow drops; stem stout, cylindrical, yellow both without and within, glandular dotted; spores rusty-ochre.—Gregarious or subcaespitose, in thin woods, often among pine needles, locally common, October and November, Wisconsin to New York and North Carolina.

B. granulatus L. (edible).   Plate 11, fig. 4.

Pileus 4-10 cm. broad, stem 2-5 cm. x 8-12 mm.; spores 7-10 x 2-3 μ.

Pileus convex to nearly plane, rusty-brown when moist, yellowish when dry, very viscid, the flesh pale-yellow, the tubes short, yellowish, adnate, with small mouths, simple and containing granules; stem pale yellow, dotted with glands above; spores orange, spindle shaped. —Under pines in woods, September until frost, more frequently found in late autumn, common, Maine to North Carolina and Minnesota to Illinois.

B. albus Peck.   White Boletus.

Pileus 3-7 cm. broad x 1 cm. thick; stem 3-8 cm. x 6-10 mm.; spores 9 x 4 μ.

Pileus convex, white where moist, dull pinkish-brown in drying, viscid, the flesh white or yellowish, the tubes rather small, subrotund, whitish becoming ochraceous, plane, short, exuding a milky, sordid, astringent fluid which dries in tubes and on stem and makes both glandular-dotted; stem white, sometimes pink-tinged toward base, glandular-dotted, cylindrical; spores ochraceous.—Woods, especially of pine and hemlock, rare, September and October, Wisconsin to New England and New York.

B. brevipes Peck. Short-stemmed Boletus (edible).

Pileus 3-6 cm. broad; stem 1-2.5 cm. x 6-10 mm.; spores 7.5 x 3 μ.

Pileus convex, thick, dark chestnut-brown covered with thick, tough gluten, fading to dingy-tawny, the margin inflexed, the flesh white, the tubes short, small, subrotund, white becoming dingy-ochraceous, nearly plane, depressed about the stem; stem whitish, not dotted.—On sandy soil in pine woods, not common, Oct.-Nov., New England to Wisconsin, Alabama.

B. collinitus Fr.

Pileus 5-10 cm.; stem 4-8 x 1 cm.

Pileus convex, thin toward margin, with brown glutinous covering, pale where gluten disappears, the flesh white, thick on disk, thin at margin, the tubes long, pale yellow becoming bright yellow, the mouths two-parted, small, adnate, without granules; stem firm, white becoming brown, somewhat reticulate with close-fitting squamules, often tapering downward, brittle.—In pine or fir woods, rare, September, New England to North Carolina and Wisconsin.

B. badius Fr. (edible)

Pileus 5-15 cm. broad; stem 4-12 cm. x 6-15 mm.; spores 11 x 5 μ.

Pileus convex, tawny-chestnut to smoky-brown, soft, smooth, viscose or glutinous, the flesh whitish to rosy becoming bluish where wounded especially near the tubes, the tubes whitish-yellow becoming green-tinged, large, angular, long, adnate or sinuate-depressed; stem subcylindrical, smooth, solid, paler than pileus, brown-pruinate. —In woods, especially of pine, not common, September, Minnesota, Wisconsin, New York.

B. rubinellus Peck.

Pileus 2-5 cm. broad; stem 2-5 cm. x 4-8 mm.; spores 13 x 4 μ

Pileus broadly conical, convex, red fading to yellow on margin, viscid when moist, subtomentose when dry, the flesh white or yellowish, the taste mild, the tubes dingy-red becoming rusty, adnate or slightly depressed about the stem; stem cylindrical, dingy-red to rusty, yellow within, often yellow at base, slender, smooth; spores rusty-brown.—Near conifers, in woods, not common, New York to North Carolina and Kentucky.

B. piperatus Bull. (edible).

Pileus 3-8 cm. broad; stem 3-8 cm. x 4-8 mm.; spores 10 x 4 μ.

Pileus convex to plane, yellowish-cinnamon or rusty, glabrous, slightly-viscid when moist, the flesh white or yellowish, very acrid, peppery, the tubes long, large, angular, reddish-rust-colored, plane or convex, adnate or subdecurrent, often unequal; stem slender, subcylindrical, tawny-yellow with bright yellow base; spores rusty-brown.—In woods and open places, along paths; not common, Wisconsin to New York and New Jersey.

B. sanguineus Peck.

Pileus 2-8 cm. broad; stem 3-5 x 3 cm.; tubes 2-4 mm. long.

Pileus scarlet, viscid, thick, firm but flexible, the tubes short, minute, pinkish then brownish-yellow, light brown where bruised; stem very thick, pale yellow, white near base and marked near apex by decurrent tube-walls.—Under beech trees, not common, Aug.-Sept., Pennsylvania to eastern Indiana, probably in the same range as the beech.

B. Russelli Frost. (edible).   Plate 10, fig. 7.

Pileus 3-10 cm. broad x 1.5-4 cm. thick; stem 8-20 cm. x 6-12 mm.; spores 20 x 9 μ.

Pileus thick, hemispherical or convex, not viscid, covered with bundles of downy red hairs, yellowish beneath hairs, often cracked into areas, the flesh yellowish not changing, the tubes dingy-yellow or tinged-greenish, rather large; stem very long, cylindrical or tapering upward, roughened by the lacerate margins of the coarse reticular depressions, red or brownish-red; spores olive-brown.—In red oak or mixed woods, common, Aug.-Oct., Minnesota to Ohio and Mississippi.

B. Morgani Peck. (edible).

Similar to the preceding but the pileus glabrous, viscid, red fading to yellow on margin, or entirely red or yellow; stem yellow, red in depressions.—On the ground, woods, not common, Aug.-Sept., Minnesota to Maine and Mississippi.

B. Betula Schw. (edible).

Pileus 3-4 cm. broad; stem 12-15 cm. x 1 cm.

Pileus convex, tawny-orange, viscose, shining when wet, tessellately cracked, small, the flesh yellowish-white, the tubes yellow, rather large, angular; stem long, narrowed downward, everywhere covered with a reticulated surface 4 mm. thick which separates like bark from the interior, pale yellow without and within.—On the ground in woods, rare, Ohio to Pennsylvania, North Carolina and Alabama.

B. Satanus Lenz.   Satanic Boletus (suspected).

Pileus 7-20 cm. broad; stem 5-8 cm. x 3-5 cm.

Pileus convex, brownish yellow or whitish, viscid, glabrous; flesh whitish becoming reddish or violaceous where wounded; tubes yellow, mouths bright red becoming orange-colored with age, free; stem thick, ovate-ventricose, red-reticulated above.—Woods, Aug.-Sept., rare, New York to North Carolina and California.

B. alveolatus Berk. and Curt. (edible)

Pileus 8-15 cm. broad; stem 7-10 cm. x 1.5-2 cm.; spores 14 x 4.5 μ.

Pileus convex, bright crimson or maroon, glabrous, shining, sometimes paler or with patches of yellow, the flesh white, blue where wounded, firm, thick, the tubes yellow with maroon mouths, adnate or subdecurrent at the surface, with alveolar depressions; stem very rough, the coarse depressions with roughened margins, reticulations bright red with yellow stains; spores yellowish-brown.—In damp woods, August, not common, New England, New Jersey to Indiana, especially in beech woods.

B. luridus Schaeff.

Pileus 5-10 cm. broad; stem 5-7 cm. x 2-3 cm.; spores 15 x 9 μ.

Pileus convex, brown-olivaceous, then sooty and somewhat viscose, tomentose, the flesh yellow becoming blue where wounded, the tubes yellow becoming greenish, the mouths small, round, vermillion becoming orange, free; stem stout, bright red or vermillion, orange-tinted toward apex, reticulate or punctate; spores greenish-gray.—In frondose or mixed woods, not common, throughout temperate North America.

B. purpureus Fr.

Pileus somewhat velvety, purplish-red, the tube mouths purple-orange, becoming blue where wounded; otherwise much as in the preceding.—In oak and chestnut woods, not common, August, Minnesota to New England and North Carolina.

B. vermiculosus Peck.

Pileus 7-12 cm. broad; stem 5-10 x 1-2 cm.; spores 11 x 4.5 μ.

Pileus thick, broadly convex, brown, yellowish or grayish-brown, often red-tinged, not viscid, dry, glabrous or minutely tomentose, firm, the flesh white, quickly becoming blue where wounded, the tubes yellow with brownish-orange mouths which become black in age, promptly changing to blue where wounded, plane, nearly free, small, round; stem firm, subcylindrical, smooth, paler than pileus; spores ochraceous-brown.—In woods, rare, August, New England to Wisconsin and Ohio.

B. Frostii Russ. (suspected)

Pileus 7-10 cm. broad; stem 5-10 cm. x 6-12 mm.; spores 14 x 5 μ.

Pileus convex, blood-red, polished, shining, the flesh medium-thick, thin on margin, scarcely changing in color, the tubes greenish-yellow, with blood-red or cinnabar mouths, becoming yellow-brown with age, large, nearly free; stem cylindrical or tapering upward, distinctly reticulate, blood-red.—On grassy places in thin woods, not common, August, Michigan to Maine to Virginia and Tennessee.

B. Sullivantii Berk. and Mont. Sullivant's Boletus.

Pileus 7-10 cm.; stem 4-8 cm. x 1 cm.; spores 15 x 5 μ.

Pileus hemispherical, tawny-red or brown, cracked into squares, glabrous, the tubes angular, free, convex, medium-sized, longer in front, with reddish mouths; stem solid, violaceous on the thickened base, red reticulate upward, expanding into pileus; spores pallid-ochraceous, oblong-fusiform.—In frondose upland woods, August, not common, Ohio and southeastern Indiana.

B. auriflammeus Berk. and Curt.

Pileus 6-8 cm. broad, 1-2 cm. thick; stem 5-9 x 0.5-1 cm.; spores 11 x 5 μ.

Pileus convex, dry, bright golden-yellow, rather thick, powdered with sulphur-dust, the flesh white, unchanging, the tubes free, plane or convex, yellow, the mouths scarlet especially when seen from one side, decurrent, large, angular; stem bright-golden, slightly tapering upward, powdered.—Woods, New York to North Carolina and Kentucky.

B. hemichrysus Berk. and Curt.

Pileus 3-5 cm. broad; stem 2-3 cm. x 6-12 mm.

Pileus convex, then plane or depressed, thick, bright golden-yellow covered with yellow powder, floccose-squamulose, sometimes cracked, the flesh yellow, the tubes adnate or decurrent, angular, large, yellow becoming reddish-brown; stem short, often eccentric, irregular, narrowed below, yellowish and tinged-red, covered with a yellow dust; spores minute, oblong, dingy-ochraceous; mycelium yellow.—On stumps of roots of pine, not common, Aug.-Sept., Wisconsin to New York and South Carolina.

B. Ravenelii Berk. and Curt.

Pileus 2-7 cm. broad; stem 3-10 cm. x 6-12 mm.; spores 11 x 5-6 μ.

Pileus convex to plane, slightly viscid when young or when moist, covered with sulphur-yellow powdery down, becoming naked and dull red on disk, the flesh whitish, the tubes adnate, pale yellow becoming brownish or umber, dingy-greenish where bruised, medium-large, subrotund, at first plane; stem clothed and colored like pileus, cylindrical, yellow within, bearing an evanescent, webby annulus; spores ochraceous brown.—Subcaespitose on ground in woods and thickets, not common, August, Wisconsin, New England, North Carolina, Alabama.

B. duriusculus Schulz. Hard Boletus (edible).

Pileus 5-15 cm. broad; stem 10-20 x 3-5 cm.; spores 15 x 5-6 μ.

Pileus hemispherical, brown to umber-brown, viscid when moist, minutely velvety, often cracking when dry and forming brown areas with pale interstices, the flesh thick, white, becoming reddish-copper where cut, the tubes 1-2 cm. long, free, shorter behind, medium-large, angular, often compound, bright yellow; stem fusiform, the largest part below the middle, yellowish, rough with black points, solid; spores cylindrical, pale umber.—In woods, often on gravelly soil, not common, Aug.-Sept., Illinois to New Jersey.

B. alboater Schw. Black and white Boletus.

Pileus 6-10 cm. broad; 2 cm. thick; stem 5-8 x 1-2.5 cm.

Pileus convex, velvety, black, the margin at first involute, the flesh thick, firm, white becoming grayish, the tubes free, white, black in young specimens, minute, round; stem tapering downward, expanding upward into the pileus, hard, sooty-black, glossy, nutty in taste. —In moist woods, frequently found, New York to Georgia and Missouri.

B. chromapes Frost.

Pileus 5-10 cm. broad; stem 5-10 cm. x 8-12 mm.; spores 13 x 4-5 μ.

Pileus convex or nearly plane, slightly and sometimes fasciculately tomentose, pale-red, the flesh white not changing, the tubes white becoming brown, subadnate, depressed about the stem; stem almost cylindrical, rough-spotted, whitish, chrome-yellow at the base both without and within, spores oblong.—In woods, not uncommon, Aug.-Sept., Wisconsin to New England and Alabama.

B. versipellis Fr. (edible). Plate 11, fig. 5.

Pileus 5-15 cm x. 1-2 cm.; stem 7-12 cm. x 1-2 cm.; spores 16 x 5 μ.

Pileus convex, orange or orange-red, dry, minutely tomentose, squamose or smooth, the margin appendiculate with the inflexed membranous veil, the flesh white or grayish, the tubes sordid-white, with gray mouths, almost free, plane or concave, minute; stem whitish or pallid, cylindrical or tapering upward, wrinkled-scaly, solid; spores oblong-fusiform.—In open places in woods, especially on sandy soil, not common, Minnesota to Maine and South Carolina, also California.

B. albellus Peck. (edible).

Pileus convex or gibbous, whitish, soft, glabrous, the flesh white, not changing in color, the tubes convex, nearly free, small, subrotund, whitish, not changing; stem glabrous or minutely branny, substriate, thickened at base or bulbous; spores brownish-ochraceous.—Wisconsin to New York and West Virginia.

B. scaber Fr. (edible).   Plate 10, fig. 6.

Pileus 3-12 cm. broad x 1-2 cm. thick; stem 5-12 cm. x 4-16 mm.; spores 16 x 5 μ.

Pileus convex, usually viscid when moist, glabrous, subvelvety, or squamulose, becoming wrinkled on surface, white, olivaceous, smoky, tan, brown, orange, or brick-red in color; tubes rather long, 8-16 mm., free, white, then darkening or sordid; stem cylindrical and narrowed near apex, very scabrous with small, dot-like, fibrous, black or red scales, solid; spores snuff-brown, oblong, fusiform.—On the ground, sandy swamps and acid flat-lands, very common, Aug.-Oct., Minnesota to Maine and in the southern states.

B. sordidus Frost.   Sordid Boletus.

Pileus 4-8 cm. broad; stem 6-8 cm. x 5-8 mm.; spores 11 x 5 μ.

Pileus convex, dirty-dark-brown, subtomentose, the flesh white or slightly greenish-tinged, the tubes long, white, changing to bluish-green, nearly free; stem tapering upward, brownish with darker streaks, generally greenish above; spores fusiform, dirty-brown.—In damp wood in tree-excavations, not common, Wisconsin to Maine and Ohio.

B. separans Peck. (edible).

Pileus 10-15 cm. broad, 2-4 cm. thick; stem 5-12 x 1-1.5 cm.; spores 13 x 5 μ.

Pileus convex, thick, glabrous, red, brown-red, or dull lilac, often pitted and disclosing the white flesh, almost shining, fading to yellowish on the margin, the flesh white and unchanging, compact, thick, the tubes plane then convex, adnate, ochraceous-yellow, at first white and stuffed, depressed about the stem or pulled away from it, often becoming brownish-yellow; stem nearly cylindrical, reticulate at least upward, colored like pileus or paler, often furfuraceous; spores brownish-ochraceous, subfusiform.—In thin grassy woods, common, Wisconsin to New England to New Jersey and Illinois.

B. variipes Peck. (edible).

Pileus 6-12 cm. broad; stem 5-10 x 1-2 cm.; spores 13 x 5 μ.

Pileus convex to plane, gray or gray-brown, soft, dry, minutely tomentose, scaly, or scaly-pointed, sometimes tinged ochraceous, the flesh white and unchanging, the tubes slightly depressed about the stem, white then greenish-yellow, small, subrotund; stem firm, reticulate, whitish or pallid; spores oblong-fusiform, ochraceous-brown tinged with green.—On ground in woods, not common, August, Wisconsin, Illinois to Pennsylvania.

B. crassipes Peck. (edible).

Pileus 5-10 cm.; stem 6-9 x 2.5-3.5 cm.

Pileus convex to centrally depressed, firm, dry, velvety-brown tinged yellow, lobed, the involute margin extending beyond the tubes, the flesh lemon-yellow, unchanging, with an odor of yeast, and a sweet taste, the tubes short, depressed behind, almost free, minute, stuffed when young, yellowish mottled with brown, stem stout, thick, swollen in the middle and sometimes bulbous, reticulate, orange tinged with brown.—On ground in rich oak woods, not common, Aug.-Sept., Illinois to Pennsylvania, New Jersey.

B. edulis Bull.   Edible Boletus.   Plate 10, fig. 8.

Pileus 10-20 cm. broad x 2-3 cm., thick; stem 5-15 x 2-5 cm.; spores 14 x 4.5 μ.

Pileus convex, variable in color, gray red, brown-red, or tawny-brown, paler on the margin, glabrous, soft, the flesh white or yellowish-reddish beneath the cuticle, the tubes white and stuffed when young, then yellow, green where bruised, minute, round, convex, nearly free, long; stem short or long, subcylindrical or bulbous, stout, usually reticulate especially upward, white, pallid, or brownish; spores oblong-fusiform.—In woods, open places, and edges of swales, common, Aug.-Oct., throughout temperate North America.

Var. *clavipes* Peck is characterized by the wholly reticulate stem tapering upward from an enlarged base.—In the same habitat and range of species, common.

B. eximius Peck. (edible).

Pileus 8-25 cm. broad x 2-4 cm. thick; stem 5-10 x 1-2.5 cm.; spores 14 x 5 μ.

Pileus hemispherical, convex, purplish-brown, or chocolate-coloring with faint tints of lilac, becoming smoky or pale-chestnut, soft, subpruinose, the tubes minute, round, colored nearly as the pileus or paler, concave or nearly plane and stuffed at first, paler and depressed about the stem in age; stem stout, usually short, abruptly narrowed at the base, minutely branny, colored as or a little paler than pileus, purplish-gray within; spores rusty.—Woods and borders of woods, not common, August, Nova Scotia to North Carolina to Wisconsin and Tennessee.

B. affinis Peck. (edible).

Pileus 5-10 cm. broad; stem 4-8 cm. x 8-16 mm.; spores 11 x 4-5 μ.

Pileus convex or nearly plane, chestnut, tawny or dingy-ochraceous, subglabrous, the tubes plane or convex, adnate or slightly depressed, white and stuffed, then glaucous-yellow or ochraceous becoming rusty-ochraceous with age or where wounded, minute, round, 1 cm. long; stem smooth, subcylindrical, glabrous, colored like pileus; spores rusty-ochraceous.—In open oak woods, July-Aug., Thornton, Illinois, Cedar Lake, Indiana, Vermont to North Carolina.

B. Peckii Frost.   Peck's Boletus.

Pileus convex, firm, red fading to buff-brown in age, the margin retaining the red color longer than disk, dry, subglabrous, the tubes minute, round, adnate or slightly decurrent, nearly plane, yellow, blue where wounded; stem cylindrical or subventricose, reticulate, red, with a yellow apex; spores oblong, pale ochraceous-brown.— In frondose woods, not common, August, Illinois to New England and North Carolina.

B. speciosus Frost. (edible).

Pileus 8-18 cm. broad x 2-4 cm. thick, stem 5-15 x 2-5 cm.; spores 11 x 4-5 μ.

Pileus subglobose, thick, red, compact, the flesh yellow, changing to blue where wounded, the tubes adnate, small, round, bright lemon-yellow, dingy with age, blue where wounded; stem stout, bright lemon-yellow outside and inside, often reddish at base, subcylindrical or bulbous, reticulate; spores pale ochraceous-brown, oblong-fusiform.—In thin woods, not common, August, Indiana and Ohio to New England and North Carolina.

B. pachypus Fr.   Thick-footed Boletus (not poisonous).

Pileus 10-20 cm. broad; stem 5-10 x 1-5 cm.; spores 13 x 5-6 μ.

Pileus convex, brownish or pale-tan, subtomentose, the flesh thick, whitish, changing slightly blue where wounded, the taste unpleasant, the tubes rather long, round, pale yellow becoming green-tinged, somewhat depressed about stem; stem thick, firm, reticulate, ovate-bulbous, then elongate-cylindrical, variegated red and pale yellow; spores ovate, pale yellowish-ochraceous.—In woods of pine or beech, Wisconsin to New York and Virginia.

B. ornatipes Peck. (edible).

Pileus 4-12 cm. broad; stem 5-10 x 1 cm.; spores 14 x 4-5 μ.

Pileus convex, grayish-brown, or yellowish-brown, firm, dry, glabrous, the flesh yellow or pale yellow, the tubes clear-yellow, small or medium-sized, plane; stem subcylindrical, firm, distinctly and beautifully reticulate, yellow without and within; spores ochraceous-brown, oblong.—In thin woods, not common, Wisconsin to New York and Alabama.

B. modestus Peck.   Modest Boletus.

Pileus 5-7 x 1 cm. broad; stem 3-5 cm. x 4-8 mm.; spores 11 x 5 μ.

Pileus convex, plane, often irregular, yellowish-brown, firm, dry, very minutely tomentose, the flesh gray or pinkish-gray, the tubes plane, adnate or subdecurrent, pale-ochraceous, the mouths angular, 1 mm. in diameter; stem cylindrical, reticulate, brown; spores elliptical.—On grassy ground in thin woods, not common, Illinois to New York and Maryland.

This is known by its small size and yellow-brown color.   The specimens found at Thornton, Illinois had angular compound tube-mouths.

B. miniato-olivaceus Frost. (edible).

Pileus 4-10 cm. broad x 5 mm. thick; stem 6-10 cm. x 6-12 mm.; spores 12 x 6 μ.

Pileus convex, plane vermillion becoming ochraceous-red or olivaceous, pruinose to glabrous, the flesh pale-yellow, blue where wounded the tubes bright-lemon-yellow, angular, of medium size, adnate or subdecurrent; stem glabrous, enlarged toward the apex, yellowish, brighter within, lurid or reddish-stained at base.—Subcaespitose or solitary in woods, common, July-Sept., Minnesota to Maine and North Carolina to Kentucky and Indiana.

B. bicolor Peck. (edible).

Pileus 5-10 cm. broad; stem 3-7 cm. x 8-12 mm.; spores 13 x 4-5 μ.

Pileus convex, dark red, firm, becoming soft, paler and sometimes yellow-stained in age, glabrous or pruinose, the flesh yellow, slowly or not at all changing to blue where wounded, the tubes nearly plane, adnate, bright-yellow, becoming duller, slowly becoming blue where wounded, the mouths subangular, small to medium sized; stem red, usually yellow at the apex, firm solid, subcylindrical; spores pale ochraceous-brown.—In open woods, common, August, Wisconsin to Maine and North Carolina.

B. parasticus Bull. Parasitic Boletus.

Pileus 2-5 cm. broad; stem 2-5 cm. x 4-8 mm.; spores 13 x 4 μ.

Pileus convex, plane, grayish or dingy-yellow, dry, silky, soon gla-brous and tessellately cracked, the tubes decurrent, medium-sized, golden-yellow; stem yellow without and within, cylindrical, rigid; spores pale brown, oblong-fusiform.—Parasitic on the tough-skinned puff-ball, *Scleroderma aurantium,* Ohio to New England and West Virginia.

B. auriporus Peck. Golden-pored Boletus (edible).

Pileus 2-7 cm. broad; stem 2-7 cm. x 4-8 mm.; spores 9 x 4-5 μ.

Pileus convex, plane, brown, grayish-brown, yellowish-brown, or reddish-brown, glabrous or pruinose-tomentose, the flesh white and unchanging, the tubes small, round, bright golden-yellow and remain-ing so when dried, adnate, plane, sometimes slightly depressed about the stem; stem viscid or glutinous when moist, subcylindrical, brown-ish; thin.—In dry woods and on shaded banks, not common, Maine, Alabama, in the Rockies.

B. alutaceus Morg. (edible).

Pileus 7 cm. broad; stem 5-8 x 1 cm.; spores 12.5 x 5 μ.

Pileus cushion-shaped, alutaceous with a tinge of red, glabrous, the flesh white, inclining toward reddish, the tubes angular, medium-sized, greenish-yellow, semi-free; stem alutaceous with a tinge of red, nearly cylindrical, striate, reticulate at the apex; spores fusiform, brownish-olive.—In rocky woods of oak and chestnut, common, Wis-consin to Pennsylvania and Kentucky.

B. pallidus Frost. (edible).

Pileus 5-10 cm. broad; stem 8-13 cm. x 8-16 mm.; spores 11 x 5-6 μ.

Pileus convex, plane then depressed, brownish-white or pallid, glabrous, soft, sometimes tinged with red, the flesh white, the tubes very pale, whitish-yellow, blue where wounded, darkening in age, plane, the mouths small; stem whitish, often brown-streaked, often red-tinged within, long, cylindrical or thickened toward the base, flexuous, glabrous; spores pale-ochraceous-brown.—In woods, not common, Wisconsin to New England and Alabama.

B. chrysenteron Fr. Golden-flesh Boletus (edible).

Pileus 2-7 cm. broad x 1 cm. thick; stem 2-7 cm. x 6-12 mm.; spores 12 x 4-5 μ.

Pileus convex or plane, soft, floccose-squamulose, brown or brick-red, often cracked into areas and disclosing the red beneath the cuticle and golden-yellow flesh beneath this, the flesh often changing slightly to blue where wounded, the tubes greenish-yellow, changing to blue where wounded, subadnate, large, angular, unequal, about 5-7 mm. long; stem red or pale yellow, fibrous-striate, rigid, subcylindrical; spores pale brown, fusiform.—In woods and on mossy banks, common, July-Oct., Indiana to Minnesota and New York to North Carolina.

B. fumosipes Peck.

Pileus 2-5 cm. broad x 8-13 mm. thick; stem 2-5 cm. x 6-8 mm.; spores 14 x 5-6 μ.

Pileus convex or plane, dark olive-brown, minutely tomentose, reticulately rivulose, the flesh whitish, the tubes plane becoming convex, the mouths white then yellowish-brown, changing to bluish-black where bruised; stem smoky-brown, minutely scurfy, cylindrical, solid; spores purplish-brown.—In woods, common, New York, North Carolina, Kentucky and southern Indiana.

This resembles the preceding but is smaller, darker-colored, and with white flesh. Like the preceding in that the surface of the flesh is red beneath the cuticle, and the surface cracks into areas.

B. radicans Pers. (edible).

Pileus 5-8 cm. broad; stem 5-6 cm. x 2 cm.; spores 11 x 5 μ.

Pileus convex, ashy-olivaceous, becoming pale yellow, dry, subtomentose, the margin thin and involute, the flesh pale yellow, instantly becoming dark blue where bruised, bitter, the tubes adnate, large, angular, unequal, lemon-yellow; stem tapering downward and radicating, with a reddish flocculose bloom, pale yellow, becoming naked and dark if touched; spores olive, fusiform.—In woods, not common, Wisconsin to Pennsylvania and southward.

B. Roxanae Frost.

Pileus 3-7 cm. broad; stem 2-5 cm. x 6-10 mm.; spores 10 x 4 μ.

Pileus broadly convex, yellowish-brown, subtomentose then covered with red hairs in bundles, the flesh yellowish-white, the tubes whitish when young, then light yellow, arcuate-adnate or slightly depressed about the stem, the mouths small; stem enlarged toward base, striate at apex, yellowish or pale cinnamon.—In borders of woods, rare, Wisconsin to New England and New York.

B. subtomentosus L.   Plate 11, fig. 14.

Pileus 2-10 cm. broad x 1-2 cm. thick; stem 3-7 cm. x 4-10 mm.; spores 11 x 4-5 μ.

Pileus convex or nearly plane, soft, dry, usually olivaceous or yellowish-brown, sometimes tawny-red or reddish-brown, villose-tomentose, often cracked into areas, color beneath cuticle same as that of cuticle, the flesh white or pallid, the tubes large, angular, sometimes compound, yellow, adnate or depressed about the stem, larger near stem; stem stout, somewhat ribbed-sulcate, scabrous with minute dots.—On decaying wood either exposed or buried, common, August, South Dakota to Maine and southward to gulf.

B. felleus Bull.   Bitter Boletus (very bitter).   Plate 10, fig. 9.

Pileus 8-25 cm. broad or larger; stem 5-12 x 1-3 cm.; spores 12-17 x 4-5 μ.

Pileus convex to nearly plane, firm becoming soft, glabrous, variable in color, gray-brown, pale-yellowish, chestnut, yellowish-brown, or reddish-brown, the flesh white sometimes becoming flesh-colored where wounded, very bitter; tubes long, adnate, convex, depressed about the stem, the mouths angular, white becoming tinged with flesh-color; stem short or long, cylindrical or tapering upward, sub-glabrous, usually reticulate upward, a little paler than pileus; spores flesh-colored, oblong-fusiform.—In thin woods, very common, July-Oct., throughout temperate North America.

B. indecisus Peck. (edible).

Pileus 7-10 cm. broad; stem 5-10 x 1 cm.; spores 13 x 4 μ.

Pileus convex or nearly plane, ochraceous-brown, often wavy or irregular on margin, dry or slightly tomentose, the flesh white, unchanging, mild in taste, the tubes grayish becoming flesh-colored, adnate, plane or convex, the mouths small, subrotund; stem reticulate above, pallid without and within, straight or flexuous, minutely furfuraceous; spores brownish-flesh-colored, oblong.—In thin oak woods, not common, August, Minnesota to New England and North Carolina to Missouri.

B. nigrellus Peck. (edible).

Pileus 8-15 cm. broad; stem 3-6 cm. x 1-2.5 cm.; spores 11 x 5-6 μ.

Pileus broadly convex or nearly plane, blackish, dry, subglabrous, the flesh white, unchanging, soft, the tubes small, subrotund, whitish becoming flesh-colored, slowly changing to brown or blackish where wounded; stem short, smooth, blackish; spores dull flesh-colored.—In woods, not common, August, Wisconsin to New York and Ohio.

B. gracilis Peck. (edible).

Pileus 2-5 cm. broad; stem 6-10 x 0.3-1.5 cm.; spores 12-17 x 5-6 μ.

Pileus convex, glabrous, ochraceous-brown or tawny, minutely tomentose, the flesh white, the tubes plane or convex, whitish becoming pale flesh-colored, the mouths round; stem long, slender, smooth or marked by long narrow reticulations, pruinose or minutely branny; spores subferruginous.—In woods, not common, Wisconsin to Nova Scotia to Georgia.

B. cyanescens Bull. (edible).   Plate 11, fig. 15.

Pileus 3-10 cm. broad; stem 5-10 x 2 cm.; spores 11 x 7 μ.

Pileus pale buff, grayish-yellow, or somewhat brownish, changing quickly to blue where handled, convex, plane, floccose-tomentose, the flesh rigid, white, quickly turning blue where exposed to air or wounded; the tubes free, white becoming yellowish, minute, round, changing to blue where bruised; stem ventricose, closely covered with fine hairs, stuffed becoming cavernous, colored as pileus; spores elliptical.—In woods and open places, common, Minnesota to New England and West Virginia.

B. castaneus Bull.   Chestnut Boletus (edible).

Pileus 3-7 x 0.7 cm.; stem 2-5 x 6-10 mm.; spores 11 x 7 μ.

Pileus convex, plane or slightly depressed, cinnamon, chestnut or reddish-brown, firm, smooth, dry, minutely velvety, the flesh white, unchanging, the tubes short, small, white becoming yellow, free; stem cylindrical or tapering upward, smooth, stuffed or hollow, clothed and colored like pileus.—Gregarious in open woods, common, June-Sept., throughout temperate North America.

AGARICACEAE

Fructifications pileate bearing the hymenium beneath on radiating gills.

See Kauffman, C. H. Mich. Geol. & Biol. Surv. Publ. 26, Ser. 5, 1918; Mich. Acad. Sci. Arts & Let. 4:311-344, 1924; 2:53-67; Mycologia 17, No. 3:113-126, 1925; Amer. Jour. Bot. 13, No. 1:11-32, 1926; Graham, V. O. Chicago Acad. Sci. Prog. of Activities 4, No. 3:42-63, 1933; Trans. Ill. Acad. Sci. 23 (3):160-168, 1931; Bot. Gaz. 33 (3):267-287, 1927; McIlvaine, C. One Thousand American Fungi, Bobbs Merrill, 1912; Moffatt, W. S. Nat. Hist. Surv. Chicago Acad. Sci. Bul. VII Pt. I, 1909; Clements, F. E., Shear, C. L. and Mrs. Clements The Genera of Fungi, H. W. Wilson & Co., 1931; Harper, E. T. Trans. Wis. Acad. Sci. Arts & Let. 17:470-502, 17 pl., 1914; 17:1011-1026, 9 pl., 1914; 17:1142-1164, 1914; Peck, C. H. N. Y. State Mus. Rep. 33:38-49, 1880; 35:150-164, 1884; 36:41-49, 1884; 39:69-73, 1886; 42:39-46, 1889; 44:38-64, 1891;; 45:32-42, 1893; 46:61-69, 1893; 49:32-55, 1896; 50:133-144, 1897; N. Y. State Mus. Bul. 2:34-43, 1887; 116:45-67, 1907; 122:141-158, 1908. 131:47-54, 1909; 139:48-77, 1910; 157:59-105, 1912; Engler, A. and Prantl, K. Die Naturlichen Planzenfamilien, 2nd ed. 6:1-290, 1928; Coker, W. C. Jour. Elish Mitchell Sci. Soc. 33:1-88, 1917; Burlingham, G. Lactariae of the United States. Mem. Torrey Bot. Club 14 (1):109 pp., 1908; Hard, M. E. Mushrooms, edible and otherwise. The Ohio Library Co., 1908; Smith, A. H. Amer. Jour. Bot. 22:858-877, 1928.

AMANITA Fr.

Carpophore composed of an orbicular, convex pileus, loosely attached to a cylindrical, central stem; both annulus and volva present; stem fleshy, usually longer than diameter of pileus; gills white, free, soft; spores oval or subglobose, white, smooth.—Terrestrial.

When young the plants are like small puff-balls in appearance, covered with a volval layer which in some species is tough, in others soft and easily broken into small particles. Such variety in the types of covering results in the widely differing appearances of plants from one species to another in this genus. *A. caesarea, A. phalloides,* and several others, because of their tough covering, have persistent cup-like volvas. *A. muscaria, A rubescens,* and others have a softer covering and consequently parts of it remain on the pileus and parts form an imperfect volva about the base of the stem. An inner veil covers the lamellae in young plants. This breaks free from the margin of the pileus as that structure expands, and drops about the stipe to form an annulus. The genus contains our most poisonous species.

1   Volva cup-like, adhering only at the base of the stem or about
     1-2 cm. along the sides of the stem-base......2
1' Volva appearing as a series of rings at top of stem-base, as
     warty scales, or as mealy patches, which are easily removed....9

2   Volva fused with stem at base only......3
2' Volva fused to 1 cm. or more above the base; stem stuffed,
     without a definite central cylinder......6

3   Pileus bright yellow, orange, or red, distinctly striate on
     the margin ....*A. Caesarea.*
3' Pileus of another color......4

4   Pileus purplish-tinged ....*A. porphyria.*
4' Pileus brown, gray, or umber......5

5   Pileus-flesh thick except at the thin margin..........*A. spreta.*
5' Pileus-flesh thin ....*A. recutita.*

6   Pileus white......7
6' Pileus smoky-olive, gray, or almost white........*A. phalloides.*

7   Annulus present at apex of stem, flocculent beneath......
     ....*A. magnivelares.*
7' Annulus lower on the stem......8

8   Annulus sometimes lacking, a veil hanging from margin of
     the pileus, volva with a collar at the top............*A. virosa.*
8' Annulus very large, volva without a collar...........*A. verna.*

9　Pileus orange or red, adorned with white, floccose, thickened
　　patches ....*A. muscaria.*
9'　Pileus otherwise colored......10

10　Pileus strongly tuberculate-striate, egg-yellow; patches
　　white ....*A. gemmata.*
10'　Pileus not tuberculate-striate......11

11　Pileus-patches yellow, flesh not changing color where bruised
　　.....12
11'　Pileus-patches brown, gray or white......14

12　Pileus and veil light yellow, bulb broad and colored by the
　　lavender remains of volva...........*A. mappa* var. *lavendula.*
12'　Pileus deep yellow, bulb neither lavender nor broad......13

13　Pileus and volval remains chrome-yellow, the volva deposited
　　on the stem as a chrome-yellow, dust-like pulverulence....
　　..*A. flavoconia.*
13'　Pileus bright yellow to orange, decorated with yellow scales
　　or warts ....*A. Frostiana.*

14　Flesh changing to reddish color where bruised......15
14'　Flesh not changing color where bruised......16

15　Warts brownish ....*A. rubescens.*
15'　Warts yellow, cap yellow-brown, stem yellow.*A. flavorubescens.*

16　Odor of chlorine present......17
16'　Odor of chlorine absent......18

17　Pileus soft, covered with mealy warts.........*A. chlorinosma.*
17'　Pileus hard, covered with thick, hard scales....*A. strobiliformis.*

18　Bulb 2 cm. broad with a flattened upper part......19
18'　Bulb not flattened above......20

19　Pileus with soft, angular, erect warts; plants white..*A. abrupta.*
19'　Pileus with floccose warts; bulb with the remnant of volva
　　often margining the upper circumference...........*A. mappa.*

20　Upper part of bulb with a sheath decorated by several rings
　　..*A. crenulata.*
20'　Bulb not so decorated; pileus with warts or floccose scales,
　　white, gray, or brown......21

21　Plants tough, cuticle not separable from the flesh..*A. solitaria*
21'　Plants soft fragile......22

22　Gills flesh-colored..............................*A. excelsa.*
22'　Gills creamy or white..........................*A. spissa.*

A. Caesarea Fr. Caesar's Amanita (edible). Plate 13, fig. 1.
A. pellucida Peck.
Pileus 5-25 cm. broad; stem 6-18 cm. x 10-25 mm.; spores 11 x 7 μ.
Pileus yellow, orange, or red, sometimes bearing a volval patch, the margin distinctly striate; gills light yellow; stem not bulbous, hollow, with pith; annulus light yellow, membranaceous, skirt-like; volva large, firm, white.—In oak woods, not common, Iowa, New York, Florida, and Louisiana.

A. spreta Peck. Plate 13, fig. 3.
A. cinerea Bres.
Pileus 6-14 cm. broad; stem 10-15 cm. x 8-17 mm.; spores 11 x 7 μ.
Pileus umber, the margin often striate, the pellicle separable; gills free but with a decurrent line, rounded in front; stem hollow, flocculent, the bulb slight or lacking and inserted in the large, thick, membranaceous, persistent, white, sheathing volva; annulus white above, tinged umber beneath, thin.—In mixed or frondose woods, common, Minnesota to Maine, Florida, and Louisiana.
This species differs from *A. phalloides* in having a distinct, hollow, central cylinder. It is said by some to be edible. Certainly its close resemblance of *A. phalloides* is sufficient to condemn it.

A. recutita Fr. Plate 13, fig. 2.
Pileus 5-8 cm. broad; stem 8-10 cm. x 5-10 mm.; spores 12 x 8 μ.
Pileus thin, the disk gray-brown dotted with white scales, the margin striate; gills narrow, free but each with a decurrent line on the stem; stem cylindrical above the small round bulb, silky white; volva thick, short, but extending higher than the bulb, white; annulus thin, collapsing.—Among conifers in sandy woods, common, Minnesota and New England to North Carolina and Louisiana.
Both *A. recutita* and *A. spreta* may have thin patches on the pileus.

A. porphyria Fr. Plate 13, fig. 4.
Pileus 3-6 cm. broad; stem 6-12 cm. x 4-7 mm.; spores 8 x 8 μ.
Pileus smoky-brown in center, lighter and purplish-tinted toward the margin, the flesh thin, white; gills slightly ventricose, broad; stem soft, stuffed then hollow, white; annulus skirt-like, white or brown tinted; volva thin; spores spherical.—In open woods, rare, Massachusetts to Minnesota to Arkansas and Virginia.

A. tomentella Krombh.
Differing from *A. porphyria* in its numerous ash-colored scales and the ash-like powder on the stem.—On the ground, in mixed woods, rare, Aug.-Oct., northern part of our area.

A. phalloides Fr.   Death-cup, Deadly Amanita (poisonous).
Plate 13, fig. 5.

Pileus 5-15 cm. broad; stem 6-20 cm. x 6-12 mm.; spores 9-12 x
8-9 μ.

Pileus smoky-gray, olive, or light citron-yellow, viscid, glabrous;
gills white, broad; stem bulbous, stuffed then hollow, without a definite central cylinder as in *A. spreta*, white; annulus skirt-like, white
membranous; volva thick, tough, lobed at top; spores apiculate, granular within.—In oak or chestnut woods, not uncommon, July-Sept.,
Minnesota and Maine to Georgia and Louisiana.

One form of *A. mappa* with large angular bulb is sometimes included with *A. phalloides*, but it does not have a distinct volval cup.

A. magnivelaris Peck.
A. elliptosperma Atkins.
Pileus 5-12 cm. broad; stem 8-15 cm. x 9-25 mm.

Stem scarcely bulbous, rooted; gills light flesh-colored, some
forked; annulus at top of stem, large, skirt-like, sometimes adhering only to gills or margin of pileus; volva thick, leathery; flesh white,
tasteless, odorless.—In open woods, rare, July-Oct., New York, Minnesota, North Carolina, Louisiana.

A. verna Fr.   White Death-cup (poisonous).   Plate 13, fig. 8.

Pileus 5-12 cm. broad; stem 8-22 cm. x 8-20 mm.; spores 8-11 x
7-9 μ.

Pileus viscid, glabrous, white; gills broad, white; stem bulbous,
white; volva thick, the margin lobed; spores apiculate.—In frondose
woods, common, June-Oct., Minnesota to Maine and Louisiana to
Florida.

A. bisporigera Atkins.

Similar to *A. verna* but smaller and more slender, with two instead
of four spores on each basidium.—On the ground, or from much
decayed wood of mixed or frondose woods, frequently found, July-
Oct., Minnesota to North Carolina.

A. hygroscopica Coker

Shaped like *A. bisporigera*, the pileus is hygrophanous, otherwise
similar to *A. verna*.—On ground of woods, rare, Aug.-Sept., in mountains of North Carolina, to southern part of our area.

A. virosa Fr.   Plate 13, fig. 10.

Annulus usually absent because it is torn into shreds while attached
to gills; stem often eccentric, the bulb with a collar at top; spores

8-9 x 7 μ; plant otherwise resembling *A. verna.*—Habitat and range as for *A. verna.*

A. gemmata Fr.   Plate 13, fig. 9.

Pileus 5-15 cm. broad; stem 5-14 cm. x 6-14 mm.; spores 8 x 10 μ.

Pileus brown or cream-colored, shining, viscid, with few to several white pyramidal patches, the margin tuberculate-striate; flesh thin, white, odorless; gills veined next to pileus, the edges floccose; annulus thin, low, often evanescent; stem tapering upward, bulbous, stuffed, white, smooth, striate near apex, the surface often splitting near base; volva with perfect or fragmented collar, which may be some distance above bulb.—In open woods, not common, Minnesota to Maine to Louisiana, to Florida.

A. nivalis Peck, *A. velutipes* Atkins., and *A. multisquamosa* Peck seem to be forms of *A. gemmata.*

A. russuloides Peck.

A. cothurnata Atkins.

Pileus pale buff in center, with irregular patches easily removable or washed away by rain, tuberculate-striate and white on margin; stem with a distinct central cylinder, stuffed, the rolled margin forming collar or sometimes two or three rings at top of bulb; spores white, elliptical, 8-11 x 7 μ.—In open woods, rare, September, locally clustered on sand flats at south end of Lake Michigan.

A. glabriceps Peck.

The white form of *A. russuloides.*—On hard soil of open woods, rare, August, throughout our area.

A. crenulata Peck.

Like *A. russuloides* but with crenulate gill-margins.—In open woods, on the ground, rare, Aug.-Sept., throughout our area.

A. flavoconia Atkins.   Chrome-dusted Amanita.   Plate 13, fig. 7.

Pileus yellow, viscid, bearing yellow powdery patches; flesh thin, white; gills close, white, the edges fimbriate; stem with chrome-yellow, powdery patches, bulbous; volva composed of powdery patches; spores oval.—Common in low rich woods, often on *Polytrichum* and *Sphagnum,* July-Sept., Minnesota to New England to North Carolina.

A. Frostiana Peck.   Plate 13, fig. 6.

Pileus 3-6 cm. broad; stem 5-10 cm. x 5 mm.; spores 7 x 10 μ.

Pileus bright yellow to orange, slightly viscid, usually decorated with yellowish scales, the margin striate; gills white or yellowish, close, broadest in front; stem light yellowish to white, stuffed, the bulb margined above with a collar-like ring; annulus thin, soon disappearing; spores globose, smooth.—Almost solitary on ground in frondose or mixed woods, not common, Aug.-Sept., Minnesota to New England and North Carolina.

A. mappa Fr.   Plate 13, fig. 11.
A. floccocephala Atkins.
Pileus 2-8 cm. broad; stem 5-8 cm. x 4-8 mm.; spores 8.5 μ.
Pileus fulvous or paler with flat, white, yellowish or brown scales; stem striate at apex, the bulb broad and abrupt; flesh white, medium thin; gills white, slightly adnexed; annulus near top of stem, membranous, white; spores globose.—Sandy marsh-edges, pine and oak woods, September, not common, Wisconsin to New York and North Carolina.
This species is known by its broad bulb on which the volva is evanescent, but patch-like remnants are present on pileus.

A. mappa var. **lavendula** Coker.
Like the typical species but with lavender volva and primrose-yellow annulus.   North Carolina, probably in our area, habitat that of species.

A. rubescens Fr.   Blushing Amanita.   Plate 14, fig. 12.
Pileus 5-14 cm. broad; stem 10-22 cm. x 8-14 mm.; spores 8 x 6 μ.
Pileus pale reddish-brown (or white in var. *alba*), with abundant floccose masses or warts, subviscid; flesh soft, white, turning slowly reddish when wounded; gills narrow; stem clavate-bulbous, the apex mealy; annulus high, membranaceous; volva merely grayish remnants or entirely lacking; spores elliptical.—In woods, common, Minnesota, New England, Florida, Louisiana.

A. flavorubescens Atkins.   Plate 14, fig. 13.
Differing from the preceding in the yellow patches on brown-yellow pileus, the yellowish flesh, and in the yellow color on upper stem; flesh changing to red as *A. rubescens*.—On the ground in woods, not as common as *A. rubescens,* Minnesota, New England, Florida.

A. muscaria Fr.   Fly Amanita, Fly mushroom (poisonous). Plate 14, fig. 14.
Pileus 6-25 cm. broad; stem 8-20 cm. x 8-26mm.; spores 10 x 7 μ.
Pileus orange-yellow, rarely red in this country, adorned with numerous, large, conspicuous, white, floccose warts, striate on margin for about 1 cm.; flesh white, separable from the cuticle; gills white, broadest in front; stem with a large oval bulb marked with partial rings above; annulus large, attached toward apex of stem, white;

spores creamy-white.—In open woods of oak, poplar, etc., locally common, July-Sept., Minnesota to Labrador to Florida, and Louisiana.

A. excelsa Fr.

Pileus 10-18 cm. broad; stem 7-15 cm. x 8-20 mm.

Pileus smoky-tan to brown or reddish-brown, convex-plane or with the margin elevated, the pellicle separable, decorated with scattered, thick, pyramidal warts; gills sometimes narrow behind, white; stem slightly bulbous, tapering upward, white or sometimes salmon; annulus large, attached near the apex, thick at the margin, flocculent below, white.—In thin oak woods on clay soil, Aug.-Sept., rare, Illinois, New England, North Carolina. The plants are shaped much as *A. muscaria,* but they have thinner flesh. Some authors treat *A. excelsa* as a form of *A. spissa.*

A. spissa Fr.   Plate 14, fig. 16.
A. Morrisii Peck.
A. submaculata Peck.

Pileus 4.5-10 cm. broad; stem 6-12 cm. x 8-12 mm.; spores 9 x 7 μ.

Pileus gray with gray-brown floccose-pulverulent scales, umber toward center, not striate; flesh thin, white, very thin on margin, gills broad, crowded, white, flocculent at edges, about 6 mm. wide; annulus large, high, striate above; stem white, gray above, with a clavate-rounded or abrupt bulb.—In oak and maple woods, rare, July-Aug., Minnesota and Maine to North Carolina.

A. strobiliformis Vitt.   Pine-cone Amanita.

Pileus hemispherical to plane, shingled with thick, hard, concentrically or spirally arranged scales. The central scales often 3 mm. thick; stem hard, usually ventricose, scale or lacking scales.—In woods and borders of marshes, August, rare, Minnesota to Maine to North Carolina.

A. chlorinosma Peck.   Chlorine Amanita.   Plate 14, fig. 15.

Pileus 5-25 cm. broad; stem 6-30 cm. x 10-30 mm.; spores 6 x 10 μ.

Pileus chalk-white to brown, with soft spines or meal in center; flesh soft, white, with an odor of chlorine; gills white, ventricose; stem bulbous, rooted, white; annulus usually lacking.—On hard ground, August, rare, Minnesota to Maine to North Carolina.

A. cinereconia Atkins. is a small race of *A. chlorinosma.*

A. solitaria Fr.   Solitary Amanita.   Plate 14, fig. 18.

Pileus 10-15 cm. broad; stem 10-15 cm. x 10-20 mm.; spores 10 x 6 μ.

Pileus covered with firm, pyramidal warts when young, soft and floccose when mature, whitish; gills narrow, crowded; annulus high, skirt-like, disappearing; flesh white.—In low woods, Aug.-Sept., rare, Minnesota to Maine and North Carolina.

A. abrupta Peck.   Plate 14, fig. 19.

Pileus 4-8 cm. broad; stem 7-12 cm. x 5-12 mm.; spores 10 x 6 μ.

Differing from *A. solitaria* in its much larger, smoother, and very abrupt bulb, its smaller stem stuffed with cottony material which when wet shows a distinct central cylinder, its pure white color and its firm and durable consistency.—In mixed woods, July-Oct., not common, Illinois to New York to North Carolina.

AMANITOPSIS Roze

Carpophore composed of an orbicular, convex pileus loosely attached to a central stipe; pileus fleshy, putrescent, soft, of different material and readily separable from stipe; stipe usually much longer than the diameter of the pileus, ten to twenty times as long as its own diameter; annulus absent; gills white, free from stem except in *A. adnata,* close, wide; spores white.—Growing mostly on the humus of the forest.

1   Pileus sulcate-striate......2
1' Pileus not so marked......3
2   With thick, floccose warts on pileus............*A. strangulata.*
2' Pileus usually smooth........................*A. vaginata.*
      See also *Amanita gemmata, A. cothurnata, A. recutita,* and *A. Caesarea.*
3   Gills free, volva large.......................*A. agglutinata.*
      See also *Amanita Caesarea.*
3' Gills adnate to stem, volva fragile, downy...........*A. adnata.*

A. strangulata Fr.   Strangled Amanitopsis (edible).   Plate 14, fig. 22.

Pileus 4-9 cm. broad; stem 8-20 cm. x 4-10 mm.; spores 9 x 12 μ.

Pileus mouse-colored, decorated with thick, gray floccose warts; gills broadest in front, white to gray; stem decorated below with fragments of the cinereous volva; spores spherical.—Solitary in conifer or deciduous forests, July-Sept., rare, Minnesota to New England and North Carolina.

A. vaginata Fr.   Sheathed Amanitopsis.   Plate 14, fig. 21.

Pileus 4-9 cm. broad; stem 8-20 cm. x 4-8 mm.; spores 8 x 11 μ.

Pileus white, var. *alba* Sacc., fulvous var. *fulva* Sacc., or mouse-colored var. *livida* Peck, usually glabrous, but occasionally with a few disappearing thin scales, sulcate-striate, the flesh white, thin toward margin; gills free, white, close, broad in front; stem usually squamulose, stuffed then hollow, without bulb; volva thin, insheathing for 2 cm.; spores globose.—In woods, common, Aug.-Sept., Minnesota to Maine and North Carolina.

A. agglutinata Berk. & Curt. (poisonous).   Plate 14, fig. 20.
A. volvata Peck.

Pileus 5-7 cm. broad; stem 5-11 cm. x 5-11 mm.; spores 9-11 x 6 μ.

Pileus whitish to brownish, slightly striate on the margin, covered with fibrillose or floccose scales or patches; gills free, close, medium broad, white; stem white to brownish, stuffed, densely flocculent; volva very large, persistent, firm, membranous, brown; spores smooth, granular within.—In open woods, occasionally on *Sphagnum,* rare, Aug.-Sept., Minnesota to New England and North Carolina.

A. adnata Smith.

Pileus 5-10 cm. broad; stem 5-10 cm. x 8-20 mm.; spores 7-8 μ in diameter.

Pileus yellow-buff, with floccose patches, the margin even, extending beyond the gills, the flesh thick; gills adnate, crowded; stem rough, fibrillose; volva white, downy, sometimes evanescent; spores globose, apiculate.—In woods, rare, Aug.-Sept., Illinois to New York and southward.

LEPIOTA Fr.

Carpophore composed of an orbicular, convex pileus loosely attached to a central stipe; pileus scaly, except in *L. naucina,* from the disassociation of the cuticle, usually white but some are pink, yellow or brown, flesh soft or firm, of different texture from that of the stipe; stipe usually longer than the diameter of the pileus, commonly about ten times as long as the diameter of the stem, stuffed or hollow, readily separated from pileus; annulus thick membranaceous and at right angles to the stem in one section, pendant in other sections, and fibrillose in others; gills free from stem, white; spores white except in *L. Morgani* in which case green.—Terrestrial species, widely distributed.

1   Pileus viscid, neither scaly nor warty......2
1' Not viscid or scaly, white, pileus smooth..........*L. naucina.*
1" Not viscid, either scaly or warty......4

2   Pileus bay-colored ....*L. glioderma.*
2' Pileus small, white to pinkish......3

3   Pileus and stem shining-white....................*L. illinita.*
3' Pileus often pinkish, in swampy woods...........*L. delicata.*

4   Pileus with red cuticle which peels and leaves a white sur-
    face ....*L. rubrotincta.*
4' Pileus distinctly grainy or scaly......5

5   Plants of gardens, pastures, or very open places in the woods,
    large; ring usually movable......6
5' Plants of forest, smaller, the pileus up to 10 cm. in diameter....8

6   Plant becoming dull red where bruised.........*L. americana.*
6' Plant not changing color where bruised......7

7   Plants taller than broad, umbonate...............*L. procera.*
7' Plants broader than tall; gills soon green.........*L. Morgani.*

8   Scales on pileus present as erect points......9
8' Scales flat, at least not erect-pointed......12

9   Under pines ....*L. hispida.*
9' In deciduous forests......10

10 Gills forked ....*L. Friesii.*
10' Gills not forking......11

11 On decayed wood, of medium size.........*L. acutaesquamosa.*
11' On decayed wood, very small....................*L. acerina.*
11" On ground in rich woods. ....*L. asperula.*

12 With some shade of blue when fresh or drying......13
12' Shades of blue absent......16

13 Plant blue only when drying, pileus brown-scaly.*L. caerulescens.*
13' Fresh plant blue or lavender......14

14 Plants foetid, pileus lavender...................*L. ecitodora.*
14' Plants not foetid......15

15 Pileus covered with heliotrope-blue powder...*L. purpureoconia.*
15' Pileus white, the margins blue...............*L. cyanozonata.*

16 Pileus covered in center with brown cuticle, scaly outward....18
16' Pileus covered with black scales....................*L. felina.*
16" Pileus covered with minute, fibrillose scales......17

17 Scales yellow on white pileus...................*L. alluviinus.*
17' Scales brownish ....*L. miamensis.*

18 Stem-base somewhat enlarged, plant caespitose...*L. cepaestipes.*
18' Stem-base not enlarged, plants not caespitose......19

19 Pileus yellowish ....*L. clypeolaria.*
19' Pileus white beneath the scales..................*L. cristata.*

L. procera Fr. Tall Lepiota, Parasol mushroom (edible). Plate 15, fig. 1.

Pileus 7-18 cm. broad; stem 10-30 cm. x 6-14 mm.; spores 15 x 10 μ.

Pileus umbonate, covered with a brown or umber-brown coat which breaks into scales and patches toward the margin, the flesh thick; gills free, broad in front, floccose at edges; stem covered with brownish scales, more or less regularly arranged, stuffed with a pith; annulus of a firm, thick texture, separating easily from the stem as a movable collar; spores subcylindrical; sterile cells present on gilledges.—In pastures and open woods, not common, July to Oct., Minnesota to New England and southward to Tennessee.

L. Morgani Peck. Morgan's Lepiota (poisonous). Plate 15, fig. 2.

Pileus 10-25 cm. broad; stem 8-20 cm. x 10-30 mm.; spores 11 x 7 μ.

Pileus hemispherical, then expanding to convex, very thick, with irregular patches and scales, some of which disappear with age; gills close, wide ventricose, free, remote from the stem, becoming greenish as the spores mature; stem very thick at base, tapering upward, glabrous, firm; annulus large, thick, soft but tough, movable.—Often in large fairy rings in meadows and open woods, Aug.-Sept., not common, Minnesota, Maine, and Tennessee.

L. americana Peck. American Lepiota (edible).

Pileus 4-9 cm. broad; stem 7-14 cm. x 4-6 mm.; spores 9 x 6 μ.

Pileus brown, umbonate, scaly, the cuticle continuous on umbo; flesh white turning dull red where bruised or with age; stem glabrous, tapering upward from the clavate base; annulus large, sometimes movable.—In open woods or around stumps, rare, August, Minnesota to New England, Alabama.

L. naucina Fr. Smooth Lepiota, Chalky Lepiota (edible). Plate 15, fig. 3.

Pileus 3-17 cm. broad; stem 5-10 cm. x 5-12 mm.; spores 8 x 5 μ.

Pileus white, smooth, without scales, soft but firm, thick; gills free, close, broad in front, white becoming pink in age, minutely floccose at edges; stem tapering upward from a bulbous or thickened base; annulus tough, movable; spores somewhat variable in shape and size.—Among grass in pastures and on golf courses, common, July-Oct., Minnesota to New England to Alabama.

L. rugulosa Peck.

Plant smaller, pileus furrowed and rugulose, and gills not changing to pink color in age, otherwise resembling *L. naucina*.—Of similar habitat and range, rare.

L. acutaesquamosa Fr.   Plate 15, fig. 9.

Pileus 5-12 cm.; stem 6-12 cm. x 6-12 mm.; spores 8 x 3 μ.

Pileus covered with tawny-brown, pointed, erect scales which are black at the tips and are crowded toward center of pileus, the margin extending beyond the gills, the flesh white; gills close, narrow, serrate at edge, not forked; stem bulbous, stuffed, white; annulus evanescent; spores elongated, smooth.—On ground or much decayed wood, common, Aug.-Oct., from Minnesota to Maine and Tennessee.

L. acutaesquamosa, L. Friesii, L. asperula, and *L. hispida* are each characterized by a marked cobwebby veil, which at length shreds vertically.

L. Friesii Lasch.

Like the preceding but with forked, very narrow, and crowded gills and spores about 8 x 2 μ.—On ground, September, Minnesota to New York and North Carolina.

L. asperula Atkins.

Pileus 1-5 cm. broad; stem 2-6 cm. x 4-6 mm.; spores 5 x 3 μ.

Pileus campanulate to expanded, olive-brown, the cuticle breaking up into pointed warts, the flesh white, fragile, scissile; gills free, somewhat narrow, crowded, the edges minutely eroded; stem cylindrical above the basal bulb, stuffed with fibrils then hollow; the arachnoid veil pulling away from the pileus to form an evanescent annulus; spores minute, smooth, white.—Gregarious on the ground in mixed or hemlock woods, Aug.-Sept., not common, Wisconsin and Michigan.

L. hispida Lasch.

Pileus 4-7 cm., broad; stem 7-11 cm. x 6-10 mm.

Pileus much as in preceding, the scale points gradually disappearing; the gills attached to a collar near the stem.—On the sand under pines, September, rare, New Jersey pine barrens and the dunes about Lake Michigan.

L. acerina Peck.

Pileus 1-3 cm. broad; stem 2-4 cm. x 2-4 mm.; spores 10 x 3 μ.

Pileus floccose with pointed scales toward center, the scales tawny or pale rufous-brown, darker on disk, the flesh thin, white; gills close, rather broad, the edges minutely fimbriate; stem covered below the

vanishing annulus with small, dark fibrillose scales; spores obliquely
apiculate and truncate at one end, smooth, white.—On much decayed
wood, in maple-beech-hemlock woods, not common, July-Sept., Wisconsin to New York.

L. clypeolaria Fr.   Plate 15, fig. 6.
L. metulispora Berk. and Broome.
Pileus 2-5 cm. broad; stem 3-9 cm. x 2-4 mm.; spores 9-16 x 4-6 μ.
Pileus thin, subumbonate, uniformly pale brown to yellowish, the
cuticle breaking into small scales, the margin sometimes striate, appendiculate; gills close, free, white, narrower in front; stem hollow,
pale, adorned with soft scales; annulus floccose and disappearing;
spores variable in size, smooth.—On ground or debris in woods, not
common, July-Oct., Minnesota to Maine and Tennessee.

L. felina Fr.
Size as in the preceding; spores 6-8 x 4-5 μ.
Pileus subumbonate, white beneath the coating of blackish scales,
the flesh thin, white; gills close, narrow; stem slender, almost cylindrical or tapering upward from a slight bulb; annulus slight, disappearing, median, sometimes with a black edge.—On the ground in
hemlock woods, and in other rich woodlands, rare, Aug.-Sept., Wisconsin, Michigan and southward.

L. cepaestipes Fr.   Onion-stemmed Lepiota (edible).   Plate
15, fig. 7.
Pileus 3-7 cm. broad; stem 5-10 cm. x 3-8 mm.; spores 9 x 6 μ.
Pileus covered with mealy, wart-like scales, at length umbonate,
with plicate striations; gills free, close, narrow, white to grayish;
stem somewhat ventricose; or shaped like the stem of a green onion,
hollow, white; annulus thin-membranaceous; spores oval.—Caespitose, often in dense clusters, in gardens, straw, or like habitats, occasionally found throughout our area, June-Sept., Minnesota to New
England and Brazil.

L. rubrotincta Peck.   Plate 15, fig. 4.
L. carneo-annulata Clem.
Pileus 3-6 cm. broad; stem 5-9 cm. x 7 mm.; spores 7 x 5 μ.
Pileus thin, plane, covered with a red, thin cuticle which cracks
or peels back from margin and rarely forms scales; gills close, white,
broadest in front; stem slender, slightly thickened below, smooth,
white, hollow; annulus entire, the margin sometimes red.—In rich
woods, especially beech-maple, not uncommon, August, Minnesota to
New England to Tennessee.

L. cristata Fr. Crested Lepiota (edible). Plate 15, fig. 8.

Pileus 1-3 cm. broad; stem 2-5 cm. x 2-4 mm.; spores 6 x 3 μ.

Pileus at first red-brown, the cuticle soon breaking toward the margin into flat appressed scales and exposing the white surface beneath, the flesh thin; stem slender, stuffed, white; annulus white, small; spores angular, wedge-shaped.—In sand under pines or in rich woods, frequently found, July-Sept., Minnesota to Maine to Georgia.

L. miamensis Morg. Miami Lepiota.

Similar to preceding species, pileus white, brownish at the center, covered with minute, fibrillose scales.—On the ground in rich woods, rare, August, throughout our area.

L. alluviinus Peck.

Similar to the two preceding but with very fine yellow scales on the white pileus.—On alluvial soil, rare, August, throughout our area.

L. caerulescens Peck.

In shape and size similar to *L. cristata,* the pileus brown-scaly, annulus membranous; the plant changing to blue when dried.—Occasionally found in woods throughout our area.

L. ecitodora Atkins. Foetid Lepiota.

In shape and size similar to *L. cristata,* the pileus lavender, not changing color in drying; stem dark brown; odor fetid.—Under shrubs, rare, throughout our area.

L. purpureoconia Atkins.

In shape and size similar to *L. cristata,* pileus white, powdered with heliotrope-colored powder, the flesh light yellow.—Under shrubs throughout our area, rare.

L. cyanozonata Longy. Blue-margined Lepiota.

In size and shape much like *L. cristata,* the pileus white with bluish margin; stem brown where bruised.—Under shrubs throughout area, rare.

L. illinita Fr. Plate 15, fig. 5.

Pileus 2-4 cm. broad; stem 5-7 cm. x 3-5 mm.; spores 5 x 3.5 μ.

Pileus and stem glutinous when moist, pure white, campanulate-expanded; gills free.—Solitary in moist woods, rare, Minnesota to New England and North Carolina.

L. delicata Fr.

Pileus 2-4 cm. broad; stem 5-9 cm. x 3-5 mm.; spores 5 x 3.5 μ.
Pileus thin, subumbonate, silky, pink; stem clavate-bulbous; gills narrow, free, white.—Gregarious in swampy elm woods, rare.

L. oblita Peck., *L. incarnata* Clem., and *L. rufescens* Morg. may be forms of *L. delicata* Fr.

L. glioderma Fr.

Pileus 2-6 cm. broad; stem 5-8 cm. x 4-6 mm.; spores 4-5 μ.
Pileus viscid, bay-red, fading, the cuticle separable, the flesh thin, white, or tinted reddish; gills free, broad, ventricose, close, white; stem covered with red floccose scales up to the small annulus.—In beech, birch, or hemlôck woods, Minnesota to Maine to North Carolina, July-Oct., common in climax forests of the range.

ARMILLARIA Fr.

Carpophore composed of a more or less orbicular, convex pileus of same material and confluent with the central, cylindrical, fleshy stipe; pileus fleshy, putrescent, soft, its context tapering into and inseparable from that of the stipe; stipe long or short; veil often cortina-like, the web at first extending from the pileus margin to the mid section of the stem, later withdrawing to form a webby annulus, in the last section the universal veil clings to the lengthening stem and expanding pileus to at length cover the pileus with a granular coat, and the lower half of the stem with a granular boot, with a flaring upper margin forming an annulus; gills variously attached, adnexed, adnate, or decurrent, white to dingy; spores white.—Either terrestrial or epixylous, widely distributed.

1   Neither pileus nor stem viscid......2
1' Pileus viscid when wet, orange.................*A. aurantia.*
2   Honey-colored, in caespitose clusters about trees and stumps
....*A. mellea.*
2' Otherwise colored, not caespitose; stem booted......3
3   Boot-like veil viscid..........................*A. ponderosa.*
3' Boot-like veil not viscid......4
4   Pileus 6-20 cm. broad......5
4' Pileus smaller, granular-scaly; stem scaly up to the annulus....6
5   Pileus bearing large chestnut-brown scales..........*A. caligata.*
5' Pileus brown, glabrous.........................*A. robusta.*
6   On decaying wood; pileus tawny, 5-8 cm. in diameter.*A. granosa.*
6' On the ground, pileus smaller......7

7   Pileus brick-red......8
7' Pileus rusty, tawny, or white......9

8   On leaves and mosses........................*A. granulosa.*
8' Under pines, in sandy woods................*A. cinnabarinus.*

9   Pileus dark dusty-red......................*A. adnatifolia.*
9' Pileus tawny ....*A. amianthina.*
9" Pileus almost white, very small..............*A. pusillomyces.*

A. mellea Fr.   Honey-colored mushroom (edible).   Plate 15, fig. 10.

Pileus 3-13 cm. broad ; stem 5-15 cm. x 6-15 mm. ; spores 9 x 6 μ.

Pileus normally honey-colored to rusty, sometimes decorated with black pointed tufts, the flesh white, medium thick, gills adnate or decurrent, not close; stem stuffed then hollow, white to yellowish-brown; veil white to membranous, collapsing to form an annulus, sometimes shredding then arachnoid.—Caespitose on stumps, living trees, or their roots, chiefly on oak and beech but sometimes on conifers, common, Sept.-Oct., Canada to the Gulf of Mexico, also around the world.

The sclerotium is in the form of yellow, shoe-string-like strands.

A. caligata Vitt.-Bres.

Pileus 6-12 cm. broad ; stem 5-10 cm. x 20-30 mm. ; spores 7 x 5 μ.

Pileus convex, expanded, light brown, bearing appressed, dark red-brown scales, the margin at first incurved, the flesh white, thick ; gills sinuate-adnate, white, crowded, broad, 7 mm. wide, the edges smooth ; stem usually tapering downward, stout, sheathed by the veil which terminates above the middle in a flaring annulus ; basidia 40 x 8 μ.—On ground near bogs, but not in them, rare, Sept.-Oct., Iowa to New York and northward.

A. aurantia Fr.   Golden Armillaria.

Pileus 5-8 cm. broad ; stem 5-8 cm. x 8-20 mm. ; spores 4.5 x 3.5 μ.

Pileus convex, expanded, often broadly umbonate, viscid when wet, ochraceous to orange-red, the cuticle breaking into crowded appressed scales, the margin at first involute, the flesh white, thick, thin at margin ; gills rounded toward stem, narrow, close, white, spotted with brown, entire, some forked ; stem tapering downward, somewhat booted up to the rather indistinct annulus ; basidium 28 x 5 μ.—On sandy soil, rare, September, Iowa to New York and northward.

A. robusta Fr.

Pileus 4-8 cm. broad; stem 2-6 cm. x 10-25 mm.; spores 7 μ in diameter.

Pileus convex-expanded or turbinate, very thick, gray to brown, fibrillose-scaly especially toward margin, the margin inrolled at first; gills nearly free, crowded, broad, 1 cm. wide; annulus large, membranous, striate floccose; stem stout, solid, tapering downward, brown-gray; spores globose.—In woods, Indiana, Ohio, eastward and southward in Appalachians.

A. ponderosa Peck.

Pileus 10-15 cm. broad; stem 10-15 cm. x 20-30 mm.; spores 4 μ.

Pileus convex, thick, glabrous, whitish, involute, gills emarginate, narrow, crowded, white to creamy; stem coated by veil up to the slight annulus; veil slightly viscid, covering the gills but finally becoming shredded, part clinging to the margin of the pileus and part to stem.—In woods, New England to Minnesota and Tennessee.

A. granosa (Morg.) Kauffm.

Pileus 5-8 cm.; stem 5-9 cm. x 8-14 mm.; spores 4x 3 μ.

Pileus ochraceous to tawny, furfuraceous-grainy, sometimes wrinkled, the flesh thick; gills narrow, adnate to stem, crowded; stem covered with floccose scales to the large flaring membranaceous annulus; stem pale above annulus; spores small.—Subcaespitose on decayed wood of deciduous trees, rare, September, Wisconsin to New York and northward.

A. granulosa (Fr.) Kauffm.
Lepiota granulosa Fr.

Pileus 3-6 cm. broad; stem 2-5 cm. x 4-9 mm.; spores 6 x 4 μ.

Pileus granular-scaled, sometimes radially wrinkled, brick-red, the flesh thin, white; gills rounded toward stem, slightly adnexed, close, medium-wide, stem booted with pale reddish scales up to the slight annulus.—Subcaespitose in woods among leaves and mosses, Aug.-Nov., local, Illinois to Michigan and New York.

A. amianthina (Fr.) Kauffm.
Lepiota amianthina Fr.

Pileus 3-6 cm. broad; stem 5-9 cm. x 4-7 mm.

Pileus usually umbonate, tawny, granular-scaly; stem booted thinly with scales up to the membranaceous annulus.

A. adnatifolia (Peck) Kauffm.   Booted Armillaria.
Lepiota adnatifolia Peck.

Pileus 2-5 cm. broad; stem 2-4 cm. x 4-7 mm.; spores 5 x 3 μ.

Pileus covered with dark rusty-red granular scales, not umbonate, the margin appendiculate; stem peronate with reddish or almost white grains and terminating in a rather indistinct annulus, the apex white. —On decaying wood, rare, September, Michigan to New York.

A. cinnabarina (Fr.) Kauffm.   Cinnabar Armillaria.
Lepiota cinnabarina Fr.
Pileus 2-5 cm. broad; stem 2-5 cm. x 5-8 mm.
Pileus covered with brick-red granular scales, appendiculate; stem booted with brick-red scales to the slight annulus.—Subcaespitose on sandy soil under pines, Aug.-Sept., Indiana and Michigan.

A. pusillomyces (Peck) Kauffm.
Pileus 4-8 mm. broad; stem 1-3 cm. x 1-2 mm.; spores 5 x 3 μ.
Pileus covered with white furfuraceous granules; stem rufous beneath white boot of granules; annulus indistinct at top of boot.— Solitary on rich soil in woods, rare, August, Wisconsin to New York.

A. mucida Fr.   Glutinous Armillaria (edible).
Pileus 3-12 cm. broad; stem 4-7 cm. x 3-7 mm.; spores 15 x 8 μ.
Pileus glutinous-viscid, hemispherical then convex-expanded, radiately wrinkled, smeared with thick gluten, usually shining white, thin; gills decurrent as striations, broad distant, rounded behind; stem white, often sooty-scaled at base; annulus attached at stem-apex, pendant and glued close to stem; pileus white, gray or olivaceous.— On trees and roots, especially of beech, in woods, September, Appalachian region west to southern Illinois.

CLITOCYBE Fr.   Plates 16 and 17.

Carpophore composed of a more or less orbicular, convex to infundibuliform pileus of same material and confluent with the central, fleshy stipe; pileus fleshy, soft, putrescent, its context tapering into the inseparable stipe; stipe long or short; annulus absent; gills mostly white, in the subgenus *Laccaria* they are brown-pink, brown or violet, broadly adnate or decurrent except in *Laccaria* in which some are adnexed.—Mostly terrestrial, but some are epixylous.

1 Pileus of mature specimens more than 8 cm. broad......2
1' Pileus smaller......10

2 Stem 2-6 cm. in diameter, pileus white to ochraceous.*C. maxima.*
2' Stem smaller or pileus orange-brown......3

3   Pileus orange or saffron, stem tapering downward, gills long decurrent ....*C. illudens.*

3'   Pileus of duller colors......4

4   Gills purple; pileus squamulose, white or pale..*C. ochropurpurea.*

4'   Gills not purple......5

5   Plants white, forming arcs of circles............*C. albissima.*

5'   Plants caespitose......6

5"   Neither caespitose nor in arcs, pileus smoky.......*C. nebularis.*

6   Pileus white, gills extending down the stem in lines...*C. piceina.*

6'   Pileus white, concave, gills not extending down the stem in lines......7

7   Plants very large, 10-20 cm. broad...............*C. gigantea.*

7'   Plants smaller, 6-10 cm. broad......8

8   Plants yellow-brown or red-brown............*C. monodelpha.*

8'   Plants white or smoky......9

9   Smoky with cartilaginous cuticle..............*C. cartilagineus.*

9'   White without such cuticle.....................*C. multiceps.*

10   Gills bright purple, plants whitish to ochraceous..........
......................................*C. ochropurpurea.*

10'   Gills otherwise colored......11

11   Pileus bright brick-red, blue, or green......12

11'   Pileus smoky, yellowish, brown, white, or flesh-colored......14

12   Plants convex to slightly depressed, blue or green.....*C. odora.*

12'   Plants brick-red......13

13   On wood or burned-over ground..................*C. sinopica.*

13'   Among moss on wet ground.................*C. sinopicoides.*

14   Growing under pines, stem not brownish......15

14'   Growing in other habitats or stem brownish......17

15   Pileus white to yellow, thick, the margin incurved........
....*C. patuloides.*

15'   Margin not incurved......16

16   Pileus tan-colored ....*C. pinophila.*

16'   Pileus white or watery-white when moist..........*C. pithopila.*

17   Pileus hygrophanous......18

17'   Pileus not hygrophanous......26

18   Gills flesh-colored, sometimes violet...............*C. laccata.*

18'   Gills otherwise......19

19   Pileus funnel-form or cup-shaped......20

19'   Pileus not funnel-form; plants small, convex or slightly depressed......24

20   Gills subdistant......21
20'   Gills crowded......23
21   Growing on lichens (Peltigera), 1 cm. or less in size......
      ....*C. peltigerina.*
21'   On debris or wood......22
22   Pileus bearing dark points, gills yellowish........*C. ectypoides.*
22'   Entire plant smoky or smoky-brown..........*C. cyathiformis.*
23   Pileus gray-brown, often zoned, caespitose........*C. caespitosa.*
23'   Not caespitose, umbilicate ....*C. albidula.*
23"   Gills long-decurrent, pileus light tan........*C. adirondackensis.*
23'" Stem attached at base by long white strands.......*C. eccentrica.*
24   Pileus, stem, and gills brownish-gray......25
24'   Pileus, stem, and gills white to tan............*C. angustissima.*
25   Farinaceous in taste, growing in bogs under tamarack
      trees ....*C. ditopoda.*
25'   Not farinaceous but mild in taste; growing in either conifer
      or frondose woods...........................*C. metachroa.*
26   Pileus symmetrical, fleshy, convex, plane or depressed; gills
      regularly adnate or adnate-decurrent; plants solitary or
      gregarious......27
26'   Pileus often asymmetrical; gills irregularly adnate or decur-
      rent, plants caespitose......33
26"   Pileus soon deep funnel-shaped; gills regularly decurrent....37
27   Pileus white to grayish......30
27'   Pileus yellowish; growing on decaying wood........*C. decora.*
27"   Pileus brown or ashy......28
28   Gills crowded, stem tapering upward.............*C. nebularis.*
28'   Gills not crowded......29
29   Stem tapering upward.........................*C. clavipes.*
29'   'Stem not tapering upward........................*C. media.*
30   Growing on wood............................*C. truncicola.*
30'   Growing on ground or among leaves......31
31   Pileus dry; often growing in fairy rings...........*C. albissima.*
31'   Pileus moist when young or in wet weather......32
32   Pileus more than 5 cm. broad, stem solid, gills close, color
      white ....*C. cerussata.*
32'   Pileus less than 5 cm. broad; stem glabrous, shining, hollow
      ....*C. candicans.*
32"   Stem pruinose or mealy above, stuffed...........*C. dealbata.*
33   Pileus white or grayish.......................*C. multiceps.*
33'   Pileus brown, yellow, or smoky......34

34   Stems tapering downward, gills very long decurrent, brown
      to bright yellow......35
34'   Stem not so tapered, smoky or pale ochraceous......36
35   Pileus reddish-yellow or saffron-yellow............*C. illudens.*
35'   Pileus brownish or reddish-brown.............*C. monadelpha.*
36   Cuticle cartilaginous, pileus smoky............*C. cartilaginea.*
36'   Cuticle soft, pileus pale ochraceous.............*C. patuloides.*
37   Pileus moist in wet weather or when young......38
37"   Pileus dry......41
38   Mature pileus funnel-shaped......39
38'   Pileus not normally funnel-shaped, growing on wood.......40
39   Pileus white, often-bowl-shaped...................*C. catina.*
39'   Pileus reddish to pale tan..............*G. infundibuliformis.*
40   Pileus glabrous, gills white, white stands present at stem-
      base ....*C. eccentrica.*
40'   Pileus dark, dotted; gills yellowish, some forked..*C. ectypoides.*
41   Dry pileus white, gills less than 6 mm. wide..*C. adirondackensis.*
41'   Dry pileus pale yellow, shining; gills white, narrow.*C. splendens.*

C. media Peck.   Medium Clitocybe.   Plate 15, fig. 11.

Pileus 5-19 cm. broad, stem 2-5 cm. x 8-16 mm.; spores 8 x 5 μ.

Pileus convex, plane or slightly depressed, fleshy, often irregularly wavy on margin, gray-brown or smoky-brown, unpolished; flesh white medium-thick, mild in taste; gills broad, adnate-decurrent, distant, white, often intervenose; stem equal, elastic, solid, concolor.— Scattered on mossy ground in woods, rare, September, Minnesota, New York and Illinois.

It differs from *C. nebularis* and *C. clavipes* in its thinner pileus and cylindrical stem.

C. nebularis (Batsch.) Fr.   Clouded Clitocybe.   Plate 15, fig. 12.

Pileus 5-10 cm. broad; stem 5-7 cm. x 10-20 mm.; spores 4.5 x 2.5 μ.

Pileus convex then plane or depressed, compact, subpruinose, smoky-brown, paler with age; flesh white; gills adnate, narrow, close, white; stem firm, tough, stout, solid, pruinose, smoky.—Subcaespitose in woods of oak and maple, September, rare, Illinois to New England and West Virginia.

C. clavipes (Pers.) Fr.   Plate 15, fig. 14.

Pileus 3-8 cm. broad; stem 1-6 cm. x 6-13 mm. at top, 15-30 mm. at base; spores 7 x 4.5 μ.

Pileus convex, almost obconic, glabrous, sooty-brown; flesh white, very thick on disk; gills subdecurrent, broad, subdistant, white or cream-colored; stem tapering from thickened base, solid, elastic, soft within, a little paler than pileus.—Usually gregarious or almost solitary in woods, July-Oct., Minnesota to New England and southward.

C. pinophila Peck. Pine Clitocybe. Plate 15, fig. 13.

Pileus 2.5 cm. broad; stem 2-5 cm. x 2-4 mm.; spores 6 x 4.5 μ.

Pileus convex then umbilicate or centrally depressed, glabrous, pale tan, the odor farinaceous; gills close, adnate, subarcuate, white; stem concolor, equal.—Gregarious under pines, July-Aug., Illinois to New England and southward.

C. decora Fr. Plate 16, fig 1.

Pileus 3-7 cm. broad; stem 3-6 cm. x 4-6 mm.; spores 5.5 x 4.5 μ.

Pileus convex to slightly depressed, fleshy, thin, dotted with minute dark brown squamules, yellow with brown tinge; gills obtusely adnate, close, narrow, yellow: stem equal, stuffed, fibrillose or dotted-squamulose.—On decaying trunks of conifers in bogs and swamps, July-Sept., rare, Illinois to New York and northward.

C. odora Fr. Plate 16, fig. 2.

Pileus 4-7 cm. broad; stem 3-6 cm. x 4-8 mm.; spores 7 x 4.5 μ.

Convex-expanded or subumbonate, fleshy, thin, regular, pale dingy-green to bluish-green, varying to white, the flesh tough, white, with an odor like anise; gills adnate, thin, close, broad, white to yellowish.—Scattered to gregarious in conifer and frondose woods, Aug.-Sept., common, Minnesota to New England and North Carolina.

C. albidula Peck. Plate 16, fig. 3.

Pileus 1-3 cm. broad; stem 2-5 cm. x 2-14 mm.; spores 6 x 3 μ.

Pileus convex-plane to umbilicate or depressed in center, thin, glabrous, white, tinged brownish in center only, faintly striate at the margin when moist; flesh white, farinaceous; gills adnate, close, narrow, thin; stem equal, glabrous or pruinose, stuffed, white.—In mixed woods, Minnesota to New England and southward.

C. truncicola Peck. Plate 16, fig. 5.

Pileus 1-3 cm.; stem 2-3 cm. x 2 mm.; spores 4.5 x 3.5 μ.

Differs from preceding in its smaller size, more globose spores, lack of pruinosity, its habitat, and the eccentric stem.—On tree trunks, Minnesota, New England and southward.

C. albissima Peck. White fairy ring. Plate 16, fig 4.

Pileus 5-7 cm. broad; stem 3-6 cm. x 4-6 mm.; spores 8 x 5 μ.

Pileus fleshy, convex-plane, soft, smooth, white, without odor; gills close, some forked, adnate, white, narrow; spores minutely echinulate; stem equal, smooth, solid, white.—Gregarious or in arcs of circles on leafy ground in woods, common, Aug.-Sept., Minnesota to New England and southward. Known by its shining whiteness, size, thick flesh, and tendency to form fairy rings.

C. cerussata Fr.   White-lead Clitocybe.   Plate 16, fig. 6.

Pileus 4-8 cm. broad; stem 3-8 cm. x 6-10 mm., spores 5 x 4 μ.

Pileus convex or plane, obtuse, smooth, moist, fleshy, white, the taste mild; gills adnate to decurrent, crowded, thin, narrow, white, unchanging; stem white, smooth, downy at base, elastic.—Scattered or gregarious in woods, infrequent, Aug.-Sept., Illinois to New England and southward.

C. pithyophila Fr.   Pine-loving Clitocybe.   Plate 16, fig. 7.

Pileus 4-7 cm. broad; stem 4-5 cm. x 3-5 mm.; spores 6.5 x 3.5 μ.

Pileus thin, fleshy, plane, umbilicate, smooth, with wavy margin, white, shining when dry; gills adnate, close, narrow; stem smooth, downy at base, hollow, often compressed, white.—Gregarious under pines, infrequent, September, Illinois, New York, southward in mountains.

C. candicans Fr.   Small white Clitocybe.   Plate 16, fig. 9.

Pileus 2-3 cm. broad; stem 2-5 cm. x 2-4 mm.; spores 6 x 4.5 μ.

Pileus convex-plane then depressed, symmetrical, shining-white when dry, the margin decurved, the flesh thin, white, the taste mild; gills adnate then decurrent, thin, narrow, crowded, white; stem equal shining, cartilaginous, smooth, stuffed or hollow, curved and hairy at base.—Subcaespitose among leaves in woods, Minnesota and southward.

C. dealbata Fr.   Ivory Clitocybe.   Plate 16, fig. 8.

Pileus 1-4 cm. broad; stem 2-3 cm. x 2-5 mm.; spores 5 x 3 μ.

Pileus convex, then depressed or umbilicate, smooth, even, dry, shining white, the margin wavy, ascending, very thin; flesh thin, white; gills adnate, white, narrow, crowded, thin, the edges minutely eroded; stem stuffed to hollow, slender, often compressed, white or pale, tough, the base villose, the apex pruinose; spores apiculate, nucleate; taste mild.—Usually in twos on decaying leaves, occasionally in grassy places in woods, Sept.-Nov., Minnesota to New York and southward.

C. monadelpha Morg.   Brotherhood Clitocybe.   Plate 16, fig. 10.

Pileus 3-8 cm.; stem 6-20 cm. x 4-8 mm.; spores 8 x 5.5 μ.

Pileus pale-brown, reddish-brown or honey-colored, convex to centrally depressed, squamose in center, the scales usually rufous-tawny, the pileus honey-colored beneath scales; gills decurrent, not close, broad in middle and narrowed at each end, intervenose, pallid to very light brown and stained darker with age; stems tapering downward to the caespitose crowded bases, the taste somewhat bitter.— Very caespitose, attached to roots or buried wood, July-Sept., Minnesota to Maine and southward.

C. patuloides Peck.   Plate 16, fig. 11.

Pileus 2-10 cm. broad; stem 2-7 cm. x 8-20 mm.; spores 7 x 5.5 μ.

Pileus pale yellow to white, firm, fleshy, convex-plane or centrally depressed, the margin when young incurved, becoming ochraceous and squamose or areolate; flesh white, mild; gills decurrent, thin, close, forked or anastomosing at base, white. Stem short, equal, solid, white, caespitose or scattered.—On cypress in swamps and in open woods especially of pine, September, not common, New York to Florida (December) and southern Illinois.

C. illudens Fr. Deceiving Mushroom, Jack O'Lantern (poisonous).   Plate 16, fig. 13.

Pileus 6-20 cm. broad; stem 8-30 cm. x 6-30 mm.; spores 4-5 μ.

Pileus orange-yellow to brown-yellow or saffron, glabrous or virgate, often irregular and lobed, convex, plane or centrally depressed, thick; flesh white or yellowish; gills decurrent, narrowed toward each end, close, colored like pileus; stem tapering downward, firm, smooth, solid or stuffed, colored as pileus or browner; spores globose. Caespitose about stumps etc., often on decayed wood, Aug.-Oct., common, Minnesota to Maine and southward.   Fresh specimens placed in dark give out a glowing light.

C. multiceps Peck. Many-headed Clitocybe (edible).   Plate 16, fig. 14.

Pileus 3-8 cm. broad; stem 5-10 cm. x 6-12 mm.; spores 5 x 8 μ.

Pileus thick, becoming abruptly thin toward margin, white to grayish-brown, convex, the flesh white, the taste oily, unpleasant; gills adnate, white, medium broad, not crowded, sometimes sinuate; stem solid, stout, cylindrical, white.—In open woods, very caespitose, common, June-Oct., Minnesota to Maine and southward to Tennessee.

C. cartilaginea Bres.

Similar to the preceding in size, differing in its cartilaginous cuticle and darker color, smoky-tan or smoky-brown.—In open woods, June-Oct., not common, Illinois, Michigan, and Ohio.

C. catina Fr.   Plate 16, fig. 12.

Pileus 4-5 cm. broad; stem 4-7 cm. x 6-9 mm.; spores 7 x 4 μ.

Pileus white, becoming funnel-shaped, occasionally bowl-shaped, flaccid, dry, glabrous, the flesh white, the odor unpleasant; gills decurrent, close, narrow, the edges entire, white; stem cylindrical, straight, stuffed or hollow, tough, white, pruinose above, tomentose below; spores ovate, smooth.—In woods of beech, oak, or occasionally white pine, Aug.-Oct., not common Minnesota to Maine and southward.

C. maxima Fr.   Plate 17, fig. 19.

Pileus 9-30 cm.; stem 5-15 cm. long x 2-5 cm. thick; spores 5 x 3.5 μ.

Pileus thick toward center, thin toward margin, convex then infundibuliform, broadly umbonate, pale tan or white; gills long-decurrent, close, 4-10 mm. broad, white, soft, narrowed at both ends but not ventricose; stem tapering at top, fibrillose, solid, white; spores subglobose.—In oak woods and open woods, not uncommon, Aug.-Sept., Minnesota to Maine and southward.

C. gigantea Fr.   Giant Clitocybe.   Plate 17, fig. 27.

Pileus 15-25 cm. broad; stem 2-6 cm. long and 2-3 cm. thick; spores 5 x 3 μ.

Pileus large, relatively thin, becoming funnel-form, glabrous, white to light tan, involute then spreading, at length coarsely sulcate; gills decurrent, often anastomosing on the stem, broad, crowded, white; stem white, cylindrical, solid; spores apiculate.—On the ground in open woods, caespitose to gregarious, infrequent, Minnesota to Michigan and Tennessee.

C. piceina Peck.   Plate 17, fig. 21.

Similar to *C. gigantea,* but differs as follows: the gills becoming yellowish, decurrent in lines down the stem, anastomosing, separable from trama of pileus as in *Paxillus.*—Found under conifers northward, under maples, southward, Minnesota and New York to Ohio and Illinois.

C. infundibuliformis Fr. Funnel Clitocybe (edible).   Plate 17, fig. 24.

Pileus 4-7 cm. broad, stem 4-7 cm. x 6-10 mm.; spores 5.5 x 3.5 μ.

Pileus convex or umbonate becoming depressed and funnel-shaped, thin, silky on margin, reddish-tan to tan or pale tan, the flesh white; gills decurrent, close, thin, narrow, pointed at both ends, the edges serrulate; stem firm, elastic, glabrous, spongy within.—On leafy ground in woods, July-Oct., Manitoba to Nova Scotia and Tennessee. It differs from *C. catina* in color. Large specimens may approach *C. maxima* or *C. gigantea* in appearance.

C. sinopica Fr. Brick-colored Clitocybe.   Plate 16, fig. 15.

Pileus 2-4 cm. broad; stem 2-4 cm. x 2-5 mm.; spores 9 x 4.5 μ.

Pileus thin, fleshy, plane, or depressed in center, or merely umbilicate, dry, becoming floccose and rivulose, ochraceous-red to brick-colored and paler with age, the flesh white; gills decurrent, whitish, becoming yellow, close, thin, broad; stem equal, fibrillose, stuffed, brick-colored to yellowish.—Open ground or burned-over places, June-Sept., Minnesota to New York and southward.

C. sinopicoides Peck.   Plate 16, fig. 16.

Differs from preceding in its arcuate gills with interspaces slightly venose.—On mosses in low wet places, June, Illinois to New York and southward.

C. eccentrica Peck.   Plate 17, fig. 29.

Pileus 2-5 cm. broad; stem 2-4 cm. x 2-4 mm.; spores 4.5 x 3 μ.

Pileus thin, umbilicate or depressed, glabrous, white, with thin margin, often lobed or very irregular on one side, subhygrophanous and shining-white when moist; gills decurrent, close, narrow, white, somewhat forked; stem slender, glabrous, tough, white, often eccentric, strigose-hairy at base with long branching strands of white mycelium continuing along and into the substratum.—Gregarious or subcaespitose on much decayed wood in open woods or clearings, July-Sept., not common, Minnesota to Maine and Tennessee.

C. ectypoides Peck.   Plate 17, fig. 30.

Pileus 2-5 cm. broad; stem 2-3 cm. x 2-4 mm.; spores 8 x 4.5 μ.

Pileus fleshy but thin, broadly umbilicate to infundibuliform, with spreading margin, virgate and with black points on the radiating fibers, moist, grayish or gray-yellow; gills decurrent, not close, narrow, yellowish, some forked; stem cylindrical, firm, solid, with white mycelium at base.—Gregarious to caespitose on decaying wood in woods and among *Sphagnum* in bogs, common in the mountains, Minnesota to New England and southward in the Appalachians.

C. adirondackensis Peck.   Plate 17, fig. 25.

Pileus 2-5 cm. broad; stem 4-7 cm. x 2-4 mm.; spores 4.5 x 3.5 μ.

Pileus thin, plane or umbilicate, then depressed or funnel-form, glabrous, moist, pale tan or white, the flesh white, edible; gills long-decurrent, close, thin, very narrow, not wider than thickness of pileus, white; stem equal, glabrous, stuffed, or hollow, white to light tan.

—Scattered or gregarious in woods, common, July-Oct., Minnesota to Maine and Tennessee.

C. splendens Fr.

Pileus 5-8 cm.; stem 4-5 cm. x 8-10 mm.; spores 4.5 μ in diameter.

Pileus thin, fleshy, plane to funnel-form, glabrous, pale yellow, and shining, the flesh white, medium thick; gills very decurrent, close, narrow, white; stem equal, solid, yellowish, glabrous; spores sub-globose.—In woods among fallen leaves, solitary, June, not common, Ohio, Indiana, New York, New Jersey .

C. cyathiformis Fr.   Cup-shaped Clitocybe.   Plate 17, fig. 26.

Pileus 3-6 cm. broad; stem 5-8 cm. x 3-7 mm.; spores 8 x 5 μ.

Pileus thin, umbilicate-depressed then deeply depressed, with spreading to almost involute margin, hygrophanous, smoky-black to smoky-brown, scissile; gills decurrent, narrow, subdistant, inter-venose, gray-brown, entire; stem tapering upward, spongy-stuffed, elastic, brown to smoky, fibrillose-reticulated, the base tomentose.—On decayed wood, Sept.-Nov., not rare, Minnesota to Maine and Tennessee.

C. caespitosa Peck.   Plate 17, fig. 22.

Pileus 2.5-5 cm. broad; stem 2-4 cm. x 4-6 mm.; spores 3 x 4 μ in diameter.

Pileus thin, funnel-form, hygrophanous, brown or gray-brown when moist, clay-colored when dry, sometimes zoned; gills decur-rent, close, narrow, branched, white; stem cylindrical, stuffed or hollow, white; spores globose.—Caespitose in rich woods, locally common, Aug.-Sept., Minnesota, New England, Tennessee.

C. ditopoda Fr.   Double-stemmed Clitocybe.   Plate 17, fig. 23.

Pileus 2-5 cm. broad; stem 2-3 cm. x 2-4 mm.; spores 5.5 x 4 μ.

Pileus thin, plane to centrally depressed, glabrous, hygrophanous, brown when moist, gray, dry, the flesh thin, farinaceous; gills slightly decurrent, brownish-gray, thin, 2 mm. wide, close stem cylindrical, hollow, brownish, compressed.—Among leaves in woods, rare, Sept.-Oct., Minnesota to Maine and Tennessee.

C. subditopoda Peck.

Similar to the preceding but with striate margin, broader and paler gills and about half the size.—On mosses in woods, rare, September, Wisconsin to New York and southward.

C. peltigerina Peck.   Plate 17, fig. 20.

Pileus 4-10 mm. broad; stem 12-20 mm. x 1-2 mm.; spores 8 x 5 μ.

Pileus thin, plane or umbilicate, hygrophanous, brown, the margin striate when moist, pale-gray when dry; gills, decurrent, subdistant, narrow, forked, intervenose, gray-brown ; stem cylindrical, firm, solid, glabrous, paler than pileus, white-tomentose at base.—On the ground, growing on the lichen Peltigera, May, rare, Minnesota to Maine and Tennessee.

C. angustissima Lasch.   Plate 17, fig. 28.

Pileus 4-5 cm. broad ; stem 3-6 cm. x 2-5 mm. ; spores 4.5 x 2.5 μ.

Pileus fleshy, depressed, watery-white when moist, shining-white when dry, the spreading margin becoming striate ; gills subdecurrent, close, narrow, thin, white ; stem slender, curved, stuffed, white, inodorous.—Low wet ground in woods September, Minnesota to New England and Tennessee.

C. ochropurpurea Berk.   Purple-gilled Clitocybe (edible).   Plate 17, fig. 17.

Pileus 5-20 cm. broad ; stem 5-18 cm. x 4-18 mm. ; spores 9 μ in diameter.

Pileus fleshy, firm convex to centrally depressed, hygrophanous, gray or pale yellow when dry, the flesh tough ; gills bright purple, thick distant, broad, adnate to decurrent ; stem cylindrical, fibrous, rigid, concolor with pileus ; spores echinulate.—In open woods or on bare ground, common, Minnesota to Maine and Alabama.

C. laccata Fr. (edible).   Plate 17, fig. 18.

Pileus 2-8 cm. broad ; stem 2-12 cm. x 2-8 mm. ; spores 9 μ in diameter.

Pileus waxy and flesh-red when moist to ochraceous-whitish when. dry ; hygrophanous, scurfy-scaly ; gills broad-emarginate, flesh-colored, mealy with spores, thick, broad, subdistant ; stem cylindrical, fibrous, firm, light flesh-colored ; spores globose.—In swamps and moist sandy or mossy places, May-Oct., very common, Minnesota to Maine and Alabama.

C. laccata var. amethystina Bolt.   Differs by having violet-colored gills.—On ground in flat, sandy woods, Thornton, Ill., throughout our area.

C. tortilis Fr.

Pileus 0.5-1.5 cm. broad ; stem 1-3 cm x 1 mm. ; spores 12-14 μ.

Pileus pale salmon-colored, thin, distinctly radiately striate from center ; gills distant, adnate-decurrent, narrow ; stem fibrous, tough, stuffed with a white pith.—On wet grounds in woods, not common, July-Sept., Illinois, New York and northward.

TRICHOLOMA Fr.

Carpophore an orbicular, convex pileus confluent with the cylindrical, central stem; pileus of the same material as the stem, veil evanescent, or fibrillose on margin; gills adnexed, adnate, or emarginate behind, sometimes with a tooth but always narrowed near stem; spores white.—Terrestrial, usually autumnal.

1 Pileus viscid when moist......7
1' Pileus not viscid......2

2 Pileus dry......3
2' Pileus moist......5

3 Pileus scaly or fibrillose......4
3' Pileus silky at least when young......20

4 Pileus with floccose or fibrillose scales......12
4' Pileus with smooth scales, the taste soapy.......*T. saponaceum.*

5 Pileus hygrophanous, thin......35
5' Pileus moist but not hygrophanous......6

6 Pileus either rivulose or adorned with watery spots, fleshy, fragile......24
6' Pileus glabrous, moist, compact, spongy......25

7 Gills becoming red-brown-spotted, pileus reddish-brown......8
7' Gills not red or brown-spotted......9

8 Stem rooting ....*T. ustale.*
8' Stem not rooting................-............*T. transmutans.*

9 Pileus white ....*T. resplendens.*
9' Pileus not white, usually of some shade of yellow......10

10 Gills and pileus yellow.........................*T. equestre.*
10' Gills not yellow......11

11 Gills crowded, pileus glabrous.................*T. terriferum.*
11' 'Gills subdistant, pileus streaked with fibrils......*T. sejunctum.*

12 Gills changing color or becoming spotted in age......13
12' Gills not changing color......18

13 Pileus with reddish or brown hues......14
13' Pileus streaked or smoky......15

14 Stem subbulbous, white ....*T. tricolor.*
14' Stem nearly cylindrical, not white..............*T. imbricatum.*

15 Gills white becoming ashy......17
15' Gills becoming black......16

16 Pileus brown ....*T. fuligineum.*
16' Pileus whitish ....*T. fumescens.*

17   Taste strongly acrid...............................*T. acre.*
17'   Taste not acrid ....*T. terreum.*
18   Pileus white 19
18'   Pileus brownish, with red tomentum or red-scales....*T. rutilans.*
19   Pileus glabrous, taste not farinaceous..........*T. Columbetta.*
19'   Pileus squamulose, taste farinaceous...............*T. grande.*
20   Pileus white or whitish, acutely umbonate........*T. subacutum.*
20'   Pileus of some other color......21
21   Gills and pileus yellow......22
21'   Gills white, pileus not yellow......23
22   With an odor of coal tar, sulphur-yellow colored........
      ....*T. sulphureum.*
22'   With no such odor, lighter yellow..........*T. chrysenteroides.*
23   Pileus flesh-colored ; gills crowded, pure white......*T. carneum.*
23'   Pileus reddish-gray, gills subdistant..............*T. infantile.*
24   Plants united at base in a fleshy mass............*T. unifactum.*
24'   Plants caespitose, flesh-colored then white..........*T. boreale.*
25   Pileus white or tinted yellowish-rust color......26
25'   Pileus of another color......32
26   Stem hollow, pileus thin...................*T. leucocephalum.*
26'   Stem solid ; pileus medium to thick......27
27   Pileus margin obscurely marked with radiating ridges......28
27'   Pileus not so marked......29
28   Pileus tinged brick red......................*T. laterarium.*
28'   Pileus buff, very bitter........................*T. acerbum.*
29   Pileus very thick (1.5-2 cm.), large..................*T. grave.*
29'   Pileus smaller, thinner......30
30   Fresh water-soaked in wet weather : gills easily separable
      from pileus......31
30'   Not as above, water-soaked pileus glabrous, white....*T. album.*
31   Plants caespitose, gills truncate-adnate.................
      ....*T. panoeolum* var. *caespitosum.*
31'   Plants gregarious, gills adnexed...............*T. cinerascens.*
32   Plants violet or faded......33
32'   Plants yellow or green......34
33   Margin involute, tomentose...................*T. personatum.*
33'   Margin naked, convex...........................*T. nudum.*
33"   Pileus conic-campanulate ....*T. ionides.*
34   Pileus dingy-greenish ....*T. virescens.*
34'   Pileus smoky-yellow ....*T. fumosoluteum.*

35   Pileus more than 2 cm. in diameter......36
35' Pileus about 1 cm. in diameter.................*T. Hebeloma.*
36   Pileus moist, striatulate on margin...............*T. sordidum.*
36' Pileus not striatulate, smoky brown...........*T. melaleucum.*

T. equestre L. Equestrian Tricholoma.   Plate 18, fig. 1.

Pileus 5-12 cm. broad; stem 2-5 cm. x 12-30 mm.; spores 7 x 5 μ.
Pileus fleshy, convex-expanded, yellow or pale yellow, the disk and central scales darker, very viscid; stem thick, solid, pale yellow to white.—On sand among fallen pine needles in the Indiana dunes, Sept.-Nov., not common, Minnesota to Maine and North Carolina.

T. sejunctum Sowerb. Separating Tricholoma.   Plate 18, fig. 2.

Pileus 2-7 cm. broad; stem 2-7 cm. x 8-16 mm.; spores 5 x 7 μ.
Pileus convex-expanded, fragile, umbonate, slightly viscid, whitish to yellowish, streaked with black fibrils, the odor slight, the flesh white, the taste bitter; gills rounded behind or emarginate, white, broad, subdistant, the edge entire; stem thick, variously thickened, solid or cavernous, glabrous, white or yellowish.—Sandy oak or pine woods, Sept.-Nov., Wisconsin, New England, southward.
The white gills and streaked pileus separate it from *T. equestre.*

T. terriferum Peck. Earth-bearing Tricholoma.   Plate 18, fig. 4.

Pileus 6-10 cm., stem 2-4 cm. x 10-25 mm.; spores 3 x 2 μ.
Pileus convex-plane, wavy and thin at margin, alutaceous, viscid, the glabrous margin at first incurved, the flesh thick; gills adnexed, crowded, narrow, whitish, never rufescent; stem solid, floccose at apex, fibrillose below, white; basidia, 2-3-spored, 22 x 4 μ.—Solitary or gregarious in deciduous forests, October, rare, Wisconsin to New England and southward.

T. resplendens Fr. Resplendent Tricholoma, Viscid, white Tricholoma.   Plate 18, fig. 7.

Pileus 4-9 cm.; stem 4-8 cm. x 10-15 mm.; spores 7 x 4 μ.
Pileus viscid, shining-white, the flesh white, thin on margin; gills narrowly adnexed, close, medium broad, ventricose, white, entire, becoming discolored or spotted; stem solid, cylindrical, glabrous, white.—Gregarious or scattered on ground in woods, Aug.-Oct., Minnesota, New England, southward.

T. transmutans Peck. (edible).   Plate 18, fig. 5.

Pileus 4-9 cm.; stem 5-10 cm. x 6-12 mm.; spores 5 x 4 μ.
Pileus viscid when moist, reddish-brown to tawny brown, glabrous, the flesh white, the taste and odor farinaceous; gills adnexed-

emarginate, narrow, close, sometimes forked, whitish becoming dingy-red and spotted with age; stem glabrous, stuffed, whitish and often marked with reddish stains.—Caespitose, forming mycorhiza on roots of *Quercus velutina* (black oak), Aug.-Oct., Minnesota, Maine, Tennessee.

T. ustale Fr. Plate 18, fig. 6.

Pileus 4-10 cm. broad; stem 5-8 cm. x 8-15 mm.; spores 7 x 5 μ.

Pileus thick, bay, viscid, naked, the margin persistently incurved, the flesh white, rufescent, taste bitter; gills emarginate, white becoming reddish-brown spotted, edge eroded, broad, crowded; stem with elongated root-like base, stuffed, white, reddish toward base.— Caespitose on much decayed wood, rare, Sept.-Oct., Minnesota to New York and southward.

T. rutilans Fr. Plate 20, fig. 27.

Pileus 4-8 cm.; stem 5-10 cm. x 10-16 mm.; spores 7 x 4 μ.

Pileus covered with a dark purplish-red tomentum on a yellowish surface, campanulate-expanded, the margin at first involute, the odor and taste mild, the flesh yellow, gills rounded-adnate, crowded, narrow, yellow, thickened and villose on edges; stem curved, cylindrical stuffed to hollow, yellow variegated with minute reddish scales. —On and about pine stumps and logs, rare, July-Oct., Minnesota, Maine, south in mountains.

T. Columbetta Fr. Dove-colored Tricholoma. Plate 18, fig. 8.

Pileus 5-10 cm.; stem 3-10 cm. x 8-20 mm.; spores 7 x 5 μ.

Pileus pure white, shining, often stained with carmine, yellow, or blue, convex-plane, the margin minutely tomentose, at first incurved; flesh white: gills emarginate, close, thin, white; stem solid, unequal, glabrous, white.—In beech and birch woods, Minnesota to Maine and Tennessee.

T. grande Peck. Grand Tricholoma. Plate 18, fig. 9.

Pileus 8-12 cm.; stem 5-10 cm. x 20-30 mm.; spores 10 x 6 μ.

Pileus thick, firm, hemispherical, then convex, dry, squamulose, silky-fibrillose toward the margin; margin inrolled at first, white; flesh thick, gray, the taste farinaceous; gills rounded toward stem, adnexed; stem stout, solid, white, cylindrical.—Among fallen leaves in woods, Illinois to New York and southward.

T. tricolor Peck.

Pileus 5-10 cm.; stem 5-8 cm. x 12-24 mm.; spores 7 x 6 μ.

Pileus convex, plane, firm, dry, striate on margin, pale alutaceous to slightly russet; gills adnexed, close, narrow, pale yellow becoming brown or purplish-brown when dried, stem firm, subbulbous, white.—On the ground in woods, August, Michigan to New York.

T. acre Peck.   Plate 20, fig. 28.

Pileus 4-9 cm.; stem 3-6 cm. x 7-15 mm.; spores 7 x 5 μ.

Pileus campanulate subexpanded, rather thin, radiately fibrillose, pale silvery-gray or mouse-gray, the flesh white, firm, the taste acrid; gills adnexed, broad, ventricose, close, white changing to ashy, the edges fimbriate, stem stuffed or hollow, white innate-silky-fibrillose.—In oak and maple woods, Minnesota to New England and southward.

T. imbricatum Fr. Shingled Tricholoma.   Plate 20, fig. 25.

Pileus 5-8 cm. broad; stem 5-10 cm. x 10-15 mm.; spores 6 x 4 μ.

Pileus convex-plane, compact, dry, brownish-red, imbricate scaly on disk, the margin innate fibrillose scaly, at first incurved and pubescent; gills adnate, close, white changing to reddish or spotted-reddish. moderately broad; stem solid like pileus.—Under conifers, and in deciduous forests, Sept.-Oct., Minnesota to Maine and North Carolina.

T. terreum Schaeff. Earth-colored Tricholoma. Plate 20, fig. 33.

Pileus 2-7 cm. broad; stem 2-5 cm. x 4-8 mm.; spores 6 x 4 μ.

Pileus thin-convex-campanulate, soft, innately fibrillose of floccose-squamose, ashy, gray-brown, or mouse-colored, the flesh white; gills adnexed or adnate and uncinate, subdistant, eroded on edges, white to ashy or yellow-stained; stem cylindrical, solid or stuffed, sometimes hollow; fibrillose, whitish.—Woods or open places, common, Aug.-Oct., Minnesota to Maine and southward.

T. fumescens Peck. Smoky Tricholoma. Plate 20, fig. 29.

Pileus 2-3 cm. broad; stem 2-3 cm. x 4-6 mm.; spores 5 x 6 μ.

Shaped as the preceding, with a very minute appressed tomentum, whitish; gills blue-black where bruised.—Woods, rare, September and October, Wisconsin to New York and southward.

T. fuligineum Peck. Sooty Tricholoma. Plate 20, fig. 32.

Like the preceding but sooty-brown, the taste farinaceous; gills uneven on edges, black when dry.—Among moss in open woods, September, rare, throughout our area.

T. saponaceum Fr. Soapy Tricholoma. Plate 20, fig. 31.

Pileus 4-8 cm. broad, stem 5-8 cm. x 15-20 mm.; spores 5 x 3 μ.

Pileus lead-gray, sometimes slightly brownish or olive-tinged, the margin at first incurved; flesh white, with soapy taste and odor; gills adnate-uncinate, broad, subdistant, white, entire; stem ventricose or subradiating below, solid, fibrous-fleshy, the apex floccose, pinkish within.—In open woods, not common, Sept.-Nov., Wisconsin to Michigan and Indiana.

T. subacutum Peck.   Plate 20, fig. 30.

Pileus 3-7 cm. broad; stem 5-10 cm. x 6-12 mm.; spores 7 x 6 μ.

Pileus broadly conical then convex, subacutely umbonate, silky, dry, covered with minute innate fibrils, whitish tinged with bluish-gray or smoky-brown, the umbo darker, the flesh white; the taste acrid; gills slightly adnexed, close, white, medium; stem cylindrical, stuffed to hollow, silky-fibrillose.—In woods, Indiana to New York and southward.

T. sulphureum Fr.   Sulphur-colored Tricholoma.   Plate 18, fig. 10.

Pileus 3-7 cm. broad; stem 4-8 cm. x 5-10 mm.; spores 9 x 5 μ.

Pileus convex-plane, usually umbonate, silky, glabrous, sulphur to olivaceous-yellow, brownish on disk, subgibbous, smooth, the margin curved upward, the flesh yellowish, thick toward disk, the odor of coal-tar, the taste disagreeable; gills adnexed-uncinate, subdistant, broad, thick, firm, yellow; stem innately fibrillose, stuffed, yellowish.—In maple-oak woods, July-Oct., infrequent, Illinois to Michigan, Indiana and southward in the Appalachians.

T. chrysenteroides Peck.   Golden-flesh Tricholoma.   Plate 18, fig. 11.

Pileus 2-5 cm. broad, stem 4-7 cm. x 6-8 mm.; spores 8.5 x 6 μ.

Pileus fleshy, convex or plane, not umbonate, firm glabrous, dry, pale yellow to buff, dingy with age, the flesh pale yellow, the taste farinaceous; gills emarginate, yellowish, close, dingy with age, with transverse veins along upper edges, the interspaces venose; stem solid, firm fibrous-striate, cylindrical.—Not common, in woods, Sept.-Oct., Indiana, New York and southward.

T. infantile Peck.   Plate 20, fig. 36.

Piles 1-2 cm. broad; stem 2-3 cm. x 2-4 mm.; spores 7 x 5 μ.

Pileus reddish-gray, moist in wet weather, thin, convex-plane, smooth, minutely silky; the margin incurved, whitish; gills subdistant but slightly ventricose, often eroded at edges; whitish; stem cylindrical, short, hollow, slightly paler than pileus.—Gravelly soil, fields, rare, June.   The pileus is sometimes papillate.

T. carneum Fr.   Flesh-colored Tricholoma.   Plate 20, fig. 34.

Pileus 1.5-2 cm. broad; stem 1-2.5 cm. x 2-3 mm.; spores 5 x 2.5 μ.

Pileus convex-plane, sometimes umbonate, flesh-colored to light tan. The margin thin, the flesh fragile, thick on disk, white, soft, with but little odor or taste; gills sinuate-adnexed, uncinate, narrow, crowded, pure white; stem cylindrical, fibrous, hollow, sometimes compressed.—On leaves in woods gregarious or subcaespitose, Aug.-Sept., rare, Indiana and Michigan.

T. unifactum Peck. United Tricholoma. Plate 19, fig. 13.

Pileus 2-5 cm. broad; stems 2-5 cm. x 6-10 mm.; spores 4 x 5 μ.

Pileus thin, convex, white, sometimes irregular or eccentric from crowding, the flesh whitish, the taste mild; gills rounded behind, white; stem cylindrical, solid, white, united at base and often fused into a large fleshy mass.—Rich hemlock woods, Wisconsin, New York and southward.

T. boreale Fr.

Pileus at first bright flesh-colored, fading to white; otherwise much as preceding.—Somewhat caespitose, Michigan, New York and northward.

T. album Schaeff. White Tricholoma. Plate 19, fig. 14.

Pileus 5-10 cm. broad; stem 5-10 cm. x 8-12 mm.; spores 5 x 6 μ.

Pileus fleshy, tough, convex-plane or depressed, obtuse, dry, smooth, white sometimes yellowish in center, the margin at first involute, the flesh white, bitter-acrid; gills emarginate, crowded, white; stem solid, cylindrical, elastic, with fibrous surface, white indistinctly pruinose at apex.—Woods, common, Indiana to New York and southward.

T. laterarium Peck. Side-marked Tricholoma. Plate 19, fig. 16.

Like *T. album* but with disk often tinged brick-red or brown and the margin marked with short subdistant ridges radiately arranged. —Woods, June-July, New York. Very close to *T. acerbum.*

T. acerbum Fr. Bitter Tricholoma. Plate 19, fig. 18.

Pileus 7-10 cm. broad; stem 4-5 cm. x 10-25 mm.; spores 4.5 μ in diameter.

Pileus buff-white or white with flesh-tinge, the margin obscurely ridged and at first involute, broad, firm, convex-expanded, obtuse, subpruinose, dry, the flesh white, thick in the middle, thin at the margin; gills emarginate, with teeth, crowded, narrow, white to cream-colored; stem tapering upward, solid, thick, with sparse white-satiny tomentum, dingy when handled; taste very bitter.—On ground in woods, June-Oct., Wisconsin, Michigan and southwards.

T. leucocephalum Fr. White-capped Tricholoma. Plate 19, fig. 19.

Pileus 2-6 cm. broad; stem 2-5 cm. x 4-8 mm.; spores 8 x 4 μ.

Pileus thin, white, slightly silky at first, plane, smooth, obtuse, moist, glabrous, the flesh white, watery in wet weather; gills free, crowded, thin, white, the edges entire; stem white, glabrous, hollow, solid at the rooting base, fibrous to subcartilaginous; taste farinaceous.—Gregarious in conifer woods, September, not common, Wisconsin to New England.

T. fumosoluteum Peck. Plate 19, fig. 20.

T. virescens Peck. (the green form of the species).

Pileus 5-12 cm. broad; stem 6-10 cm. x 8-20 mm.; spores 4 x 6 μ.

Pileus convex-expanded, moist, glabrous, smoky-yellow or dingy-green; gills rounded behind, broad, close, white; stem hollow, white, sometimes tinged like pileus.—In thin woods, gregarious to caespitose, rare, October, Michigan to New York and southward.

T. personatum Fr. Masked Tricholoma. Plate 20, fig. 37.

Pileus 2-12 cm. broad; stem 2-8 cm. x 12-24 mm.; spores 9 x 5 μ.

Pileus at first violet, fading when moist to pale ashy with wet appearance, compact, thick on disk, rather thin toward margin; margin violaceus, solid, fibrillose, or villose; spores sordid white.—Among fallen leaves in woods, common, Sept.-Nov., Minnesota to New England and southward.

T. nudum Fr. Plate 20, fig. 38.

Pileus broad, thin, purplish, violet or lavender, fading to pale brown, the margin at first incurved and naked; gills truncate-adnate, crowded, narrow, violaceous; stem slightly enlarged at base, colored like pileus.—Gregarious in woods, common, Sept.-Oct., Minnesota to New England and southward.

T. ionides Fr. Plate 20, fig. 39.

Pileus 3-5 cm. broad; stem 4-8 cm. x 4-8 mm.; spores 7 x 5 μ.

Pileus conic-campanulate, at first floccose on margin, thick, thin toward margin; stem stuffed to hollow; gills and spores white.—In woods, May-Nov., Illinois to Michigan and southward.

T. grave Peck. Heavy Tricholoma. Plate 19, fig. 17.

Pileus 12-20 cm. broad; stem 8-12 cm. x 20-35 mm.; spores 8 x 5 μ.

Pileus 2-4 cm. thick, hemispherical then convex, compact, thick, heavy, grayish-tawny, spotted when moist, pale when dry, the margin paler, involute, covered with gray silky tomentum, the flesh grayish;

gills adnexed, subdistant, whitish then pale ochre or tawny; stem stout, solid, penetrating the soil deeply.—Mixed woods, Wisconsin, New York.

T. cinerascens Fr. Ashy Tricholoma.   Plate 20, fig. 40.

Pileus 5-10 cm. broad; stem 5-8 cm. x 10-15 mm.; spores 5 x 3 μ.

Pileus white or buff, then gray, moist, convex-expanded, smooth, the margin thin, naked, the flesh white, thick in center; gills adnexed, close, dingy-white, medium wide, easily separable from pileus; stem cylindrical, mycelioid at base, stuffed to hollow, white then ashy, pruinose at apex; taste farinaceous.—Gregarious to caespitose among decayed leaves in woods, October, southern Michigan.

T. panoeolum var. **caespitosum** Bres.   Plate 19, fig. 21.

Pileus 5-15 cm. broad; stem 3-8 cm. x 8-15 mm.; spores 6 x 3.5 μ.

Pileus convex-expanded, irregular, sometimes eccentric, whitish, buff, gray-brown, dingy-tan, or shining-white, glabrous, the cuticle subcartilaginous, the margin persistently incurved, the flesh firm, moist in wet weather, or water-soaked, fragile; gills truncate-adnate, very crowded, easily separable from pileus, white soon dingy-flesh-colored; stem solid, pruinose-white then fibrillose; taste peppery or unpleasant.—Conifer or deciduous woods, Sept.-Nov., Illinois to Michigan.

T. melaleucum Fr.   Plate 19, fig. 22.

Pileus 3-7 cm. broad; stem 3-8 cm. x 3-7 mm.; spores 8 x 4.5 μ.

Pileus convex-plane, glabrous, the cuticle somewhat separable, smoky-brown (when moist), tan (when dry), the umbo darker, the flesh scissile, light gray to whitish; gills adnexed, subventricose, close, thick, pure white to dingy; stem straight, cylindrical, with dark fibrils on surface.—In grass, on lawns, etc., June-Oct., Michigan to Ohio.

T. sordidum Fr. Sordid Tricholoma.   Plate 19, fig. 24.

Pileus 2-6 cm. broad; stem 2-5 cm. x 4-6 mm.; spores 7 x 4 μ.

Pileus campanulate to plane or centrally depressed, often irregular or eccentric, brown with a violaceous tint, striatulate on margin when moist, subcinereous when dry, the flesh white; gills adnate, thin, close, whitish or smoky-violaceous; stem fibrillose-striate, cylindrical, solid, white within, colored like pileus.—On manured ground, not common, May-Sept., Illinois to New York.

T. Hebeloma Peck.

Pileus 1 cm. broad; stem 2 cm x 2 mm.; spores 6 x 4 μ.

Pileus conic to campanulate, brown with darker disk (when wet), striatulate, gray (when dry); gills rounded behind, broad, yellowish;

stem equal, hollow, pale.—Woods, July, not common, New York to Illinois.

HYGROPHORUS Fr.

Carpophore composed of a more or less orbicular, conical, convex, or depressed pileus of same material and confluent with the central stipe; pileus fleshy, putrescent, soft, somewhat waxy or watery: stipe usually cylindrical, similar in texture to pileus, often watery and fragile; annulus absent; gills translucent or waxy-watery in appearance, edge acute but gradually the gill thickens toward its attachment with the pileus, thus narrowly triangular in section, distant or subdistant; spores white.—Growing on the ground.

1   Pileus red, bright green, orange, or yellow......2
1' Pileus white, disk sometimes yellowish......10
1" Pileus not red, bright green, yellow, or white......29
2   Plants brilliant red, pink, flesh-colored, or rufous......3
2' Plants bright green, yellow, or orange......21
3   Pileus viscid......4
3' Pileus not viscid......9
4   Stem stout and pileus thick......5
4' Stem slender, pileus thin, fragile......7
5   Gills becoming reddish-spotted..................*H. Russula.*
5' Gills not so marked......6
6   In tamarack swamps, stem viscid, pileus scarlet or
    orange ....*H. speciosus.*
6' In open woods, pileus tinged with flesh color, stem
    dry ....*H. pudorinus.*
7   Pileus small (1-2 cm. broad), flesh-colored; stem slender,
    viscid ....*H. Peckii.*
7' Pileus 3-7 cm. broad, scarlet or vermillion; stem not viscid....8
8   Gills arculate-adnate; stem-base yellowish........*H. coccineus.*
8' Gills almost free, slightly adnexed; stem-base white.*H. puniceus.*
8" Plant becoming black where bruised...............*H. conicus.*
9   Pileus 1-3 cm. broad, scarlet or vermillion; plants of low
    wet ground ....*H. miniatus.*
9' Pileus 3-7 cm. broad, tawny-flesh-colored.........*H. pratensis.*
10 Pileus viscid or glutinous......13
10' Pileus and stem not viscid......11
11 Pileus and stem compact, stout; disk thick......12
11' Pileus 1-3 cm. broad, stem slender..............*H. borealis.*

12   Pileus white ....*H. virgineus.*

12′ Pileus almost white, with a fulvous tinge..............
.................................*H. pratensis* var. *pallidus.*

13   Pileus entirely white......17

13′ Pileus white with yellowish or reddish tints......14

14   Upper part of stem decorated with yellowish granular dots...16

14′ Upper part of stem decorated with white scaly dots......15

15   Pileus disk pale reddish-brown...................*H. Laurae.*

15′ Pileus disk yellow to orange.................*H. flavodiscus.*

16   Pileus covered with yellowish or brownish gluten..*H. paludosus.*

16′ Pileus white with numerous golden dots toward margin....
....*H. chrysodon.*

17   Stem viscid or glutinous......19

17′ Stem dry......18

18   Pileus small (1-3 cm.), tough, thin...............*H. niveus.*

18′ Pileus very large (8-15 cm.), stem stout..........*H. sordidus.*

19   Stem with white squamules near top, gills adnate-decurrent...20

19′ Stem without dots; gills almost free, adnexed; pileus at first
conical ....*H. purus.*

20   Annulus glutinous, becoming red dotted near apex of stem
....*H. glutinosus.*

20′ Annulus and rings around stem absent...........*H. eburneus.*

21   Pileus viscid or glutinous......23

21′ Pileus not viscid......22

22   Pileus orange, fading, fragile; gills deep orange.*H. marginatus.*

22′ Pileus pale yellow, very small (6-12 mm. broad)...*H. parvulus.*

23   Pileus bright green, usually conical; gills yellowish or
green ....*H. psitticinus.*

23   Pileus not bright green......24

24   Pileus orange-red or yellow to tawny, becoming black where
bruised, conical ....*H. conicus.*

24′ Pileus orange, yellow, or tawny; not becoming black where
bruised......25

25   Gills adnexed, pileus golden-yellow..........*H. chlorophanus.*

25′ Gills adnate-decurrent......26

26   Pileus becoming yellow or whitish when frozen,
3-8 cm. broad...............................*H. speciosus.*

26′ Pileus small (1-3 cm.)......27

27   Plant tough, pileus tawny-yellow..................*H. laetus.*

27′ Plant fragile, pileus wax-yellow......28

28   Gills decurrent, plants fading to whitish in age......*H. nitidus.*
28' Gills adnate-decurrent, plants not fading...........*H. ceraceus.*
29   Both pileus and stem viscid or glutinous......30
29' Stem dry, solid; pileus subviscid, smoky-brown..*H. fusco-albus.*
30   Pileus grayish-brown or smoky-brown, gills pure white......31
30' Pileus dark brownish-olivaceous.............*H. olivaceoalbus.*
31   Stem hollow ....*H. unquinosus.*
31' Stem solid ....*R. fuligineus.*

H. flavodiscus Frost. (edible).   Plate 26, fig. 7.

Pileus 3-7 cm. broad; stem 3-7 cm. x 6-12 mm.; spores 7 x 4.5 μ.

Pileus convex to plane, glutinous, white, pale yellow to reddish-yellow on disk, smooth, glabrous, the margins of young specimens involute; gills adnate or slightly decurrent, subdistant, white or slightly flesh-colored, stem cylindrical, solid, very glutinous, apex bearing white scabrous points, white or yellowish below; spores inequalateral.—In red oak, hard maple, beech, or hemlock forests, gregarious, common, September, Olympia fields, Illinois to Wisconsin, New York, southward.

H. Laurae Morg.   Laura Hygrophorus (edible).   Plate 26, fig. 4.

Pileus 3-10 cm. broad; stem 3-8 cm. x 6-12 mm.; spores 8 x 4.5 μ.

Pileus convex to plane, umbonate, irregular, white with purplish-brown on disk, glutinous, glabrous, the margins of young plants involute; gills adnate-decurrent, narrow, white to cream; stem cylindrical or tapering downward, glutinous, solid, white or yellowish, the upper half scabrous-squamulose, the apex with scabrous points; spores apiculate.—Gregarious to caespitose among leaves on ground in deciduous thickets, Aug.-Nov., frequently found, Wisconsin to New York and southward.

H. eburneus Fr. Ivory Hygrophorus (edible).   Plate 26, fig. 1.

Pileus 2-7 cm. broad; stem 6-15 cm. x 3-8 mm.; spores cylindrical, 7 x 5 μ.

Pileus pure white, shining, convex-plane, glutinous, the margin at first involute, floccose pubescent, the flesh white, thick, firm; gills adnate to decurrent, white, broad behind, narrowed in front, somewhat venose, stem white, elongated, cylindrical or tapering downward, often flexuous, glutinous, shining, spotted when dry, the apex bearing white squamulous dots, stuffed to hollow.—Gregarious to subcaespitose in thickets or grassy woods, Oct.-Nov., frequently found, Minnesota to New England and southward to Tennessee.

H. speciosus Peck.   Showy Hygrophorus (edible).   Plate 26, fig. 2.

Pileus 2-8 cm. broad; stem 3-10 cm. x 8-20 mm.; spores 9 x 5.5 μ.

Pileus subconic to convex, plane, sometimes broadly umbonate, glutinous, bright red or orange when young and fading in age or when frozen, often virgate, rugulose from drying gluten, the margin soon spreading, the flesh white, often orange beneath the separable cuticle, thick, soft; gills decurrent, distant, broad in middle, thick, intervenose, white or tinged yellowish; stem stout, watery-white (hyaline), floccose-fibrillose up to the disappearing annulus.—In groups in tamarack swamps, Oct.-Nov., common locally, in bog near Fox Lake, Volo, Illinois, Minnesota and New England and northern Indiana.

H. olivaceoalbus Fr.   Olive Hygrophorus.   Plate 26, fig. 5.

Pileus 4-8 cm. broad; stem 4-7 cm. x 8-15 mm.; spores 11 x 7 μ.

Pileus rounded, convex, often umbonate, the margin at first involute, covered with thick gluten, olive-gray or smoky-olive, becoming ferrugineous and wrinkled from drying gluten, the flesh white, thick, soft; gills adnate to decurrent, rather broad, subdistant, white; stem stout, subequal, peronate at first, solid, curved and partly rooting, floccose-scaly because of the glutinous veil, finally marked by fulvous-rusty annular stains, the apex at first bearing bead-like drops, later densely white-scaly dotted.—On the ground in oak woods, rare, Sept.-Oct., Lake Villa, Illinois, Michigan, and New York.

H. Russula Fr. (edible).   Plate 26, fig. 3.

Tricholoma Russula Schaeff.

Pileus 5-12 cm. broad; stem 3-7 cm. x 15-20 mm.; basidia 4.5 x 6 μ; spores 7 x 4 μ.

Pileus convex, plane or finally depressed, firm, viscid when moist, pale pink to rosy-red, the disk often scaly dotted, the margin at first inrolled and floccose, the flesh thick especially on disk, becoming decurrent by the upturning of the pileus, white then red-spotted; stem stout, cylindrical or subventricose, white becoming reddish in age, the apex white, floccose; spores narrow, apiculate.—Often in groups among leaves on ground in woods, common, Sept.-Oct., Minnesota to New England and southward.

H. pudorinus Fr.   Blushing Hygrophorus (edible).   Plate 26, fig. 8.

Pileus 2-10 cm. broad; stem 3-8 cm. x 5-20 mm.; spores 6-9 x 3.5-5 μ.

Pileus convex-campanulate to expanded, firm, compact, thick, viscid when moist, pale, tan, tinged incarnate, or pinkish-buff, smooth, glabrous, the margin at first involute, minutely downy; gills pointed, subdecurrent, subdistant, narrow, venose, thickish, usually connected to stem by a narrow border; stem stout, compact, solid, dry, cylindrical, white to pinkish-buff, floccose-scabrous at apex, fibrillose downward.—Gregarious or caespitose on ground in frondose or hemlock woods, frequently found, Sept.-Nov., Wisconsin to New York and southward.

H. sordidus Peck. Sordid Hygrophorus (edible).   Plate 26, fig. 10.

Pileus 8-16 cm. broad; stem 6-10 cm. x 1.5-3 cm.; spores 7 x 4.5 μ.

Pileus convex-expanded to plane, thick, firm, compact, viscid when moist, pure-white or rarely tinged yellowish-buff, glabrous, smooth, the margin at first incurved and slightly floccose; gills adnate-decurrent, subdistant, broad in middle, waxy, white; stem stout, short, solid, dry, white, cylindrical, smooth, obscurely mealy at apex.—Gregarious among leaves on ground in deciduous forests, common, Sept.-Nov., Wisconsin to New York and southward.

H. pratensis Fr. Meadow Hygrophorus (edible).   Plate 26, fig. 6.

Pileus 2-8 cm. broad; stem 4-7 cm. x 7-12 mm.; spores 7 x 5 μ.

Pileus convex-expanded or somewhat turbinate, obtuse or broadly. umbonate, glabrous, smooth, reddish-fulvous to pale tawny, moist when fresh but not viscid, the disk thick, the margin thin, the flesh white to tawny; gills decurrent, distant, thick, whitish to yellowish, very broad in middle, intervenose; stem short, cylindrical, glabrous, stuffed, white or tinged like pileus.—Solitary or caespitose in grassy places and on the ground in woods, July-Oct., common, New England to Minnesota and southward.

In var. *pallidus* the plants are whitish; in var. *cinereus* they are cinereous.

H. virgineus Fr. (edible).   Plate 27, fig. 14.

Pileus 2-5 cm. broad; stem 2-4 cm. x 6-10 mm.; spores 7 x 3.5 μ.

Pileus convex, often plano-depressed, often turbinate and obscurely pruinose, smooth, white, the disk thick, the margin thin, not viscid; gills decurrent, subdistant, medium broad, thickish, white, at length tinged with cream-flesh-color; stem short, thick, cylindrical or narrowed downward, glabrous, white.—Solitary to caespitose on sandy ground in mixed open woods of beech, hard maple and pine, Sept.-Oct., common, New England to North Dakota and southward.

H. niveus Fr. Snowy Hygrophorus (edible). Plate 27, fig. 16.

Pileus 1-3 cm. broad; stem 2-8 cm. x 2-5 mm.; spores 8 x 5 μ.

Pileus convex or campanulate at first, finally plane, umbilicate. hygrophanous-white, slightly viscid, glabrous, striate when moist, thin; gills decurrent, distant, narrow, thin, venose, white; stem white, glabrous, cylindrical.—On moist ground, in low woods or on moss in bogs, Aug.-Sept., not common, Illinois to New York and northward.

H. borealis Peck. (edible). Plate 27, fig. 15.

Pileus 1-3.5 cm. broad; stem 2-5 cm. x 2-5 mm.; spores 8 x 5 μ.

Pileus convex, expanded, obtuse, moist, smooth, glabrous, thick on disk and thin at margin, white; gills decurrent, arcuate, white, intervenose, distant; stem slender, firm, subcylindrical straight or flexuous, glabrous, stuffed, white.—On moist ground in swamps or mixed woods, Aug.-Oct., not common, northern Illinois to Michigan, New York and northward.

H. ceraceous Fr. Waxy Hygrophorus (edible). Plate 27, fig. 12.

Pileus 1-4 cm. broad; 2-5 cm. x 2-4 mm.; spores 7 x 4 μ.

Pileus convex campanulate, soft, fragile, viscous, pale lemon-yellow, sometimes tinged with orange, pellucid-striate, glabrous; gills broadly adnate to subdecurrent, subdistant, thickish, pale yellow to whitish; stem cylindrical, round or compressed, hollow, shining, undulate, waxy-yellow, slightly viscid.—On moist ground in conifer and frondose woods, July-Sept., common, Dunes State Park, Indiana, Michigan, New York.

H. miniatus Fr. Vermillion Hygrophorus (edible). Plate 26, fig. 9.

Pileus 1-3 cm. broad; stem 2-7 cm. x 3-5 mm.; spores 8 x 5 μ.

Pileus vermillion-red, reddish-yellow, fading, convex to expanded-plane, at length umbilicate, never viscid, minutely tomentose-scaly or glabrous, smooth, fragile, watery-wax aspect, thin, the flesh pale yellowish; gills adnate or subdecurrent, subdistant, orange, red, or yellow, thickish; stem cylindrical, orange-red or yellow, becoming hollow, dry, glabrous.—On bare ground in woods and swamps, common, Minnesota, to New England and southward.

H. miniatus var. **Cantherellus** Schw.

H. Cantherellus Schw.

Stem longer, gills more decurrent, pileus smaller.—Habitat and range that of species.

H. miniatus var. **sphagnophilus** Peck.

Pileus subconic to convex, centrally depressed.—On sphagnum in bogs, Illinois to New York and northward.

H. puniceus Fr. (edible). Plate 27, fig. 11.

Pileus 3-7 cm. broad; stem 5-8 cm. x 6-12 mm.; spores 9-12 x 4-5 μ.

Pileus campanulate, obtuse, at length expanded and wavy-lobed, bright red, fading, viscid, glabrous, fragile, the flesh white, yellow under cuticle, the taste mild; gills almost free, narrowly adnexed, thick, distant, intervenose, hollow, yellow to scarlet, white at base, fibrillose striate; spores smooth.—Gregarious or solitary on the ground in moist places, or bare ground in thickets and sandy swales, Aug.-Oct., not frequent, Illinois to New York, northward and southward.

H. coccineus Fr. (edible).

Very close to *H. puniceus,* not quite as viscid, cherry red; gills arcuate; adnate; stem compressed and furrowed.—In low meadows and moist woods, rare, Illinois to New York and northward.

H. chlorophanus Fr. (edible). Plate 27, fig. 13.

Pileus 2-5 cm. broad; stem 3-7 cm. x 4-8 mm.; spores 6-8 x 4-5 μ.

Pileus convex or campanulate, later nearly plane, viscid sulphur to golden-yellow, glabrous, often pellucid-striate on margin, fragile, not black when bruised; gills adnexed to emarginate, ventricose, thin, subdistant, broad, pale citron-yellow; stem cylindrical, concolor, unicolorous, viscid, not compressed.—Gregarious on ground and often among mosses in low moist woods, June-Sept., common, Illinois to New York and northward, and south in Appalachian mountains.

H. marginatus Peck. Plate 27, fig. 21.

Pileus 1-4 cm. broad; stem 2-5 cm. x 3-8 mm.; spores 7-8 x 4-5 μ.

Pileus fragile, campanulate to convex, sometimes gibbous, finally plane, sometimes broadly umbonate, hygrophanous, glabrous, golden-yellow to orange or tinted olivaceous, fading to pale yellow, striate or cracked on margin, thin; gills adnate to emarginate, arcuate, ventricose, broad, deep yellow, not fading, intervenose; stem fragile, hollow, not viscid, often flexuous, irregularly compressed, glabrous, orange, fading to straw.—Gregarious or caespitose in moist places in conifer or frondose swampy woods, July-Aug., rare, Illinois to New York, northward and southward.

H. conicus Fr. Conic Hygrophorus (suspected). Plate 27, fig. 20.

Pileus 1-3 cm. broad and high, stem 3-9 cm. x 2-6 mm.; spores 9 x 6 μ.

Pileus conical, subacute at apex, splitting-expanded or lobed at the margin, viscid when moist, shining, glabrous, orange-red, orange, yellow, virgate, stained black where bruised or in age, very thin; gills almost free, broad, ventricose, sulphur-yellow becoming black; stem fibrillose striate, dry, twisted, hollow, golden yellow, black staining, splitting.—Gregarious or solitary in low moist sandy swales, grassy places, and low woods, May-Oct., common, Minnesota to Maine and southward.

H. nitidus Berk. and Curt. Shining Hygrophorus. Plate 27, fig. 17.

Pileus 1-2.5 cm. broad; stem 3-7 cm. x 2-4 mm.; spores 6.5 x 3.5 μ.

Pileus convex, umbilicate, fragile, viscid when moist, wax-yellow, whitish when dry, pellucid-striate and shining when moist, glabrous; gills decurrent, arcuate, distant, not broad, pale yellow, intervenose; stem cylindrical, slender, hollow, fragile, viscid and wax yellow to dry and white.—Gregarious on ground in coniferous bogs, July-Sept., Northern Illinois to New York and northward, common locally.

H. laetus Fr. Pleasing Hygrophorus. Plate 27, fig. 18.

Pileus 1.5-3 cm. broad; stem 3-5 cm. x 3-6 mm.; spores 6-7 x 4 μ.

Pileus convex, plane, obtuse, viscid when moist, shining, tawny not fading, pellucid-striate, tough, thin; gills broadly-adnate, subtriangular, distant, thin, yellow, greenish-yellow, grayish-yellow, or finally orange; stem tough, slender, glabrous, very viscid, cylindrical, tawny, wavy uneven.—Gregarious in swamps and meadows, July-Aug., northern Indiana to New York, northward and southward in mountain regions.

H. Peckii Atkins. Peck's Hygrophorus. Plate 27, fig. 19.

Pileus 1-2 cm. broad, stem 3-8 cm. x 2-4 mm.; spores 7 x 5 μ.

Pileus convex-plane, broadly umbilicate, glutinous when moist, pale yellow, flesh-colored or vinaceous-buff, rarely tinged greenish, glabrous, pellucid-striatulate when moist, somewhat faded when dry; gills arcuate-decurrent, distant, broad, whitish or pale flesh-colored; stem concolor, very viscid, hollow, round, smooth.—Gregarious or solitary on moss in wet places, especially in bogs, July-Sept., frequent locally, Illinois to New York, northward and southward in the mountains.

H. psitticinus Fr. Parrot Hygrophorus. Plate 27, fig. 22.

Pileus 1-3 cm. broad; stem 4-7 cm. x 2-5 mm.; spores 7 x 4-5 μ.

Pileus campanulate, finally expanded, glutinous, parrot-green becoming flesh or yellowish, pellucid-striate, thin; gills adnate, ventricose, thick, of same color as the pileus; stem toughish, very viscid, smooth, glabrous, undulate-uneven, subpellucid, green to reddish orange or yellow, hollow.—Gregarious or subcaespitose in rich moist mossy woods, July-Oct., Minnesota to Maine and southward.

RUSSULA Fr.

Pileus orbicular, on a central stem of same material and confluent with it, fleshy, rigid-brittle, of bladder-like oval cells held together by hyphae, putrescent, without milky juice, acrid or mild in taste; gills white, becoming ochraceous if the spores are ochraceous; spores globose, echinulate, white, cream-colored, or ochraceous.—terrestrial, common during August.

Species are similar to those of the related genera *Hygrophorus* and *Lactarius* except that the former has thicker and wax-appearing gills, and the latter has milky juice, which it exudes where broken. The gills are adnate or almost free in one species, in others adnate or adnexed. The plants are comparatively short and compact.

1　Gills unequal, alternately long and short; margin of the pileus thick, not striate......2
1′　Gills dichotomously forked throughout; pileus pale purple-olivaceous then umber ....*R. variata.*
1″　Gills mostly equal, the shorter ones scattered among the longer......7

2　Flesh white, unchanging......3
2′　Flesh becoming reddish or black......6

3　Entire plant white......4
3′　Plant changing to reddish or smoky in age or when bruised....5

4　Odor strongly alkaline, pileus 10-30 cm. broad....*R. magnifica.*
4′　Odor absent......5

5　Gills subdistant, pileus 8-15 cm. broad.............*R. delica.*
5′　Gills distant, pileus 4-8 cm. broad................*R. brevipes.*

6　Flesh finally black, gills rather distant...........*R. nigricans.*
6′　Flesh red then black, gills crowded............*R. densifolia.*
6″　Flesh becoming rusty, gills not distant..........*R. compacta.*

7　Mature pileus red to violet or red and yellow mixed......8
7′　Mature pileus of some shade of green, yellow-brown, or white......31

8　Violet shades predominant......9
8′　Other colors predominant......11

9   Pileus large (5-10 cm. broad), thick; stem white. *R. cyanoxantha.*
9'   Small (3-6 cm. broad)......10

10   Plant growing under conifers, silky-shining....*R. sericeonitens.*
10'   Plant purplish on disk, very fragile, growing in wet mossy
places ....*R. fallax.*

11   Red color present......12
11'   Red color scarcely present......31

12   Taste very acrid......13
12'   Taste mild 22

13   Mature pileus small (2-7 cm. broad)......14
13'   Mature pileus large (7-12 cm. broad)......19

14   Stem very fragile, spores pure white......15
14'   Stem not fragile, or gills colored by yellowish spores......16

15   Pileus rosy on margin, purplish or pale toward center; plants
growing in wet mossy habitats....................*R. fallax.*
15'   Pileus uniformly rose-red.......................*R. fragilis.*

16   Margin of pileus striate, cuticle separable......17
16'   Margin of pileus not striate, dry; cuticle adnate. .*R. subpunctata.*

17   Pileus red-buff to red-purple, plants growing in swamps. .
....*R. palustris.*
17'   Pileus rosy-red to scarlet......18

18   Gills white to cream-colored...................*R. sanguinea.*
18'   Gills straw-yellow ....*R. veternosa.*

19   Plant fragile, rosy red to scarlet......20
19'   Plant rigid; pileus dark red, with smooth margin.........
....*R. atropurpurea.*

20   Gills deep ochraceous................. ....*R. tenuiceps.*
20'   Gills white......21

21   Taste very acrid, pileus not rugulose..............*R. emetica.*
21'   Taste slowly acrid, pileus rugulose..............*R. rugulosa.*

22   Pileus pruinose, velvety.....................*R. mariae.*
22'   Pileus not markedly pruinose......23

23   Gills with crenulate edges; pileus viscid, shining, blood-red;
stem reddish ....*R. purpurina.*
23'   Gills not crenulate......24

24   Spores white; gills remaining white......25
24'   Gills becoming yellowish with colored spores......28

25   Pileus with silky sheen, red-purple to violet-purple,
flexible ....*R. sericeonitens.*
25'   Pileus without silky sheen....26

26   Small (1-6 cm. in diameter)......27
26' Large (6-14 cm. in diameter), tuberculate striate, red spotted
     with yellow; a northern species..............*R. subdepallens.*
27   Cuticle extending not quite to the edge of the pileus so that
     a narrow white margin is formed; gills staining brown.*R. vesca.*
27' Pileus pink beneath the separable cuticle, gills not staining
     brown ....*R. uncialis.*
28   Stem staining ashy or black where bruised.........*R. obscura.*
28' Stem not staining ashy......29
29   Plants small (2-5 cm. in diameter)......30
29' Plants medium to large (5-10 cm. broad or larger)......42
30   Pileus umbonate, plant growing on Sphagnum..*R. sphagnophila.*
30' Pileus not umbonate, plant growing in other habitats......
     ....*R. Chamaeleontina.*
31   Pileus of some shade of green......32
31' Pileus without green shades......34
32   Cuticle separable, not scaly....................*R. aeruginea.*
32' Cuticle not separable, cracked into scales or areas......33
33   Pileus viscid ....*R. crustosa.*
33' Pileus not viscid..............................*R. virescens.*
34   Pileus white, taste acrid........................*R. albidula.*
34' Pileus yellow or brown......35
35   Margin of pileus strongly tuberculate-striate......36
35' Margin of pileus not strongly striate......40
36   Odor aromatic......37
36' Odor not aromatic......38
37   Pileus large, 7-12 cm. broad....................*R. foetens.*
37' Pileus 2-7 cm. broad, stem-base with rusty-red stains.....
     ....*R. foetentula.*
38   Taste acrid; plant small to medium (3-6 cm., broad); pileus
     grayish-brown, substriate ....*R. sororia.*
38' Taste mild......39
39   Pileus small, sulphur-yellow becoming dingy-brown, not
     ashy beneath cuticle ....*R. pulverulenta.*
39' Pileus small to medium, ashy beneath cuticle..*R. pectinatoides.*
40   Taste acrid, pileus slightly striate................*R. sororia.*
40' Taste mild, pileus not striate......41
41   Stem ashy-stained where bruised..............*R. decolorans.*
41' Stem staining brownish where bruised............*R. squalida.*
42   Pileus viscid, becoming striate on margin, dark purple, red
     to olive; gills rounded toward stem..............*R. alutacea.*
42' Pileus dry, not striate, dark purple-red.........*R. ochrophylla.*

R. nigricans, Fr. Umber Russula (edible).   Plate 33, fig. 2.

Pileus 7-15 cm. broad; stem 2-6 cm. x 10-30 mm.; spores 8 x 10 μ.

Pileus convex then depressed, often wavy, white clouded with umber, soon smoky, glabrous, somewhat viscid when young, the flesh white changing to red then black, the taste mild or slowly and slightly acrid; gills narrowed behind, adnexed, thick, firm, subdistant, short and long gills alternating, white becoming grayish; stem stout, solid, hard, glabrous, cylindrical, red then black where bruised, colored as pileus.—In coniferous or deciduous forests on ground, common, July-Sept., Wisconsin, New York, Michigan, chiefly northern.

This species is parasitized by another gilled-mushroom, *Nyctalis asterophora.*

R. densifolia Secr. (edible).

Pileus 5-12 cm. broad; stem 5-6 cm. x 1-3 cm.; spores 7 x 9 μ.

Pileus dull white at first, soon clouded with smoky-brown, pruinose when dry, the flesh compact, grayish, changing to red then black, the taste slowly acrid; gills narrow, adnate to decurrent, crowded; stem rigid, spongy-solid, turning reddish then blackish where bruised; otherwise as preceding.—Gregarious or solitary on ground in oak forests; rare, southern Michigan to New England and southward.

R. magnifica Peck.

Pileus 10-25 cm. broad; stem 5-12 cm. x 1.5-4 cm.; spores 8 x 10 μ.

Pileus convex then depressed and funnel-form, glabrous, viscid, smooth, squamose in center, whitish becoming pale rusty-ochraceous, the flesh white, alkaline, strong and disagreeable in taste; gills adnate-decurrent, close, narrow, white and faintly pink, becoming reddish-brown where wounded, reddish-cinamon when dried; stem cylindrical or tapering downward, spongy-solid to cavernous.—Among fallen leaves in rich woods, July-Aug., not common, dunes of northern Indiana, New York, local.

This is the largest known *Russula.*

R. compacta Frost.   Compact Russula (edible).   Plate 22, fig. 29.

Pileus 6-12 cm. broad; stem 3-6 cm. x 1-3 cm.; spores 9 x 7 μ.

Differing from *R. magnifica* in its smaller size, the absence of odor in fresh plants; pileus dry, unpolished, becoming sordid pale pink or ochraceous, the flesh changing to red where bruised; stem brittle, becoming reddish-brown from handling.—On the ground in beech-maple forest, rare, Aug.-Sept., northern part of our area.

R. delica Fr. (edible)

Pileus 8-15 cm. broad; stem 2-5 cm. x 1.5-2 cm.; spores 10 x 11 μ.

Pileus convex-umbilicate later funnel-form, dull white, unpolished, occasionally stained brownish, dry, when young the margin involute, the flesh white not changing color when bruised; gills adnate-decurrent, narrowed toward stem, subdistant, white, the edges often greenish; stem short, solid, stout, white becoming dingy.—Gregarious on sandy soil in birch-conifer woods, July-Oct., locally common in the Great Lakes region.

R. brevipes Peck.   Short-stemmed Russula.

Gills crowded; pileus 4-6 cm. broad.—On hard soil.   Kauffman believed this to be an ecological variety of the preceding.

R. variata Bann. (edible).   Plate 21, fig. 12.

Pileus 5-12 cm. broad; stem 4-7 cm. x 1-3 cm.; spores 8 x 10 μ.

Pileus rather thick, firm convex to depressed, viscid, not striate on margin, purplish-rose when young becoming olive or umber of various shades when mature, rarely greenish, under lens reticulate-wrinkled, the cuticle separable at margin only, the flesh white, tinged gray beneath the cuticle, firm but with cheesy structure, the taste mild to slowly acrid; gills persistently white, adnate-decurrent, thin, close, narrow toward each end, dichotomously forked, intervenose; stem firm, white, solid, cylindrical; spore print white.—On ground in either deciduous or conifer forests, July-Sept., frequent, Wisconsin to New England and southward.

R. crustosa Peck. (edible).   Plate 22, fig. 19.

Pileus 5-12 cm. broad; stem 3-5 cm. x 1-2 cm.; spores 8 x 10 μ.

Pileus thick, firm, hemispherical then expanded or slightly depressed, cracked except in center into brownish or ochraceous crust-like areas, green beneath cuticle, viscid on disk, the flesh and spores white; gills white on cream-white, broad toward pileus-margin, narrowed and almost free toward stem, thick, not crowded, brittle; stem, stout, spongy, stuffed, white.—Scattered in open woods, July-Sept., common, Illinois to New England and Alabama.

R. virescens Fr. Green Russula (edible).   Plate 22, fig. 31.

Differing from the preceding in the dry, not viscid pileus, the central disk especially broken into pulverulent or floccose patches, gray-green, the margin rarely striate.—In open woods, common, July-Aug., Minnesota, Maine and Alabama.

Peck states that *R. crustosa* may be distinguished from *R. virescens* by its unbroken but warty center and usually striate margin.   Green specimens of *R. variata* have pure white gills which are much more forked than those of *R. virescens*.

R. aeruginea Lindb. (edible).   Plate 21, fig. 2.

R. graminicolor Quel.

Pileus 5-8 cm. broad; stem 3-5 cm. x 1-1.5 cm.; spores 6 x 9 μ.

Pileus firm, convex to slightly depressed, dingy-green, smoky-green, or dark green, viscid when moist, the margin often faintly striate when old, the dry surface having a slight luster of velvet; the flesh thick on disk, thin at margin, white, often ashy-green beneath the cuticle; gills almost free, not close, rather narrow, white to creamy, almost equal; spores cream-colored.—Scattered on ground in rich woods, July-Sept., rare, Indiana dunes and northward.

R. cyanoxantha, Fr., var. (edible).   Blue Russula.   Plate 21, fig. 9.

Pileus 4-8 cm. broad; stem 3x7 cm. x 1-2 cm.; spores 7 x 9 μ.

Pileus compact, thick, convex to slightly depressed, somewhat irregular, viscose, variable in color from lilac to dark bluish-purple, the disk whitish, yellowish or pink, the cuticle thin, adhering closely, separable and seldom striate on margin, the taste mild, the flesh white; gills rounded behind, broad, not close, stem white, cylindrical or wavy, spongy-stuffed.—Scattered, on ground in open woods, July-Aug., not infrequent, Illinois to New York, southward.

R. foetens Fr.   Fetid Russula (not edible).   Plate 22, fig. 23.

Pileus 7-12 cm. broad; stem 4-6 cm. x 1-2 cm.; spores 7 x 10 μ.

Pileus yellowish or dingy-ochraceous, fleshy, hard becoming fragile, convex to somewhat depressed, viscid when moist, the margin tuberculate-sulcate, the cuticle adnate, the flesh thin, rigid-fragile, dull white; gills white, exuding drops of water when young, dingy when bruised, adnexed, close, few-forked, intervenose; stem stout, stuffed to cavernous, whitish.—In mixed or deciduous forest on ground, not common, July-Sept., Minnesota to New England and southward.

R. foetentula Peck.   Plate 22, fig. 21.

Pileus 3-7 cm. broad; stem 3-5 cm. x 6-12 mm.; spores 8 x 6 μ.

Pileus hemispherical becoming plane or depressed, thin, viscid, dusky-ochraceous with russet tinge, the disk darker and granular, striate halfway or more to center in most plants, the taste slightly acrid, the slight odor of bitter almonds, the flesh whitish; gills nearly free, relatively narrow, close, broadest towards margin of pileus, thin; stem spongy-stuffed to cavernous, sordid-white, stained at the base with cinnabar-red stains; spores creamy white in mass.—Scattered on grounds in woods, July-Sept., frequent locally, Illinois to New England and southward.

R. pectinatoides Peck.   Plate 21, fig. 14.

Pileus 3-7 cm. broad; stem 2-5 cm. x 5-10 mm.; spores 6 x 8 μ.

Pileus fragile, thin, viscid, convex-plane to slightly depressed; the cuticle thin and separable, radiately sulcate from margin halfway to center of pileus, straw colored or brownish to umber-brown, the flesh white, soon fragile, ashy beneath the cuticle, unchanging; the taste mild or slowly and slightly acrid; gills narrow behind, broadest in front, white, thin, not crowded, equal, moderately broad; stem whitish, cylindrical, glabrous, stuffed then hollow; spores light cream-colored in mass.—In grassy places in open woods or lawns, July-Aug., common, Wisconsin to New England and southward.

R. pulverulenta Peck.   Plate 22, fig. 25.

Pileus 3-5 cm. broad; stem 3-5 cm. x 1-1.5 cm.; spores 6 x 8 μ.

Pileus thin, rigid then fragile, convex-expanded and finally centrally depressed, the margin soon sulcate-striate, the cuticle adnate, viscid, sulphur-yellow becoming ochraceous to dingy yellow-brown, dotted with numerous pale yellow flocculent granules, the flesh firm but soon soft, white; gills narrowly adnate, narrow, close, broader toward front, white unchanging, forked near stem, intervenose; stem rigid-fragile, at first with sulphur-yellow flocculent granules near base, spongy-stuffed to cavernous; spores, apiculate, white in mass. —In thin woods and lawns, not common, Illinois to New York and southward.

This species is often confused with *R. foetentula* and *R. pectinatoides*.

R. sororia Fr.   Plate 22, fig. 16.

Pileus 3-6 cm. broad; stem 2-5 cm. x 1-2 cm.; spores 7 x 8 μ.

Pileus thin especially toward margin, the margin becoming substriate, olivaceous-brown or gray-brown, the flesh white, unchanged, the taste acrid; gills adnate, subdistant, narrow, white, then discolored-dingy, the interspaces venose; stem white unchanging, spongy-stuffed, spores white.—Solitary in woods, rare, Indiana to Michigan to New York and southward.

R. vesca Fr.

Pileus 5-10 cm. broad; stem 2-5 cm. x 8-16 mm.; spores 8 x 10 μ.

Cuticle not extending to margin of pileus radiately or venosely wrinkled, pink or red-flesh-colored to blackish-green in center, the flesh thin toward margin, white, the taste mild; gills adnate, thin, close, staining rusty, forked or anastomosing at base, narrow especially toward stem, white at first; stem hard, white, solid, rivulose, often with rusty stains; spores white.—On the ground in woods, rare, Illinois to New York and southward.

R. subpunctata Kauffm.   Plate 22, fig. 30.

Pileus 2-5 cm. broad; stem 2-4 cm. x 4-10 mm.; spores 8 x 10 μ.

Pileus rigid, subviscid, pale dull red to rosy-red, white spotted where cuticle has disappeared, minutely rivulose, the margin smooth, acute, the flesh firm, compact, abruptly thick, thin toward margin, taste very acrid; gills adnate or subdecurrent, not broad, not crowded or subdistant, white then pale cream, pruinose, intervenose; stem slightly tapering down or cylindrical, spongy-stuffed to cavernous, white or rosy, unchanging, forming mycorrhiza on roots; spores rough-reticulate.—On ground in frondose woods, Ann Arbor, Michigan, July-Aug., infrequent.

R. atropurpurea Maire.   Plate 21, fig. 15.

Pileus 5-14 cm. broad; stem 4-8 cm. x 1-2.5 cm.; spores 8 x 10 μ.

Pileus firm, medium-thick, thinner toward margin, dark crimson becoming purplish, blackish-red, or olivaceous-purple pruinose in drying, the margin smooth or slightly striate, the flesh white, unchanging, dark red beneath cuticle, the taste acrid; gills white, dingy in age, adnexed, rather narrow, not close except near stem, intervenose, a few short ones intermingled; stem cylindrical, white, pruinose, punctate at apex with flocculent clusters of dots; spores, white.—On ground or decayed logs in rich woods of beech and pine, red oak, etc., common, Illinois to Michigan and southward.

R. Mariae Peck.   Mary Peck's Russula (edible).   Plate 21, fig. 8.

Pileus 3-9 cm. broad; stem 3-8 cm. x 8-15 mm.; spores 8 μ in diameter.

Pileus round-convex, plane then depressed, dry, or subviscid when wet, densely pruinose-velvety, the surface with an unmistakable sheen, dark-crimson or red-purple, the flesh thick, thinned toward margin, white, often reddish beneath cuticle, the taste mild to slightly acrid; gills adnate, narrow, close, forked at base, becoming cream-colored; stem cylindrical or tapering downward, pruinose, red, firm then fragile, spongy-stuffed.—Gregarious on the ground in oak woods, not infrequent, July-Aug., northern Illinois to New York and southward.

R. squalida Peck. (suspected).   Plate 21, fig. 4.

Pileus 7-11 cm. broad; stem 5-9 cm. x 1-2 cm., spores 7.5 x 10 μ.

Pileus convex then plane-depressed, firm soon subflaccid, the margin smooth becoming slightly tuberculate-striate, thick on disk, thin elsewhere, the cuticle continuous but not easily removed, subviscid in wet weather, usually dry and pruinose-velvety, red-purple, to yellowish-olive or tan, sometimes variegated, the flesh white, grayish-purple beneath cuticle, the taste mild, the odor unpleasant; gills inter-venose, cream, broad, subdistant, soon fragile, broadest in front; stem white, changing to ochraceous if bruised, brown when handled.— Solitary or gregarious in rich woods of hard maple, hemlock, red oak, etc. July-Sept., not common, Illinois to New England and southward.

R. alutacea Fr.   Plate 21, fig. 3.

Pileus 8-15 cm. broad; stem 7-10 cm. long, 3-4 cm. thick; spores 9 x 11 μ.

Pileus convex then depressed, dull in color, red-purple or sordid-red, the cuticle separable, subviscid when wet, soon dry and pruinose, subgranulose, the margin smooth or short-striate in age, the flesh thick, white, the taste mild; gills ochraceous from beginning, broad, broader in front, subdistant, rounded behind, intervenose, the edges often reddish; stem white often tinged red in places, firm, spongy-stuffed, solid.—Solitary in deciduous forests, not very common, Illinois to Michigan and southward.

R. obscura Romm.   Obscure Russula (edible).   Plate 22, fig. 17.

Resembling *R. alutacea,* but the stem white becoming ashy or smoky where bruised; pileus smaller (4-7 cm. in diameter), dark blood-red, darker toward center, gills broad, yellowish, narrowly adnate.—In low woods, southern Wisconsin to New York and southward.

R. ochrophylla Peck.   Plate 21, fig. 3.

Differing from *R. alutacea* in its dark purple-red non-viscid pileus, darker in center, the flesh red beneath adnate cuticle.—Oak woods, rare, Illinois to New York and southward.

R. emetica Fr.   Emetic Russula.   Plate 21, fig. 10.

Pileus 5-10 cm. broad; stem 4-7 cm. x 1-2 cm.; spores 8 x 10 μ.

Pileus convex, rosy to blood-red, fading to white, the margin tuberculate-striate, viscid and shining, the flesh white, red beneath cuticle, the taste very acrid; gills pure white, narrow, adnexed to free, broad, equal, venose; stem white often tinged red, spongy-stuffed, cylindrical.—On ground or much decayed wood, often on moss, usually on acid soil in woods, July-Oct., Minnesota to Maine and southward to Alabama.

R. rugulosa Peck.   Plate 21, fig. 5.

Differing from the preceding in its radiately rugulose pileus, slowly but very acrid in taste.—Aug.-Sept., Minnesota to New York.

R. fragilis Fr.   Fragile Russula.   Plate 21, fig. 7.

Pileus 2-5 cm. broad; stem 2-5 cm. x 5-10 mm.; spores 8 x 9 μ.

Pileus very thin, fragile, convex to plane-depressed, tuberculate-striate, the cuticle viscid, rosy to white, the flesh white beneath the cuticle, the taste quickly very acrid ; gills adnexed, ventricose, crowded, broad, thin; stem spongy to hollow, cylindrical, fragile.—Scattered on ground in moist woods, July-Aug., not common, Illinois to New York and southward.

R. fallax Cooke. Plate 21, fig. 6.

Pileus 3-7 cm. broad; stem 3-4 cm x 6-10 mm.; spores 7.5 μ in diameter.

Pileus soon plane, thin, fragile, pale rose, the disk olive or livid sometimes purplish, quite viscid, the margin striate, the cuticle minute-rugulose, the flesh white, promptly acrid in taste ; gills very narrowly adnexed, subdistant, narrow ; stem soon hollow, minutely and longitudinally wrinkled.—Common in sphagnum bogs, July-Oct., Illinois to New York and northward.

R. albidula Peck. Plate 22, fig. 26.

Pileus 3-5 cm. broad; stem 3-4 cm. x 8-12 mm.; spores 7-10 μ in diameter.

Pileus white, viscid, broadly convex, not striate, subfragile, the taste acrid; gills adnexed, white, crowded, not broad, equal in length ; stem white, cylindrical, spongy-stuffed, smooth.—Solitary on ground in oak woods, July-Aug., rare, Illinois to New York and southward.

R. sanguinea Fr. Plate 22, fig. 28.

Pileus 3-6 cm. broad; stem 4-6 cm. x 6-12 mm.

Pileus firm, subfragile, convex-plane or depressed, rosy-red, viscid, the margin tuberculate-striate, acute, thin, the flesh thin, white, red beneath cuticle, the taste slowly acrid; gills adnate, not close, equal, creamy; stem tapering downward, often eccentric, white or tinged rosy, spongy-stuffed to cavernous, fragile, glabrous, smooth; spore mass cream-colored.—Gregarious among grass in open woods, not common, Illinois to Michigan and southward.

Small forms of this are easily mistaken for *R. fragilis*.

R. veternosa Fr. Languishing Russula.   Plate 21, fig. 1.

Pileus 5-8 cm. broad; stem 5-7 cm. long x 1-1.5 cm. thick; spores 8-9 μ in diameter.

Pileus deep rose-red (as in *R. emetica*), the margin faintly striate, viscid when moist, convex to expanded, the cuticle separable, flesh white, red beneath cuticle, the taste acrid; gills white then straw-ochraceous, adnate, narrow, close, broader in front, venose; stem white, never red, cylindrical, spongy-stuffed, slender, fragile hollow. —Scattered in oak woods July-Aug., Illinois to New England and southward.

R. tenuiceps Kauffm. Plate 22, fig. 18.

Pileus 7-12 cm. broad; stem 5-9 cm. x 2-2.5 cm.; spores 6-8 μ in diameter.

Pileus on margin striate, deep rose-red or blood-red, sometimes blotched with orange spots or fading, minutely rugulose, the flesh white, red beneath cuticle, thin, fragile, the taste slowly but very acrid; gills becoming yellow-ochraceous.—Gregarious on ground in mixed forest, July-Aug., not common, Wisconsin to Michigan and southward.

R. paulstris Peck. Swamp Russula. Plate 22, fig. 27.

Pileus 4-8 cm. broad; stem 3-7 cm. x 6-12 mm.; spores 7-10 μ in diameter.

Pileus hemispheric to plane, fragile, viscid, the cuticle separable, the striae obscure, red-buff, purple-red on disk, the flesh white, thin, tinged red-buff beneath the cuticle, the taste slowly acrid; gills intervenose, narrow, becoming yellow, entire, subdistant, stem white or rosy, spongy-stuffed or hollow, fragile.—Scattered in low woods and swamps, Aug.-Sept., not common, Wisconsin to New York and southward.

R. purpurina Quel. and Schultz. (edible). Plate 21, fig. 13.

Pileus 3-7 cm. broad; stem 5-8 cm. x 8-12 mm.; spores 8-10 μ in diameter.

Pileus thin, fragile, red beneath cuticle, brilliant rosy-red to dark blood-red, the cuticle separable, expanded or plane or centrally slightly depressed, the margin striate only when fully expanded, the flesh white, the taste mild; gills white sometimes yellowish in age, adnexed, not distant, broadest in front, medium broad, equal, seldom or few-forked, the edges flocculose-crenulate; stem comparatively long, cylindrical usually flecked rosy-pink, spongy-stuffed, fragile.— In oak woods, often among mosses, Aug.-Sept., common locally, northern Illinois and the Indiana dunes to New York and northward.

R. uncialis Peck. Inch Russula (edible). Plate 22, fig. 24.

Pileus 2-5 cm. broad; stem 1-3 cm. x 4-10 mm.; spores 7-8 μ in diameter.

Like the preceding but smaller, the pileus thin, fragile, slightly viscid, pink or bright flesh-colored, the margin striate in age, the taste mild; gills pure white, unchanging, rather broad, stem white, spongy-stuffed.—On ground in oak woods, common locally, southern Wisconsin to New York and southward.

R. sericeo-nitens Kauffm.   Silky Russula (edible).   Plate 21, fig. 11.

Pileus 4-6 cm. broad; stem 3-7 cm. x 6-15 mm.; spores 6 x 8 μ.

Pileus thin especially toward margin, very regular, convex then plano-depressed, dark violet-purple or red-tinted-purple, the cuticle slightly viscid and separable, not striate, the surface with silky sheen, the taste mild; gills white, intervenose, narrowed behind, medium-broad, equal, few-forked at ‘base; stem white, cylindrical but thickened near apex, spongy-stuffed.—In maple, hemlock and birch woods of northern Michigan and near bog edges in northern Illinois.

R. chamaeleontina Fr. The Chameleon (edible). Plate 22, fig. 22.

Pileus 2-5 cm. broad; stem 2-5 cm. x 4-6 mm.

Pileus thin, plane-depressed, viscid, the cuticle separable, the margin finally striate, red, purple-red or light-red fading to yellowish on the disk, the flesh white; gills almost free, close, rather broad, thin, venose, ochraceous; stem slender, white, spongy-stuffed, somewhat clavate or centrally enlarged.—Scattered on ground in conifer or deciduous woods, not common, July-Aug., Illinois to New York and northward.

R. integra Fr.

Larger (5-10 cm. high), the pileus tuberculate-striate thin on margin; gills white then cream-colored.—Occasional, Wisconsin to New England and southward.

R. sphagnophila Kauffm.   Plate 22, fig. 20.

Pileus 2-4.5 cm. broad; stem 4-5 cm. x 7-12 mm.; spores 6 x 7 μ.

Pileus convex-umbonate, very fragile, the disk purplish-red or rosy red, the margin pale olive-brown with viscid cuticle, glabrous, slightly striate, reddish beneath the cuticle; gills white then pale ochraceous, adnate-decurrent, narrow, close, narrowed toward ends, few-forked; stem rosy, irregularly swollen, spongy-stuffed then cavernous, very fragile, rivulose.—Scattered on sphagnum in swamps, Aug.-Sept., rare, Illinois to Michigan and northward.

LACTARIUS Fr.

Carpophore composed of an orbicular, convex or depressed pileus on a short, central stipe; pileus brittle, fleshy, exuding where broken a milky or colored juice; context of round or oval cells with few hyphae; stipe short, cylindrical, brittle; gills fragile, emarginate, adnate or decurrent; spores white or ochre, globose, echinulate.—Terrestrial, most common during August.

1   Milk white, unchanging in color......2
1'   Milk at first white, changing color when exposed to the air....23
1"   Milk brightly colored when fresh......32
2   Pileus viscid at least when moist......3
2'   'Pileus not viscid......9
3   Pileus distinctly zonate......4
3'   Pileus not zonate or obscurely so......5
4   Margin of pileus distinctly hairy; zones of pileus flesh-
     colored ....*L. torminosus.*
4'   Margin of pileus not hairy, pileus copper-orange....*L. insulsus.*
5   Pileus large, usually much more than 8 cm. in diameter......6
5'   Pileus usually smaller than 6 cm. in diameter......7
6   Pileus pale yellow, the gills broad.................*L. affinis.*
6'   Pileus lilac-smoky ....*L. trivialis.*
7   Pileus drab-lilac-gray, tinged with flesh-color.........*L. vietus.*
7'   Pileus putty-colored ....*L. mucidus.*
7"   Pileus reddish......8
8   Pileus papillate, 1-2 cm. broad...................*L. oculatus.*
8'   Pileus umbilicate, 5-7 cm. broad.................*L. hysginus.*
9   Pileus tomentose or with velvety bloom......10
9'   Pileus glabrous......16
10   Pileus white......11
10' Pileus of another color......12
11   Pileus velvety-tomentose on both disk and margin..*L. vellereus.*
11' Pileus densely wooly on margin only.............*L. deceptivus.*
12   Pileus reddish-brown to pale tawny......13
12' Pileus smoky to gray-brown......14
13   Gills close, pileus roughened-wrinkled, reddish-brown......
     ....*L. corrugis.*
13' Gills distant, pileus smooth and tawny.......*L. hygrophoroides.*
13" Plant growing in swamps and bogs...............*L. helvus.*
14   Pileus 1-3 cm. broad, gray.......................*L. griseus.*
14' Pileus 2-7 cm. broad, flesh reddish where bruised......15
15   Pileus sooty-brown with velvet sheen............*L. lignyotus.*
15' Pileus gray-brown ....*L. fuliginosus.*
16   Pileus white; gills crowded, much forked; plant large.....
     ....*L. piperatus.*
16' Pileus of some shade of gray or brown......17
16" Pileus of some shade of red or yellow......18
17   Pileus 1-3 cm. broad, pale lilac-umber; gills becoming dingy
     greenish-brown ....*L. parvus.*
17' Pileus 4-6 cm. broad, zoned, gray to brown-gray; gills yel-
     lowish ....*L. pyrogalus.*

18   Gills distant, pileus pale brownish-orange....*L. hygrophoroides.*
18' Gills moderately close......19
19   Pileus bay-red or brown-red......20
19' Pileus fulvous, orange, or pale tan......21
20   Taste acrid, pileus bay-red........................*L. rufus.*
20' Taste mild, odor aromatic..................*L. camphoratus.*
21   Taste acrid, pileus pale yellowish..................*L. affinis.*
21' Taste not acrid......22
22   Pileus 5-12 cm. broad, brownish-orange ; stem solid..*L. volemus.*
22' Pileus 2-5 cm. broad, light brown-red to tan.......*L. subdulcis.*
23   Milk becoming violet or lilac on bruised flesh at least near
       gills ....*L. uvidus.*
23' Milk becoming pink to red on bruised flesh, pileus with velvet
       sheen......25
23'' Milk becoming yellow on bruised flesh......26
23''' Milk becoming green, gray or brown on bruised flesh......24
24   Milk becoming greenish on bruised flesh......30
24' Milk staining gills gray where bruised......31
24'' Milk becoming brown on bruised flesh.............*L. luteolus.*
25   Pileus chocolate-sooty-brown, usually roughened....*L. lignyotus.*
25' Pileus gray-brown to tan, usually smooth.......*L. fuliginosus.*
26   Pileus very wooly-hairy, buff ....*L. cilicioides.*
26' Pileus hairy on margin only, stem spotted......*L. scrobiculatus.*
26'' Pileus margin smooth or nearly so......27
27   Pileus zonate especially toward margin......28
27' Pileus not zonate......29
28   Pileus orange-yellow, very viscid when moist.......*L. croceus.*
28' Pileus spotted, zoned, dull orange ; milk acrid...*L. chrysorheus.*
28' Pileus faintly zoned, dull orange ; milk slowly acrid......
      ....*L. theiogalus.*
28''' Pileus viscid, dingy-greenish-gray..............*L. blennius.*
29   Odor disagreeable, pileus 3-10 cm. in diameter...*L. theiogalus.*
29' Odor absent, pileus very viscid, greenish-gray......*L. blennius.*
29'' Odor slight, pileus substriate on margin, 2-5 cm. in diameter
      ....*L. isabellinus.*
29''' Odor slight ; pileus reddish-brown, 2-6 cm. in diameter....
      ....*L. colorascens.*
30   Pileus dark olive-green, rigid, zonate............*L. atroviridis.*
30' Pileus smoky-gray with violet tinge, not zonate.....*L. trivialis.*
       var. *viridilactis.*
31   Pileus olive-brown, umber, rigid, 6-12 cm. in diameter.*L. turpis.*
31' Pileus lilac-gray or drab, 3-6 cm. in diameter........*L. vietus.*

32 Plants indigo-blue, milk indigo.....................*L. indigo.*
32' Young gills and milk dark red...............*L. subpurpureus.*
32" Young gills and milk orange...................*L. deliciosus.*

L. torminosus Fr. Griping Lactarius (poisonous). Plate 23, fig. 1.

Pileus 4-10 cm. broad; stem 3-7 cm. x 1-3 cm.; spores 9 x 7 μ.

Pileus thick, rather soft, convex then depressed, buff tinged with rose color, with spotted zones, involute at first and persistently fringed with hairs on margin, the disk glabrous, the flesh white, tinged with flesh color; gills narrow-decurrent, close, thin, some forked at base, whitish or creamy becoming reddish-yellow; stem smooth, stuffed to hollow, flesh-colored, sometimes spotted; milk very acrid, white, unchanging.—In mixed forests; July-Sept., not uncommon, Minnesota, Maine, Alabama, Nebraska.

This species is known by its fringed margin, large size and colored zones. It is to be separated from *L. deliciosus* with naked margin and orange milk.

L. cilicioides Fr. Wooly Lactarius (poisonous). Plate 23, fig. 6.

Differing from *L. torminosus* in its pileus covered with long, matted hairs, not zonate, viscid when moist, white to reddish-buff; its gills white or tinged yellow; its stem pruinose, not spotted, whitish, its milk white, slowly changing to pale yellow, acrid.—In pine woods and on moist sand flats, Sept.-Oct., Minnesota to New York and southward.

L. vellerius Fr. Velvety Lactarius (suspected). Plate 23, fig. 2.

Pileus 6-12 cm. broad; stem 1.5 cm. x 1-3 cm.; spores 8 μ in diameter.

Differing from *L. torminosus* in its pileus dry, white, entirely covered with minute tomentum, velvety to the touch; gills subdistant, moderately broad, white to cream, staining brown; its stem short, stout, pubescent, white, solid; its spores nearly smooth, its milk acrid.—Gregarious in frondose or mixed forests, locally abundant, Minnesota, Maine, Alabama.

L. deceptivus Peck. Deceptive Lactarius (edible). Plate 23, fig. 4.

Differing from *L. torminosus* in its pileus white or whitish, often with dingy rusty stains, the margin densely cottony-tomentose, involute then spreading, elevated and fibrillose; gills rather broad, sub-distant, some forked, white or cream; stem solid, pubescent, white; spores 9 x 12 μ, echinulate; milk white, unchanging, acrid.—Gregarious on ground, July-Sept., abundant northward, usually in conifer forests, Michigan, Maine, Alabama.

L. scrobiculatus Fr. (poisonous).   Plate 23, fig. 3.

Differing from *L. torminosus* in its pileus straw-yellow becoming subferruginous, the surface cracked into areas when dry, the margin tomentose-hairy or densely fringed; gills sometimes anastomose on stem, white to yellowish, darker where wounded; stem straw-colored, pitted with brightly colored spots.—Gregarious on moss at margins of swamps, mostly near conifers, not common, Illinois to New York and Alabama.

L. turpis Fr. Base Lactarius (edible).   Plate 25, fig. 3.

Pileus 6-12 cm. broad; stem 3-4 cm. x 2 cm.; spores 7 μ.

Pileus rigid, olive-brown, darker on disk, not zoned, slightly floccose at first and at length glabrous, the fibers glutinous when moist, the margin involute and yellowish-villous at first, the flesh thick, white, firm; gills adnate to decurrent; narrow, cream-colored, stained gray to black where bruised; stem stout, firm, colored like pileus, often spotted with darker colors, stuffed; milk acrid, white, unchanging or making gray stains on gills.—A northern species in woods of hemlock, balsam, maple, and poplar, rare, Michigan to Maine and in the mountains to North Carolina.

L. atroviridis Peck. Dark Green Lactarius (edibility not tested). Plate 25, fig. 1.

Pileus 7-15 cm. broad; stem 2-6 cm. x 1-3 cm.; spores 8 μ in diameter.

Pileus similar to the preceding but dry, scabrous-hairy, dark olive-green to almost black, sometimes zoned toward margin, gills stained with dark-green where bruised, intervenose; stem dark-greenish; milk causing green stains on gills.—On the ground in frondose woods, not common, Illinois to Connecticut and Virginia.

L. blennius Fr. Slimy Lactarius.

Pileus 7-12 cm. broad; stem 2-5 cm. x 2-4 cm.; spores 8 μ in diameter.

Differing from the preceding in the pileus, glutinous, dingy-gray, somewhat zonate, with drop-like markings, the milk staining gills ochraceous; stem viscid.—Woods, Indiana, Ohio and New York to Tennessee.

L. piperatus Fr. Peppery Lactarius (edible).   Plate 24, fig. 21.
Pileus 4-15 cm. broad; stem 2-7 cm. x 1-3 cm.; spores 6-7.5 μ in diameter.

Pileus white, convex then expanded-depressed and infundibuliform, azonate, the flesh white, thick, firm; gills subdecurrent, narrowed toward stem, crowded, narrow, dichotomously forked, white to cream, stem cylindrical or tapering downward, firm, solid, white; spores nearly globose, almost smooth.—Woods, July-Sept., Minnesota, Maine, Alabama.

The very acrid taste disappears when these plants are cooked, but a somewhat bitter taste remains.

L. pergamenus Fr.

Like *L. piperatus,* but with a longer stem, a less deeply depressed pileus, and adnate and narrower gills.—On the ground, in woods, northern Illinois.

L. controversus Fr.

Plants very large, resembling those of *L. piperatus;* pileus and gills in age bearing flesh-colored spots.—On the ground in low woods, northern Illinois and southern Michigan.

L. pyrogalus Fr. (poisonous)

Pileus 4-6 cm. broad; stem 3-6 cm. x 6-10 mm.; spores 6-8 μ in diameter.

Pileus gray to brown-gray, the margin zoned, the flesh white, compact, thick; gills adnate to decurrent, distant, thin, firm, medium-broad, yellowish; stem cylindrical or tapering downward, becoming hollow, glabrous, paler than the pileus, white-mycelioid at base; spores echinulate; cystidia 70 x 9 μ, abundant; milk very acrid, remaining as coagulated drops on gills.—On ground in woods, July-Aug., not common, Minnesota to New York and southward.

L. theiogalus Fr.

Pileus 3-10 cm. broad; stem 4-7 cm. x 7-15 mm.; spores 7 x 9 μ.

Pileus obtuse or depressed, dry or subviscid, pale tawny to ochre with flesh tint, obscurely zoned, the flesh medium-thick, firm, white then yellow, the milk white, changing to sulphur-yellow, slowly acrid; gills adnate-decurrent, close, narrow, some forked, pale yellow to light flesh-colored, reddish-brown where bruised, the odor strong, pungent; stem strigose at base.—July-Oct., on ground in conifer woods, Minnesota, Maine and Alabama.

An ecological form occurs on Sphagnum in tamarack swamps. *L. chrysorheus* Fr. differs mainly in the lack of odor and in the presence of more distinct zones.

L. insulsus Fr. (suspected). Plate 23, fig. 5.

Pileus 5-9 cm. broad; stem 3-6 cm. x 1-1.5 cm.; spores 8 μ in diameter.

Pileus copper-orange, zoned, viscid, convex to depressed, at first involute then elevated, the margin naked, the flesh thick, white, not very firm; gills adnate to decurrent, narrow, thin, not crowded, some forked at bases, white to pale; stem nearly cylindrical, paler than pileus; spores deeply echinulate; milk pale yellow, very acrid.— Gregarious or occasionally caespitose on ground in deciduous woods, July-Oct., common, Minnesota to Maine and Alabama.

L. affinis Peck. (edibility unknown). Plate 23, fig. 10.

Pileus 7-15 cm. broad; stem 5-10 cm. x 1-2 cm.; spores 9 x 11 μ.

Pileus obtuse then depressed, ochraceous, not zoned, viscid, the surface sometimes becoming areolate, the flesh white, thick; gills adnate-decurrent, subdistant, broad, forked at bases; cream-yellow; stem cylindrical, glabrous, stuffed to hollow, pale ochre, sometimes spotted; milk acrid, white, unchanging.—On ground in frondose or mixed woods, rare, July-Sept., Wisconsin, New York, southward in mountains.

L. trivialis Fr. Worthless Lactarius (suspected). Plate 23, fig. 9.

Pileus 5-12 cm. broad; stem 4-10 cm. x 1-2 cm.; spores 8 x 10 μ.

Pileus convex, plane, and depressed, viscid, not zoned, variable in color, gray or smoky with violet, lilac, or brown tints, the margin thin, pruinose, the flesh medium-thick, fragile, pale; gills adnate-decurrent, close, thin, medium in width, some forked, cream becoming greenish, dingy-stained in age; stem cylindrical, firm, becoming hollow, paler than pileus, spores yellowish, echinulate; milk white or cream, unchanging, acrid.—On ground in deciduous and conifer woods, common, July-Oct., Michigan to Vermont, to North Carolina and Tennessee.

L. hysginus Fr. (edible). Plate 23, fig. 7.

Pileus 5-7 cm. broad; stem 3-5 cm. x 6-15 mm.; spores 9-10 μ in diameter.

Pileus tan, reddish-tan or reddish-brown, zoned or not zoned convex-plane to slightly depressed, viscid, the margin thin and involute, the flesh medium in thickness; gills adnate-decurrent, close, medium in width, white to cream; stem cylindrical, glabrous, becoming hollow, paler than pileus; milk acrid, white.—On ground in mixed woods, not common, July, Illinois to Vermont and southward in mountains to Virginia.

L. uvidus Fr. Grape-colored Lactarius (poisonous).

Pileus convex, plane to slightly depressed, firm, often subumbonate, viscid, usually zoneless, ashy-lilac, gray-purple, or reddish-gray, the margin pruinose, thin, spreading, the flesh white becoming lilac when cut, soft, moist; gills adnate-decurrent, close, thin, narrow, cream-colored becoming violet if bruised; stem glabrous, viscid, becoming hollow, white to dingy-yellow; milk white, changing quickly to lilac in contact with flesh, bitter-acrid.—Gregarious on moss in swamps, Aug.-Sept., Illinois to New York and northward.

L. subpurpureus Peck. Purple-spotted Lactarius (edible). Plate 25, fig. 6.

Pileus 5-8 cm. broad; stem 3-8 cm. x 6-10 mm.; spores 9 x 7 μ.

Pileus convex, plane then somewhat depressed, slightly viscid when moist, pink-zonate, purplish-gray becoming green-stained where wounded, the flesh becoming red when broken near gills, the taste slightly acrid when fresh; gills adnate to decurrent, purplish-red becoming tinged dull yellow or greenish with age, close, medium-broad, narrowed at each end; stem cylindrical, hollow, glabrous, dark red, spotted more deeply red, hairy at base; milk dark red.—Among mosses and fallen leaves in swamps, July-Oct., rare, Minnesota to Vermont and North Carolina.

L. deliciosus Fr. Delicious Lactarius (edible). Plate 25, fig. 7.

Pileus 5-12 cm. broad; stem 4-7 cm. x 1-2 cm.; spores 9 x 7 μ.

Pileus convex then depressed-infundibuliform, viscid when moist, orange fading to gray when old, zoned with brighter orange or red, the flesh white soon stained orange or greenish near gills; gills adnate-decurrent, close, narrow, intervenose, forked, bright orange becoming greenish where bruised; stem cylindrical becoming hollow, orange-yellow to greenish variegated; milk orange, mild.—Moist mossy woods, bogs and swamps, July-Sept., local, Minnesota to Maine and Alabama.

L. indigo Schw. Indigo Lactarius (edible). Plate 25, fig. 8.

Pileus 4-12 cm. broad; stem 2-5 cm. x 1-3 cm.; spores 7 μ in diameter.

Entire plant deep indigo-blue fading when dry to a gray lustre; pileus zonate, glabrous; milk dark indigo-blue, mild.—On ground in forests of oak, maple or pine, Aug.-Sept., Minnesota to Maine and Alabama, rare northward, common locally.

L. lignyotus Fr. (poisonous). Plate 25, fig. 4.

Pileus 3-8 cm. broad; stem 4-10 cm. x 5-12 mm.; spores 8 μ in diameter.

Pileus almost plane, umbonate, dry, pruinose-velvety, uneven-rugu-lose, chocolate to dark smoky, the margin with wavy elevations in age, the flesh white and slowly turning pink where wounded, medium-thick; gills adnate-decurrent, not close, broad, pure-white becoming ochre or pink where bruised; stem cylindrical, velvety, sooty-stuffed; milk white slowly changing to pink.—On ground in rich frondose or conifer woods, not common, Minnesota to Maine and North Carolina.

This species differs from L. *fuliginosus* Fr. in its darker color, its longer stem, and its rougher pileus.

L. fuliginosus Fr. Smoky Lactarius (suspected). Plate 25, fig. 5.

Pileus 2-6 cm. broad; stem 2-6 cm. x 3-10 mm.; spores 8 μ in diameter.

Differing from the preceding in the smooth pileus, which is tawny or gray-brown with a smoky tinge.—Gregarious on ground in woods of maple, oak, etc., Illinois to New York and North Carolina.

L. helvus Fr. Tawny Lactarius. Plate 24, fig. 16.

Pileus 4-12 cm. broad; stem 5-15 cm. x 5-15 mm.; spores 7-9 μ in diameter.

Pileus convex-plane then depressed, with or without a broad umbo, dry, floccose-scaly, light tawny, the margin at first involute, the flesh watery; gills slightly decurrent, thick, narrow, not close, broadest behind, white then flesh-colored, pruinose; stem greatly elongated, rigid-fragile, the base white-mycelioid, becoming cavernous, milk scarce, watery, mild or slightly acrid in taste; odor somewhat fragrant like that of L. *camphoratus*.—Frequent in sphagnous bogs, mossy borders of lakes, etc., July-Sept., Minnesota to Maine to Ohio and northern Illinois.

L. rufus Fr. Red Lactarius (poisonous). Plate 24, fig. 13.

Differing from the preceding in the pileus umbonate, bay red, floc-culose-silky, not fading, the flesh soft when wet, medium-thin; gills adnate-decurrent, close, narrow, ochre then rufous; stem reddish or paler, often strigose-hairy at base; odor none.—On ground in hem-lock or pine woods, Wisconsin to Vermont and southward in mountains.

L. Boughtoni Peck.

Pileus without umbo, otherwise as above.—In swamps, Wisconsin to Vermont and southward.

L. griseus Peck. Gray Lactarius. Plate 24, fig. 20.

Pileus 1-4 cm. broad; stem 1-6 cm. x 2-5 mm.; spores 8 x 6 μ.

Pileus convex, later funnelform with a small sharp umbo, not zonate, tomentose, brownish-gray to gray or smoky-shaded, the flesh thin, white; gills adnate-decurrent, not close, relatively broad, pruinose, white to cream; stem gray, glabrous, becoming hollow; milk white, unchanging, slowly acrid.—On ground or much decayed wood of conifers, Wisconsin, New York and southward.

L. camphoratus Fr. Aromatic Lactarius (edible). Plate 24, fig. 17.

Pileus 1-4 cm. broad; stem 1-6 cm. x 3-8 mm.; spores 7 μ in diameter.

Pileus convex to depressed, often umbonate, light orange-brown to dark reddish-brown, dry, glabrous, uneven, opaque, thin, the flesh reddish-brown, with the aromatic odor of slippery elm; gills narrow, dull yellow to reddish-brown; stem often compressed or fluted; milk white, unchanging, mild.—On ground in swamps or borders of swamps, common, July-Aug., Minnesota to Maine and southward.

L. subdulcis Fr. Sweet Lactarius (edible). Plate 24, fig. 18.

Pileus 2-4 cm. broad; stem 4-6 cm. x 2-8 mm.; spores 7-8 μ in diameter.

Pileus convex to depressed, sharp-umbonate, azonate, dry, glabrous, brown-red to clay-red, the flesh white or tinged fulvous; gills sometimes forked, narrow, white to flesh-colored, stem becoming hollow, smooth or wrinkled, flesh-brown; milk white or watery, unchanging, mild.—In low woods, sand swales, etc., June-Oct., Minnesota to Maine and Tennessee.

L. oculatus (Peck). Burl. Plate 24, fig. 11.

Pileus 1-2 cm. broad; stem 2-4 cm. x 2-5 mm.; spores 7-8 μ in diameter.

Pileus abruptly papillate-umbonate, viscid when moist ,fulvous, fading to pink-fulvous; gills broad.—In moist mossy woods or bogs, July-Oct., not common, Minnesota, to Maine and Ohio.

Peck considered this a small variety of the preceding.

L. volemus Fr. (edible). Plate 24, fig. 14.

Pileus 5-12 cm. broad; stem 3-10 cm. x 1-2 cm.; spores 8 μ in diameter.

Pileus firm, convex to depressed, glabrous, dry, orange-fulvous to brownish-orange, involute at first, the flesh rigid, white to brown; gills close, rather broad, yellowish, brown where bruised, some forked; stem solid, usually paler than pileus; milk white, unchanging, mild, abundant; odor slight.—On ground in oak woods, etc., Minnesota to Maine and Tennessee.

L. corrugis Peck.   Plate 24, fig. 15.

Differing from the preceding in the rugose or corrugated pileus and brown spicules on sides of gills. Both are found from July-Sept.

L. hygrophoroides Berk. and Curt.   edible).   Plate 24, fig. 19

Pileus 3-7 cm. broad; stem 2-4 cm. x 7-15 mm.; spores 9-11 μ in diameter.

Pileus convex to expanded then somewhat depressed, minutely pubescent, dry, tawny-orange to orange-brown, the margin at first involute, the flesh fragile, white, thick; gills distant, narrow, often intervenose, white or cream-yellow; stem short, cylindrical or tapering downward.—On ground in open woods, July-Aug., not common, Wisconsin to Maine and Mississippi.

L. luteolus Peck.

Differing from the preceding in the close gills; the thin white flesh which becomes brown where bruised; the more slender stem, 3-7 mm. thick; the slightly smaller size; the copious milk, mild, changing to brown on the flesh.

Even partly dried specimens exude milk when broken.

L. vietus Fr. (suspected).   Plate 23, fig. 8.

Pileus 3-6 cm. broad; stem 3-8 cm. x 5-10 mm.; spores 6-8 μ in diameter.

Pileus convex then depressed, viscid when moist, azonate, minutely silky-tomentose, drab-lilac-gray to brown-lilac-gray, the margin involute then elevated, the flesh whitish, not thick; gills close, narrow, pruinose, cream-colored, stained gray where bruised; stem cylindrical or tapering upward, becoming hollow, wrinkled; milk white unchanging, slowly acrid in taste.—Beech-maple forest, rare, August, Michigan to New York.

L. mucidus Burl.

Pileus 1-3 cm. broad; stem 2-6 cm. x 6-12 mm.

Similiar to the preceding but the pileus more viscid, putty-colored with sepia center.—In hemlock woods, July-Sept., not common, Wisconsin to New York and Maryland.

L. croceus Burl. (suspected).   Plate 25, fig. 2.

Pileus 5-10 cm. broad; stem 3-6 cm. x 0.5-2 cm.; spores 6-8 μ in diameter.

Pileus soon infundibuliform, thin, viscid, micaceous when dry, saffron-yellow, glabrous, at first involute, the margin downy, the flesh white, staining clay-yellow when cut; milk white, slowly changing to yellow, bitter; gills medium-close, moderately broad, pale yellow to flesh-tinged, changing to cadmium-yellow where bruised; spores echinulate, pale-yellow.—On ground in rich woods, local, not common, Aug.-Sept., Wisconsin to Vermont to North Carolina.

L. isabellinus Burl.

Pileus 2-5 cm. broad; stem 2-4 cm. x 4-6 mm.; spores 8 x 7 μ.

Pileus convex-expanded or slightly depressed, subumbonate, azonate, wrinkled on disk, red-fulvous where moist, paler on margin, paler when dry, the margin short-striatulate, the flesh white, staining yellowish; milk white or watery, at length sulphur-yellow on flesh, abundant, slowly acrid or astringent in taste; gills close, thin, narrow, forking near bases; pale yellow.—On ground among conifers and under tamaracks in bogs, northern Illinois to Vermont and northward.

L. colorascens Peck.

Like *L. camphoratus,* but the milk turning sulphur-yellow.—Under conifers, Aug.-Sept., rare, Indiana Dunes to Michigan and New York.

L. parvus Peck.

Pileus 1-3 cm. broad; stem 2-3 cm. x 3-5 mm.; spores 7 μ in diameter.

Pileus broadly convex to slightly depressed, more or less papillate, azonate, pale lilac-umber, fading, the margin at first involute; gills close, narrow, dingy or ochraceous, becoming dingy-greenish then dingy-brown where bruised; stem cylindrical, glabrous, becoming hollow, often compressed, colored like pileus; milk white, unchanging or but slightly changed on flesh, acrid, without odor.—On ground or much decayed wood in swampy places, Aug.-Sept., Wisconsin, New York and northward.

CANTHARELLUS Fr. Plate 33.

Pileus narrow, obconical to broad funnel-form or turbinate; gill-edge very thick or gills ridge-form; stem central, confluent with pileus; spores white to ochraceous.

Plants are similar in form and habit to *Craterellus* of the Thelephoraceae and to the decurrent-gilled genera, *Clitocybe* and *Hygrophorus.*

1 Pileus brownish-red ....*C. cinnabarinus.*
1' Pileus orange to yellow......2
1" Pileus of some other color, ashy, brownish-gray, buff, etc.......4
2 Gills ridge-form......3
2' Gills knife-blade-form, crowded................*C. aurantiacus.*

3   Plants large (6-15 cm. high) gills much anastomosing......
    ....*C. floccosus.*
3'   Plants smaller, gills not anastomosing.............*C. cibarius.*
4   Gills knife-blade-form, pileus brownish-gray, plants growing
     in moss ....*C. umbonatus.*
4'   Gills ridge-form......5
5   Pileus narrowly obconic, gills flesh-colored, stem solid.....
     ....*C. clavatus.*
5'   Pileus spreading, usually perforated into the hollow of the
     stem .... *C. infundibuliformis.*

C. clavatus Fr.   Plate 33, fig. 11.

Plant 4-10 cm. high ; pileus 5-8 cm. broad ; stem 1-2 cm. x 8-15 mm. ;
spores 10-13 x 4-5 μ.

Pileus narrowly obconic, turbinate, truncate, depressed, ochraceous-buff, glabrous, narrowed downward into stem, the margin thin,
erect ; gills near margin, wrinkled downward, pruinose with spores,
light vinaceous-drab, drying drab, spores pale ochraceous in mass.—
Solitary or caespitose on ground in conifer woods, rare, July-Aug.,
New England to Minnesota and southward.

This has been considered as a species of either *Craterellus* or *Cantharellus*. The presence of gills like those of other species of *Cantharellus* seems to justify its placement here.

C. floccosus Schw.   Floccose Cantharellus (edible).   Plate 33,
fig. 9.

Plant 6-15 cm. high ; pileus 5-10 cm. broad ; stem 1-2 cm. x 1-3 cm. ;
spores 13 x 7 μ.

Pileus at length deeply funnel-shaped, thick, floccose to scaly, yellow becoming rufescent-orange, the flesh white ; gills deep-decurrent,
ridge-form, anastomosing and dichotomously forked throughout,
orange-yellow ; stem short, solid, glabrous, pale-ochraceous, white at
the base, firm ; spores smooth, ochraceous in mass.—On ground in
conifer woods, especially hemlock, rare, July-Aug., probably from
Minnesota to New England and southward in mountains.

C. cibarius Fr.   Chantarelle (edible).   Plate 33, fig. 1.

Pileus 3-7 cm. broad ; stem 3-6 cm. x 6-12 mm. ; spores 8 x 4 μ.

Pileus convex, soon expanded and depressed, compact, thick, the
margin becoming elevated, thick, at first involute, chrome-yellow to
egg-yellow, glabrous, non-striate, often turbinate, the flesh white ;
gills long-decurrent, thick, dichotomously forked, some anastomosing,

distant, chrome-yellow, blunt at edges; stem orange, solid, glabrous; spores smooth, faintly ochraceous.—Gregarious on ground in rich woods, July-Sept., common, Minnesota to Maine and southward.

C. cinnabarinus Schw.   Cinnabar Cantharellus (edible).   Plate 33, fig. 4.

Pileus convex-obtuse or becoming depressed, not thick but firm, irregular, glabrous, brown-red or cinnabar, fading, the flesh tinged reddish; gills long-decurrent, distant, forked dichotomously, narrow, ridge-form, intervenose, colored like pileus; stem cylindrical, solid to cavernous, tough, glabrous, smooth, colored like pileus; spores smooth, white.—Gregarious in open or rich woods, attaining larger size in more open woods, locally frequent, July-Oct., Indiana Dunes State Park, Michigan, New England, and southward.

C. infundibuliformis Fr. (edible).   Plate 33, fig. 7.

Pileus 2-5 cm. broad; stem 4-10 cm. x 3-7 mm.; spores globose, 10 x 8 μ.

Pileus umbilicate, plano-depressed usually perforated into the hollow of the stem, the margin irregularly lobed, thin, pliant, ashy-yellow, watery-brown; gills decurrent, ridge-form, irregularly forked, distant, pruinose, ashy with a bluish cast; stem slender, cylindrical, compressed, yellow, hollow; spores smooth, pale yellow.—Common in bogs, sometimes in conifer forests, Aug.-Oct., Fox Lake, Volo, Illinois to New York and northward

C. umbonatus Fr. (edible).   Plate 33, fig. 5.

Pileus 2-4 cm. broad; stem 3-9 cm. x 4-7 mm.; spores 10 x 4 μ.

Pileus convex to plane or depressed, with or without a slight umbo, top-shaped, brownish-gray to smoky, pruinose to flocculose, dry, pliant, the margin smooth or wavy, the flesh thin, white becoming reddish with age; gills decurrent, narrow, thick, dichotomously forked, not ridge-form, close, white, soon stained yellowish or reddish; stem cylindrical, elastic, pale gray, smoky upward, silky, stuffed; spores smooth, white.—Gregarious, attached to moss at borders of peat bogs, usually with *Polytrichum*, July-Oct., common in the Great Lakes region.

C. aurantiacus Fr.   Golden Cantharellus (edible).   Plate 33, fig. 6.

Pileus 2-7 cm. broad; stem 3-5 cm. x 4-10 mm.; spores 6 x 3-4 μ.

Pileus convex-plane then deep-concave, the margin at first involute then elevated, orange-yellow to brownish-orange, the disk subtomentose, pliant, thick, thin toward margin; flesh soft, ochraceous, mild in taste; gills decurrent, arcuate, thin with blunt edges, crowded, forked dichotomously, narrow but not ridge-form, bright-orange, sometimes salmon-tinged; stem spongy, subcylindrical, stuffed or hollow, tomentose, pale orange to brownish-orange; spores smooth, white in mass.—Gregarious in conifer woods, or in frondose woods where conifers have been, July-Oct., not rare, Illinois to New York and northward.

This species is known by the thin crowded gills and orange color.

NYCTALIS Fr.   Plate 33.

Carpophore with an orbicular, convex pileus on a central stem; gills thick, obtuse on edges; stem central; plants parasitic on other gilled mushrooms; fleshy, decaying; spores white, the chlamydospores abundant, connected; brownish, elliptical, long-spined, 12-18 μ in diameter, formed by the surface hyphae of pileus; basidia dwarfed.

Nyctalis asterophora Fr.   Plate 33, fig. 2.

Pileus 1-2 cm. broad; stem 2-3 cm. x 3-7 mm.; spores when present 6 x 4 μ.

Pileus subglobose to hemispheric, floccose to pulverulent, whitish, becoming dingy-brown, thick, the flesh pallid, moist; gills adnate, distant, thick, narrow, sometimes not developed; stem stout, stuffed to hollow, silky, whitish becoming brown; chlamydospores borne on the surface of the pileus, spiny.—On *Russula nigricans*, etc., Illinois to New York, and southward.

Other parasites on fungi are *Boletus parasiticus, Volz aria Loveana, Stropharia epimyces* and *Cordyceps agariciformis*.

PLEUROTUS Fr.

Carpophore orbicular, reniform or flabelliform, convex to plane, with or without stipe; stipe fleshy, lateral, eccentric, rarely central, or lacking; flesh putrescent; gills soft, adnate, adnexed or decurrent; spores white, lavender in *P. sapidus*.—Growing on living or dead wood.

1   Stem eccentric, plants 4-20 cm. in diameter......2
1'   Stem very short or lacking, plants medium-sized to small......6
2   Pileus and stem yellow........................*P. sulfuroides*
2'   Pileus white when fresh......3
3   Stem very tough, large, gills rounded behind, plants growing
     on elm ....*P. ulmarius*
3'   Stem not tough, gills adnate to decurrent......4

4   Gills decurrent in lines, anastomosing.............*P. ostreatus*
4' Gills not anastomosing......5
5   Spore-print lavender, stem short...................*P. sapidus*
5' Spore-print white; stem slender, 2-5 cm. long......*P. lignatilis*
6   Gills conspicuously orange-yellow, pileus involute.........
    ....*Claudopus nidulans*
6' Gills not so colored, pileus not involute......7
7   Pileus viscid, smoky-colored.....................*P. serotinus.*
7' Pileus not viscid, in many cases gelatinous......8
8   Cuticle gelatinous, pileus hairy or scaly......9
8' Cuticle not gelatinous, gill-edges fimbriate........*P. petaloides.*
9   Pileus dark gray-brown, paler toward margin, villose, often
    bluish ....*P. atrocaeruleus.*
9' Pileus deep brown, erect-squarrose-scaly........*P. mastrucatus.*

P. ulmarius Fr.   Elm tree Pleurotus (edible).   Plate 34, fig. 4.
Pileus 4-15 cm. broad; stem 3-15 cm. x 1-3 cm.; spores 4-7 μ in diameter.
Pileus thick, convex, firm, obtuse, glabrous, tomentose or rarely appressed-scaly, white with brownish shades, cracked in age, the flesh white; gills adnexed, becoming rounded behind, broad, rather close, white; stem stout, solid, tough, firm, straight or curved, glabrous, scaly or tomentose; spores minute, spherical.—On living wood of elm, box elder, cottonwood, maple and hickory, often growing from the position of a removed branch, Sept.-Nov., Minnesota to Maine and southward

P. sulfuroides Peck.
Pileus 2-7 cm. broad; stem 3-8 cm. x 5-7 mm.; spores 8 x 5.5 μ.
Pileus convex, umbonate, pale yellow, thin, soft; gills soon rounded behind, sulphur-yellow or yellow, white-floccose on the edges; broad, close; stem eccentric, rigid-elastic, pale yellow, the apex floccose.—Gregarious on logs and stumps, not common, Aug.-Sept., mostly northern.

P. ostreatus Fr.   Oyster mushroom (edible).   Plate 34, fig. 5.
Pileus 4-15 cm. broad; stem 0-2 cm. x 1-2 cm.; spores 8 x 4 μ.
Pileus firm, shelf or shell-shaped, convex to depressed, white becoming brownish-ashy, glabrous, thick with thin margin, soft; gills decurrent down stem in anastomosing lines, broad, narrowed at ends, white; stem lateral, short or lacking, often hairy, white, stout and firm, the taste pleasant.—Caespitosely overlapping on dead wood, logs

or trunks of various deciduous trees, rarely on conifers, July-Nov., or wintering through to May, common, Minnesota to Maine and southward.

P. sapidus Kalchb. Lavender-spored Pleurotus (edible). Plate 34, fig. 3.

Very similar to the preceding in general appearance, but the stem often eccentric; pileus depressed toward stem, wavy on the margin, often tinted with tan; gills decurrent, rarely anastomosing; spore-print lilac.—Caespitosely overlapping on dead wood, trunks, or logs, May-Nov., common, Minnesota, Maine, southward.

P. lignatilis Fr. Plate 34, fig. 1.

Pileus 3-5 cm. broad; stem 3-4 cm. x 3-4 mm.; spores 4 x 2.5 μ.

Pileus convex or depressed, tough, irregular, flocculose-pruinose to glabrous, white; gills somewhat decurrent, narrow, close, white; stem slender, stuffed to hollow, curved, eccentric, minute-hairy; odor farinaceous.—Gregarious on logs not common, Aug.-Sept., Minnesota to New England and southward.

P. fimbriatus Fr.

Similar to *P. lignatilis* but the pileus somewhat hygrophanous and the odor not farinaceous.

P. circinatus Fr.

Similar to *P. lignatilis,* but the pileus very regular.

P. astrocaerulens Fr. var. **griseus** Peck.

Pileus 2-5 cm. broad; spores 7 x 3.5 μ

Pileus at first resupinate then horizontal, with gelatinous and tough cuticle, dark gray-brown shaded with dark blue or black, coarse-hairy toward base, the flesh breaking into layers, thin toward margin; gills broad, close, decurrent at the bases, white to yellowish with fimbriate edges.—Caespitose and somewhat overlapping, on deciduous trees, infrequent, Wisconsin to New York.

P. applicatus Fr.

Pileus minute, thin, soon horizontal from a resupinate tubercle, dark gray, 3-6 mm. in diameter; the gills subdistant.—On rotten wood, June-Sept., rare.

P. mastrucatus Fr.

Pileus 3-10 cm. broad; spores 9 x 5 μ.

Pileus at first resupinate then reflexed, sessile, obovate, flaccid, with an upper gelatinous layer, mouse-colored, bearing black hair-tuft squamules, the margin incurved; gills whitish, broad, not close.

—Caespitose and overlapping on decaying logs, not common, Sept.-
Nov., Illinois to New York, southward.

P. serotinus Fr. (edible)
Pileus 3-6 cm. long x 3-8 cm. wide x 7 mm. thick; spores 5 x 1.5 μ.

Pileus nearly plane, orbicular to reniform, with a gelatinous cuticle,
viscid when wet, olivaceous-umber, sometimes shaded with yellow-
brown or greenish, often covered with dense tomentum, firm, thick;
gills whitish, yellowish, or tan, close, narrowed in front; stem short,
5-20 mm. long, 8-10 mm. thick, solid.—Caespitose-overlapping or
solitary on fallen timbers, especially of elm, locally common, Aug.-
Nov., Minnesota to Maine, southward

P. petaloides Fr. Petaloid Pleurotus. Plate 34, fig. 2.
Pileus 2-10 cm. long x 1.5 cm. wide x 4 mm. thick; spores 4 μ.

Pileus wedge-shaped or spatulate, tapering to stem-like base, white,
tan, or reddish-brown, finely striate on the margin, thin; gills decurrent, very narrow, fimbriate on the edges, crowded, yellowish or
white.—Caespitose on decaying stumps, etc., July-Sept., not common,
Minnesota to Michigan and northern Indiana.

PANUS Fr.

Carpophore almost stemless, reniform, flabelliform, or twisted,
plane or depressed, not putrescent but arid, leathery, reviving as in
the genera *Lentinus* and *Marasmius;* pileus eccentric, or lateral,
erect forms often crowded and very irregular in form; gills with
entire edge, becoming dry and tough with age; spores smooth, white.
—Growing on wood.

1 Stem eccentric, set off from pileus by a distinct margin behind. . 2
1' Pileus stemless or prolonged laterally to a stem-like base,
   very astringent; plants many in clusters...........*P. stipticus.*
2 Pileus creamy-white, densely strigose-hairy........*P. strigosus.*
2' Pileus reddish-brown to tan......3
3 Pileus bearing tufted hairs, tawny...................*P. rudis.*
3' Pileus nearly glabrous or bearing a few scales......*P. torulosus.*

P. torulosus Fr. (edible)
Pileus 5-10 cm. broad; stem 2-3 cm. x 1-3 cm. thick; spores 6 x 3 μ.

Pileus fleshy, pliant to tough, thin, plane to funnel-form, eccentric
to lateral, livid-flesh-colored tinged violet or reddish, when young
covered with a delicate tomentum, soon glabrous or slightly scaly in
center; gills decurrent, somewhat forked or anastomosing, narrow,

pallid rufescent or violaceous, the edges smooth; stem tough, solid, gray-tomentose.—Caespitose on decaying stumps, rare, Sept.-Oct., Illinois to New York and Kentucky.

P. strigosus Berk. and Curt.   Strigose Panus (edible).

Pileus 10-40 cm. broad; stem short 2-15 cm. long, 2-4 cm. thick; spores 12 x 4 μ.

Pileus large, usually eccentric to lateral, fleshy-fibrous to leathery, convex, reniform, bearing a dense, thick, strigose-villose covering of hairs to 2 mm. long, creamy-white, becoming yellow when dry, the odor agreeable; gills broad, somewhat decurrent, of various lengths, subdistant, thick, white becoming yellowish, with entire edges; stem stout, strigose-villose, whitish, ashy, or yellowish.— Solitary or somewhat clustered on wounds of maple, birch, etc., not common, Aug.-Sept., Minnesota to New York and southward to Tennessee.

P. rudis Fr.   Rudy Panus (edible).

Pileus 2-7 cm. broad; stem 2-3 cm. x 1-2 cm.; spores 5.5 x 2.5 μ.

Pileus irregular, eccentric, vase-shaped, tough, villose to strigose, alutaceous-brown to reddish-brown, the margin ascending and often lobed, incurved, the taste slightly bitter, the odor none; gills decurrent, crowded, narrow, pale or reddish-brown, with entire edges; stem very short, sometimes lacking, villose, alutaceous-brown.— Caespitose on stumps, logs, and trunks of frondose trees, common, May-Nov., Minnesota to Maine, southward to Tennessee.

P. stipticus Fr.   Stiptic Panus.

Pileus 1-3 cm. broad; stem very short; spores 4.5 x 2 μ.

Pileus convex then depressed, subreniform, abruptly narrowed to stem-base, the surface soon furfuraceous-scaly, smooth, very tough, the taste very astringent; gills pale-cinnamon, venose, connected; stem lateral, short, solid, often compressed, pruinose, pale cinnamon; spores smooth, white.—Caespitose on wood, logs, etc., common, May-Oct., Minnesota to Maine and Tennessee.

LENTINUS Fr.   Plate 34.

Plant fleshy-tough, reviving when moistened, hard when old, orbicular and central stemmed to dimidiate or reniform; stem eccentric, lateral, or not present, confluent with pileus; spores white; gills thin, concrete with pileus, membranaceous, the edges serrate or laceratetoothed.—Growing on wood.

The species are numerous in tropics, and occupy a position between those of *Pleurotus* and *Panus.*

1   Pileus sessile, dimidiate, or fan-shaped......2
1' Pileus on a distinct stem......3
2   Pileus large, 5-15 cm. broad, coarsely hairy, rough-striate..
....*L. vulpinus.*
2' Pileus small, less than 5 cm. broad, thick, at first whitish becoming reddish-brown ....*L. ursinus.*
3   Pileus scaly......4
3' Pileus glabrous, reddish-ochraceous or brown, twisted......
....*L. cochleatus.*
4   Stem short, stout; pileus convex to plane, bearing brownish
subconcentric scale-blotches ....*L. lepideus.*
4' Stem slender, tapering; pileus umbilicate, bearing pointed
dark scales especially in center; gills often aborted...*L. tigrinus.*

L. tigrinus Fr.   Tiger Lentinus (edible).

Pileus 2-5 cm. broad; stem 1-3 cm. x 3-7 mm.; spores 6 x.3 μ.

Pileus fleshy, leathery, orbicular, convex then umbilicate, white, covered with dark brown hairy scales especially toward center, the flesh white, thin; gills decurrent, narrow, close, white, the edges eroded-serrate; stem whitish, slender, solid, minutely scaly.—On hard dead wood, common, Minnesota to New England and Tennessee.

A monstrosity with gills destroyed or inhibited by a white mycelial growth occurs even more commonly than the form with gills.

L. lepideus Fr.   Scaly Lentinus (edible).   Plate 34, fig. 12.

Pileus 5-20 cm. broad; stem 2-3 cm. x 1-3 cm.; spores 12 x 5 μ.

Pileus convex, compact, firm, tough, often irregular, buff, with more or less concentric brown blotches of adpressed scales, the cuticle often cracking into areas; gills sinuate behind, decurrent, broad, white staining ferruginous, covered at first by a membranaceous veil; stem hard, short, thick, solid, scaly, at first bearing a ring near apex.—On coniferous logs and timbers, ties, posts, etc., exposed to the sun, throughout our area, common, May-Oct., Minnesota to Maine and Tennessee.

L. cochleatus Fr.   Twisted Lentinus (edible)

Pileus 2-5 cm. broad; stem 3-7 cm. x 3-7 mm.; spores sub-globose, 4 x 5 μ.

Pileus depressed to funnel-form, irregularly compressed or lobed, tough, glabrous, pale reddish-brown to tan, the flesh thin, whitish, the odor aromatic; gills decurrent, broad, close, whitish tinged flesh-colored, serrate; stem glabrous, central to lateral, confluent at base, deeply sulcate; spores subglobose.—Confluent-caespitose on stumps, occasionally on buried wood, in mixed and frondose woods, July-Sept., not uncommon, Minnesota to Maine, and southward.

L. vulpinus Fr.   Fox Lentinus.

Pileus 5-15 cm. broad; stem none; spores 2.5 x 3.5 μ.

Pileus dimidiate, conchate-reniform, joined to others at base, multiple-imbricate, coarsely hairy, radiately rough, ribbed, dull yellowish, alutaceous, the margin incurved, thin, tough-fleshy, white within, the odor and taste peppery; gills decurrent, broad in front, narrowing toward rear, crowded, white or tinged flesh-colored, coarsely serrate. —On decaying wood, not common, July-Oct., Minnesota to Maine and southward.

L. ursinus Fr.-Bres.   Bear Lentinus

Pileus 1-7 cm. broad, without stem; spores 5.5 x 4 μ.

Pileus pale reddish-brown, somewhat tomentose or pruinose, sub-reniform, thick, tough, very thin at margin; gills subdecurrent, radiating from stem-like base, rather broad, close, whitish-tan, lacerate-dentate on edges.—On logs in woods of beech and hemlock, not common, September, Minnesota to Maine and southward.

SCHIZOPHYLLUM Fr.

Carpophore sessile, dimidiate to suborbicular, tough, reviving in wet weather; gills with split edges, the gill structure continued upward through trama of pileus to the thin pellicle; spores white; veil absent.

S. commune Fr.   Split-gilled bracket.   Plate 34, fig. 11.

Pileus 1-3 cm. broad; spores 4 x 5 μ.

Pileus sessile, suborbicular, thin, pliant, tough, narrowed at the base, densely white-hairy or tomentose, the margin incurved and lobed; gills radiating from the point of attachment, very narrow, split on the obtuse edges, white, gray, lavender, or pink.—Very common on dead branches of deciduous trees, persistent throughout the year, North Dakota to Maine and Tennessee.

TROGIA Fr.

Carpophore resupinate-reflexed or sessile, tough, arid, reviving when moist, growing on logs and sticks; pileus often becoming infolded on margin and hiding gills; gills obtuse, arid.

The species are related to those of *Cantharellus* in the obtuse fold-like gills and to those of *Schizophyllum* by the texture and the ability to revive when moistened.

T. crispa Fr.

Pileus 1-2 cm. broad; spores 4 x 1.5 μ.

Pileus sessile, shelf-like or resupinate, tough, persistent, white-hairy, becoming buff-brown when dry, the flesh thin; gills vein-like, often forked, bluish gray, crisped, very narrow, fold-like, obtuse.— On logs and branches of deciduous trees, common, persistent throughout the year, North Dakota to Maine and Tennessee.

MARASMIUS Fr.

Carpophores composed of an orbicular, campanulate or convex pileus on a tough, often horny central stem; pileus fleshy to membranaceous, tough, reviving when moistened, Collybia-like to Mycena-like in form; stem confluent with pileus but of different material, central, veil absent; spores white, smooth.—On bark, wood, or on the ground, among grass, or on dead leaves.

1   Stem inserted at base (mycelium hidden), not radicating......2
1' Stem radicating or attached by floccose, strigose, or mycel-ioid base......9
2   Stem filiform, horny, rigid; pileus convex-campanulate, membranaceous......3
2' Stem not filiform, 1 mm. or more in diameter; pileus sub-membranaceous or thicker......7
3   Plants minute, attached to grass; pileus 2-4 mm. in diameter ....*M. gramineum.*
3' Plants larger, attached to dead leaves or sticks......4
1   Pileus 4-10 mm. broad, radiate-plicate, white with dark de-pression in center; stem black....................*M. rotula.*
4' Pileus without dark depression......5
5   Usually on pine needles; pileus about 1 cm. in diameter.... ....*M. androsaceus.*
5' On deciduous leaves or sticks......6
6   Pileus with white central depression, elsewhere darker.... ....*M. capillaris.*
6' Pileus milk-white, without central depression; gills very distant ....*M. epiphyllus.*
7   Stem entirely glabrous; odor garlic-like........*M. scorodonius.*
7' Stem minute-velvety or pruinose; garlic-like odor not present..8

8   Pileus rufescent, 1-1.5 cm. in diameter ; plant of beech-maple
     woods .... *M. olneyi.*
8'   Pileus pure white, sulcate, 4-8 mm. in diameter, plant at-
     tached to sedges in marshes.................... *M. caricicola.*
8"   Pileus comparatively large, 2-5 cm. in diameter with thick
     flesh ; plants attached to grass roots, gregarious in circles..
     .... *M. oreades.*

9   Stem covered with easily removed villous hairs, not radi-
     cating......10
9'   Stem smooth or the hairs not easily removed, often rooting..13

10   Plants growing among grass, often many in a fairy ring..
     .... *M. oreades.*
10' Plants on ground in frondose woods, among leaves, etc.......11

11   A mass of brown hairs at stem base......12
11' A mass of white hairs at stem-base................. *M. urens.*

12   At bases and on sides of living trees............. *M. fagineus.*
12' Growing among leaves....................... *M. peronatus.*

13   Gills arcuate-decurrent ; plants white, glandular pubescent..
     .... *M. resinosus.*
13' Gills not decurrent......14

14   Gills reddish-brown with abundant colored cystidia ; stem
     bay, horny, subvelvety .... *M. cohaerens.*
14' Gills without such cystidia, lacking the red-brown color......15

15   Stem hairy above base......16
15' Stem glabrous, or hairy at very base......20

16   Stem-pubescence dark-colored......17
16' Stem-pubescence grayish or whitish......19

17   With odor of garlic.......................... *M. prasiosmus.*
17' Without odor......18

18   Stem minutely pruinose, horny................. *M. erythropus.*
18' Stem densely tomentose..................... *M. semihirtipes.*

19   On mossy logs, slender, papillate............... *M. papillatus.*
19' Among fallen leaves, not papillate.............. *M. velutipes.*

20   Pileus sulcate, membranaceous, campanulate, orange.. *M. siccus.*
20' Pileus rufescent .... *M. felix.*
20" Pileus white or dingy-ochraceous......21

21   Pileus, gills, and upper part of stem white ; stem dark brown
     below apex, attached to substratum by a spreading mycelium
     .... *M. delectans.*
21' Pileus tawny, striate, stem reddish-brown........ *M. glabellus.*
21" Pileus tawny, plicate-striate, stem wine-color .... *M. bellipes.*

M. oreades Fr. Fairy-ring (edible). Plate 30, fig. 13.

Pileus 2-5 cm. broad; stem 4-8 cm. x 3-5 mm.; spores 8 x 4-5 μ.

Pileus convex, obtuse, or broadly umbonate, thick, dull brick-red when moist, yellow-buff when dry, glabrous, smooth or substriate when moist, the odor fragrant, the taste pleasing; gills rounded behind, broad, subdistant, whitish with a yellowish tinge, commonly intervenose; stem cylindrical, tough, solid, covered with close, fine pubescence.—Gregarious in arcs of circles in open grassy places, attached to grass or herb roots, more abundant in sandy regions, common, Minnesota, Maine and southward.

M. urens Fr. (poisonous). Plate 30, fig. 1.

Pileus 2-5 cm. broad; stem 4-9 cm. x 1-3 mm.; spores 8 x 3 μ.

Pileus thin, convex then plane, obtuse or subumbonate, red-brown to tan with darker disk, smooth then wrinkled, glabrous, tough, pliant; gills withdrawing from stem, thick, intervenose, narrow, close, whitish then tinged reddish; stem cylindrical, solid, terete, blackish at base, pale reddish-brown above base, clothed with a close white pubescence of minute hairs, attached by a one-sided substrigose base; taste acrid. —Gregarious on ground and among leaves, sticks, or grass in frondose woods, July-Oct., not infrequently found, Minnesota to Maine and southward.

M. peronatus Fr. Peronate Marasmius (poisonous). Plate 30, fig. 2.

Pileus 2-6 cm. broad; stem 5-8 cm. x 2-4 mm.; spores 7 x 4 μ.

Pileus convex-plane, thin, pliant, leathery, pale brick-red fading to tan, finally lacunose, the margin striate at first, wrinkled later; gills subdistant, thin, whitish then rufescent; stem fibrous-stuffed, yellowish-rufescent, yellow-brown strigose hairs enlarging the base; taste acrid.—Gregarious among leaves and sticks in frondose woods, infrequent, July-Oct., Minnesota to Maine and southward.

This species is sometimes confused with *Collybia hariolorum*.

M. fagineus Morg. Beech Marasmius. Plate 30, fig. 3.

Pileus 1-3 cm. broad; stem 1-2 cm. x 1-2 mm.; spores 11 x 3.5-4 μ.

Pileus submembranaceous, convex then plane, obtuse, pliant, tan, striatulate when moist, whitish to brown; stem short, curving, dilated at the apex, light chestnut, with white villous covering, brown strigose-hairy at base.—Subcaespitose on bark near bases of living beech, maple, or elm trees, or on stumps, not common, Wisconsin to New York and Ohio.

M. glabellus Peck.   Plate 30, fig. 4.

Pileus 1-2 cm. broad; stem 2-5 cm. x 0.5-1 mm.; spores 10 x 4.5 μ.

Pileus convex-expanded, membranaceous, obtuse, often striate, tan or dull ochraceous, the disk uneven; gills distant, broad, ventricose, white, intervenose; stem horny, tubular, shining, white at apex, chestnut elsewhere, mycelioid-thickened at base.—On fallen leaves, not comomn, Aug.-Sept., Illinois, Indiana, Michigan.

M. bellipes Morg.

Pileus pale tawny brown, sulcate-plicate; stem white to wine-purple, dilated at the apex.—On fallen leaves, not common, Aug.-Sept., Minnesota to New York and southward.

This has been considered a variety of *M. glabellus*.

M. delectans Morg.   Delightful Marasmius.   Plate 30, fig. 5.

Pileus 1-4 cm. broad; stem 3-7 cm. x 1-1.5 mm.; spores 8 x 3 μ.

Pileus convex-expanded, thin, tough, white to pale tan, rugulose-striate; gills adnexed, subdistant, white, venose; stem slender, cylindrical, glabrous, shining-pure-white above, dark-brown below, the mycelioid base forming a wide white arachnoid mat on substratum of fallen leaves; taste mild.—In frondose woods, not uncommon in wet weather, Aug.-Oct., Minnesota to Maine and southward.

M. semihirtipes Peck.   Hairy-stemmed Marasmius.   Plate 30, fig. 6.

Pileus 2-3 cm. broad; stem 3-8 cm. x 1.5 mm.; spores 9 x 4.5 μ.

Pileus convex, plane, then depressed, submembranaceous, hygrophanous, pliant, red-brown when moist, tan when dry, the disk darker, the taste mild; gills whitish subfimbriate on edges, venose, adnate-seceding, narrow, not distant; stem dark-reddish-brown the entire length, tubular or compressed, substriate, densely velvety almost to apex, the tomentum concolor.—Among leaves and sticks in frondose woods, common, July-Sept., Minnesota to Maine and southward.

M. prasiosmus Fr.   Garlic Mushroom (edible).   Plate 30, fig. 7.

Pileus 2-2.5 cm.; stem 5-8 cm. x 2-3 mm.; spores 14 x 3.5 μ.

Pileus convex-plane then depressed, pale brown to tan with flesh-tinge, sulcate, glabrous, submembranaceous, toughish, the odor strongly of garlic; gills narrow, paler than pileus; stem hollow, horny, white and glabrous above, dark reddish-brown and short-villose below.—On fallen oak leaves, not common, Minnesota to New York and southward.

M. velutipes Berk. & Curt.   Velvet-stemmed Marasmius.   Plate 30, fig. 8.

Pileus 1.5-4 cm. broad; stem 7-12 cm. x 2-4 mm.; spores 6 x 4 μ.

Pileus thin, convex or plane, grayish-brown or grayish-rufous, ashy when dry; gills gray, very narrow, crowded; stem slender, tough, cylindrical, hollow, densely gray-velvety-tomentose.—Among fallen leaves in frondose woods, locally common, Wisconsin to New York and Indiana.

M. resinosus (Peck). Sacc.   Plate 30, fig. 9.

Pileus 5-12 mm. broad; stem 2-6 cm. x 0.5-1 mm.; spores 7 x 3.5 μ.

Pileus convex, thin, submembranaceous, tough, dull white, glandular-pubescent, the odor and taste mild; gills arcuate-decurrent, narrow, not distant, white, veined, flocculent at edges; stem tough, glandular-pruinose, tubular, whitish, attached by floccose base.—Subcaespitose on grass, sticks, and leaves in frondose woods, July-Sept., common locally in wet weather, Minnesota to New York and southward.

M. erythropus Fr. var.   Red-stemmed Marasmius.   Plate 30, fig. 10.

Pileus 1-2.5 cm. broad; stem 5 cm. x 1.5 mm.; spores 8 x 3 μ.

Pileus hemispheric-campanulate then plane, thin, dark orange or dark rose-madder, the disk darker, rugulose when dry, the margin at first incurved, the flesh white; gills subdistant, ventricose, broad to medium, white or ochraceous-tinged, entire; stem horny, dark red-brown, darker below, flexuous, pale at apex, minutely pruinose, enlarged-mycelioid at base.—On decaying leaves and sticks in beech woods, rare, July-Sept., Illinois, New England and southward.

M. scorodonius Fr.   Garlic Mushroom.   Plate 30, fig. 11.

Pileus 5-15 mm. broad; stem 2-3 cm. x 1-2 mm.; spores 7 x 4 μ.

Pileus thin submembranaceous, pliant, convex, plane or elevated at the margin, whitish with rufous tinge, glabrous, becoming wrinkled, with an odor of garlic where bruised; gills adnate, narrow, whitish at the apex, inserted by naked dark base.—Attached to grass-roots in grassy places, June-Sept., abundant locally, Minnesota to Michigan and southward.

M. Olneyi Berk. & Curt.   Plate 30, fig. 12.

Pileus 1-1.5 cm. broad; stem 2-4 cm. x 1 mm.; spores 10 x 4-5 μ.

Pileus convex, pliant, at length depressed, rufescent, striate when moist, radiately rugose when dry, membranaceous; gills attached to a seceding collar, crenulate at the edges, white; stem dilated at apex,

narrowed downward, inserted at base, minutely hairy; odor absent.
—Gregarious on fallen leaves and sticks in beech-maple woods, September, rare, Minnesota to Michigan and Illinois.

M. caricicola Kauffm.

Pileus white, 4-8 mm. in diameter, radiately sulcate.—On *Carex* stems in marshes.

M cohaerens Fr.-Bres.   Brown-gilled Marasmius.   Plate 30, fig. 14.

Pileus 1-2 cm. broad; stem 5-12 cm. x 4-6 mm.; spores 7 x 4 μ.

Pileus campanulate, obtuse, often umbonate, vinaceous-buff or vinaceous-cinnamon to chestnut-colored, fading to tan, thin but not membranaceous; gills moderately broad, rounded behind, rather broad, ventricose, brownish to brick-red with abundant cystidia; stem horny, tubular, shining, glabrous, smooth, bay-brown paler at the expanded apex, the base darker and densely floccose with attaching hairs.—Caespitose on ground or rotten wood in frondose woods, frequently found, July-Sept., Maine to Minnesota and Tennessee.

M. papillatus Peck.   Plate 30, fig. 17.

Pileus 5-15 mm. broad; stem 2-6 cm. x 1 mm.; spores 10 x 3.5 μ.

Pileus convex-expanded, striatulate on margin, with an erect umbo, markedly papillate, slightly fleshy-membranaceous, dingy-white with rufus tinge; gills decurrent by a tooth, narrowed toward front, not distant, whitish; stem cylindrical, elastic, toughish, hollow, pallid, pruinose, rooting.—Gregarious on mossy rotten logs in conifer woods, rare, July-Sept., Minnesota to New York.

M. siccus (Schw.) Fr.   Orange pin-wheel.   Plate 30, fig. 18.

Pileus 1-2.5 cm. broad; stem 4-8 cm. x 0.5 mm.; spores 13-18 x 3-5 μ.

Pileus broadly campanulate, membranaceous, orange to ochraceous or rose-madder, radiately striate-sulcate from margin to disk; gills narrowed toward stem, distant, venose, whitish; stem horny, glabrous, shining, brownish-black, whitish at apex.—Gregarious on fallen leaves and sticks in woods, June-Oct., common, Minnesota to Maine and southward.

M. felix Morg.   Plate 30, fig. 19.

Pileus 3-8 mm. broad; stem 3-7 cm. x 0.5 mm.; spores 7 x 4 μ.

Pileus convex, buff or rufescent, membranaceous, wrinkled-striate; gills adnate, distant, white, venose, sometimes forked; stem brownish-black often whitish at apex, minutely velvety, slightly brown-hairy or naked at base.—Attached to veins of leaves in frondose woods, not common, Iowa to New York and southward.

M. rotula Fr. Pin-wheel. Plate 30, fig. 15.

Pileus 4-12 mm. broad; stem 2-5 cm. x 0.5 mm.; spores 8 x 3.5 μ.

Pileus membranaceous, convex, whitish, with dark umbilicus in center, radiately-plicate with crenate margin; gills attached to free collar behind, distant, whitish; stem horny, tubular, black, whitish at apex, glabrous.—On leaves, sticks, etc., very common in woods, May-Sept., Minnesota to Maine and southward.

M. androsaceus Fr. Plate 30, fig. 20.

Pileus 6-12 mm. broad; stem 3-8 cm. x 0.5 mm.; spores 7 x 3 μ.

Pileus hemispherical, then plane or umbilicate, buff, reddish-brown or tinged-purplish, radiately wrinkled or sulcate, glabrous; gills adnate, distant, buff or flesh-colored; stem capillary-tubular, tough, glabrous, shining, black, paler at apex.—Gregarious on pine needles and fallen leaves and sticks, July-Sept., common, Minnesota to Maine and southward.

M. gramineum Libert. Plate 30, fig. 16.

Pileus 2-4 mm. broad; stem 3 cm. long, hair-like; spores 14 x 3-4 μ.

Pileus minute, umbonate, pale reddish brown, sulcate, the umbo darker; gills few, cream-colored, venose, attached to a free collar; stem capillary, black, shining, the apex white.—Gregarious among grass, attached to the blades, rare, June-Sept., Iowa to New York and southward.

M. capillaris Morg. Plate 30, fig. 21.

Pileus 2-5 mm. broad; stem 4 cm. x 0.5 mm.; spores 9 x 5 μ.

Pileus membranaceous, convex-umbilicate, plicate, sulcate, dull-buff or alutaceous with white center, glabrous; gills adnate to a free collar, distant, white; stem capillary, black, shining, tough, tubular.—Gregarious on fallen leaves and sticks in frondose woods, rare, September, Minnesota, New England and southward.

M. epiphyllus Fr. Plate 30, fig. 22.

Pileus 2-7 mm. broad; stem 2-4 cm. x 0.5 mm.; spores 10 x 3.5 μ.

Pileus convex, plane, or umbilicate, glabrate, white, wrinkled, membranaceous; gills adnate, very distant, white, few; stem filiform, red-brown, whitish at apex; pruinose, pubescent toward base.—Scattered on fallen leaves, where they are attached to midvein, October, not uncommon, Minnesota to New England and southward.

HELIOMYCES Lev.

Similar to *Marasmius,* but flesh tremelloid, subcoriaceous, reviving in wet weather; pileus sulcate, rugose; stem central; gills with acute edges; spores white.

H. nigripes (Schw.) Morg.

Pileus 1-2 cm. broad; stem 2-4 cm. x 1-2 mm.; spores 8 x 4 μ.

Pileus convex, plane, very thin, chalk-white, pruinose, rugulose; gills subdistant adnate to slightly decurrent, intervenose, white; basal mycelium hidden; stem black beneath the white-pruinose covering, black within, hollow with minute central cavity.—On sticks and debris in low woods, Sept.-Oct., common, Minnesota to Maine and southward.

COLLYBIA Fr.   Plate 28.

Carpophore an orbicular, convex or plane pileus on a central, cylindrical stem; pileus not very fleshy, nor very putrescent, soon expanded, at first incurved at the margin; stem cartilaginous or with a cartilaginous cuticle; gills adnate to almost free but never decurrent; annulus and volva lacking; plants mostly growing on wood and slow of growth.   With the exception of one group of species which includes *C. radicata,* they are medium-sized or small.

A mature *Collybia* is usually expanded, while one of *Mycena* remains campanulate.

1   Plants large, commonly 6-10 cm. in diameter......2
1′ Plants smaller, under 5 cm. in diameter......4.
2   Pileus viscid, stem long, radicating..............*C. radicata.*
2′ Pileus not viscid, stem not radicating......3
3   Pileus gray-brown, bearing dark fibers; plant growing on decayed wood; gills very broad...............*C. platyphylla.*
3′ Pileus white to yellow; stem bulbous, plant growing on ground ....*C. albiflavida.*
4   Stem tomentose, velvety to pruinose throughout....5
4′ Stem glabrous, or pruinose at apex, or hairy at base......13
5   More or less reviving when moistened......6
5′ Not reviving when moistened......7
6   Pileus zonate ....*C. zonata.*
6′ Pileus umbilicate or papillate...................*C. stipitaria.*
6″ Pileus not umbilicate, nor zonate, hygrophanous; stem densely white-pubescent ....*C. confluens.*

7   Stem with brown-velvet covering; plants caespitose, on wood
    ....*C. velutipes.*
7' Stem not densely velvety......8

8   Pileus small, less than 2 cm. in diameter......9
8' Pileus larger......11

9   Growing on partly buried pine cones...........*C. conigenoides.*
9' On decaying vegetation......10

10 Stem with tuber; plant growing on decayed mushrooms..
    ....*C. tuberosa.*
10' Stem bearing minute black dots (as seen under magnifying
    lens) ....*C. floccipes.*

11 Flesh becoming dark where bruised...............*C. succosa.*
11' Flesh not becoming black where bruised......12

12 Stem long, rooted...............................*C. longipes.*
12' Stem short, 2-4 cm. long, white-hairy...........*C. hariolorum.*

13 Stem deeply rooting......14
13' Stem not radicating......15

14 Pileus viscid ....*C. radicata.*
14' Pileus not viscid, hygrophanous............*C. hygrophoroides.*

15 Gills white or whitish......16
15' Gills of another color......22

16 Gills broad; plants dark red-brown, obtuse, growing in
    beech-hemlock woods ....*C. succinea.*
16' Gills narrow......17

17 Plants caespitose on decaying wood......18
17' Plants not markedly caespitose, usually gregarious......20

18 Pileus hygrophanous......19
18' Pileus not hygrophanous.....................*C. abundans.*

19 Pileus red-brown ....*C. acervata.*
19' Pileus buff-brown ....*C. familia.*

20 Pileus markedly thickening in center, the moist surface hav-
    ing a fatty lustre; stem striate..................*C. butyracea.*
20' Pileus not so thickened; stem straight, white, shining, pel-
    lucid ....*C. strictipes.*
20'' Pileus markedly thickened in center, the surface not having
    this lustre......21

21 In swamps ....*C. lentinoides.*
21' Among fallen leaves ....*C. dryophila.*

22 Gills dark lilac, narrow, very crowded........*C. myriadophylla.*
22' Gills soon rufous or smoky......23

23   Pileus striatulate, moist; odor farinaceous. . . . .*C. expallens.*
23' Pileus not striate, odor none. 24
24   On burnt ground; pileus black. . . . .*C. atrata.*
24' On mossy places. 25
25   Pileus blackish-chestnut when moist, stem 3-5 cm. long. . . .
. . . .*C. plexipes.*
25' Pileus grayish-brown, stem 2-3 cm. long. . . . .*C. atratoides.*

C. radicata Fr.   Rooting Collybia (edible).   Plate 28, fig. 13.

Pileus 3-12 cm. broad; stem 5-25 cm. x 4-12 mm.; spores 16 x 10 μ.

Pileus convex, plane or umbonate, viscid, glabrous, gray-brown to smoky-umber or nearly white, the flesh white, not thick; gills broad, adnexed, subdistant, white; stem elongated into a tapering root-like projection, firm, rigid, glabrous, striate to sulcate, cartilaginous.— On ground in woods, common, June-Oct., Minnesota to Maine to South Carolina and Mississippi.

C. longipes Fr.

Similar to the preceding, but the pileus not viscid.

C. platyphylla Fr.   Broad-gilled Collybia (edible).   Plate 28, fig. 14.

Pileus 6-12 cm. broad; stem 6-12 cm. x 1-2 cm.; spores 9 x 6.5 μ.

Campanulate then convex-plane, gray-brown or gray-white, streaked with dark radiating innate fibrils or scales, the margin commonly wavy, the flesh scissile, fragile, white, thin; gills broad, adnexed, white, subdistant; stem stout, fibrous-fleshy, fibrillose-striate, white.—Solitary to caespitose on rotten wood, stumps, and humus, common after heavy rains, Minnesota to Maine, to Tennessee and Virginia.

C. velutipes Fr.   Velvet-stemmed Collybia (edible).   Plate 28, fig. 1.

Pileus 2-5 cm. broad; stem 2-7 cm. x 3-6 mm.; spores 8 x 3.5 μ.

Pileus medium-sized to small, convex, viscid, obtuse, the cuticle separable, tawny, tan, or reddish-yellow, thickish with white flesh; gills adnexed, subdistant to close, whitish, the edges fimbriate, rather broad or medium; stem tough, stuffed to hollow, velvety with dense short brown or blackish-brown hairs, yellow at apex.—Caespitose on decaying stumps, logs, roots, etc., or on bark of living trees, common throughout the year whenever sufficient moisture and several days above freezing occur, North Dakota to Maine and southward.

C. succosa Peck.   Plate 28, fig. 2.

Pileus 1-3 cm. broad; stem 2-5 cm. x 2 mm.; spores 3 x 4 μ.

Pileus campanulate-convex, subcartilaginous, ashy-brown or smoky, minutely pubescent, the thickish white flesh becoming purple-black where bruised; gills adnate, each with a decurrent tooth, broad tapering in front, colored as the flesh; stem cartilaginous, cylindrical, clothed with smoky fine hair, soon dark-colored.—Caespitose or scattered on decaying logs, etc., especially in hemlock woods, not common, July-Sept., Minnesota to New England, southward in range of hemlock.

C. floccipes Fr.   Plate 28, fig. 3.

Pileus 0.5-2 cm. broad; stem 3-8 cm. x 0.5-2 mm.; spores 4 x 5 μ.

Pileus small, conic-campanulate to papillate-plane, gray-brown or smoky-brown with darker umbo, glabrous, faintly striatulate when moist, thin; gills narrowly attached, medium-broad, subdistant, white, the edges pulverulent; stem tough, filiform, smooth, flexuous, hollow, white, minutely black-dotted (as seen with lens), the base covered with spreading white fibrils.—Gregarious on humus, decayed leaves, and rotten wood, May-June, common locally, Minnesota to New York and southward.

C. tuberosa Fr.   Tuberous Collybia.   Plate 28, fig. 4.

Pileus 0.5-1 cm. broad; stem 2-4 cm. x 1 mm.; spores 5 x 2.5 μ.

Pileus small, plane, whitish or yellowish, thin; gills minutely pubescent, adnate, close, white; stem slender, hollow, whitish or reddish-tinged, clothed with webby pulverulence, arising from a tuberous black or brown sclerotium which is 2 cm. long x 2 mm. wide.—On remains of decayed mushrooms or damp humus, frequently found, July-Sept., Minnesota to Maine and southward.

C. conigenoides Ellis.   Plate 28, fig. 5.

Similar to the preceding in size, the pileus cream or tan-colored and covered with minute pubescence, convex-plane.—Attached to buried white pine cones, very rare, in the range of *Pinus Strobus*.

C. hariolorum Fr. (edible).   Plate 28, fig. 6.

Pileus 2-5 cm. broad; stem. 2-5 cm. x 3 mm.; spores 7 x 3 μ.

Pileus convex-plane, flexible, thin, soon soft in moist weather, white with reddish-brown disk, fading to white, flesh soft, collapsible; gills very narrow, crowded, almost free, thick, collapsing; stem covered with white tomentum, cartilaginous becoming soft when wet.—Scattered to caespitose among fallen leaves, infrequent, Minnesota to Michigan and southward.

C. confluens Fr. (edible). Plate 28, fig. 7.

Pileus 2-5 cm. broad; stem 5-10 cm. x 2-5 mm.; spores 6 x 3 μ.

Pileus obtuse, convex-plane, tough, hygrophanous, reddish-brown when moist, gray when dry, rather thin, with white flesh; gills narrow, whitish, crowded, free; stem hollow, tough, red beneath the dense white pubescence, often several joined at base by dense floccose mycelioid web.—Gregarious or caespitose, often in partial rings, on fallen leaves, common, July-Oct., Minnesota to Maine and southward.

C. stipitaria Fr. Plate 28, fig. 8.

Pileus 0.5-1 cm. broad; stem 2-5 cm. x 0.5-1 mm.; spores 7 x 3.5 μ.

Pileus small, convex-plane, umbilicate, with minute papillae in center of umbilicus, grayish, minutely radiately fibrillose-hairy or strigose, when dry radiately wrinkled, submembranaceous, soft; gills adnexed, narrow, white; stem filiform, dark-red when moist, gray when dry, tough, cylindrical, tubular, the mycelium hidden, clothed with gray tomentum.—Abundant in woods, June-Oct., Minnesota to Maine and southward.

C. zonata Peck. Plate 28, fig. 9.

Pileus 2-3.5 cm. in diameter covered with coarse, tawny, densely matted hairs arranged in zones.—On decaying wood, rare, Aug.-Sept., Illinois to New York, northward.

This plant has the aspect of a large *Collybia stipitaria,* and some believe it may eventually be proven to be a variety of that species.

C. albiflavida Peck. Cream-colored Collybia (edible). Plate 28, fig. 15.

Tricholoma albiflavidum Peck.

Pileus 5-10 cm. broad; stem 6-16 cm. x 5-8 mm.; spores 9.5 μ.

Pileus large, convex-plane, obtuse or broadly umbonate, whitish or creamy-yellow, smooth, glabrous, the flesh white; gills adnexed, narrow, crowded, white; stem cylindrical above the bulbous base, long, solid, fibrous within, the cuticle cartilaginous, white.—Solitary, scattered, or subcaespitose, frequent on ground in deciduous forests, June-Sept., Minnesota to Maine and southward.

C. abundans Peck. Abundant Collybia. Plate 28, fig. 10.

Pileus 1-3 cm. broad; stem 3-5 cm. x 2 mm.; spores 5-6 μ.

Pileus small, convex-plane, subumbilicate, not hygrophanous, pale gray-brown, with darker disk, innate-fibrillose, thin; gills adnate, close, narrow, white; stem hollow, glabrous, cylindrical, short, easily splitting, whitish or gray-brown.—Caespitose on rotten wood in woods, not common, Aug.-Oct., Minnesota to Maine and southward.

C. succinea Fr. (edible). Plate 28, fig. 11.

Pileus 1-3 cm. broad; stem 2-3 cm. x 2-3 mm.; spores 8 x 3 μ.

Pileus convex-campanulate, smoky-red-brown, moist, glabrous, rather thin, taste farinaceous; gills adnexed, broad, subdistant, ventricose, whitish, the edges minutely serrulate; stem glabrous, tough, cylindrical, dark-red-brown, the apex pruinose; cystidia ventricose.— Gregarious on ground in beech-hemlock woods, not common, Wisconsin to New York.

C. dryophila Fr. Oak-loving Collybia. Plate 28, fig. 17.

Pileus 3-5 cm. broad; stem 3-6 cm. x 2-5 mm.; spores 6 x 3.5 μ.

Pileus convex-expanded, obtuse, often irregular, smooth, glabrous, subhygrophanous, tan to brown with yellowish cast, darker on disk, thin and pliant, the odor and taste mild; gills narrow, crowded, whitish; stem reddish-brown, cylindrical, tough, white-mycelioid at base. —Gregarious or subcaespitose in oak woods, common, July-Oct., Minnesota to Maine and southward.

C. lentinoides Peck.

Like the preceding, but the pileus hygrophanous, the stem white, and the gills serrated.—In swamps, rare but found throughout our area.

C. butyracea Fr. Buttered Collybia (edible). Plate 28, fig. 12.

Pileus 3-7 cm. broad; stem 3-7 cm. x 4-6 mm.; spores 6 x 3 μ.

Pileus convex-expanded, umbonate, glabrous, reddish-brown, fading with age, with a fatty lustre when moist, subhygrophanous or watery, and soft in wet weather, the flesh thick on disk; gills adnexed, almost free, crowded, narrow, white, the edges crenulate; stem narrowed upward, striate, mycelioid at base.—Solitary or gregarious, very common, July-Oct., on ground in pine woods in the north, in red-cedar woods southward.

C. strictipes Peck. Plate 28, fig. 20.

Differing from *C. dryophila* in the pellucid white stem, the subhygrophanous rugose pileus, and in the clear-waxy-shining colors.— In moist rich frondose woods.

C. familia Peck. (edible). Plate 28, fig. 21.

Pileus 1-3.5 cm.; stem 4-8 cm. x 2-4 mm.; spores 3 x 4 μ.

Pileus fragile, convex, hygrophanous, glabrous, brown-buff when moist, creamy-buff when dry, splitting on margin and substriatulate, thin, the flesh concolor; gills crowded, white, almost free; stem slender, whitish, confluent at base by white-mycelioid tomentum.—Caespitose on tamarack and hemlock logs, not common, Aug.-Oct., Minnesota to Maine and southward.

C. acervata Fr.   Plate 28, fig. 22.

Differing from *C. familia* in the gills refuscent in age and in the stem reddish-brown or purplish-brown.—Caespitose on decaying trunks and logs, May-Oct., not common, Minnesota to New York and southward.

C. hygrophoroides Peck.   Hygrophorus-like Collybia.   Plate 28, fig. 23.

Young unopened pileus resembling *Hygrophorus conicus* in color and shape, the margin straight as in *Mycena;* mature pileus 2-4 cm. broad, obtuse-conical then plane, hygrophanous, rufous-tan when moist, dull-tan when dry, glabrous, thin ; gills arcuate, toothed, close, broad, dingy-white, ventricose, finally tinged with flesh-color ; stem 5-12 cm. long, 2-5 mm. thick.—Solitary or subcaespitose in moist ravines with red oak and hard maple, May-Aug., rare, Illinois to Michigan and New York.

C. atrata Fr.   Black Collybia.   Plate 28, fig. 24.

Pileus 1-2 cm. broad; stem 2-3 cm. x 2-5 mm.; spores 6 x 4 μ.

Pileus tough, glabrous, umbilicate, pitch-black and shining when moist, smoky when dry, rather thick, firm ; gills adnate, rather broad, subdistant, gray then fuscous ; stem short, glabrous, tough, fuscous without and within.—On burned-over ground about stumps, June-Oct., not common, Illinois to New York and southward.

C. plexipes Fr.   Smoky Collybia.   Plate 28, fig. 19.

Pileus 1-2.5 cm. broad; stem 3-5 cm. x 1-3 mm.; spores 6 x 3 μ.

Pileus campanulate or convex, obtuse, smoky-chestnut drying rufous, hygrophanous, glabrous, not shining, very thin at margin, with dark flesh ; gills narrow, adnexed, brown, glaucous ; stem tough, black, lighter upwards.—Caespitose to solitary on very rotten mossy wood in frondose woods, not common, Michigan to New York.

C. atratoides Peck

Like the preceding in size ; the pileus subumbilicate, blackish-brown, the margin often crenate, gills rather broad, subdistant, gray.—In habitats similar to those of the preceding.

C. expallens Peck.   Plate 28, fig. 18.

Pileus 1-2.5 cm. broad; stem 2 cm. x 3 mm.; spores 4 x 5 μ.

Pileus convex-plane, subumbilicate, hygrophanous, black then brown or fuscous, glabrous, striatulate on margin when moist, thin ; gills adnate, fuscous, medium-broad, with entire edges ; stem tapering downward, tough, fuscous-brown or blackish, pruinose ; odor and taste farinaceous.—Gregarious among fallen pine needles, not common, Minnesota to Maine.

C. myriadophylla Peck. Plate 28, fig. 16.

Pileus 2 cm. broad; stem 2-3 cm. x 1.5 mm.; spores 3 x 2 μ.

Pileus plane or depressed, hygrophanous, smooth, flexible, umbilicate to papillate, dull lilac-umber-brown when moist, buff when dry, very thin; gills very crowded, narrow, thickish, dark-lilac; stem cylindrical, terete or compressed, stuffed to hollow, dull lilac or brown, pruinose.—Gregarious on mossy logs of tamarack or other conifers, July-Oct., not common, Wisconsin to New York and Indiana.

MYCENA Fr. Plate 25.

Carpophore a deeply campanulate pileus on a long, slender, cylindrical, central stem; pileus conical to campanulate, the margin at first straight and adpressed to stem; gills adnexed or adnate, decurrent in *M. vulgaris;* spores white; stem cartilaginous, slender, hollow. These are small putrescent plants which grow on wood, the ground, or herbs. They differ from those of *Collybia* in the unexpanding pileus with the straight margin, from those of *Marasmius* in not reviving when moistened after drying.

1   Stem with red or brown juice......2
1'   Stem without colored juice......3

2   Edges of gills deeply colored; pileus 4-6 mm. broad.....
    ....*M. sanguineolenta.*
2'   Edges of gills not distinctly colored; pileus 1-3 cm. broad
    ....*M. haemotopa.*

3   Stem viscid......4
3'   Stem not viscid......7

4   Both pileus and stem viscid......5
4'   Pileus not viscid, stem viscid, slender..........*M. clavicularis.*

5   Whole plant bright orange-yellow, 2-4 cm. broad, caespitose
on decaying wood..............................*M. leajana.*
5'   Plant colored otherwise, smaller......6

6   Brownish plants with decurrent gills, on fallen white pine
needles ....*M. vulgaris.*
6'   Gills not decurrent........................*M. epipterygia.*

7   Base of stem dilated into a disk or bulb; pileus white or delicately tinted, up to 10 mm. broad...............*M. crystallina.*
7'   Base of stem not so diluted......8

8   Edges of gills dark-colored with cystidia......9
8'   Edges of gills not distinctively colored......10

9   Pileus large, 2-6 cm. broad; gills violet to brown. .*M. pelianthina*.
9' Pileus small, conic-campanulate, less than 2 cm. broad; gills
    flesh-colored, the edges deeper....................*M. rosella*.

10 Stem inserted on the bark of trees with naked base. .*M. corticola*.
10' Stem attached by a more or less hairy base......11

11 Gills remaining pure-white; plant growing on ground, small,
    up to 10 mm. high, pure-white or bright-colored......12
11' Gills ashy, fuscous in age......14

12 Pileus large, 2-5 cm. broad, thick, rose to pale lilac, with a
    radish-like odor ....*M. pura*.
12' Pileus small, with no such odor......13

13 Pileus papillate ....*M. minutula*
13' Pileus not papillate, stem pellucid.............*M. immaculata*.

14 Stem firm, mostly attached to wood and caespitose......16
14' Stem not especially firm and rigid......15

15 Stem fragile, slender; pileus hygrophanous; plants often
    with marked odor......18
15' Stem filiform, pileus not hygrophanous, plants growing on
    ground or on mossy logs......21

16 Pileus large, not blue, 1-4 cm. broad......17
16' Pileus bluish, 5-12 mm. broad.....*M. subcaerulea f. cyanobasis*.

17 Pileus gray or whitish, gills not flesh-colored.....*M. parabolica*.
17' Pileus brown or dark-fuscous, gills becoming flesh-colored
    ....*M. galericulata*.
17" Pileus gray, gills soon flesh colored, odor nitrous.........
    ....*M. polygramma*.

18 Odor nitrous or alkaline......19
18' Odor otherwise; plant growing on sphagnum....*M. praelonga*.

19 Pileus glaucous-pruinose when dry...........*M. leptocephala*.
19' Pileus not glaucous......20

20 Stem slippery when moist......................*M. alcalina*.
20' Stem not lubricous, growing in bogs..............*M. metata*.

21 Pileus orange, red, yellow, or blue......22
21' Pileus dull, gills attached to stem by a collar......*M. collariata*.

22 Base of stem adorned with blue mycelial threads, pileus
    bright blue when young..........*M. subcaerulea f. cyanothrix*.
22' Plant without blue tints......23

23 Pileus orange-red or red.......................*M. acicula*.
23' Pileus yellow or dull-red...................*M. pulcherrima*.

M. leajana Berk.   Golden Mycena.   Plate 29, fig. 1.

Pileus 2-4 cm. broad; stem 3-8 cm. x 2-5 mm.; spores 9 x 5 μ.

Pileus convex-expanded, bright orange, with viscid separable cuticle, glabrous, rather thick; gills narrow, close, orange, the edges red; stem cylindrical, hollow, tough, viscid, orange.—Caespitose on logs, common, July-Sept., Minnesota to Maine and southward.

M. epipterygia Fr.   Gray Mycena.   Plate 29, fig. 2.

Pileus 0.5-2 cm. broad; stem 3-8 cm. x 1-2 mm.; spores 9 x 6 μ.

Pileus conical to campanulate, obtuse, viscid, thin, with separable cuticle, yellowish-gray to grayish-brown or fuscous; gills white to grayish-rufescent, arcuate, uncinate; stem slender or filiform, tough, viscid, yellow or brownish.—On decaying wood or humus, September, not rare.

Three kinds are recognized: (1) plants hygrophanous, yellowish-gray then gray or fuscous, stem 2 mm. thick; (2) plants with similar colors but more slender, and (3) plants grayish-brown, obscurely striate, with filiform stem.

M. vulgaris Fr.   Plate 29, fig. 3.

Pileus 5-15 mm. broad; stem 2-5 cm. x 1 mm.

Pileus convex, umbilicate, gray-brown to fuscous, striate up to the umbilicus, darker in the center, soft, slightly hygrophanous, membranaceous; gills broad behind, decurrent, white to gray; stem very viscid when moist, tough, hollow, glabrous.—Caespitose or scattered, attached to fallen pine needles, locally common, Aug.-Sept., Minnesota to Maine and Indiana.

This plant with the aspect of an *Omphalia* is known by its habitat on pine needles, and by its small size and smoky-brown, striate, umbilicate pileus.

M. clavicularis Fr.   Plate 29, fig. 4.

Pileus 0.5-1.5 cm. broad; stem 5-8 cm. x 0.5-1.5 mm.; spores 11 x 17 μ.

Pileus campanulate, white, yellow or dull gray-brown, not viscid, membranaceous; gills adnate, broad, close, white, or yellowish-rufescent; stem slender or filiform, viscid, rooting.—On ground in moss and on debris, nut-shells, etc., not common, September, Minnesota to New York and southward.

Var. *luteipes* Kauffm. is sulphur-yellow with olivaceous or green shades; the gills are arcuate-subdecurrent, yellowish-flesh-colored.

M. pelianthina Fr.   Violet Mycena.   Plate 29, fig 5.

Pileus 2-5 cm. broad; stem 5-8 cm. x 2 mm.

Pileus campanulate, obtuse, sordid-brown-violet, striate, thin; gills rounded behind, becoming sinuate, with purple edges, close, narrow, dull-violet then brownish; stem glabrous, smooth, hollow, fragile, whitish streaked with violaceous fibrils.—Scattered among fallen leaves in deciduous woods, common, July-Oct., Wisconsin to New York and southward.

M. rosella Fr.   Rose Mycena.   Plate 29, fig. 6.

Pileus 3-15 mm. broad; stem 5-6 cm. x 1 mm.; spores 8 x 5 μ.

Pileus campanulate-convex, obtusely umbonate, or obtuse, sulcate-striate, pale rose, glabrous, membranaceous toward margin; gills broadly adnate, broad, pale-rose with darker edges; stem pellucid-flesh-colored, glabrous, filiform, hollow, base covered with white mycelium.—Caespitose, two or three together, among fallen leaves or pine needles, locally abundant, Wisconsin to Michigan, northern Illinois, perhaps widely distributed.

M. haematopa Fr.   Bleeding Mycena.   Plate 29, fig. 7.

Pileus 1-3 cm. broad; stem 4-8 cm. x 2 mm.; spores 9 x 5 μ.

Pileus campanulate, obtuse, purplish-red-brown or paler, striate, thin, the sterile crenate margin extending beyond the gills; gills adnexed, narrow, concolor, the edges flocculose; stem fragile, hollow, rufous, exuding juice when broken, the base hairy.—subcaespitose on decaying wood, June-Oct., Minnesota to Maine and southward.

M. sanguineolenta Fr.   Plate 29, fig. 8.

Pileus 4-6 mm. broad; stem 4-7 cm. x 0.5 mm.; spores 9 x 4.5 μ.

Pileus small, campanulate, obtuse, glabrous, striate, pale-red then smoky, soft, membranaceous; gills narrowly adnate, broader in front, light reddish with dark purple edges; stem filiform, soft, glabrous, exuding reddish juice where broken.—Among leaves in broad-leaved forests and tamarack swamps, rare, Minnesota to Ontario and northern Illinois.

M. corticola Fr.   Bark Mycena.   Plate 29, fig. 10.

Pileus 4-8 mm. broad; stem 0.6-1.2 cm. x 2 mm.

Pileus hemispherical, obtuse, strongly striate, pruinose, blackish, ashy, or ochraceous-gray, thin to membranaceous; gills distant, each adnate by a tooth, broad, pale; stem minutely furry, paler than pileus.—Common on trunks of deciduous trees, Minnesota to New York and southward.

M. pura Fr.   Pure Mycena.

Pileus 2-4 cm. broad; stem 5-10 cm. x 3 mm.; spores 7 x 3.5 μ.

Pileus campanulate to plane, broad-umbonate, moist, bright rosy-red or violet, the margin striate, thin, the odor radish-like; gills sinuate, broad, ventricose, rose, violet, or white, intervenose; stem

glabrous, hollow, somewhat tough, cylindrical, paler than pileus.—
Caespitose or scattered on humus decayed logs, and moss or in bogs,
common, June-Oct., throughout our area.

M. immaculata Peck.   Immaculate Mycena.   Plate 29, fig. 9.

Pileus 4-8 cm. broad; stem 1.5-3.5 cm. x 0.5 mm.; spores 8 x 3 μ.
Pileus small, pure-white, conical to hemispherical, glabrous, slightly
striate on the margin, membranaceous; gills distant, white, each
adnate with a tooth, rather broad; stem pellucid-white, often strigose-
hairy at base.—On leaves and mosses on ground in woods, Iowa to
New York and southward.

M. minutula Peck.

Pileus papillate, striatulate to the center; stem covered with microscopic hairs its full length, inserted.—On wood and twigs, Sept.-
Oct., northern Illinois and northward.

M. crystallina Peck.

Pileus pruinose (as seen under lens) with minute glandular hairs
and particles.—On cedar or tamarack twigs in swamps, northern
Illinois and northward.

M. galericulata Fr.   Brown Mycena.   Plate 29, fig. 13.

Pileus 2-4 cm. broad; stem 4-12 cm. x 2 mm.; spores 9 x 6 μ.
Pileus obtusely conic-campanulate, striate up to the umbo, glabrous,
brown or darker on the umbo, lighter to buff toward the margin,
the flesh thin, somewhat tough; gills arcuate-adnate, toothed, dull-
tinged with rufous, reddish-brown in age; stem tough, pale to red-
brown-stained, paler at apex.—Very caespitose on rotten wood, common, Mar.-Nov., manitoba to Newfoundland and southward.

M. parabolica Fr.   Plate 29, fig. 17.

Pileus 1-3 cm. broad; stem 3-10 cm. x 2 mm.; spores 9 x 6 μ.
Pileus conic-campanulate, then margin turning upward, obtuse,
with a broad umbo, coarse-striate, moist, glabrous, blackish then
pearl-gray, thin; gills narrow, without tooth, whitish to ashy; stem
smooth, ashy, curving, white hairy at the rooting base.—Subcaespitose
or scattered on rotten wood of pine, beech, etc., common, locally,
Minnesota to Maine and Michigan to Indiana.

M. polygramma Fr.   Gray Mycena.   Plate 29, fig. 14.

Pileus 2-5 cm. broad; stem 5-10 cm. x 3 mm.; spores 9 x 5.5 μ.
Pileus campanulate, obtuse-subumbonate, sulcate-striate on the margin, gray to white, glabrous, thin, the odor nitrous; gills without

teeth, subdistant, white, medium-broad, white or tinted-pink, the cystidia abundant, fusiform-acuminate; stem cylindrical, cartilaginous, hollow, striate at apex or throughout, firm, fragile, glabrous, shining, white, hairy at the base.—Caespitose or scattered on rotting deciduous logs, May-June, locally common, Minnesota to New York.

M. subcaerulea (Peck) Sacc. Blue Mycena.

Pileus 0.5-2 cm. broad; stem 5-9 cm. x 1-2 mm.; spores 6-9 μ.

Pileus oval then campanulate, dark greenish brown or blue, then paler with a blue margin, tough, firm, glabrous, striatulate on the margin; gills ascending, narrow, close, whitish or gray, edge minute fimbriate; stem cylindrical, flexuous, slender, tubular, tough, elastic, pruinose, grayish-brown, hairy and rooting at the base; spores subspherical, smooth.—On fallen leaves and rotten wood in frondose forests, somewhat caespitose, locally common, June and October, throughout our area, but more common northward.

"Collections having bluish or aeruginous tints at first, in some portion of the fruiting body, a thick gelatinous pellicle, a rather flexible-cartilaginous consistency, and a densely pruinose stipe can be referred to one of two species. If the spores are ellipsoid and measure 7-9 x 4-5 μ the species is properly placed in *M. amica*. If the spores measure 7-8 x 6-8 μ and are globose to subglobose, the collection should be placed in *M. subcaerulea*. All measurements should be made on spores from 4-spored basidia. The spores of both species turn pale blue with iodine and chloral hydrate." (A. H. Smith in Myc. 28, 418, 1936.)

Form **cyanothrix** Atkins. Plate 29, fig. 24.

Is at first bright blue and viscid.—Found in northern part of our area.

Form **cyanobasis** Peck. Plate 29, fig. 18.

Is at first greenish brown to bluish, and not viscid.—Found throughout our area.

M. alcalina Fr. Plate 29, fig. 19.

Pileus 1-2.5 cm. broad; stem 3-7 cm. x 1.5 mm.; spores 10 x 6 μ.

Pileus grayish-brown or darker when moist, gray with darker center when dry, campanulate, usually obtusely-umbonate, the odor nitrous; gills whitish, narrowly adnate, becoming gray, close to subdistant; stem rigid, fragile, slippery when moistened, pale brown, fading, rooting, hollow, smooth, the rooting base covered with white hairs.—Usually scattered in bogs and swamps ,May-June, Minnesota to New York and Indiana.

M. metata Fr. is similar to *M. alcalina* but differs as follows: Pileus striate, ashy-brown; edges of gills flocculose.—On sphagnum in bogs.

M. leptocephala Fr.   Plate 29, fig. 16.

Pileus 0.5-2 cm. broad; stem 5-10 cm. x 1 mm.; spores 9 x 6 μ.

Pileus scarcely hygrophanous, grayish-white to smoky, with an obtuse umbo, subsulcate or striate, glaucous, thin, the odor nitrous; gills adnate, ventricose, narrowed behind, whitish then pale-brown; stem filiform, elastic, hollow, smooth, glabrous, darker than cap, lighter above.—Scattered among mosses and on leaves on ground in woods, not common, Iowa to New York and southward.

M. praelonga Peck.   Plate 29, fig. 15.

Pileus 0.5-1.5 cm. broad; stem 15-20 cm. x 0.5-1 mm.; spores 9 x 6 μ.

Pileus oval then conical to convex, umbonate, striate, glabrous, dark lead-brown; gills narrow, white; stem very long, filiform, firm, striatulate, red-brown.—Rooting in peat moss, gregarious, in tamarack bogs, May-June, Minnesota to Maine and southward.

M. collariata Fr.   Collared Mycena.   Plate 29, fig. 23.

Pileus 6-12 mm. broad; stem 2-3 cm. x 2 mm.; spores 9 x 5 μ.

Pileus campanulate-convex, striate, fuscous to gray, membranaceous; gills joined to a collar behind, crowded, whitish; stem filiform, tough, glabrous, shining.—On decayed logs, rare, Wisconsin to New York and southward.

It resembles *M. vulgaris* but lacks the viscid stem of that species.

M. pulcherrima Peck.   Beautiful Mycena.   Plate 29, fig. 21.

Pileus 5-10 mm. broad; stem 3-5 cm. x 0.5-1 mm.; spores 8 x 6 μ.

Pileus campanulate, faint-striatulate on margin, dull-yellow to reddish-glaucous, paler at the margin, membranaceous; gills ventricose, yellowish; stem filiform, flaccid, cylindrical, pellucid-white, shining, the base white-hairy.—Scattered or clustered in twos or threes on rotten wood or debris under hemlock trees.

M. subincarnata Peck.

Similar to the preceding but the pileus pale flesh-colored; spores 6 x 4 μ.—On ground or mossy hemlock logs.

M. acicula Fr.   Vermillion Mycena.   Plate 29, fig. 22.

Pileus 2-4 mm. broad; stem 2-5 cm. long, filiform; spores 8 x 3 μ.

Smaller than the preceding, vermillion, red, orange, or yellowish with red center; stem pellucid-yellow; gills subdistant, yellowish.— In grass, on leaves and on rotten wood in woods, common, May-June and September, Minnesota to Maine and southward.

OMPHALIA Fr

Carpophores composed of an orbicular, usually umbilicate pileus with an inrolled margin, confluent with a central stem; pileus conical, hemispherical, campanulate or expanded, usually umbilicate which is widened to infundibuliform in some species; stem cartilaginous, usually hollow or stuffed, slender, widening above into the pileus; gills decurrent or widely adnate; spores white.—In low moist places, on the ground or much decayed wood, from spring until fall, widely distributed.

1 Plants wholly white......2
1′ Plants not wholly white......5
2 Gills broad......3
2′ Gills narrow......4
3 Plants snow-white, stem tubular................O. gracillima.
3′ Plants whitish, stem solid......................O. albidula.
4 Plants pure-white ....O. scyphoides.
4′ Plants dull ....O. scyphiformis.
5 Pileus viscid, brownish, or white; plant growing on pine
   needles ....Mycena vulgaris.
5′ Pileus not viscid......6
6 Pileus yellow or orange......7
6′ Pileus of another color......8
7 Pileus 1.5-2.5 cm. broad; plant growing among mosses on dry
   soil ....O. fibuloides.
7′ Pileus 5-10 mm., plant growing in moist mossy places..O. fibula.
7″ Pileus 5-15 mm. broad, plant growing on decaying logs....
   ....O campanella.
8 Pileus dotted with black points; plant growing on sphagnum
   ....O. Gerardiana.
8′ Pileus not dotted......9
9 On gravelly soil; pileus dull to rusty................O. rustica.
9′ On hemlock logs; pileus wrinkled on disk.........O. rugodisca.
9″ On decaying logs of frondose trees; pileus silky or flocculose
   ....O. epichysium.

O. campanella Fr. Bell Omphalia, Golden trumpets. Plate 32, fig. 30.

Pileus 1-2.5 cm. broad; stem 2-3 cm. x 1 mm.; spores 7 x 3.5 μ.

Pileus bright orange-yellow becoming dull and brown with age, convex, umbilicate, thin, striate up to the umbilicus; gills thick, veiny, decurrent, arcuate, rather distant, pruinose; stem horny, tubular, date-brown, yellowish at apex and within, bearing fulvous hairs at the thickened base; odor mild.—Extensive clusters often covering decaying logs or rotten stumps, May-Nov., Minnesota to Maine and southward.

O. fibuloides Peck. Plate 32, fig. 34.

Pileus 1-2 cm. broad; stem 3-5 cm. x 2 mm.; spores 7 x 5 μ.

Pileus convex, deeply umbilicate, hygrophanous, yellowish-orange or lighter, striatulate when moist, thin; gills strongly decurrent, arcuate, intervenose, close, white; stem glabrous, hollow, yellow.—Gregarious among Ceratadon purpureus, a moss which grows on burned-over ground, May-June infrequently found, Minnesota to New England and southward. Many were found in Deer Grove Forest Preserve near Palatine, Illinois, May 25. 1924.

O. fibula Fr. Plate 32, fig. 31.

Pileus 3-8 cm. broad; stem 3-8 cm. x 0.5-1 mm.; spores 5 x 2 μ.

Pileus hemispherical or cucullate, umbilicate, striate, often unexpanded, pale yellow-orange, fading, minutely pubescent under lens, thin; gills narrow, arcuate, creamy-yellow, subpruinose; stem flexuous, white to straw-colored, toughish, somewhat hollow.—Gregarious on mosses in bogs, swamps, and low wet woods, common, May-Oct., Minnesota to New York and northern Illinois.

O. gracillima Fr. Plate 32, fig. 29.

Pileus 3-10 mm. broad; stem 2-5 cm. x 0.5 mm.; spores 7 x 3.5 μ

Pileus hemispherical, papillate, snow-white, pellucid-striate, fragile, membranaceous; gills triangular, broad, distant, thin, white, with fimbriate edges; stem filiform, tubular, minute-pruinose, white, floccose, or smooth at base.—Gregarious among fallen leaves or grass in deciduous forests, June and Sept.-Oct., not common, Minnesota to Maine and southward.

O. scyphoides Fr.

Pileus 4-8 mm. broad; stem 8-20 mm. x 0.5 mm.; spores 6 x 4.5 μ.

Pileus minute, convex-umbilicate then funnel-form, pure-white, irregular, silky, very thin; gills white, crowded, narrow; stem short, white, stuffed.—On mossy or grassy places or on dead leaves in woods, July, rare, northern part of our area.

O. scyphiformis Fr.

Similar to the preceding, but the pileus minute, dull-white, membranaceous; gills and stem whitish.—On moist ground and on mosses, rare, August, northern part of our area.

O. rugodisca Peck.

Pileus 1-2.5 cm.; stem 2-3 cm. x 1-2 mm.; spores 6 x 4 μ.

Pileus rugose, convex-plane, umbilicate, hygrophanous, watery-cinnamon-brown, striatulate when moist, paler when dry, thin; gills narrow, close, whitish, short-decurrent; stem glabrous, hollow, cinnamon-brown, paler at the apex, cartilaginous.—On prostrate rotten hemlock logs, July, probably in the same range as the hemlock, not common.

O. pyxidata Fr.

Pileus 2 cm. broad, deep-umbilicate, brick-red, striate when moist, paler when dry; gills narrow-decurrent.—Very rare, on ground by roadsides.

O. epichysium Fr.   Plate 32, fig. 35.

Pileus 1-4 cm. broad; stem 1-3 cm. x 1-3 mm.; spores 7.5 x 4 μ.

Pileus dark ashy-brown, convex-umbilicate to depressed, striate, decurrent on margin, thin, soft; gills ashy-white, narrow, thin, close; stem smoky-ashy, solid, cylindrical, glabrous.—On decaying logs in deciduous or mixed forests, July-Sept., not common, Minnesota to Maine and southward.

O. albidula Peck.

Pileus 3-8 mm. broad; stem 1-4 cm. x 0.5 mm.; spores 9 x 3 μ.

Pileus hemispherical, glabrous, striate, pure-white becoming dingy, membranaceous; gills of the same color as the pileus, decurrent, distant, broad; stem toughish, solid, very slender, white.—On leaves and bark in deciduous forests, rare, Minnesota to Maine and southward.

O. stellata Fr.   Plate 32, fig. 28.

Similar to *O. albidula* but the stem fragile.—On decaying logs.

O. papillata Peck.

Similar to *O. albidula* but the pileus pure white and papillate, conical.—On dead leaves in deciduous forest in the northern part of our area.

O. Gerardiana Peck.   Plate 32, fig. 33.

Pileus 1-2 cm.; stem 4-6 cm. x 1-2 mm.; spores 9 x 4 μ.

Pileus convex-plane to funnel-form, ashy-brown, dotted with dark scurvy points, hygrophanous, fragile, paler when dry, the flesh thin, brownish; gills narrow, subdistant, decurrent; stem hollow, tough, darker-colored than pileus.—On sphagnum in bogs, May-Aug., local, Minnesota to Maine and northern Illinois.

O. rustica Fr.   Rustic Omphalia.   Plate 32, fig. 32.

Pileus 0.5-1.2 cm. broad; stem 1.5 cm x 2 mm.; spores 10 x 5 μ.

Pileus membranaceous, broadly umbilicate, striate, fuscous then gray when moist, white to brownish when dry; gills decurrent, thick, somewhat distant, gray, arcuate; stem slender, stuffed, cylindrical or thickened upward, at length hollow only where so thickened, gray-brown.—On gravelly soil among short grasses, west and northwest of Chicago, May-July.

VOLVARIA Fr.

Carpophore composed of a hemispherical to convex pileus loosely attached to a central stipe; pileus fleshy, putrescent, soft, of different material and readily separable from the stipe; stipe usually longer than the diameter of the pileus, cylindrical, glabrous, silky, or villous, fitted at base into a cup-shaped, membranaceous, or thicker, almost fleshy volva; gills free from stem, soon pink from spores, soft, broad; spores smooth, rose-colored.—Terrestrial or epixylous, mostly rare.

1   Growing on tree trunks, pileus very silky, volva large......
....*V. bombycina*.
1'   Growing on the ground......2
2   Pileus viscid......4
2'   Pileus scarcely viscid......3
3   Pileus dark grayish-brown with black fibrils, darker on disk
....*V. volvacea*.
3'   Pileus white, volva brown........................*V. Taylori*.
4   Pileus smoky-gray, the margin striate..........*V. gloiocephala*.
4'   Pileus white, the margin not striate...............*V. speciosa*.

V. bombycina Fr.   Silky Volvaria (edible).   Plate 31, fig. 1.

Pileus 8-20 cm. broad; stem 8-20 x 1-1.5 cm.; spores 7 x 5.5 μ.

Pileus hemispherical, campanulate then convex, not umbonate, white, very silky, floccose at edge, rather thin, soft; gills free, remote, crowded, broad, ventricose, eroded; stem white, solid, usually curved, with a large, thick, loose, somewhat splitting volva which is occasionally half the diameter of pileus.—In wounds on living or decayed trees, not common, July-Sept., Minnesota to Maine and Tennessee.

V. volvacea Fr.   Plate 31, fig. 2.

Pileus 5-8 cm. broad; stem 5-10 cm. x 5-8 mm.; spores 7 x 4 μ.

Pileus campanulate, expanded, thick on disk, thin elsewhere, soft, grayish-yellow, streaked with black fibrils, not umbonate; gills free, 4-5 mm. broad; stem cylindrical, white, solid; volva loose, large, white, much smaller than in preceding.—On ground on roadsides, in cellars, rare, Aug.-Sept., Minnesota to New England to North Carolina.

V. Taylori Berk. Taylor's Volvaria.

Pileus 4 cm. high, 4-5 cm. broad; stem 6 cm. x 6 mm.

Pileus conic-campanulate, penciled, cracked, similar to that of *V. volvacea* but lighter in color and the margin lobed; volva dark brown, smaller than in preceding species.—In much decayed stumps, rare, July-Sept., Indiana to Pennsylvania.

V. gloiocephala Fr. Viscid Volvaria (poisonous).

Pileus 5-10 cm. broad; stem 8-15 cm. x 1-2 cm.; spores 12 x 7 μ.

Pileus campanulate-plane, sometimes umbonate, very viscid, smoky-gray to pearl-gray, lustrous, glabrous, the margin striate, thin, fragile; gills free, close, broad in front, subventricose; stem solid, glabrous above, villose downward; volva thin, adhering, tomentose, often three-lobed from splitting; odor and taste strong, disagreeable.—Solitary on decaying vegetation in low woods, August, rare, Minnesota to New England, South Carolina, Mississippi.

V. speciosa Fr. Handsome Volvaria (poisonous). Plate 31, fig. 6.

Pileus 5-10 cm. broad; stem 10-20 x 1-2 cm.; spores 12-18 x 10-12 μ.

Pileus hemispherical then plane and subumbonate, very viscid, white, glabrous, not striate, sometimes gray-tinged, thin, soft; gills free, broad, ventricose, crowded, rosy; stem cylindrical, villose, the base tomentose, white; volva large, membranaceous, splitting, flaccid, downy, close-fitting; odor rather strong and disagreeable.—Solitary or gregarious on leaf-mould in woodland or in rich cultivated fields, not common, May-July; Iowa to New York. southward and in California.

PLUTEUS Fr.

Carpophore composed of an orbicular, convex pileus loosely attached to a central stipe; pileus fleshy, soft, of different texture from that of the stipe; stipe usually longer than diameter of pileus, commonly about ten times as long as its own diameter, fleshy, usually solid, easily separable from pileus; gills free, soft, white to yellowish, soon tinged pink by spores, sterile cells and cystidia present; spores rosy, minute, smooth, broadly oval to subglobose.—Terrestrial or epixylous, spring until fall.

1   Pileus large, seldom as small as 5 cm. broad......2
1'   Pileus small, seldom as large as 5 cm. broad......3

2   Gill-edges smoky-brown ....*P. umbrosus.*
2'   Gill-edges colored like gills......................*P. cervinus.*

3   Pileus white ....*P. tomentosulus.*
3'   Pileus gray, brown, cinnamon, yellow, etc.......4

4   Pileus smoky-umber, plants growing on wood in alder-willow
     swamps ....*P. salicinus.*
4'   Plants growing in other habitats......5

5   Pileus yellow to brown, with granulose-villose (plush-like)
     surface ....*P. granularis.*
5'   Pileus not granulose-villose......6

6   Pileus brownish ashy, long-striate ....*P. longistriatus.*
6'   Pileus not striate or striate on margin only......7

7   Pileus cinnamon, the margin striate............*P. chrysophaeus.*
7'   Pileus brownish-ashy, not striate....................*P. nanus.*
7''' Pileus vermillion, orange or yellow......8

8   Pileus vermillion to orange......................*P. caloceps.*
8'   Pileus yellow......9

9   Pileus small 1-2 cm. broad; hygrophanous; stem with myce-
     loid base ....*P. admirabilis.*
9'   Pileus 2-5 cm. broad, stem cylindrical or enlarged below....
     ....*P. leoninus.*

P. cervinus Fr. Fawn-colored Pluteus (edible). Plate 31, fig. 5.
Pileus 5-12 cm. broad; stem 5-15 x 0.6-2 cm.; spores 5-8 x 4-5 μ.
Pileus campanulate-convex to expanded, dark grayish brown,
dingy-tan, or white, glabrous to fibrillose, with a somewhat separable
often subviscid pellicle, the flesh rather thick, white; gills white then
flesh-colored, free, close, broad, rounded behind; stem cylindrical or
tapering upward, straight or curved, dingy-white or brownish, fibrillose-striate to almost glabrous, firm, solid; spores flesh-colored in
mass; odor and taste somewhat disagreeable.—On stumps, logs, sticks,
roots, sawdust, etc., very common, June-Oct., throughout temperate
North America.
     Var. *alba* Peck includes whitish plants which grow on sawdust piles.
In var. *viscosus* Lloyd the pileus very viscid and has narrow gills. In
var. *petasatus* Fr. the pileus is striate to the center. *P. cervinus* and
its varieties are known by the free flesh-colored gills, the large size
of the plants, the types of habitat, and the innately dark-fibrillose stem.

P. umbrosus Fr.   Smoky-gilled Pluteus (edible).   Plate 31, fig. 12.

Pileus 5-10 cm. broad; stem 3-8 cm. x 4-8 mm.; spores 5-7 x 3-4 μ.

Pileus campanulate, convex-expanded, broadly umbonate, smoky-umber or blackish-brown, rugose-reticulate and floccose-scaly on disk, smooth and fibrillose on margin, the flesh rather thick, white; gills free, whitish then flesh-colored, with smoky-brown fimbriate edges, close, broad, ventricose; stem solid, firm, cylindrical or larger toward base, dingy-white covered with smoky-brown fibrils; spores oval, smooth, flesh-colored in mass; odor and taste slightly disagreeable. —On decaying wood, especially of conifers, common, June-Sept., Wisconsin to New York and North Carolina.

The species is known by smoky edges of the gills, but intermediate forms grade into *P. cervinus*.

P. salicinus Fr.   Willow Pluteus.   Plate 31, fig. 9.
Leptonia salicinus Fr.
Pileus 2-5 cm. broad; stem 2-4 cm. x 2-4 mm.; spores 8 x 5-6 μ.

Pileus convex-plane, broadly umbonate, smoky-umber, pruinose-velvety, the disk floccose; gills free, white then flesh-colored, close, not broad, extending to margin of the pileus, the edges concolor; stem cylindrical, curved, bulbillose, shining, whitish, silky-fibrillose, covered with smoky fibrils, the base smoky-olive; spores oval, smooth, flesh-colored.—Solitary on rotten wood in alder-willow swamps, July-Aug., rare.

Green and blue tints are sometimes present on the pileus and the base of the stem. This species resembles a small form of *P. umbrosus* but does not have darker gill-edges. It was originally described as a species of *Leptonia* but the free gills are a character of *Pluteus*, not of *Leptonia*.

P. tomentosulus Peck.   Plate 31, fig. 4.

Pileus 3-7 cm. broad; stem 5-10 cm. x 4-8 mm.; spores 6 x 5 μ.

Pileus thin, convex, expanded, umbonate or obtuse, white or tinged-pink, floccose-tomentose, smooth on the margin, the flesh white; gills free, white then rosy, fimbriate on edges, crowded, broad; stem white, fibrillose-striate, cylindrical, solid, subbulbous at base; spores sub-globose, smooth, rose-flesh-colored in mass; cystidia 90 x 24 μ, not horned, bottle-shaped on slender stalk.—Solitary or scattered on rotten logs in hemlock, tamarack, and cedar swamps, Wisconsin to New York and Ohio.

P. longistriatus Peck.   Plate 31, fig. 8.

Pileus 2-5 cm. broad; stem 3-5 cm. x 2-3 mm.; spores 6 x 5 μ.

Pileus very thin, convex, plane, brownish-ashy or pale brownish-gray, minutely scaly on disk, long-striate or subsulcate in age; gills free, close, broad, not ventricose, rounded behind, white then flesh-colored, the edges pulverulent; stem white, pulverulent, fibrous, innately striatulate, cylindrical, solid; spores globose, granular within, smooth, pale flesh-colored; cystidia ventricose, not horned, 75-90 μ long.—Solitary on rotten wood, not common, June-July, Minnesota to New York and Illinois.

It is known by its long-striate ashy-brown pileus with free flesh-colored gills.

P. granularis Peck. (edible). Plate 31, fig. 11.

Pileus 2-5 cm. broad; stem 4-7 cm. x 2-4 mm.; spores 7 x 6 μ.

Pileus convex, plane, subumbonate, yellow to brown, with a plush-like granulose villose surface, rugose-wrinkled; gills free, crowded, rather broad, ventricose, white then flesh-colored, the edges concolor; stem velvety-pubescent, rarely scaly, cylindrical, solid, yellow to brown, paler at apex, often brown-scaly toward the base; spores broadly oval or globose.—On decaying wood in mixed woods, more frequently found in hemlock regions, not common, June-Oct., Wisconsin to New York and southward in mountains to Virginia.

P. caloceps Atkins. Plate 31, fig. 7.

Pileus 2-4.5 cm. broad; stem 3-6 cm. x 3-5 mm.; spores 5-8 x 4-6 μ.

Pileus convex, umbonate, orange to vermillion, glabrous or slightly granular, or somewhat rimose on margin, the flesh white, thin; gills free, rounded behind, broadly elliptical to subventricose, pale-dull-flesh-colored, the edges flocculose; stem pallid, fibrous-striate.—Solitary on rotten wood or on ground in woods, Illinois and Michigan, rare.

P. nanus Fr. Plate 31, fig. 10.

Pileus 2-3 cm. broad; stem 2-3 cm. x 2-3 mm.; spores 5 μ in diameter.

Pileus thin, convex, plane or obtuse, umber then brownish-ashy, radiately rugose on disk, nearly even on margin, velvety pruinose, pulverulent, or granulose; gills free, white then flesh-colored, fimbriate at edges, close, ventricose, narrowed toward ends; stem solid, glabrous, pellucid-white, cylindrical, rigid, often curved, striatulate or innately fibrillose; spores subglobose, smooth, flesh-colored in mass; cystidia 75 μ long, fusiform, bottle-shaped, not horned, vacuolate.—Solitary or scattered on decaying logs, sticks, etc. in low woods and swamps, June-Oct., not common, Michigan to Kentucky, eastward and westward.

In var. *lutescens* Fr. the stem and sometimes the gills are yellow; stem is solid and striate; plants are found in the same habitat as the type.

P. leoninus Fr.   Plate 32, fig. 13.

Pileus 2-5 cm. broad; stem 5-7 cm. x 2-5 mm.; spores 6-7 x 5 μ.

Pileus campanulate-convex-subumbonate, yellow, not rugulose, glabrous, moist, striate on margin, thin; gills free, white then deep flesh-colored, close, moderately broad; stem pellucid-white or whitish, cylindrical or enlarged below, solid, glabrous, striatulate; spores sub-globose, smooth, rose-colored; cystidia not abundant, fusiform, 60 μ long.—On rotting wood, Aug.-Sept., not common, Illinois, Michigan, Kentucky.

P. admirabilis Peck.

Pileus 1-2 cm. broad; stem 3-5 cm. x 1-2 mm.; spores 5.5-.7 x 5-6 μ.

Pileus thin, convex-campanulate, expanded, usually umbonate, ochraceous-yellow to luteus, glabrous, rugose-reticulate, hygropha-nous, brownish when young, striatulate on the margin when moist, almost smooth when dry; gills free, whitish or yellowish, then rosy-flesh-colored, rounded behind, moderately broad, ventricose, close; stem slender, yellow, stuffed then hollow, cylindrical, subrigid, glab-rous, white-myceloid at base; spores subglobose, smooth, rosy-flesh-colored in mass.—Scattered on decaying wood in conifer and fron-dose woods, rare, July-Sept., Michigan to Kentucky.

P. chrysophaeus Schaeff.   Golden Pluteus (edible).

Pileus 3-6 cm. broad; stem 5-8 cm. x 4-6 mm.; gills 4-6 mm. wide; spores 5 μ in diameter.

Pileus very thin, campanulate, expanded, cinnamon-colored, glab-rous, slightly wrinkled, the margin striate; gills free, white then pale-salmon; stem whitish, glabrous, cylindrical, becoming hollow.—On beech trunks, not common, June-Oct., Michigan to New Jersey.

ENTOLOMA Fr.

Carpophore an orbicular, convex pileus of same material and con-fluent with the central, cylindrical, fleshy stipe; pileus fleshy, soft, putrescent; stipe usually longer than diameter of pileus, fleshy or fibrous; gills emarginate to sinuate; spores rosy, usually angular.— Growing on the ground.

1   Pileus dry, flocculose or squamulose......4
1'   Pileus hygrophanous, moist or viscid......2

2   Pileus thin, hygrophanous, somewhat silky when dry......6
2'   Pileus moist or viscid, not hygrophanous, glabrous......3
3   Pileus convex or nearly plane, large..............*E. lividum.*
3'   Pileus conic or subcampanulate, plant growing in bogs......14
4   Pileus umbonate, grayish-brown or mouse-colored..*E. jubatum.*
4'   Pileus not umbonate......5
5   Pileus with violaceous tints....................*E. cyaneum.*
5'   Pileus white ....*E. sericellum.*
5"   Pileus dark brown........................*E. scabrinellum.*
6   Gills pale yellow at first....................*E. flavifolium.*
6'   Gills never yellow......7
7   Fresh plants with an alkaline or nitrous odor, fragile....
     ....*E. nidorosum.*
7'   Fresh plants lacking this odor......8
8   Odor and taste farinaceous, pleasant......9
8'   Odor and taste not farinaceous......12
9   Gills gray at first; pileus dark brown, 2-5 cm. broad, the
     margin striate when moist....................*E. sericeum.*
9'   Gills white at first; pileus lurid-brown or gray. the margin
     smooth......10
10   Pileus conic-campanulate or umbonate, sometimes radiately
     streaked or spotted with fibrils.................*E. clypeatum.*
10' Pileus convex, plane, subumbonate, not virgate......11
11   Stem white, gills narrow, pileus fading to whitish..*E. sericatum.*
11' Stem gray-tinged; pileus not fading, with a delicate sepa-
     rable cuticle ....*E. griseum.*
12   Pileus white when moist, fragile.................*E. speculum.*
12' Pileus watery-white, tinged yellowish when moist..*E. grayanum.*
12" Pileus umber, smoky, or cinnamon when moist......13
13   Pileus umbonate, 2-6 cm. broad; stem twisted, brownish to
     grayish-white ....*E. strictius.*
13' Pileus obtuse to plane, 4-8 cm. broad; stem pure-white; gills
     rather broad ....*E. rhodopolium.*
14   [See errata]

E. jubatum Fr. Crested Entoloma. Plate 35, fig. 1.

Pileus 2-5 cm. broad; stem 5-8 cm. x 4-6 mm.; spores 7-11 x 6 μ.

Pileus campanulate, then expanded-umbonate, mouse-colored, vil-
lose-scaly or fibrillose, thin; gills adnexed, seceding readily from
stem, smoky-brown, close, ventricose; stem cylindrical, brownish,
fragile, fibrous, stuffed or hollow, clothed with smoky fibrils; spores
very irregular-shaped.—On the ground in woods, rare, Illinois to
Michigan and New York.

E. cyaneum Peck.   Violaceous Entoloma.   Plate 35, fig. 2.

Pileus 2-3.5 cm. broad; stem 3-6 cm. x 2-4 mm.; spores 8 x 5 μ.

Pileus convex-campanulate, umbonate, brown or brownish-violaceous, dry, fibrillose-squamulose, the flesh thin except on the disk, white; gills adnate, close, rather broad, whitish often tinged-vinaceous, then flesh-colored-tinged-ashy, the edges white, fimbriate; stem subcylindrical, solid, often twisted, fibrillose-striate, furfuraceous-squamulose upward, vinaceous above, pallid below, white within, the fibrous flesh covered with a subcartilaginous cuticle; spores angular-tuberculate, subelliptical.—Scattered on low, wet sandy soil and humus or much decayed wood, June-Sept., rare, Indiana to Michigan and New Hampshire.

E. sericellum Fr.   Silky Entoloma.   Plate 35, fig. 4.

Pileus 5-15 mm. broad; stem 2-5 cm. x 1-2 mm.; spores 9-12 x 7 μ.

Pileus thin, convex-plane then centrally depressed, white or shining-pellucid-white, silky or minutely squamulose, smooth on margin, the margin at first incurved and floccose; gills broadly adnate, each slightly decurrent by a tooth, rather distant, broad, white, cylindrical, smooth, soft, pruinose at the apex, stuffed then hollow; spores angular-tuberculate.—Scattered on debris or humus in cedar swamps or low woods, locally common, Aug.-Sept., Minnesota to New York and southward.

E. scabrinellum Peck.   Scabrous Entoloma.

Pileus 1-3 cm. broad; stem 3-8 cm. x 2-3 mm.; spores 7-10 x 6 μ.

Pileus broadly convex, expanded, and subumbonate, dry, scabrous, densely covered with minute, erect spine-like scales, dark mouse-brown or smoky-brown, the thin incurved margin slightly surpassing gills; flesh thin, pallid; gills adnexed, rounded behind, broad, ventricose, grayish-white becoming pink, the edges white-flocculose; stem tapering upward from thicker base, pruinose at apex, white-myceloid at base, pallid or brownish-tinged, fibrillose, glabrescent, stuffed then hollow; spores coarsely tuberculate-angular, elliptic in outline.—Gregarious on ground in low mossy woods, September, rare, Illinois, Michigan, New York.

E. nidorosum Fr.   Nitrous Entoloma.

Pileus 2-7 cm. broad; stem 4-7 cm. x 4-6 mm.; spores 9 x 6-7 μ.

Pileus convex, obtuse, grayish-brown when moist, silky and shining when dry, hygrophanous, fragile, the margin incurved, the flesh thin, white, fragile; gills adnexed, emarginate or nearly free, subdistant, broad, often wavy, pallid becoming pale flesh-colored; stem subcylindrical, stuffed soon hollow, pruinose at apex, whitish, slightly fibrillose; spores ovate, somewhat angular especially at the prominent apiculus.—On mosses in sphagnous bogs, rare, Sept.-Oct., Illinois to Michigan and New York.

E. clypeatum Fr. Shield Entoloma (edible). Plate 35, fig. 6.

Pileus 3-10 cm. broad ; stem 4-6 cm. x 6-12 mm. ; spores 9 x 7 μ.

Pileus campanulate with broad obtusely conic umbo, hygrophanous, lurid-brown when moist, brownish-ashy when dry, often virgate with darker lines, glabrous, often wavy, the flesh thin ; gills adnexed, seceding, rounded behind, moderately broad, serrulate on the edges, whitish then sordid-rose-colored ; stem often rather stout and short, white, fragile, silky-fibrillose, subpruinose at the apex, sometimes compressed, stuffed or hollow ; spores subglobose, angular, rosy in mass ; taste and odor farinaceous.—Gregarious to subcaespitose on ground in low woods among moss or in grassy places in woods, spring and autumn, not common, Wisconsin to New York and southward.

E. sericeum Fr. Plate 35, fig 3.

Pileus 2-6 cm. broad ; stem 2-6 cm. x 3-5 mm. ; spores 9 x 6-7 μ.

Pileus convex-expanded, more or less umbonate, umber-brown with darker umbo when moist, fading to grayish-brown and silky-shining when dry, glabrous, hygrophanous, the margin striatulate when moist, at first smooth then wavy, the flesh thin, moist, concolor, the odor farinaceous ; gills adnexed-emarginate, usually broadest behind, grayish-white becoming salmon-colored, rather broad, subdistant, the edges entire ; stem grayish or grayish-brown, innately silky-fibrillose, subcylindrical, sometimes compressed or twisted, stuffed then hollow ; spores angular.—Gregarious, among grass in open woods and meadows, rare, June-July, Illinois to Michigan and New York.

E. sericatum (Britz) Kauffm. Plate 35, fig. 5.

Pileus 3-8 cm. broad ; stem 5-10 cm. x 5-10 mm. ; spores 9 x 6-8.5 μ.

Pileus campanulate then plane, subumbonate, grayish-brown when moist, fading to creamy-buff or whitish when dry, darker on the umbo while drying, hygrophanous, smooth, glabrous, silky-shining when dry, the margin striatulate when moist, at length splitting or upturned, the flesh thin, concolor, scissile, the taste and odor farinaceous ; gills white, at length pale flesh-colored, eroded at the edges, narrow, to a point at margin of pileus, close, thin, adnexed becoming emarginate ; stem long, slender, pure-white, shining, obscurely undulate, innately silky-striatulate, glabrous, cylindrical or narrowed below, fibrous-stuffed then partly hollow, splitting longitudinally when dry, pruinose at the apex.—Gregarious among leaves in conifer or frondose woods, abundant locally, September, Michigan and surrounding states.

E. griseum Peck. Grayish Entoloma. Plate 35, fig. 7.

Pileus 3-7 cm. broad; stem 3-8 cm. x 5-10 mm.; spores 8 x 7 μ.

Pileus campanulate-convex, obtuse or slightly umbonate, grayish brown fading but little when dry, firm then fragile, glabrous, smooth on the margin, subhygrophanous, sometimes pale-umber, the cuticle somewhat differentiated, thin, separable, the margin decurved, the flesh moderately thin, the odor and taste farinaceous, very scissile; gills adnexed, emarginate, each decurrent with a tooth, about 4 mm. broad, whitish-gray, slowly flesh-colored, sometimes veined; stem cylindrical, whitish, pruinose at the apex, silky-fibrillose; spores sub-globose, angular, pale-flesh-colored.—On ground in low conifer and frondose woods, common locally, May and October, Wisconsin to New York and Indiana.

E. speculum Fr. Shining-white Entoloma. Plate 35, fig. 8.

Pileus 2-6 cm. broad; stem 3-9 cm. x 3-8 mm.; spores 7-9 x 7 μ.

Pileus convex-expanded, plane, or slightly depressed about the umbo, hygrophanous, pinkish-white when moist, white and silky-shining when dry, the umbo obtuse and when moist whiter than other parts of pileus, the flesh thin, fragile, white; gills emarginate, broad behind, subdistant, white becoming deep-rose-colored, suberoded at the edges, sometimes veined; stem cylindrical, fragile, shining-white, soon hollow, sometimes compressed, pruinose at the apex, silky-fibrillose or striatulate; spores globose-angular, apiculate, nucleate.—Solitary to subcaespitose in grass, on leaf-mould, or on debris in woods, not common, Indiana and Michigan.

E. grayanum Peck. Plate 35, fig 9.

Pileus 5-12 cm. broad; stem 6-12 cm. x 1-2 cm.; spores 8 x 7 μ.

Pileus campanulate-convex, then expanded, firm, glabrous, hygrophanous, whitish or slightly yellow when moist, shining white when dry, flesh thin to medium in thickness, white or tinged yellowish, scissile; gills adnexed becoming emarginate, broad, ventricose, white then rosy, edge smooth; stem cylindrical, stout, fibrous-stuffed, silky shining, watery-white or tinged yellowish; spores 5-10 angled, apiculate, flesh-color in mass.—Solitary to subcaespitose-gregarious on the ground in the woods, occasionally found, Aug.-Oct., northeastern part of our area.

E. grande Peck (Plate 36, fig. 17) differs from the preceding but little. The hygrophanous flesh and thinner pileus of *E. grayanum* are the points for separation.—Michigan to New York.

E. strictius Peck. (suspected). Plate 35, fig. 10.

Pileus 2.5-6 cm. broad; stem 6-10 cm. x 3-7 mm.; spores 11 x 7 μ.

Pileus obtusely conic-campanulate to broadly campanulate, then expanded and often strongly umbonate, umber to watery-cinnamon when moist, pearl-gray and silky-shining when dry, glabrous, hygrophanous, the flesh thin, scissile, concolor; gills adnexed, broad, ventricose, almost distant, narrowed in front, white or pallid becoming rosy-flesh-colored, the edges minutely eroded; stem slender, cylindrical, strict, obscurely bulbous, rigid-fragile, twisted, easily splitting, fibrillose, pallid to grayish-white; spores elongated, angular, curving toward apiculus.—Subcaespitose in low woods or near sphagnum swamps, on much decayed wood, etc., not common, June-Oct.

E. rhodopolium Fr.   Rosy Entoloma (suspected).   Plate 35, fig. 11.

Pileus 4-7 cm. broad; stem 4-10 cm. x 4-6 mm.; spores 6-9 μ.

Pileus subcampanulate, nearly plane or slightly depressed in center, fibrillose when young, soon glabrous, hygrophanous, brownish, and striatulate on margin when moist, silky-shining and pale-gray when dry; the flesh thin but fleshy, fragile, white; gills adnate, sinuate, subdistant, white becoming rosy; stem cylindrical or tapering upward, pruinose at apex, white, hollow, glabrous, with a fibrous subsartilaginous rind; odor and taste none; spores subglobose, 5-6 angled, deep-rose-colored in mass.—Solitary or subcaespitose on the ground in mixed or deciduous woods, not common, Aug.-Sept., Minnesota, New England, Illinois, Ohio.

E. lividum Fr.   Livid Entoloma (poisonous).   Plate 36, fig. 12.

Pileus 7-10 cm. broad; stem 6-8 cm. x 1.5-2.5 cm.; spores 8-10 μ in length.

Pileus campanulate then expanded, glabrous, pelliculose, the cuticle composed of subgelatinous hyphae about 6 μ in diameter, fibrillose when dried, viscid when very wet, pale-livid-tan fading when dry, wrinkled-rugose, the margin striate; gills adnexed, broad, subventricose, subdistant behind, pallid then bright-flesh-colored; stem stout, white, glabrous, subpruinose at the apex, stuffed then hollow; spores globose, angular; odor faint, taste farinaceous.—Gregarious on the ground in white pine and beech woods of western Michigan, Indiana Dunes State Park, rare

E. salmoneum Peck.   Salmon Entoloma.   Plate 36, fig. 15.

Pileus 1.5-3 cm. broad; stem 8-15 cm. x 2-4 mm.; spores 11 μ.

Pileus conical or campanulate, subacute or with a minute papilla or small cusp at apex, thin, glabrous, moist, salmon-colered; gills adnexed, broad, subdistant, ventricose, salmon-colored; stem slender, cylindrical, hollow, salmon-colored, glabrous, pruinose at apex, innately silky-striatulate.—Gregarious among mosses under balsam fir, spruce, and other conifers, Aug.-Sept., infrequently found and local, Minnesota to Maine, Michigan and New York.

E. cuspidatum Peck.

Differing from *E. salmoneum* in its pale yellow pileus, gills, and stem, and in the distinct cusp present on pileus.—In sphagnous swamps, northern Illinois.

E. Peckianum Burt. Peck's Entoloma.

Pileus 1.5-3 cm, broad; stem 5-10 cm. x 2-4 mm.; spores 7.5-10 μ long.

Pileus thin, conical becoming subcampanulate, moist, brown or blackish and shining, paler in drying, umbonate, obscurely roughened by the matted ends of minute fibrils; gills adnexed, abruptly rounded behind, broad, whitish becoming pink; stem slender, cylindrical, hollow, fibrillose-striate, pale-brown, often with white mycelium at base, white within; spores angular uninucleate.—In sphagnous swamps, rare, August, Minnesota to New England, Illinois and Michigan.

CLITOPILUS Fr.

Carpophore composed of a more or less orbicular, convex to infundibuliform pileus of same material and confluent with the central fleshy stipe; pileus fleshy, soft, putrescent, its context tapering into the inseparable stipe; stipe long or short, annulus absent; gills mostly white or dingy, soon tinged pink by spores, decurrent or broadly adnate; spores angular or rounded, varying light to deep rose-color. —Terrestrial, or on rotting wood.

1 Pileus viscid when moist, compact, fleshy, soft, 3-9 cm. in diameter ....*C. orcella.*
1' Pileus not viscid......2
2 Pileus 5 cm. or more in diameter......3
2' Pileus small, 1-5 cm. in diameter......☞ 5
3 Very caespitose, firm but brittle, whitish.........*C. caespitosus.*
3' Not markedly caespitose......4
4 Spores not angular, flesh thick, pileus pruinate......*C. prunulus.*
4' Spores angular, pileus brownish, some plants in each group commonly much deformed......................*C. abortivus.*
5 Spores and mature gills rosy-red......6
5' Spores and mature gills flesh-colored or very pale; pileus concentrically rivulose; stem white-mycelioid at base..........
......................................*C. noveboracensis.*

6 Pileus deeply umbilicate, dark smoky-gray; gills broad in
    middle ....*C. undatus.*
6' Pileus hemispheric, gray with pink-tinge; gills narrow....
    ....*C. erythrosporus.*

C. undatus Fr.

Pileus 1.5-3.5 cm. broad; stem 1.5-2 cm. x 1.5-3 mm.; spores 8 x 6 μ.
Pileus fragile, deeply umbilicate to subinfundibuliform, dark
smoky-gray when moist, fading, opaque, silky when dry, splitting
radially in age, sometimes obscurely zonate, the margin wavy, the
flesh concolor; gills decurrent, broad in middle, close, dark-ashy then
tinged-reddish-flesh-colored; stem cylindrical,. smooth, brownish-
ashy to pale-brown, glabrous, solid, tough-elastic; spores angular,
nucleate, subglobose or oval, reddish-flesh-colored in mass; odor none.
—On mossy ground or rotten wood in open woods, Michigan.

C. abortivus Berk. & Curt. Abortive Clitopilus (edible). Plate 36, fig. 14.

Pileus 5-10 cm. broad; stem 3-9 cm. x 6-10 mm.; spores 9 x 5-6 μ.
Pileus firm, convex, plane or depressed, grayish-brown, dull, becoming pale-tan (isabelline), dry, covered at first with silky tomentum, the margin smooth, the flesh white; gills decurrent to merely
adnate, each with a tooth, close, thin, rather narrow, pale-gray becoming rosy to salmon-colored; stem pale-grayish-brown to pale tan.
minutely floccose, subcylindrical, fibrous, solid; spores irregular, angular, nucleate, pale-rose-colored or almost salmon in mass; odor
and taste somewhat farinaceous.—Subcaespitose or gregarious on
ground or very much decayed wood in woods, Iowa to New England
and Tennessee.
Commonly diseased plants of this species are found as abortive
masses with the appearance of irregular puff-balls.

C. erythrosporus Peck. Red-spored Clitopilus (edible).

Pileus 2.5-5 cm. broad; stem 2.5-4 cm. x 4-6 mm.; spores 5 x 3-4 μ.
Pileus thin, hemispherical or strongly convex, pinkish-gray, glabrous or pruinose, the flesh white-tinged with pink; gills deeply decurrent, arcuate, crowded, narrow, colored like pileus; stem subcylindrical, hollow, slightly pruinose at apex, concolor; spores elliptical;
taste farinaceous.—Sparsely gregarious on decayed wood and among
fallen leaves in woods, Sept.-Nov., not common, Pennsylvania, New
York, Indiana.

C. caespitosus Peck. Tufted Clitopilus. Plate 36, fig. 21.

Pileus 5-15 cm. broad; stem 3-7 cm. x 5-12 mm.; spores 5 x 3 μ.

Pileus convex, soon expanded and then plane to depressed, somewhat firm but brittle, very fragile when moist, glabrous, whitish to gray-tinged when young, watery-dingy-white when moist, dull-whitish to pale-tan and silky-shining when dry, smooth, the margin at first inrolled, often recurved and split in age, the flesh pallid, white, thin, subhygrophanous, somewhat scissile; gills adnate-decurrent, very crowded and narrow, thin, dingy-pale-flesh-colored; stem cylindrical or tapering downward, pallid,, silky-fibrillose, scurfy at apex, stuffed, fragile and easily splitting in age; spores smooth, sordid-white with pink tinge in mass; odor slightly fragrant.—Very caespitose, on ground in woods, not common, Aug.-Oct., Illinois to New York.

C. noveboracensis Peck. New York Clitopilus. Plate 36, fig. 18.

Pileus 2.5-5 cm. broad; stem 2.5-5 cm. x 2-6 mm.; spores 4-5 μ in diameter.

Pileus thin, convex, expanded, or slightly depressed, dingy- white, cracked in areas or concentrically rivulose, sometimes obscurely zonate; gills deeply decurrent, sometimes forked, white, becoming dingy, tinged-yellow or flesh colored, narrow, close; stem cylindrical, forming white branching root-like fibers; spores globose; odor farinaceous; taste bitter.—Gregarious or caespitose on ground in woods and pastures, not common, Aug.-Oct., Minnesota to Maine and southward.

C. prunulus Fr. (edible). Plate 36, fig. 20.

Pileus 5-10 cm. broad; stem 3-8 cm. x 5-15 mm.; spores 11 x 6 μ.

Pileus convex then nearly plane, firm, dry, pruinate, white to dark-gray, often eccentric, the margin smooth, often wavy, the flesh white, thick on disk; gills deeply decurrent, narrow, subdistant, white then flesh-colored; stem solid, naked, striate, subcylindrical, white, sometimes ventricose, spores subfusiform, smooth, with three deep longitudinal furrows, tinged salmon; odor and taste farinaceous.—On the ground in open woods, not common, July-Sept., Minnesota to New England, Illinois and Pennsylvania.

C. orcella Fr.

Pileus 3-9 cm. broad; stem 3-5 cm. x 4-10 mm.; spores 10 x 5 μ.

Similar to preceding but with viscid pileus when moist, closer gills and with soft texture.—On the ground in sugar-maple woods, rather common, Wisconsin, New York and Tennessee.

CLAUDOPUS W. G. Smith.

Carpophore orbicular, reniform or flabelliform, convex to plane, with or without a stipe; stipe fleshy, lateral, or lacking, flesh putrescent; gills soft, adnate, adnexed or decurrent; spores rosy in mass. Growing on wood.

Claudopus nidulans Fr. (edible).   Plate 34, fig. 7.

Pileus 2-5 cm. long x 2-7 cm. wide x 5-9 mm. thick; spores 7 x 4 μ.

Plants narrowed to short stem-like base, orbicular to reniform, convex or plane, with incurved margin, yellow or buff, coarsely tomentose-hairy, firm tough; gills bright-orange-yellow, adnate, close, rather broad; stem-like base tomentose beneath; odor disagreeable in fresh plants.—Gregarious or caespitose, overlapping, on decaying logs in frondose forest, especially of *Acer saccharum* (sugar maple) and *Fagus* (beech), July-Oct., common, Minnesota to Maine and Alabama.

LEPTONIA Fr.   Plate 32.

Pileus at length subexpanded and usually depressed in center, the margin at first incurved, the umbilicus minutely squamulose; stem cartilaginous, confluent with the pileus, stuffed but soon hollow usually glabrous and polished but some species are dotted with colored squamules, often compressed, furrowed, or twisted; gills adnexed or adnate-seceding; spores pink and angular except in *L. seticeps* Atkins., which may more properly belong to the genus *Pluteus*. A peculiar lustre of stem and pileus is due, according to Patouillard, to the presence of air between the hyphae in the surface layer.

1   Pileus hygrophanous or subhygrophanous, dark-colored, umber or blue-black......2
1'   Pileus not hygrophanous......3
2   Pileus striatulate when moist, watery or whitish.....*L. asprella.*
2'   Pileus never striatulate, the flesh bluish-black.....*L. lampropoda.*
3   Stem and pileus rosy, white, waxy-yellow-greenish or violaceous......4
3'   Stem and pileus of another color......5
4   Colors rosy; plants growing on sphagnum............*L. rosea.*
4'   Colors white; pileus striate..................*L. transformata.*
4"   Colors waxy-yellowish; pileus scaly or fibrillose......*L. formosa.*
4''' Pileus, stem, and gills violaceous, stem dotted with purple fibrils ....*L. euchroa.*
4''''Pileus, stem and gills greenish, with an odor of mice....*L. incana.*
5   Pileus and stem brown to leather-colored......6
5'   Pileus walnut-brown, gills but slightly adnexed, plants growing on rotten wood..............................*L. seticeps.*

6 Stem marked with dark dots at least above......7
6' Stem not so marked, pileus bluish-black.........*L. lampropoda.*

7 On the ground; gill-edges dark and serrulate......*L. serrulata.*
7' On rotten wood; gill-edges concolor, pileus smoky, squamulose; stem lavender-tinged, squamulose.............*L. placida.*

L. asprella Fr. Plate 32, fig. 14.

Pileus 2-4 cm. broad; stem 3-8 cm. x 2-3 mm.; spores 9-13 x 7 μ.

Pileus convex then expanded and umbilicate-depressed, pale umber
to grayish-brown, striatulate-glabrous or fibrillose when moist, silky-
shining and not striatulate when dry, the margin thin and fragile,
becoming split; gills adnexed to adnate-seceding, rather broad behind, narrowed in front, subdistant, whitish to grayish then rosy,
the edges entire, concolor; stem slender, straight, fuscous or pale,
rigid-elastic but fragile, stuffed then hollow, glabrous, the apex
pruinose, the base white-mycelioid; spores sharp-angled; odor and
taste mild.—On the ground in woods, especially near decaying wood,
Aug.-Sept., not common, in conifer regions, northern Illinois,
Michigan.

L. serrulata Fr. Plate 32, fig. 15.

Pileus 1-3 cm. broad; stem 2-5 cm. x 1-2 mm.; spores 11 x 7 μ.

Pileus convex then plane, umbilicate-depressed, bluish-black, smoky,
not striate, the flesh thin, whitish; gills adnate, whitish, the edges
black, serrulate, ventricose; stem blackish or steel-blue, black dotted
at the apex, glabrous, cartilaginous, rigid, stuffed then hollow, the base
white-mycelioid; spores elongated, nodular-angular; sterile cells on
gill-edge filled with dark coloring matter.—On the ground in low,
wet woods of elm, ash, etc., locally common, July-Sept., Wisconsin
to New England, and Illinois.

This species is known by its black, serrulate gill-edges and its dark
colors. It superficially resembles *Eccilia atrides.*

L. euchroa Fr. Violet Leptonia. Plate 32, fig. 16.

Pileus 1-2 cm. broad; stem 2-3 cm. x 2 mm.; spores 11 x 6 μ.

Pileus convex then plane, violaceous to wine-colored, covered with
fibrillose squamules, not striate, the margin fibrillose-scaly; gills narrowly adnate, violet becoming pallid, subdistant, very ventricose, narrowed at ends; stem slender, cylindrical, dark violet with purple
fibrils, glabrous, toughish, becoming hollow; spores nodose-angular.
—Subcaespitose on rotten wood or sawdust, rare, July-Sept., Minnesota, Michigan and Illinois.

L. formosa Fr.   Plate 32, fig. 17.

Pileus 1-3 cm. broad; stem 4-5 cm. x 2 mm.; spores 11 x 6 μ.

Pileus convex then plane and umbilicate, yellow-wax-colored, minutely fuscous-squamulous, the margin striate, the flesh membranaceous, tough, thin, yellow; gills adnate, each with a tooth, tinged yellow then flesh-colored, subdistant, rather broad, tinged-yellow then flesh-colored, subdistant, rather broad, the edges entire, concolor; stem yellow, striatulate, cylindrical, cartilaginous, becoming hollow, glabrous, shining; spores somewhat rectangular in outline, with oblique apiculus, flesh-colored in mass; odor and taste mild.—In low wet, rich woods, July-Sept., locally common, Minnesota to New York and Illinois.

L. incana Fr.   Hoary Leptonia.   Plate 32, fig. 20.

Pileus 2-3 cm. broad; stem 3-5 cm. x 2-4 mm.; spores 8-9 μ.

Pileus convex, plane, umbilicate, greenish, submembranaceous, smooth with silky lustre, the margin striate; gills adnate, broad, subdistant, white then greenish; stem hollow, smooth, shining, brownish-green; spores irregular, dull yellowish-pink, rough; odor strongly of mice.—In pastures after warm rains, locally common, July-Sept., Indiana and Ohio.

L. placida Fr.   Plate 32, fig. 18.

Pileus 3-5 cm. broad; stem 2-5 cm. x 3-8 mm.; spores 10 x 6 μ.

Pileus campanulate, then convex, obtuse, pale-smoky, covered with dark brown or black silky scales which are darker and more abundant on disk, sometimes obscurely violet-tinged, not striate, the flesh thin, pallid with slight pink tinge; gills adnexed, broad behind, not thin, crowded, whitish then flesh-colored, the edges concolor; stem dotted with lavender, dark blue or blackish squamules, thickened at the apex, white-mycelioid at the base, cartilaginous, becoming hollow, rather thick, often compressed and grooved, curved, sometimes twisted; spores tuberculate-angular, with oblique apiculus.—Gregarious on rotten wood, locally common, June-Oct., common, Minnesota, Michigan and southward.

L. lampropoda Fr.   Black Leptonia.   Plate 32, fig. 21.

Pileus 1-3 cm. broad; stem 2.5-5 cm. x 2-4 mm.; spores 11 x 6 μ.

Pileus convex then plane, umbilicate, or depressed, bluish-black or jet-black when young, fading to smoky and becoming minutely squamulose in age, never striate, not papillate, margin at first curved downward, then upward, the flesh at first bluish-black then grayish, subhygrophanous, thin; gills adnate-seceding, white then rose-colored, moderately broad, ventricose, subdistant, the edges-entire and concolor; stem bluish-black becoming smoky, glabrous, smooth, firm, elastic, soon hollow, the base white and mycelium-covered; spores rosy in mass, tuberculate-angular; odor and taste none.—Gregarious on the ground in conifer or frondose forests, somewhat common, July-Sept., Minnesota to New England and Illinois.

L. rosea Longyear.   Rosy Leptonia.   Plate 32, fig. 22.

Pileus 1.5-3.5 cm. broad; stem 5-8 cm. x 1-1.5 mm.; spores 11 x 7 μ.

Pileus convex then expanded, depressed or subumbilicate, not striate, rose-colored when young, fading to pale tan with reddish umbilicus, minutely fibrillose-scaly especially in the center, the flesh thin and white; gills adnate, each with slight tooth, white then flesh-colored, close, ventricose, broad behind; stem slender, cylindrical, cartilaginous, stuffed, pale rose, subpellucid,striatulate, white and mycelium-covered at the base; spores flesh-colored in mass, angular.— Scattered, on sphagnum in tamarack and cedar swamps and on burned-over sandy soil, rare, July-Sept., Wisconsin to Michigan and Indiana.

L. seticeps Atkins.   Plate 32, fig. 19.

Pileus 1-3 cm. broad; stem 1-2 cm. x 2-3 mm.; spores 7 x 6 μ.

Pileus convex to expanded, umber to brownish-gray, darker on disk, faintly and finely long-striate, minutely granulose under a lens, the margin at first somewhat incurved, the flesh whitish, very thin, composed of two layers; gills slightly adnexed or free, white then flesh-colored, eroded on the edges, broad, elliptical in outline; stem short, glabrous or villose-dotted, whitish to brownish, subcartilaginous, solid, fibrous-striate, sometimes with bulb, sometimes slightly eccentric; spores not angular, pale flesh-colored in mass; odor and taste slight.—Scattered on rotten logs usually near hemlocks or tamaracks, not common, July-Sept., Minnesota to New York and Illinois.

This species is known by the long, fine striations on the umber pileus, and by its growth on rotten wood. Its characters are intermediate between those of *Pluteus* and *Leptonia*.

NOLANEA Fr.   Plate 32.

Pileus thin, campanulate, usually papillate, the margin at first straight and adpressed to stem; stem cartilaginous or tough, slender, hollow; gills adnate, adnexed, or almost free, seceding, not decurrent; spores angular, pink. These small, slender, putrescent plants, without volva or annulus, grow on the ground.

1   Pileus lavender to violet............*N. caelestina* var. *violacea*.
1'   Pileus of another color......2

2   Pileus very shining, greenish-tinged, brownish-smoky......

    ....*N. versatilis.*

2′   Pileus neither greenish-tinted nor lustrous......3

3   Pileus umber-brown, obtuse; spores cruciate-four-angled....

    ....*N. pascua.*

3′   Pileus cinnamon to umber, umbonate......4

4   Pileus cinnamon when moist, paler when dry, without odor..

    ....*N. conica.*

4′   Pileus umber, with an odor of rancid meal; gills gray......

    ....*N. mammosa.*

N. pascua Fr.   Plate 32, fig. 27.

Pileus 2-4 cm. broad, stem 4-10 cm. x 2-4 mm.; spores 8 x 11 μ.

Pileus fragile, conic-campanulate, sometimes umbonate, hygrophanous, umber-brown and striatulate when moist, fading and not striatulate when dry, glabrous, silky, shining, thin, the flesh concolor; gills adnexed, rounded behind, broad, ventricose, close, grayish becoming flesh-tinged; stem pallid-grayish-brown, fragile, often twisted, fibrillose-striate; spores almost cross-shaped, deep flesh-colored in mass.—Gregarious on low mossy ground near lakes, September, not common, Michigan, New York and Ohio.

N. versatilis Fr.   Plate 32, fig. 25.

Pileus 1-3 cm. broad; stem 3-6 cm. x 1-4 mm.; spores 10 x 7 μ.

Pileus elongated-oval then campanulate, fragile, obtuse, becoming subumbonate when fully expanded, silky-fibrillose, lustrous, smoky or olive-brown, subhygrophanous, thin, submembranaceous, the flesh grayish; gills narrowly adnexed, ventricose, broad in front, subdistant, gray becoming flesh-colored, the edges minutely fimbriate; stem cylindrical, hollow, often twisted or compressed, splitting longitudinally, fibrillose-striate, shining, pallid then smoky; spores tuberculate-angular; odor and taste none or slight.—Among grass in low moist woods, July-Aug., infrequently found, Minnesota to New York.

N. mammosa (Fr.) Bres.   Plate 32, fig. 26.

Pileus 2-4 cm. broad; stem 5-9 cm. x 2-5 mm.; spores 10 x 5-7 μ.

Pileus conical to broadly campanulate, with decurved margin, mammilately umbonate, umber, faintly striate when moist, soon grayish-brown or fuscous, innately fibrillose and shining when dry; the flesh thin, dingy, brownish near surface, subscissile; gills narrowly adnate but seceding, rounded behind, rather broad, subdistant, thickish, pale gray becoming flesh-tinged; stem tinged-fuscous, white, white-pruinose at the apex, cartilaginous, otherwise glabrous, hollow; spores tuberculate-angular, deep flesh-colored; odor and taste that of rancid meal.—Gregarious on the ground in woods, common, July-Oct., Minnesota to New York, southward.

N. conica Peck.   Plate 32, fig. 24.

Pileus 5-15 mm. broad; stem 2-5 cm. x 1-2 mm.; spores 7-9 μ.

Pileus conical then expanded and papillate, hygrophanous, watery-cinnamon and striatulate when moist, paler and silky shining when dry, thin; gills slightly adnexed, narrowed behind, moderately broad, close, white then bright-flesh-colored; stem slender, tubular, cylindrical, elastic, tinged-ashy-brown, the base white-mycelium-covered; spores tuberculate-angular with prominent apiculus.—On moss in wet places in conifer or mixed woods, rare, July-Sept., Wisconsin to New York and northward.

This species is known by its conical, shining, watery-cinnamon, hygrophanous pileus.

N. caelestina var. **violacea** Kauffm.   Plate 32, fig. 23.

Pileus 8-10 mm. broad; stem 5 cm. x 1 mm.; spores 9-11 x 6-7 μ.

Pileus conico campanulate, lavender, acutely papillate, innately silky-fibrillose, the margin smooth; gills adnexed, rather narrow, subdistant, white then flesh-colored, not extending to the pileus-margin; stem slender, smooth, glabrous, pruinose at the apex, cylindrical, lavender, darker than the pileus; spores tuberculate, elliptical; cystidia none; odor none.—Solitary in low woods and elm swamps, rare, usually hidden among debris, Elk Grove, west of Chicago, throughout our area.

ECCILIA Fr.

Carpophore composed of an orbicular, usually umbilicate pileus on a central, slender stem; pileus umbilicate or depressed, margin at first incurved; gills decurrent, either attenuated behind, or broadly adnato-decurrent; stem slender, hollow or stuffed, cartilaginous; spores angular, rose-colored.—On the ground and on rotting wood, rare, widely distributed.

1   Flesh of pileus appearing water-soaked when wet......2
1'   Flesh of pileus not water-soaked when wet......5

2   Gills close or crowded....................*E. pentagonospora.*
2'   Gills subdistant or distant......3

3   Growing in cedar-swamps.................:............*E. griseo-rubella.*
3'   Growing on ground in rich woods......4

4   Pileus finely striate, the margin darkened with micaceous
     particles ....*E. carneo-grisea.*
4' Pileus not striate, tough, 2-5 cm. broad.............*E. mordax.*
5   Growing on sphagnum......................*E. sphagnicola.*
5' Growing on rotten wood, pileus dark umber.........*E. atrides.*

E. griseo-rubella Fr.

Pileus 1-2.5 cm. broad; stem 2-4 cm. x 1-2 mm.: spores 8-9 x
5-6 μ.

Pileus campanulate, umbilicate, hygrophanous, brownish-ashy and
striate when moist, with darker umbilicus, minutely squamulose, elsewhere bearing innate white fibrils, the flesh thin, concolor; gills
broadly adnate, slightly decurrent, broad, subdistant, pallid then flesh-
colored, the edges smooth; stem glabrous, pallid to buff, cylindrical,
smooth, cartilaginous, hollow; spores tuberculate-angular.—Scattered on the ground in cedar swamps, not common, September, in the
range of Arbor-Vitae swamps.

E. pentagonospora Atkins.   Plate 36, fig. 13.

Pileus 5-20 mm. broad; stem 1-2.5 cm. x 1-1.5 mm.; spores 7 x
9.5 μ.

Pileus fragile convex-plane, umbilicate, hygrophanous, blackish-
gray fading to steel-gray and shining, smooth, minutely tomentose-
flocculose later appressed-scurfy, thin-membranous; gills adnate-
subdecurrent, grayish then dark flesh-colored, thickish, close to
subdistant, somewhat crisped, the edges concolor; stem cylindrical,
glabrous soon hollow, metallic-gray, white-mycelium-covered at base;
spores obtusely tuberculate-angular, deep flesh-colored in mass; cystidia none; basidia 30 x 10 μ.—Gregarious in moist places in frondose woods, rare, August, Michigan to New York, southward.

E. mordax Atkins.

Pileus 2-5 cm. broad; stem 3-6 cm. x 3-5 mm.; spores 6-7 x 4-5 μ.

Pileus tough, convex, umbilicate, hygrophanous, dull reddish-brown,
light sordid-tan when dry, glabrous, smooth, margin inrolled, thin,
the flesh dirty-white; gills adnate, subdecurrent, dingy-brown then
flesh-colored, close, narrow; stem tough, cylindrical, concolor, fibrous-
cartilaginous, often compressed, glabrous or pruinose, white-mycelium-covered at base; spores oval, smooth, pale flesh-colored.—
Gregarious on ground on springy sides of ravines, not common,
August.

This species approaches *Clitocybe cyathiforme* in external appearance, but differs in its flesh-colored spores, umbilicate pileus, and
habit of growth on ground.   This is our largest *Eccilia.*

E. carneo-grisea Berk. and Broome.   Plate 36, fig. 16.

Pileus 2-3 cm. broad; stem 3-5 cm. x 1-2 mm.; spores 7 x 5 μ.

Pileus convex plane, umbilicate, dark gray or grayish-flesh-colored, finely striate, the margin darkened with micaceous particles; gills adnate, decurrent, distant, slightly undulate, the edges darkened irregularly, rosy; stem slender, smooth, glabrous, wavy, hollow, concolor, white-tomentose at base; spores irregularly oblong, rough.— In rich woods, ravines, and hillsides, rare, July-Sept., Nova Scotia to Ohio and Indiana.

E. sphagnicola Peck.   Plate 36, fig. 19.

Pileus 8-12 mm. broad; stem 3-5 cm. x 1 mm.; spores 7-12 x 6-7 μ.

Pileus hemispherical or umbonate-turbinate, glabrous, striate on margin, dark-brown; gills very decurrent, whitish becoming slightly pink, broad, distant; stem slender, glabrous, concolor; spores angular.—On sphagnum in bogs, rare, August, Minnesota to Maine, southward.

E. atrides Fr.   Dark Eccilia.

Pileus 1-2 cm. broad; stem 2-3 cm. x 1-2 mm.; spores 12 x 6.5 μ.

Pileus deeply umbilicate, dark-umber, with darker umbilicus, striate up to the umbilicus, pruinose, somewhat streaked, thin; gills decurrent, narrowed behind, close, pallid, the edges black; stem brownish, paler and floccose-dotted at the apex, glabrous below, cylindrical, slender; spores tuberculate-angular, elongated, bright flesh-colored in mass.—Solitary or gregarous on very rotten wood, not common, July-Aug., Minnesota to New York, mainly northern.

This species is known by its dark colors and decurrent gills. It is very close to *Leptonia serrulata*. Ricken considers the two identical.

HEBELOMA Fr.

Carpophore composed of an orbicular, convex pileus of same material and confluent with the central, fleshy stipe; pileus fleshy, soft, putrescent, glabrous, somewhat viscid, mostly pale colored, fibrillose veil or cortina visible when young; stipe cylindrical, with thick outer rind and central pith which breaks down leaving the stem hollow; gills at length emarginate as in *Tricholoma* and *Entoloma*, gill-edge often white-fimbriate from long sterile cells, somewhat liquid drops give a beaded appearance under lens; spores pale ochraceous or pale brown, smooth or slightly roughened.—Terrestrial.

1   Stem solid......2
1'   Stem stuffed with pith or hollow......6

2   Pileus very large, tan or sordid-gray-brown; stem stout, scaly-torn ....*H. sinapizans.*
2' Without this combination of characters......3

3   Cortina present when young......4
3' Veil always absent......5

4   Pileus 3-7 cm. broad; convex-plane, pale yellowish-tan; gills beaded with drops of liquid in wet weather........*H. fastibile.*
4' Pileus conical, 2-3 cm. broad, dull yellow......*H. mesophaeum.*
4" Pileus soon convex-umbonate, brownish-clay or rusty, plants growing on bare ground in open woods.........*H. pascuense.*

5   Stem silky-fibrillose, with bulb of adhering sand; pileus tan, 2-7 cm. broad ....*H. Colvini.*
5' Stem scaly-torn, pileus thick compact, 6-15 cm. broad, tan or gray-brown ....*H. sinapizans.*

6   Cortina present but quickly disappearing; pileus 2-3 cm. broad, tan; stem slender......................*H. gregarium.*
6' Cortina never present......7

7   Edges of gills beaded with drops of liquid in moist weather, odor strong, plants often growing on sphagnum.........
    ....*H. crustuliniforme.*
7' Edges of gills not beaded......8

8   Stem short, 2-4 cm. long; plants small............*H. sociale.*
8' Stem longer......9

9   Gills narrow......10
9' Gills rather broad, stem fragile..............*H. longicaudum.*

10 Stem bulbous, pileus whitish..................*H. albidulum.*
10' Stem not bulbous, pileus whitish.................*H. album.*

H. fastibile Fr.   Plate 37, fig. 1.

Pileus 3-7 cm. broad; stem 4-6 cm. x 6-10 mm.; spores 11 x 5.5 μ.

Pileus viscid, glabrous, convex-plane, compact, obtuse, often wavy, dull ochraceous to light clay-colored, the margin pubescent, incurved, the flesh white; gills emarginate, not close, of various lengths, the edges white-fimbriate, beaded with drops of water in damp weather, whitish then silvery-cinnamon; stem firm, bulbous, solid or partly hollow, fibrillose, white, the remains of the cortina on upper part sometimes slightly annular; cystidia clavate; taste bitter, odor disagreeable, radish-like.—In woods and borders of woods and in sandy, shrubby swales, not common, September, Minnesota to Illinois and Pennsylvania.

H. mesophaeum Fr.   Plate 37, fig. 2.

Pileus 1-3 cm. broad; stem 4-7 cm. x 4 mm.

Pileus conical then campanulate and convex with a broad umbo, slightly viscid, chestnut-brown on disk, buff to white on margin, often wavy, glabrous with a silky sheen, the margin commonly bearing the whitish remains of the webby cortina; gills adnate then emarginate, close, broad, ventricose, white becoming rusty-ochraceous, white-fimbriate on edges; stem slender, silky-fibrillose, white to dingy, fleshy-fibrous, becoming twisted, mealy at the apex; odor and taste slight.—Subcaespitose on bare ground in woods or sandy grassy soil, locally common, October, Wisconsin to Michigan and southward.

H. pascuense Peck.   Pasture Hebeloma.   Plate 37, fig. 3.

Pileus 3-5 cm. broad; stem 3-5 cm. x 5 mm.; spores 10 x 6 μ.

Pileus convex, plane, viscid, obtuse, brownish-clay-colored, darker on disk, subhygrophanous, pale when dry, innately streaked with fibrils, the margin at first white with the webby cortina, the flesh whitish, the odor that of radishes; gills adnexed, ventricose, broad, pallid becoming ochraceous-cinnamon, the edges white-fimbriate at first; stem whitish, cylindrical, firm, slightly mealy at the apex.—Subcaespitose or gregarious in stony pastures, open pastured woods, etc., common locally, May, June and October, Minnesota to New York and southward.

H. sinapizans Fr.   Giant Hebeloma.   Plate 37, fig. 5.

Pileus 6-16 cm. broad; stem 6-12 cm. x 2-3 cm.; spores 12 x 8 μ.

Pileus large, compact, thick, lobed, obtuse, convex, plane, ashy-brown to clay-colored or tan, sordid, the flesh soft in age, firm when young, radish-like in odor and taste; gills broad, pale then dull-yellowish-cinnamon, the edges of the same color; stem very stout, rigid, often striate above, stuffed then cavernous, white, dingy, fibrillose, the torn cuticle breaking into large, thick, curving scales, the apex flocculose.—In troops on margins of sandy swales or on wooded hillsides, locally common, September, Michigan, Illinois and eastward.

H. crustuliniforme Fr. (poisonous).   Plate 37, fig. 6.

Pileus 4-6 cm. broad; stem 4-5 cm. x 6-10 mm.; spores 11 x 6 μ.

Pileus fleshy, convex, plane, obtusely umbonate, smooth, glabrous, slightly viscid, light tan to brick-red, or pale whitish-tan with reddish disk, the margin incurved at first, the flesh firm, white, the odor radish-like, the taste disagreeable; gills adnexed, narrow, close, thin, whitish then clay-colored becoming cinnamon-brown, the edge crenulate and beaded with drops when young and moist.—On ground in open places, Sept.-Oct.

Form **sphagnophilum** Kauffm. (Plate 37, fig. 4) grows on sphagnum, has a longer stem; occurs in May and June as well as in autumn, Minnesota to Maine and southward, Illinois, Michigan, etc.

H. longicaudum Fr.   Long-stemmed Hebeloma.   Plate 37, fig. 8.

Pileus 3-6 cm. broad; stem 5-10 cm. x 5-8 mm.; spores 13 x 7 μ.

Pileus convex, expanded, glabrous, viscid, smooth or irregular, pale ochraceous-tan or whitish, brownish on disk, the flesh soft, white, mild in taste but with little odor; gills adnexed, sinuate, close, whitish becoming clay-colored, the edges serrulate and white-fimbriate, medium-broad; stem cylindrical, white, stuffed to hollow, fragile, fibrillose-striate, mealy at least toward apex.—Gregarious in tamarack swamps or their borders, not frequently found, Sept.-Nov., Minnesota to Maine and southward.

H. albidulum Peck.   Whitish Hebeloma.   Plate 37, fig. 10.

Pileus 3-6 cm. broad; stem 3-8 cm. x 4-8 mm.; spores 11 x 6 μ.

Pileus firm, fleshy, broadly convex, expanding, obtuse, glabrous, viscid when moist, dingy-white, buff, or grayish, smooth, thick on disk, the flesh odorless, mild in taste, white; gills adnexed, emarginate, crowded, narrow, whitish becoming pale-brownish, the edges minutely white-fimbriate, stem cylindrical, firm, glabrous, mealy at apex, hollow, whitish, silky-shining.—Gregarious on ground in woods, found infrequently, Sept.-Oct., Maine to Minnesota and Indiana.

H. album Peck.   White Hebeloma.   Plate 37, fig. 7.

Pileus 2.5-5 cm. broad; stem 4-7 cm. x 5 mm.; spores 14 x 7 μ.

Pileus firm, fleshy, convex, plane or concave by upturning margin, glabrous. sub-viscid, white or yellowish-white, the flesh white, thin, thicker on disk; gills adnexed, sinuate, narrow, close, thin, whitish becoming rusty-brown; stem cylindrical, firm, long, solid or stuffed, white, slightly mealy at apex; spores pointed at both ends.—Among fallen leaves in woods, not common, October, Minnesota to Maine and southward.

H. colvini Peck.   Sand Hebeloma.   Plate 37, fig. 11.

Pileus 3-7 cm. broad; stem 5-9 cm. x 5-8 mm.; spores 11 x 7 μ.

Pileus convex to nearly plane, sometimes thicker on one side, often broadly umbonate, glabrous, grayish or with dull yellow tint, fleshy; gills adnexed, sinuate, broad, close, whitish becoming brownish-ochraceous; stem silky-fibrillose, whitish, cylindrical, flexuous, stuffed to hollow above, solid below.—On sandy soil, the mycelium binding the sand into a globose mass at the base of the stem, not common, May-Aug., Minnesota to Maine and Indiana.

H. sociale Peck.   Social Hebeloma.   Plate 37, fig. 12.

Pileus 2-3 cm. broad; stem 2-3.5 cm. x 3-6 mm.; spores 7 x 5 μ.

Pileus fleshy, thin, convex, plane, glabrous, subviscid, yellowish-white, the flesh yellowish-white, with a nauseous taste; gills adnexed, close, thin, whitish then yellowish becoming rusty-brown; stem white, short, fibrous, hollow, floccose-fibrillose.—Gregarious in short grass in pastures, infrequently found, October, throughout our area.

H. gregarium Peck.   Gregarious Hebeloma.   Plate 37, fig. 6.

Pileus 2-3.5 cm. broad; stem 3-5 cm x 3 mm.; spores 11 x 6 μ.

Pileus hemispheric-convex, thin, subviscid, glabrous with slightly silky margin, pale-ochraceous, often darker or tawny in center, the flesh whitish; gills adnate, close, thin, whitish becoming cinnamon; stem stuffed or hollow, slender, fibrillose, white, mealy at apex. —On sandy soil in swales of small bushes, etc., not common, October, Indiana to Michigan and New York.

PHOLIOTA Fr.

Carpophore composed of a more or less orbicular, convex pileus of same material and confluent with the usually central, cylindrical, fleshy stipe; pileus putrescent, fleshy, soft, its context tapering into and inseparable from that of the stipe; stipe long or short, fleshy or fibrous, provided with a membranaceous annulus which is either persistent or may break into shreds which disappear during wet weather; gills adnexed, adnate or slightly decurrent, seceding from stem to become emarginate at maturity; spores smooth, brown, rusty brown, or rusty fuscous.—Terrestrial or on wood.

1 Pileus viscid when moist......20
1' Pileus not viscid......2
2 Pileus hygrophanous, changing color in drying......3
2' Pileus not hygrophanous......8
3 Growing on moss, pileus striate..............:*P. mycenoides.*
3' Growing on wood......4
4 Solitary on rotten wood lying on very moist ground, gills broad, pileus soon wrinkled.....................*P. rugosa.*
4' Without this combination of characters......5
5 Gills at first of some shade of yellow............*P. unicolor.*
5' Gills never with yellow tints......6
6 Annulus soon disappearing, pileus watery-brown, gills narrow ....*P. marginata.*
6' Annulus membranaceous, large, persistent......7

7   Pileus floccose, fragile, brick-red..............*P. confragosa.*
7'   Pileus glabrous, rusty-yellow..................*P. acericola.*
8   Growing on ground, pileus not scaly......9
8'   Growing on wood, pileus scaly......11
9   In rich woods......10
9'   In grassy places, lawns, etc............................
     ....*P. praecox, P. dura,* and *P. temnophylla.*
10   Pileus large, covered with woolly units; annulus large, persistent, movable ....*P. caperata.*
10' Pileus medium-sized to large, glabrous; annulus large; a northern species growing under willows and poplars......
     ....*P. aegerita.*
11   Gills yellow at least until old......12
11' Gills never yellow......16
12   Pileus bright orange-yellow, with pilose sulphur-yellow scales
     ....*P. flammans.*
12' Pileus bright-orange yellow with innate scales; annulus ample, apical ....*P. spectabilis.*
12" Without this combination of characters......13
13   Gills broad......14
13' Gills narrow; pileus innately scaly, 2-4 cm. in diameter....
     ....*P. curvipes.*
14   Pileus with green shades.....................*P. aeruginosa.*
14' Pileus without green shades......15
15   Pileus bearing rusty, pointed scales; gills close.....*P. muricata.*
15' Pileus pale red or yellowish, gills rather distant...*P. luteofolia.*
16   Pileus and stem densely brown-squarrose-scaly.*P. squarrosoides.*
16' Scales on pileus and stem appressed or fibrillose......17
17   Stem bulbous-radicate; pileus light yellow, very large....
     ....*P. destruens.*
17' Stem cylindrical, stuffed then hollow......18
18   Pileus small, 2-3 cm. broad......19
18' Pileus 6-12 cm. broad, tawny..............*P. fulvosquamosa.*
19   Pileus bearing erect spine-like scales.............*P. erinaceela.*
19' Pileus bearing innate minute scales..............*P. curvipes.*
20   Pileus scaly......21
20' Pileus glabrous......24
21   Pileus bright yellow......22
21' Pileus but slightly or not at all yellow, large......23
22   Pileus large, very viscid, very scaly...............*P. adiposa.*
22' Pileus somewhat viscid, medium-sized; gills bright yellow ....*P. lucifera.*

23   Pileus and stem bearing dense recurved erect tawny-brown
      scales ....*P. squarrosoides.*
23'   Pileus tawny, scales easily removed...........*P. albocrenulata.*
23"   Pileus yellowish-white or darker; stem bulbous-radicate...
      ....*P. destruens.*
24   Pileus dark-smoky; plant growing on ground in woods,
      rather small ....*P. aggericola.*
24'   Pileus whitish-buff; plant growing on ground in grass,
      medium-sized ....*P. praecox.*
24"   Pileus hygrophanous; plant growing on stumps, etc., cinna-
      mon when moist, tan when dry.................*P. discolor.*

P. destruens (Fr.) Bres. Destructive Pholiota. Plate 38, fig. 8.
P. comosa Fr.
P. heteroclita Fr.
Pileus 6-15 cm. broad; stem 4-15 cm. x 2-3 cm.; spores 9 x 5 μ.
Pileus convex, subviscid, yellowish-white, covered with white-floccose scales, involute, very thick; gills rounded-adnexed, decurrent by a line, broad, close, white becoming dark cinnamon; stem thick, solid, curving, often eccentric, bulbous-radicate, white squamose becoming smooth, yellowish-white; odor strong.—Solitary or sub-caespitose on poplar, birch, and willow, not common, Sept.-Nov., Minnesota to Maine and Illinois, southward.

P. fulvosquamosa Peck. Tawny-scaled Pholiota. Plate 38, fig. 5.
Pileus 6-12 cm. broad; stem 5-8 x 1 cm.; spores 7 x 4 μ.
Pileus convex, plane, rather thin for size, not viscid, bearing numerous appressed tawny scales, the disk concentrically cracking, the flesh white, brown where bruised; gills attached to collar behind, narrow, close, narrowed behind, white becoming pinkish-cinnamon; stem rigid, cylindrical, stuffed to hollow, erect-floccose-tawny-scaly below, white above; annulus ample, persistent, membranaceous.—On oak trees, near their bases, rare, Aug.-Oct., Wisconsin to New York.

P. albocrenulata Peck. Plate 38, fig. 7.
Pileus 3-12 cm. broad; stem 6-15 cm. x 5-10 mm.; spores 13 x 6 μ.
Pileus convex, very viscid, orange-fulvous, becoming rusty-tawny, adorned with numerous darker fibrillose scales, the margin involute, often bearing remnants of the veil, the flesh white, thick; gills adnate to rounded behind, very broad, white then gray finally smoky-rusty, the crenulate edges beaded with white drops of liquid; stem stuffed, firm, covered with squarrose brown scales up to the fugaceous annulus, the apex white, pruinose; spores smooth rusty-umber.—On

wounds of trees, especially sugar-maple, yellow-birch, and hemlock, rare, July-Sept., Minnesota to New York to southern Wisconsin.

P. squarrosoides Peck.   Squarrose Pholiota (edible). Plate 38, fig. 6.

Pileus 4-10 cm. broad; stem 6-10 cm. x 1 cm.; spores 5 x 3 μ.

Pileus viscid when moist, densely covered with terete, erect, tawny, pointed scales on the whitish cuticle, thick; gills adnate, close, white becoming rusty-brown, rather narrow; stem firm, cylindrical, stuffed, booted with numerous floccose tawny scales which terminate in a torn floccose annulus, the apex white and smooth.—On trunks of living maple, birch, and beech or rarely on buried wood, up to 50 in a cluster, Aug.-Sept., frequent northward.   Minnesota to New York, to southern Wisconsin.

P. curvipes Fr.   Plate 39, fig. 12.

Pileus 1-3 cm. broad; stem 2 cm. x 3 mm.; spores 7 x 3.5 μ.

Pileus convex, expanded, tawny-yellow, floccose when young becoming minutely scaly, incurved at the margin, thin; gills adnate, broad, white or yellowish then rusty-cinnamon; stem curving, cylindrical, stuffed to hollow, fibrillose; annulus soon disappearing.— Solitary or gregarious on logs of elm, oak, etc.   Minnesota to New York to Illinois and southward.

P. erinaceëlla Peck.   Plate 38, fig. 2.

Similar in aspect to the preceding but the pileus covered with tawny-brown, erect, densely arranged, spine-like scales which are easily rubbed off; gills broad; stem densely squamulose below the slight annulus.—On logs, rare, August, northern part of our area.

P. muricata Fr.   Plate 38, fig. 15.

Similar to the preceding in size and aspect, but the pileus covered with dense-clustered or granular, pointed, tawny-yellow scales, the disk rusty, thin; gills broad, adnate-seceding, close, yellow becoming rusty, the edges minutely yellow-fimbriate; stem curved, stuffed to hollow, tawny, floccose-fibrillose or granular-scaly up to disappearing annulus.—Gregarious on decaying logs, rare, Aug.-Sept., Wisconsin to New York and Illinois.

P. flammans Fr.   Flaming Pholiota.   Plate 38, fig. 1.

Pileus 4-7 cm. broad; stem 6 x 0.5-1 cm.; spores 4 x 2 μ.

Pileus plane, fiery-yellow to orange or orange-red, not viscid, covered with squarrose, easily rubbed off, sulphur-yellow scales, the flesh thin, bright yellow, bruising red-brown; gills adnexed, very narrow, crowded, bright yellow becoming rusty; stem bright yellow, cylindrical, not viscid, squarrose-scaly up to the torn but membranaceous annulus; odor radish-like.—On decaying conifer stumps, northern Michigan, Wisconsin, in northern part of our area only.

P. spectabilis Fr.   Showy Pholiota.   Plate 38, fig. 17.

Pileus 5-10 cm. broad; stem 6-9 x 1-1.5 cm.; spores 8 x 6 μ.

Pileus convex, not viscid, tawny-orange, thick, compact, glabrous then minute-fibrillose-scaly; the flesh yellowish, thin at margin; gills adnate, narrow, crowded, yellow then rusty, the edges floccose; stem stout, firm, hard, solid, subventricose, booted with scales up to the persistent membranaceous annulus near the apex, concolor; spores rough; taste bitter.—On the bases of yellow birch trees, not common, August, northern Wisconsin to Maine, southward into northern part of our area.

P. adiposa Fr.   Fatty Pholiota (edible).   Plate 38, fig. 3.

Pileus 5-12 cm. broad; stem 4-8 x 1 cm.; spores 8 x 5 μ.

Pileus convex, very viscid, bright yellow to orange, with numerous separable, orange, concentric, darker-in-age scales, the margin at first incurved and decorated with the veil, the flesh thick, yellowish becoming rusty, tough; stem firm, solid, yellow becoming rusty-stained with spores, usually scaly, the annulus slight and quickly disappearing.—Caespitose on rotting logs and in wounds of living sugar-maple and ash, common, June-Oct., Minnesota to Maine and southward to Alabama.

P. aurivella Batsch.

Resembling *P. adiposa,* but the pileus only slightly viscid when moist, gibbous, splitting on margin, smooth, almost glassy when dry, bright yellow or orange, decorated with dark tufts of tawny fibers; annulus shreddy and tawny-scaly below; spores rusty brown, 4-6 x 8-9 μ.—On decaying logs, River Forest, Illinois (Harper).

P. lucifera (Lasch) Bres.   Plate 38, fig. 9.

Pileus 3-5 cm. broad; stem 3-4 cm. x 6 mm.; spores 8 x 5 μ.

Pileus convex, plane, umbonate, viscid, sulphur-yellow to orange-yellow, the disk covered with tawny thin scales, the margin incurved, appendiculate, the flesh white, yellow beneath the cuticle; gills subdecurrent, bright yellow, rather narrow, crowded, crenulate on the edges; stem yellow, fibrillosely booted up to the rusty-yellow, narrow, disappearing annulus; spores rusty.—On decaying wood, rare, Aug.-Oct., northern Wisconsin to Ontario and at Thornton, Illinois.

P. luteofolia Peck.   Plate 38, fig. 16.

Pileus 2-5 cm. broad; stem 3-6 cm. x 6 mm.; spores 8 x 5 μ.

Pileus convex, expanded, not viscid, obtuse, with red-brown scales, scattered on disk, areolate-cracking toward margin, the margin covered with adpressed ochraceous-brown scales, the flesh rather thin, white; gills emarginate, broad, subdistant, serrate, yellow becoming rusty; stem firm, cylindrical, stuffed to hollow, yellowish, pruinose above the slight disappearing annulus.—Subcaespitose on decaying oak, September, rare.

P. aeruginosa Peck. Green Pholiota. Plate 38, fig. 10.

Similar to *P. luteofolia* but the pileus dark green or yellow stained with green.—On railroad ties and boards, infrequently found, June-Oct., Minnesota to New York and southward.

P. discolor Peck. Plate 38, fig. 12.

Pileus 2-4 cm. broad; stem 5-8 x 3 mm.; spores 8 x 5 μ.

Pileus convex, plane, viscid, hygrophanous, ochraceous-yellow when dry, rusty-brown and striate when moist, thin, glabrous; gills subdecurrent, white, close, the edges minutely crenulate, becoming rusty; stem pale, soon hollow; annulus membranous, persistent, apical.—Caespitose on rotting wood, common, May-Oct., Wisconsin to New York and Kentucky.

This species has the aspect of *Collybia velutipes*.

P. marginata Fr. (suspected). Plate 38, fig. 13.

Of the same size and aspect as the preceding but the pileus watery-tan when moist, darker when dry, striate on margin; gills dark red-brown at maturity; annulus distant from the apex of the stem, disappearing.—On decaying logs and limbs, common, May-Nov., Minnesota to Maine and Kentucky.

P. unicolor Fr. Plate 38, fig. 11.

Similar to *P. marginata* but the pileus watery-brown when moist, ochraceous when dry, the margin extending beyond the gills; gills triangular behind, broad, ochre-cinnamon; stem often white-mycelium-covered at base, the annulus persistent.—Habitat similar to that of the preceding.

P. confragosa Fr. Plate 38, fig. 4.

Pileus slightly larger than that of the preceding, brick-red when moist, dotted with white, covered with an easily-removed flocculose coating, pale tan when dry, striate on the margin when moist, thin, fragile; gills tawny-brick-colored; stem silky, peronate at least when young, reddish; annulus membranous, persistent, apical.—On logs, rare, Aug.-Sept., northern Wisconsin to northern Michigan, and possibly in extreme northern part of our area.

P. acericola Peck. Maple-loving Pholiota. Plate 39, fig. 7.

Pileus 2-7 cm. broad; stem 4-10 x 0.5-1 cm.; spores 10 x 6 μ.

Pileus convex, plane, hygrophanous, not viscid, glabrous, yellow-ish-cinnamon when moist, not striate, paler when dry, rugose-reticulate under lens, rather thin; gills pale becoming cinnamon, rather narrow, close, adnate; stem fibrillose-striate, cylindrical, stuffed to hollow, white, smoky at the base; annulus membranous, persistent, large, flabby; spores obscurely 5-angled, rusty-cinnamon in mass. —On rotten logs of maple and beech, not uncommon, June-Aug., Minnesota to Maine and Kentucky.

P. caperata Fr. Goat Pholiota. Plate 39, fig. 11.

Pileus 5-10 cm. broad; stem 7-12 x 1-2 cm.; spores 13 x 8 μ.

Pileus ovoid, campanulate-expanded, obtuse, straw-colored, superficially floccose, at length glabrous, the flesh white, thick on disk; gills adnate, close, white, crisped on the edges, becoming pale rusty; stem stout, firm, solid, glabrous, dingy-white; annulus membranous, persistent, white, reflexed, near middle of stem.—On ground in conifer or mixed woods, Aug.-Sept., infrequently found, Minnesota to Maine and following conifers southward.

P. praecox Fr. (edible). Plate 39, fig. 5.

Pileus 2-6 cm. broad; stem 4-8 cm. x 3-5 mm.; spores 11 x 7 μ.

Pileus convex, soft, white, yellowish or leather-colored, the margin incurved at first, thick; gills adnate, seceding, close, medium-broad, white, gray then rusty-brown, crenulate on the edges; stem slender, cylindrical, straight, white, glabrous, the apex pruinose; annulus whitish, disappearing, often hanging from the edge of the pileus; spores rusty-brown in mass.—Among grass, common during May and June, Minnesota to Maine and Kentucky.

P. dura Fr. Plate 39, fig. 6.

Like the preceding, but with a tough and tan pileus, which cracks into areas; otherwise as preceding.

P. temnophylla Peck. Plate 39, fig. 10.

Similar to *P. praecox* but with broad gills and dingy-ochraceous pileus.

P. Howeana Peck. Plate 39, fig. 4

Pileus 1.5-5 cm. broad; stem 3-7 cm. x 2-4 mm.; spores 10 x 5.5 μ.

Pileus convex-expanded, not viscid, subumbonate, glabrous, pale ochraceous, fragile; gills adnate each with a tooth, white becoming rusty-brown, close, narrow, the edges of the same color; stem smooth, rigid, glabrous, whitish to dull ochraceous; annulus high, membranous, easily removed, very thin; spores more or less 5-angled.—Gregarious among grass, June, not common.

P. aggericola Peck.　Plate 39, fig. 3.

Pileus 1.5-4 cm. broad; stem 3-6 cm. x 4-7 mm.; spores 14 x 6 μ.

Pileus convex, then plane with recurved margin, viscid, dark-smoky fading brownish, the margin faintly striate, glabrous, rugose or smooth; gills adnate to subdecurrent, rather broad, narrowed toward the margin of the pileus, gray becoming rusty-brown; stem fibrillose-striate, dark-smoky, paler toward apex; annulus thin, fragile, smoky, striate above, sometimes clinging to edge of pileus.—Gregarious in paths and among debris in moist ground, July-Oct., Minnesota to Maine, Lisle, Illinois, found frequently locally.

P. rugosa Peck.　Plate 39, fig. 2.

Pileus 0.5-3 cm. broad; stem 4 cm. x 2-3 mm.; spores 11 x 5 μ.

Pileus conical to campanulate, thin, expanding-umbonate, hygrophanous, striatulate on margin, rusty-ochraceous when moist, tan or yellowish when dry, rugose when drying, the flesh with no distinctive taste; gills adnexed, pale ochre becoming rusty-brown, the edges white, fimbriate; stem hollow, white-mealy near apex, fibrillose below the annulus; annulus persistent, membranous, striate, removed from the apex.—On rotting wood and on ground in wet places, not uncommon, Aug.-Oct., Minnesota to New York and southward.

P. mycenoides Fr.　Plate 39, fig. 1.

Pileus 2-3 cm. broad; stem 4-5 cm. x 2 mm.; spores 9 x 5 μ.

Pileus campanulate to convex, membranaceous, hygrophanous, rusty-tawny, striate, tan when dry; gills adnate, distant, narrow, soon rusty; stem hollow, glabrous, rusty, slender; annulus high, white, membranous.—On moss in bogs and swamps, local, rare, Minnesota to eastern Ontario and southward.

FLAMMULA Fr.

Carpophore composed of a more or less orbicular, convex or plane pileus of same material and confluent with the central, fleshy stipe; pileus soft, putrescent, fleshy, often very viscid, usually yellowish, olive or smoky, usually with scattered fibrillose scales when young, glabrous in age; stem fleshy or fibrous, becoming darker with age, straight or curved depending on position of substratum, often shorter than the diameter of the pileus; gills adnate or decurrent; spores dark brown, rusty-brown, or yellow-rusty, oval, smooth. —Mostly on wood.

The presence of a fibrillose cortina on many species reminds one
of *Cortinarius*. Such species are most readily separated from *Cortinarius* by their habitat on wood.

1   Pileus viscid or lubricous......2
1' Pileus not viscid, covered with minute scales; gills bright yel-
     low; plants growing on conifer wood..............*F. sapinea.*
2   Gills soon olive-purplish; pileus orange or yellow, olive to-
     ward margin, scaly ....*F. polychroa.*
2' Gills without gray or purple hues......3
3   Pileus large, 6-12 cm. broad, the flesh white.........*F. lubrica.*
3' Pileus small, 2-7 cm. broad, the flesh yellow......4
4   Gills yellowish......5
4' Gills smoky-brown, the edges white; pileus 2-6 cm. in diam-
     eter; plants growing in swampy places......*F. carbonaria* var.
5   Plants viscid, growing in conifer regions, bright yellow....
     ....*F. spumosa.*
5' Plants lubricous cadmium-yellow, growing on stumps of
     alder, willow, etc.; stem-base rooting..............*F. alnicola.*

F. polychroa Berk.

Pileus 3-8 cm. broad; stem 3-7 cm. x 5-12 mm.; spores 7 x 4 μ.

Pileus convex, expanded then slightly concave, sometimes with a
broad umbo, very viscid, orange-yellow on disk, yellow outward
and olive or greenish at margin, adorned with concentrically arranged, triangular, creamy to light purple-brown scales, the outer
circle of which fringes the pileus, the margin incurved then straight,
the flesh yellowish-white, thick toward center, thin toward margin,
soft; gills adnate, seceding or appearing decurrent as pileus turns
upward, broader behind, close, buff then smoky-gray, finally dark
olive-purple-gray, the edges flocculose, white; stem slender, tough,
rigid, subcylindrical, curved, fibrillose with small recurved scales up
to the fibrillose evanescent annulus, yellow above, concolor below but
becoming reddish-brown; spores smoky-brown with purple tinge in
mass.—Solitary to subcaespitose on wood of frondose or conifer
trees, common, July-Oct., Minnesota to Maine and Illinois to Indiana.

F. lubrica Fr.

Pileus 6-12 cm. broad; stem 4-6 cm. x 8-15 mm.; spores 5 x 3 μ.

Pileus convex, expanded, tawny-orange with yellowish margin,
with separable viscid cuticle covered with small loose scales, the flesh
rather thick, whitish, yellowish beneath the cuticle; gills adnate, soon
seceding, sometimes each with tooth, close, medium-broad, sulphur-

yellow or greenish-tinted becoming ochraceous and olive-brown, the edges minutely fimbriate; stem subbulbous, spongy within, whitish or tinged-rusty at base, fibrillose.—Gregarious or subcaespitose on decaying wood in mixed or deciduous low woods, infrequently found, September, Minnesota to Maine and southward.

F. spumosa Fr.   Plate 39, fig. 8.

Pileus convex-plane, viscid, with separable cuticle, sulphur yellow or greenish-tinged, the center fulvous, the flesh yellowish, rather thin, often green-tinged; gills adnate, each with tooth, sulphur-yellow or with greenish tint then rusty, close, medium-wide; stem slender soon hollow, fibrillose, yellow becoming rusty toward base; odor faintly of radish.—Scattered on ground among debris or on mossy logs in moist places in conifer regions, July-Sept., common in range of pine-hemlock forests.

F. alnicola Fr.   Plate 38, fig. 14.

Pileus 5-7 cm. broad; stem 6-10 cm. x 6-12 mm.; spores 9 x 4 μ.

Pileus convex-expanded, lubricous, not truly viscid, fibrillose toward the margin or minutely fibrillose-scaly, bright cadmium-yellow becoming rusty or greenish, compact; gills adnate, decurrent or rounded behind, broad, plane, pale yellow then rusty; stem bright-yellow then rusty, rooting, commonly curved, fibrillose, the cortina webby; odor and taste strong, pungent, bitter.—On old stumps of deciduous trees, especially alder and willow, not uncommon, Iowa to New York and southward to Kentucky.

F. sapinea Fr.   Plate 39, fig. 13.

Pileus 2-7 cm. broad; stem 5-7 cm. x 6-12 mm.; spores 7 x 4-5 μ.

Pileus convex-expanded, obtuse, tawny or golden-yellow, paler on the margin, minute-scaly, fading and rimose-cracking, the flesh thick, yellowish; gills adnate, narrow, thin, chrome-yellow becoming rusty, minutely fimbriate on the edges; stem innately fibrillose, yellowish, brownish toward base, stuffed to hollow, often compressed or irregular; odor strong.—Scattered on conifer wood northward and on tamaracks in bogs, not common, Aug.-Oct., Minnesota to Maine and Illinois.

INOCYBE Fr.   Fiber-heads.

Carpophore a conic-campanulate, thin, innately-fibrillose pileus, confluent with and of same material as the central, cylindrical stem; pileus fibrillose scaly or radiately silky; fibrillose cortina extending from the cuticle of the pileus to the stem in young plants; stem fibrous fleshy; gills soft, spores ochre-brown, angular or rounded.—Growing on the ground in woods.

1 Pileus viscid, tawny; spores large-tubercular.....*I. trechispora.*
1' Pileus not viscid; spores not tuberculate......2

2 Pileus white or lilac...............*I. geophylla, I. albodisca.*
2' Pileus straw-colored to cream-colored......3
2" Pileus brown, red-brown, or smoky......7

3 Pileus soon rimosely cracked, fibrillose or silky......4
3' Pileus not rimosely cracked, smoky-yellow.........*I. scabella.*

4 Disk white; pileus glabrous, gray on margin, small.*I. albodisca.*
4' Disk of same color as margin; pileus creamy-white, large
....*I. fibrosa.*
4" Pileus straw-colored, medium-sized......5

5 Pileus very small, averaging 2 cm. broad, chestnut when
young ....*I. eutheloides.*
5' Pileus averaging 3-6 cm. broad......6

6 Gill-edges white-fimbriate, pileus about 3 cm. broad..*I. Curreyi.*
6' Gill-edges not white-fimbriate, pileus much larger..*I. fastigata.*

7 Pileus erect-scaly or squarrose-scaly......8
7' Pileus appressed-scaly, innately fibrillose, or silky......9

8 Pileus tawny to rufous-scaled on the ochraceous cuticle..
....*I. caesariata.*
8' Pileus covered with dense smoky-umber scales....*I. leptophylla.*

9 Pileus silky, tan to rufous-brown, the cuticle not torn, plant
growing on wet moss.........................*I. scabella.*
9' Pileus rimose, lacerate, or scaly......10

10 Pileus soon rimose or splitting......11
10' Pileus not rimose-splitting......13

11 Pileus brown, fibrillose-virgate...................*I. rimosa.*
11' Pileus, if brown, then not fibrillose-virgate......12

12 Pileus rich-yellowish-smoky, typically very conical, large
....*I. fastigata.*
12' Pileus brown or red-brown, small or medium-sized, very
rimose   stem mealy-pubescent; plant growing in sandy
woods ....*I. asterophora.*

13 Pileus brown or red-brown, small with upcurving scales;
gill-edges white, fimbriate; plant growing in low woods....
....*I. calospora.*
13' Pileus gray-brown, small, fibrillose-scaly, the umbo umber-
cinnamon; gill-edges not white, fimbriate; plant growing on
wet soil ....*I. infelix.*

I. caesariata. Fr.   Caesar's Fiber Head.   Plate 40, fig. 1.

Pileus 2-5 cm. broad; stem 2-4 cm. x 3-6 mm.; spores 9 x 5.5 μ.

Pileus convex-obtuse, at first covered with erect ochre or fulvous tomentose scales or warts, not splitting on the margin, the disk thick, the margin incurved and connected with stem by the dingy fibrillose cortina, thin; gills rounded behind, rather broad, ventricose, dull ochraceous becoming rusty, the edges white-floccose; stem usually short, scaly or floccose-fibrillose, colored like pileus, soon hollow, light ochraceous within; spores ochraceous-cinnamon, smooth; taste mild. —In troops on moist naked soil or among short grass on low ever moist sandy flats along dunes, Indiana, locally common, spring and autumn, near the Great Lakes.

I. leptophylla Atkins.   Plate 40, fig. 2.

Similar in size to *I. caesariata,* the pileus covered with dense, erect, umber, pointed, squarrose scales; gills pale with white, crenulate edges; stem floccose-fibrillose.—On the ground in conifer woods, not common, extreme northern part of our area.

I. calospora Quel.   Plate 40, fig. 3.

Pileus 1-3 cm. broad; stem 4-6 cm. x 2 mm.; spores 9-12 μ.

Pileus conical then convex-umbonate, smoky-reddish, fading, darker on the umbo, covered with recurved fibrillose scales, thin; gills narrow, pale, the edges white-fimbriate; stem pale reddish-brown, pruinose, terminating in a small bulb; spores covered with blunt spines.—Gregarious on ground in frondose woods, common locally, Minnesota to New York and southward.

I. infelix Peck. (poisonous).   Plate 40, fig. 4.

Pileus 1-2.5 cm. broad; stem 3-5 cm. x 2-3 mm.; spores smooth, 12 x 5 μ.

Pileus plane-umbonate, grayish-brown with dark brown umbo, fibrillose-scaly or floccose-scaly, thin; gills adnexed, ventricose, close, white becoming cinnamon; stem whitish becoming brown below, white within.—On ground in low wet woods, common, May-July, Michigan to Illinois and Indiana.

I. lacera Fr.   Plate 40, fig. 5.

Differing from the preceding in its slightly larger size and in the reddish internal part of the stem; spores 12 x 5 μ.—On sand in dunes, long mycelial threads extending from the base of the stem and binding the sand together, not common, October, around the southern part of Lake Michigan.

I. pyriodora Fr. Plate 40, fig. 6.

Similar to *I. infelix* in size, the pileus whitish becoming clay-colored and faintly streaked; odor sweet and spicy; gills staining red where broken.—On the ground in oak woods, not common, throughout our area.

I. rimosa Peck. Rimose fiber-head. Plate 40, fig. 7.

Pileus 2-6 cm. broad; stem 3-8 cm. x 4-7 mm.; spores 8 x 6 μ.

Pileus brown becoming yellow-tinged in age, ovoid, campanulate then expanded, usually with a broad umbo, silky-fibrillose becoming virgate and split on margin, finally upturned, the flesh fragile, strong and nauseating in odor where crushed; gills almost free, crowded, narrow, ashy-clay-colored with white-fimbriate edges; stem cylindrical or tapering upward, solid, pale with white-mealy apex; spores reniform, smooth.—Gregarious on the ground in low frondose woods, not common, Aug.-Oct., northern part of our area.

I. fastigata Bres. Plate 40, fig. 8.

Pileus 2-7 cm. broad; stem 4-8 cm. x 4-9 mm.; spores 11 x 6 μ.

Pileus conic-campanulate, often with a broad umbo, deep-smoky-yellow, radially fibrillose, rimose splitting, virgate, the flesh white; gills adnexed, narrow, ventricose, close, white, gray or olive, then darker; stem cylindrical, solid, somewhat fibrillose, white or smoky-tinted; spores smooth, subreniform (not angular).—Gregarious in low conifer or deciduous woods, common, July-Sept. and southward.

I. Curreyi Berk. Plate 40, fig. 9.

Pileus 2-4 cm.; stem 2-4 cm. x 3-7 mm.; spores 8 x 5 μ.

Pileus obtuse, irregularly campanulate, appressed-fibrillose, pale tawny-yellowish, undulate on the margin, the flesh white; gills narrowly adnexed, broad, close, grayish becoming smoky-olivaceous, the edges white-fimbriate; stem clavate at base, solid, whitish, scaly at apex; spores subreniform, smooth, smoky-cinnamon; odor strongly earthly.—Among grass in open frondose woods, somewhat common, Minnesota to Maine and southward.

I. Cookei Bres. Plate 40, fig. 10.

Pileus straw-yellow; gills white soon ochraceous, then cinnamon; stem terminating in a marginate distinct bulb.—On ground in frondose and conifer woods, not common, northern part of our area.

I. eutheloides Peck. Plate 40, fig. 11.

Pileus 1-2.5 cm.; stem 2-5 cm. x 3 mm.; spores 9 x 5 μ.

Pileus small, conical then expanded-umbonate, fawn-colored, chestnut when young, darker on umbo; gills adnexed, broad, ventricose, close, whitish becoming cinnamon, the edges white-fimbriate; stem cylindrical or with bulb, at first densely fibrillose.—Gregarious on ground in low woods, common, June-Sept., Illinois to New York and southward.

I. fibrosa Bres. (poisonous). Plate 40, fig. 12.

Pileus 4-8 cm. broad; stem 4-8 cm. x 6-15 mm.; spores 11 x 6 μ.

Pileus large, obtusely campanulate, cream-tinted or straw-colored, silky, the margin split and lobed, the flesh white, thick, thin toward margin, with an earthy odor; gills free, rounded behind, ventricose, broader in front, close, whitish becoming cinnamon, white-fimbriate on the edges; stem white to sordid, splitting lengthwise, subcylindrical to long-bulbous, striate, the apex pruinose; spores angular.—On ground in low frondose woods, June-Aug., not common, throughout our area.

I. albodisca Peck. Plate 40, fig. 13.

Pileus small, whitish, pale lilac when young, 1.5-3.5 cm. broad with a glabrous, whitish, obtuse umbo; stem terminating in a submarginate bulb.—In beech and hemlock woods, not common, Aug.-Sept., northern part of our area.

I. asterospora Quel. Plate 40, fig. 17.

Pileus 2-5 cm.; stem 4-6 x 3-5 mm.; spores 10 μ.

Pileus campanulate to convex-umbonate, rufous-brown, fibrillose-scaly, thin, very rimose; gills adnexed, close, ventricose, grayish-brown; stem cylindrical, terminating in a rounded bulb, innately striate, fibrous, solid, red-brown, pruinose; spores spiny-tuberculate. —Gregarious in low sandy woods, June-Aug., not uncommon in such habitats.

In general characters this species is similar to *I. calospora* but differs from it in its rimose scaly pileus.

I. scabella Fr. Plate 40, fig. 15.

Pileus 2 cm. broad; stem 3-6 cm. x 1-3 mm.; spores 12 x 6 μ.

Pileus campanulate with small glabrous obtuse umbo, silky, dry, dull-yellowish to rufous or cinnamon, thin; gills sinuate-adnexed, not close, ventricose, gray with white-fimbriate edges, becoming cinnamon; stem cylindrical, stuffed, pale; spores almond-shaped.—On low mossy wet soil of dunes and in cedar-hemlock woods, common, autumn, northern part of our area.

I. geophylla Fr. White Inocybe. Plate 40, fig. 14.

Pileus 2 cm. broad; stem 2-5 cm. x 2-3 mm., spores 9 x 5 μ.

Pileus conical then expanded and umbonate or plane, white to light tan, silky-glossy, thin; gills adnexed, broad, close, ventricose, white, becoming gray-clay-colored, the odor slightly nauseating; stem cylindrical slender, firm, white, silky; spores subreniform, smooth.—On the ground in frondose or conifer woods, common, July-Oct., Minnesota to Maine and southward.

I. geophylla var. *lilacina* Pat., with lilac to smoky-purple pileus and pale lilac stem, is otherwise similar to the typical variety.—On the ground in frondose and conifer woods, not common, throughout our area.

I. trechispora Berk. Plate 40, fig. 16.
Pileus 1-3 cm. broad; stem 2-5 cm. x 2-3 mm.; spores 6 x 5 μ.

Pileus viscid, with a tawny and naked umbo, tawny-ochraceous elsewhere; gills sinuate-adnexed, ventricose, the edges white-fimbriate; stem marginate-bulbous at base, white; cystidia ventricose, flask-shaped, crystallate at apices, 50 μ long.—On ground in moist deciduous or conifer woods, not common, July-Sept., extreme northern part of our area.

CORTINARIUS Fr.

Carpophore an orbicular, convex, fleshy pileus, confluent with the central fleshy stem; pileus putrescent, glutinous or dry, glabrous or decorated; stem often marked by the remnant of the cortina, without volva or annulus; gills adnate becoming emarginate, changing color with spore development; cortina web-like connecting the pileus margin and stem; spores cinnamon.—On the ground in woods.

1   Gills bright-red or bright-cinnabar-red......2
1' Gills of another color......4
2   Pileus tawny-yellow ....*C. semisanguineus.*
2' Pileus red......3
3   Pileus cinnabar-red ....*C. cinnabarinus.*
3' Pileus and stem blood-red.....................*C. sanguineus.*
3" Pileus vermilion-red to orange....................*C. rubens.*
4   Pileus covered with a glutinous cuticle, always more or less viscid, at least when moist......5
4' Pileus not viscid......11
5   Stem terminating at base in an abrupt marginate bulb......6
5' Stem cylindrical, clavate or round-bulbous......7
6   Pileus yellow, flesh and gills violet.........*C. Atkinsonianus.*
6' Pileus tawny, gills pale then rusty..............*C. corrugatus.*
6" Pileus, gills, and stem pale violaceous.......*C. michiganensis.*

7   Stem viscid with the universal veil......8
7' Stem not viscid......10
8   Pileus dark violet ....C. iodes.
8' Pileus of another color......9
9   Stem marked with interrupted rings.............C. mucifluus.
9' Stem scarcely marked, gills at first violaceous....C. cylindripes.
10 Pileus tawny, stem stout-clavate-bulbous..........C. coloratus.
10' Pileus yellow, gills at first bluish...............C. claricolor.
10" Pileus yellow to tawny, stem slender, gills cinnamon....
    ....C. vibratilis.
11 Pileus distinctly scaly......12
11' Pileus not distinctly scaly......15
12 Stem marked with red zones.................C. armillatus.
12' Stem not marked with red zones......13
13 Pileus, gills, and stem dark violet...............C. violaceus.
13' Plant not dark violet......14
14 Pileus of some shade of yellow and covered with tawny erect
    scales ....C. annulatus.
14' Pileus brownish, hygrophanous, bearing whitish-fibrillose
    scales ....C. flexipes.
15 Either pileus or gills violet or purplish......16
15' Plant without violet, purple or lilac shades......20
16 Pileus large, 6-10 cm. broad......17
16' Pileus medium-sized; pileus and stem violaceous-white....
    ....C. alboviolaceus.
17 Pileus pale violaceous; gills narrow, close.......C. argentatus.
17' Gills broad, subdistant......18
18 Pileus, gills, and stem lilac.................C. lilacinus Peck.
18' Pileus different in color from gills......19
19 Pileus buff, gills purple...................C. subpulchrifolius.
19' Pileus violaceous-fulvous becoming rusty-fulvous....C. caninus.
20 Gills bright-yellow......21
20' Gills of another color......22
21 Pileus medium-sized, cinnamon ....C. cinnamomeus.
21' Pileus large, 5-15 cm. broad; cream-buff or tawny........
    ....C. flavifolius.
21" Pileus tawny, small, 2-5 cm. broad; gills saffron yellow..
    ....C. croceofolius.
22 Pileus large, 5-10 cm. broad......23
22' Pileus small or medium-sized, 1-5 cm. broad......26

23   Pileus tawny-yellow, erect-scaly on disk..........*C. annulatus.*
23'   Pileus not erect-scaly......24
24   Pileus streaked with rusty fibrils...............*C. autumnalis.*
24'   Pileus not streaked with rusty fibrils......25
25   Stem white ....*C. duracinus.*
25'   Stem brown or fuscous, annulate with white bands......
      ....*C. brunneus* Fr.
26   Stem not slender, 3 mm. or more thick......27
26'   Stem slender......31
27   Stem clavate ; plant growing on mosses...........*C. gracilis.*
27'   Stem cylindrical, or not clavate......28
28   Pileus brown to chestnut-colored......29
28'   Pileus and stem olive......................*C. raphanoides.*
29   Gills distant, brownish......30
29'   Gills close, stem bearing veil remnants, young pileus dark
      with white margin...........................*C. nigrellus.*
30   Stem marked with a white zone, gills distant........*C. distans.*
30'   Stem not zoned ; pileus brown, 2-5 cm. broad, smoky-chest-
          nut ; plant growing among moss in spruce-balsam woods
      ....*C. uraceus.*
31   Stem almost rooting, whitish...................*C. scandens.*
31'   Stem not rooting, pileus canescent............*C. hemitrichus.*

C. mucifluus Fr.   Glutinous Cortinarius (edible).   Plate 41,
fig. 1.
     Pileus 3-7 cm. broad ; stem 6-10 x 7-12 mm. ; spores 11 x 6 μ.
     Pileus convex to plane, glutinous when moist, with thick cuticle,
tawny, straw to almost white or rusty-stained, medium-thick, the
margin incurved ; gills grayish becoming clay then rusty-colored, adnate, close, of medium width ; stem tapering downward, stout, rigid,
stuffed, whitish, covered with a thick glutin, which forms scaly bands
or broken rings on stem.—On sandy soil, among mosses, and common on rich loam in oak woods and swamps, Aug.-Oct., Minnesota
to Maine and near Thornton, Illinois.

C. cylindripes Kauffm.   Plate 41, fig. 2.
     Pileus 3-6 cm. broad ; stem 6-10 cm. x 6-10 mm. ; spores 14 x 7 μ.
     Pileus convex-plane, very glutinous and shining, lavender, then
brownish-ochraceous and not shining, the margin incurved, striate,
the flesh thin, thick on disk, violaceous to pale cinnamon with spores,
close, the edges floccose and paler, serrulate ; stem very cylindrical,
the violaceous glutinous veil persisting in the form of patches on the

stem; spores almond-shaped.—Gregarious on rich ground in conifer or deciduous forests, common, July-Oct., Minnesota to Michigan, Illinois and the dunes of Indiana.

C. vibratilis Fr.   Plate 41, fig. 3.

Pileus 2-5 cm. broad ; stem 3-7 cm. x 4-7 mm. ; spores 7 x 4-5 μ.

Pileus convex, obtuse, gibbous, ochre-yellow to fulvous-yellow, with a glutinous surface, the flesh soft, bitter, whitish ; gills adnate to slightly decurrent, close, narrow, pallid then pale ochraceous-cinnamon ; stem soft, pure-white, clothed when young with the glutinous, hyaline veil ; taste of every part intensely bitter.—Among leaves or humus in conifer or frondose woods, not common, Aug.-Sept., northern part of our area.

C. iodes Berk. and Curt.   Violet Cortinarius.   Plate 41, fig. 5.

Pileus 2-6 cm. broad ; stem 5-7 cm. x 4-15 mm. ; spores 9 x 6 μ.

Pileus campanulate-convex, dark violet, tough, viscid, with separable cuticle, yellowish on disk, at length glabrous, smooth, thick on disk and abruptly thin toward margin, the flesh violaceous or paler ; gills adnate, violaceous then gray-cinnamon, broad, close ; stem clavate or fusiform, viscid, solid, fibrillose, the cortina violaceous, pale ; taste and odor mild or none.—On ground in low woods, gregarious, August, Minnesota to New York and southward.

C. iodeoides Kauffm.   Plate 41, fig. 6.

Similar to the preceding but with a bitter taste.—Among fallen leaves of maple and oak, not common, Sept.-Oct., northern part of our area.

C. heliotropicus Peck.   Plate 41, fig. 4.

Similar to *C. iodes,* but the pileus generally spotted, purple in color. —On ground in woods, rare, August, northern part of our area.

C. Atkinsonianus Kauffm.   Atkinson's Cortinarius.   Yellow and violet Cortinarius (edible).   Plate 41, fig. 8.

Pileus 6-9 cm. broad ; stem 6-8 cm. x 1-2 cm. ; spores 14 x 8 μ.

Pileus convex, expanded, smooth, glabrous, yellow with viscid separable cuticle, tawny in parts, the flesh violet, thick ; gills violet, at length cinnamon, the edges yellow ; stem stout, deep violet, with a broad-turbinate bulb, the webby cortina yellow.—Gregarious on leaf-mould in mixed or deciduous woods, not common, Minnesota, Michigan and Indiana dunes.

C. rubens Kauffm.   Red Cortinarius.   Plate 41, fig. 9.

Pileus 3-7 cm. broad ; stem 4-7 cm. x 1-1.5 cm. ; spores 15-18 x 8 μ.

Pileus hemispherical then convex-expanded, vermilion-red to

orange-fulvous, with a viscid separable toughish pellicle, the flesh thick, whitish; gills adnexed, rather broad, pale drab then silvery-cinnamon; stem pale straw to whitish-yellow within, cylindrical above the rounded marginate depressed bulb which is clothed by the vermilion veil, the cortina white or red-tinged.—Gregarious or subcaespitose on ground in oak and maple woods, October, rare; Wisconsin and Michigan.

C. purpurascens Fr. Purple Cortinarius. Plate 41, fig. 12.

Pileus 5-7 cm. broad; stem 2-5 x 1-2 cm.; spores 9 x 5 μ.

Pileus at first dark purple or violet then in age variegated clay-colored or brown, viscid, the pellicle separable, the flesh thick, firm, tinged-purplish; gills adnexed, rounded behind, narrow, close, azure changing to purple where bruised; stem short, stout, solid, fibrillose with remnants of the cortina, the bulb small, usually emarginate; odor and taste mild.—Gregarious, solitary, or caespitose on the ground, often on packed soil, not common, Sept.-Oct., throughout our area.

C. calochrous Fr.

Pileus 3-6 cm. broad; stem 3.5 cm. x 5-9 mm.; spores 9 x 5 μ.

Pileus ochre-yellow then fading, viscid, with thick compact flesh; gills emarginate-adnexed, narrow, at first rosy-purple, later clay-colored, the edges serrulate; stem pale violet to whitish becoming dingy-yellowish with the veil; bulb small, marginate-depressed; spores inequilateral.—Solitary or gregarious in maple or beech woods during Sept.-Oct., northwest of Chicago, Minnesota, Michigan, and northern Illinois.

C. michiganensis Kauffm. (edible). Plate 41, fig. 7.

Pileus 8-14 cm. broad; stem 4-7 x 1.5-3 cm.; spores 9 x 5 μ.

Pileus broadly convex, then expanded, smooth, glabrous, viscid to glutinous, pale violet to lilac, margin inrolled, silky, flesh thick, unchanging; gills adnexed, rounded behind, acuminate in front, narrow, crowded, pale violaceous-white to ashy becoming colored by the spores, edge serrulate; stem concolor with pileus, decorated by the bluish white cortina, with a large marginate bulb, 4 cm. across; spores long-ovate, ochraceous-cinnamon in mass.—On the ground among leaves in beech-maple forests, caespitose, not common, Aug.-Oct., throughout our area.

C. caesius Clements. Blue Cortinarius.

Similar to *C. michiganensis* but the pileus not viscid, averaging about two-thirds as large.—Probably in the western part of our area.

C. caerulescens Fr.

Smaller than *C. michiganensis* and of similar aspect, the pileus 3-6 cm. in diameter; spores 13 x 6 μ.—On the ground in woods, not common, Aug.-Sept., northern part of our area.

C. corrugatus Peck. Wrinkled Cortinarius.   Plate 41, fig. 10.

Pileus 5-10 cm. broad; stem 7-12 cm. x 5-15 mm.; spores 12 x 8 μ.

Pileus campanulate, obtuse, viscid, thin toward margin, radiately wrinkled, tawny to ochraceous, the flesh white; gills adnate, broad, close, transversely striate, pale then rusty-cinnamon, eroded on the edges; stem long-cylindrical, fibrillose, stuffed, flocculose or scurfy at the apex, tawny-yellow. terminating in a small round bulb, clothed with viscid remains of universal veil, the cortina evanescent; spores rough-tuberculate; odor pleasant.—Gregarious on moist mossy ground in low woods, July, October, frequently found, Minnesota, New York, southward.

The margin of the bulb is present in the button-stage only.

C. coloratus Peck. Tawny Cortinarius.   Plate 41, fig. 11.

Pileus 5-10 cm. broad; stem 6-12 cm. x 8-14 mm.; spores 10 x 6.5 μ.

Pileus convex, plane, bright-tawny-orange, becoming dull, glabrous, smooth or radially cracked, viscid, the margin at first involute, the flesh thick, white, thin at margin; gills adnate, broad, close, whitish-clay then cinnamon; stem clavate-bulbous, firm, solid, white, silky-fibrillose, attached at base by white-mycelioid strands, the bulb 2-3 cm. broad, the cortina cobwebby, white, not copious; odor and taste slight; spores almond-shaped.—Gregarious among leaves in deciduous forests, not common, Sept.-Oct., Minnesota to Maine and Indiana.

C. claricolor Fr.   Plate 41, fig 13.

Pileus 5-10 cm. broad; stem 5-8 cm. x 1-1.5 cm.; spores 9 x 5.5 μ.

Pileus plane, glutinous when moist, shining when dry, smooth, glabrous, orange-buff, the margin incurved and webby; the flesh thick on disk, compact, white; gills narrow, pale bluish or brownish then clay-colored, the edges eroded; stem round or clavate-bulbous, white, firm, solid, fibrillose, the bulb 2 cm. thick; spores almond-shaped; odor and taste mild.—Among spruce and white pine needles, northern.

C. alboviolaceous Fr. (edible).   Plate 43, fig. 14.

Pileus 3-6 cm. broad; stem 4-8 cm. x 7 mm. above, 2 cm. below; spores 7 x 5 μ.

Pileus convex, broadly umbonate, pale violaceous, silky-shining becoming silvery, smooth, the margin decurved, the flesh thin toward margin, violet-tinged or bluish; gills adnate to emarginate, close, broad, pale ashy-purplish becoming cinnamon, the edges crenulate; stem clavate-thickened toward base, spongy-stuffed, usually clothed below with the silky soft veil, violaceous, the cortina white; spores variable in size.—Gregarious among leaves in mixed or deciduous forests, occasional, Aug.-Oct., Minnesota to Maine and Kentucky.

C. subpulchrifolius Kauffm.   Plate 43, fig. 16.

Pileus 4-10 cm. broad; stem 5-10 cm. x 10-15 mm.; spores 10 x 6 μ.

Pileus convex, obtuse, innately silky-fibrillose, smooth, buff becoming rusty-stained, thick, compact, the margin broad; gills subdistant, purple, finally cinnamon-umber; stem stout, firm, sheathed with the dingy veil to above the middle, the apex violaceous or pale drab, the cortina copious, white; spores rough.—Gregarious or subcaespitose among fallen leaves in deciduous forests, somewhat common, Sept.-Oct., northern part of our area.

C. annulatus Peck.   Plate 43, fig. 17.

Pileus 4-9 cm. broad; stem 4-8 cm. x 8-15 mm.; spores 7 x 6 μ.

Pileus convex-expanded, obtuse, covered with minute pointed erect floccose tawny scales on the golden-tawny cuticle, with bronze lustre, the margin incurved, thick; gills 4-9 mm. broad, subdistant, pale ochraceous then rusty, the edges paler; stem clavate, solid, yellow within, clothed to considerably above the middle with the tawny veil which terminates in an obscure ring, the cortina white; spores rough, globose; odor radish-like.—Scattered on ground in woods, Aug.-Oct., Minnesota to Maine and Kentucky.

C. flavifolius Peck.   Plate 43, fig. 15.

Pileus 5-15 cm. broad; stem 5-12 cm. x 5-15 mm. above; 15-30 mm. below; spores 8 x 5 μ.

Pileus convex-expanded, cream-buff then tawny, appressed-hairy or minute-fibrillose-scaly, the margin incurved at first, the flesh thick, abruptly thin toward margin, whitish, moist; gills subdistant, yellow then rusty-yellow; stem clavate, covered with the silky universal veil, finally naked, the cortina silky, white, copious; spores minutely rough, each with an abrupt long apiculus.—Gregarious on humus or fallen leaves in oak and maple forests, common, Aug.-Oct., Minnesota to Maine and southward to Ohio.

C. violaceus Fr.   Plate 43, fig. 18.

Pileus 5-12 cm. broad; stem 7-12 cm. x 10-15 mm.; spores 14 x 8 μ.

Pileus convex, obtuse, dark violet, covered with minute villose tufts, shining, not viscid, thick, the flesh gray or dark violet; gills adnate, subdistant, broad, dark violet, at length ashy-cinnamon; stem stout, long, dark violet, clavate-bulbous, fibrillose; spores rough.—

Scattered among moss, fallen leaves, etc. in conifer woods, not common; Minnesota to Maine and southward.

C. lilacinus Peck. Similar to the preceding. The pileus 5-9 cm. in diameter, lilac colored minutely silky; gills lilac then cinnamon.—Gregarious in low places in woods, not common, Aug.-Sept., northern part of our area.

C. argentatus Fr. Similar to *C. violaceus,* but the pileus silvery-violaceous-white, appressed-silky, 5-9 cm. broad, gills close, pale violaceous then alutaceous-cinnamon.—On ground in white pine and beech woods, not common, September, northern part of our area.

C. autumnalis Peck. Plate 43, fig. 19.
Pileus 5-9 cm. broad; stem 6-10 cm. x 1 cm.; spores 8 x 4.5 μ.
Pileus convex to expanded, dull rusty-yellow, streaked with innate, rusty fibrils, the flesh white; gills adnate broad, becoming rusty-yellow, stem cylindrical above the oval bulb, pale rusty-yellow, firm, solid.—In pine woods, Illinois to Pennsylvania, infrequently found.

C. gracilis Peck. Plate 43, fig. 22.
Pileus 1-4 cm. broad; stem 5-15 cm. 3-8 mm.; spores 11 x 6 μ.
Pileus conical then campanulate with prominent acute umbo, vinaceous-cinnamon, subhygrophanous, smooth, the margin at first webby and incurved, silky-shining with innate fibrils, very thin; gills adnate, close, pale then cinnamon; stem long, cylindrical, flexuous, solid, the cortina white, rarely forming a ring.—Base of stem deeply sunken in sphagnum in bogs, not common, September, northern part of our area.

C. caninus Fr. Plate 43, ng. 23.
Pileus 6-10 cm. broad; stem 7-10 x 1-2 cm.; spores 9 x 8 μ.
Pileus violaceous-fulvous then rusty-fulvous, micaceous-glistening, convex-plane, obtuse, thin, thicker on disk, the flesh pale with a lilac tinge; gills lilac-clay then cinnamon, broad, subdistant; stem pale to rusty-fibrillose, stuffed then hollow, the veil often forming a partial ring; odor and taste mild.—In open sandy woods, not common, September, Minnesota to Vermont and Indiana.

C. cinnamomeus Fr. var. Cinnamon Cortinarius. Plate 43, fig. 20.
Pileus 2-6 cm. broad; stem 5-9 cm. x 4-6 mm.; spores 8 x 5 μ.
Pileus hemispheric or campanulate, umbonate, obtuse, regular then wavy-margined, fragile, cinnamon-brown, tinged olivaceous, rufous

on disk, innately and minutely fibrillose-scaly or silky, the margin incurved, the flesh light yellowish; gills adnate, narrow, yellow, eroded on the edges; stem somewhat enlarged below, fibrillose-striate, pale yellow tinged with olive, hollow, of the same color within; odor and taste mild.—Among mosses in cedar and tamarack bogs and in flat, poorly drained oak woods, Aug.-Oct., local, Minnesota to Maine and Illinois.

C. cinnamomeus Fr. Similar to the preceding but the pileus lacking rufous tints and the gills rather broad.—In bogs and wet conifer woods, common, Aug.-Oct., northern part of our area.

C. croceofolius Peck. Plate 43, fig. 21.
Pileus 2-5 cm. broad; stem 2-4 cm. x 3-5 mm.; spores 7 x 5 μ.
Pileus convex to plane, obtuse or broad-umbonate, brownish-cinnamon often saffron-yellow toward margin, thin, thicker on disk; the flesh pale yellow or gray; gills close, thin, saffron-yellow or orange-tinted becoming cinnamon, crenulate on the edges; cortina yellow.—On mossy ground in spruce-fir woods, rarely in oak woods, not common, Aug.-Sept., Illinois to New York, Cedar Lake, Indiana.

C. semisanguineus Fr. Plate 43, fig. 25.
Pileus 2-7 cm. broad; stem 3-8 cm. x 3-8 mm.; spores 6 x 4 μ.
Pileus convex-campanulate to hemispheric, obtuse or broad-umbonate, tawny-yellow; gills adnate, narrow, crowded, red or cinnabar; stem subcylindrical, yellow or tawny; cortina elastic.—In low ground near blueberry plants or among sphagnum, locally common, Aug.-Oct., Minnesota to Maine, Illinois and the Indiana Dunes.

C. cinnabarinus Fr.
Similar to preceding in dimensions; pileus and gills bright-cinnabar-red; stem cinnabar, stuffed then hollow, the cortina red; spores 8 x 5 μ, rough-punctuate.—On ground in oak woods, locally common, Minnesota to Michigan and Illinois.

C. sanguineus Fr.
About two-thirds as large as *C. semisanguineus*, pileus blood-red, the flesh red, the stem blood-red, the gills dark blood-red.—In deep beds of sphagnum in conifer woods, infrequently found, Minnesota and Michigan.

C. raphanoides Fr.
Similar to *C. semisanguineus*, the pileus light brownish-olive, obtuse; gills green then darker; stem cylindrical olivaceous, mycelioid at the base.—Attached to sphagnum, rare, northern part of our area.

C. flexipes Fr.   Plate 43, fig. 26.

Pileus 1-3 cm. broad; stem 4-5 cm. x 2-4 mm.; spores 7 x 4.5 μ.

Pileus conic-campanulate, hygrophanous, cinnamon-brown, densely covered with grayish-white, fibrillose scales up to the apex of the acute umbo, the scales easily rubbed-off; gills brown with purplish tint, the edges whitish, broad; stem often flexuous, dark violaceous at apex, gray-brown with remnants of the annulus near or above middle, and marked with white patches below, violet within.—On mosses in bogs and in spruce swamps, frequently found locally; New York to Illinois; in bog near Fox Lake, Illinois.

C. armillatus Fr. (edible).

Pileus 5-12 cm. broad; stem 7-14 x 1-2 cm.; spores 11 x 6 μ.

Pileus convex with decurved margin, brick-red, not truly hygrophanous, the flesh spongy, rather thin for the size of the pileus; gills broad, distant, pale cinnamon becoming rusty-brown; stem elongated-bulbous, 3 cm. thick on bulb, brownish, encircle by several red zones or partial rings of the membrane-like red universal veil; spores rough-tuberculate.—Solitary or scattered on humus or very rotten wood in northern forests, Minnesota to Maine and southward.

C. nigrellus Peck.   Black Cortinarius.   Plate 43, fig. 24.

Pileus 2-5 cm. broad; stem 5-8 cm. x 3-6 mm.; spores 7 x 3.5 μ.

Pileus conical to convex, often umbonate, minute-silky, hygrophanous, blackish-chestnut, the margin white when young; gills close, narrow, ochre-brown becoming cinnamon; stem silky-fibrillose, pale, marked in subannulate patches with remnants of the whitish veil.— On moss (*Polytrichum*) in flat poorly drained woods, local, Oct.- Nov., Illinois to New York.

C. duracinus Fr. var.

Pileus 4-10 cm. broad; stem 4-12 x 0.6-1.5 cm.; spores 9 x 5 μ.

Pileus convex, obtuse, hygrophanous, watery-cinnamon when moist, buff when dry, glabrous, smooth, the margin incurved, silky, rigid-brittle, thin, scissile; gills adnate, subdistant, rather broad, pale then watery-cinnamon; stem tapering downward, fusiform, subradicate, rigid, stuffed to hollow, shining-white, sometimes compressed, at first fibrillose with remnants of the cortina; spores almond-shaped. —Gregarious in grassy places, not common, Aug.-Oct., Minnesota to New York and southward to Indiana.

C. scandens Fr.

Pileus 1-3 cm. broad; stem 3-8 cm. x 2-5 mm.; spores 7 x 4.5 μ.

Pileus rigid, conical-campanulate then covnex-umbonate, rusty- fulvous when moist and striate, honey-colored when dry, thin; gills adnate, narrow, subdistant, pale brown becoming cinnamon; stem tapering downward, flexuous, rigid, stuffed or hollow, fulvous when moist to shining-white when dry.—Scattered among fallen leaves in deciduous and conifer woods, Oct.-Nov., common northward, Wisconsin, Michigan and Indiana.

PAXILLUS Fr.   Plate 33.

Carpophore composed of a more or less orbicular, convex, turbinate pileus, of same material and confluent with the fleshy central or eccentric stipe; pileus thick at disk, thinning to the usually involute margin; stipe confluent with the pileus, fleshy, tending to be eccentric or lacking; gills decurrent, forked behind, often anastomosing on the stem, easily separable from the trama of the pileus; spores ochraceous.—On ground and on decaying wood.

These plants are similar in shape to *Hygrophorus* and *Gomphidius*.

1   Stem covered with dense black hairs.........*P. atrotomentosus.*
1' Stem not hairy......2
2   Pileus orange-brown, gills bright yellow, not persistently
    involute ....*P. rhodoxanthus.*
2' Pileus of a duller color; gills dingy becoming brown where
    bruised, involute until aged....................*P. involutus.*

P. atrotomentosus Fr. (edible).

Pileus 5-10 cm. broad; stem 3-10 cm. x 8-25 mm.; spores 5 x 3 μ.

Pileus convex then plane and depressed, tough, dark rusty brown to almost black, smooth, the margin involute or finally incurved, the flesh thick, spongy or compact, the odor and taste mild; gills slightly decurrent, narrow, close, forked behind, often anastomosing or porose on the stem; stem thick, often eccentric, solid, tough, covered with a black velvety tomentum; spores smooth, yellowish in mass.—On decaying wood in conifer forests, locally common, July-Sept., northern part of our area.

P. involutus Fr. (edible)   Plate 33, fig. 12.

Pileus 4-8 cm. broad; stem 4-5 cm. x 1-2.5 cm. broad; spores 8 x 5 μ.

Pileus dull ochraceous-brown, olive-brown, or rusty, somewhat cottony, the margin markedly involute at length spreading, convex to expanded-depressed, firm, thick; the flesh pallid, tinged brownish-yellow where bruised; gills arcuate-decurrent, crowded, olive-yellow, anastomosing on the stem, brown where bruised.—On ground in conifer or mixed woods, July-Oct., common northward, Minnesota to Indiana and east to the Atlantic Ocean.

P. rhodoxanthus Schw.   Plate 33, fig. 13.

Pileus 3-10 cm. broad; stem 3-8 cm. x 6-15 mm.; spores 11 x 4 μ.

Pileus orange-brown to chestnut, not viscid, commonly rimosely cracked in the surface, convex to depressed or turbinate, not viscid, glabrous or minutely tomentose, the disk thick, the flesh pale with yellow tinge; gills long-decurrent, broad, golden-yellow or chrome-yellow, intervenose, sometimes reticulate-porose toward stem, sometimes not at all anastomosing; stem cylindrical or ventricose or tapering downward, orange, yellow at base; spores almost fusiform.—On ground in frondose or conifer woods, July-Aug., not common, Minnesota, Maine and Indiana.

CREPIDOTUS Fr.   Plate 34.

Carpophore composed of a dimidiate or lateral pileus attached either to a short stem or stemless and sessile, fleshy, putrescent. Pileus when young often resupinate, of same material and confluent with the fleshy stem when present; veil lacking; spores globose or elliptical, ochre-brown to rusty in color.—Growing on wood.

1   Pileus viscid, white ....*C. haerens.*
1'   Pileus not viscid, in some cases gelatinous......2
2   Upper layer of pileus gelatinous......3
2'   Pileus without gelatinous cuticle......4
3   Pileus glabrous, gills becoming yellow with spores....*C. mollis.*
3'   Pileus hairy or scaly.................*Pleurotus mastrucatus.*
4   Pileus hygrophanous......5
4'   Pileus not hygrophanous......7
5   Pileus covered with thin tawny tomentum....*C. fulvotomentosus.*
5'   Pileus glabrous or white-tomentose......6
6   Pileus gray-white, with white tomentum; gills broad......
    ....*C. malachius.*
6'   Pileus white-cottony on basal half............*C. croceophyllus.*
6'' Pileus white, glabrous; gills very narrow........*C. applanatus.*
7   Gills yellow then rusty........................*C. dorsalis.*
7'   Gills white then rusty, plants white-villose.........*C. versutus.*

C. haerens Peck.

Pileus 1-3 cm. long x 1-5 cm. wide x 4 mm. thick; spores 3 x 5.5 μ.

Pileus sessile, plane, reniform to dimidiate, hygrophanous, viscid with the thin gelatinous tough cuticle, the cuticle separable, glabrate, watery gray-brown when moist, whitish when dry, the base villose, thin; gills narrow, close, whitish becoming brown-tinged with rusty-cinnamon spores.—On decaying wood of deciduous trees, not common, June-Sept., Minnesota to New York and Indiana.

C. mollis Fr.   Soft Crepidotus.

Pileus 1-5 cm. long x 1-4 cm. wide x 4 mm. thick; spores 8 x 4.5 μ.

Pileus sessile, reniform or obovate, plane, the cuticle gelatinous, subviscid when moistened, flaccid, glabrous, substriate on the margin, dirty white when moist, tan when dry, thin; gills decurrent, crowded, narrow, white then cinnamon with spores; odor absent.—Caespitose-overlapping or solitary, rare, September, Wisconsin to New York and Indiana.

C. versutus Peck.

Pileus 5-20 mm. broad, reniform or dimidiate, sessile. white, clothed with soft down, the margin incurved; gills rounded behind, rather broad, subdistant, white then rusty with spores.—On decaying wood, June-Oct., common, Minnesota to New York and southward.

C. herbarum Peck.

Like the preceding except the pileus 3-10 mm. wide and long; gills narrow.—On dead stems of herbs, common, Wisconsin to New York, northward and southward.

C. cinnabarinus Peck.

Pileus 5-10 mm. broad, scarlet or cinnabar-red, sessile or short-stemmed, sparingly villose; gills scarlet on edges, fimbriate.—On decaying logs, rare, in Great Lakes region.

C. fulvo-tomentosus Peck.

Pileus 1-5 cm. long x 1-4 cm. wide x 0.5 cm. thick; spores 9 x 5.5 μ.

Pileus orbicular-dimidiate to reniform, plane, firm, thin, sessile or with short tubercle, hygrophanous, densely tawny-tomentose when young, the tomentum becoming small tawny scales in age, the cuticle ochraceous beneath the tomentum; gills soon rusty, broad, close, white-fimbriate on the edges.—Gregarious on rotten wood, common, June-Oct., Minnesota to Maine and southward.

C. malachius Berk. and Curt.

Pileus 1-4 cm. long, fan-shaped to subreniform, sessile or with a very short white-tomentose stem, hygrophanous, water-soaked in wet weather, glabrous, whitish, striate on the margin, firm then soft; gills broad, abruptly narrowed behind, ventricose, whitish, flesh-colored, then rusty with spores.—On decaying wood of deciduous trees, common, June-Nov., Minnesota to Maine and southward.

C. applanatus Fr.

Differing from the preceding in the very narrow gills, which are almost line-like where decurrent, crowded, and white then cinnamon.—On rotten wood, July-Sept., rare, Wisconsin to Michigan and Illinois.

C. dorsalis Peck. Plate 34, fig. 6.

Pileus 1-3 cm. broad, convex, sessile, dimidiate-orbicular to reniform, adorned with tawny fibrillose scales on a tawny background, down-curved at the margin, pliant, thin; gills rounded, radiate from the villose point; spores 6 μ in diameter.—On decaying wood in swamps, July-Sept., not common, Minnesota to Maine and Indiana.

C. croceophyllus Berk.

Pileus 1-3 cm. broad, fan-shaped to reniform, narrowed to the stem-like base, white-cottony-tomentose on basal half, pale yellow when dry, watery-yellowish when wet; gills yellow-buff becoming rusty-ochraceous with spores, close, thick, rather broad; spore with a cavity or depression on one side.—On rotten logs especially of beech, September, rare, Michigan to Ohio, probably eastward and westward.

NAUCORIA Fr. Plate 34.

Carpophore composed of an orbicular, hemispherical, conical or convex pileus on a central cylindrical stem; pileus slightly fleshy, its margin at first incurved, putrescent; stipe subcartilaginous, hollow or stuffed; partial veil fugaceous or absent; gills adnate or adnexed, usually with sterile cells on the edge causing the color to be pale to white; spores ochre-brown or rusty brown, smooth.—Growing on the ground or on wood.

1   Growing on wood......2
1' Growing on the ground or on herbaceous plants......4
2   Gill-edges crenulate with yellow-green flecks......*N. centuncula.*
2' Gill-edges not so marked......3
3   Pileus small, 3-10 mm. broad, acutely umbonate, chestnut-brown.—Growing on decayed wood in beech-hemlock woods
....*N. triscopoda.*
3' Pileus 5-20 mm. broad, becoming depressed about the umbo, hygrophanous ....*N. lignicola.*
4   Pileus tobacco-colored when moist, hygrophanous, small, 6-18 mm. broad; stem slender, 2-3 cm. long.—Growing on cultivated ground ....*N. tabacina.*
4' Pileus dull yellow, or else stem booted with scales......5

5   Pileus slightly viscid or else brown-scaly......6
5' Pileus not viscid, silky at least toward margin; gills light
    brown then sordid-brown ....*N. pediades.*
6   Pileus hemispherical-convex, stem round, gill-edges white
    fimbriate ....*N. semiorbicularis.*
6' Pileus convex-expanded, stem hollow or compressed, gill-
    edges pallid-fimbriate ....*N. platysperma.*

N. semiorbicularis Fr.   Half-globe Naucoria.   Plate 34, fig. 9.

Pileus 1-3 cm. broad; stem 4-6 cm. x 2 mm.; spores 12-15 x 9 μ.

Pileus hemispherical-convex, obtuse, slightly viscid when wet, ful-vous-yellow with darker center, glabrous, not striate, without veil, thin, the disk thicker; gills adnate, broad, close, alutaceous becoming rusty-brown, the edges white-fimbriate; stem cylindrical or thickened toward ends, tough, subrigid, terete, dull yellow, often silky-shining, stuffed; spores rusty-brown in mass.—Gregarious in grassy places, May-Sept., common, Minnesota, New England, Kentucky, North Carolina.

N. pediades Fr.   Plate 34, fig. 10.

Pileus 2-6 cm. broad; stem 4-9 cm. x 2-3 mm.; spores 11 x 7 μ.

Pileus campanulate-hemispherical then plane, obtuse, dry, not shin-ing, fulvous-ochraceous becoming dull tan, tomentose toward margin, silky on the margin, slightly fleshy; gills broadly adnate, broad-ventricose, pale brown finally sordid-brown; stem mealy-flocculose, yellowish or fulvous, silky, stuffed, often twisted; spores silver-brown in mass.—In grassy places, on lawns, etc., June, Minnesota, Maine, Kentucky.

N. platysperma Peck.   Flat-spored Naucoria.

Pileus 2-4.5 cm. broad; stem 3-5 cm. x 3 mm.; spores 14 x 8 μ.

Pileus convex, ochraceous, viscid when moist, glabrous, with a slight veil, the flesh white, thick on disk; gills adnate, broader be-hind, close, thin, dull yellow then smoky-brown, the edges pallid-fimbriate, stem hollow and often compressed, dull yellow, slightly flocculose, often striate at apex; some of the spores flattened on one side.—Gregarious on dung hills, in grassy woods and pastures, frequently found, May, June and September, Minnesota to Maine to Kentucky.

N. centuncula Fr.   Plate 34, fig. 8.

Pileus 1.5-2.5 cm. broad; stem 2-3 cm. x 2-3 mm.; spores 6.5 x 4 μ.

Pileus convex then plane, obtuse, hygrophanous, smoky-olive-brown and striate when moist, dull yellow when dry, silky under lens, the

margin covered with sulphur pulverulence, submembranaceous; gills
adnate, broad, thick, crowded, yellow-gray or olive-brown, the edges
marked with yellowish-green crenations; stem often eccentric, curved,
hollow, pale olive, white-granular above, the base mycelioid; spores
kidney-shaped.—On decayed wood in deciduous forests, July-Sept.,
infrequently found, Michigan.

N. lignicola Peck.

Pileus 5-20 mm. broad; stem 2-4 cm. x 1 mm.; spores 7-8 x 3-4 μ.

Pileus convex-campanulate, umbonate, at length depressed about
the umbo, hygrophanous, watery-cinnamon and striatulate when
moist, dull yellow when dry, glabrous, thin; gills adnate, plane, narrow, brown, the edges concolor; stem tough, cylindrical, glabrous or
fibrillose; spores smooth, rusty-brown.—On decayed wood, July, infrequently found, Wisconsin to New York.

BOLBITIUS Fr.   Plate 43.

Carpophore composed of an oval, conical, or campanulate pileus
on a slender, cylindrical, central stem; pileus thin, usually split on
margin, margin at first straight as in *Mycena*, flesh very thin, soft,
putrescent; gills narrowly attached to stipe, dissolving somewhat in
wet weather as in *Coprinus*; stipe long, fragile; spores ochre-brown
to rusty ochraceous, smooth, elliptical.—On dung, among grass, and
on the ground in fields.

These plants are with difficulty separated from *Pluteolus*. It is
advisable in identifying species of *Bolbitius* to compare the specimens
with members of the genera *Pluteolus* and *Galera*.

1   Pileus less than 2 cm. broad, not umbonate, gills quickly
    dissolving ....*B. tener*.
1' Pileus larger, 2-5 cm. broad, umbonate, gills very slowly,
    if at all, dissolving......2
2   Stem yellow, pileus-margin striate, plants growing on culti-
    vated ground ....*B. fragilis*.
2' Stem white, pileus-margin plicate, plants growing on cow's
    dung ....*B. vitellinus*.

B. tener Berk.   Tender Bolbitius.   Plate 42, fig. 12.

Pileus 1-1.5 cm. high; stem 6-12 cm. x 1-2 mm.; spores 14 x 9 μ.

Pileus conical, dull white, creamy-yellow upward, smooth or dis-
tantly striate, glabrous, atomate when dry, the flesh very thin; gills
free, close, narrow, ochre, dissolving quickly; stem slender, hollow,

glabrous, bulbilate at the base, pure white, soon collapsing.—In grass on lawns, in parks, etc., especially where manure has been applied, July-Aug., rare, temperate North America.

Galera lateritia resembles this species but has a larger pileus, a rigid-fragile stem, and non-dissolving gills.

B. fragilis Fr. Fragile Bolbitius. Plate 42, fig. 11.

Pileus 2-5 cm. broad; stem 8 cm. x 2 mm.; spores 12 x 7 μ.

Pileus conical, expanding-umbonate, viscid, light yellow, with a deeper yellow umbo and a striate margin, pellucid, glabrous, membranaceous, thin; gills sometimes free, yellow becoming pale cinnamon, somewhat dissolving; stem fragile, glabrous, yellow, hollow.— Gregarious in cultivated ground, May-July, rare, throughout our area.

B. vitellinus Fr. Plate 42, fig. 10.

Differing from the preceding in the plicate pileus, white stem which is pruinose at apex, white edges of the young clay-colored gills.—On cow dung, May-July, common, throughout our area.

PLUTEOLUS Fr. Plate 42.

Carpophore composed of a conical to convex, orbicular pileus attached to a slender, cylindrical stem; pileus thin, viscid, margin at first straight, putrescent; gills free from stipe, not dissolving in wet weather; stipe distinct from pileus, of different material and readily separable from the pileus, subcartilaginous; spokes rusty-yellow to ochre-brown.—Growing on various substrata, very rotten wood, among grass, or on ground in open fields.

1   Pileus decorated with reticulations; plants growing on decay-ing wood ....*P. reticulatus*.
1' Pileus not so decorated; plants growing on dung, straw, and ground......2
2   Pileus yellow, stem deep yellow.................*P. expansus*.
2' Pileus gray, stem not deep yellow.............*P. coprophilus*.

P. reticulatus Fr.

Pileus 2-5 cm. broad; stem 4-7 cm. x 3-6 mm.; spores 10 x 5-6 μ.

Pileus campanulate then expanded, obtuse, with gluten which dries to form reticulate veins on surface, radiately rugose on disk, violaceous-gray becoming smoky, the margin pale, the flesh medium to thin; gills free or nearly so, rounded behind, crowded, ventricose, broad, white then rusty or cinnamon with white-fimbriate edges; stem cylindrical, elastic, somewhat tough, white, minutely floccose, fibrillose-striate, hollow; spores elliptical rusty-brown, smooth.—Clustered about the bases of stumps or trees and on decayed wood, rare, October and May, northern part of our area. This species is commonly associated with our beech-maple forest.

P. expansus Peck. Plate 42, fig. 15.

Pileus 3-6 cm. broad; stem 5-10 cm. x 3-6 mm.; spores 11 x 7 μ.

Pileus oval then expanded-plane, fragile, viscid, ashy-ochraceous tinged brownish or greenish, the margin sulphur yellow, striate-sulcate, thin submembranaceous; gills free, narrow, close white becoming ochraceous-cinnamon, the edges minutely flocculose; stem citron-yellow, pruinose, fragile, hollow or compressed, yellow within; hymenium composed of inflated sterile cells and basidia.—Gregarious on manured fields and lawns or in woods, May-July, infrequent, Illinois to New York, northward and southward.

P. coprophilus Peck. Orchard Pluteolus. Plate 42, fig. 13.

Pileus 2-4 cm. broad; stem 6-11 cm. x 3 mm.; spores 14 x 8 μ.

Pileus conic-campanulate then expanded, viscid, striatulate on the margin, whitish, soon rosy-gray, thin; gills free, narrow, close, pale rusty-cinnamon; stem slender, pure white, hollow.—Gregarious in orchards on straw and manure, common, May-June, Minnesota to New England and southward.

GALERA Fr.   Plate 42.

Carpophore composed of an oval, conical or campanulate pileus on a long, slender, cylindrical stem; pileus thin, the margin at first straight and appressed on the stem, putrescent, fragile, small; gills narrowly adnate or adnexed, usually narrow, mature gills usually pale rusty yellow; stipe slender, hollow, cylindrical, usually fragile; spores ochre-brown or rusty-yellow, smooth, elliptical or oval.—Growing on the ground, among grass, mosses, on dung, on lawns, in pastures or in woodlands.

1   Growing in wet mossy places......2
1' Growing on dung......4
1'' Growing in glassy places......3
2   Stem blue ....G. cyanopes.
2' Stem yellowish or brownish....................G. Hypnorum.
3   Gills crisped and veined, stem white..................G. crispa.
3' Gills not crisped or veined, stem cream-colored.......G. tenera.
4   Stem rooting ....G. antipus.
4' Stem not rooting......5

5   Stem-base bulbous ....*G. bulbifera.*
5'   Stem-base not bulbous......6
6   Stem distinctly striatulate; plant growing on cow's dung....
     ....*G. pubescens.*
6'   Stem scarcely striatulate......7
7   Pileus very soft and very fragile, expanded.......*G. teneroides.*
7'   Pileus membranous, longer than wide..............*G. lateritia.*

G. antipus Lasch. Rooting Galera. Plate 42, fig. 3.

Pileus 1.5-2.5 cm. broad (rarely 5 cm.); stem 4 cm. x 3 mm.; spores 9 x 6 μ.

Pileus broadly campanulate, hygrophanous, rusty-cinnamon when moist, buff-yellow when dry, not striate, the flesh very thin, thickened on disk; gills crowded, narrow, pale, dull-cinnamon-yellow becoming dark rusty-colored; stem subfusiform with a very long horizontal white root-like extension, striate or twisted, ochraceous; spores lemon-shaped, obscurely 6-angled.—Gregarious on dung in woods, September, locally abundant, northward, northern part of our area.

G. lateritia Fr. Plate 42, fig. 6.

Pileus 2-3 cm. high; stem 6-10 cm. x 2-3 mm., spores 13 x 8 μ.

Pileus cylindric-conical to conic-campanulate, pale buff, finely striate on the margin, glabrous, hygrophanous, membranaceous; gills nearly free, rusty-fulvous, linear, crowded, not dissolving; stem rigid, fragile, pure white, pruinose, hollow; spores rusty, smooth.—On dung or manured grassy places, June-Sept., infrequently found, North Dakota, Maine, North Carolina.

G. bulbifera Kauffm. Bulbous Galera. Plate 42, fig. 4.

Pileus 0.5-2.5 cm. broad; stem 6-15 cm. x 1.5-3 mm.; spores 13 x 8 μ.

Pileus oval-campanulate, obtuse, rusty-cinnamon when moist, ochraceous when dry, hygrophanous, rivulose-reticulate; gills ascending-adnate, narrow, close, rusty-cinnamon; stem pale rusty, hollow, bulbous at the base; spores smooth, rusty in mass.—On horse-dung, not common, Aug.-Sept., Indiana, Michigan, Ohio.

G. pubescens Gill. Pubescent Galera. Plate 42, fig. 5.

Pileus 1-4 cm. broad; stem 4-10 cm. x 1-3 mm.; spores 11 x 6 μ.

Pileus oval-campanulate, rusty-cinnamon to rufous-brown when moist, tan when dry, hygrophanous, sometimes reticulate-rivulose or wrinkled, submembranous; gills adnate, narrow, close, cinnamon-ochraceous; stem cylindrical, often striatulate, minutely pubescent to glabrous, hollow, brown-ochraceous, shining.—Common on cow-dung, June-Sept., Minnesota to New England and southward.

G. tenera Fr. Plate 47, fig. 7.

Pileus 8-16 mm. broad; stem 4-7 cm. x 1.5 mm.; spores 11-16 x 6-9 μ.

Pileus obtuse, conic-campanulate, pale rusty and striate when moist, cream-colored and atomate when dry, glabrous, submembranous; gills adnate, rather close, cinnamon, rather narrow; stem slender, fragile, straight, hollow, colored like pileus, pruinose at the apex; spores smooth.—In manured lawns and fields or on dung hills, very common, May-Oct., Minnesota, Maine, Tennessee. In aspect this species is similar to *Bolbitius tener* but it does not collapse at maturity. Both are often found in same habitat.

G. crispa Longyear. Plate 42, fig. 8.

Pileus 1.5-3 cm. broad; stem 6-9 cm. x 1-2 mm.; spores 12-15 x 8-13 μ.

Pileus persistently conic-campanulate, subacute, rivulose-striate, brownish-ochre at apex, buff-white elsewhere when moist, buff-atomate when dry, glabrous, sometimes minutely wrinkled, membranous; gills adnexed, close, narrow, white becoming rusty-brown, crisped and veined; stem pure white, fragile, hollow, slightly bulbous.—Among grass, June-July, not common, Minnesota, Michigan, Ohio, Illinois.

G. teneroides Peck. Plate 42, fig. 9.

Pileus 5-20 mm. broad; stem 3-6 cm. x 1 mm.; spores 8 x 5 μ.

Pileus soft-watery and fragile, separating readily from the tough persistent stem, sublubricous, hygrophanous, striatulate and brown-cinnamon when moist, paler when dry, glabrous, the flesh membranous; gills narrow, adnate.—On horse dung or on decayed debris in woods, Aug.-Sept., not common, Minnesota to New York and southward. The stems are seen in place after the caps have disappeared.

G. cyanopes Kauffm. Blue-stemmed Galera. Plate 42, fig. 1.

Pileus 8-12 mm. broad; stem 5-7 cm. x 1-1.5 mm.; spores 8-9 x 6.5-7 μ.

Pileus convex-campanulate, pale watery-cinnamon and striatulate when moist, whitish-buff and atomate when dry, membranous; gills adnate, linear, pale-cinnamon-ochraceous, the edges· minutely flocculose; stem pale greenish-gray to bluish, elastic, pruinose at the apex, hollow; spores ochraceous, smooth.—On moss (*Polytrichum*) in a poplar swamp, Ann Arbor, Michigan, July, rare. (after Kauffman).

G. Hypnorum Fr.   Moss Galera.   Plate 42, fig. 2.

Pileus 4-12 mm. broad; stem 3-6 cm. x 1-2 mm.; spores 9 x 5-6 μ.
Pileus campanulate, cinnamon-yellowish to ochraceous and striate
when moist, glabrous, buff, not striate when dry, membranaceous;
gills adnate, broad, subdistant, fulvous-cinnamon, the edges minutely
flocculose; stem short, slender, cylindrical, hollow, pruinose at the
apex, colored like pileus, flexuous.—Gregarious on mosses, common
May-Oct., Wisconsin, Michigan, Illinois.

AGARICUS Fr.   Plate 44.
Psalliota Fr.

Carpophores mostly large, each composed of a convex, orbicular,
fleshy pileus on a central, fleshy stipe; pileus glabrous to scaly, of
different material and readily separable from the stipe; gills free,
usually pink when young becoming purple-brown with age; stipe
fleshy, provided with a persistent or evanescent annulus, usually
shorter than the diameter of the pileus; spores purple-brown.—
Growing on the ground in woods among fallen leaves, on cultivated
ground, among grass of lawns and golf fairways, and about hay
stacks in meadows.

1   Flesh soon turning red where broken or rubbed......2
1' Flesh not becoming red......3

2   Plant growing in hot houses, small, 1-3 cm. broad...*A. echinata.*
2' Plant growing in woods, large, 5-10 cm. broad, with a large
    pendulous annulus ....*A. haemorrhoidaria.*

3   Annulus double, bearing floccose patches on lower side;
    pileus large, 4-20 cm. broad......4
3' Annulus simple, without floccose scales on lower side; pileus
    small (except in *A. campestris*)......9

4   Annulus a broad band often with two rims; plants growing
    along city streets.............................*A. Rodmanii*
4' Annulus otherwise......5

5   Growing in forests......6
5' Growing in fields, open places, lawns, pastures, etc., plants
    very large 8

6   Pileus soon scaly with numerous appressed pale tawny scales,
    the disk reddish-brown; plants often very large.........
    ....*A. subrufescens.*
6' Pileus glabrous, or fibrils present......7

7   Pileus white, yellowish on disk where rubbed; stem termina-
      ting in an abrupt bulb.....................*A. abruptibulba.*
7'   Disk of pileus blackish, fibrils present..........*A. placomyces.*
8   Pileus white, yellowish on disk when rubbed.......*A. arvensis.*
8'   Disk reddish-brown, many light tawny scales present on
      pileus ....*A. subrufescens.*
9   Growing in forests, pileus small, 2-5 cm. broad......10
9'   Growing in open places......11
10   Pileus creamy-white ....*A. comptula.*
10'   Pileus with reddish-brown tint...............*A. diminutiva.*
11   Gills at first gray, pileus gray-brown........*A. micromegetha.*
11'   Gills at first deep pink, pileus white (scaly forms are
      brownish) ....*A. campestris.*

A. arvensis Fr. Horse mushroom (edible). Plate 44, fig. 1.

Pileus 6-18 cm. broad; stem 6-18 cm. x 1-3 cm.; spores 6 x 4 μ.

Pileus very large, hemispherical then convex-expanded, glabrous, shining, or bearing appressed scales, white becoming ochraceous when rubbed, the disk plane, the flesh white, thick; gills free, broad, crowded, whitish, gray-pink then dark brown, the edges entire; stem stout, white, becoming yellow-stained where rubbed, stuffed with loose pith then hollow, glabrous; annulus ample, thick, double, radially cracked below into large ochraceous patches; odor like that of anise.—Scattered on ground in meadows, about old hay or straw stacks, etc., common, July-Oct., Minnesota to Maine and North Carolina.

A. subrufescens Peck. (edible). Plate 44, fig. 3.

Pileus 8-16 cm. broad; stem 7-14 x 1-1.5 cm.; spores 7 x 4-5 μ.

Pileus large, hemispherical then convex, plane and.wavy, split on margin, silky-fibrillose at first, the cuticle breaking up into numerous appressed, tawny scales, the disk remaining tawny without scales, not striate, the flesh medium-thick to thin, white, not changing; gills free, narrow, crowded, white, pink, then dark brown; the edges minutely white-fimbriate; stem white above the annulus, tawny-scaly below, stuffed then hollow, often clavate, the annulus very large, double, reflexed, distant from the apex, smooth and white above, floccose and tawny below; odor that of almonds when crushed.—Caespitose on humus and decaying leaves in woods, not common, temperate North America.

A. campestris Fr. Commercial mushroom (edible). Plate 44, fig. 2.

Pileus 4-8 cm. broad; stem 3-7 x 1-2 cm.; spores 8 x 5 μ.

Pileus flattened-hemispherical to convex or plane, glabrous or minute-scaly, dry, white, or brownish if scaly, the margin extending
beyond the gills, the flesh white, unchanging, thick; gills free, rounded
behind, close, not broad, delicate-pink and purplish-brown then dark
brown, with smooth edges; stem white, firm, solid, glabrous, the
annulus near the middle of the stem, with torn edge, evanescent;
odor and taste pleasant.—On lawns, pasture, etc., often growing in
circle five to twenty feet in diameter, common, July-Oct., throughout
temperate North America.   This is the mushroom of cultivation and
commerce.

A. Rodmanii Peck.   Rodman's mushroom (edible).   Plate 44,
fig. 5.

Similar to preceding but the annulus present as a broad band-like,
double ring, with spreading edges or merely grooved, near or below
the middle of the stem; spores 6 x 4.5 μ.—On lawns or along city
streets, caespitose, May and October, common, temperate North
America.

A. haemorrhoidaria Fr.   Red-flesh Agaricus (edible).   Plate
44, fig. 6.

Pileus 5-10 cm. broad; stem 5-10 x 1-1.5 cm.; spores 6-7 x 4 μ.

Pileus almost ovate, campanulate-expanded then nearly plane,
covered with dense fibrillose brownish-gray appressed scales, the
margin incurved, the flesh white becoming quickly red when broken,
thick on the disk, thin at the margin; gills free, crowded; stem stuffed
to hollow, whitish, glabrescent; annulus large, single, superior, persistent, pendulous, white then colored with spores; odor and taste
pleasing.—In rich woods near bases of trees, caespitose, Aug.-Oct.,
Iowa, New England, southward.

A. abruptibulba Peck. (edible).   Plate 44, fig. 7.

A. abruptus Peck.

Pileus 7-15 cm. broad; stem 8-17 x 1-1.5 cm.; spores 6 x 3.5 μ.

Pileus convex then plane, brittle, glabrous, white, covered with
silky appressed white fibrils or scales, the disk bearing yellowish
stains, the flesh rather thick, staining yellow, more so beneath the
cuticle; gills remote, free, crowded, narrow, pink then dark brown,
the edges entire; stem cylindrical, terminating in an abrupt bulb at
base, creamy-white, staining yellowish, stuffed then hollow, the
annulus double, ample, cracking on the lower side, somewhat evanescent, the remnants persisting as patches on the stem; odor and taste
pleasant.—Among fallen leaves in woods, May-Oct., throughout
temperate North America.

A. placomyces Peck. (edible).   Plate 44, fig. 8.

Pileus 5-10 cm. broad; stem 7-12 cm. x 4-8 mm.; spores 6 x 4 μ.
Pileus ovate expanding to plane, often somewhat umbonate,
squamulose, whitish except for dark brown dotting scales, and the
blackish-brown disk covered with abundant scales, the flesh thin
except on disk, white, yellowish beneath the cuticle; gills free,
crowded, white, pink then blackish-brown, smooth on the edges, stem
tapering upward or long-bulbous, glabrous, whitish, stuffed to hollow, the annulus high, double, large, cracking radially on the lower
side.—Scattered or few and caespitose in mixed woods, rarely on
lawns, not common, July-Sept., Minnesota, Maine, Illinois, Indiana.

A. comptula Fr. (edible).   Plate 44, fig. 9.

Pileus 2-4 cm. broad; stem 3-5 cm. x 3-5 mm.; spores 4-5 x 3 μ.
Pileus convex, sometimes subumbonate, grayish-white, silky, the
disk yellowish-tinted or rufous-tinged, the flesh thickish on disk,
ochraceous beneath the cuticle; gills free, broader in front, dingy-
incarnate then smoky, 5-6 mm. broad; stem innately silky, pallid,
hollow, the annulus attached near the middle of stem, thin membranaceous, somewhat evanescent, whitish; spores dark purple-
brown.—Among fallen leaves in conifer and beech woods, infrequent,
September, Minnesota, Michigan, Indiana.

A. diminutiva Peck. (edible).   Plate 44, fig. 10.

Pileus 2-5 cm. broad; stem 3-6 cm. x 2-5 mm.
Pileus convex then plane, silky, covered with fibrils which become
delicate red-brown scales, paler on margin, white beneath the fibrils,
the flesh thin, whitish; gills free, close, ventricose, with entire edges;
stem cylindrical or tapering upward, glabrous, silky, whitish, stuffed
or hollow, the annulus thin, delicate, narrow, white, somewhat persistent; odor and taste none.—Solitary or gregarious on mossy
ground or leaf mould in woods, temperate North America, more
common northward. This species is known by its pink or red fibrils.

A. micromegetha Peck. (edible).   Plate 44, fig. 4.

Pileus 2-7 cm. broad; stem 2-5 cm. x 6-10 mm.; spores 5 x 4 μ.
Pileus convex, plane, fibrillose-scaly, brownish-gray, brown on disk,
rusty-stained, the flesh white-unchanging; gills free, close, gray, pink
then brown; stem tapering upward or cylindrical, sometimes terminating in a bulb, white, stuffed to hollow, the annulus slight, evanescent.—Solitary or gregarious on sandy or clay soil or among grass,
northern part of our area and eastward to New York.

STROPHARIA Fr. Plate 45.

Carpophore composed of a convex, hemispherical, or almost plane, orbicular, fleshy pileus on a central, fleshy stipe; pileus usually viscid, putrescent; gills adnate; stipe fleshy, confluent with the pileus, cylindrical; annulus present, membranaceous, or fibrillose-floccose; spores purple-brown.—On dung, on debris, or among grass.

1   Growing on ground or among debris......2
1' Growing on dung......4
1" Growing parasitic on *Coprinus*...................*S. epimyces.*
2   Pileus and stem greenish......................*S. aeruginosa.*
2' Pileus and stem of another color......3
3   Annulus with radiating gill-like folds, gills violaceous-purple
    ....*S. bilamellata.*
3' Annulus not so marked, pileus white............*S. albonitens.*
4   Pileus conic-campanulate ....*S. umbonatescens.*
4' Pileus persistently hemispheric................*S. semiglobata.*
4" Pileus convex; plants growing on dung heaps......*S. stercoraria.*

S. stercoraria Fr. (edible). Plate 45, fig. 11.

Pileus 2-6 cm. broad; stem 6-15 cm. x 3-6 mm.; spores 18 x 10 μ.

Pileus soon broadly convex, viscid, ochre or buff, often spore-stained, thin toward margin; gills very broad, the edges white-flocculose, cystidia present; stem long, stuffed with white pith then hollow, dull yellowish-white, floccose-scaly below the narrow annulus; taste of cuticle of pileus slightly bitter.—On dung heaps, common, May-Oct., Minnesota, Maine, Kentucky.

S. semiglobata Fr. Half-globe mushroom (edible). Plate 45, fig. 12.

Pileus 1-3.5 cm. broad; stem 5-12 cm. x 2-4 mm.; spores 16 x 9 μ.

Pileus persistently hemispherical, very viscid, yellow, shining, glabrous, thick on disk, thin on margin, soft; gills very broad, adnate, the edges minutely white-flocculose; stem cylindrical, straight, slender, rigid, hollow, flocculose below the narrow annulus, buff.—In grassy places and on dung, common, May-Oct., Minnesota, Maine, Alabama.

S. umbonatescens Peck. Umbonate Stropharia (suspected).

Pileus 1-2.5 cm. broad; stem 5-10 cm. x 2-4 mm.; spores 18 x 10 μ.

Pileus conic-campanulate, often mamillately umbonate, viscid, pale brownish-tan, with bright-ochraceous-brown to reddish-brown umbo, glabrous, thin, the flesh with odor of radishes or fetid; gills adnate or slightly decurrent, broad to subtriangular, close, whitish then gray, finally dark purplish-brown or blackish; stem slender, cylindrical, stuffed then hollow, toughish, pallid, tinged ochraceous; the annulus easily removed and soon disappearing; spores dark purplish in mass.—Gregarious on dung heaps, not common, Sept.-Oct., Minnesota, New York, southward.

S. epimyces (Peck) Atkins. Parasitic Stropharia. Plate 45, fig. 15.

Pileus 2-6 cm. broad; stem 2-7 x 0.5-1.5 cm.; spores 8 x 4 μ.

Pileus globose then convex or elevated at the margin, whitish, thick, the margin thin; gills narrow, broader in front, grayish then blackish-brown, the edges white-fimbriate; stem solid, stuffed then hollow, soft, mealy, striate; the annulus low, floccose, white, the base of the stem often almost volva-like where it is inserted into the host; spores almost black in mass.—Parasitic one to several on *Coprinus atramentarius* or *C. comatus,* rare, Iowa to New York.

S. bilamellata Peck. Double-gilled Stropharia. Plate 45, fig. 16.

Pileus 2-6 cm. broad; stem 3-6 cm. x 3-5 mm.; spores 11 x 7 μ.

Pileus convex-expanded, white or yellowish, subviscid, the flesh white, thickish; gills present on the upper surface of the pileus, adnate, rounded behind, moderately broad, close, violaceous then purplish; stem cylindrical, white, stuffed then hollow; the annulus broad, membranous, white or violaceous with spores.—On sandy ground in orchards, cultivated fields, etc.; Aug.-Sept., rare, Minnesota to New York and southward.

S. coronilla Bres. Like the preceding but smaller, the annulus bearing radiating striae, the spores 9 x 4-5 μ.—In woods, northern part of our area.

S. albonitens Fr. Plate 45, fig. 17.

Pileus 1-3 cm. broad; stem 3-7 cm. x 2-3 mm.; spores 8 x 4-5 μ.

Pileus campanulate then plane and subumbonate, viscid, white to buff, glabrous, smooth, thin, the flesh white, moist; gills adnate, subdistant, rather broad, ventricose, gray to purplish-gray, the edges minutely white-fimbriate; stem whitish, cylindrical, soon hollow, yellowish within, pruinose, the annulus high, white, soon disappearing, colored with spores; spores purple-brown in mass.—On ground in open grassy woods, October, Wisconsin to New York, and southward.

This species is known by the gray tinge of its gills and the yellow tints of its stem when old.

S. aeruginosa Fr. Green Stropharia (suspected). Plate 45, fig. 14.

Pileus 2-4 cm. broad; stem 3-7 cm. x 3-5 mm.; spores 8 x 4-5 μ.

Pileus convex, plane, subumbonate, very viscid with green slime, the cuticle yellowish, the flesh soft, thickish on disk; gills adnate, plane, rather broad, close, whitish-gray then purplish-brown, the edges minutely white-flocculose; stem viscid, greenish-blue, soft, hollow, at first fibrillose-scaly below the annulus; the annulus narrow, distant from apex, submembranous.—On the ground in rich forests of beech and maple, or beech and hemlock, rare, Aug.-Oct., Minnesota to Pennsylvania and South Carolina.

HYPHOLOMA Fr. Plate. 45.

Plants putrescent, each with a campanulate or convex, orbicular pileus on a cylindrical, central stem; pileus thick and compact in one section, thin and fragile in another, margin at first incurved, decorated with the veil remnants; gills adnexed or emarginate, variously colored; stipe confluent with the pileus, fleshy, cylindrical; spores purple-brown, elliptical.—Growing on the ground or on decaying wood.

1   Pileus firm, rather thick, brick-red to deep yellow; plants caespitose......2
1' Pileus rather fragile, neither brick-red nor deep yellow......4
2   Pileus brick-red......3
2' Pileus yellow................................H. capnoides.
3   Young stem stuffed, gills at first whitish......H. sublateritium.
3' Young stem hollow, gills at first yellow.........H. perplexum.
4   Pileus hygrophanous, not over 6 cm. broad......7
4' Pileus not hygrophanous......5
5   Pileus hairy or fibrillose, brownish......6
5' Pileus partly or wholly glabrous............H. rugocephalum.
6   Pileus whitish, covered with brownish scales............
    ....H. lachrymabundum.
6' Pileus tawny, appressed-scaly.................H. velutinum.
7   Pileus whitish or yellowish......8
7' Pileus of another color......9
8   Growing in lawns or grassy places..............H. incertum.
8' Growing in woods...............H. incertum var. sylvestris.
9   Pileus when moist watery-dark-brown, gills at first gray-brown ....H. hydrophilum.
9' Pileus honey-brown or else very thin and fragile......10
10 Plants terrestrial, gregarious.............H. hymenocephalum.
10' Plants commonly on wood and caespitose.....H. appendiculatum.

H. incertum Peck. Uncertain Hypholoma. Plate 45, fig. 23.

Pileus 3-6 cm. broad; stem 3-7 cm. x 3-6 mm.; spores 7 x 4 μ.

Pileus fragile, broadly campanulate, obtuse, hygrophanous, pale honey-colored when moist, buff to whitish when dry, white-flocculent to glabrous, with loose shreds hanging from margin in age, thin and radially splitting, the flesh white; gills adnate-seceding, rosy-brown, at length dark purplish, the edges white-fimbriate; stem slender, cylindrical, hollow, easily split, white, innately silky, often mealy above.—Among grass, on lawns and in pastures, common, spring, summer and autumn, Minnesota, New England and Alabama.

The commonly encountered var. *sylvestris* Kauffm. is similar except for the longer stem and habitat in rich forests.

H. hymenocephalum Peck. Thin-capped Hypholoma.

Pileus 2.5-5 cm. broad; stem 5-10 cm. x 2-3 mm.; spores 8 x 4 μ.

Pileus very thin and fragile, campanulate or convex then expanded, sometimes umbonate, hygrophanous, brown and striatulate when moist, pallid or whitish and radiately rugulose when dry, subatomate; gills thin, narrow, close, dingy-white becoming purplish-brown; stem slender, fragile, hollow, striate, slightly mealy at the apex, white.—Gregarious on ground among fallen leaves under bushes and small trees, not common, July-Aug., Minnesota to Maine, and Kentucky.

H. appendiculatum Fr. Appendiculate Hypholoma (edible). Plate 45, fig. 19.

Pileus 2-4 cm. broad; stem 5-10 cm. x 3-6 mm.; spores 10 x 4-5 μ.

Pileus hemispheric-campanulate, hygrophanous, dark-honey-brown when moist, dull tan when dry, the flesh thin, pallid; gills adnate, crowded, 6-7 mm. broad, remaining whitish for a long time then grayish-purplish, at length purplish-brown; stem fragile, nearly cylindrical, striate and mealy at the apex, silky, flexuous, the veil webby, white, attached to stem and margin of pileus at first but soon disappearing.—Densely caespitose on rotten wood, more commonly in beech woods, Aug.-Oct., Iowa, New York, North Carolina.

H. hydrophilum Fr. (suspected). Plate 45, fig. 22.

Pileus 2-6 cm. broad; stem 4-6 cm. x 3-6 mm.; spores 6 x 3 μ.

Pileus fragile, campanulate-convex then expanded, chestnut-brown when moist, ochraceous-buff when dry, often pellucid-substriate on the margin, wavy, silky-bordered with the veil, the flesh thin, brown to ochraceous; gills adnate-seceding, thin, narrow, ventricose, crowded, gray-brown then purplish-umber-brown, the edges minutely white-fimbriate when young; stem slender, cylindrical, hollow, splitting, glabrous except at the pruinose apex, shining-white, the base mycelioid; spores minute, smooth; sterile cells present on edges of gills, inflated-saccate, short, 30 μ long; odor and taste none.—Caespitose in extensive clusters on decaying wood or at the bases of stumps or living trees, not common, Minnesota, Maine, southward.

H. sublateritium Fr.   Brick-top (edible).   Plate 45, fig. 21.

Pileus 3-8 cm. broad; stem 8-12 cm. x 5-14 mm.; spores 7 x 4 μ.

Pileus convex, firm, obtuse, dark brick-red, smooth, decurved on the margin which is white silky with remnants of the veil, the flesh whitish, thick, firm; gills adnate, narrow, crowded, white then gray, finally dark purple-brown, the edges minutely white-crenulate; stem rather stout, stuffed, white toward apex, rusty below, floccose-fibrillose on surface; spores smooth, dark purplish in mass; taste mild or bitter.—Densely caespitose at bases of stumps and trees or on buried roots, very common, Sept.-Nov., North Dakota, Maine, Alabama.

H. perplexum Peck.   Perplexing Hypholoma.

Similar to the preceding, but the gills yellow at first, and the pileus more yellow.—In the same habitat and range as the preceding of which it may be a variety.

H. capnoides Fr.   Similar to *H. sublateritium*, but the pileus ochraceous (Peck states that in American plants the disk may be orange), 2.5-4 cm. broad; stem 4-7 cm. x 4-6 mm.; spores 7-8 x 4-5 μ. —Singly or caespitose on or near pine or spruce stumps or living trees, May-Sept., rare.

H. lachrymabundum (Fr.) Quel.   Weeping Hypholoma (edible).   Plate 45, fig. 20.

Pileus 4-10 cm. broad; stem 6-12 cm. x 5-10 mm.; spores 7 x 3.5 μ.

Pileus convex then campanulate, whitish to buff, decorated except on disk with rather large, appressed, brownish hairy scales, the margin incurved and appendiculate with remnants of the rather thick, floccose, white veil, the flesh thick, thin toward margin, white, firm; gills adnate-seceding, narrow, crowded, distilling bead-like drops of liquid, white finally purplish-brown with white-floccose edges; stem striate above, hollow, fibrillose-scaly below, whitish or dirty-white, yellowish where bruised, the base white-mycelioid; spores slightly curved, elliptical, smooth.—In forests, rare, Minnesota to New England and southward.

H. velutinum (Fr.) Quel. (edible).   Plate 45, fig. 18.

Pileus 3-10 cm. broad; stem 2-8 cm. x 4-10 mm.; spores 9-12 x 7 μ.

Pileus convex, broadly campanulate, finally plane, hairy-tomentose then appressed-fibrillose-scaly, not striate, tawny to yellowish, dark on disk, often radially rugulose, the margin at first appendiculate with

326   THE CHICAGO ACADEMY OF SCIENCES

remnants of the veil, splitting, the flesh thick on disk, watery-brown
or sordid-yellowish, soft; gills adnate-seceding, broad behind,
crowded, not extending to the margin of pileus, pale yellowish then
umber and dotted with spore masses, the edges white-floccose and
beaded with drops of liquid; stem tawny up to the obsolete annulus,
whitish above; spores tuberculate.—Caespitose or scattered on alluvial soil in woods, July-Oct., occasionally found, Minnesota to Maine
and southward.

H. rugocephalum Atkins.

Pîleus 6-10 cm. broad; stem 7-12 cm. x 6-10 mm.; spores 8-11 x 7 μ.

Pileus convex then expanded, broadly umbonate, glabrous, radiately rugose, tawny, the thin margin often upward-curved, the flesh
thick on disk, yellowish; gills adnate-seceding, slightly sinuate,
spotted-purplish-black with spore masses when mature, close, 5-7
mm. broad, the edges white-fimbriate; stem cylindrical, subbulbous,
smooth, glabrous, hollow, tawny below, paler above, obscurely annulate by thread-like remnants of the veil which are marked by blackish spore-stains; spores ventricose, abruptly pointed at each end,
minutely tuberculate, inequilateral, black in mass; odor and taste
mild.—On ground in low swampy deciduous forests, rare, July-Sept.,
Minnesota, Maine, Illinois.

PSILOCYBE Fr.   Plate 46.

Plants putrescent, each composed of an orbicular, convex pileus on
a central, cylindrical stipe; pileus convex or campanulate, expanding
to almost plane; gills adnexed to adnate-decurrent; stipe rigid-fragile
or tough, cortex cartilaginous; spores purple-brown.—Growing on
much decayed wood, on buried roots, sticks, and wood debris, often
around stumps in the woods.

1   Pileus hygrophanous......2
1' Pileus not hygrophanous......11
2   Spores in mass brick-red....................*P. connissans.*
2' Spores brown or purple-brown......3
3   Growing in sandy soil........................*P. arenulina.*
3' Growing in woods or among grass......4
4   Pileus large, 5-14 cm. broad, brown when moist.......*P. larga.*
4' Pileus smaller, 4 cm. or less broad (in *P. spadicea* occasionally
    6 cm.)......5
5   Stem 10-15 cm. long, pale smoky; plants growing on sphag-
    num ....*P. atrobrunnea.*
5' Stem shorter......6

6   Pileus dull brownish when moist, spotted......*P. submaculata.*
6' Pileus not spotted......7

7   Plants growing among grass, tan to rufous-brown........
....*P. foenisecii.*
7' Plants of other habitats......8

8   Plants growing on low wet ground in woods......9
8' Plants growing on decaying wood or around stumps.......10
8" Plants growing on sphagnum.................*P. fuscofulva.*

9   Pileus dark bay-brown when moist, 2-4 cm. wide...*P. murcida.*
9' Pileus pale rufous or umber-brown when moist, 1-3.5 cm.
wide ....*P. agrariella.*

10 Pileus bay, 2.5-6 cm. wide; plants found around stumps or
on leaf mould................................*P. spadicea.*
10' Pileus 1-4 cm. wide, livid-brown when moist, striate; plants
found around bases of stumps in woods.............*P. cernua.*
10" Pileus 2.5-4 cm. broad; plants found around stumps and in
crevices of rocks in woods...................*P. fuscofolia.*

11 Pileus with white fibrillose-hairy scales on its umber-colored
surface, 1-3 cm. wide, 6-8 cm. high............*P. canofaciens.*
11' Pileus tawny-bay when moist, 1-2 cm. wide and high....*P. uda.*

P. arenulina Peck.   Sand-loving *Psilocybe*.   Plate 46, fig. 1.
Pileus 1-3 cm. broad; stem 3-5 cm. x 2 mm.; spores 11 x 5-6 μ.
Pileus convex, at length plane or depressed, rarely with an umbo,
glabrous, hygrophanous, dark brown and with coarsely striate margin
when moist, dingy-whitish when dry; gills adnate, close, cinnamon
then darker, to purplish-brown; stem often clavate and radicating
at base, whitish, hollow.—Gregarious on sandy soil, Sept.-Oct., rare,
Wisconsin, New York, especially around the Great Lakes.

P. conissans Peck.   Dusty Psilocybe.   Plate 46, fig. 3.
Clitopilus conissans Peck.
Pileus 2.5-5 cm. broad; stem 3.5-5 cm. x 2-4 mm.; spores 8-10 x
4-5 μ.
Pileus broadly convex, at length plane, glabrous, hygrophanous,
pale chestnut or rusty and with striatulate margin when moist, pale
dull yellow or buff and sometimes slightly rugose when dry, the flesh
white, fleshy but thin; gills rounded behind, adnexed, close, thin, bay
verging to dark purple or liver-colored; stem firm, rather slender,
white, glabrous, cylindrical, curved, hollow, without veil; spores red
or brick-red or wine-colored.—Caespitose about bases of deciduous
trees, Sept.-Oct., not common, Minnesota, Maine and southward.

P. larga Kauffm.   Large Psilocybe.   Plate 46, fig. 11.

Pileus 4-14 cm. broad; stem 5-10 cm. x 5-15 mm.; spores 8-9.5 x 4-5 μ.

"Pileus large, oval-campanulate at first, at length expanded-plane and radially cracked or split on margin, fragile, hygrophanous, bay-brown to ochraceous-brown and smooth when moist, whitish-tan and radiately rugulose when dry, at first dotted with scattered small snow-white floccose superficial scales, quickly denuded, often glabrous except for the white-silky margin, the flesh rather thin, white when dry, scissile, homogeneous, with large cells; gills adnate, rounded behind, rather broad, close to subdistant, white at first then pale-fuscous finally umber, the edges minutely white-fimbriate; stem stout, cylindrical or tapering upward, soon hollow, terete or compressed, rather firm, usually striate to sulcate, furfuraceous but glabrescent, then shining white, the cortex subcartilaginous; spores elliptical, smooth, obtuse, purple-brown under microscope, umber in mass; cystidia abundant." (Kauffman, Agaricaceae of Michigan, p. 279.) —Gregarious or caespitose around old stumps, buried roots, etc. in grassy clearings in woods, southern Michigan, May-Sept. (more frequent in spring), not infrequently found in swamps.

P. spadicea Fr.   Bay Psilocybe.   Plate 46, fig. 4.

Pileus 2-6 cm. broad; stem 5-8 cm. x 5 mm.; spores 9 x 5 μ.

Pileus convex becoming nearly plane, obtuse, scabrous, hygrophanous, bay-brown when moist, pallid when dry, the flesh rigid, fleshy; gills adnexed-rounded behind, close, whitish becoming pinkish-brown; stem whitish, rather tough, cylindrical, glabrous, hollow; spores brown.—Commonly caespitose on ground, fallen leaves, or around bases of trees, in woods, not common, September, New York to Illinois.

P. atrobrunnea Fr.   Plate 46, fig. 5.

Pileus 1-4 cm. broad; stem 5-15 cm. x 1.5-4 mm.; spores 11 x 6 μ.

Pileus campanulate-convex, obtusely umbonate, hygrophanous, umber when moist, dingy-ochraceous when dry, smooth, glabrous, the flesh thin, of the same color; gills adnate-rounded behind, seceding, subdistant, rather broad, brownish-gray then smoky, the edges whitish; stem long, slender, flexuous, smooth, pale smoky, covered with white-silky fibrils, stuffed; spores large, smooth, dark purple-brown; odor and taste slightly farinaceous.—Among spagnum in tamarack bogs, Sept.-Nov., locally common, Minnesota, Michigan, Illinois.

P. murcida Fr.   Plate 46, fig. 6.

Pileus 2-4 cm. broad; stem 6-8 cm. x 2 mm.; spores 10-12 x 6 μ.

Pileus fragile, not umbonate, campanulate-convex then expanded, hygrophanous, dark bay-brown and striatulate when moist, light fulvous when dry, atomate and subrugulose, glabrous, the flesh fragile, thin; gills adnate, narrow, narrowed in front, subventricose, whitish becoming smoky-purple, the edges white-flocculose; stem white then pallid, fragile, slender, with white pith then hollow, undulate on the surface, slightly fibrillose; veil none; spores obtuse, purplish-black in mass; cystidia scattered on sides and edges of gills, 55 x 9 μ.—On ground in low moist woods, May-June, frequently found, Wisconsin and Michigan.

P. fuscofolia Peck.   Plate 46, fig. 7.

Pileus 2.5-5 cm. broad; stem 2.5-4 cm. x 2-4 mm.; spores 6-8 x 3-4 μ.

Pileus conical or hemispherical becoming convex-plane or centrally depressed, glabrous, not striate, hygrophanous, pale dull-yellow when moist, subochraceous and rugose when dry, the flesh whitish or yellowish, thin; gills narrow, adnate, thin, close, sometimes forked, pale brown becoming reddish-brown; stem white, silky-fibrillose, slender, cylindrical, thickened or subbulbous at base, hollow, the base covered with white mycelioid tomentum; spores brown in mass, ellipsoid.—Solitary, gregarious, or caespitose on or about stumps, on the ground, on decaying wood, and in rock crevices, Oct.-Nov., common, New York and westward.

P. submaculata Atkins.   Spotted Psilocybe.

Pileus 4-10 mm. broad; stem 2-3 cm. x 2-3 mm.; spores 6-7 x 3-4 μ.

Pileus very small, convex, glabrous, hygrophanous, dull brownish then dull white and bearing dark watery and yellowish spots, the margin at first incurved, the flesh with surface layer of subpyriform cells; gills adnate, emarginate, rather crowded, brownish with purple fringe, the edges whitish; stem white and shining, fistulose; spores purple-brown under microscope; cystidia few on sides of gills, numerous on edges, ventricose, the apices crystalline.—On very rotten wood, rare, Michigan and perhaps in surrounding states.

P. foenisecii Fr.   Haymaker's Psilocybe (edible).   Plate 46, fig. 9.

Pileus 1-2.5 cm. broad; stem 4-8 cm. x 1.5-2 mm.; spores 12-17 x 8 μ.

Pileus campanulate-convex or subhemispheric, obtuse, glabrous, hygrophanous, dark reddish-brown or grayish-brown when moist, paler when dry, the flesh thin, pallid; gills adnate, subdistant, broad, ventricose, smoky-brown, variegated, the edges white; stem pallid or subrufescent, pruinose at the apex, slender, nearly straight, rigid, fragile, glabrous, smooth, without veil, hollow; spores slightly tuberculate, variable in size, apiculate, purplish-brown.—Gregarious in grassy places, May-June, rarely July-Sept., Minnesota, Maine, Alabama.

P. agrariella Atkins.

Pileus 1-3.5 cm. broad; stem 4-6 cm. x 3-4 mm.; spores 7-9 x 4-5 μ.

Pileus campanulate-convex then expanded, without umbo, glabrous, at first incurved and white-silky on margin, hygrophanous, fragile, umber-brown to pale rufous and obscurely striatulate or rivulose when moist, duller, whitish-ochraceous when dry, the flesh thin, concolor, the odor and taste mild; gills adnate, seceding, ventricose, close, medium-broad, finally purplish-umber, the edges white-fimbriate; stem white, fragile, pruinose at the apex, glabrous, stuffed soon hollow, the base white-mycelioid; spores inequilateral, blackish-purple in mass; cystidia scattered, more numerous on edges of gills, 45-55 x 10-15 μ, lanceolate, the apices obtuse.—Gregarious or scattered in wet places in frondose woods, May, June, Sept., not common, in northern states.

P. cernua Fr.   Plate 46, fig. 10.

Pileus 1-4 cm. broad; stem 2-5 cm. x 2-4 mm.; spores 6-7 x 3-4 μ.

Similar to the preceding but pileus livid watery-brown and striate when moist, areolate-cracked and rugulose in age, the veil and cystidia lacking; stem white, rigid-cartilaginous, flexuous or variously curved.—Caespitose-gregarious at the bases of trees, infrequently found, northern states.

P. fuscofulva Peck.

Pileus 1.2-2.5 cm. broad; stem 3-5 cm. x 2-4 mm.; spores 11 x 7 μ.

Pileus convex or subcampanulate, subumbonate, hygrophanous, with striatulate margin and dark brown color when moist, dull ochraceous when dry, glabrous; gills adnate, subventricose, close, rather broad, becoming purplish-brown; stem reddish-brown, slightly silky, flexuous.—Solitary or scattered in sphagnum, chiefly northern.

P. canofaciens Cooke.   Plate 46, fig. 13.

Pileus 1-3 cm. broad; stem 5-7 cm. x 2-4 mm.; spores 10-15 x 4-5 μ.

Pileus rather small, campanulate-convex then expanded, sometimes subumbonate, smooth, umber-brown, at first decorated with scattered white fibrils, at length appressed-fibrillose-scaly, the fibrils concolor, the flesh rather thick in center, concolor; gills adnate, subdistant, dark umber, rather broad, venticose; stem dark umber, darker at base, covered with long fibrils, toughish, soon hollow; spores very variable in size, curved in one plane, purple-brown under microscope, umber in mass.—On ground in woods, August, rare, Michigan.

P. uda (Pers.) Fr. Moist Psilocybe. Plate 46, fig. 14.

Pileus 2-3 cm. broad; stem 5-8 cm. x 2-3 mm.; spores 16-20 x 7-9 μ.

Pileus convex becoming plane, tawny-bay becoming whitish or yellowish and rugulose when dry, the flesh thin but fleshy; gills adnexed, subdistant, ventricose, whitish then purple-brown or darker; stem tough, pale above, ferruginous below, cylindrical, elongated, fibrillose, hollow; spores purplish-brown in mass.—Gregarious in swamps among sphagnum and other mosses, Sept.-Oct., Minnesota to Maine, and northern part of our area.

In var. *elongata* (Pers.) Sacc. the margin of the pileus is striate when moist; the pileus is livid or greenish yellow, pale yellow when dry. It occupies the same habitats and range as the typical variety during the period July to September.

PSATHYRA Fr.   Plate 46.

Plants putrescent, each composed of a campanulate, orbicular pileus on a central cylindrical stipe; pileus hygrophanous, thin, permanently campanulate, margin at first straight; gills adnate or adnexed; stem cartilaginous in the outer part, rigid-fragile, hollow, slender; veil if present persisting in the form of delicate fibrils over the surface of the young plant; spores purple-brown.—Terrestrial or on decayed wood.

1 Pileus glabrous or atomate, veil none......2
1' Pileus and stem at first floccose or fibrillose with remnants of the veil......4
2 Caespitose in dense clusters on wood, pileus striate when moist ....*P. umbonata.*
2' Not in dense clusters......3
3 Pileus smoky-umber ....*P. obtusata.*
3' Pileus rufous-tinged, brown...................*P. persimplex.*
4 Caespitose in dense clusters, stems short........*P. microsperma.*
4' Gregarious ....*P. vestita.*

P. umbonata Peck. Umbonate Psathyra. Plate 46, fig. 18.

Pileus 2-5 cm. broad x 2-3 cm. high; stem 4-9 cm. x 1.5-3 mm.

Pileus subcylindrical at first then conic-campanulate, at length with a rather large obtuse umbo, hygrophanous, dark bay-brown to purplish-brown when moist, the flesh thin, concolor; gills adnate-seceding, 3-4 mm. broad, narrowed in front, soon dark purple-brown, then blackish, the edges white-fimbriate; stem slender, cylindrical, rigid-fragile, hollow, shining-white.—Caespitose on rotten wood, common, June-Sept., Minnesota, Maine, southward.

P. obtusata Fr. Obtuse Psathyra. Plate 46, fig. 17.

Pileus 1-3 cm. broad; stem 5-8 cm. x 1-3 mm.; spores 8 x 4 μ.

Pileus campanulate-convex, obtuse, hygrophanous, umber and sometimes faintly striate, buff and atomate when dry, the flesh thin; gills adnate, rather broad, umber, the edges white-fimbriate; stem white then pallid, cylindrical, glabrous, rigid-fragile, hollow; spores dark purple-brown.—Solitary or a few together on very rotten wood, rare, Minnesota, Maine, southward.

P. persimplex Britz. Plate 46, fig. 19.

Similar to the preceding but the spores larger, 11 x 6 μ; margin of the pileus more spreading.—On sticks and decayed wood, rare, September, in the range of *P. obtusata*.

P. semivestita Berk. and Broome. Half-clothed Psathyra. Plate 46, fig. 20.

Pileus 1-2 cm. broad; stem 4-6 cm. x 1.5-2 mm.; spores 9-12 x 6 μ.

Pileus sprinkled with white superficial remnants of the veil when young, ovate-campanulate, subobtuse, hygrophanous, rufous-umber and pellucid-short-striate when moist, pale tan when dry, very thin; gills broadly adnate, dark smoky-fuscous, triangular by being narrowed in front; stem closely sprinkled over with white-fibrillose flecks, cylindrical, pale smoky.—Gregarious on horse dung, Minnesota, New York, southward.

P. vestita Peck. Clothed Psathyra. Plate 46, fig. 21.

Similar to the preceding but wholly clothed when young with white floccose fibrils, reddish becoming almost white in color.—Among fallen leaves and grass, rare, September, Minnesota, New York, southward.

P. microsperma Peck.

Pileus 1-2.5 cm. broad; stem 2-4 cm. x 2-3 mm.; spores 7 x 4 μ.

Pileus ovate or subhemispherical then convex-campanulate, usually irregular, smooth, hygrophanous, pale watery-brown when moist, ashy-buff when dry, bearing white-floccose scales when young, thin, with a slight cuticle; gills adnate-seceding, close, not broad, subventricose, narrow in front, white-gray then gray-purplish-brown, the edges white-fimbriate; stem cylindrical, pure-white, rigid-fragile, covered at first with minute white fibrils.—Very caespitose on or about stumps in woods, October, rare, Ohio, Indiana and Michigan.

DECONICA W. G. Smith.   Plate 46.

Plants small, putrescent, each with a conical, hemispherical to convex pileus attached to the expanded apex of a more or less cylindrical, central stipe; pileus often subumbonate, subviscid, yellow to brown; gills broadly adnate to somewhat decurrent; stipe cylindrical or thickest at apex and tapering downward, often decorated with the remnants of the veil; spores purple brown.—On dung, among grass, or on moss.

1   Pileus viscid at least when moistened......2
1' Pileus dry, the whole plant rufous-brown..........*D. atrorufa.*
2   Plants growing on dung, 1-3 cm. broad............*D. merdaria.*
2' Plants growing in pastures or among moss, very small, 5-15 mm. broad ....*D. subviscida.*

D. merdaria (Fr.) W. G. Smith.   Plate 46, fig. 15.

Pileus 1-3 cm. broad; stem 2-4 cm. x 1-3 mm.; spores 15 x 18 μ.

Pileus hemispherical at first, at length plane, livid-brown to lividyellowish, smooth, subviscid, glabrous, at first bearing slight flecks on the margin, the flesh pallid, thin; gills broadly adnate to subtriangular-decurrent, broad, at first yellowish, subdistant, then colored with the purple-brown spores, at length dark-brown; stem cylindrical, pale yellow, stuffed then hollow, slightly ridged at apex by the decurrent gills, often bearing a slight remnant of the annulus; spores smooth, large; odor mild; cystidia absent.—On horse-dung in company with *Stropharia stercoraria,* not common, May-June, Michigan to Wisconsin and northern Illinois.

D. subviscida Peck.   Viscid Deconica.

Pileus 5-15 mm. broad; stem 2-4 cm. x 1-2 mm.; spores 7 x 5 μ.

Pileus small, fragile, thin, ovate-campanulate then subexpanded and obtusely umbonate, at first viscid, hygrophanous, chestnut or rufous-brown and striatulate when moist, buff when dry, subviscid and glabrous; gills broadly adnate, subtriangular, broad, rather thick, whitish then umber; stem slender, cylindrical, pallid to smoky or chestnut-brown, covered at first with white fibrils; spores pale brown, tinged wine-colored under microscope.—Among grass or moss or on dung, in pastures, Apr.-June, infrequently found, Minnesota, New York, southward.

D. atrorufa Fr.   Dark-red Deconica.   Plate 46, fig. 16.

Similar in size and shape to the preceding but the pileus umber-brown then rufous-brown and striatulate when moist, pale alutaceous when dry, not viscid; stem bay-brown throughout; spores 5-8 x 5 μ, pointed at each end, smooth, reddish-brown under microscope.— Gregarious on ground, in woods, June-July, Michigan.

COPRINUS Pers. Plate 47.

Plants putrescent, each composed of a dome-shaped pileus on a cylindrical, central stipe; pileus ovoid to dome-shaped, variously decorated with squamose, minute innate, superficial white, floccose, or micaceous scales or with a superficial downy coat resembling white meal, fleshy, of different material and readily separable from fleshy stipe; gills white becoming brown or purplish gray then black, soon deliquescing, dripping ink-like fluid, free or but slightly attached; stipe fleshy-fibrous, stuffed or hollow; annulus sometimes present; spores black or dark gray.—Growing on dung, sand or wood, and among grass on lawns, or one species on concrete walls.

Massee* divided the genus into two groups: Pelliculosi with fleshy, large pilei, including the species here treated from *C. comatus* to *C. radians;* and Veliformes with pilei thin and small, including the remainder of the species here treated.

1   Pileus fleshy, usually more than 3 cm. broad (Pelliculosi)....2
1' Pileus thin, small, less than 3 cm. broad (Veliformes)......15
2   Cuticle torn into distinct scales; pileus commonly ovate......3
2' Cuticle not so torn into scales; pileus decorated with superficial granules or patches......4
2" Pileus almost smooth, or bearing innate fibrils......5
3   Pileus cylindrical: plants found in autumn.........*C. comatus.*
3' Pileus cylindrical; plants found in spring.......*C. sterquilinus.*
3" Pileus ovate ....*C. ovatus.*
4   Veil breaking up into felt-like patches or areas......6
4' Veil differently disposed......7
5   Spores smooth; plants found on rich soil, or about stamps ....*C. atramentarius.*
5' Spores warted; plants found about trees in woods...*C. insignis.*
6   Plants growing from rhizomorphs; pileus 5-8 cm. broad.. ....*C. quadrifidus.*
6' Plants growing from yellow ozonium, on wood; pileus 2-3 cm. broad ....*C. laniger.*
7   Veil composed of fibrillose scales or a dense coat of white, mealy clusters of scales......8
7' Veil composed of small granules or mica-like particles......14

*Massee, Revision of the Genus Coprinus: Ann. Bot.. Vol. 10, p. 123, 1896.

8   Growing on sand...............................*C. arenatus.*
8' Growing on concrete or tile walls.................*C. jonesii.*
8" Growing in other habitats......9
9   Disk livid, veil-particles connected by webby strands......
....*C. lagopides.*
9' Disk without cobwebby strands......10
10 Gills free......11
10' Gills attached......13
11 Pileus cylindrical ....*C. tomentosus.*
11' Pileus never cylindrical......12
12 Stem rooting.................*C. fimetarius* var. *macrorhizus.*
12' Stem not rooting; plants found in troops on dung..*C. fimetarius.*
13 Disk red-brown, obtuse......................*C. domesticus.*
13' Disk not colored, narrow; veil composed of mealy cluster
....*C. niveus.*
14 Densely caespitose; felt-like ozonium absent.......*C. micaceus.*
14' Singly or rarely caespitose; ozonium present........*C. radians.*
15 Veil composed of superficial scales or meal-like particles......16
15' Veil absent 21
16 Annulus present ....*C. bulbilosus.*
16' Annulus absent; pileus covered with white-floccose or mealy
coat......19
16" Annulus absent; pileus covered with mica-like scales.......17
17 Growing on lawns, around trees, etc..............*C. micaceus*
17' Growing on dung......18
18 Pileus 1-3 cm. broad, spores ovate-triangular....*C. Patouillardii.*
18' Pileus 2-15 mm. broad, spores elliptical...........*C. radiatus.*
19 Plants growing from black sclerotia on dung..*C. sclerotigenus.*
19' Sclerotia absent 20
20 Pileus covered with a downy, cottony layer......*C. stercorarius.*
20' Pileus covered with snow-white, floccose down.......*C. niveus.*
21 On dung, pileus striate-plicate.................*C. ephemerus.*
21' On the ground in the woods, pileus striate-plicate..*C. silvaticus.*
21" Among grass, gills distant, pileus sulcate...........*C. plicatilis.*

C. comatus Fr. Shaggy mane (edible). Plate 47, fig. 1a.

Pileus 7-12 cm. long; gills 8-12 mm. wide; stem 10-15 x 1-2 cm.; spores 15 x 8 μ.

Pileus cylindrical, expanded in age, at first smooth then the cuticle breaking into torn adpressed scales, some ochraceous brown, some dark brown, the surface white between scales; gills free, white or pinkish then black; stem cylindrical, white, hollow, bulbous, the ring movable; spores black, elliptical.—Gregarious on lawns and in fields, very common, autumn, sometimes spring and summer, throughout our area.

C. ovatus Fr. (edible). Plate 47, fig. 1b.

Pileus 5-6 cm. long; gills 4 mm. wide; stem 5-10 cm. x 8-12 mm.; spores 11 x 7 μ.

Pileus at first smooth and covered with an ochraceous cuticle which breaks into concentric scales, the apical part not breaking, the margin striate, the flesh thin, white, soft at first; gills free, distant from the stem, white at first then black; stem rooting, narrowed toward apex, flocculose or fibrillose, white, hollow; spores elliptical, black.—On lawns and in pastures, rare, summer and autumn, throughout our area.

C. sterquilinus Fr. Shaggy mane (edible). Plate 47, fig. 1c.

Pileus 5-8 cm. high; gills 7-10 mm. wide; stem 9-15 cm. x 1-1.5 cm.; spores 18-25 x 12-15 μ.

Pileus cylindrical, conical, then expanded, cuticle at first silky, white tinged-brown or smoky-brown on disk, becoming broken into scales much as in *C. comatus* but more squarrose especially on disk, sulcate on margin, the flesh thin, white; gills free, close, white then purplish-black; stem cylindrical, white, often blackened with spores, hollow, the base thickened, solid, peronate with the free margin of the volval sheath; spores smoky to black.—On manure or manured ground, common, June, throughout our area.

C. atramentarius Fr. Gray ink-cap (edible). Plate 47, fig. 2.

Pileus 5-8 cm. broad when expanded; stem 7-12 cm. x 1-2 cm.; spores 12 x 6 μ.

Pileus ovate then expanded, grayish, fibrous-silky, brownish at the apex, the flesh thin; gills free, crowded, broad, ventricose, white becoming black and ink-like; stem cylindrical, white, silky, shining, hollow, the annulus evanescent, basal.—Caespitose about stumps or on rich ground, common, summer and autumn, throughout temperate North America.

C. insignis Peck.

Pileus 5-7 cm. broad when expanded; stem 10-14 x 1 cm.; spores 10 x 7 μ.

Pileus ovate then campanulate, thin, sulcate-striate to the disk, glabrous, gray or gray-brown, the disk sometimes cracked into scalelike areas; gills free, broad, crowded; stem cylindrical, white, striate, hollow; spores with roughened-warty surface.—About trees in low woods, rare, southern Michigan.

C. quadrifidus Peck. Plate 47, fig. 3a.

Pileus 5-8 cm. broad when expanded; stem 6-10 x 0.7 cm.; spores 8 x 10 μ.

Pileus oval then companulate, thin, covered with a veil which soon becomes flaky and disappears, finely striate, whitish to gray-brown; gills free, crowded, thin, broad, white, to purple then black; stem white, hollow, floccose.—Caespitose or gregarious about decaying stumps, growing from root-like rhizomorphs, not common, throughout our area.

C. laniger Peck. Plate 47, fig. 3c.

Pileus 1-2.5 cm. broad; stem 2-3 cm. x 3 mm.; spores 7-10 x 4 μ.

Pileus conic-campanulate, tawny, sulcate-striate, covered with tawny floccose scales which partly disappear; gills narrow, crowded, becoming brownish-black; stem hollow, white, pruinose.—Caespitose or gregarious, growing from profusely developed yellow ozonium on decaying wood, not common, throughout our area.

It resembles *C. radians* but the patches on the pileus are not minute as in that species.

C. ebulbosus Peck. Plate 47, fig. 3b.

Pileus 5-7 cm. broad when expanded; stem 7-15 x 1-1.5 cm.; spores 9 x 5 μ.

Pileus campanulate gray-brown, the margin at length revolute, the cuticle breaking into broad white scales; gills free, crowded, narrow, slate-colored becoming black; stem cylindrical, hollow, white; spores elliptical.—Caespitose, near or upon decaying stumps, not common, Illinois to New York.

C. fimentarius Fr. Plate 47, fig. 4a.

Pileus 2-5 cm. broad when expanded; stem 12-15 cm. x 5 mm.; spores 12 x 5 μ.

Pileus clavate then conical-expanded, grayish, brownish at the apex, covered at first with white floccose scales, then naked and rimose-sulcate, thin; gills free, narrow, rapidly becoming fluid; stem hollow, solid at the thickened base, white, squamulose; cystidia numerous, large.—On dung heaps, common, spring to autumn, throughout our area.

This plant emerges in late afternoon and but little remains of it the following morning.

C. fimetarius var. **macrorhiza** Fr.

Pileus at first covered with feathery squamules which often form a crown on the disk by becoming squarrose; stem short, subbulbous, elongated at the base, villous, hollow.—On dung heaps, very common, throughout our area.

C. tomentosus Fr.   Tomentose Coprinus.   Plate 47, fig. 4c.

Pileus 2-5 cm. broad when expanded; stem 5-8 cm. x 5 mm.; spores 12 x 7 μ.

Pileus cylindrical to narrowly conical, membranaceous, splitting at the margin when expanded, striate, at first floccose, then adorned with persistent patches or flakes, pale gray; gills free, narrow; stem cylindrical, hollow, velvety-white or light gray; spores elliptical.— On dung or manure-debris, solitary or gregarious, April and May, not uncommon, throughout our area.

C. lagodipus Karst.   Plate 47, fig. 4b.

Pileus 4-7 cm. broad when expanded; stem up to 17 cm. long; spores 7 x 5 μ.

Pileus campanulate, very thin, grayish to dark livid, ornamented with white scales connected by hairs; gills free, remote, crowded, soon black; stem cylindrical, hollow, white; spores apiculate.—On very rotten wood in forests, rare, in northern part of our area.

C. Jonesii Peck.   Plate 47, fig. 4d.

Pileus 2-5 cm. broad when expanded; stem 5-9 cm. x 5-6 mm.; spores 8 x 6 μ.

Pileus campanulate, grayish, buff on disk, at first covered with ashy floccose scales; gills free, crowded; stem cylindrical, hollow, white; spores oval.—On stone or tile walls, rare, in Chicago.

C. arenatus Peck.   Sand Coprinus.   Plate 47, fig. 4e.

Pileus 2-5 cm. broad when expanded; stem 2-5 cm. x 2-5 mm.; spores 8 x 6 μ.

Pileus broadly ovate, soon expanded and convex, whitish-gray, becoming gray-brown with age; gills free, crowded, broad, gray-white becoming black; stem cylindrical, white, hollow; spores ovate. —On sand in dune regions, locally common, about the Great Lakes.

C. domesticus Fr.   Domestic Coprinus.   Plate 47, fig. 4f.

Pileus 3-5 cm. broad when expanded; stem 5-7 cm. x 5 mm.; spores 15 x 8 μ.

Pileus thin, ovate, soon campanulate, obtuse, squamulose, furry, pale gray with brownish disk, sulcate, splitting; gills adnexed, crowded, narrow, at first reddish-white then brown-black; stem white, somewhat silky, hollow.—Caespitose on vegetable debris, common, throughout our area.

C. semilanatus Peck.

Pileus 2-2.5 cm. broad when expanded; stem 10-15 cm. x 5-8 mm.; spores 13 x 10 μ.

Pileus convex, striate, white then gray-brown, mealy-tomentose; stem white, cottony below the middle; spores broadly elliptical.—On cow dung in woods and shaded pastures, not uncommon, throughout our area.

C. niveus Fr.   Snowy Coprinus.   Plate 47, fig. 4g.

Pileus 1.5-2.5 cm. broad when expanded; stem 4-8 cm. long; spores 16 x 12 μ.

Pileus long-oval then campanulate when expanded, submembranaceous, persistently covered with snowy-floccose material, the margin white-villose; gills narrowly attached, narrow; stem white, villose with remains of tomentose veil, hollow.—On dung heaps, sweepings, and manured ground, not common, temperate North America.

C. micaceus Fr.   Common ink-cup.   Plate 47, fig. 5a.

Pileus 4-6 cm. across when expanded; stem 3-7 cm. x 5 mm.; spores 8 x 5 μ.

Pileus ovate then expanded, coarse-striate, with smooth disk, very thin, ochraceous or tan, bearing minute glistening flakes which soon disappear; gills adnexed, lanceolate, white to brown then black; stem white, silky, cylindrical, hollow —Densely caespitose about stumps and trees, very common throughout the year, Minnesota, Maine, Alabama.

C. radians (Desm.) Fr.   Radiate-strand Coprinus.   Plate 47, fig. 5b.

C. pulchrifolius Peck.

Pileus 2-5 cm. broad when expanded; stem 3-6 cm. x 3 mm.; spores 7 x 4 μ.

Pileus ovate, conic-campanulate, fulvous, soon paler, striate to the disk, bearing small brown granules which are more numerous on the disk; gills rather narrow; stem white, hollow, smooth or minutely mealy, with yellow or white mycelial strands radiating from base; spores elliptical, smooth.—On wood, rubbish, or humus, rather common, throughout our area.

C. bulbilosus Patouill.   Plate 47, fig. 6a.

Pileus 8-10 mm. broad when expanded; stem 3 cm. x 1 mm.; spores 9 x 7 or 8 x 5 μ.

Pileus convex, gray, covered with white meal, very thin, the disk yellow, the margin striate; gills narrow, gray; stem slender, white, bulbous, the ring loose, white; spores compressed, oval to subglobose. —On horse dung, not common, throughout our area.

C. stercorarius Fr.   Plate 47, fig. 7a.

Pileus 1-2.5 cm. high; stem 7-12 cm. x 5 mm.; spores 7 x 4 μ.

Pileus ovate, campanulate, then expanded, very thin, densely covered with glistening white meal, the margin rolling up, striate; gills adnexed, 2-3 mm. wide, subventricose; stem ovate-bulbous at base, hollow, white, mealy at first; spores elliptical.—On cow dung, not common, throughout our area.

C. sclerotigenus Ell. and Everh.   Plate 47, fig. 7b.

Pileus very small and thin, 4-12 mm. broad and high; stem slender, 2-10 cm. long, growing from a subglobose black sclerotium which is internally white.—On sheep dung, occasionally found, throughout our area.

C. Patouillardi Quel.   Plate 47, fig. 8a.

Pileus 1-3 cm. high, 1-2 cm. broad; stem 3-5 cm. x 1-2 mm.; spores 7 x 5 μ.

Pileus ovate or oblong, at length expanded and revolute, at first finely striate, finally plicate, ashy with pulverulent particles, yellow-brown on disk, very thin; gills narrow, white at first, soon smoky-brown; stem white, cylindrical, glabrous or somewhat tomentose or pulverulent near base; spores angled.—Growing on dung, common, spring, summer, and autumn, throughout our area.

C. radiatus Fr.

Pileus 2-15 mm. high, 2-10 mm. wide; stem 3-7 cm. x 1-2 mm.; spores 12 x 9 μ

Pileus at first ovate-cylindrical, finally plane or depressed in the center, very thin, deeply plicate, adorned with a few scattered brownish granular scales or flecks, pruinose with a few gland-tipped hairs, gray or darker; gills free, narrow, distant; stem cylindrical, hollow, fragile, white, pruinose with glandular hairs; spores very dark, elliptical.—On dung, very common, from early summer to autumn, throughout our area

C. ephemerus Fr.   Ephemeral Coprinus.   Plate 47, fig. 9a.

Pileus 1-2 cm. broad; stem 4-5 cm. x 1-2 mm.; spores 16 x 8 μ.

Pileus expanded, striate, plicate, very thin, yellowish-brown or red-brown on disk, at first pruinose with minute hairs; gills very narrow, linear; stem white, hollow, slender; spores elliptical.—Common on dung, throughout our area.

C. silvaticus Peck.   Forest Coprinus.   Plate 47, fig. 9c.

Pileus 1-3 cm. broad when expanded; stem 5 cm. x 1 mm.; spores 12 x 8 μ.

Pileus dark brown, membranaceous, the disk thin but fleshy, the margin plicate-striate; gills adnexed, narrow, subdistant, brown then black; stem white, slender, hollow, fragile; spores gibbous, ovate.—On the ground in woods, rare, northern part of our area.

C. plicatilis Fr.   Plate 47, fig. 9b.

Pileus 1-2 cm. broad when expanded; stem 5-8 cm. x 1-2 mm.; spores 10 x 7 μ.

Pileus narrow-ovate then campanulate, membranaceous, sulcate to the apex; gills attached to a collar, narrow, distant; stem cylindrical, hollow, smooth, white; spores broadly ovate, compressed.—Among grass, occurring in troops or singly, not uncommon, throughout our area.

PANAEOLUS Fr.   Plate 47.

Plants symmetrical, putrescent, each composed of a hemispherical to campanulate pileus attached to a long, slender, cylindrical, straight, central stipe; pileus firm, thin, not striate, often appendiculate or white silky on margin with the more or less evanescent veil; gills grayish black, mottled gray and black, more or less attached but seceding; stem subrigid, polished; spores dark gray or black.—Growing on dung.

1   Stem 5-15 mm. in diameter, solid..................*P. solidipes.*
1'   Stem 6 mm. or less in diameter, hollow......2
2   Pileus reticulately veined on disk, usually moist.....*P. retirugis.*
2'   Pileus not so marked......3
3   Cuticle of the pileus at length breaking up into scales or areas, neither viscid nor moist....................*P. papilionaceus.*
3'   Cuticle of the pileus neither veined nor scaly......4
4   Pileus with dark zone near margin.................*P. fimicola.*
4'   Pileus not zoned, persistently conic-campanulate.*P. campanulatus.*

P. solidipes Peck.   Solid-stemmed Panaeolus (edible).   Plate 47, fig. 10.

Pileus 4-8 cm. broad; stem 8-20 cm. x 5-15 mm.; spores 17 x 10 μ.

Pileus large, firm, hemispherical to convex, not umbonate, glabrous, moist, white, smooth becoming rimose-scaly and yellowish on disk; gills adnate, broad, ventricose, soon variegated white, ashy, and black, the edges white-flocculose; stem firm, solid, long, white, striate at the apex; odor and taste slight.—On dung heaps and in manured fields, common, May-July, Maine, Minnesota, Kentucky.

P. retirugis Fr.   Reticulate Panaeolus (suspected).   Plate 47, fig. 11.

Pileus 1-3 cm. broad; stem 5-16 cm. x 2-6 mm.; spores 17 x 10 μ.
Pileus firm, oval then broadly hemispherical or campanulate, without an umbo, dark smoky when wet, grayish to clay-colored and shining-micaceous when dry, the surface commonly reticulate-veined on disk, glabrous, the veil membranous and clinging to the margin of the pileus, the flesh thin; gills adnate, broad, ventricose, close, variegated, the edges white-floccose; stem whitish, tinged reddish or purplish within and on surface, darker toward base, sometimes covered with white bloom, bulbate, hollow.—Gregarious on dung hills, very common, May-Oct., Minnesota to Maine and southward.

P. papilionaceus Fr.   Butterfly Panaeolus (suspected).   Plate 47, fig. 12.

Pileus 2-4 cm. broad; stem 6-8 cm. x 2-5 mm.; spores 17 x 10 μ.
Pileus hemispherical then convex-expanded, neither viscid nor hygrophanous, at length bearing scaly areas where the cuticle has cracked, smoky-gray or brownish, the veil clinging to the margin, the flesh white, thickish; gills adnate, broad, ventricose, variegated; stem toughish, whitish, hollow, brownish at the base, the apex striate and white-pruinose.—Common on dung heaps and manured ground, Maine to Minnesota and southward.

P. fimicola Fr.   Plate 47, fig. 13.

Pileus 2-4 cm. broad; stem 5-10 cm. x 2-4 mm.
Pileus campanulate to convex, smoky-gray when wet, clay-hoary when dry, fleshy, thin, smooth, glabrous, bearing a narrow smoky zone around the margin and a white zone within, the flesh grayish, thin; gills adnate, broad, ventricose, variegated; stem soft, fragile, cylindrical, dingy, white-pruinose and substriate at apex.—On horse dung, June, not common, Illinois.

P. campanulatus Fr. (suspected)   Plate 47, fig. 14.

Pileus 2-4 cm. broad; stem 7-10 cm. x 1-2 mm.; spores 17 x 11 μ.
Pileus persistently conic-campanulate, brownish-gray or yellowish-gray, thin, neither hygrophanous nor viscid; gills adnate, broad, close, variegated, the edges white-floccose; stem reddish-brown, black-dotted and striate at the apex, straight, rigid-fragile, pruinose.—On dung heaps, common, Minnesota to Maine and southward.

ANELLARIA L.

Differing from *Panaeolus* in the presence of a more or less persistent membranaceous annulus; spores dark.

A. separata L.

Pileus 2-4 cm. broad; stem 8-15 cm. x 2-5 mm.; spores 16-22 x 10-12 μ.

Pileus ovate-campanulate, clay-white, slightly fleshy, smooth, viscid; gills adnate, ashy-black, somewhat variegated; stem fistulose, straight, rigid, slightly attenuated from the thickened base, whitish, smooth, striate under lens, naked, the ring distant, white, entire, persistent.—On horse dung in woodland pastures, May-Sept., throughout our area.

GOMPHIDIUS Fr.   Plate 47, fig. 16.

Plants putrescent, each composed of a more or less fleshy, turbinate pileus, centrally attached to a downward-tapering stipe; pileus fleshy, viscid; gills thick, decurrent, waxy in consistency, with acute edges, subdistant, forked; stem confluent with pileus; spores black to smoky-olive, elongated, fusiform; cystidia abundant.—Growing on the ground, usually under pines.

G. maculatus Fr.   Plate 47, fig. 16.

Pileus 2-5 cm. broad; stem 4-7 cm. long x 5-12 mm. at apex; spores 15-23 x 6-7.5 μ.

Pileus convex, obtuse, then plane or depressed, with viscid separable cuticle, brown-flesh-colored to pale clay-colored, rugulose, spotted and shining when dry, the flesh thick, soft, white or faintly flesh-colored; gills decurrent, thickish, rather distant, soft-waxy, forked dichotomously, whitish then pale olive-gray, finally smoky; stem tapering downward, solid, firm, whitish above, dotted at first with reddish scurf, becoming black-spotted in age or when handled, yellow at base, the veil absent; taste mild.—Gregarious in pine woods or under tamarack trees, Oct.-Nov., rare, Minnesota to New York and Illinois.

G. vinicolor Peck.   Wine-colored Gomphidius.

Pileus 1-2 cm. broad; stem 3-4 cm. x 2-4 mm.; spores 13-16 x 6 μ.

Pileus convex, sometimes umbonate, then plane, with viscid or glutinous separable cuticle, wine or red-cinnamon with smoky center, paler at the margin, the flesh thick, pale flesh colored; gills decurrent, thickish broad in middle, rarely forked, olive-brown sprinkled with dark spores; stem slender, cylindrical, smooth, solid, viscid, vinaceous, not yellow at base, silky fibrillose; odor slight but disagreeable.

—Solitary or gregarious in low conifer woods, September, rare, Michigan to New York and Indiana.

PSATHYRELLA Fr.

Plants small, putrescent, each composed of a thin, conical to campanulate pileus attached to a slender, cylindrical, central stipe; pileus membranaceous, striate, the margin at first straight, not exceeding the gills; gills adnate or adnexed, at length uniformly dark colored, neither deliquescent as in *Coprinus* nor variegated as in *Panaeolus;* stipe straight or curved depending on position of substratum; spores black or purple-black, elliptical, smooth.—On debris or on the sides of stumps and tree trunks.

P. disseminata Fr.   Plate 47, fig. 15.

Pileus 5-10 mm. broad; stem 2-4 cm. x 0.5-1 mm.; spores 8 x 4 μ.

Pileus soon campanulate, sulcate-plicate, white then gray or grayish-brown, small with a buff umbo, at first covered with microscopic one-celled hairs, the flesh very thin; gills adnate, ventricose, white, ashy then uniformly black; stem slender, white, hollow, minutely hairy at base.—On debris on the ground and about bases of trees, common, May-Oct., throughout temperate North America.

PHALLACEAE

Plants at first puff-ball-like, a volva surrounding the vertically compressed stem, nutrient layer, and gleba; stem suddenly elongating at maturity and bearing the gleba near its apex and the volva about its base; spores minute, elliptical.—Growing on ground, or much decayed wood.

MUTINUS Fr.   Plate 48.

Plants at first enclosed in a puff-ball-like volva and composed of a much shortened stem, the red or orange gleba, clinging about it, the inner volva a soft, gelatinous nutrient-layer, the outer volva tougher and peridium-like; mature plant a columnar stem fitting into a basal volva and smeared near apex with the pink gleba.

1   Stem differentiated where gleba is borne............*M. caninus.*
1'   Stem not differentiated......2
2   Gleba rosy-red; plant growing in old fields.......*M. Ravenelii.*
2'   Gleba rosy to orange; plant growing on or about decaying
    logs ....*M. elegans.*

M. Ravenelii (Berk. and Curt.) Fisher.   Rosy Stinkhorn.

Plants enclosed within a puff-ball-like volva 2-3 cm. high and wide, the much shortened stem pure white and surrounded by the rosy-red gleba, which in turn is surrounded by the soft gelatinous inner volva and the firmer outer volva; mature plant produced by the expanding stem breaking through the volva and extending upward 6-8 cm; gleba surrounding upper third of stem, bright rosy-red, fading toward lower part, strong and offensive in odor; volva persistent at maturity about the base of the stem.—In old fields devoid of humus, very rare, eastern and southern part of our area.

M. caninus Fr.   Dog stinkhorn.   Plate 48, fig. 1.

Similar to *M. Ravenelii,* but the stem distinctly different where gleba is borne, 6-15 cm. high, the gleba rosy-red.—On the ground in grassy or sedgy places near marshes, not common, throughout our area.

M. elegans Mont.   Plate 48, fig. 2.
M. Curtisii Berk.
M. bovinus Morg.

Plants inclosed in a puff-ball-like volva 2-3 cm. high and wide, the much shortened stem pure white and surrounded by the rosy-red gleba, which in turn is surrounded by the soft gelatinous inner volva and the firmer outer volva; mature plant produced by the expanding stem breaking through the volva and extending upward 10-17 cm.; gleba rosy-red, surrounding upper one-third of the tapering, apically perforated stem; volva white, spherical, then elongated, collapsing about the stem, rooted by a strong cord.—On or about decaying logs or on wood humus, not uncommon, eastern part of our area.

ANTHURUS Kalchb.

Plants at first inclosed in a puff-ball-like volva and composed of a much shortened apically branched stem, the gleba dark, borne on sides and inner faces of the branches; the stem growing through the volva and carrying upward its several branches, the branches remaining connivent at tips or bending more or less strongly outward.

A. borealis Burt.   Plate 48, fig. 6.
Lysurus borealis (Burt) Henn.

Plants at first 3-4 cm. high and 2-3 cm. wide, whitish; the lengthening stem growing through the volva to 8-12 cm. high; gleba clinging to the inner and lateral surfaces of the several apical branches; branches meeting and adhering at their apices.—In gardens and flower-beds, probably introduced from tropics, very rare, eastern part of our area (after Burt).

DICTYOPHORA Desv.

Plants at first enclosed in a more or less globe-shaped volva, containing a much shortened stem about which clings the gleba; inner volva a soft gelatinous nutrient-layer, the outer volva tougher and peridium-like; stem rapidly elongating and bursting through the upper part of the volva to a height of 10 to 20 cm., carrying upward about its apex the gleba and indusium; indusium large, veil-like, campanulate.

D. duplicata (Bosc.) Ed. Fisch.

Mature plants 10-20 cm. high; pileus 3-5 cm. long and wide, strongly chambered by anastomosing plates, the slime brownish olive, the indusium light pink, net-like, extending below the pileus 3-5 cm., its perforations regular, 1-2 mm. broad, smaller toward margin; stem hollow, the walls chambered; volva subspherical, white, plicate below, pale brownish, flesh-colored above, with large fleshy root from below; odor strong but not as offensive as *Mutinus* or *Phallus*.—On the ground about stumps in woods, rare, throughout our area.

PHALLUS Michel. Stinkhorn.

Plants at first inclosed in a more or less spherical volva; the stem growing upward to a height of 7-15 cm.; pileus a thin, campanulate membrane attached to the apex of the stem and bearing on the outside the dark green slimy gleba; volva remaining about the base of the stem.—Usually on wood, humus, or soil.

P. impudicus (L.) Fr. Plate 48, fig. 4 and 5.

Pileus 4-5 cm. high and wide; stem 7-20 cm. x 2-3 cm.

Pileus conical-campanulate, apically attached to the non-perforated stem tip, covered with dark olive-green, reticulately ridged gleba, the odor very putrid; stem pure white, slightly pitted on surface, cylindrical or tapering upward, the base surrounded by the cup-like volval remnant; spores minute.—Growing on lawns, on sand among tall grass, and about trees, often found, summer and autumn, throughout our area.

P. Ravenelii (Berk. and Curt.) E. Fisch. Stinkhorn.

Dictyophora Ravenelii Berk. and Curt.

Pileus conical, attached around the terminal raised ring of the stem, covered with dark olive-green smooth gleba, the odor putrid; stem pure white, slightly pitted on surface, cylindrical or tapering toward apex, the base surrounded by the cup-like voval remnant; volva pinkish, tough, thick, wrinkled below and bearing purplish root-like strands; spores minute.—Growing on decaying logs, sawdust, and wood humus in woods, common, summer and autumn, throughout our area.

HYMENOGASTRACEAE

Plants hypogean usually bearing tramal plates; gleba fleshy to cartilaginous or somewhat gelatinous, not powdery but more or less putrescent.

PHALLOGASTER Morg.

Plants puff-ball-like in shape, spherical to pyriform, stipitate, covered by a one-layered peridium with more or less regularly arranged thickened areas which later become perforated, each perforation connected with one of the internal divergent lobes of the gleba; entire contents deliquescent at maturity, adhering in distinct masses to inner surface of peridium.

P. saccatus Morg.

Plants 2-5 cm. long, 1-2.5 cm. broad; spores 5 x 2 μ.

Plants spherical or pyriform, stipitate to nearly sessile, smooth, whitish or tinted dull flesh-colored at maturity; gleba dark sage-green, adhering in irregular masses to the inner face of the peridial wall; spores greenish, globose, 6-8 on each basidium.—Solitary or rarely subcaespitose on sandy soil in pine or in mixed woods, not common, Aug.-Oct., eastern part of our area.

LYCOPERDACEAE. Plate 48.

Plants mostly globose, subglobose, or pyriform, sessile or stalked; peridium membranaceous-coriaceous, usually two-layered and breaking irregularly or by a mouth at the apex; gleba fleshy-cellulose, commonly pulverulent at maturity; spores subglobose, smooth or warted, hyaline or colored.—Growing on the ground or on decaying wood.

See Moffatt, W. S. Higher Fungi of the Chicago region, Bul. 7 (Pt. 2) Nat. Hist. Surv., Chicago Acad. Sci. 1923; Peck, C. H. N. Y. State Mus. Rep. 32:58-72, 1879; McIlvaine, C. One Thousand American Fungi, 568-617, 1912; Coker, W. C. and J. N. Couch The Gasteromycetes of eastern United States and Canada, 123 pl., 201 pp., The Univ. of N. Car. Press, 1923.

SECOTIUM Kunze

Plants subglobose to conical-ovoid, stipitate with a columella up through center to the apex; gleba cellulose; capillitium lacking; spores colored.

S. acuminatum Mont. Plate 48, figs. 9 and 10.

S. Warnei Peck.

S. rubigenum Harkn.

S. agaricoides Czern.

Plants 2-3 cm. broad; spores 8 x 6 μ.

Plants subglobose to ovoid, whitish becoming brownish, smooth or squamose, sessile or short stipitate, rupturing about base by several longitudinal fissures; columella extending through peridium from the base to the apex; spore-mass tobacco-brown; spores globose or broadly elliptical, often apiculate.—On the ground, in fields and pastures, infrequently found, throughout our area.

CALVATIA Fr.

Peridium large, globose or turbinate with a stem-like base, the outer layer thin, smooth or granular, soon falling away, the inner layer thick but fragile, at maturity breaking into fragments from above downward; subgleba prominent, definitely limited above; capillitium dense, composed of long, slender, branched threads; spores globose, colored.

All species except *C. saccata* are quite large, ranging from 7 cm. broad to several times that size. The color of the spore-mass at maturity is the most conspicuous differentiating character.

1   Plants large, 7 cm. or more in diameter....2
1'   Plants small, 5 cm. or less in diameter......5
2   Capillitium maturing purple-brown, plants growing in meadows ....*C. cyathiformis.*
2'   Capillitium maturing yellowish or olive......3
3   Plants very large, 15-40 cm. or more in diameter, plants growing in grassy woods or pastures...................*C. gigantea.*
3'   Plants smaller, seldom more than 12 cm. in diameter......4
4   Capillitium soon greenish-yellow, at length olivaceous; plants growing in thin woods..................,..............*C. caelata.*
4'   Capillitium soon greenish-yellow, at length dull, dingy-yellow ....*C. craniiformis.*
5   Orange inner peridium soon exposed, capillitium deep orange ....*C. rubro-flava.*
5'   Peridium white to brownish, stem-like base longer than the diameter of peridium, plants growing in swamps....*C. saccatus.*

C. gigantea (Pers.) Lloyd. Giant puff ball (edible).
C. Bovista (L.) McBride
C. maxima Schaeff.
L. giganteum Batsch.
Plants 15-40 cm. broad or larger, according to reports, to over 5 ft.
Plant very large, globose or flattened from its own weight, sessile, white or slightly yellowish, dingy with age, glabrous or slightly floc-

culose; capillitium and spores greenish-yellow, then dingy-olivaceous, spores globose.—In troops in grassy places in pastures or open woods, Aug.-Sept. infrequently found, Minnesota to Maine, Alabama.

C. caelata Bull. Carved puff ball (edible).

Plants 7-12 cm. broad; spores 4-4.5 μ in diameter.

Plants obovoid or turbinate, flattened above, each with a thick base and cord-like root, the outer layer thickish, bearing coarse warts or spines above, whitish, then ochraceous, finally brown and breaking into areas, the inner layer fragile, thick, thinner at apex where it ruptures and forms a large torn opening; capillitium and spores compact, farinaceous, greenish-yellow or olivaceous, becoming pale to dark-brown.—On the ground in fields and thin woods, not common, Aug.-Oct., Colorado, North Dakota, New York, Ohio, Iowa and Illinois.

C. cyathiformis Bosc. Cup-shaped puff ball (edible).

C. lilacina Berk. and Mont.

Plants 7-15 cm. in diameter; spores 5-6 μ in diameter.

Peridium globose or depressed globose, white, ashy, or pinkish-brown, glabrous to scaly, often becoming cracked into areas, commonly with a short stem-like base, the falling away of upper part of plant leaving a cup-shaped base with ragged margin; capillitium and spores purple-brown, spores globose, rough.—On ground in pastures and meadows, common after heavy rains, July-Oct., Dakota, Maine, Florida.

C. craniiformis Schw. Brain puff ball (edible). Plate 48, fig. 18.

Plants 7-18 cm. in diameter; spores 3-3.5 μ in diameter.

Peridium obovoid or turbinate, with a thick stout stem-like base and a cord-like root, white, pallid, or grayish, the outer peridium thin, breaking into small areas, the inner peridium thin, ochraceous to bright brown, the upper surface of plant commonly convoluted like a brain; capillitium and spores greenish-yellow becoming dingy-ochraceous.—On the ground in rich woods, common, Sept.-Nov., Minnesota, Maine, Alabama, and Texas.

C. rubro-flava Cragin. Orange puff ball.

Plants 2-10 cm. wide and 1-5 cm. high; spores 3-3.5 μ in diameter.

Peridium obconic, tapering to the rooting mycelium, the outer layer thin, furfuraceous or granulose, with few, short, scattered spinules above, the inner peridium thin, fragile, whitish becoming orange-red to orange-brown, becoming exposed above with falling away of outer layer; capillitium and spores reddish-ochre becoming olivaceous-orange.—On the ground in fields and in sand by drainage ditches, not common, Missouri, New York southward to Brazil.

C. elata Masse.

Plants 2.5-5 cm. in diameter, 7.5-12 cm. high; spores 5-6 μ in diameter.

Plant depressed-globose above, abruptly contracted into a long, stout, stem-like base, which is 2-4 cm. in diameter, 6-9 cm. long, often lacunose, subequal, bearing a fibrous mycelium, the outer peridium very thin, composed of minute, persistent granules, the inner peridium white or gray becoming brownish, thin, fragile, in age breaking up; spores and capillitium brownish-olivaceous, the spores globose, warted.—Among mosses in tamarack swamps, Minnesota, New England, Ohio and Illinois.

LYCOPERDON Tourn. Plate 48.

Plants globose or pyriform, stem-like at the base, the outer peridium soon breaking up into subpersistent granules, warts, or spines, the inner peridium smooth, opening by a small apical mouth, the subgleba varying from almost none to about one-third the contents of the peridium; capillitium dense, the threads branched or simple; spores colored subglobose.

1   On decaying wood......2
1' On ground in pastures or woods, or among moss on decaying wood......3

2   Outer layer of pinkish-brown granules, plants normally globose ....*L. subincarnatum.*
2' Outer layer of reddish-brown granules, plants pyriform...
    ....*L. pyriforme.*

3   On ground in woods, on leaf mould, etc.......4
3' Among moss......10
3'' Among grass in pastures......7

4   Under pines, inner layer tan to golden, outer layer granular
    ....*L. umbrinum.*
4' In deciduous forests, inner layer brown or pale, outer layer long spiny......5

5   Spines shedding, exposing a smooth pale surface..*L. gemmatum.*
5' Spines shedding, exposing smooth brown surface......6

6   Spines white, very long...................*L. pulcherrimum.*
6' Spines creamy then brown...................*L. echinatum.*

7   With a cord-like root at base......8
7' Without such a root......9

8   Outer layer persistent.........................*L. pusillum.*
8' Outer soft layer deciduous, exposing a light brown inner
    covering ....*L. cepaeforme.*
9   Soft, fragile, white spines present on the straw-colored inner
    layer; plants small ....*L. Wrightii.*
9' Pyramidal warts present on the dark brown inner layer,
    plants 2.5-5 cm. in diameter.................*L. marginatum.*
10 Plants seldom over 2 cm. in diameter; apex often pointed;
    soft, white, outer layer persistent..............*L. acuminatum.*
10' Plants 1-3 cm. in diameter, common among Polytrichium;
    spindules minute, larger at apex; inner layer pale brown
    ....*L. molle.*

L. pulcherrimum Berk. and Curt. Beautiful puff ball. Plate
48, fig. 20.
L. Frostii Peck.
L. pedicellatum Peck.
Plants 2-7 cm. in diameter; spores 4.5-5.5 μ in diameter.

Plants obovoid, with short stout base and thick cord-like root, the
outer layer of very long white spines convergent at apex, these finally
falling away and exposing the smooth, shining purplish-brown inner
peridium, the subgleba filling about one-third of peridium; capillitium and spores olivaceous then brownish-purple; spores globose,
minutely warted; odor strong but not unpleasant.—On low ground
in woods, infrequently found, Kansas, Illinois, Vermont, and southward to southern Ohio.

L. echinatum Pers.
Like *L. pulcherrimum* but the creamy-white then deep brown spines
which fall away expose a brown inner layer, the capillitium purplish-
brown to dull brown, the subgleba small.—On deciduous leaf-mould,
not common, Wisconsin, New York, and North Carolina.

L. umbrinum Pers.
L. hirtum Mart.
L. glabellum Peck.
Plants 2-3.5 cm. wide, 3-4.5 cm. high; spores 4 μ in diameter.

Plants depressed-globose-pyriform, white or light brownish-gray,
turning to tawny buff or rarely golden-yellow, the surface lightly
persistent granular or the granules mingled with slender minute
spines, the subgleba present in stalk-like base and extending up the
widest part of plant in chambers; gleba pale olivaceous then darker
olivaceous-brown at maturity.—In pine woods, sometimes in grass of
shaded lawns, Wisconsin to Ontario and Florida.

L. gemmatum Batsch. Gemmed puff ball (edible).
L. perlatum Pers.
Plants 2-5 cm. wide, 2-7 cm. high; spores 4.5 μ in diameter.
Plant top-shaped, depressed above, the base short and obconic, arising from a fibrous mycelium, covered with long, thick, erect, whitish or gray spines of irregular shape intermixed with smaller ones, the largest spines at length falling away and exposing the pale inner peridium, the subgleba occupying more than one-third of peridium; capillitium and spores greenish-yellow becoming pale brown, the threads few-branched, about as thick as spores, the spores globose, finely granulated.—Gregarious on ground in woods, common, Minnesota, Maine, Alabama.

L. pyriforme Schaeff. Pear-shaped puff ball (edible). Plate 48, fig. 23.
Plants 1.5-3 cm. wide, 2.5-5 cm. high; spores 4 μ in diameter.
Plant obovoid or pyriform with an abundance of long white cord-like rhizomorphs at the base, the peridium buff to brownish, covered with persistent reddish-brown granules, the subgleba small, white; capillitium and spores greenish-yellow then brownish-olivaceous, the threads branched, larger than spore-thickness, the spores smooth, globose.—Often in clusters on rotten logs or on wood-humus, very common, spring, summer, autumn, Minnesota, Maine, Florida.

L. subincarnatum Peck. Pink puff ball.
Plants 0.6-1.5 cm. wide; spores 4-5 μ in diameter.
Plant small, subglobose, sessile, the outer layer pinkish-brown composed of minute short spinules which fall away at maturity and expose the pitted ashy-gray inner peridium; the subgleba small, capillitium and spore-mass greenish-yellow then brownish-olive, the threads unbranched, the spores subglobose, minutely warted.—Sometimes abundant on decaying logs, old stumps, and on ground covered with decayed wood, Aug.-Oct., Wisconsin, Maine, North Carolina.

L. marginatum Vitt.
L. cruciatum Rostk.
Plants 2.5 cm. high, 2.5-5 cm. in diameter; spores 4 μ in diameter.
Plant medium to large, globose or flattened above, covered with dense pyramidal, substellate warts which peel off in patches and expose the dark brown minutely furfuraceous inner peridium, the subgleba about one-fourth of peridium volume; capillitium and spore-mass dingy-olivaceous, the spores globose, smooth.—In pastures, not common, Aug.-Oct. Wisconsin, Connecticut, Florida.

L. Wrightii Berk. and Curt.

L. Curtisii Berk.

Plants 0.8-1.8 cm. in diameter; spores 4 μ in diameter.

Plant globose, small, sessile, covered above with soft, fragile, white spines which soon fall away and expose the pale tan or straw-colored smooth inner peridium, the subgleba small, convex; spore-mass and capillitium greenish-yellow then pale-olive, the threads long, simple, hyaline, much thicker than spores, the spores globular, finely granular.—Clustered in short grass in fields, Sept.-Oct., common, Wisconsin, New York, Virginia.

L. cepaeforme Bull.   Onion puff ball.

L. polymorphum Vitt.

L. coloratum Peck.

Plants 1.2-2.5 cm. in diameter; spores 3.5-4 μ in diameter.

Plants small, globose or depressed-globose, plicate underneath and with cord-like root, covered with a thin, white, minutely furfuraceous coat, which is soon rimulose in small patches and scales, finally falling away and exposing pale brown inner peridium, the subgleba slight; spore-mass and capillitium greenish-yellow then pale olivaceous, the threads much branched, their main axes much thicker than the spores, the spores globose, smooth.—In sandy soil and in meadows and pastures, not common, Wyoming, Indiana, New York, North Carolina.

L. pusillum (Batsch) Fr.

Plants 0.5-2-5 cm. in diameter; spores 4 μ in diameter

Plants globose, sessile, radicating, the outer peridium white when old, falling away and exposing the brownish inner peridium which is rimose-squamulose or minutely roughened with minute floccose warts; capillitium and spore-mass greenish-yellow becoming dingy-olivaceous, the spores smooth.—Caespitose in short grass in pastures or sandy soil, June-Oct., North Dakota, Wyoming, New York, Florida, Indiana dunes.

L. acuminatum Bosc.   Pointed puff ball.

Plants 0.6-1.2 cm. wide; spores 3 μ in diameter.

Plants small, globose or ovoid, often pointed above, with abundant mycelium at the base, the outer peridium white, soft, thin, the subgleba none; capillitium and spore-mass pale greenish-yellow then dingy-gray, the threads simple, hyaline, much thicker than the spores, the spores round, smooth.—Gregarious among moss in woods and on moss-covered logs, not common, Missouri, New Jersey, South Carolina.

The outer peridium dries as a thin persistent layer.

L. molle (Pers.) Morg. Soft puff ball.

Plants 1-3 cm. wide; spores 4-4.5 μ in diameter.

Plants globose or depressed-globose or turbinate, narrowed below
to a stem-like base, the outer peridium whitish, composed of nearly
uniform persistent minute weak spinules or granular warts, sometimes with a few larger papilliform ones toward the apex, sometimes tinged with yellow, falling away when mature, then the inner
peridium pale brownish or pale olivaceous-brown, nearly smooth,
furfuraceous, somewhat shining, capillitium and spore-mass dingy-
olive; columella present; spores minutely rough, globose.—Among
moss, especially *Polytrichum,* in old meadows and low pastures; Illinois, New York, West Virginia.

BOVISTELLA Morg.

Plants globose or broadly obovoid, often flattened or depressed
above, plicate beneath, bearing a thick cord-like root, cortex a dense
floccose coat; inner peridium thin, strong, elastic, opening by an
apical mouth; subgleba present, cup-shaped, threads free and separate,
branched; spores subglobose with long, hyaline, persistent pedicels.—
Growing on the ground.

B. radicata (Mont.) Patouill. Plate 48, fig. 17.

B. Ohiensis Ell. and Morg.

Plants rather large, 2.5-7.5 cm. in diameter, globose or broadly
ovoid, convex or more commonly concave above, plicate beneath and
bearing a thick cord-like root; the outer coat composed of soft warts
or spines, white or grayish, drying buff and at length falling away;
the inner coat smooth, shining, pale brown or yellowish; subgleba
large, occupying one-half of peridium, cup-shaped and persistent;
spores clay-brown.—On the ground in pastures and grassy open
woods, common, Illinois, New York, Florida.

BOVISTA Dill.

Plants globose or broadly obovoid, often somewhat flattened above,
peridium in two layers, the outer fragile and falling away, except
for a small portion about the base; inner peridium thin, membranaceous, becoming papyraceous, dehiscent by a definite irregularly torn
apical mouth; capillitium colored, dense, originating within the tissue
of the gleba, the threads several times dichotomously branched;
spores minute, globose, smooth, brown.—Growing on the ground in
open woods or pastures.

B. pila Berk. and Curt. (edible).

Plants 2.5-10 cm. in diameter; spores 4 x 5 μ.

Plants irregularly globose, bearing a stout cord-like root, the outer peridium thin, soon falling away; inner peridium buff, dark gray, or purplish-brown, commonly persisting through the winter without opening, at length forming an irregular torn aperture near the apex; capillitium pale brown or olivaceous, at length dark purple-brown, the threads much branched; spores smooth, globose.—On the ground in open grassy woods, Aug.-June, common, Wyoming, Wisconsin, New York, North Carolina.

B. plumbea Pers. (edible).
Plants 1.2-2.5 cm. in diameter; spores 7 x 6 μ.
Plants small, irregularly globose, or depressed above in age, the outer peridium flaking off, dull white, the inner peridium lead-colored, smooth, opening at the apex by a round or oblong aperture; capillitium olivaceous then purplish-brown, the threads much branched; spores smooth, subglobose, apiculate, brown.—On the ground in pastures, common, Wyoming, Wisconsin, Massachusetts, and North Carolina.

MYCENASTRUM Desv.

Plants subglobose, without a thickened base, the outer peridium thin, smooth, continuous, at first closely adnate to the inner peridium, at length flaking away, the inner peridium thick, tough, coriaceous, becoming hard, rigid and corky, the upper part at length breaking up into irregular lobes or fragments; capillitium originating in the gleba, the threads short, sparingly branched, bearing scattered prickles; spores large, globose, brown.—On dry sandy soil.

M. corium Desv.
M. spinulosum Peck.
Plants 5-10 cm. in diameter; spores 9-12 μ in diameter.
Plants large, depressed-globose, often irregular and elongated, bearing a thick cord-like root, the outer peridium soft, white, smooth, continuous, at length flaking away in large polygonal patches, the inner peridium almost woody, very thick, breaking up into irregular lobes; capillitium and spore mass bright olivaceous then dark purple-brown, the threads subhyaline, flexuous, sparsely spinulose; spores rough, subglobose.—On sandy soil, Wyoming, Canada, New Jersey, Indiana dunes.

ASTRAEUS Morg.

Plants subglobose; mycelium fibrous, proceeding from all parts of the surface; outer peridium thick, at first united to the inner then splitting away in stellate fashion; spores large, globose, minutely warted, brown.

A. hygrometricus (Pers.) Morg.   Water-measuring earthstar.
Plate 49, fig. 15.

Geaster hygrometricus Pers.

Expanded plant 5-8 cm. across; inner peridium 1-2 cm. in diameter; spores 8-11 μ in diameter.

Outer peridium deeply parted into 7-20 acute, hygrometric segments, reflexed when moist, strongly incurved when dry; inner
peridium depressed-globose, sessile, whitish becoming gray or
brownish; aperture stellate, scarcely protruding, torn; threads of
capillitium thinner than the spores; spores large, globose, rough.—In
sand in pine woods, Minnesota, Maine, Florida, frequent.

GEASTER Michel.   Plate 48.

Peridium subglobose, composed of three layers, the two outermost
usually not separable and splitting from the apex in a stellate manner; inner peridium sessile or on a pedicel, opening by a single apical
aperture; subgleba prominent or rudimentary; spores globose, rough,
colored.

1   Exoperidium strongly incurved when dry......2
1' Exoperidium not incurved when dry......4
2   Mouth bordered by a fringe....................*G. minimus.*
2' Hair-like fringe absent from aperture......3
3   Exoperidium thickish; expanded plant 3-5 cm. broad......
    .... *Astraeus hygrometricus.*
3' Exoperidium thin; expanded plant 2-2.5 cm. broad........
    ....*G. floriformis.*
    ered with sharp sand...............................*G. asper.*
4   Inner subglobose peridium appearing under lens as if cov-
4' Inner peridium not so decorated......5
5   Mouth sulcate......6
5' Mouth not sulcate; plant growing in woods or about the bases
    of trees......7
6   Growing in grassy places.....................*G. Schmidlei.*
6' Growing where wood has decayed.................*G. Archerii.*
7   Unexpanded plant acute, at the apex......8
7' Unexpanded plant globose......9
8   Exoperidium saccate ....*G. saccatus.*
8' Exoperidium not saccate, plant when expanded often appear-
    ing to have a cup-like middle layer..................*G. triplex.*
9   Plants reddish-brown ....*G. rufescens.*
9' Plants blackish or dark brown...................*G. limbatus.*

G. floriformis Vitt.   Plate 48, fig. 14.

G. delicatus Morg.

Plants 2 cm. across when expanded, 1 cm. in diameter when closed; spores 5-6 μ in diameter.

Outer peridium thin, splitting into 6-10 unequal segments; inner peridium sessile, subglobose, pallid to pale brown; mouth lacerate, plane; spores pale brown, minutely warted.—In sandy woods, locally common, North Dakota, Canada, Florida.

G. Schmidlei. Vitt.

G. Rabenhorstii Kunze.

Plants 3-4 cm. across when expanded, 1 cm. when closed; spores 3.5-5 μ in diameter.

Outer peridium brown, pedicellate, splitting into 6-8 multifid segments, strongly reflexed; mouth conical, sulcate; spores minutely warted, globose.—Gregarious, in grassy places, locally common, Sept.-Nov., Nebraska, Illinois, New Jersey, North Carolina, Texas, Cuba.

G. minimus Schw.   Least earthstar.

G. coronatus Schaeff.

G. marginatus Vitt.

Plant expanding to 3-4 cm. across; inner peridium 0.5-1.5 cm. in diameter.

Outer peridium splitting into 8-12 acute segments which are divided to the equator, generally shaggy with fragments of leaves or grass; pedicel short but distinct; inner peridium ovoid, white to pale-brown or almost black; mouth lifted on a single cone and bordered with a hairy fringe; columella slender; spores globose, minutely warted, brown.—In pastures, common, summer and early autumn, California, Wisconsin, New York, Florida, South America, Japan, and New Zealand.

G. asper Michel.   Rough earthstar.

G. campestris Morg.

Plant expanding to 3 cm. across; inner peridium 1-1.5 cm. in diameter; spores 3-6 μ in diameter.

Outer peridium revolute, splitting to about the middle in 8-10 segments the mycelial and fleshy layers closely adherent; pedicel short and thick; inner peridium subglobose, verrucose, beset with grainy particles; mouth conical, beaked, sulcate, seated on a depressed zone; columella prominent, persistent; capillitial threads simple, long-tapering; spores globose, rough.—On sandy ground, Wyoming, North Dakota, to Ohio and Texas.

358 THE CHICAGO ACADEMY OF SCIENCES

G. Archeri Berk.

Plant expanded to 4-6 cm. across; inner peridium 2-3 cm. in diameter; spores 4 μ in diameter.

Plants reddish-brown, acute at the apex when unopened; outer peridium splitting beyond the middle into 7-9 acute segments, the mycelial layer closely adherent, the fleshy layer thin, closely adhering; inner peridium globose, sessile, mouth indefinite, sulcate; columella globose-clavate; threads of capillitium thicker than spores; spores almost smooth.—On the ground where wood has decayed, not common, Illinois, Massachusetts, Kentucky.

G. saccatus Fr. Saccate Geaster.

Plant expanding to 4-5 cm. across; inner peridium 2-3 cm. in diameter; spores 3-5 μ in diameter.

Plant globose when unexpanded; outer layer splitting into 6-9 recurved segments; inner peridium globose, sessile; mouth conic, seated in definite circular area; spores globose, smooth.—In woods, common, Kansas, Missouri, Illinois, Wisconsin, Canada, North Carolina.

G. triplex Jungh. Three-layered Geaster. Plate 48, fig. 24.

Plant expanding to 7-10 cm. across; inner peridium 2-4 cm. in diameter, spores 3-6 μ in diameter.

Unexpanded plant subglobose, acute at the apex; outer peridium a thick fleshy layer which splits away from the apex to the equator or to two-thirds of the distance to the base into 5-8 segments and breaks away from the fleshy layer at about the middle, leaving a cup-like structure; inner peridium subglobose, sessile, pallid or brownish; mouth broadly conic, ciliate-fimbriate, seated in a definite circular area; capillitium-threads thicker than spores; spores globose, minutely warted, pale-brown.—Gregarious under trees in rich woods, common, Washington, Canada, Minnesota, Maine, Florida and New Zealand.

G. rufescens Pers. Red earthstar.

Plant expanding to 6-8 cm. across; inner peridium 2-3 cm. across; spores 3-6 μ in diameter.

Outer peridium splitting into 6-8 segments, recurved; inner peridium globose or ovoid, subsessile, reddish-brown; mouth indefinite; fibrillose capillitium threads thicker than spores; spores globose, minutely warted.—On the ground under oak trees, often buried by fallen leaves, not common, Aug.-Nov., Missouri, Wisconsin, New York, Alabama, Mexico, Japan.

G. limbatus Fr.

Plant very similar to *G. rufescens* except for dark brown color.

Outer peridium composed of 8-10 segments, recurved; inner peridium globose or broadly obovoid, dark brown, pedicellate; mouth elevated, ciliate-fimbriate and lacerate; threads of capillitium thicker than spores; spores globose, brown, minutely warted, 4-5 μ.—About trees and stumps on ground, not common, Minnesota, Massachusetts, Kansas, Illinois, New York.

MYRIOSTOMA Desv.

Outer peridium as in *Geaster*, coriaceous, pliable, splitting stellately, the segments expanded or reflexed; inner peridium bearing several short stalks, rarely one, membranous, papery, opening by many mouths.

Myriostoma coliformis Dicks.   Pepper-box.   Plate 48, fig. 16.

Plant expanding to 2-4 cm. across; inner peridium 1-1.5 cm. across, spores 3-6 μ in diameter.

Exoperidium thickish, splitting to about the equator, the lobes 6-10, recurved when first open, rather firm and rigid, when exposed to weather and easily separating into thin layers; inner peridium subglobose, supported on several more or less confluent pedicels; mouths several, round, plane or slightly elevated; columellae several, filiform; spores globose, roughened; threads one-half the diameter of spores.—In sandy soil, Colorado, Dakota, Ohio, Ontario, Florida, infrequently found.

TYLOSTOMA Pers.   Plate 48, fig. 8.

Plants composed of a more or less globose peridium on a stem usually several times as high as the diameter of the peridium; peridium opening by an apical aperture; outer layer deciduous; stem elongated, distinct, scaly or lacerate; capillitial threads nodulose at the prominent septa; mycelium much branched, often forming a sand bulb.—Species chiefly western.

1   Plants dark reddish-brown......................*T. rufum*
1' Plants not reddish......2

2   Plants small, 2-3 cm. high...................*T. mammosum.*
2' Plants taller, 3-10 cm. high......3

3   Mouth irregular, lacerate or fimbriate......4
3' Mouth entire, plants 5-10 cm. high.............*T. verrucosum.*

4   Mouth shield-shaped, fimbriate.................*T. poculatum.*
4' Mouth irregular, lacerate......................*T. campestre.*

T. verrucosum Morg. Warted Tylostoma.

Peridium 1-1.5 cm. in diameter; stem 5-10 cm. x 2-6 mm.; spores 5-6 μ.

Peridium depressed-globose, thickish becoming firm and rigid, covered with a dense brown cortex of persistent warts and scales; mouth circular, entire, small; stem lacerate-scaly, with central pith of long fibers, with a large mycelial bulb at the base; spores irregularly globose, pale-brown, minutely warted.—Growing in sand, not common, Oct.-Nov., Indiana dunes.

T. campestre Morg. Field Tylostoma. Plate 48, fig. 8.

Peridium 1-2 cm. in diameter; stem 2-7 cm. x 5-7 mm.; spores 5 μ

Peridium depressed-globose, the brown-scaly cortex gradually falling away; inner peridium thickish, becoming smooth and whitish; mouth plane, irregular, lacerate, not fimbriate; stem subequal, brown-scaly, white within, fibrillose-stuffed; spores pale-brown, minutely warted, subglobose.—In troops on sand, common, Colorado, Canada, Virginia, dunes of Great Lakes area.

T. poculatum White.

Peridium 1-1.5 cm. in diameter; stem 2-3 cm. x 3-4 mm.

Peridium reddish-brown, smooth, depressed-globose; mouth strongly raised, shield-shaped, fimbriate; cortex thick, persistent at base of peridium as a cup; stem smooth, obscurely striate, whitish, thickened below.—On sandy soil, October, not common, Indiana dunes, and about the Great Lakes.

T. mammosum Fr. Umbonate Tylostoma.

Peridium subglobose, the brown-scaly cortex falling away first from apex and leaving the greater part of the inner peridium exposed; inner peridium ochraceous becoming chalky-white, smooth membranaceous; mouth short-tubular with a circular opening; stem irregularly striate, cream-colored, sparsely scaly, white within, stuffed. —On sand in the Great Lakes region, August, not common; reported from North Dakota, Wisconsin, Kansas, Ohio.

T. rufum Lloyd. Red Tylostoma.

Peridium depressed-globose, 1-1.5 cm. in diameter; stem slender, dark reddish-brown, up to 3 cm. long, 1-2 mm. thick, tapering and scaly toward the apex; inner peridium brown to red-brown; gleba cinnamon, capillitium threads 3.5-5 μ.—On sandy soil, Urbana, Illinois, and Florida to Texas and Iowa.

CATASTOMA. Morg. Plate 49.

Small puff-ball-like plants, growing just beneath the ground and attached by very small threads which issue from every part of the thick cortex; cortex breaking away at maturity in a circumscissle manner, the lower part remaining in the ground, the upper remaining as a cap on the inner peridium.

C. circumscissum Berk. and Curt. Plate 48, fig. 7.

Plants 1-2 cm. in diameter, depressed-globose, thin, pallid becoming gray with branny scales; mouth small, basal; spore-mass olivaceous changing to pale-brown, the spores globose, minutely warted, 4-5 μ.—In or along paths, in pastures, not common, Maine to Wyoming and southward.

CALOSTOMA Morg.

Plants at first irregularly globose or elongated; outer layer of the peridium thick, gelatinous, white, the middle layer tough, cartilaginous and usually brightly colored, early forming at apex a stellate, red-edged mouth, endoperidium a thin-walled sac; with elongation the outer peridium becomes so watery as to break away exposing the spore bearing endoperidium suspended from the stellate mouth within the middle layer, with enlargement and rupture the powdery spore mass is discharged.—On the ground about stumps and decaying wood.

C. cinnabarina Desv. Plate 48, fig. 12.

Peridium composed of three layers, outermost a thick, white gelatinous tissue, 1-3 cm. broad, 3-5 cm. high; the middle layer tough, cartilaginous, bright red, hollow, spherical, with a stellate, apical opening; the inner layer, the endoperidium which at maturity hangs from the apex as a thin-walled sac containing the developing spores; mature stipe elongated to 1-2 cm., at which time the gelatinous, watery outer peridium falls away exposing the brightly colored layers within.—Growing on the ground, about stumps and logs, southern part of our area.

SCLERODERMATACEAE

Peridium thick, tough, coriaceous, sessile or stipitate, opening irregularly at the apex; gleba containing numerous cavities, the tramal plates disappearing, or persistent and inclosing peridiola; capillitium scanty or lacking.

SCLERODERMA Fr.   Plate 48.

Plants subglobose, usually much broader than high.

Peridium firm, the outer covering persistent as warts or granules; endoperidium indehiscent or splitting in a stellate manner at the apex; gleba and the walls of the trama present on every part of the peridium; spores large, globose, rough.—Terrestrial.

1   Plant splitting open and spreading, irregularly star like....
....*S. Geaster.*
1′ Plant not so splitting......2
2   Peridium thin, 0.5-0.8 mm. thick; spore-mass watery-cream
then deep brown ....*S. lycoperdoides.*
2′ Peridium much thicker......3
3   Plant coarsely warted, pale golden-brown; spore-mass blue-
black ....*S. aurantium.*
3′ Plant squamulose or granular; spore-mass of some shade of
brown......4
4   Plants light yellow, internally tobacco-brown, somewhat plicate below, bearing a yellow mass of roots..........*S. flavidum.*
4′ Peridium brittle, sordid-yellow; gleba dark yellowish-brown
....*S. Bovista.*
4″ Peridium smooth, reddish-yellow, strongly rooted with fine
rootlets ....*S. Cepa.*

S. aurantium Pers.   Golden Scleroderma.   Plate 48, fig. 21, 22.
S. vulgare Fr.

Plants 2.5-7 cm. in diameter, sessile, irregular, hard, warted, pale golden-brown or whitish, internally blue-black; spores 9-11 μ, globose, warted.—On the ground in open woods, common, Aug.-Nov., Wisconsin, Illinois, Canada, New York, North Carolina.

S. flavidum Ell. and Everh.   Yellow Scleroderma.

Plants 2.5-6 cm. in diameter depressed-globose, light yellow, internally tobacco-brown, firm, tough, coriaceous, stellately dehiscent, roughened with innate granules or minute warts above, smoother and somewhat plicate below, bearing strongly developed yellowish roots which form a mass in sand as large as the peridium itself; spores globose, echinulate, 7-12 μ.—In sand about the Great Lakes and in Florida.

S. Bovista Fr.

Plants 3-5 cm. wide; spores 11-18 μ in diameter.

Plant irregularly globose, depressed above, deeply and broadly plicate beneath, sordid-yellow, the peridium rigid and brittle when dry, 1 mm. thick, slightly to very squamulose with scales formed by the irregular cracking of the outer surface, later minutely areolate, rooted by a dense mass of cords; gleba dark yellowish-brown; tramal plates yellow-persistent; spores coarsely reticulated.—In sandy soil, not common, Canada to North Carolina.

S. Cepa (Vaill.) Pers.   Onion-shaped Scleroderma.

Distinguished from preceding by its less rigid peridium lighter-colored spore-masses, and smaller spiny spores.—On the ground in open woods, not common, Wisconsin to North Carolina.

S. lycoperdoides Schw
S. tenerum Berk. and Curt.

Plants 1-5 cm. wide; broader than thick, light brown or yellowish-brown, dotted with minute dark brown or red-brown scales; peridium thin, 0.5-0.7 mm. thick; spore-mass watery-cream-colored then deep brown, and faintly purplish; spores asperulate, 8-18 μ broad, deep brown, globose.—In damp shady places, locally common, Wisconsin, Massachusetts, Florida.

S. Geaster Fr.   Earthstar Scleroderma.

Plants 4-8 cm. in diameter, subglobose, thick with a very short stem or sessile, hard, rough, splitting into irregular stellate limbs, each limb becoming reflexed; internal mass dark brown to blackish, often purplish-tinged.—On hillsides etc., Sept.-Nov., not common, Ohio to Florida, in southern part of our area.

PISOLITHUS Alb. and Schw.
Polysaccum D. C.

Plants irregularly globose, usually higher than broad, attenuated downward into a thick stem-like base; gleba divided into distinct sack-like cells.

P. tinctorius Pers.   Many-chambered puff-ball.   Plate 48, fig. 19.
Polysaccum pisocarpium Fr.

Plants 3-4 cm. in diameter, irregularly globose, attenuated downward to a stem-like base, obscurely nodulose, olivaceous-black; internally dark sac-like peridioles irreguarly angular, 5 x 3 mm.; spores globose, tuberculate, coffee-brown, 9-13 μ broad.—In pine or mixed woods, on sandy soil, rare, Aug.-Oct., Ohio to Alabama and Florida.

NIDULARIACEAE.   Plate 48.

Spores developed within distinct subglobose or lenticular sporangia formed within a more or less cup-shaped peridium, which opens by dehiscence of an operculum, membrane, or by falling away of part of peridium.

CYATHUS Pers. Bird's nest fungi. Plate 1, fig. 42.

Peridium tubular, trumpet-shaped, or goblet-shaped, composed of three adnate layers, at first closed by a white membrane (epigragm), then widely open at the top; peridioles flattened, disk-shaped, umbilicate beneath and attached to the peridium by a compound funiculus.

1 On manure or manured ground, peridioles blackish.*C. stercoreus.*
1' On wood, peridioles ashy to whitish......2
2 Peridium dark brown............................*C. striatus.*
2' Peridium ashy-gray to light brown..............*C vernicosus.*

C. stercoreus (Schw.) De Toni.

Plants 0.5-1.5 cm. high, 4-8 mm. wide at top, 1-3 mm. at base.

Peridium thin, narrowly obconical, tapering to a slender base, the outer surface fulvous-brown, hirsute, finally naked, the inner surface lead-colored, glabrous, shining; peridioles blackish, smooth, discoid, depressed beneath; spores hyaline, subglobose, 22-35 µ broad. —On dung or manured ground in fields and pastures, common Minnesota, New York, Florida.

C. striatus Hoffm. Plate 48, fig. 11.

Plants 1-2 cm. high; 0.5-1 cm. in diameter, externally dark rusty-brown and tomentose, the inner surface lead-colored or brownish, glabrous, striate with longitudinal plications, at length opening at the top by detachment of the epigragm; peridioles ashy becoming whitish, globose then angular by mutual pressure; spores hyaline, broadly cylindrical, 12-15 x 6-8 µ.—On sticks, nut shells, trunks of trees, etc., Minnesota, Maine, Alabama.

C. vernicosus (Bull.) D. C.

Plants 8-12 mm. high; 5-15 mm. wide; peridioles 2-3 mm. broad; spores 12 x 9 µ.

Peridium campanulate with wide-expanded or recurved mouth, externally silky-hairy or smooth, ashy-gray or brownish, the inner surface dark gray to lead-colored, shining; peridioles ashy, globose, flattened beneath.—On partly buried sticks and chips about barnyards, gardens, and stubble fields, common, summer and autumn, Wisconsin, New York, Tennessee.

CRUCIBULUM Tul.

Peridium at first globose, composed of one layer which is continuous up to the mouth and forms a lid-like structure, the lid at length disappearing and the entire plant becoming crucible-shaped; peridioles numerous, disk-shaped, whitish, smooth, each with a globular process beneath, the lower part of which is attached to inner wall of peridium.

C. vulgare Tul. Crucible bird's nest.

Plants 5-7 mm. high and broad; peridioles 1.5-2 mm. broad; spores 9 x 5 μ.

Peridium at first globose and closed, sessile, at length opening and becoming cylindric-crucibuliform, outwardly fulvous, velvety when young, grayish and furfuraceous in age, the inner surface whitish-satiny-shining; peridioles globose, crowded, flattened by pressure.—On dead sticks in crevices, very common, Wyoming, Illinois, New York, Florida.

NIDULARIA Fr.

Plants subglobose, not opening regularly to form a perfect cup but thin and fragile and breaking up irregularly, the peridioles being left exposed on the substratum; peridioles dark brown to reddish-brown, shining, embedded in mucus when fresh.

N. pulvinata (Schw.) Fr.
N. pisiformis Roth.
Plants 6 mm. in diameter, subglobose, cinnamon-brown, tomentose, without a thin inner layer; peridioles small, up to 0.8 mm. wide, dark brown, somewhat adherent with mucus when dry; spores hyaline, smooth, 5 x 7 μ.—On old logs, sometimes on leaves, not common, July-Sept., Maine, Alabama, Iowa.

TUBARIA W. G. Smith

A yellow-spored genus (Agaricaceae), not yet found within our area. In form it corresponds to *Omphalia* of the white-spored division. In all characteristics except spore color it corresponds to the genus *Omphalia*.

DICTIONARY OF TERMS

aberrant—differing from the usual.

abrupt—with an obtusely conical or flat top, not rounded.

acerose—pointed and stiff like spruce needles.

acicular—very slender and bristle-shaped.

aculeate—slender-pointed.

adpressed—in close contact but not adherent.

aeruginose—verdigris-green.

agglutinate—glued together, cohering.

aggregate—crowded together but not cohering.

allantoid—sausage-shaped.

alutaceous—pale tan, light leather-colored.

alveolate—deeply pitted.

amphigenous—not confined to one surface.

amygdaline—like cherry or peach stones or cherry bark in taste and odor.

anastomosing—branching in an irregular pattern, the branches connected to make pits or pores.

anterior—in front or toward the margin.

apiculus—point of attachment of a spore.

apothecium—the open cup-shaped fructification of the discomycetes and lichens.

appendiculate—decorated with hanging fragments.

applanate—expanded horizontally.

appressed—closely pressed against the surface.

approximate—approaching but not touching an object.

arachnoid—cobwebby.

arcuate—bow-shaped.

areolate—divided into small areas or patches.

argillaceous—clay-colored.

arid—dry.

ascus—(pl., asci)—spore-sac bearing usually eight spores.

aseptate—without partitions, without cross-walls.

atomate—sprinkled with minute particles.

attenuate—gradually narrowed.

auriculate—ear-shaped.

azonate—without zones or parallel bands.

beaded—decorated with rows of droplets.

bibulous—capable of absorbing moisture

bifurcate—forking.

biseriate—arranged in two rows.

bister—blackish-brown.

bloom—a minutely velvety substance.

byssoid—composed of a fine net of hyphal strands.

caespitose—grouped, often in tufts.

calyptra—the portion of the veil covering the pileus.

campanulate—bell-shaped.

canaliculate—furrowed.

candidous—shining-white.

canescent—clothed with hoary down.

capillary—hair-like.

capillitium—spore-bearing threads filling the inside of puffballs and other fungi.

carbonaceous—with the texture of charcoal.

carinate—keeled, boat-shaped.
carneous—fleshy, flesh-colored.
cartilaginous—firm and tough.
castaneous—chestnut-colored, tawny-brown.
caulicolous—growing upon stems of herbs.
centimeter—0.3937 inch; 5 centimeters is approximately 2 inches.
cepaeform—onion-shaped.
ceraceous—wax-like
cerebriform—like the brain.
cervine—deep tawny.
chlamydospore—thick-walled resting spore.
chrome-yellow—deep yellow.
ciliate—bearing a hair-like fringe.
cinereous—light bluish-gray-colored, ash-gray.
cinnabar—brownish-red.
circumscissile—opening or dividing along a transverse circular line.
citrine—lemon-yellow.
clavate—club-shaped.
colliculose—covered with hill-like elevations.
columella—sterile tissue rising column-like into the spore-bearing capil-
    litium.
conchate—resembling a clam-shell or an oyster-shell.
concolor—of the same color.
confervoid—much branched, loose, and thread-like.
conglobate—collected into a globose mass.
connate—grown permanently together.
connivent—converging.
context—texture, substance, trama.
coriaceous—leathery texture.
corneous—horny texture.
cortex—outside covering.
cortina—a veil of web-like structure.
costate—ribbed with ridges (of gills or of pileus of *Morchella*).
cretaceous—like chalk.
crisped—strongly and finely undulate.
cucullate—shaped like a high hat.
cuspidate—with spear-like point.
cyaneous—bright blue.
cyathiform—cup-shaped, shape of a drinking glass somewhat widened at top.
cyst—a bladder-like cell.
cystidium—special, usually projecting hyaline cells among basidia, or in a
    surface.
dealbate—whitened.
decorticate—destitute of cortical layer.
decurrent—prolonged down the stem.
decurved—bent down with more or less curving.
deflexed—bent down.
dehiscent—opening by valves or slits when a certain development is attained.
deliquescent—referring to mushrooms which at maturity become liquid.
dendroid—branched as a tree
depauperate—development arrested in some way.
diaphanous—nearly transparent.
difformed—irregular in form, literally in two-forms.
digitate—dividing like fingers of the hand.

dilated—enlarged.

dilute—reduced in strength.

dimidiate—literally divided in two, (of gills) reaching about half way to stem; (of pileus) more or less semicircular in outline.

discocarp—ascocarp in which the hymenium is exposed while the asci are maturing as in Pezizaceae and Elvelaceae.

discrete—not coalescent; e.g., scales on the pileus are discrete with pileus.

dissepiments—partitions, the walls between pores of a polypore, etc.

distal—pertaining to apex or to outer extremity.

distant—relatively far apart; e.g., when gill-edges are clearly a millimeter or more apart.

divaricate—diverging widely.

echinate—bearing sharp-pointed projections such as pointed scales.

echinulate—very fine, or microscopic sharp projections.

effused—spread over and without regular form.

effuso-reflexed—effused with upper margin bent out to form a pileus.

egg—young stage before rupture of volva; e.g., *Phallus, Amanita.*

emarginate—(of gills) notched near stem.

endoperidium—the inner layer of the covering of a Gasteromycete.

epiphragm—the delicate membrane closing the cup-like receptacle of the Nidulariaceae.

epiphytal—growing on leaves.

epispore—outer covering of a spore.

epithecium—a layer sometimes formed over the asci by the concrescent tips of the paraphyses.

epixylous—growing upon wood.

eroded—edge ragged, as if gnawed.

erumpent—originating beneath and breaking through.

exoperidium—the outer layer of the covering of a Gasteromycete.

falcate—sickle shaped.

farinaceous—like meal (of odor, taste, or covering).

ferrugineous, or ferruginous—(color) rusty red.

fibrillose—with small strands of fibrous hyphae.

fimbriate—(of pileus) with margin jaggedly cut; (of gills) minutely fringed on edge.

flaccid—soft and limber, flabby.

flaring—spreading away from stem.

friable—easily crumbling into powder.

frondose—said of broad leaved trees.

front—(of gills) end toward margin of pileus.

fugacious—disappearing or fading early.

fuliginous, fuligineous—(color) smoky sooty.

fulvous—tawny, yellowish brown.

funiculus—(L. a small rope) in Nidulariaceae the cord attaching the peridiole to inner wall of nest-like peridium.

furcate—forked.

furfuraceous—with bran-like scales.

fuscous—smoky-gray-brown.

Gasteromycetes—(Gr. stomach-fungus) fungi with hymenium enclosed in a sack-like covering called the peridium.

gibbous, gibbose—more swollen on one side than other.

gill-trama—the tissue of the gill between the hymenial layers.

gilvous—yellowish leather color.

glabrous—smooth, without hairs.

glandular—with sticky drops or dots.
glaucous—covered with a white bloom or white powder.
gleba—spore-bearing tissue composed usually of chambers lined or not
with hymenium and enclosed by a sack-like peridium.
gluten—the dissolved gelatinous hyphae.
gregarious—several scattered over a small area.
guttate—bearing or containing droplets of water or sap.
guttulate—containing an oily globule.
gyrate, gyrose—circling in wavy folds.
hirsute—hairy with stiff hairs.

hispid—bristly.
hyaline—colorless, transparent.
hygrophanous—of watery appearance when moist, changing color when
drying.
hygroscopic—the property of absorbing moisture from the air.
hymenium—the spore-bearing surface.
Hymenomycetes—the group of fungi having unenclosed basidia-bearing
hymenium.

incrassated—thickened, as stem or foot of an agaric.
incurved—(of pileus) bent downward and curved inward.
innate—immediately under the surface, a part of surface tissue.
isabelline—(color) nearly same as alutaceous, color of sole-leather.
inserted—(of base of stem) attached directly without roots or fibrils.
instititious—same as inserted.
invagination—the pushing of one layer into another.
involute—rolled inward.

labyrinthine—with pore mouths curving and sinuous.
laciniate—deeply or irregularly cut.
lactiferous—milk-bearing, having white or colored sap.
lacuna—a pit or hollow.
lamella—a gill, one of the radiating hymenial plates.
lanate—wooly.
latex—a thick milky juice, white or colored.
lenticular—lentil-shaped like a double convex lens.
ligulate—strap-shaped.
livid—like the black and blue of a bruise, leaden.
lurid—smoky reddish gray.
luteous—dull egg-yellow.

mammiform—(of umbo and of perithecia) portion of surface enlarged toward a hemispherical shape.
marginate—(of bulb at base of stem) having a well defined horizontal
platform on upper side.
mauve—light violet.
melanosporous—(Gr.-black-spore) having black spores.
micaceous—covered with flat glistening particles.
mitrate—shaped like a miter or a bonnet.
mucronate—tipped with an abrupt sharp point.
multifid—having many divisions.
multipartite—divided into many parts.
muricate—rough with short firm projections.

navicular—boat-shaped.
nigrescent—becoming black.

obsolete—(of parts of a fungus) very imperfectly or not developed.

ochraceous—ochre yellow; yellow with brownish tinge.

olivaceous—(color) a dull yellowish green color, color of an unripe olive.

paraphyses—slender, sterile threads among the spore-bearing organs.

partial veil—the inner veil extending from margin of pileus to the stem.

pellicle—skin, cuticle.

pellucid—translucent, nearly transparent, waxy-translucent.

peridiolum—an interior peridium containing the hymenium; e.g., the "egg-like structures in the nest" of the Nidulariaceae.

peridium—the enveloping coat of a fungus-fruit, as of a puff-ball.

peristome—the ring around the opening of a peridium.

peronate—a stem with a sock-like covering enclosing its base usually to above the middle is said to be peronate or booted.

piliferous—covered with soft hair.

pilose—covered with hairs.

pip-shaped—shape of an apple seed.

pisiform—pea-shaped.

plicate—folded like a fan; plaited.

poculiform—cup-shaped.

procumbent—in a horizontal position.

protobasidium—basidium divided by transverse walls into four cells each producing a spore on an exserted sterigma, or basidium divided by walls crossing at right angles to form four cells each terminating in a long tubular sterigma.

pruinate—as if finely powdered.

pulverulent—covered with powder.

pulvinate—cushion-shaped.

reflexed—(margin) turned up.

repand—margin of pileus wavy and turned up.

resupinate—attached to substratum by the back, the hymenium facing outward.

resupinate-reflexed—(of pileus) part of fungus against and parallel to substratum and part perpendicular to substratum like a shelf.

reticulate—marked with net-like ridges.

revolute—rolled back and up, compare "repand."

rimose—cracked with clefts.

rivulose—marked by sinuous lines like rivulets.

rugose—wrinkled.

rugulose—minutely wrinkled.

scissile—(scissilis to cleave) capable of being easily split into layers or plates.

sclerotium—a resting body usually of small size composed of compact hyphae from which fruiting bodies may arise.

scrobiculate—marked with small pits.

scutellate—shield-shaped, saucer-shaped.

secede—(gills) at first attached to stem but later pulling away.

seriate—arranged in rows.

sericeous—silky.

seta—a stiff bristle-like hair.

sigmoid—by bending of ends appears slightly S-shaped.

sinuate—a concave indentation of gill near stem.

sinuous—wavy, serpentine.

spicule—a bristle-like projection.

squamose—covered with scales.

squarrose—covered with recurved scales.

sterigma—one of four projections on the club-shaped basidium to which spores are attached.

strigose—rough with long, stiff hairs.

stuffed—(of stem) filled with pith which often later disappears leaving stem hollow.

subgleba—the basal portion of hyphal material within a puffball, beneath the gleba.

subiculum—(an under layer) a more or less compact layer of hyphae on the substratum from which the fruiting body arises.

superficial—(of scales, etc.) easily removable.

superior—(annulus) near apex of stem

testaceous—(color) brick-red.

trama—fleshy portion of pileus or hyphal layer between the hymenial sides of the gill.

tuberculiform—shaped like a tuber, like a potato in shape.

tuberculose, tubercular, tuberculate—covered with tubercles.

turbinate—shaped like a broad inverted cone.

umbilicate—with a central rounded depression.

umbonate—(of pileus) with a central, mound-like elevation.

umbo—a convex knob on center of pileus.

uncinate—provided with a narrow downward extension of gill at stem, hook-like.

ungulate—shaped like the hoof of a horse.

uniseriate—in one series or row.

universal veil—the volva, the outer surrounding veil.

urceolate—shaped like a pitcher with a contracted mouth.

vacuolate—provided with vacuoles that contain or have contained water, air or secretions in or among the cells.

veins—swollen wrinkles are called veins.

ventricose—swollen in middle, widest in middle.

verrucose—covered with warts.

villose—covered with long, soft, weak hairs.

virgate—(of pileus) streaked with fibrils.

vitelline—(color) egg-yellow.

volva—(a wrapper) same as universal veil; when ruptured it may remain as a cup about the stem base, or be carried partly or wholly as fragments on the aerial parts of the fungus.

ERRATA

p. 196, couplet 31', read *H. fuligineus.*

p. 203, couplet 22, read *R. Mariae.*

p. 212, for **"R. paulstris"** read **R. palustris.**

p. 229, for **"P. astrocaerulens"** read **P. atrocaeruleus.**

p. 235, couplet 8, read *M. Olneyi.*

p. 248, couplet 7', for "diluted" read dilated.

p. 264, add the following to key:

14 Gills salmon-colored	. . . .	*E. salmoneum.*
14' Gills pale yellow	. . . .	*E. cuspidatum.*
14'' Gills whitish or pink	. . .	*E. Peckianum.*

p. 318, couplet 11, read *A. micromegatha.*

p. 335, couplet 9, read *C. lagodipus.*

p. 337, for **"C. fimentarius"** read **C. fimetarius.**
for "var. **microrhiza**" read **microrhizus.**

INDEX

PLATES 1 - 49

Plate 1

Various Types of Fungi

1, 2 Agaricaceae: 1 lower side of pileus, 2 lengthwise section of fructification.

3–6 Polyporaceae: 3, 4 *Boletus*, 5, 6 *Boletinus*.

7–13a Hydnaceae: 7–11 *Hydnum*, 12 *Radulum*, 13 *Odontia*, 13a *Phlebia*.

14–23 Polyporaceae: 14 *Polyporus*, 15 *Fomes*, 16 *Fistulina*, 17 *Poria*, 18 *Merulius*, 19 *Trametes*, 20 *Daedalea*, 21 *Lenzites*, 22 *Favolus*, 23 *Cyclomyces*.

24, 25 Clavariaceae: *Clavaria*.

26–35 Thelephoraceae: 26 *Craterellus*, 27 *Stereum*, 28 *Thelephora*, 29 *Tremellodendron*, 30 *Aleurodiscus*, 31, 32 *Solenia*, 33 *Coniophora*, 34 *Corticium*, 35 *Hymenochaete*.

36, 37 Tremellaceae: 36 *Tremella*, 37 *Tremellodon*.

38, 39 Lycoperdaceae: 38 *Lycoperdon*, 39 *Calvatia*.

40, 41 Phallaceae: 40 *Mutinus*, 41 *Phallus*.

42 Nidulariaceae: *Cyathus*.

43 Lycoperdaceae: *Tylostoma*.

44–47 Elvelaceae: 44 *Morchella*, 45 *Verpa*, 46, 47 *Elvela*.

48 Pezizaceae: *Peziza*.

49 Hypocreaceae: *Cordyceps*.

50, 51 Xylariaceae: 50 *Daldinia*, 51 *Xylaria*.

52–54 Geoglossaceae: 52 *Leotia*, 53 *Spathularia*, 54 *Geoglossum*.

PLATE 1

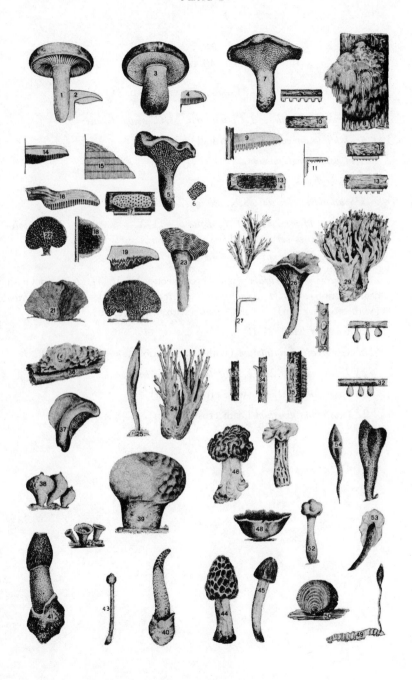

PLATE 2

HYPOCREACEAE, GEOGLOSSACEAE, AND XYLARIACEAE

1 *Cordyceps herculea*, 2 *C. militaris*, 3 *C. agariciformis*.

4 *Daldinia concentrica* (cut in half).

5 *Hypoxylon rubiginosum*.

6 *Trichoglossum velutipes*.

7 *Spathularia clavata*, 8 *S. velutipes*.

9 *Xylaria Hypoxylon*, 10 *X. digitata*, 11 *X. polymorpha*, 12 *X. polymorpha* (in cross-section), 13 *X. corniformis*.

14 *Mitrula phalloides*.

15 *Microglossum rufum* (with cross-section), 16 *M. fumosum* (with cross-section), 17 *M. longisporum* (with cross-section), 18 *M. olivaceum* (with cross-section), 19 *M. viride* (with cross-section).

20 *Cudonea lutea*, 21 *C. circinans*.

22 *Gloeoglossum glutinosum* (with cross-section).

23 *Leotia lubrica*, 24 *L. stipitata*, 25 *L. chlorocephala*.

26 *Geoglossum glabrum* (with cross-section).

27 *Geoglossum nigritum* (with cross-section).

PLATE 2

Plate III

Pezizaceae and Phaeobulgaria

1 *Pseudoplectania fulgens,* 2 *P. nigrella,* 3 *P. vogesiaca.*

4 *Plectania floccosa,* 5 *P. coccinea.*

6 *Aleuria rutilans,* 7 *A. rhenana.*

8 *Scodellina leporina.*

9 *Bulgaria rufa.*

10 *Phaeobulgaria inquinans.*

11 *Urnula craterium.*

12 *Paxina leucomelas,* 13 *P. sulcata.*

14 *Wynnea americana.*

15 *Paxina Acetabulum.*

16 *Peziza badia.*

17 *Geopyxis catinus.*

18 *Peziza pustulata,* 19 *P. succosa,* 20 *P. venosa.*

21 *Aleuria aurantia,* 22 *A. wisconsinensis.*

23 *Aleurina atrovinosa.*

24 *Paxina fusicarpa,* 25 *P. semitosa.*

26 *Melastiza Charteri.*

27 *Plectania hiemalis,* 28 *P. occidentalis.*

29 *Bulgaria melastoma.*

30 *Paxina hispida,* 31 *P. macropus.*

32 *Peziza vesiculosa,* 33 *P. sylvestris,* 34 *P. violacea,* 35 *P. repanda.*

36 *Geopyxis cupularis.*

Plate III

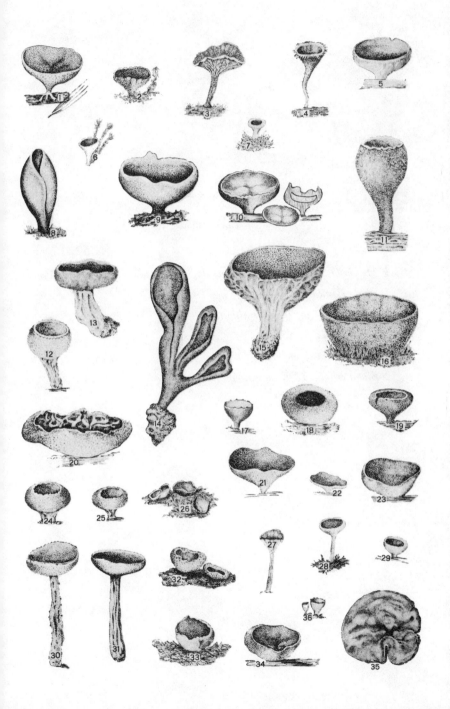

Plate 4

Elvelaceae

1 *Verpa bohemica,* 2 *V. conica.*

3 *Morchella angusticeps,* 4 *M. hybrida,* 5 *M. deliciosa,* 6 *M. esculenta.*

7 *Elvela elastica.*

8 *Morchella conica,* 9 *M. crassipes.*

10 *Elvela infula.*

11 *Underwoodia columnaris.*

12 *Elvela crispa,* 13 *E. mitra,* 14 *E. Underwoodii.*

PLATE 4

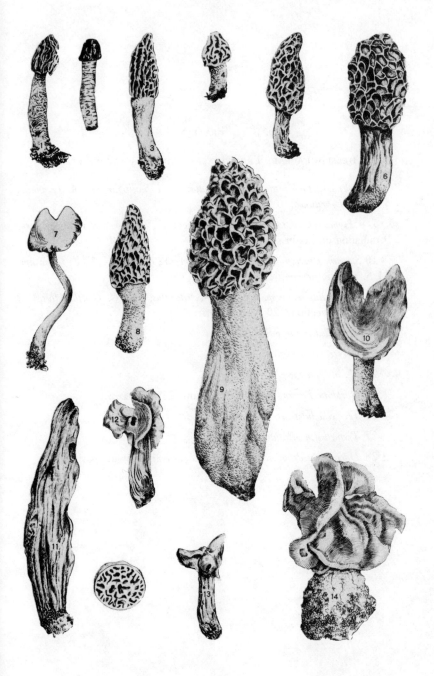

PLATE 5

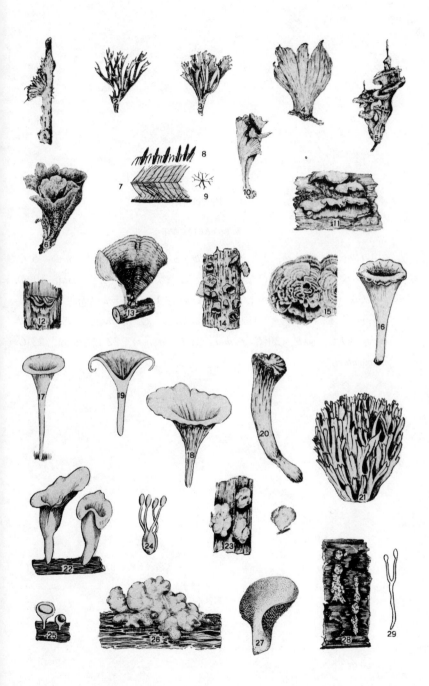

PLATE 6

CLAVARIACEAE

1 *Clavaria Botrytis*, 2 *C. holorubella*, 3 *C. formosa*, 4 *C. flava*, 5 *C. densa*, 6 *C. albida*, 7 *C. crassipes*, 8 *C. abietina*, 9 *C. cristata*, 10 *C. pyxidata*, 11 *C. amethystina*, 12 *C. Kunzei*, 13 *C. corniculata*, 14 *C. lentofragilis*, 15 *C. rugosa*, 16 *C. inaequalis*, 17 *C. fusiformis*, 18 *C. pistillaris*, 19 *C. ligula*, 20 *C. foetida*, 21 *C. fistulosa*, 22 *C. juncea*, 23 *C. vermicularis*.

PLATE 6

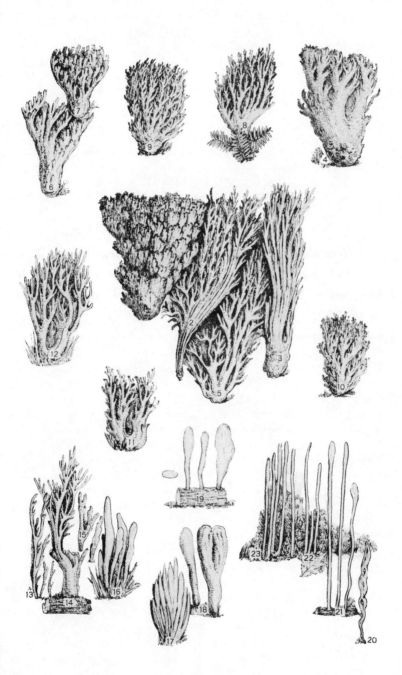

PLATE 7

PLATE 8

POLYPORACEAE

1 *Polyporus arcularius*, 2 *P. brumalis*, 3 *P. cristatus*, 4 *P. Berkeleyi*, 5 *P. graveolens* (x 1/4), 6 *P. radicatus*, 7 *P. Tsugae*, 8 *P. lucidus*, 9 *P. Curtisii*, 10 *P. umbellatus*, 11 *P. picipes*, 12 *P. perennis*, 13 *P. cinnamomeus*, 14 *P. conchifer*, 15 *P. versicolor*, 16 *P. Schweinitzii* (x 1/10), 17 *P. betulinus*, 18 *P. squamosus*.

19 *Cyclomyces Greenii*.

20 *Polyporus sulphureus* (x 1/10), 21 *P. gilvus*, 22 *P. cinnabarinus*.

PLATE 8

PLATE 9

POLYPORACEAE
EACH ABOUT ONE-FOURTH NATURAL SIZE UNLESS OTHERWISE MARKED

1 *Polyporus dichrous,* 2 *P. crispus,* 3 *P. abietinus,* 4 *P. amorphus,* 5 *P. pergamenus,* 6 *P. fragilis,* 7 *P. guttulatus,* 8 *P. borealis,* 9 *P. fibrillosus,* 10 *P. volvatus* (lateral view), 11 *P. volvatus* (lengthwise section), 12 *P. alboluteus,* 13 *P. chioneus,* 14 *P. albellus,* 15 *P. tephroleucus,* 16 *P. caesius,* 17 *P. croceus,* 18 *P. sanguineus.*

19 *Fomes applanatus* (x 1/8).

20 *Polyporus hirsutus,* 21 *P. frondosus* (x 1/5), 22 *P. humilis.*

PLATE 9

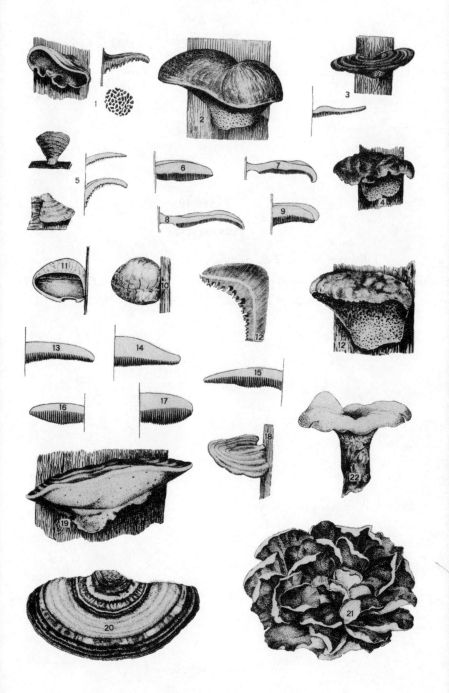

PLATE 10

POLYPORACEAE

1 *Boletinus porosus,* 2 *B. spectabilis.*

3 *Boletus sphaerosporus,* 4 *B. americanus,* 5 *B. luteus,* 6 *B. scaber,* 7 *B. Russelli,* 8 *B. edulis,* 9 *B. felleus.*

PLATE 10

PLATE 11

POLYPORACEAE

1 *Favolus canadensis.*

2 *Polyporus circinatus.*

3 *Fistulina hepatica.*

4 *Boletus granulatus,* 5 *B. versipellis.*

6 *Daedalea unicolor* (under side).

7 *Boletinus pictus.*

8 *Daedalea confragosa,* 9 *D. quercina* (section, upper and underside).

10 *Lenzites saepiaria* (under and upper side).

11 *Fomes applanatus* (section), 12 *F. fomentarius* (section).

13 *Trametes Peckii* (section).

14 *Boletus subtomentosus,* 15 *B. cyanescens.*

PLATE 11

Plate 12

Key to the Agaricaceae

1–4 General types of gilled mushrooms: the variations of that in fig. 1 are shown in fig. 5–9, variations of that in fig. 2 are shown in fig. 10–12, variations of that in fig. 3 are shown in fig. 13–15, and variations of that in fig. 4 are shown in fig. 17–19.   Each of fig. 5–19 represents one or more genera which differ from one another in color of spores as indicated below by the following symbols: (b) black, (p) purple or purple-brown, (r) red, (w) white, (y) yellow or yellow-brown.

   5 *Amanita* (w).

   6 *Lepiota* (w), *Agaricus* (p), *Coprinus* (b).

   7 *Amanitopsis* (w), *Volvaria* (r).

   8 *Pluteus* (r), *Bolbitius* (y).

   9 *Coprinus* (b).

  10 *Armillaria* (w), *Cortinarius* (y), *Stropharia* (p), *Annellaria* (b).

  11 *Tricholoma* (w), *Russula* (w, y), *Lactarius* (w, y), *Hygrophorus* (w), *Entoloma* (r), *Hebeloma* (y), *Hypholoma* (p).

  12 *Panaeolus* (b).

  13 *Clitocybe* (w), *Clitopilus* (r), *Paxillus* (y), *Gomphidius* (b), *Hygrophorus* (w), *Russula* (w, y), *Lactarius* (w, y), *Flammula* (y), *Cantharellus* (w).

  14 *Pholiota* (y).

  15 *Inocybe* (y).

  16 *Pleurotus* (w), *Schizophyllum* (w), *Panus* (w), *Crepidotus* (y), *Claudopus* (r).

  17 *Collybia* (w), *Leptonia* (r), *Psilocybe* (p), *Marasmius* (w), *Naucoria* (y).

  18 *Mycena* (w), *Nolanea* (r), *Galera* (y), *Pluteolus* (y), *Psathyra* (p), *Psathyrella* (b).

  19 *Omphalia* (w), *Eccilia* (r), *Tubaria* (y), *Deconica* (p).

PLATE 12

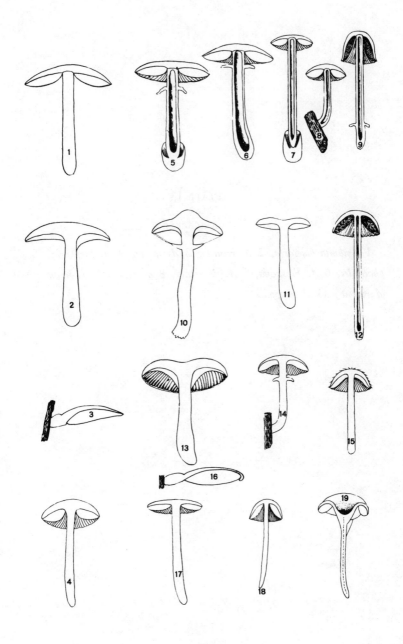

PLATE 13

AGARICACEAE

1 *Amanita Caesarea,* 2 *A. recutita,* 3 *A. spreta,* 4 *A. porphyria,* 5 *A. phalloides,* 6 *A. Frostiana,* 7 *A. flavoconia,* 8 *A. verna,* 9 *A. gemmata,* 10 *A. virosa,* 11 *A. mappa.*

PLATE 13

AGARICACEAE

PLATE 14

12 *Amanita rubescens*, 13 *A. flavorubescens*, 14 *A. muscaria*, 15 *A. chlorinosma*, 16 *A. spissa*, 17 *A. strobiliformis*, 18 *A. solitaria*, 19 *A. abrupta*.

20 *Amanitopsis agglutinata*, 21 *A. vaginata*, 22 *A. strangulata*.

PLATE 14

PLATE 15

PLATE 16

AGARICACEAE

1 *Clitocybe decora*, 2 *C. odora*, 3 *C. albidula*, 4 *C. albissima*, 5 *C. truncicola*, 6 *C. cerrusata*, 7 *C. pithophila*, 8 *C. dealbata*, 9 *C. candicans*, 10 *C. monadelphia*, 11 *C. patuloides*, 12 *C. catina*, 13 *C. illudens*, 14 *C. multiceps*, 15 *C. sinopica*, 16 *C. sinopicoides*.

PLATE 16

PLATE 17

PLATE 18

AGARICACEAE

1 *Tricholoma equestre*, 2 *T. sejunctum*, 3 *T. portentosum*, 4 *T. terriferum*, 5 *T. transmutans*, 6 *T. ustale*, 7 *T. resplendens*, 8 *T. columbetta*, 9 *T. grande*, 10 *T. sulphureum*, 11 *T. chysenteroides*, 12 *T. fallax*.

PLATE 18

PLATE 19

AGARICACEAE

13 *Tricholoma unifactum,* 14 *T. album,* 15 *T. nobile,* 16 *T. laterarium,* 17 *T. grave,* 18 *T. acerbum,* 19 *T. leucocephalum,* 20 *T. fumosiluteum,* 21 *T. panaeolum* var. *caespitosum,* 22 *T. melaleucum,* 23 *T. brevipes,* 24 *T. sordidum.*

PLATE 19

PLATE 20

AGARICACEAE

25 *Tricholoma imbricatum*, 26 *T. sculpturatum*, 27 *T. rutilans*, 28 *T. acre*, 29 *T. fumescens*, 30 *T. subacutum*, 31 *T. saponaceum*, 32 *T. fuligineum*, 33 *T. terreum*, 34 *T. carneum*, 35 *T. panaeolum*, 36 *T. infantile*, 37 *T. personatum*, 38 *T. nudum*, 39 *T. ionides*, 40 *T. cinerascens*.

PLATE 20

PLATE 21

PLATE 22

AGARICACEAE

16 *Russula sororia*, 17 *R. obscura*, 18 *R. tenuiceps*, 19 *R. crustosa*, 20
R. sphagnophylla, 21 *R. foetentula*, 22 *R. chamaeleontina*, 23 *R. foetens*,
24 *R. uncialis*, 25 *R. pulverulenta*, 26 *R. albidula*, 27 *R. palustris*, 28
R. sanguinea, 29 *R. compacta*, 30 *R. subpunctata*, 31 *R. virescens*.

PLATE 22

PLATE 23

AGARICACEAE

1 *Lactarius torminosus*, 2 *L. vellerius*, 3 *L. scrobiculatus*, 4 *L. deceptivus*, 5 *L. insulsus*, 6 *L. cilicioides*, 7 *L. hysginus*, 8 *L. vietus*, 9 *L. trivialis*, 10 *L. affinis*.

PLATE 23

11 *Lactarius oculatus*, 12 *L. cinereus*, 13 *L. rufus*, 14 *L. volemus*, 15 *L. corrugis*, 16 *L. helvus*, 17 *L. camphoratus*, 18 *L. subdulcis*, 19 *L. hygrophoroides*, 20 *L. griseus*, 21 *L. piperatus*.

PLATE 24

Plate 25

Agaricaceae

1 *Lactarius atroviridis*, 2 *L. croceus*, 3 *L. turpis*, 4 *L. lignyotus*, 5 *L. fuliginosus*, 6 *L. subpurpureus*, 7 *L. deliciosus*, 8 *L. indigo*.

PLATE 25

PLATE 26

AGARICACEAE

1 *Hygrophorus eburneus*, 2 *H. speciosus*, 3 *H. Russula*, 4 *H. Laurae*, 5 *H. olivaceoalbus*, 6 *H. pratensis*, 7 *H. flavodiscus*, 8 *H. pudorinus*, 9 *H. miniatus*, 10 *H. sordidus*.

PLATE 26

PLATE 27

AGARICACEAE

11 *Hygrophorus puniceus*, 12 *H. ceraceus*, 13 *H. chlorophanus*, 14 *H. virgineus*, 15 *H. borealis*, 16 *H. niveus*, 17 *H. nitidus*, 18 *H. laetus*, 19 *H. Peckii*, 20 *H. conicus*, 21 *H. marginatus*, 22 *H. psitticinus*.

Plate 27

PLATE 28

AGARICACEAE

1 *Collybia velutipes*, 2 *C. succosa*, 3 *C. floccipes*, 4 *C. tuberosa*, 5 *C. conigenoides*, 6 *C. hariolorum*, 7 *C. confluens*, 8 *C. stipitaria*, 9 *C. zonata*, 10 *C. abundans*, 11 *C. succinea*, 12 *C. butyracea*, 13 *C. radicata*, 14 *C. platyphylla*, 15 *C. albiflavida*, 16 *C. myriadophylla*, 17 *C. dryophylla*, 18 *C. expallens*, 19 *C. plexipes*, 20 *C. strictipes*, 21 *C. familia*, 22 *C. acervata*, 23 *C. hygrophoroides*, 24 *C. atrata*.

Plate 28

PLATE 29

AGARICACEAE

1 *Mycena leajana*, 2 *M. epipterygia*, 3 *M. vulgaris*, 4 *M. clavicularis*, 5 *M. pelianthina*, 6 *M. rosella*, 7 *M. haematopa*, 8 *M. sanguineolenta*, 9 *M. immaculata*, 10 *M. corticola*, 11 *M. setosa*, 12 *M. minutula*, 13 *M. galericulata*, 14 *M. polygramma*, 15 *M. praelonga*, 16 *M. leptocephala*, 17 *M. parabolica*, 18 *M. subcaerulea* form *cyanobasis*, 19 *M. alcalina*, 20 *M. ammoniaca*, 21 *M. pulcherrima*, 22 *M. acicula*, 23 *M. collariata*, 24 *M. subcaerulea* form *cyanothrix*.

PLATE 29

PLATE 30

AGARICACEAE

1 *Marasmius urens*, 2 *M. peronatus*, 3 *M. fagineus*, 4 *M. glabellus*, 5 *M. delectans*, 6 *M. semihirtipes*, 7 *M. prasiosmus*, 8 *M. velutipes*, 9 *M. resinosus*, 10 *M. erythropus*, 11 *M. scorodonius*, 12 *M. Olneyi*, 13 *M. oreades*, 14 *M. cohaerens*, 15 *M. rotula*, 16 *M. gramineum*, 17 *M. papillatus*, 18 *M. siccus*, 19 *M. felix*, 20 *M. androsaceus*, 21 *M. capillaris*, 22 *M. epiphyllus*.

PLATE 30

Plate 31

Agaricaceae

1 *Volvaria bombycina*, 2 *V. volvacea*.

3 *Pholiota praecox*.

4 *Pluteus tomentulosus*, 5 *P. cervinus*.

6 *Volvaria speciosa*.

7 *Pluteus caloceps*, 8 *P. longistriatus*, 9 *P. salicinus*, 10 *P. nanus*, 11 *P. granularis*, 12 *P. umbrosus*.

PLATE 31

PLATE 32

AGARICACEAE

13 *Pluteus leoninus*.

14 *Leptonia asprella*, 15 *L. serrulata*, 16 *L. euchroa*, 17 *L. formosa*, 18 *L. placida*, 19 *L. seticeps*, 20 *L. incana*, 21 *L. lampropoda*, 22 *L. rosea*.

23 *Nolanea caelestina* var. *violacea*, 24 *N. conica*, 25 *N. versatilis*, 26 *N. mammosa*, 27 *N. pascua*.

28 *Omphalia stellata*, 29 *O. gracillima*, 30 *O. campanella*, 31 *O. fibula*, 32 *O. rustica*, 33 *O. Gerardiana*, 34 *O. fibuloides*, 35 *O. epichysium*.

PLATE 32

1 *Cantharellus cibarius.*

2 *Nyctalis asterophora*, growing on *Russula nigricans.*

3 *Cantharellus lutescens,* 4 *C. cinnabarinus,* 5 *C. umbonatus,* 6 *C. aurantiacus,* 7 *C. infundibuliformis,* 8 *C. rosellus,* 9 *C. floccosus,* 10 *C. tubaeformis,* 11 *C. clavatus.*

12 *Paxillus involutus,* 13 *P. rhodoxanthus.*

PLATE 33

Plate 34

Agaricaceae

1 *Pleurotus lignatilis*, 2 *P. petaloides*, 3 *P. sapidus*, 4 *P. ulmarius*, 5 *P. ostreatus*.

6 *Crepidotus dorsalis*.

7 *Claudopus nidulans*.

8 *Naucoria centuncula*, 9 *N. semiorbicularis*, 10 *N. pediades*.

11 *Schizophyllum commune*.

12 *Lentinus lepideus*.

PLATE 34

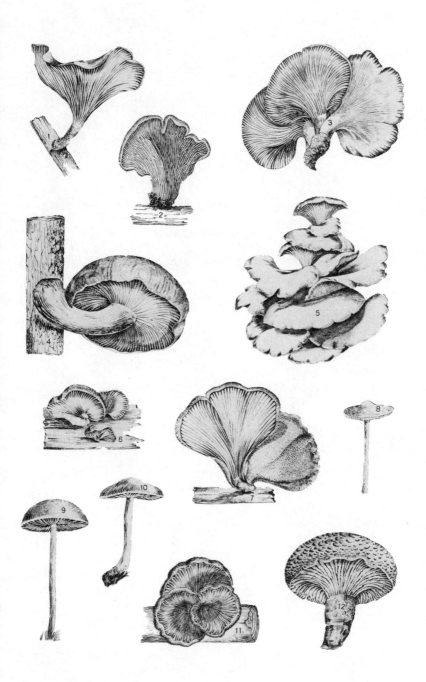

PLATE 35

AGARICACEAE

1 *Entoloma jubatum*, 2 *E. cyaneum*, 3 *E. sericeum*, 4 *E. sericellum*, 5 *E. sericatum*, 6 *E. clypeatum*, 7 *E. griseum*, 8 *E. speculum*, 9 *E. Grayanum*, 10 *E. strictius*, 11 *E. rhodopolium*.

PLATE 35

PLATE 36

PLATE 37

AGARICACEAE

1 *Hebeloma fastibile*, 2 *H. mesophaeum*, 3 *H. pascuense*, 4 *H. crustulini-forme* form *sphagnophilum*, 5 *H. sinapizans*, 6 *H. gregarium*, 7 *H. album*, 8 *H. longicaudum*, 9 *H. crustuliniforme*, 10 *H. albidulum*, 11 *H. colvinii*, 12 *H. sociale*.

Plate 37

PLATE 38

AGARICACEAE

1 *Pholiota flammans*, 2 *P. erinaceella*, 3 *P. adiposa*, 4 *P. confragosa*, 5 *P. fulvosquamosa*, 6 *P. squarrosoides*, 7 *P. albocrenulata*, 8 *P. destruens*, 9 *P. lucifera*, 10 *P. aeruginosa*, 11 *P. unicolor*, 12 *P. discolor*, 13 *P. marginata*.

14 *Flammula alnicola*.

15 *Pholiota muricata*, 16 *P. luteofolia*, 17 *P. spectabilis*.

PLATE 38

PLATE 39

AGARICACEAE

1 *Pholiota mycenoides*, 2 *P. rugosa*, 3 *P. aggericola*, 4 *P. Howeana*, 5 *P. praecox*, 6 *P. dura*, 7 *P. acericola*.

8 *Flammula spumosa*.

9 *Pholiota aegerita*, 10 *P. ptemnophylla*, 11 *P. caperata*, 12 *P. curvipes*.

13 *Flammula sapinea*.

PLATE 39

PLATE 40

AGARICACEAE

1 *Inocybe caesariata*, 2 *I. leptophylla*, 3 *I. calospora*, 4 *I. infelix*, 5 *I. lacera*, 6 *I. pyriodora*, 7 *I. rimosa*, 8 *I. fastigata*, 9 *I. Curreyi*, 10 *I. Cookei*, 11 *I. eutheloides*, 12 *I. fibrosa*, 13 *I. albodisca*, 14 *I. geophylla*, 15 *I. scabella*, 16 *I. trechispora*, 17 *I. asterospora*.

PLATE 40

PLATE 41

AGARICACEAE

1 *Cortinarius mucifluus*, 2 *C. cylindripes*, 3 *C. vibratilis*, 4 *C. heliotrop-icus*, 5 *C. iodes*, 6 *C. iodeoides*, 7 *C. michiganensis*, 8 *C. Atkinsonianus*, 9 *C. rubens*, 10 *C. corrugatus*, 11 *C. coloratus*, 12 *C. purpurascens*, 13 *C. claricolor*.

PLATE 41

1 *Galera cyanopes*, 2 *G. Hypnorum*, 3 *G. antipus*, 4 *G. bulbifera*, 5 *G. pubescens*, 6 *G. lateritia*, 7 *G. tenera*, 8 *G. crispa*, 9 *G. teneroides*.
10 *Bolbitius vitellinus*, 11 *B. fragilis*, 12 *B. tener*.
13 *Pluteolus coprophilus*, 14 *P. aleuriatus* var. *gracilis*, 15 *P. expansus*.

PLATE 42

PLATE 43

AGARICACEAE

14 *Cortinarius alboviolaceus*, 15 *C. flavifolius*, 16 *C. subpulchrifolius*, 17 *C. annulatus*, 18 *C. violaceus*, 19 *C. autumnalis*, 20 *C. cinnamomeus*, 21 *C. croceofolius*, 22 *C. gracilis*, 23 *C. caninus*, 24 *C. nigrellus*, 25 *C. semisanguineus*, 26 *C. flexipes*.

PLATE 43

PLATE 44

AGARICACEAE

1 *Agaricus arvensis*, 2 *A. campestris*, 3 *A. subrufescens*, 4 *A. micro-megatha*, 5 *A. Rodmanii*, 6 *A. haemorrhoidaria*, 7 *A. abruptibulba*, 8 *A. placomyces*, 9 *A. comptula*, 10 *A. diminutiva*.

PLATE 44

PLATE 45

AGARICACEAE

11 *Stropharia stercoraria*, 12 *S. semiglobata*, 13 *S. stercoraria*, 14 *S. aeruginosa*, 15 *S. epimyces*, 16 *S. bilamellata*, 17 *S. albonitens*.

18 *Hypholoma velutinum*, 19 *H. appendiculatum*, 20 *H. lachrymabundum*, 21 *H. sublateritium*, 22 *H. hydrophillum*, 23 *H. incertum*.

PLATE 45

PLATE 46

AGARICACEAE

1 *Psilocybe arenulina*, 2 *P. caerulipes*, 3 *P. connissans*, 4 *P. spadicea*, 5 *P. atrobrunnea*, 6 *P. murcida*, 7 *P. fuscofolia*, 8 *P. camptopoda*, 9 *P. foenisecii*, 10 *P. cernua*, 11 *P. larga*, 12 *P. fuscofulva*, 13 *P. canofaciens*, 14 *P. uda*.

15 *Deconica merdaria*, 16 *D. atrorufa*.

17 *Psathyra obtusata*, 18 *P. umbonata*, 19 *P. persimplex*, 20 *P. semivestita*, 21 *P. vestita*, 22 *P. conica*.

PLATE 46

PLATE 47

Plate 48

Gasteromycetes

1 *Mutinus caninus*, 2 *M. elegans*, 3 *M. elegans* (section of a young plant).

4 *Phallus impudicus*, 5 *P. impudicus* (lengthwise section of a young plant).

6 *Anthurus borealis*.

7 *Catastoma circumscissum*.

8 *Tylostoma campestre*.

9, 10 *Secotium acuminatum*.

11 *Cyathus striatus*.

12 *Calostoma cinnabarinum*.

13 *Calvatia saccata*.

14 *Geaster floriformis*.

15 *Astreaeus hygrometricus*.

16 *Myriostoma coliformis*.

17 *Bovistella radicata*.

18 *Calvatia craniformis*.

19 *Pisolithus tinctorius*.

20 *Lycoperdon pulcherrimum*.

21 *Scleroderma aurantium*, 22 *S. aurantium* (section).

23 *Lycoperdon pyriforme*.

24 *Geaster triplex*.

25 *Lycogala epidendron*.

PLATE 48

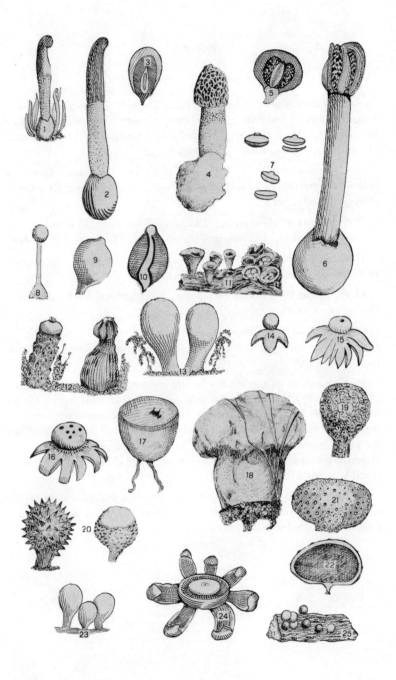

PLATE 49

ILLUSTRATED GLOSSARY

1-17 Shapes of pilei: 1 hemispherical, 2 ovoid, 3 conical, 4 convex, 5 campanulate, 6 umbonate, 7 umbilicate, 8 infundibuliform, 9 turbinate, 10 tubiform, 11 dimidiate, 12 flabellate, 13 reflexed, 14 resupinate, 15 applanate, 16 ungulate, 17 spathulate.

18-42 Shapes of gills: 18 free, 19 emarginate, 20 adnate, 21 receding, 22 decurrent, 23 adnexed, 24 uncinate, 25 ascending, 26 anastomosing, 27 bifurcate.

28-36 Shapes of gill-margins: 28 entire, 29 serrate, 30 serrulate, 31 dentate, 32 crenate, 33 crenulate, 34 undulate, 35 sinuate, 36 eroded.

37-42 Shapes of ends of gills: 37 acuminate, 38 acute, 39 obtuse, 40 rounded, 41 mucronate, 42 cuspidate.

43-47 Shapes of stipes: 43 attenuate, 44 cylindrical, 45 ventricose, 46 clavate, 47 with an abrupt bulb.

48-53 A cup-fungus showing: the apothecium (48), asci (51), a portion of the stipe (49), and (52) a spore-containing ascus (53), with paraphyses (50).

54-47 Growth of a gilled mushroom showing the very young plant (54) surrounded by the universal veil, which breaks (55) as the mushroom expands upward and forms patches on the pileus above and becomes the volva below (56, 57); the partial veil below and extending across the young pileus (in figures 55, 56) breaks as the pileus enlarges and becomes the annulus in the mature mushroom (57). Here it hangs skirt-like around the stipe.

58 Longitudinal section of a puff-ball, the gleba and columella at the base, the capillitium in the center, and the three-layered peridium surrounding the whole.

PLATE 49

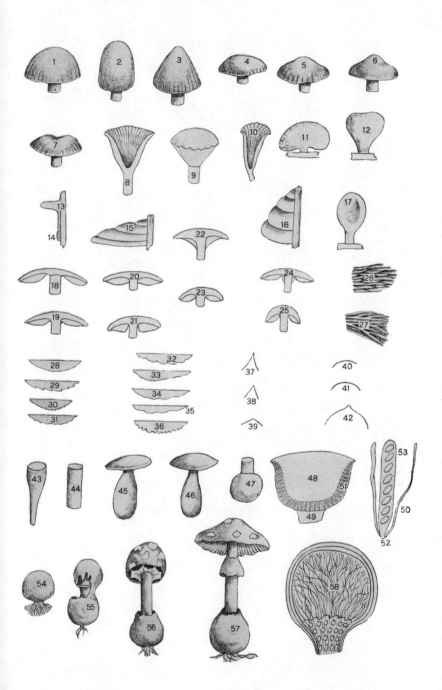

A CATALOGUE OF SELECTED DOVER BOOKS
IN ALL FIELDS OF INTEREST

A CATALOGUE OF SELECTED DOVER BOOKS
IN ALL FIELDS OF INTEREST

AMERICA'S OLD MASTERS, James T. Flexner. Four men emerged unexpectedly from provincial 18th century America to leadership in European art: Benjamin West, J. S. Copley, C. R. Peale, Gilbert Stuart. Brilliant coverage of lives and contributions. Revised, 1967 edition. 69 plates. 365pp. of text.

21806-6 Paperbound $3.00

FIRST FLOWERS OF OUR WILDERNESS: AMERICAN PAINTING, THE COLONIAL PERIOD, James T. Flexner. Painters, and regional painting traditions from earliest Colonial times up to the emergence of Copley, West and Peale Sr., Foster, Gustavus Hesselius, Feke, John Smibert and many anonymous painters in the primitive manner. Engaging presentation, with 162 illustrations. xxii + 368pp.

22180-6 Paperbound $3.50

THE LIGHT OF DISTANT SKIES: AMERICAN PAINTING, 1760-1835, James T. Flexner. The great generation of early American painters goes to Europe to learn and to teach: West, Copley, Gilbert Stuart and others. Allston, Trumbull, Morse; also contemporary American painters—primitives, derivatives, academics—who remained in America. 102 illustrations. xiii + 306pp. 22179-2 Paperbound $3.00

A HISTORY OF THE RISE AND PROGRESS OF THE ARTS OF DESIGN IN THE UNITED STATES, William Dunlap. Much the richest mine of information on early American painters, sculptors, architects, engravers, miniaturists, etc. The only source of information for scores of artists, the major primary source for many others. Unabridged reprint of rare original 1834 edition, with new introduction by James T. Flexner, and 394 new illustrations. Edited by Rita Weiss. 6⅝ x 9⅝.

21695-0, 21696-9, 21697-7 Three volumes, Paperbound $13.50

EPOCHS OF CHINESE AND JAPANESE ART, Ernest F. Fenollosa. From primitive Chinese art to the 20th century, thorough history, explanation of every important art period and form, including Japanese woodcuts; main stress on China and Japan, but Tibet, Korea also included. Still unexcelled for its detailed, rich coverage of cultural background, aesthetic elements, diffusion studies, particularly of the historical period. 2nd, 1913 edition. 242 illustrations. lii + 439pp. of text.

20364-6, 20365-4 Two volumes, Paperbound $6.00

THE GENTLE ART OF MAKING ENEMIES, James A. M. Whistler. Greatest wit of his day deflates Oscar Wilde, Ruskin, Swinburne; strikes back at inane critics, exhibitions, art journalism; aesthetics of impressionist revolution in most striking form. Highly readable classic by great painter. Reproduction of edition designed by Whistler. Introduction by Alfred Werner. xxxvi + 334pp.

21875-9 Paperbound $2.50

POEMS OF ANNE BRADSTREET, edited with an introduction by Robert Hutchinson. A new selection of poems by America's first poet and perhaps the first significant woman poet in the English language. 48 poems display her development in works of considerable variety—love poems, domestic poems, religious meditations, formal elegies, "quaternions," etc. Notes, bibliography. viii + 222pp.
22160-1 Paperbound $2.00

THREE GOTHIC NOVELS: THE CASTLE OF OTRANTO BY HORACE WALPOLE; VATHEK BY WILLIAM BECKFORD; THE VAMPYRE BY JOHN POLIDORI, WITH FRAGMENT OF A NOVEL BY LORD BYRON, edited by E. F. Bleiler. The first Gothic novel, by Walpole; the finest Oriental tale in English, by Beckford; powerful Romantic supernatural story in versions by Polidori and Byron. All extremely important in history of literature; all still exciting, packed with supernatural thrills, ghosts, haunted castles, magic, etc. xl + 291pp.
21232-7 Paperbound $2.00

THE BEST TALES OF HOFFMANN, E. T. A. Hoffmann. 10 of Hoffmann's most important stories, in modern re-editings of standard translations: Nutcracker and the King of Mice, Signor Formica, Automata, The Sandman, Rath Krespel, The Golden Flowerpot, Master Martin the Cooper, The Mines of Falun, The King's Betrothed, A New Year's Eve Adventure. 7 illustrations by Hoffmann. Edited by E. F. Bleiler. xxxix + 419pp.
21793-0 Paperbound $2.50

GHOST AND HORROR STORIES OF AMBROSE BIERCE, Ambrose Bierce. 23 strikingly modern stories of the horrors latent in the human mind: The Eyes of the Panther, The Damned Thing, An Occurrence at Owl Creek Bridge, An Inhabitant of Carcosa, etc., plus the dream-essay, Visions of the Night. Edited by E. F. Bleiler. xxii + 199pp.
20767-6 Paperbound $1.50

BEST GHOST STORIES OF J. S. LeFANU, J. Sheridan LeFanu. Finest stories by Victorian master often considered greatest supernatural writer of all. Carmilla, Green Tea, The Haunted Baronet, The Familiar, and 12 others. Most never before available in the U. S. A. Edited by E. F. Bleiler. 8 illustrations from Victorian publications. xvii + 467pp.
20415-4 Paperbound $3.00

THE TIME STREAM, THE GREATEST ADVENTURE, AND THE PURPLE SAPPHIRE— THREE SCIENCE FICTION NOVELS, John Taine (Eric Temple Bell). Great American mathematician was also foremost science fiction novelist of the 1920's. *The Time Stream,* one of all-time classics, uses concepts of circular time; *The Greatest Adventure,* incredibly ancient biological experiments from Antarctica threaten to escape; The *Purple Sapphire,* superscience, lost races in Central Tibet, survivors of the Great Race. 4 illustrations by Frank R. Paul. v + 532pp.
21180-0 Paperbound $3.00

SEVEN SCIENCE FICTION NOVELS, H. G. Wells. The standard collection of the great novels. Complete, unabridged. *First Men in the Moon, Island of Dr. Moreau, War of the Worlds, Food of the Gods, Invisible Man, Time Machine, In the Days of the Comet.* Not only science fiction fans, but every educated person owes it to himself to read these novels. 1015pp.
20264-X Clothbound $5.00

EAST O' THE SUN AND WEST O' THE MOON, George W. Dasent. Considered the best of all translations of these Norwegian folk tales, this collection has been enjoyed by generations of children (and folklorists too). Includes True and Untrue, Why the Sea is Salt, East O' the Sun and West O' the Moon, Why the Bear is Stumpy-Tailed, Boots and the Troll, The Cock and the Hen, Rich Peter the Pedlar, and 52 more. The only edition with all 59 tales. 77 illustrations by Erik Werenskiold and Theodor Kittelsen. xv + 418pp. 22521-6 Paperbound $3.00

GOOPS AND HOW TO BE THEM, Gelett Burgess. Classic of tongue-in-cheek humor, masquerading as etiquette book. 87 verses, twice as many cartoons, show mischievous Goops as they demonstrate to children virtues of table manners, neatness, courtesy, etc. Favorite for generations. viii + 88pp. 6½ x 9¼. 22233-0 Paperbound $1.25

ALICE'S ADVENTURES UNDER GROUND, Lewis Carroll. The first version, quite different from the final *Alice in Wonderland,* printed out by Carroll himself with his own illustrations. Complete facsimile of the "million dollar" manuscript Carroll gave to Alice Liddell in 1864. Introduction by Martin Gardner. viii + 96pp. Title and dedication pages in color. 21482-6 Paperbound $1.25

THE BROWNIES, THEIR BOOK, Palmer Cox. Small as mice, cunning as foxes, exuberant and full of mischief, the Brownies go to the zoo, toy shop, seashore, circus, etc., in 24 verse adventures and 266 illustrations. Long a favorite, since their first appearance in St. Nicholas Magazine. xi + 144pp. 6⅝ x 9¼. 21265-3 Paperbound $1.75

SONGS OF CHILDHOOD, Walter De La Mare. Published (under the pseudonym Walter Ramal) when De La Mare was only 29, this charming collection has long been a favorite children's book. A facsimile of the first edition in paper, the 47 poems capture the simplicity of the nursery rhyme and the ballad, including such lyrics as I Met Eve, Tartary, The Silver Penny. vii + 106pp. 21972-0 Paperbound $1.25

THE COMPLETE NONSENSE OF EDWARD LEAR, Edward Lear. The finest 19th-century humorist-cartoonist in full: all nonsense limericks, zany alphabets, Owl and Pussycat, songs, nonsense botany, and more than 500 illustrations by Lear himself. Edited by Holbrook Jackson. xxix + 287pp. (USO) 20167-8 Paperbound $2.00

BILLY WHISKERS: THE AUTOBIOGRAPHY OF A GOAT, Frances Trego Montgomery. A favorite of children since the early 20th century, here are the escapades of that rambunctious, irresistible and mischievous goat—Billy Whiskers. Much in the spirit of *Peck's Bad Boy,* this is a book that children never tire of reading or hearing. All the original familiar illustrations by W. H. Fry are included: 6 color plates, 18 black and white drawings. 159pp. 22345-0 Paperbound $2.00

MOTHER GOOSE MELODIES. Faithful republication of the fabulously rare Munroe and Francis "copyright 1833" Boston edition—the most important Mother Goose collection, usually referred to as the "original." Familiar rhymes plus many rare ones, with wonderful old woodcut illustrations. Edited by E. F. Bleiler. 128pp. 4½ x 6⅜. 22577-1 Paperbound $1.25

AGAINST THE GRAIN (A REBOURS), Joris K. Huysmans. Filled with weird images, evidences of a bizarre imagination, exotic experiments with hallucinatory drugs, rich tastes and smells and the diversions of its sybarite hero Duc Jean des Esseintes, this classic novel pushed 19th-century literary decadence to its limits. Full unabridged edition. Do not confuse this with abridged editions generally sold. Introduction by Havelock Ellis. xlix + 206pp.   22190-3 Paperbound '$2.00

VARIORUM SHAKESPEARE: HAMLET. Edited by Horace H. Furness; a landmark of American scholarship. Exhaustive footnotes and appendices treat all doubtful words and phrases, as well as suggested critical emendations throughout the play's history. First volume contains editor's own text, collated with all Quartos and Folios. Second volume contains full first Quarto, translations of Shakespeare's sources (Belleforest, and Saxo Grammaticus), Der Bestrafte Brudermord, and many essays on critical and historical points of interest by major authorities of past and present. Includes details of staging and costuming over the years. By far the best edition available for serious students of Shakespeare. Total of xx + 905pp.
21004-9, 21005-7, 2 volumes, Paperbound $7.00

A LIFE OF WILLIAM SHAKESPEARE, Sir Sidney Lee. This is the standard life of Shakespeare, summarizing everything known about Shakespeare and his plays. Incredibly rich in material, broad in coverage, clear and judicious, it has served thousands as the best introduction to Shakespeare. 1931 edition. 9 plates. xxix + 792pp.   (USO) 21967-4 Paperbound $3.75

MASTERS OF THE DRAMA, John Gassner. Most comprehensive history of the drama in print, covering every tradition from Greeks to modern Europe and America, including India, Far East, etc. Covers more than 800 dramatists, 2000 plays, with biographical material, plot summaries, theatre history, criticism, etc. "Best of its kind in English," *New Republic.* 77 illustrations. xxii + 890pp.
20100-7 Clothbound $8.50

THE EVOLUTION OF THE ENGLISH LANGUAGE, George McKnight. The growth of English, from the 14th century to the present. Unusual, non-technical account presents basic information in very interesting form: sound shifts, change in grammar and syntax, vocabulary growth, similar topics. Abundantly illustrated with quotations. Formerly *Modern English in the Making.* xii + 590pp.
21932-1 Paperbound $3.50

AN ETYMOLOGICAL DICTIONARY OF MODERN ENGLISH, Ernest Weekley. Fullest, richest work of its sort, by foremost British lexicographer. Detailed word histories, including many colloquial and archaic words; extensive quotations. Do not confuse this with the Concise Etymological Dictionary, which is much abridged. Total of xxvii + 830pp. 6½ x 9¼.
21873-2, 21874-0 Two volumes, Paperbound $6.00

FLATLAND: A ROMANCE OF MANY DIMENSIONS, E. A. Abbott. Classic of science-fiction explores ramifications of life in a two-dimensional world, and what happens when a three-dimensional being intrudes. Amusing reading, but also useful as introduction to thought about hyperspace. Introduction by Banesh Hoffmann. 16 illustrations. xx + 103pp.   20001-9 Paperbound $1.00

THE RED FAIRY BOOK, Andrew Lang. Lang's color fairy books have long been children's favorites. This volume includes Rapunzel, Jack and the Bean-stalk and 35 other stories, familiar and unfamiliar. 4 plates, 93 illustrations x + 367pp.
21673-X Paperbound $2.50

THE BLUE FAIRY BOOK, Andrew Lang. Lang's tales come from all countries and all times. Here are 37 tales from Grimm, the Arabian Nights, Greek Mythology, and other fascinating sources. 8 plates, 130 illustrations. xi + 390pp.
21437-0 Paperbound $2.50

HOUSEHOLD STORIES BY THE BROTHERS GRIMM. Classic English-language edition of the well-known tales — Rumpelstiltskin, Snow White, Hansel and Gretel, The Twelve Brothers, Faithful John, Rapunzel, Tom Thumb (52 stories in all). Translated into simple, straightforward English by Lucy Crane. Ornamented with headpieces, vignettes, elaborate decorative initials and a dozen full-page illustrations by Walter Crane. x + 269pp.
21080-4 Paperbound $2.50

THE MERRY ADVENTURES OF ROBIN HOOD, Howard Pyle. The finest modern versions of the traditional ballads and tales about the great English outlaw. Howard Pyle's complete prose version, with every word, every illustration of the first edition. Do not confuse this facsimile of the original (1883) with modern editions that change text or illustrations. 23 plates plus many page decorations. xxii + 296pp.
22043-5 Paperbound $2.50

THE STORY OF KING ARTHUR AND HIS KNIGHTS, Howard Pyle. The finest children's version of the life of King Arthur; brilliantly retold by Pyle, with 48 of his most imaginative illustrations. xviii + 313pp. 6⅛ x 9¼.
21445-1 Paperbound $2.50

THE WONDERFUL WIZARD OF OZ, L. Frank Baum. America's finest children's book in facsimile of first edition with all Denslow illustrations in full color. The edition a child should have. Introduction by Martin Gardner. 23 color plates, scores of drawings. iv + 267pp.
20691-2 Paperbound $2.25

THE MARVELOUS LAND OF OZ, L. Frank Baum. The second Oz book, every bit as imaginative as the Wizard. The hero is a boy named Tip, but the Scarecrow and the Tin Woodman are back, as is the Oz magic. 16 color plates, 120 drawings by John R. Neill. 287pp.
20692-0 Paperbound $2.50

THE MAGICAL MONARCH OF MO, L. Frank Baum. Remarkable adventures in a land even stranger than Oz. The best of Baum's books not in the Oz series. 15 color plates and dozens of drawings by Frank Verbeck. xviii + 237pp.
21892-9 Paperbound $2.00

THE BAD CHILD'S BOOK OF BEASTS, MORE BEASTS FOR WORSE CHILDREN, A MORAL ALPHABET, Hilaire Belloc. Three complete humor classics in one volume. Be kind to the frog, and do not call him names . . . and 28 other whimsical animals. Familiar favorites and some not so well known. Illustrated by Basil Blackwell. 156pp.
(USO) 20749-8 Paperbound $1.25

PLANETS, STARS AND GALAXIES: DESCRIPTIVE ASTRONOMY FOR BEGINNERS, A. E. Fanning. Comprehensive introductory survey of astronomy: the sun, solar system, stars, galaxies, universe, cosmology; up-to-date, including quasars, radio stars, etc. Preface by Prof. Donald Menzel. 24pp. of photographs. 189pp. 5¼ x 8¼.
21680-2 Paperbound $1.50

TEACH YOURSELF CALCULUS, P. Abbott. With a good background in algebra and trig, you can teach yourself calculus with this book. Simple, straightforward introduction to functions of all kinds, integration, differentiation, series, etc. "Students who are beginning to study calculus method will derive great help from this book." Faraday House Journal. 308pp.
20683-1 Clothbound $2.00

TEACH YOURSELF TRIGONOMETRY, P. Abbott. Geometrical foundations, indices and logarithms, ratios, angles, circular measure, etc. are presented in this sound, easy-to-use text. Excellent for the beginner or as a brush up, this text carries the student through the solution of triangles. 204pp.
20682-3 Clothbound $2.00

TEACH YOURSELF ANATOMY, David LeVay. Accurate, inclusive, profusely illustrated account of structure, skeleton, abdomen, muscles, nervous system, glands, brain, reproductive organs, evolution. "Quite the best and most readable account,' Medical Officer. 12 color plates. 164 figures. 311pp. 4¾ x 7.
21651-9 Clothbound $2.50

TEACH YOURSELF PHYSIOLOGY, David LeVay. Anatomical, biochemical bases; digestive, nervous, endocrine systems; metabolism; respiration; muscle; excretion; temperature control; reproduction. "Good elementary exposition," The Lancet. 6 color plates. 44 illustrations. 208pp. 4¼ x 7.
21658-6 Clothbound $2.50

THE FRIENDLY STARS, Martha Evans Martin. Classic has taught naked-eye observation of stars, planets to hundreds of thousands, still not surpassed for charm, lucidity, adequacy. Completely updated by Professor Donald H. Menzel, Harvard Observatory. 25 illustrations. 16 x 30 chart. x + 147pp.
21099-5 Paperbound $1.25

MUSIC OF THE SPHERES: THE MATERIAL UNIVERSE FROM ATOM TO QUASAR, SIMPLY EXPLAINED, Guy Murchie. Extremely broad, brilliantly written popular account begins with the solar system and reaches to dividing line between matter and nonmatter; latest understandings presented with exceptional clarity. Volume One: Planets, stars, galaxies, cosmology, geology, celestial mechanics, latest astronomical discoveries; Volume Two: Matter, atoms, waves, radiation, relativity, chemical action, heat, nuclear energy, quantum theory, music, light, color, probability, antimatter, antigravity, and similar topics. 319 figures. 1967 (second) edition. Total of xx + 644pp.
21809-0, 21810-4 Two volumes, Paperbound $5.00

OLD-TIME SCHOOLS AND SCHOOL BOOKS, Clifton Johnson. Illustrations and rhymes from early primers, abundant quotations from early textbooks, many anecdotes of school life enliven this study of elementary schools from Puritans to middle 19th century. Introduction by Carl Withers. 234 illustrations. xxxiii + 381pp.
21031-6 Paperbound $2.50

LAST AND FIRST MEN AND STAR MAKER, TWO SCIENCE FICTION NOVELS, Olaf Stapledon. Greatest future histories in science fiction. In the first, human intelligence is the "hero," through strange paths of evolution, interplanetary invasions, incredible technologies, near extinctions and reemergences. Star Maker describes the quest of a band of star rovers for intelligence itself, through time and space: weird inhuman civilizations, crustacean minds, symbiotic worlds, etc. Complete, unabridged. v + 438pp. 21962-3 Paperbound $2.50

THREE PROPHETIC NOVELS, H. G. WELLS. Stages of a consistently planned future for mankind. *When the Sleeper Wakes,* and *A Story of the Days to Come,* anticipate *Brave New World* and *1984,* in the 21st Century; *The Time Machine,* only complete version in print, shows farther future and the end of mankind. All show Wells's greatest gifts as storyteller and novelist. Edited by E. F. Bleiler. x + 335pp. (USO) 20605-X Paperbound $2.25

THE DEVIL'S DICTIONARY, Ambrose Bierce. America's own Oscar Wilde—Ambrose Bierce—offers his barbed iconoclastic wisdom in over 1,000 definitions hailed by H. L. Mencken as "some of the most gorgeous witticisms in the English language." 145pp. 20487-1 Paperbound $1.25

MAX AND MORITZ, Wilhelm Busch. Great children's classic, father of comic strip, of two bad boys, Max and Moritz. Also Ker and Plunk (Plisch und Plumm), Cat and Mouse, Deceitful Henry, Ice-Peter, The Boy and the Pipe, and five other pieces. Original German, with English translation. Edited by H. Arthur Klein; translations by various hands and H. Arthur Klein. vi + 216pp. 20181-3 Paperbound $2.00

PIGS IS PIGS AND OTHER FAVORITES, Ellis Parker Butler. The title story is one of the best humor short stories, as Mike Flannery obfuscates biology and English. Also included, That Pup of Murchison's, The Great American Pie Company, and Perkins of Portland. 14 illustrations. v + 109pp. 21532-6 Paperbound $1.00

THE PETERKIN PAPERS, Lucretia P. Hale. It takes genius to be as stupidly mad as the Peterkins, as they decide to become wise, celebrate the "Fourth," keep a cow, and otherwise strain the resources of the Lady from Philadelphia. Basic book of American humor. 153 illustrations. 219pp. 20794-3 Paperbound $1.50

PERRAULT'S FAIRY TALES, translated by A. E. Johnson and S. R. Littlewood, with 34 full-page illustrations by Gustave Doré. All the original Perrault stories—Cinderella, Sleeping Beauty, Bluebeard, Little Red Riding Hood, Puss in Boots, Tom Thumb, etc.—with their witty verse morals and the magnificent illustrations of Doré. One of the five or six great books of European fairy tales. viii + 117pp. 8⅛ x 11. 22311-6 Paperbound $2.00

OLD HUNGARIAN FAIRY TALES, Baroness Orczy. Favorites translated and adapted by author of the *Scarlet Pimpernel.* Eight fairy tales include "The Suitors of Princess Fire-Fly," "The Twin Hunchbacks," "Mr. Cuttlefish's Love Story," and "The Enchanted Cat." This little volume of magic and adventure will captivate children as it has for generations. 90 drawings by Montagu Barstow. 96pp. (USO) 22293-4 Paperbound $1.95

TWO LITTLE SAVAGES; BEING THE ADVENTURES OF TWO BOYS WHO LIVED AS INDIANS AND WHAT THEY LEARNED, Ernest Thompson Seton. Great classic of nature and boyhood provides a vast range of woodlore in most palatable form, a genuinely entertaining story. Two farm boys build a teepee in woods and live in it for a month, working out Indian solutions to living problems, star lore, birds and animals, plants, etc. 293 illustrations. vii + 286pp.

20985-7 Paperbound $2.50

PETER PIPER'S PRACTICAL PRINCIPLES OF PLAIN & PERFECT PRONUNCIATION. Alliterative jingles and tongue-twisters of surprising charm, that made their first appearance in America about 1830. Republished in full with the spirited woodcut illustrations from this earliest American edition. 32pp. $4\frac{1}{2}$ x $6\frac{3}{8}$.

22560-7 Paperbound $1.00

SCIENCE EXPERIMENTS AND AMUSEMENTS FOR CHILDREN, Charles Vivian. 73 easy experiments, requiring only materials found at home or easily available, such as candles, coins, steel wool, etc.; illustrate basic phenomena like vacuum, simple chemical reaction, etc. All safe. Modern, well-planned. Formerly *Science Games for Children*. 102 photos, numerous drawings. 96pp. $6\frac{1}{8}$ x $9\frac{1}{4}$.

21856-2 Paperbound $1.25

AN INTRODUCTION TO CHESS MOVES AND TACTICS SIMPLY EXPLAINED, Leonard Barden. Informal intermediate introduction, quite strong in explaining reasons for moves. Covers basic material, tactics, important openings, traps, positional play in middle game, end game. Attempts to isolate patterns and recurrent configurations. Formerly *Chess*. 58 figures. 102pp.   (USO) 21210-6 Paperbound $1.25

LASKER'S MANUAL OF CHESS, Dr. Emanuel Lasker. Lasker was not only one of the five great World Champions, he was also one of the ablest expositors, theorists, and analysts. In many ways, his Manual, permeated with his philosophy of battle, filled with keen insights, is one of the greatest works ever written on chess. Filled with analyzed games by the great players. A single-volume library that will profit almost any chess player, beginner or master. 308 diagrams. xli x 349pp.

20640-8 Paperbound $2.75

THE MASTER BOOK OF MATHEMATICAL RECREATIONS, Fred Schuh. In opinion of many the finest work ever prepared on mathematical puzzles, stunts, recreations; exhaustively thorough explanations of mathematics involved, analysis of effects, citation of puzzles and games. Mathematics involved is elementary. Translated by F. Göbel. 194 figures. xxiv + 430pp.   22134-2 Paperbound $3.00

MATHEMATICS, MAGIC AND MYSTERY, Martin Gardner. Puzzle editor for Scientific American explains mathematics behind various mystifying tricks: card tricks, stage "mind reading," coin and match tricks, counting out games, geometric dissections, etc. Probability sets, theory of numbers clearly explained. Also provides more than 400 tricks, guaranteed to work, that you can do. 135 illustrations. xii + 176pp.

20338-2 Paperbound $1.50

How to Know the Wild Flowers, Mrs. William Starr Dana. This is the classical book of American wildflowers (of the Eastern and Central United States), used by hundreds of thousands. Covers over 500 species, arranged in extremely easy to use color and season groups. Full descriptions, much plant lore. This Dover edition is the fullest ever compiled, with tables of nomenclature changes. 174 full-page plates by M. Satterlee. xii + 418pp. 20332-8 Paperbound $2.75

Our Plant Friends and Foes, William Atherton DuPuy. History, economic importance, essential botanical information and peculiarities of 25 common forms of plant life are provided in this book in an entertaining and charming style. Covers food plants (potatoes, apples, beans, wheat, almonds, bananas, etc.), flowers (lily, tulip, etc.), trees (pine, oak, elm, etc.), weeds, poisonous mushrooms and vines, gourds, citrus fruits, cotton, the cactus family, and much more. 108 illustrations. xiv + 290pp. 22272-1 Paperbound $2.50

How to Know the Ferns, Frances T. Parsons. Classic survey of Eastern and Central ferns, arranged according to clear, simple identification key. Excellent introduction to greatly neglected nature area. 57 illustrations and 42 plates. xvi + 215pp. 20740-4 Paperbound $1.75

Manual of the Trees of North America, Charles S. Sargent. America's foremost dendrologist provides the definitive coverage of North American trees and tree-like shrubs. 717 species fully described and illustrated: exact distribution, down to township; full botanical description; economic importance; description of subspecies and races; habitat, growth data; similar material. Necessary to every serious student of tree-life. Nomenclature revised to present. Over 100 locating keys. 783 illustrations. lii + 934pp. 20277-1, 20278-X Two volumes, Paperbound $6.00

Our Northern Shrubs, Harriet L. Keeler. Fine non-technical reference work identifying more than 225 important shrubs of Eastern and Central United States and Canada. Full text covering botanical description, habitat, plant lore, is paralleled with 205 full-page photographs of flowering or fruiting plants. Nomenclature revised by Edward G. Voss. One of few works concerned with shrubs. 205 plates, 35 drawings. xxviii + 521pp. 21989-5 Paperbound $3.75

The Mushroom Handbook, Louis C. C. Krieger. Still the best popular handbook: full descriptions of 259 species, cross references to another 200. Extremely thorough text enables you to identify, know all about any mushroom you are likely to meet in eastern and central U. S. A.: habitat, luminescence, poisonous qualities, use, folklore, etc. 32 color plates show over 50 mushrooms, also 126 other illustrations. Finding keys. vii + 560pp. 21861-9 Paperbound $3.95

Handbook of Birds of Eastern North America, Frank M. Chapman. Still much the best single-volume guide to the birds of Eastern and Central United States. Very full coverage of 675 species, with descriptions, life habits, distribution, similar data. All descriptions keyed to two-page color chart. With this single volume the average birdwatcher needs no other books. 1931 revised edition. 195 illustrations. xxxvi + 581pp. 21489-3 Paperbound $3.25

MATHEMATICAL PUZZLES FOR BEGINNERS AND ENTHUSIASTS, Geoffrey Mott-Smith. 189 puzzles from easy to difficult—involving arithmetic, logic, algebra, properties of digits, probability, etc.—for enjoyment and mental stimulus. Explanation of mathematical principles behind the puzzles. 135 illustrations. viii + 248pp.
20198-8 Paperbound $1.75

PAPER FOLDING FOR BEGINNERS, William D. Murray and Francis J. Rigney. Easiest book on the market, clearest instructions on making interesting, beautiful origami. Sail boats, cups, roosters, frogs that move legs, bonbon boxes, standing birds, etc. 40 projects; more than 275 diagrams and photographs. 94pp.
20713-7 Paperbound $1.00

TRICKS AND GAMES ON THE POOL TABLE, Fred Herrmann. 79 tricks and games— some solitaires, some for two or more players, some competitive games—to entertain you between formal games. Mystifying shots and throws, unusual caroms, tricks involving such props as cork, coins, a hat, etc. Formerly *Fun on the Pool Table*. 77 figures. 95pp.
21814-7 Paperbound $1.00

HAND SHADOWS TO BE THROWN UPON THE WALL: A SERIES OF NOVEL AND AMUSING FIGURES FORMED BY THE HAND, Henry Bursill. Delightful picturebook from great-grandfather's day shows how to make 18 different hand shadows: a bird that flies, duck that quacks, dog that wags his tail, camel, goose, deer, boy, turtle, etc. Only book of its sort. vi + 33pp. 6½ x 9¼. 21779-5 Paperbound $1.00

WHITTLING AND WOODCARVING, E. J. Tangerman. 18th printing of best book on market. "If you can cut a potato you can carve" toys and puzzles, chains, chessmen, caricatures, masks, frames, woodcut blocks, surface patterns, much more. Information on tools, woods, techniques. Also goes into serious wood sculpture from Middle Ages to present, East and West. 464 photos, figures. x + 293pp.
20965-2 Paperbound $2.00

HISTORY OF PHILOSOPHY, Julián Marias. Possibly the clearest, most easily followed, best planned, most useful one-volume history of philosophy on the market; neither skimpy nor overfull. Full details on system of every major philosopher and dozens of less important thinkers from pre-Socratics up to Existentialism and later. Strong on many European figures usually omitted. Has gone through dozens of editions in Europe. 1966 edition, translated by Stanley Appelbaum and Clarence Strowbridge. xviii + 505pp. 21739-6 Paperbound $3.00

YOGA: A SCIENTIFIC EVALUATION, Kovoor T. Behanan. Scientific but non-technical study of physiological results of yoga exercises; done under auspices of Yale U. Relations to Indian thought, to psychoanalysis, etc. 16 photos. xxiii + 270pp.
20505-3 Paperbound $2.50

Prices subject to change without notice.
Available at your book dealer or write for free catalogue to Dept. GI, Dover Publications, Inc., 180 Varick St., N. Y., N. Y. 10014. Dover publishes more than 150 books each year on science, elementary and advanced mathematics, biology, music, art, literary history, social sciences and other areas.